The North-West Frontier
(KHYBER PUKHTUNKHWA)

ESSAYS ON HISTORY

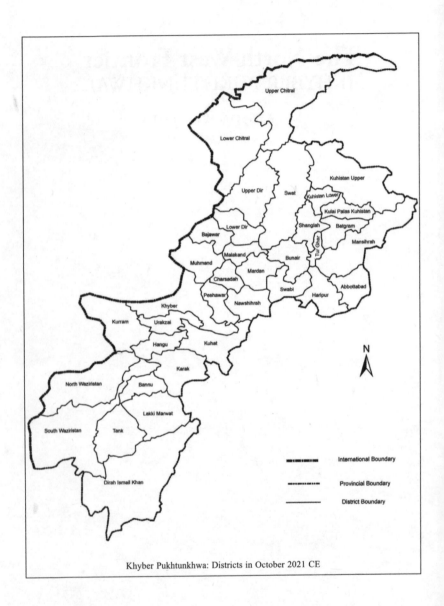

Khyber Pukhtunkhwa: Districts in October 2021 CE

The North-West Frontier (KHYBER PUKHTUNKHWA)

ESSAYS ON HISTORY

SECOND REVISED EDITION

SULTAN-I-ROME

OXFORD

UNIVERSITY PRESS

OXFORD
UNIVERSITY PRESS

Oxford University Press is a department of the University of Oxford.
It furthers the University's objective of excellence in research, scholarship,
and education by publishing worldwide. Oxford is a registered trade mark of
Oxford University Press in the UK and in certain other countries

Published in Pakistan by
Oxford University Press
No. 38, Sector 15, Korangi Industrial Area,
PO Box 8214, Karachi-74900, Pakistan

ISBN 978-0-19-070790-3

Typeset in Times New Roman
Printed on 68gsm Offset Paper

Printed by The Times Press (Pvt.) Ltd., Karachi

To
my elder brothers
Alamzeb Bacha and Sultan Mahmud

Contents

Author's Note

ALTHOUGH the diacritical marks are not used, I have tried, in this edition, to write the local names and non-English words and terms to their greater conformity with their local pronunciation and rendering, and to the transliteration rules. Therefore, in many cases, the spellings of such names and terms, and titles of books, etc., in this edition are different from those generally written. For instance:

Chakdarah	instead of Chakdara
Hazarah	instead of Hazara
Jargah	instead of *jarga/jirga/jirgah*
Khail	instead of Khel
Kuhistan	instead of Kohistan
Landakay	instead of Landakai
Malak	instead of *malik*
Mardrasah	instead of *madrasa/madrassa*
Mingawarah	instead of Mingora and Mingawara
Mula	instead of *mulla* and *mullah*
Sahibzadah	instead of Sahibzada
Swarah	instead of *swara*
Turangzi	instead of Turangzai
Yusufzi	instead of Yusufzai/Yusufzais

However, in direct quotes, and where the authors have spelled their names as such, they have been retained. But in some such cases, and also in some other cases, they have been included in parenthesis when first appeared, so that non-local readers can comprehend and pronounce them properly and correctly. This was also required for consistency throughout the book.

In the first edition of the book, the spelling of 'Pukhtunkhwa' was adopted and it remained so till the final proof that I checked and approved. But, it was later changed by the project coordinator in OUP, despite my refusal to give my consent and approval, which really was a shock for me when the book was published. I expressed my disagreement with and disapproval of this change also in my talk at the launching ceremony of the book at the first Islamabad Literature Festival held in 2013. Later I communicated it to the Managing Director OUP, Pakistan, who agreed to change the spelling in the next edition of the book. Hence, this edition carries the spelling as 'Pukhtunkhwa'—save in direct quotes.

I have adopted the spelling 'Pukhtunkhwa', instead of 'Pakhtunkhwa', because the Pukhtuns, in general, pronounce it so and it sounds technically correct. There are two variants of Pukhtu or Pashto, i.e. hard and soft—in the former the alphabet خ 'khin' is used and in the later ش 'shin'. In the 'hard' form for the 'Pathans' in Pukhtu the singular is 'Pukhtun' and 'Pukhtan' and the plural 'Pukhtanah', whereas in the soft form the singular is 'Pushtun', 'Pashtun', and 'Pashtin' and the plural 'Pushtanah' and 'Pashtanah'. All those, save the Afridi and Bangash, who use and speak the 'khin' variant, pronounce the name 'Pukhtunkhwa' and 'Pukhtankhwa' and not 'Pakhtunkhwa'. Therefore, 'Pakhtunkhwa' is technically or dialectically unsound. Going by the soft variant the word 'Pashtunkhwa' sounds technically and dialectically correct.

Preface

IN 1999, the University of Peshawar introduced a new graduate level course, dealing with the history of the North-West Frontier Province (now Khyber Pukhtunkhwa), titled 'A Short History of NWFP'. However, the majority of the recommended books are not available in the shops or in college libraries—to the great inconvenience of the students. Therefore, both teachers and the students have keenly felt the need for a book that covers the topics in the syllabus.

My students have frequently urged me to write such a book; Dr Syed Minhaj ul Hassan also suggested the same. So I took on the task and wrote a few chapters along the pattern of a regular textbook. However, when I gave the draft of chapter 8 to advocate Abdul Halim (of Ghaligay, Swat) for his comments, his feedback was that it was not a reflection of my writing, because of its lack of references, and suggested that I write it as a research project. Dr Syed Minhaj ul Hassan also suggested the same. While this increased my workload, it also gave a new dimension to the book, changed its pattern, and made it into a research-oriented one—which, in turn, increased its worth and made it authentic and of interest for a larger and wider audience.

It took me more than seven years to bring this work to completion. It was, initially, tentatively titled *A History of NWFP*, *A History of NWFP: Selected Topics*, and *The Frontier Perspectives: Essays in Historical Studies*, and, hence, mentioned as such in some of my writings. But the title needed to be changed as the book deals with various topics, most chapters have already been published in research journals, and the name of the province has been changed. Therefore, after considering a number of titles, the book was titled: *The North-West Frontier (Khyber Pukhtunkhwa): Essays on History*.

Work of this nature cannot be carried out and completed without the support of others, especially in a remote area like Swat where the required source material and other facilities are not always at hand. A number of people took interest in this work by morally supporting me, cooperating with me, providing source material, and giving their input. They include advocates Abdul Halim (Ghaligay, Swat) and Shah Salam Khan (Gulkadah, Swat); Dr Syed Minhaj ul Hassan (Department of History, University of Peshawar); Dr Altaf Qadir (Department of

History, University of Peshawar); Dr Ishtiaq Ahmad (Galuch, Swat); Dr Asfandyar Durrani (Khwishkay); Dr Himayatullah Yaqubi (Department of History, Quaid-i-Azam University); Dr Rafiullah Khan (Taxila Institute of Asian Civilizations, Quaid-i-Azam University); Prof. Muhammad Amin (Mingawarah, Swat); Prof. Shaukat Ali (Charbagh, Swat); Prof. Abdul Wahab Khan (Runryal, Swat); Prof. Anwar Ali Shah (Damghar, Swat); Tahira Tanweer (National Archives, Islamabad); Dr Ansar Zahid Khan (Karachi); my teachers at the Department of General History, University of Karachi: Prof. Sayyad Abdur Rahman (Karachi) and Dr Tahera Aftab (Karachi); Dr Urs Geiser (Department of Geography, Zurich University); Islamuddin (Khwaza Khilah, Swat); Gauhar Ali (Hazarah, Swat); architect Shaukat Ali Sharar (Sapal Bandai, Swat); Nawsherawan Khan advocate (Kutah, Swat); Prof. Khurshid (Kanju Township, Swat); Farman Ali aka Farman (Hazarah, Swat); Ali Akbar (librarian); Khwajah Samiullah aka Tuta; and Rahmat Ali (Library of Government Jahanzeb College, Saidu Sharif, Swat); Shah Wazir Khan and Hamayun Iqbal (Government Jahanzeb College, Saidu Sharif, Swat); Sharif Hussain (Director General, Provincial Disaster Management Authority, Khyber Pukhtunkhwa); Prof. Subhani Gul (Aligramah, Swat); Prof. Attaur Rahman (Faizabad, Ulandar, Shanglahpar); Prof. Ihsan ur Rahman (Shinkad, Swat); Dr Robert Nichols (The Richard Stockton College, New Jersey); Aftab Ali (Hazarah, Swat); Dr Lal Baha (Peshawar); Akhtar Ayub advocate (Saidu Sharif, Swat); Ikramullah (Saidu Sharif—Suhail Computers, Mingawarah, Swat); Abdul Wali Khan aka Wali Khan (Amankut, Swat) and Abdul Haseeb (librarian, Department of History, University of Peshawar). Dr Mohammad Usman FRCS (Consultant Surgeon, Saidu Sharif, Swat), went through the draft thoroughly and gave immense input.

This work would not have been possible without the support extended to me, throughout my research, by my elder brothers, Alamzeb Bacha and Sultan Mahmud. My nephews, Irfanullah Khan, Dr Abdullah, and Ihsanullah, shared the burden of some of my domestic responsibilities and facilitated me in continuing my work. My dear children and my wife have suffered as I have not been able to give them enough time on various occasions; and my wife has shouldered a lot of my responsibilities, as well.

I am thankful to all those mentioned above, and to anyone whose name might inadvertently remain unmentioned. This book owes a lot to those whose works and writings have been consulted and utilised, and I am grateful to all of them.

While working on this study, I used to give drafts of various chapters to my students because of the non-availability of relevant material for some of the topics of the abovementioned course. Unfortunately, a hard copy of chapter 3 got lost somewhere in Mingawarah. To ensure that the drafts given to my students, and the one that got lost, were not pirated and published by someone else, I sent these versions to research journals to be published under my name, and the risk of piracy was thus minimised.

As mentioned earlier, versions of ten of the fourteen chapters have been published in research journals, i.e. chapters 1, 6, and 12 in *Pakistan Perspectives* (Karachi); chapter 2 (divided in three articles) in *Journal of the Pakistan Historical Society* (Karachi); chapter 3 in *Pakistan Vision* (Lahore); chapter 5 in *Journal of the Research Society of Pakistan* (Lahore); chapters 7 and 11 in *Afghan Research Journal* (Lahore); chapter 8 in *Journal of Law and Society* (Peshawar); and chapter 9 in *Hamdard Islamicus* (Karachi). However, where necessary, new material has been added and modifications have been made. Hence, in case of difference in the versions published as research articles and this book, the version in this volume should be considered as authoritative.

In this edition, not only the errors in the first edition (noticed after publication), have been rectified but some queries, raised during this period, have also been addressed. Besides, modifications and additions have been made, where required, especially in light of the changes caused as a result of the 25th Amendment in the Constitution of Pakistan, 1973.

The contents of some books that I came across, and which are relevant to this book, have not been quoted and critically evaluated as that would have brought no significant contribution to, and change in, the existing contents of the book, except for making it bulkier. I, however, have included them in the Bibliography for the readers' information—the omission in quoting or critical evaluation of such books is for the reason underlined.

Abbreviations and Acronyms

AIML	All India Muslim League
AINC	All India National Congress
APH	Azeem Publishing House
AS	Alayhi-Salam
AWI	Almqvist & Wiksell International
BCE	Before Common Era (also Before Christian Era), also called BC
BT	Book Traders
c/c./ca.	about (in dating)
CAP	Carolina Academic Press
CE	Common Era (also Christian Era), also called AD
cf.	*confer*, compare
Chap.	Chapter
Chaps.	Chapters
comp.	compiler, compiled by
CPL	Curzon Press Ltd
DAT	Daily Afghanistan Times
DM	Dawlati Matba
e.g.	*exempli gratia*, for example
EAC	Extra Assistant Commissioner
ed.	editor, edited, edited by (one person)
edn.	edition
eds.	Editors, edited by (more than one person)
etc.	etcetera, and so forth (of things)
f.n.	footnote
FATA	Federally Administered Tribal Areas
FCR	Frontier Crimes Regulation
ff.	and the following pages
FFL	Faber and Faber Ltd.
FH	Fiction House
FR	Frontier Region
GA	Gosha-e-Adab
HK	Hind Kitabs
i.e.	*id est*, that is
ibid.	*ibidem*, in the same place

ICHP	Indian Council of Historical Research
IIC	Institute of Islamic Culture
IIS	Idarah Ishaat-i Sarhad
impr.	impression
IP	Indus Publications
JNMF	Jawaharlal Nehru Memorial Fund
JPHS	*Journal of the Pakistan Historical Society*
LPP	Low Price Publications
n.	note
n.d.	no date
n.p.	no place, no publisher, no page
NCHCR	National Commission on Historical and Cultural Research
NIHCR	National Institute of Historical and Cultural Research
No.	number
Nos.	numbers
NT	Nisa Traders
NWFP/	
N-WFP/	
N.W.F.P.	North-West Frontier Province
OLL	Orient Longmans Ltd
OUP	Oxford University Press
p.	page
PA	Pashto Academy/Pukhtu Academy
PASR	Pushto Adabi Society (Rgd)
passim	here and there
PATA	Provincially Administered Tribal Areas
pp.	pages
PP	Popular Prakashan
RA	Raziyallahu Anhu
RBC	Royal Book Company
repr.	reprint
rev.	revised, revised by, revision
RSP	Research Society of Pakistan
S.A.W.	Sallalahu Alaihi wa Alihi wa Sallam
SAFRON	States and Frontier Regions (Ministry of)
SBB	Saeed Book Bank
SCC	S. Chand & Co.
sic	thus (to show that an obvious error is an exact reproduction of the original)
SMP	Sang-e-Meel Publications

trans.	translation
UBA	University Book Agency
UK	University of Karachi
VB	Vanguard Books
vis-à-vis	in relation to or in comparison with something or someone
viz.	*videlicet*, namely, that is to say
vol.	volume
vols.	volumes
WB	Wali Bagh

1 Geography: Some Historical Aspects

> The geography of a country shapes its history
> just as surely in the East as in the West.
> – Thomas Holdich

> The North-West Frontier is a well-defined region
> with a long and unique history.
> – David Dichter

KHYBER PUKHTUNKHWA (North-West Frontier Province till 2010)—formerly part of British India and now of Pakistan—is of significant geostrategic importance. It is located at the juncture of three prominent and significant geographical regions of Asia—South Asia, Central Asia, and China. The settled area of the province became an integral part of British India in 1849, when the Britons (*see* Chapter 4, n. 6) annexed it as part of the then-Sikh kingdom of Punjab.[1] The tribal areas, both the later-day Federally Administered Tribal Areas (FATA) and the Provincially Administered Tribal Areas (PATA), that remained so till May 2018, were later brought under the loose control of the British as a protectorate. Nevertheless, the then Indian States/Princely States (as they were generally referred to by the British) that existed in the areas that comprise the later-day PATA held a somewhat different status. The settled area remained a part of the province of Punjab until its separation was decided upon during Lord Curzon's tenure as viceroy,[2] and when it was given the status of a separate province—the North-West Frontier Province—in November 1901.

LOCATION

The province is situated between latitude 31°4' N and 36°57' N and between longitude 69°16' E and 74°7' E. The length of the province, at its greatest, between the parallels is 408 miles; the maximum breadth between the meridians is 279 miles.[3] According to James W. Spain, the distance between the Indus River and the mountain crest 'in the focal central section' is hardly 100 miles.[4] David Dichter points out that the minimum breadth is 'something less than 60 miles in Kohat District'.[5] All these, however, apply to the then settled area of the province, i.e. excluding the then tribal area or till the 25th Amendment in the Constitution of Pakistan in May 2018.

The sources do not state the actual area of the province, nor are the given areas the same. This applies to the settled and now former tribal areas. For instance, according to Dr Lal Baha, the total area of the province is 'approximately 39,000 square miles', out of which the total area of the settled districts was '13,419 square miles' and that of the now former tribal agencies '25,500 square miles'.[6] On the other hand, the *Imperial Gazetteer of India* has stated that the approximate area of the province 'is 38,665 square miles, of which only 13,193' were settled districts and the remaining, i.e. 25,472 square miles, were the (now former) tribal areas.[7] According to James W. Spain, the total area of the province 'is approximately 39,259 square miles', in which the tribal areas covered '25,140 square miles' and the settled districts '14,119 square miles'.[8] Qaiyum Khan states that according to the census report of 1941, the tribal areas covered 'an area of 24,986' square miles and the settled districts an area of 14,263 square miles,[9] totalling 39,249 square miles. The tribal agencies and the Frontier Regions, or all the tribal areas, were commonly considered to be a part of the province, but technically and constitutionally this was not so. 'The Constitution (Twenty-fifth Amendment) Act, 2018', made the area of the erstwhile tribal agencies and Frontier Regions an integral part of the province since 31 May 2018.

At its inception, the Hindu Kush Range (and Afghanistan) formed the province's boundary to the north, Baluchistan and the Dirah (Dera) Ghazi Khan area of Punjab to the south, Kashmir and Punjab to the east, and Afghanistan to the west.[10] Currently, the Hindu Kush Range and Afghanistan remain the boundary to the north, but the Zub (Zhob; Jub) and Musa Khail (Khel) districts of Baluchistan and the Dirah Ghazi Khan District of Punjab form the boundary to the south. The Layah (Leiah), Bhakkar, Mianwali, Attak (Attock), and Rawalpindi districts of Punjab,[11] Kashmir and Gilgit Baltistan form the boundary to the east, while Afghanistan remains the boundary to the west. Parts of the Indus Kuhistan (Kohistan) and Hazarah (Hazara) areas of the province lie in the cis-Indus region or, in other words, are located on the left side of the Indus, while the remaining area is in the trans-Indus region or, on the right side of the Indus.

POLITICAL DIVISION

Although the tribal agencies and Frontier Regions did not, constitutionally and technically, form a part of the province, they were generally considered to be a part of it; hence, it was thought that the province was divided into two political divisions—namely, the settled area or administrative districts and the political agencies or tribal area. At the time of its formation, the settled districts comprised the five districts of Hazarah, Peshawar, Kuhat (Kohat), Bannu, and Dirah (Dera) Ismail Khan, whereas the political agencies were the Agency of Dir, Swat and Chitral; the Khyber Agency; the Kurram Agency; the North Waziristan Agency; and the South Waziristan Agency. Besides its boundaries with the neighbouring areas, the province also had an internal political and administrative boundary that separated the settled and tribal areas.[12]

The Agency of Dir, Swat and Chitral included the princely states of Chitral, Dir, and later the newly emerged Swat State, as well as the Malakand Protected Area or, as it is commonly called, the area of the Malakand Agency or Malakand District, Bajawar, and Utman Khail. The above-mentioned areas of the Agency of Dir, Swat and Chitral (excluding Bajawar and Utman Khail), along with the area of the former Amb State, the cis-Indus tribal area of Tur (Toor) Ghar or Black Mountain or Kala Dhakah, and Kuhistan Area were defined as the Provincially Administered Tribal Areas (PATA) under the Interim Constitution of the Islamic Republic of Pakistan, 1972,[13] and their status was retained under the Constitution of the Islamic Republic of Pakistan, 1973.[14] Unlike the other tribal areas, the territory of the now former PATA, although a tribal area, was constitutionally part of the province and hence represented in the provincial legislature.

There was another type of tribal area till May 2018, known as the Frontier Regions (FRs). They were not part of the province but connected to the adjoining settled or administrative districts for administrative purposes. FR Kurram, later called Central Kurram, however, was a third subdivision of the Kurram Agency. On 16 February 2004, the governor of the province, Iftikhar Hussain Shah, 'formally informed tribal leaders from the region' that 'it had become necessary to rename the area as calling the agency's third sub division [subdivision] simply Frontier Region was causing a number of legal complications'.[15] Some areas of the Frontier Regions, such as Urakzai (Orakzai) and Muhmand (Mohmand; also pronounced as Mumand and Mamand), were later made separate agencies. These areas (Frontier Regions), however, were not made subservient to the formal laws and administrative system employed in the settled districts, with which they were connected; but were governed by the special laws applicable to the tribal areas, i.e. the Agencies. They were under the deputy commissioners (DCs)—called district coordination officers (DCOs) during 2001–2012 CE—of the respective districts. Later the Frontier Regions were: FR Peshawar, FR Kuhat, FR Kurram, FR Bannu, FR Lakki Marwat, FR Tank, and FR Dirah Ismail Khan.[16] It is noteworthy that FR Kurram was not mentioned in article 246 of the Constitution of 1973, while the tribal areas were; perhaps, because, as stated above, it was a subdivision of the Kurram Agency, which was mentioned as part of the Federally Administered Tribal Areas (FATA). The Frontier Regions, too, were part of the FATA. This political division of the settled and tribal areas was brought to an end on 31 May 2018, under the 25th Amendment in the Constitution of 1973.

GEOGRAPHICAL DIVISION AND PHYSICAL FEATURES

The province was divided 'into three main geographical divisions': (1) the cis-Indus, Indus Kuhistan and Hazarah region; (2) 'the comparatively narrow strip between the Indus and the hills', constituting the then trans-Indus settled districts of Peshawar, Kuhat (Kohat), Bannu, and Dirah (Dera) Ismail Khan; (3) 'the rugged mountainous regions on the north and west', between the then four trans-Indus settled districts and the border of Afghanistan,[17] namely the tract that comprised the erstwhile tribal areas, later divided into FATA and PATA. At this point, it is pertinent to underline that, as stated above, FATA was not part of the province, neither technically nor constitutionally. However, for some administrative purposes and from some counts, these areas were linked and tied to the province with which they were commonly identified.

The physical features of the province vary vis-à-vis the different localities. The northern area of the cis-Indus Hazarah region 'forms a wedge extending north-eastwards', 'tapering to a narrow point at the head of the Kaghan Valley'. 'The mountain chains' that 'enclose the Kaghan defile sweep southwards into the broader portion' of the district. 'Towards the base of the wedge', adjoining Punjab, 'the hills open out and fertile plains' replace 'the terraced hill-sides [hillsides] and forests of the northern uplands' of the district.[18]

The four settled districts in the trans-Indus region, from north to south, were Peshawar, Kuhat, Bannu, and Dirah Ismail Khan. Each of these districts formed a minor natural division. Peshawar District, situated in the north, was a plain, mostly 'encircled by hills'. To its south lay the Kuhat District, 'a rugged table-land broken by low ranges of hills', some relatively fertile valleys, and the Salt Range—which made internal communication difficult—beyond which lay a sandy plain. The Juwaki (Jowaki) Range separated it from Peshawar. To the south of Kuhat, lay Bannu District, situated 'in the broad basin of the Kurram river and completely surrounded by low ranges'. Despite the arid character of the surrounding area, irrigation and crop rotation allowed for a good agricultural yield. The southernmost district of the province, Dirah Ismail Khan, stretched out in the south of Bannu—a vast, barren, and stony plain, enclosed between the Sulaiman (Sulayman) Range and the Indus, 'and tapering to a blunt point at its southern extremity'. There was also a fertile strip along the Indus, as well as clayey deposits called *daman* (plain) along the lower slopes. These five districts were mainly plains comprising both cultivable and non-cultivable and irrigated and non-irrigated lands.[19]

The areas of the five districts now (in 2021) constitute the districts of Batgram (also pronounced as Batagram), Mansihrah (Mansehra), Abbottabad, Haripur (formed out of Hazarah District), Swabi (Swabai), Mardan, Nawshihrah (Nowshera), Charsadah (Charsada), Peshawar (formed out of Peshawar District), Kuhat, Hangu, Karak (formed out of Kuhat District), Lakki Marwat, Bannu (formed out of Bannu District), Tank, and Dirah Ismail Khan (formed out of Dirah Ismail Khan District). Indus Kuhistan, comprising the right and left flanks of the Indus Kuhistan, was also given the status of a district in 1976. It was later divided into two districts: Kuhistan [Kohistan] Upper and Kuhistan Lower. In 2017, a new district called Kulai Palas Kuhistan (Kolai Pallas Kohistan) was created out of the existing District Kuhistan Lower; and thus the area of the Kuhistan District created in 1976 now comprises three districts. In 2011, the Tur Ghar or Black Mountain area was given the status of a district with the name of Tur Ghar (Toor Ghar).

The erstwhile tribal territory, lying between the Indus and the settled districts on the one side and the Durand Line on the other, is varied in composition and is wilder and more rugged in character. It contains rugged and rocky terrain and wild lofty mountains with narrow, deep, remote, and less accessible fertile valleys. In the erstwhile tribal areas to the north, in the Agency of Dir, Swat and Chitral, the territory of Chitral is mountainous with deep valleys and lofty ranges. Most parts of Chitral are bare and treeless. In the south of Chitral, one finds the hilly areas of Dir and Bajawar, with their thickly wooded hills, and the fertile valleys of the Swat and Panjkurah (Panjkorah/Panjkora) rivers, which have

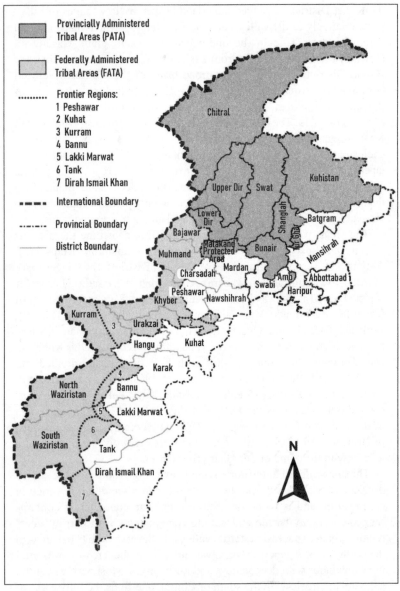

Khyber Pukhtunkhwa and FATA till May 2018
Courtesy: Dr Urs Geiser

become famous for their high yields of grains and fruits as well as a variety of medicinal plants. The territory that fell in the previous Agency of Dir, Swat and Chitral penetrates further into the Himalayas more than the Hazarah District on the left side of the Indus.[20] The territories of Swat Kuhistan, Shanglahpar (Shanglah, Shangla), and the right hand of Indus Kuhistan are mountainous and were thickly forested. Bunair (Buner, Bunir), however, is mostly plain but with a lower yield because of scarcity of water. The areas of the former Agency of Dir, Swat and Chitral now (in 2021) constitute the districts of Upper Chitral, Lower Chitral, Upper Dir, Lower Dir, Swat, Shanglah (Shangla), Bunair (Buner), Malakand, and Bajawar (Bajaur).

To the southwest of the then-Agency of Dir, Swat and Chitral lies the Muhmand (Mohmand) country, 'a rough and rocky tract', which also extends into Afghanistan; an area that is mostly without vegetation and difficult for communication. To its south lies the territory of Khyber (Khaibar), wherein the famous Khyber Pass is situated. South of the Khyber area, one comes across the rugged and mountainous area of Tirah, which also has fertile little valleys. Its north-western extremity is bordered by the Safaid Kuh (Safed Koh; White Mountain). Most of the Tirah highlands are not easily accessible. To the west of the Tirah (which is situated in the former Khyber Agency, now Khyber District), lies the fertile Kurram Valley. It stretches south-eastwards, along the Kurram River, from the peak of the Sikaram and the Piwar Kutal (Piwar Kotal, Piwar Pass) 'to the western extremity' of the Miranzai Valley. Divided into an upper and lower Kurram Valley by a spur of hills, the Kurram Valley has been famous for its 'bumper crops of' fruits 'and the medicinal plant, artemesia'.[21]

To the south of the Kurram Valley lies the territory of Waziristan, formerly divided into the political agencies of North and South Waziristan: now the districts of North and South Waziristan. The Waziri country comprises a mass of hilly areas, the Tuchi (Tochi) Valley, and the plain of Wana. The Tuchi Valley is divided into upper and lower parts by a spur of hills which extend to the bed of the Tuchi River—from which the valley took its name. Further south, from Kaniguram in South Waziristan, 'a series of steep gorges' lead into the 'hills, to the Wana Plain'. The Gumal (Gomal) River 'intersects the hills in the southern area', thus providing the famous route from Afghanistan to Dirah Ismail Khan, Baluchistan, and the Lower Punjab. The valleys of North and South Waziristan broaden out into plains and form fertile and well-irrigated dales; while some of the higher hills are wooded, the hills are mostly barren and treeless—from the border of the Kurram Valley in the north until they merge with the Sulaiman Range in the south.[22] As mentioned earlier, the territories of the then Agency of Dir, Swat and Chitral were made a part of PATA, but instead of remaining four agencies, by 1973 the number of the political agencies was raised to seven—the agencies of Bajawar (Bajaur), Muhmand (Mohmand), Khyber, Urakzai (Orakzai), Kurram, North Waziristan, and South Waziristan—which were also called FATA along with the Frontier Regions and held a separate status under the Constitution of 1973 till 'The Constitution (Twenty-fifth Amendment) Act, 2018', in May 2018, in the Constitution of 1973 through which the special tribal status of both FATA and PATA was brought to an end.

MOUNTAINS

There is a confusing 'mass of mountains formed by the meeting of the Outer and Mid-Himalayan ranges', in the cis-Indus part of the province. Two mountain ridges run from this mass of mountains, which enclose Kaghan, in unbroken lines until they meet at the Babusar Pass (13,589 feet high). On the western side of the Indus, the mighty range of the Hindu Kush 'runs almost due east and west along the north-eastern and northern frontiers of the Province'. The Hindu Kush Range meets, 'at its north-eastern corner', with 'a continuation of the Outer Himalayan chain which crosses the Indus above the Kaghan valley'. Minor ranges descend from this chain, 'in a north-westerly direction', traversing Bajawar and Swat, 'until they meet the curved range of hills' which connect the Mid-Himalayas with the Safaid Kuh (Safed Koh) and encircle the Peshawar Valley to the north.[23]

'A long broken line of mountains run almost due south' from the Durah (Dorah) Pass in the Hindu Kush, separating the province from Kafiristan and, further south, from other parts of Afghanistan. The Hindu Kush, and the two ranges which run southwards from it, enclosed the Agency of Dir, Swat and Chitral. The minor ranges that descend from these ranges filled the intervening spaces. The western lines of these ranges merge 'in the Khyber hills', forming 'the eastern extremity of the Safed Koh'.[24]

'The Safed Koh…runs almost due east and west, forming the watershed between the Kabul and Kurram rivers.' Minor ranges descend from the southern slopes of the Safaid Kuh, eastwards to the Indus, forming the Chirat hills. The Sulaiman Range, wherein lay the famous Takht-i Sulaiman (Solomon's Throne), 'runs up [along] the western border of the Province to meet the Safed Koh'. It 'also throws out a series of parallel spurs to the east', which traverse the entire Kuhat (Kohat) District (the latter Kuhat Division). The Sheikh Budin Range, 'the southern extremity of the Salt Range, forms the boundary between Bannu and Dera Ismail Khan', eventually merging into the Sulaiman Range.[25]

The Tur Ghar or Black Mountain, 'A mountain range on the north-western border' of the Hazarah region of the province, is 25 to 30 miles long 'from north to south and [has] an elevation of 8,000 feet above the sea-level'. Another famous hill is the Mahabanr (locally called Mabanr), which is situated on the right-bank of the Indus at the eastern end of a spur of the Ilam Range.[26]

There are also the low mountains of the Khyber hills, running southwards, wherein lies the Tartarah (Tatara) Peak (about 6,800 feet high); the Juwaki (Jowaki) Range, an extension of the Safaid Kuh, where the Kuhat Pass separates the Peshawar and Kuhat regions; the spur of hills that divide the Kurram Valley into its upper and lower portions; the low ranges of hills and the extension of the Salt Range that intrude into the southern and eastern portions of the Kuhat region; the rough and broken Wazir hills of both North and South Waziristan; and the western Sulaiman hills in the Dirah Ismail Khan region.[27] Besides, there are hills that extend down into Dir, Swat, Shanglahpar, Bunair, and Bajawar, among whom the famous ones are the Murah (Morah) and the Ilam ranges. James W. Spain has aptly observed:

> Perhaps the most important point to be made about the Frontier hills is that, although they are a barrier, they are a barrier with many and major qualifications. First, they are occupied…. Second[ly], there are many natural routes through the barrier, of which the Khyber is only one. Thirdly, no power—including that of British India at its height—has ever been able to establish full control over the people and the passes of the hills. Lord Curzon, Viceroy of India at the beginning of the twentieth century, accepted these facts and formally divided the tribal area off from the rest of India as a marchland. This has been its role throughout history.[28]

PASSES

H.C. Verma has stated that 'like other natural geographical features', mountain passes 'contribute towards [the] moulding and shaping' of the 'historical pattern' of a region. 'The frequent movements of people through' the mountain passes 'break the isolation of different ways of life' and also broaden man's political horizon, allowing him an understanding of other cultures. Battles for the passes, 'in the regions now forming

Afghanistan and Pakistan', were not only a prelude to encroachment over the interior of these regions, but over the Indian subcontinent as well, because 'whosoever captured these passes had an edge over their opponents'.[29]

The mountains that lie to the north and northwest of the Khyber Pukhtunkhwa form the boundary between Afghanistan and the province, and contain some of the very important passes. As mountain passes have played an important role throughout history, the passes in the mountains of these areas gave great strategic and political importance to the province, not only after its formation as a separate province but also to the region throughout its known history. These passes ended the seclusion of the areas, exposing them to external cultural and political influences and serving as routes for trade between Central and South Asia as well as for invasion from Central Asia over India, and vice versa. James W. Spain observes: 'Since these passes and river valleys have played such a great part in history and are so essential to the maintenance of any kind of life in the wild mountain barrier through which they run, they are still worthy of note.'[30]

Among these passes, the Barughil (Baroghil; 12,000 feet high) and Durah (Dorah) passes lie in Chitral, 'in the northern zone of the Hindu Kush' Range, and lead into the Pamir and Afghanistan, respectively. Towards the south, there is the route from the Kunar Valley into Bajawar, Swat, and the plains of the province,[31] through the Malakand, Shahkut (Shahkot), Murah (Morah), and Karakar passes. Alexander of Macedonia led a contingent of his forces, for an attack on the subcontinent, through this route. In the Khyber area, in the south zone of the Hindu Kush, lies the famous Khyber Pass (3,373 feet high) which, in James W. Spain's opinion, is perhaps the most historic 'of all the passes of the world'. The Khyber Pass stretches through the Khyber hills for 32 miles, in 'an almost direct line between Peshawar and Kabul', and is the leading pass and main route of communication between Afghanistan and South Asia.[32]

The Piwar Kutal (Kotal) and the Shutargardan Pass lie further south in the Kurram Valley. These passes lead to Kabul and Ghazni, respectively, but have been mainly used for ordinary or local communication. The Tuchi (Tochi) and Gumal (Gomal) passes further south also play their strategic, political, and commercial role. Although James W. Spain has termed the Gumal Pass as 'the wildest and most isolated of the routes through the Frontier hills', it is no less significant for its role in trading and for providing access to Lower Punjab and Sindh.[33] It was through the

Gumal Pass that Mahmud of Ghazna[34] and Muhammad Ghauri made most of their invasions[35] into Punjab, Sindh, and further into India.

In addition to these main passes, which are mostly situated in the hills bordering Afghanistan, there are many other passes in the same hills that have not achieved fame or historic significance but have been a link for their local communities.

Within the province, too, there are several passes that have played a significant strategic, commercial, and communication's role. They include:

- Babusar Pass (13,589 feet high), which connects the Kaghan Valley with Gilgit.
- Luwari (Lowari; Lwarai) Pass (more than 10,000 feet high), which links Chitral with Dir, Swat, and onwards with the Peshawar plain and the subcontinent.
- Katgalah (Katgala) Pass, which links Bajawar and Dir with Swat, and with the plains of the subcontinent through the Malakand Pass in one direction, and with Afghanistan in the other direction.
- Malakand Pass, which is the main link between Chitral, Dir, and Swat on one side and with the province and the subcontinent on the other—where the British were strongly resisted in 1895, and again in 1897 for seven days.[36]
- Murah (Morah) and Shahkut (Shahkot) passes in the Murah Hill on the southern border of Swat, which held great strategic and commercial importance in the past. The newly constructed Swat Express Way passes through the Shahkut Pass
- Karakar Pass, which is the main pass between Bunair and Swat, and where the mighty forces of the Mughal Emperor Akbar (emperor of India from 1556 to 1605) met with disaster in 1586 at the hands of the tribesmen.[37]
- Kutkay (Kotkay) Pass, which links Swat with Shanglahpar, and onwards with China through the present-day Qaraquram (Karakoram) Highway.
- Ambilah (Ambela) Pass, which links Bunair with Mardan. In 1863, the mighty British forces were strongly resisted here, for about two months, at the time of the Ambilah Campaign. About one-tenth of the British soldiers that took part in the campaign were either killed or wounded in the pass; an additional number was invalidated 'from exposure or who died of disease', resulting in a record loss to the British during their wars in India.[38]

- Kuhat (Kohat) Pass or Kuhat Kutal, which links Peshawar Valley and the upper parts of the province with Kuhat and other southern parts of the province, and also onwards with Lower Punjab, Sindh, and Baluchistan.

RIVERS

Rivers play a pivotal role in preserving life and the development and progress of civilisations. The Khyber Pukhtunkhwa has been blessed with this natural resource, which not only contributes to the livelihood of the inhabitants of the province but also those outside the province. The main rivers of the province are the Indus, Kabul River, Swat River, Kurram River, and the Gambila or Tuchi (Tochi) River. There are several smaller rivers, or rivulets, as well.

Indus: With its head in Tibet, and tail in the Arabian Sea, the Indus is one of the significant rivers of the world. Its total length is '2,000 miles, depending on meanders'.[39] From its head, it flows through Kashmir and enters the Khyber Pukhtunkhwa near Bhasha. It drains the entire province (only the Kunhar River—flowing through the Kaghan Valley into the Jhelum River—does not form its tributary). In the north, the Indus divides the province from Chilas. Towards the south, it divides the Indus Kuhistan into two parts, and then separates the Hazarah region from the rest of the province. Further south, it separates the province from Punjab and forms its eastern boundary for about 200 miles. However, the Isa Khail (Khel) *tahsil* of the Mianwali (Myawali) District of the province of Punjab lies on its western side. The Indus has been the great natural waterway of the province. Besides its other tributaries, which feed into it before it enters the province, it has tributaries within the province as well. Its tributaries in the province include the Uran, Siran, Dur (Dor), and Haruh (Harroh) on the eastern side in the Hazarah region; Barandu which flows from Bunair and joins the Indus near Amb; and the Landay and Kurram rivers, which are its significant tributaries in the province, on its western side.[40]

The multi-purpose Tarbilah (Tarbela) Dam—which provides water for irrigation, is a source of fish, and is used for generating hydroelectric power—has been constructed in the province over the Indus. Similarly, the Ghazi-Barutha Canal has been taken from the Indus, with its headwork at Ghazi in the province—it is used to generate hydroelectric power at Barutha in Punjab.

Kabul River: Rising in the lofty Hindu Kush Range, 'about 45 miles west of Kabul', the Kabul River flows eastwards and enters the province from Afghanistan; after crossing the Muhmand hills, it enters the territory of the Peshawar District at Warsak. In addition to being an important source of water, it also forms a natural waterway for the province. Also known as Landay below its junction with the Swat River, it joins the Indus at Attak, draining Swat, Dir, Chitral, Tirah, and the Peshawar Valley. Its principal tributaries are the Yarkhun, Chitral, Kunar, Panjkurah (Panjkora), Swat, and Barah (Bara) rivers.[41] The Kabul River Canal, constructed in the 1880s, with its headwork at Warsak, provides water for irrigation. The Warsak Dam, constructed on the Kabul River, is used for the production of hydroelectric power.

Swat River: The Swat River originates at Kalam, at the confluence of the Ushu and Gabral rivers—both of which rise in the lofty ranges bordering Chitral—and drains the Swat Valley. It is one of the valuable natural resources of the area, as it is the source of water and irrigation, not only for Swat but for further afield as well and has also been widely used to transport timber. In addition to some small tributaries, the Panjkurah River joins it at Busaq, a few miles below Qalangai (Qulangai). It joins the Kabul River at Nisatah (Nisatta).[42] The Lower Swat Canal and Upper Swat Canal—completed in 1885 and 1913, respectively,[43] and fed by the Swat River—irrigate vast tracts of land outside Swat in the Charsadah, Samah, and Swabi regions; electricity is also generated at the Jabanr and Dargai power stations on the Upper Swat Canal. Another branch below Jabanr, called Malakand Three, was completed in 2008; it supplies water for irrigation and the generation of hydroelectric power. The Fatihpur Irrigation Canal provides water for irrigation in the Jinki Khail and Azi Khail tracts of Swat. This canal was first constructed during Miangul Abdul Wadud's reign, when Swat was a State, as a civil canal but was taken over by the provincial irrigation department in the 1970s, after the merger of Swat State. The Nikpi Khail Irrigation Canal, with its headwork at Ningwalai (the first phase was inaugurated in 1982), provides water for irrigation in Nikpi Khail tract of Swat. And the Bagh Dhirai Irrigation Canal, inaugurated in 2020, provides water for irrigation in the Shamizi tract of Matta *tahsil*.

One hydroelectric power generation project, the Daral Khwar Hydro Power Project, has been completed, and was inaugurated in 2019, by diverting the water of Daral Khwar, a tributary of the Swat River. Work on the second, called Matiltan-Gurkin Hydro Power Project, is in progress by diverting the water of Ushu River, a tributary of the Swat River, in a tunnel. The foundation stone of the construction work of Muhmand (Mohmand) Dam, on the Swat River, has also been laid on 2 May 2019, which is planned to be completed in five years. The Dam will provide water for irrigation and will also generate hydroelectric power.[44]

Barah River: The Barah (Bara) River rises in the Tirah hills and flowing through the Afridi country, supplying water for irrigation, it falls into the Kabul River, to the east of Peshawar, after a journey of 100 miles.[45]

Kurram River: The Kurram River rises in the Afghan territory, near Ahmad Khail, on the southern slope of the Safaid Kuh (Safed Kuh). It enters the Kurram Valley near Kharlachi and passes through the Kurram Valley and the Lower Waziri hills into Bannu District. Traversing the district, it enters the Isa Khail plain, joining the Indus opposite Mianwali. Besides its tributaries in the Kurram Valley, which are mainly streams, it is joined by the Tuchi River below Lakki.[46] It provides water for irrigation along its course, both in the Kurram Valley and further downstream in the province.

Tuchi River: The Tuchi (Tochi) or Gambila River rises in Afghanistan and flows through North Waziristan and Bannu. Running through the Dawar Valley in North Waziristan, it drains North Waziristan and irrigates considerable areas in the Dawar Valley and Bannu region. It joins the Kurram River below Lakki, having journeyed 100 to 150 miles.[47]

Gumal River: The Gumal (Gomal) River is the only significant river in South Waziristan. It rises near Sarwandi, on the Kuh (Koh) Nak Range, in Afghanistan. While its bed runs from Afghanistan to the Indus near Dirah Ismail Khan, its water is used in Dirah Ismail Khan and 'does not reach the Indus'. It receives numerous tributaries but most are mere torrents that remain dry for most of the year. However, the Tank Zam, its tributary the Shahur, and the Wana Tui (Toi) are perennial streams.[48] The Gumal Zam Dam project, which is being built over the Gumal River, will provide water for irrigation to areas in Dirah Ismail Khan and Bannu districts.

Other Rivers: The Yarkhun, Chitral, Kunar, and Panjkurah rivers drain the territories of Chitral, Dir, and Bajawar, and supply water to some other areas. The Barandu and Kalpanrai are the two main streams, sometimes referred to as rivers, in Bunair.[49]

ETHNICITY

Ethnically, the population of the province has different origins. The ethnological problem of the province, according to C.C. Davies, 'is more complicated and intricate'. Even the 'folklore, traditions and legends are singularly silent about the races who inhabited the frontier prior to the

Pathan invasions'.[50] 'The "Pathans" and "Afghans" are interchangeable terms' that are used for the major ethnic group of the province, but most call themselves Pukhtun (also Pukhtan) or Pushtun (also 'Pashtun' and 'Pashtin') 'in their own language' (Pukhtu or Pushtu or Pashtu or Pashto).[51]

Although the Pukhtu-speaking people of the province are known as Pukhtuns/Afghans/Pathans outside the province, the situation in the province is different.[52] Inside the province, Pukhtuns refer to a specific segment of the population that belongs to the ethnicity by a genealogical line. The artisans and religious segments are not considered Pukhtuns (Pukhtanah). The progeny of those who lose their share in the landed property of the concerned tribe, section, or subsection in some way, or who acquire a religious education and adopt a religious occupation, lose their identity as Pukhtuns after a generation or two as well as their say in the tribal councils or *jargah*s (in Pukhtu: *jargay*).[53] Similarly, there have been cases in which those who were not considered Pukhtuns have been ranked in the segment, over time, after acquiring a share in the tribal landed property in some way.[54]

The Pukhtun population of the province belongs to various tribes. The main tribes are the Yusufzi (formerly pronounced as Isafzi and Yusafzi; now incorrectly as Yusufzai. It is plural: Yusufzi, singular male: Yusufzay, female: Yusufzai), Mandanr, Utman Khail, Safi, Shalmani, Mamund, Muhmand (Mohmand, also Mamand/Mumand), Mulaguri (Mulagori), Dawudzi, Muhammadzi, Gigyani (Gagyani; Gugyani), Khalil, Afridi, Shinwari, Urakzi (Orakzi), Bangash (also Bangakh), Zaimukht, Khatak, Marwat, Banuchi, Turi, Chamkani, Wazir, Mahsud, Bitani, Dawar, Urmar, Dutani (Dotani), Kundi, Luhani (Lohani), Shirani, Mian Khail, Babar, Gandapur, and Sulaiman Khail. It is noteworthy that these tribes reside in the trans-Indus area of the province. The Pukhtuns of the erstwhile tribal and settled areas have been considered 'similar, culturally, linguistically, and racially'.[55]

The Yusufzi and Mandanr have occupied the areas of Dir, Swat, Shanglahpar, Bunair, the Malakand Protected Area (commonly known as the Malakand Agency, and now Malakand District), a large part of the formerly Mardan District till the bank of the Indus, and the western slopes of the Tur Ghar. The Utman Khail, Safi, and Mamund are mainly in Bajawar and in a part of the Malakand Protected Area commonly called Malakand Agency, now Malakand District. The Muhmand (Mamand, Mumand) mainly occupy the Muhmand area, although they are also settled in the Malakand Agency, the Samah area, and the Peshawar region. The Muhammadzi, Dawudzi, Gigyani, and Khalil occupy the Ashnaghar and Peshawar regions. The Shalmani, Mulaguri, Shinwari, and Afridi inhabit the former Khyber Agency (now district). The Urakzi occupy the former Urakzai (Orakzai) Agency (now district). The homeland of the Bangash (also Bangakh) is the Miranzai (Meranzai) Valley in the Kuhat region and the upper Kurram Valley. The Turi and Chamkani reside in the Kurram Valley. The Khatak (Khattak) mainly occupy the Karak and Nawkhar (Nawshirah, Nowshera) regions, and also reside in Samah and the Malakand Protected Area, now Malakand District. The Banuchi occupy the Bannu area, and the Marwat inhabit the Lakki Marwat region. The Wazir, Dawar, Urmar, Bitani (Bittani), Mahsud, Dutani, and Sulaiman Khail inhabit the North and South Waziristan regions. The Kundi, Luhani, Gandapur, Mian Khail, Shirani, and Babar reside in Dirah Ismail Khan.[56] Parts of these tribes also live among other tribes, but they neither have a dominant position in those areas nor do they constitute major groups there. The majority of these tribes inhabit the areas mentioned above, where they constitute the major groups and are dominant.

However, some Pukhtun tribes also inhabit the cis-Indus Hazarah region; they are the Yusufzi, Jadun, and Swati. The Swati are those Pukhtuns who had occupied and inhabited the Swat Valley for centuries, before their departure from Swat at its occupation by the Yusufzi in the sixteenth century. However, it is noteworthy that in a later study Muhammad Akhtar questions the ethnicity of these Swatis as Pukhtuns. He believes that these Swatis were Gabri (Gabari) by religion and Tajak by origin.[57] He successfully proves his hypothesis to the extent that these Swatis were Gabri (fire worshippers) by religion before their conversion to Islam. But, as far his contention about their Tajak origin is concerned, he fails to prove his claim.[58]

People of other ethnic groups also inhabit the province. These include the Awan, Gujar, Tinawli, Dhund, Tajak, and Kashmiri who mostly reside in the cis-Indus Hazarah region. The Gujar inhabit the trans-Indus areas as well. Although Pukhtun tribes also inhabit the Dirah Ismail Khan region of the province, the Baluch and Jat predominate.[59] The Sayyad (Sayyid) are spread throughout the province. It should be noted that Denzil Ibbetson has not ranked the Dalazak, Swati, Jadun, Tinawli, and Shalmani tribes as Pukhtuns but termed them 'allied races, who though not usually acknowledged as Pathans, have by long association become closely assimilated with them in manners, customs, and character', who chiefly reside in the Hazarah area of the province.[60] As already mentioned, the Shalmani are also found in great numbers in the former Khyber Agency (now district) and the Jadun in the trans-Indus Gadun area and on the southern slopes of the Mahabanr Mountain. Hindki (locally called Hindkyan) also inhabit the province: mostly in Peshawar, Kuhat, and Hazarah. Their language is called Hindku. The Parachkan (Parachgan) also inhabit the province, who are a separate ethnic group.[61]

Chitral, too, is inhabited by non-Pukhtun tribes. The occupants of the northern mountainous regions of Dir, Swat, and both sides of the Indus are commonly called Kuhistani (mountain-dwellers), because of the mountainous nature of the area they inhabit. The areas they occupy are known as Dir Kuhistan, Swat Kuhistan, and Abasin (Indus) Kuhistan. They are regarded as 'remnants of the population which existed in Buddhist times'.[62]

GEOSTRATEGIC SIGNIFICANCE

As stated in the beginning, the Khyber Pukhtunkhwa region is of significant geostrategic importance. It has played a remarkable role throughout known history. David Dichter observes:

> Few areas in the world have played so notable a role as a transitional zone between peoples and cultures as the North-West Frontier Region of Pakistan. From a physiographical point of view, the NWF [North-West Frontier] lies between the highland massif of central Asia and the plains of Hindustan. The physical structures which separate these two areas from each other, such as the Hindu Kush range, as well as those structures, which provide access between the areas, such as the Khyber Pass, are located on the Frontier. As a result, the NWF has been the site for a continual cultural flow across its territory. When populations themselves did not move through the Frontier's passes, armies seeking to conquer or control central Asia and northern India have been almost irresistibly attracted to this region. In their language, customs, and features the Pathans themselves reflect the history of the area.[63]

The province is part of the geographical area that includes the passes and routes that have proven to be not only the gateways to India,[64] but also to Central Asia and China. Having been the gateways to India for most of the region's known history, frequent migrations and invasions from Central Asia and the West, to India and further, took place through this area—from the so far believed Aryan migration and invasion which began in about 1900 BCE (the Aryan migration has now been questioned and contested by some circles) to the Greeks, Scythians or Saka, Parthians, Kushans, White Huns, Muslim invasions under the Ghaznavids, the Ghauris, Mongols, Turks (Mughals), Iranians, and on to Ahmad Shah Abdali.

Invasions and expansionist expeditions to Central Asia, from the subcontinent, have also taken place through this area. The expansion of the Mauryan Empire and the Hindu Shahis' encroachments into Afghanistan, Muhammad bin Tughluq's projected expedition into Central Asia, the Indian Mughal rulers' invasions and expeditions into Afghanistan and Central Asia, and the British advances into Afghanistan (in the nineteenth century) are evident examples of the area playing the role of a gateway to Central Asia as well. This role was not limited to the remote past, but was evident in the recent past too—the area remained a base for the anti-Soviet proxy war in Afghanistan in the last quarter of the twentieth century. The war culminated in the failure of the communist revolution in Afghanistan, the withdrawal of Soviet forces from that country, the disintegration of the Soviet Union, and the emergence of the modern Central Asian states and several other states.

The area has continued to play the same role in America and her allies' anti-Taliban and anti-Al-Qaida post 9/11 (2001) war. The consequent military operations, actions, and crackdowns against members of Al-Qaida and its allies in the erstwhile tribal areas, and the unprecedented concentration and posting of a large number of Pakistani armed forces in these areas and along the Pak-Afghan border, is proof of the area's role and significance, even in this age of advanced technology and communication.

In light of the new global political environment and changing scenario on the international stage, the area is becoming a gateway to China as well. It will continue to be so, especially when seen in the context of the USA's endeavours to encircle China; due to its geostrategic location, the area will play a prominent role in any potential Sino-American tussles. In the projected Kashghar-Gwadar transit route, called China Pakistan Economic Corridor (CPEC), too, the province plays the role of gateway to China and vice versa.

As stated earlier, H.C. Verma remarks that battles for the passes, in the regions that now form Afghanistan and Pakistan, were not only a prelude to encroachment over the interior of those regions but over the Indian subcontinent as well, because 'whosoever captured these passes' got 'an edge over their opponents'.[65] But, we have seen that the converse also applied—whosoever captured and held the passes from the Indian/ Pakistani side had an edge over their enemies in Afghanistan and Central Asia—as is evident from the Anglo-Afghan wars of the nineteenth century, the anti-Soviet war in Afghanistan in the twentieth century, and the post 9/11 (2001) war against the Al-Qaida and Taliban suspects and their leaders in these passes and rugged areas.

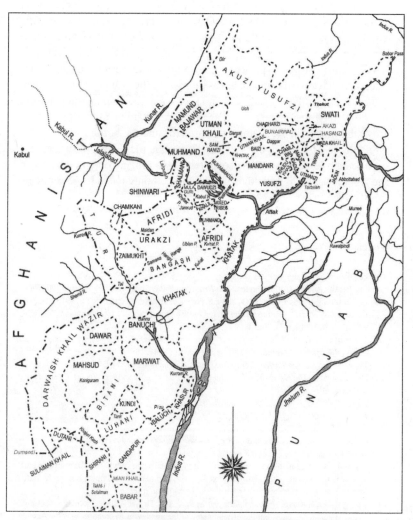

General Pukhtun Tribal Map of Khyber Pukhtunkhwa

James W. Spain rightly states that 'no power—including that of British India at its height—has ever been able to establish full control over the people and the passes of the hills'[66] of this area. Spain's statement holds true even in later time, as is borne out by the post-9/11 situation. In spite of the actions and operations of the Pakistani armed forces in the erstwhile tribal areas and the installation of a large number of Pakistani armed forces on the one side of the Durand Line, and of Afghan, American, and NATO (North Atlantic Treaty Organisation) armed forces on the other side, there have been frequent accusations—by the Afghan and American authorities as well as by the Pakistani side—that the Taliban's actions and activities in Afghanistan, as well as in the Pakistani and other territories, prove that they and their supporters are crossing the border.

The area of the Khyber Pukhtunkhwa has played a prominent and significant role because of its geostrategic location, not only in the remote and recent past but is still doing so and will certainly retain its geostrategic significance in times to come.

Notes

1. For details, see chap. 4 of this book.
2. For details, see C. Collin Davies, *The Problem of the North-West Frontier, 1890–1908: With a survey of policy since 1849*, 2nd edn., rev. and enlarged (London: CPL, 1975), chap. 6; Lal Baha, *N.-W.F.P. Administration under British Rule, 1901–1919* (Islamabad: NCHCR, 1978), chap. 1; chap. 7 of this book.
3. *Imperial Gazetteer of India: Provincial Series; North-West Frontier Province* [henceforward *Imperial Gazetteer of India, NWFP*], repr. (Lahore: SMP, 1991), 1.
4. James W. Spain, *The Pathan Borderland*, repr. (Karachi: IP, 1985), 21.
5. David Dichter, *The North-West Frontier of West Pakistan: A Study in Regional Geography* (London: OUP, 1967), 8.
6. Baha, *N.-W.F.P. Administration under British Rule*, 1–2.
7. *Imperial Gazetteer of India, NWFP*, 1.
8. Spain, *The Pathan Borderland*, 21–2.
9. Abdul Qaiyum, *Gold and Guns on the Pathan Frontier* (Bombay: HK, 1945), 5.
10. *Imperial Gazetteer of India, NWFP*, 1.
11. It should be noted that on the eastern side, it is basically the Indus that, for a greater part, separates the province from Punjab. However, the said districts of Punjab border the Indus in the respective areas, and hence border the province in a sense.
12. Baha, *N.-W.F.P. Administration under British Rule*, 1–2. Dr Lal Baha has sometimes referred to the Malakand Agency, but the official name of the agency, at its creation, was the Agency of Dir and Swat; later, when Chitral was affiliated with the agency in March 1897, it was renamed the Agency of Dir, Swat and Chitral—the name by which she has referred to the agency on occasions.
13. See 'Article 260, The Interim Constitution of the Islamic Republic of Pakistan, 1972', in Safdar Mahmood, *Constitutional Foundations of Pakistan (Enlarged and Revised)* (Lahore: Jang Publishers, 1997), 752.

14. See 'The Constitution of the Islamic Republic of Pakistan [Passed by the National Assembly of Pakistan on the 10th April, 1973 and Authenticated by the President of the National Assembly on the 12th April, 1973]', in Mahmood, *Constitutional Foundations of Pakistan (Enlarged and Revised)*, 969.

15. *Dawn, The Internet edition*, http://www.dawn.com/2004/02/17/local31.htm, accessed: 15 January 2009.

16. For details, see Sher Muhammad Mohmand, *FATA (Federally Administered Tribal Areas of Pakistan): A Socio-Cultural and Geo-Political History* (n.p., n.d.).

17. *Imperial Gazetteer of India, NWFP*, 1.

18. Ibid.

19. Ibid., 2; Spain, *The Pathan Borderland*, 23.

20. Baha, *N.-W.F.P. Administration under British Rule*, 2; *Imperial Gazetteer of India, NWFP*, 2; Spain, *The Pathan Borderland*, 23–4.

21. *Imperial Gazetteer of India, NWFP*, 2; Spain, *The Pathan Borderland*, 24.

22. Spain, *The Pathan Borderland*, 24–5; *Imperial Gazetteer of India, NWFP*, 2.

23. *Imperial Gazetteer of India, NWFP*, 3.

24. Ibid.

25. Ibid., 3–4.

26. Ibid., 107–8.

27. Spain, *The Pathan Borderland*, 22–5.

28. Ibid., 27.

29. H.C. Verma, *Medieval Routes to India: Baghdad to Delhi; A Study of Trade and Military Routes* (Lahore: BT, n.d.), 261.

30. Spain, *The Pathan Borderland*, 25.

31. Baha, *N.-W.F.P. Administration under British Rule*, 3.

32. Spain, *The Pathan Borderland*, 25–6.

33. Ibid., 26–7; Baha, *N.-W.F.P. Administration under British Rule*, 3.

34. For Mahmud of Ghazna or Sultan Mahmud Ghaznavi and his exploits in India, see Muhammad Nazim, *The Life and Times of Sultan Mahmud of Ghazna*, with foreword by Thomas Arnold (Cambridge: At the University Press, 1931); Mohammad Habib, *Sultan Mahmud of Ghaznin*, 2nd edn. (Delhi: SCC, n.d.).

35. For Muhammad Ghauri and his exploits in India, see S.M. Ikram, *A History of Muslim Civilization in India and Pakistan: A Political and Cultural History*, 6th edn. (Lahore: IIC, 1994), chap. 3.

36. For some details of the Malakand wars of 1895 and 1897, see Sultan-i-Rome, 'The Malakand Jihad (1897): An Unsuccessful Attempt to oust the British from Malakand and Chakdara', *JPHS* (Karachi), vol. 43 (Part 2, April 1995), 171–86. Also see H.L. Nevill, *Campaigns on the North-West Frontier*, repr. (Lahore: SMP, 2003), chaps. 12–16.

37. See Khwajah Nizamuddin Ahmad, *The Tabaqat-i-Akbari of Khwajah Nizamuddin Ahmad: (A History of India from the early Musalman invasions to the thirty-eight year of the reign of Akbar)*, vol. 2, trans: Brajendra Nath De, rev. and ed. Baini Prashad (Delhi: LPP, 1992), 609–10. Also see Nizam-ud Din Ahmad Bakhshi, *Tabakat-i Akbari*, trans. and ed. H.M. Elliot and John Dowson, repr. (Lahore: SMP, 2006), 285–6; Mahomed Kasim [Muhammad Qasim] Ferishta, *History of the Rise of the Mahomedan [Muhammadan] Power in India, till the year A.D. 1612*, trans. from the original Persian of Mahomed Kasim Ferishta by John Brigge, vol. 2, repr. (Lahore: SMP, 1977), 259–60; Ahmad Hasan Dani, *Peshawar: Historic City of the Frontier*, [2nd edn.] (Lahore: SMP, 1995), 102. It is to be mentioned that some of the writers have stated that Akbar's forces met this disaster in Malandrai (Mlandarai) Pass. For such contention, see Abu-l-Fazl, *The Akbar Nama of Abu-l-Fazl (History of the reign of Akbar including an Account of His Predecessors)*, trans. from the original Persian by H. Beveridge, vol. 3, repr. (Lahore: SMP, 2005), 573–4; Henry George Raverty, *Notes on*

Afghanistan and Baluchistan, vol. 1, 2nd edn. in Pakistan (Quetta: NT, 1982), 263–4; Vincent A. Smith, *Akbar: The Great Mogul [Mughul], 1542–1605*, 2nd edn., rev. Indian repr. (Delhi: SCC, 1958), 168; Olaf Caroe, *The Pathans: 550 B.C.–A.D. 1957*, repr. (Karachi: OUP, 1976), 215–17; Saranzeb Swati, *Tarikh Riyasat-i Swat* (Pukhtu) (Pikhawar: APH, 1984), 68. Sayyad Bahadar Shah Zafar Kaka Khail, *Pukhtunah da Tarikh pah Ranra kay* (Pukhtu), (Pikhawar: UBA, n.d.), 552–3; Himayatullah Yaqubi, *Mughal-Afghan Relations in South Asia: History and Developments* (Islamabad: NIHCR, 2015), 132. This contention, however, is not sound as the Malandrai debacle was the second one which Akbar's forces sustained two days after that of the Karakar's. See Ahmad, *The Tabaqat-i-Akbari*, vol. 2, 610; Bakhshi, *Tabakat-i Akbari*, 286. See also, Sultan-i-Rome, *Swat Through the Millennia: From Prehistory to the Early Twentieth Century* (Karachi: OUP, 2021), chap. 8.

38. For some details about the significance of the Ambela (Ambilah) Campaign for the British, the fighting, and the significant losses, see W.W. Hunter, *The Indian Musalmans*, with introduction by Bimal Prasad, repr. (New Delhi: Rupa & Co, 2002), chap. 1. Also see Lord Roberts, *Forty-one Years in India: From Subaltern to Commander-in-Chief*, new edn. in one volume, with forty-four illustrations (London: Macmillan and Co., Limited, 1898), chap. 35; Caroe, *The Pathans*, chap. 22.

39. Jean Fairley, *The Lion River: The Indus*, with introduction by Monte Porzio, 1st edn. in Pakistan (Lahore: S.I. Gillani, 1979), 273.

40. *Imperial Gazetteer of India, NWFP*, 4, 109–10, 223; Baha, *N.-W.F.P. Administration under British Rule*, 3. Also see Raza Ali Abidi, *Shir Darya* (Urdu) (Lahore: SMP, 1998); Fairley, *The Lion River*.

41. Baha, *N.-W.F.P. Administration under British Rule*, 3; *Imperial Gazetteer of India, NWFP*, 4.

42. Sultan-i-Rome, 'Swat State under the Walis (1917–69)' (Unpublished PhD Dissertation, Department of History, University of Peshawar, 2000), 21; Sultan-i-Rome, *Swat State (1915–1969): From Genesis to Merger; An Analysis of Political, Administrative, Socio-Political, and Economic Developments* (Karachi: OUP, 2008), 18; *Imperial Gazetteer of India, NWFP*, 4, 116, 216.

43. For details, see Baha, *N.-W.F.P. Administration under British Rule*, chap. 6.

44. For the Mohmand Dam, see *Roznamah Aaj* (Urdu daily, Peshawar), 3 May 2019.

45. Baha, *N.-W.F.P. Administration under British Rule*, 3; *Imperial Gazetteer of India, NWFP*, 4, 118–19.

46. *Imperial Gazetteer of India, NWFP*, 4, 119, 237–8. Also see Baha, *N.-W.F.P. Administration under British Rule*, chap. 6.

47. Spain, *The Pathan Borderland*, 26; *Imperial Gazetteer of India, NWFP*, 4, 119; Baha, *N.-W.F.P. Administration under British Rule*, 3.

48. *Imperial Gazetteer of India, NWFP*, 119–20, 249.

49. Baha, *N.-W.F.P. Administration under British Rule*, 3; *Imperial Gazetteer of India, NWFP*, 223.

50. Davies, *The Problem of the North-West Frontier*, 37–8.

51. Qaiyum, *Gold and Guns on the Pathan Frontier*, 17.

52. For different theories and viewpoints about the origin of the Pukhtuns/Afghans/Pathans, see Khwajah Nimatullah Harwi, *Tarikh Khan Jahani wa Makhzan-i Afghani*, Urdu trans. Muhammad Bashir Husain (Lahore: Markazi Urdu Board, 1978), 31–127; Khwajah Nimatullah Harwi, *History of the Afghans: Translated from the Persian of Neamet Ullah*, trans. Bernhard Dorn, 3rd edn. (Karachi: IP, 2001); Khan Roshan Khan, *Tazkirah (Pathanu ki Asliyat aur un ki Tarikh)* (Urdu), 4th impr. (Karachi: Roshan Khan and Company, 1983), 33–114; Caroe, *The Pathans*, chaps. 1–8; Ghani Khan, *The Pathans: A Sketch*, repr. (Islamabad: PASR, 1990), 3–5; Khushal Khan Khattak, *Dastar Namah* (Pukhtu), with *pishlafz* by Muhammad Nawaz Tair, *pijandgalu* by Purdal Khan Khattak (Pikhawar: PA, 1991), 153–7; Kaka Khail, *Pukhtanah da Tarikh pah Ranra kay*, 14–125; Sayyad Bahadar Shah Zafar Kaka

Khail, *Pushtun: Apni Nasal kay Aayinay mayn* (Urdu) (Peshawar: UBA, 1994); Shaheer Niazi, 'The Origin of the Pathans', *JPHS* (Karachi), vol. 18 (Part 1, January 1970), 23–38; Preshan Khattak, *Pushtun Kaun? (Tarikh, Tahqiq, Tanqid)*, rev. Muhammad Nawaz Tair and Jahanzeb Niyaz (Urdu) (Peshawar: PA, 1984); Mujawar Ahmad Zyar, *Pukhtu aw Pukhtanah da Jabpuhanay pah Ranra kay (Lah Saki Makhinay Sarah)* (Pukhtu) (Pikhawar: Da Sapi Pukhtu Siranu aw Parakhtya Markaz, 2001); chap. 2 of this book.

53. For an example, see A.H. McMahon and A.D.G. Ramsay, *Report on the Tribes of the Malakand Political Agency (Exclusive of Chitral)*, rev. R.L. Kennion (Peshawar: Government Press, North-West Frontier Province, 1916), 17; A.H. McMahon and A.D.G. Ramsay, *Report on the Tribes of Dir, Swat and Bajour* [Bajawar] *together with the Utman-Khel and Sam Ranizai*, repr., ed. with introduction by R.O. Christensen (Peshawar: SBB, 1981), 42.

54. For an example, see Makhdum Tasadduq Ahmad, *Social Organization of Yusufzai Swat: A Study in Social Change* (Lahore: Panjab University Press, 1962), 14, 21–2.

55. Baha, *N.-W.F.P. Administration under British Rule*, 4.

56. For the location of the areas occupied by each one of these tribes, see the map 'The North-West Frontier Province (Approximate Tribal Distribution)' at the end of Davies, *The Problem of the North-West Frontier*. Also see the map in this book, p. 19.

57. See Muhammad Akhtar, *Tajak Swati wa Mumlikat-i Gabar Tarikh kay Aayinah mayn* (Urdu) (Abbottabad: Sarhad Urdu Academy, 2002).

58. Although Muhammad Akhtar has worked hard, and his study is a valuable contribution, it suffers from clearly contradictory statements and contentions because of which his findings and conclusions cannot be accepted in their entirety.

59. Baha, *N.-W.F.P. Administration under British Rule*, 4.

60. Denzil Ibbetson, *Punjab Castes*, repr. (Delhi: LPP, 1993), 64.

61. See Ashraf Faiz, *The Parachgan* (Lahore: The Frontier Post Publications, 1994).

62. Davies, *The Problem of the North-West Frontier*, 39.

63. Dichter, *The North-West Frontier of West Pakistan*, 3.

64. For a viewpoint and discussion of the gates of India, see Thomas Holdich, *The Gates of India: Being an Historical Narrative*, 1st edn. published in Pakistan (Quetta: GA, 1977).

65. Verma, *Medieval Routes to India*, 261.

66. Spain, *The Pathan Borderland*, 27.

2 Origin Of The Pukhtuns: The Bani Israelite, Aryan, and Mixed Race Theories

> O mankind! We created you from a single (pair) of a male
> and a female, and made you into nations and tribes, that ye
> may know each other (not that ye may despise each other).
> Verily the most honoured of you in the sight of Allah is
> (he who is) the most righteous of you. And Allah has full
> knowledge and is well acquainted (with all things).
> – *Al-Quran*, 49:13

THE MAJORITY of the inhabitants of Khyber Pukhtunkhwa are ethnically Pukhtun (Pukhtanah)—also spelled and pronounced as Pakhtun, Pakhtoon, Pashtun, Pashtoon, Pushtun, Pushtoon, and Pashtin. The majority of the inhabitants of Afghanistan, and a significant portion of the population of Baluchistan, Sindh, and Punjab are also ethnically Pukhtun. A large number of the Pukhtuns have merged with the populations of India and other parts of the world. They are also called Afghans and Pathans. Different writers, Pukhtun and non-Pukhtun, have used these three names—Afghans, Pukhtuns, and Pathans—for the same people. The question is: who are the Pukhtuns or Afghans or Pathans by origin or ethnicity?

C. Collin Davies observes that 'no ethnological problem is more complicated and intricate than' the one 'presented by the North-West Frontier of India'.[1] The question of the origin or ethnicity of the Pukhtuns has recently become quite complicated. A number of scholars, writers and historians have spent their lives trying to untangle this problem. They have either put forth their own theories and contentions or endorsed those of others. As a result, over the course of time, a number of theories have been presented. Three of these, namely, the Bani Israelite Theory, the Aryan Race Theory, and the Mixed Race Theory, are prominent.

Of the other theories, a few are: the Banu Qaturite Theory, according to which Pukhtuns are the descendants of Prophet Ibrahim (Alayhi-

Salam: henceforward AS) by his wife Qaturah and, hence, Banu Qaturah;[2] Khushal (Khushhal) Khan Khattak's Theory, according to which they are the descendants of the brother of Prophet Ibrahim (Abraham [AS]);[3] the Saka Origin Theory, which is based on philological arguments and evaluation, and according to which they are Saka by origin;[4] and the Greek Origin Theory, according to which they are Greek by origin or ethnicity. Here, in this chapter, we will discuss the Bani Israelite, Aryan, and Mixed Race theories.

THE BANI ISRAELITE THEORY[5]

Israel, meaning night-runner, was the surname of Prophet Yaqub (Jacob [AS]), while Bani means progeny; hence, Bani Israel means the progeny of Prophet Yaqub (AS). The Bani Israelite Theory, about the origin of the Pukhtuns, is the first and best-known theory. It has been known of, presented, and preserved in written form since it was put on paper between 1609–1612 CE by Khwajah Nimatullah bin Habibullah of Herat, also known as Khwajah Nimatullah Harwi.

It has been contended that this theory was written at the command of Khan Jahan Ludi (Lodi), during the reign of the Mughal Emperor Jahangir, to negate the propaganda against the Pukhtuns.[6] But Nimatullah Harwi has put forth his reason for writing the history and the theory as follows:

> Yet of the prosperous state of the affairs of the Afghan Nation, relative to their number, increase of Tribes, and conversion to Islamism [Islam], nothing at all has hitherto been satisfactorily recorded in any book or history; owing to which circumstance, the links of their genealogy, as well as the cause of their transmigration [emigration] to the countries of Roh [Ruh] and Koh Suleiman [Kuh Sulaiman], have remained quite unknown and unnoticed.[7]

Also, that 'the history of this exalted nation has not been written by any Historian of the time', and that none of those who have written in the last period 'had sufficiently and satisfactorily traced the pedigree of the nation in question, to exhibit it in perfect clearness'.[8]

Nimatullah Harwi has further stated that he undertook to write the history of the Afghans from the beginning of their origin, going as far back as their ancestor, Prophet Yaqub (AS), with the assistance of Haibat Khan Kakar bin Salim Khan of Samana, who was an attendant of Khan Jahan Ludi and who collected and arranged the scattered and confused genealogy of the Afghans for him. Harwi states that he had tried to fully and clearly elucidate, to the greatest possible extent, the events during the reign of Talut up to the time of Abdur Rashid; and that, in this work, he had made selections from authentic histories, such as *Tarikh Tabari*, *Majma-ul-Ansab*, *Guzaidah Jahankushayi*, *Mutla-ul-Anwar*, and *Madan Akhbar Ahmadi*; and that he had named his work *Makhzan-i Afghani*.[9]

Starting from Adam (AS), Nimatullah Harwi has given the history and genealogical narration in descending order until Prophet Nuh (Noah [AS])—and then to Yaqub (AS), surnamed Israel. He further states that Yaqub (AS) was blessed with twelve sons, born to his 'two wives and two concubines'. They were Yahuda, Ruyel, Simeon (Shamun), Levi (Lavi), Manun, and Isashar (Yashjar) 'from his chief consort Lea' (Liyyah); Yusuf and Benjamin (Bin Yamin) from Rahil; Koslan (Fuzlan) and Dan from Zilfa; and Ziad (Ziyad) and Shari (Shiri) from another concubine. The twelve tribes that sprung from Yaqub's (AS) twelve sons were called Bani Israel, or the Children of Israel, from Yaqub's (AS) surname 'Israel' which the Almighty 'had conferred upon him'.[10]

The lineage of the Afghans (Pukhtuns) descends from Yaqub's (AS) eldest son Yahuda. Sarugh (Asru) was the eldest son of Yahuda and became his successor. He had a son called Knokh (Akhnuj), whose son was Muhalab, whose son was Kali (Fali), whose son was Qays, whose son was Sarul who became famous by the name Talut[11] and to whom the genealogy of the Afghans has been traced.

Over the course of time, as the Bani Israel grew in number, they disregarded the teachings of the Divine Law, and so earned the condemnation of the Almighty and were subjected to Pharaoh's atrocities. Although they were restored to their former glory at the end of the punishment, they again resorted to insubordination of the Divine orders and, hence, were subjected to the rule and atrocities of the Amalekites (Amaliqah). During this time, the Almighty sent Prophet Ismuel (AS), with prophetic responsibilities, to the Israelites. They asked Ismuel (AS) to solicit the Almighty to send a king for them under whose command they might fight against Jalut (Goliath), the Amalekite King, and their other enemies. Consequently, under the instructions of the Almighty, Prophet Ismuel (AS) appointed Sarul, surnamed Talut, as the King of the Israelites. He was said to be the son of Qays, who in turn was said to be the descendant of Bin Yamin (Benjamin) son of Yaqub (AS); according to another version, he was the descendant of Yaqub's (AS) son, Yahuda.[12]

The Israelites were not ready to recognise Talut as their king and argued with Ismuel (AS) at length, but in vain. Faced with Ismuel's (AS) remonstrations and continuous threats about the vengeance and wrath of the Almighty, the Israelites became apprehensive and declared their willingness to recognise Talut as their ruler, but with some conditions. When their conditions were met, the Israelites 'offered up prayers to the Almighty; and conferring, in obedience to Ismuel, the royal title upon Talut, placed him' on the throne and all twelve tribes submitted completely to his authority.[13]

After many years, the Almighty asked Ismuel (AS) to tell Talut to declare war on Jalut's people. At this, Talut called the chiefs of the empire and informed them of the Divine injunction. The Israelites assembled, without objection or reluctance from any quarter, 'an army of seventy thousand of the bravest cavalry' under the command of the king. All joined the army except the old, the sick, and the children. On the other side, Jalut had 'eight hundred thousand' horses under his command. Skirmishes continued between the opposing forces for eleven days, during which they retreated to their entrenchments at night. Then Jalut sent a proposal to Talut: 'How long shall we sacrifice human life, by carrying on war in this way? Come out in the morning, that we may meet in single combat; on condition' that if you should 'kill me, my whole possessions belong to' you 'but in case I should take' your life, your kingdom becomes mine; should you, however, 'not like to stand forward in person, send another one to fight me'.[14]

This proposition Talut disclosed to Ismuel; who being perplexed by it, was informed, by divine intimation, that there was a person amongst the Israelites, a father of twelve sons, the youngest of whom, called Davud [Dawud], was destined to put Jalut to death; in remuneration of which, Talut should be obliged to make him his son-in-law, and to resign to him part of the monarchy. Ismuel, extremely rejoiced at this agreeable intelligence, began to enter upon a diligent search, and succeeded in finding him. On his standing forward with his twelve sons, the Prophet asked which was Davud, in whose hand God had placed Jalut's death; and being pointed out to him, he seized his hand, put it into Talut's, and at the same time mentioned the partition of the power about to be made: after which, Davud, with his father and brothers, repaired to their home, agitated with apprehension and hope. On their arrival, however, they cheered their spirits, convinced that Ismuel's command would be in entire conformity with the divine will; and in the same night Davud heard a voice saying, 'Davud, Jalut is to be killed by thee with the stone of a sling: take, therefore, these three stones, and preserve them,' which he did accordingly. The next day Jalut proceeded to the field of combat, clad in complete armour, with a helmet upon his head, and seated upon a Mankulusian elephant; and Talut, after having furnished Davud likewise with a complete armour, sent him forth to meet his opponent. Having first pronounced the name of the All-powerful God, he put a stone into his sling; and taking aim at Jalut, lodged it in his forehead: the second stone struck him behind the ear, and the third he directed against the forehead of the elephant; and both Jalut and the animal fell down on the ground, and the former delivered his soul to the guardians of hell. At this very moment Talut ordered a general attack upon the hostile army, who were either slain or taken prisoners; and such a quantity of effects, jewels, and cattle fell into the hands of the army of the faithful, that it baffled all description. Davud seating himself upon Jalut's throne, rode back to his camp in triumph and glory, and the whole hostile kingdom was subjugated to the true believers.[15]

'In fulfilment of the command' of the Almighty and 'the Prophet', Talut married his daughter to Dawud (AS), gave him a share in his kingdom, entrusted him with 'uncontrolled administration of the most important affairs', and bestowed Jalut's kingdom upon him. The Israelites were pleased with Dawud (AS) because of his 'excellent conduct'. Not only did they praise him lavishly, they also placed themselves under his protection in vast numbers. All this made Talut jealous of Dawud (AS), and so he hatched a plot to murder him. The plan, however, was disclosed to Dawud (AS) by a relative of Talut's who bore him a grudge. Dawud's (AS) wife also told him about Talut's visit to their house, inquiring about the location of Dawud's (AS) bedroom and inspecting his 'sleeping apartment'. Hence, Talut's attempt failed. On the other hand, Dawud (AS) demonstrated that while he could take Talut's life, he refrained from doing so because of what he owed to Talut and, instead, fled. Dawud's (AS) escape made Talut more apprehensive and repressive. In a short period, he had 'thirty thousand' people killed; his repressive measures and atrocities abounded.[16]

However, while on a hunting expedition, an event occurred that changed his outlook on life. Seeking salvation, he was told that despite the burden of his sins, his repentance would be accepted and he would achieve salvation, 'after having resigned' his 'kingdom to Davud' (AS), and his marching out, along with his ten sons, to die as martyrs in combat against the infidels—martyrdom was the route that could ensure salvation for him. On returning from the hunting expedition, he apprised the Israelites of the means for his salvation, as was revealed to him, and asked them to search for Dawud (AS). He was ready to hand-over 'all his power to him', and then to leave to die in a battle against the infidels. Dawud (AS) was found, and placed on Talut's throne. Among the information imparted to him (by Talut) was the disclosure that two of Talut's wives were pregnant, and that Ismuel (AS) had revealed that two male children would be born to Talut (one to each wife) whose descendants, besides other facts, would 'be registered in the Book of Time' until 'the day of resurrection'. 'This done', Talut 'invaded the frontier of the infidels' and, 'together with his ten sons', died a martyr's death.[17]

Dawud (AS) treated the two bereaved widows with great kindness; both of them gave birth to one son each 'at the same hour'. One of them was named Barkhya (Berkhia), and the other Armya (Ermia). Dawud (AS) arranged for their education. When they came of age, each one was entrusted with the government of a tribe of Israelites. They distinguished themselves, by dint of their merit and services, under Dawud (AS). He put Barkhya in charge of 'civil affairs' (minister) and Armya in charge 'of the military department' (commander-in-chief). Each of them was blessed with a son. Barkhya's son was named Asif, and Armya's son was named Afghana. 'Splendid festivals' were arranged at their births and endeavours were made to educate them properly. When Asif and Afghana reached adulthood, their fathers died, upon which Dawud (AS) bestowed Barkhya's designation on his son Asif, and Armya's on his son Afghana.[18]

On Dawud's (AS) death, his son Sulayman (Sulaiman AS) succeeded him, both onto the throne and in prophethood. He assigned the duties of civil administration to Asif who distinguished himself in performing the duties of the *wazarat* (ministership). He made Afghana, who had won the hearts of the 'people by his vigilance and military abilities', the commander-in-chief of the army. Sulayman (AS) also wanted to complete work on the al-Aqsa mosque, the foundation of which had been laid by Dawud (AS). Afghana, who was assigned the responsibility for supervising its construction, commanded 'eighty thousand porters, janitors, and assistants' to complete the edifice. Construction was completed in forty years under his supervision. Both Asif and Afghana became men of great repute. Sulayman (AS) 'never undertook any thing [anything] without their advice and co-operation'. Asif had eighteen, and Afghana forty sons. The descendants of Afghana increased to such an extent 'that no tribe of the Israelites equalled them'. Asif and Afghana held their posts at Jerusalem and exercised an absolute authority over the Israelites until their deaths, and even then, their descendants remained in the land.[19]

With the passage of time, the Israelites deviated from the righteous path and so were subjected to the wrath of the Almighty. The Almighty let Bukhtunasar (Nebuchednezzar, 630–562 BCE) 'subjugate the territories of Sham' (Syria), raze Jerusalem (586 BCE) and 'vanquish the Israelites', 'carry their families into captivity and slavery, and drive all those who had faith in the Tora [*Taurat*] into exile'. The Israelites, especially the descendants of Asif and Afghana, settled in the mountainous districts of Ghaur, Ghazni, Kabul, Qandahar, Kuh Firuzah, and 'the parts lying within the fifth and sixth climates' (Aqalim). They continually grew in number, declared war on the surrounding infidels and held the areas till the time of Mahmud of Ghazna (998–1030 CE) and Shahabuddin Ghauri (d. 1206 CE).[20]

After the expulsion of the descendants of Asif and Afghana, by Bukhtunasar, from Sham, 'some sought shelter in Arabia' and took up their abode in the vicinity of Makkah; 'the Arabs calling them Israelites' and the 'Children of Afghana'. After the passage of 'one thousand five hundred years' after Sulayman (AS), Allah Almighty blessed Muhammad (*Sallalahu Alaihi wa Alihi wa Sallam*: henceforth S.A.W.) with prophethood. Among the descendants of Afghana, who settled in Makkah, was Walid bin Utbah bin Akramah. Walid had two sons, Khalid bin Walid and Walid bin Walid. Khalid bin Walid was among those who were staunch opponents of Islam at the beginning, and even fought against the Muslims (in the Battle of Uhud, 625 CE), but then embraced Islam after the Treaty of Hudaybiyah (concluded between the Prophet Muhammad [S.A.W.] and the Quraysh in 628 CE), becoming an ardent follower and great champion of Islam. He 'sent a letter to the Afghans who had been settled in the mountainous countries' about Ghaur, informing them of the appearance of the Last Prophet (S.A.W.). At this, several chiefs of the Ghaurid Afghans left for Madinah, the chief one being Qays, 'whose pedigree ascends in a series of thirty-seven degrees [steps] to Talut, of forty-five to Ibrahim [AS], and of six hundred and three to Adam [AS]'.[21]

On arrival at Madinah, the deputation embraced Islam under Khalid's (*Raziyallahu Anhu*: henceforth RA) guidance and the Prophet (S.A.W.) 'lavished all sorts of blessings upon' its members. The Prophet (S.A.W.) retained the names of all the members, except that of Qays. He stated that while they were Arabs, Qays was a Hebrew name, and so gave Qays the name of Abdur Rashid. The Prophet (S.A.W.) told them that being the progeny of King (Malik) Talut, 'whom the Almighty had mentioned in the sublime' Quran, they too should be called *malik* (in Pukhtu: *malak*). When the Prophet (S.A.W.) left Madinah for Makkah, to annihilate the army of Makkah, he placed Khalid bin Walid (RA) and Qays (Abdur Rashid), at the head of a force which distinguished itself by its great feats. The Prophet (S.A.W.) predicted that the Almighty would give Abdur Rashid so many children that they 'would outvie all other people', in establishing the Faith. The angel Gabriel (Jabrail) revealed, to him, that the strength of their adherence to the Faith would 'be like the wood upon which they lay the keel when constructing a ship': the wood 'seamen call Pathan'. Hence, the Prophet (s.a.w.) conferred, upon Abdur Rashid, 'the title of Pathan also'.[22]

The Prophet (s.a.w.), 'at length', asked Abdur Rashid 'to return to' Ghaur and 'the adjacent Kohistan...to propagate the new faith' there, and 'to direct the infidels' towards it. He died in 41 AH (661 CE) at the age of eighty-seven years. Abdur Rashid had three sons. He named the eldest, Sarbani (سربني); the second, Bitani (بيتني); and the third, Ghurghusht (غورغشت). From each of these three, 'descended sons and tribes, on such a scale as to surpass all conception'.[23]

AKHUN DARWIZAH'S VERSION

Another writer, Akhun Darwizah, wrote *Tazkiratul Abrar-i wal Ashrar*,[24] in 1021 AH[25] (1612 CE): a contemporary work of *Tarikh Khan Jahani wa Makhzan-i Afghani*. We need to examine it in order to assess and judge the validity of the theory in perspective.

Writing about the genealogy of the Afghans, Akhun Darwizah has stated that Prophet Ibrahim (AS) had two sons, Ismail (AS) and Ishaq (AS). Ishaq (AS) had a son named Yaqub (AS) who had twelve sons, one of whom was Yahuda in whose family rested the kingship of the Israelites. When the Bani Israel (Israelites)—the descendants of Yaqub (AS)—disregarded the teachings of their Prophet (AS) and began leading increasingly sinful lives, Jalut, an enemy who was strong both in power and personal strength, conquered, suppressed, and tyrannised them. Finally, they requested their Prophet, Samuel (AS), to appoint a king among them so that they might fight under his command against the enemy. On their pledge that they would obey the command of the king and would accompany him to fight the enemy, the Prophet (AS) prayed to the Almighty. His prayer was honoured and, per the command of the Almighty, the Prophet (AS) appointed Talut, a descendant of Bin Yamin, as their king. After some hesitation and discussion, the Israelites recognised Talut as their king. Talut, too, had reservations about the kingship but became relieved by the solace offered by the Prophet (AS).[26]

Talut led the Israelites against Jalut but, having defied his instructions—about not drinking from a stream on their way to battle—only 313 of the 70,000 men reached the battlefield. One of the 313 was Dawud (AS), a very strong young man who had just reached adolescence and was not yet blessed with prophethood. On the way, a stone spoke to him and asked him to pick it up for it would help him. Two other stones did the same.

He picked them up and placed them in his bag, upon which all the three united into one.[27]

Both the armies faced each other: Jalut's forces comprised 700,000 people, while Talut had 313. Jalut offered to duel but there was no one of his stature and strength, among Talut's followers, to enter into combat with him. At this, Dawud (AS) offered to face him. Talut told Dawud (AS) that he did not possess the strength and power that were required. But, Dawud (AS) insisted that he was sufficiently able and skilled. When Talut retorted that a child also considers himself to be sufficiently skilled, Dawud (AS) asked Talut how he would be rewarded should he kill Jalut. Talut offered his daughter in marriage and half of his kingdom. Dawud (AS), dressed in war attire and armed with the stone and a catapult, stood before Jalut. Placing the stone in the catapult, he hit Jalut in the head with full force. The stone bulleted into Jalut's forehead and split into three: one went through the right side of his head, one through the left, and one straight through. Jalut was knocked down and his forces soon defeated.[28]

Dawud (AS) now asked Talut to fulfil his promise. Talut married his daughter to Dawud (AS) but did not keep his word about half the kingdom. This remained a point of dispute between the two until Talut decided to murder Dawud (AS). Talut's daughter (Dawud's [AS] wife) discovered and disclosed the plot to Dawud (AS). On confirmation of the plot, Dawud (AS) fled to the mountains. After some time, he came back and the Almighty blessed him with both the entire kingdom and prophethood, on Talut's death.[29]

Dawud (AS) was succeeded by Sulayman (AS). Malik (*malak* in Pukhtu) Talut had left two sons: Asif and Afghan. Asif was appointed Wazir (minister), because of his qualities of head and heart, while Afghan was made jailer (Akhun Darwizah's Persian words are سجانش گردانید *sajanash gardanid*), because of his qualities. The descendants and tribes of the progeny of Afghan (Talut's son) are said to be the lost tribe of Bani Israelites, but are considered dead. The Afghans, because of their pride and self-consciousness, did not recognise the kingship of one of their own race as they considered themselves equals and were not prepared to serve and obey a relative of theirs. It is for this reason that Afghans are called '*malik*' in their country. The second reason for the title '*malik*' is that the Almighty had termed Talut as *malik* in the Holy Quran, after which all Afghans are called *malik*.[30]

This group of Afghans resided in the Sulaiman Range (due to which they are called Sulaymani in Arabia) until the prophethood of the Prophet Muhammad (S.A.W.). When people from Arabia and Ajam came to the

Prophet (s.a.w.) and accepted Islam, a delegation of seventy Afghan *maliks* also visited him and embraced Islam. Afterwards, they took the news of the prophethood of the last Prophet (s.a.w.) to their own people and all of them, in unison along with their families, embraced Islam. In the fighting with the infidels, the Afghan women joined the war on the Muslims' side. They collected arrows for, and carried water to, those fighting for the Almighty. The Holy Prophet (s.a.w.) did not prohibit them from doing so.[31]

Once the Prophet (s.a.w.) remarked that all Afghans would be thrown into Hell on the Day of Judgement. When the Afghans learnt of this, they were infuriated and concerned and asked to be allowed to go to their homeland to apprise their people about the remarks. When this news was brought to the Prophet (s.a.w.), he asked them the reason for their resentment and dissension. The Afghans told him that if, in spite of their sacrifices for the cause of Islam, their destiny was Hell then there was no reason for them to fight. The Prophet (s.a.w.) told them that he had not spoken about them, but about their descendants, and then explained his reason to them. The Afghans chose to stay in Qandahar area and did not go to any other country until their departure for India with Mahmud of Ghazna.[32]

OTHER POINTS

There are other points which, although not found in the interpretations of the theory by Nimatullah Harwi (whom critics of the theory consider its founder and main proponent) and Akhun Darwizah, have been brought up in other interpretations of the theory, such as that relating to the marriage of Khalid bin Walid's (RA) daughter with Qays, and the origin of the Pukhtu language. It is claimed that after Qays embraced Islam, Khalid bin Walid (RA) gave his daughter, Sarah, in marriage to him.[33] It is also said that the Pukhtu language, introduced by Afghana, is a changed form of Hebrew; it was in this language that Prophet Sulayman (AS) used to converse with Asif and Afghana, in the presence of other people, about confidential matters.[34]

Another important and noteworthy point relating to the Bani Israelite Theory about the origin of the Pukhtuns is the taunt that the Pukhtuns are the progeny of the demon (Diw, Dev, Dio[35]). It is claimed that Mughal court historians invented obscenities and baseless stories to debase and demoralise the Pukhtuns. The latter were the rivals of the Mughals in India. Once a Persian envoy of Emperor Shah Abbas Safawi remarked, to the amusement of the courtiers, in the court of the Mughal Emperor Jahangir and in the presence of a large number of courtiers, including some Pukhtuns as well, that he had read that the Pukhtuns were the progeny of Diw.[36] This was seen as a wilful attempt to debase the Pukhtuns. Consequently, the Pukhtun *umara* (nobles) resolved to negate the assertion and prove themselves racially superior, resulting in the invention of the Bani Israelite Theory, compiled by Nimatullah Harwi.[37]

Related to this narrative about the demon is the story that a tyrannical ruler of Iran, Zahak, was told that there was a place towards the west where the women were as beautiful as fairies. So, Zahak sent a general, named Nariman, there. After a great battle, Nariman took possession of 1,000 girls. Night fell while they were still on a mountain where an ill-natured demon lived. That night, the demon attacked the army. As a result of which some soldiers were killed, while others fled. Then, having violated the chastity of the girls, the demon disappeared. In the morning, Nariman collected his remaining army and the girls to take them to Zahak. But, when Zahak heard what had happened, he got angry and ordered that the girls be left on the mountain. There, they gave birth to children who later multiplied. These are the people who are called the Afghans.[38]

There is also the issue of Asli Afaghinah and Wasli Afaghinah. The progeny of the three sons of Qays, also known as Abdur Rashid, namely Sarban (سربن), Ghurghusht (غورغشت), and Bitan (بیتن), are considered Asli Afaghinah (اصلی افاغنه real Afghans), and the Matuzi (متوزي) and Karlanri (کرلانی) tribes are considered Wasli Afaghinah (وصلی افاغنه allied or adopted Afghans).[39] This resembles the Arabs who are considered Arab Aribah—real Arabs—and Arab Mustaribah—adopted or naturalised Arabs.

KHUSHAL KHAN'S VERSION

It is imperative to give Khushal (Khushhal) Khan Khattak's version about the origin of the Pukhtuns, in order to critically evaluate the Bani Israelite Theory with a proper and true perspective.

Khushal Khan Khattak states that he had heard and read a number of opinions about the origin of the Pukhtuns; and had gone beyond the bounds of research on the topic—examining histories and genealogical tables. While, in one book the Pukhtuns have been identified as the descendants of Yafas bin Nuh (AS), in another they have been identified as Qibtis, the people of Firun (Pharaoh), and in a third as the offspring of Yaqub's (AS) son, Yahuda. Yet others have included them with the Kurds.

Khushal Khan Khattak claims that no one would have taken greater pains than him to determine the genealogy of the Pukhtuns and that, beyond all doubt, all Pukhtuns are the progeny of the brother of Prophet Ibrahim (AS).[40]

Khushal Khan Khattak states that Pukhtuns are too numerous to give details of their tribes and sub-tribes. However, should he be released from Rantanbur (Ranthambore: a strong fort on a hill in Rajasthan, India), he would write a detailed history. In the summarised version, starting with his own grandson—Afzal Khan—he has worked upwards. According to him, Burhan (later also known as Bahram and Barahim) had three sons: Luqman, also known as Khattak; Sulayman, the Afridi; and Utman, the Utman Khail. The Burhan and Zidran are the descendants of the Kaudi, and are more numerous than the Karranri. The Dalazak and the Urakzi are from one father. Abdur Rahman, Shairzad, Hizar Khail, and all the Khugyani are from another father. Shitak, Halim, and all the Kiwi are from yet another father. Suranray and Dawar are close to one another. The Turay and the Zazi are close. All the Wazir, Wardak, Dakhail, Hunay, Mingli, and Dani are Karranri. Kaudi had six sons; all the mentioned tribes among the Pukhtuns are their offspring. The Karlanri is Dani, and brought up by Urmar, meaning they are the progeny of Sarabani (Sarbani). All the Pukhtuns are descendants of Sharkbun and Kharshbun.[41]

Continuing, Khushal Khan Khattak states that, he saw in authentic history, the infant Prophet Danyal (AS)—Daniel—was separated from his mother in a desert due to an incident. The Almighty made a lioness look after him. She took him on her cave, suckled him with her milk, and nourished the exalted Prophet (AS) with her breasts till he grew up as a lion. Once a king, on a hunting expedition, saw Danyal (AS) at the mouth of the lioness' cave. Surprised, the king took him to his house and began to educate him. With the passage of time, Danyal (AS) was blessed with prophethood and was distinguished with a state and kingship. He engraved the figure of a lion on his stamp. When [Bukhtunasar, accursed] conquered [quarter of][42] the inhabited world, he conquered Bait-ul-Muqadas (Masjid al-Aqsa in Jerusalem). Prophet Danyal (AS) was caught by the vicious king and imprisoned. Expelled from that country, along with his nation, he was forced to live in Kirman and Sistan. A group of his followers remained in Arabia, in the vicinity of Makkah. Khalid bin Walid (RA) is from that group. In short, Arabia remained their abode until the time when Prophet Muhammad (S.A.W.) was blessed with prophethood. They continued to bear the highhandedness and tyrannies of the Zoroastrians. When, during the Umayyad reign, the army of Islam invaded Khurasan, the whole nation became the advance guard of the army of Islam due to the affinity with Khalid's progeny, and conquered the country till the land of Sindh. Their origin is from Prophet Danyal (AS) and they embraced Islam during the Khilafat of the Umayyads.[43]

Khushal Khan has further contended that Danyal (AS) was a descendant of Malak Talut who, in turn, was a descendant of the brother of Prophet Ibrahim (AS). The bravery and valour found in the Pukhtuns are the effects of the milk of that lioness. The title *malak* is because of the relationship with Malak Talut. When the Arabs came to Khurasan, they were aware of the lineage of the Pukhtuns, so, when the Pukhtuns accepted Islam, the Arabs told them that, as they were the progeny of Malak Talut, they can retain their title, viz. *malak*. The descendants of Subuktigin, who were the rulers of Ghazni, bestowed the title of Pathan upon them. Sultan Mahmud went to Gujrat in the *ghaza* (holy war) of Sumnat (Somnath). During this expedition the Pukhtuns showed gallantry. The Sultan told them that they were the Patan (پتان) of his army. Patan is a timber upon which ships were built. Arkhya, Malak Talut's son, won the title of Afghan during the days of king Sulayman (AS). In Hebrew, Af (اف) means catching; Ghan (غان) was the name of a demon (Diw), viz. *diwgir*, so *diwgir* is the one who caught the Ghan demon. The Ghan demon was caught by Arkhya, which is why the Uzbaks (Uzbeks) say that they are the progeny of Barkhya and the Pukhtuns are of Arkhya. Allah knows the facts best.[44]

It is noteworthy that those, whether Pukhtun or non-Pukhtun, who wrote about the origin and ethnicity of the Pukhtuns/Pathans/Afghans did not mention Khushal Khan's theory and have ignored his contention. Only in Bahadar Shah Zafar Kaka Khail's book *Pushtun: Apni Nasal kay Aayinay mayn*[45] (in which he too dealt with the question of the origin of the Pukhtuns/Afghans/Pathans) and Preshan Khattak's book *Pushtun Kaun? (Tarikh, Tahqiq, Tanqid)*[46] are there stray references to Khushal Khan's version.

The main points to be inferred from Khushal Khan's versions are:

1. There are different viewpoints about the origin of the Pukhtuns, at least since the seventeenth century.
2. The Pukhtuns are the progeny of Prophet Ibrahim's (AS) brother. Hence, they are not Bani Israel, although Semitic in origin.
3. The Pukhtuns are the progeny of Malak Talut from his son Arkhya (Armya of the Bani Israelite Theory).
4. Khushal Khan, too, has mentioned and believed in the forced migration or transportation and settlement of the progeny of Talut

to the east, along with the settlement of a group of them in the vicinity of Makkah, whose descendant was Khalid bin Walid (RA).

5. The name Afghan has not been given by the Arabs or Iranians (Persians), but is a Hebrew word and hence an ancient one.

6. The Arabs knew the Pukhtuns' origin and, hence, retained the title *malak* for them.

7. The title Pathan was not given by Prophet Muhammad (S.A.W.) nor by the Indians but by Mahmud of Ghazna, referring to the Pukhtuns as the rudder and keel of his forces.

8. Pukhtuns have relationship with lions, and possess a lion's qualities, because a lioness had been Prophet Danyal's (AS) foster mother and wet nurse.

9. Khushal Khan has considered the lioness' story true, having read in authentic history. (Although he did not mention the name of the book, he calls it authentic history).

10. The Pukhtuns embraced Islam in the Umayyads' reign.

11. All the Pukhtuns are the offspring of Sharkbun (شرکبون) and Kharshbun (خرشبون).

CRITICAL EVALUATION

It is evident, from the above, that the Pukhtuns are considered the progeny of Talut. According to common belief, Talut was a descendant of Prophet Yaqub (AS), also known as Israel; hence, the Pukhtuns are Bani Israel by origin. This theory was commonly believed for centuries, if not for millennia, until it was questioned by European scholars in the nineteenth century. Since then, the theory has remained a bone of contention between those who discard it outright or at least do not believe in it in its given form, and those who still believe in it and defend it. Below are the main points, and the evaluation of the points, of those who do not agree with the theory, and then some points of those who defend the theory.

Those who advocate that the Bani Israelite Theory is not sound contend, besides other things, that:

1. The portions of the theory related to the Israelites do not corroborate entirely with the contentions of *Taurat* (*Tora* or *Old Testament*). For instance, there are discrepancies between the contentions of the theory, and that of the *Taurat* regarding Dawud's (AS) marriage to Talut's daughter; the giving of a share of his kingdom to Dawud (AS) by Talut; Dawud's (AS) flight and subsequent return; Talut's

repentance followed by his fighting the infidels along with his ten sons, leaving his two pregnant wives in the guardianship of Dawud (AS); and the construction of the al-Aqsa mosque under the supervision of Afghana.

2. There was no one named Afghana during the entire reign of Prophet Sulayman (AS).

3. The theory refers to the attack by Bukhtunasar (Nebuchadnezzar) after the reign of Prophet Sulayman (AS) but does not refer to the approximately 400 intervening years.

4. Before Bukhtunasar, the Sumerian kingdom of the Israelites was attacked by the Assyrian (Achaemenid) king, Salman Sar (Salmanasar), who imprisoned the Israelites and then expelled them from their homeland. The expelled Israelites were settled in the cities of Medes. Hence, there is no possibility of flight by the ten tribes of Israelites as a result of Bukhtunasar's ravages.

5. Bukhtunasar's Babul kingdom was destroyed by Cyrus (Kurush), who freed the Israelites. They then returned to Palestine where they were busy with the reconstruction of their homeland; hence their settlement in the mountains of Ghaur does not corroborate.

6. The contentions about the Pukhtu language and the remarks of the Prophet Muhammad (S.A.W.) about Pukhtu are not sound, and reveal that the writers of the theory did not know the Pukhtu language; otherwise, they would not have made such a contention.[47]

Sadullah Jan Barq raises a question about this portion of the theory, and also attempts to compare the nature and behaviour of the Pukhtuns and the Jews, to disprove the theory.[48]

Besides, critics have also taken into account the portion of the theory that is related to the Muslims period and history. The main points inferred from their arguments are:

1. Khalid bin Walid (RA) was an Arab, from the Bani Makhzum branch of the Quraysh tribe. As the Bani Makhzum descended from Prophet Ismail (AS), the son of Prophet Ibrahim (AS) and half-brother of Prophet Ishaq (AS), the connection between the Bani Israel of Ghaur and Khalid bin Walid (RA) is baseless.

2. There is no proof from the history of the Muslims that a delegation from Ghaur visited Prophet Muhammad (S.A.W.) in Madinah and embraced Islam; or that the delegates took part in the conquest of Makkah; or that Khalid bin Walid (RA) married his daughter to

Qays, the head of the delegation; or that the Prophet (s.a.w.) sent them back to Ghaur; or that, on the return of the delegation, all the Bani Israel residing in Ghaur embraced Islam *en masse*.

3. The Pukhtuns did not embrace Islam *en masse*, but slowly and gradually. Hence, during the reigns of Mahmud of Ghazna and Muhammad Ghauri, the Muslim Pukhtuns (Afghans) fought alongside the Muslims, while the non-Muslim Pukhtuns fought alongside the Hindus.

4. The name Qays was familiar among Arabs. As the Prophet (s.a.w.) had not changed the names of others who had embraced Islam, there was no need to change his name from Qays to Abdur Rashid either.

5. The name Abdur Rashid is uncommon in Arabia and is an Indian or non-Arab name. So, why would the Prophet (s.a.w.) change a familiar name to an unfamiliar one?

6. Pukhtu resembles Sanskrit, Zend, etc. languages but not Hebrew.[49]

Moreover, there is a gap of 1,200 years in the account, from the time of the dislocation of the Israelites at the hands of Bukhtunasar and the prophethood of Prophet Muhammad (s.a.w.) until the conversion of the Ghauri Israelites to Islam.[50]

Also, the nomenclature 'Afghan' and 'Pathan' have been brought into question. It has been argued that 'Afghan' was first used by the Arabs and Persians, while Pathan was first used by the Indians. Although the innovators of the theory were racially Pukhtun, they were born and grew up in India or who had spent a major part of their lives in India because of which they neither knew their own tongue—Pukhtu—nor did they know their proper name—Pukhtun. So, to explain their nomenclature—Afghan—they invented the story of Armya and Afghana.[51]

If the Pukhtuns had no relationship with the Bani Israel by origin, the question arises as to why did they invent a story to prove that they were from Israelite stock? The reason behind this, according to its critics, was an attempt by the Mughals, who had not only usurped the throne of Delhi from the Pukhtuns but also tried to deride the Pukhtuns—to demoralise them and expunge their sense of superiority. For this purpose, Mughal court historians wrote novels about Pukhtuns and their origin. The Mughals were joined by another imperialist power of the age—the Safwis of Iran (Persia)—in this exercise, and so, the story of the progeny of the demon was related, at the court of Emperor Jahangir, by the Persian envoy.[52]

APPRAISAL OF VIEWS OF SOME CRITICS

While evaluating the contentions and assessment of the critics, we see that there is no consistency in their writings and most of them suffer from contradictions. For instance, Sayyad (Sayyid) Bahadar Shah Zafar Kaka Khail has stated, on the authority of *Shaukat-i Afghani*, that it was due to the exigency of the time (due to the abovementioned reason) that Khan Jahan Ludi (Lodi) sent his nobles (*umara*), such as Qutab Khan, Sarmast Khan Abdali, Hamzah Khan Tukhi, Umar Khan Kakar, and Zarif Khan Yusufzay, to Afghanistan and confirmed that the Afghans were Bani Israel whose roots reached Sam bin Nuh (AS), the elder brother of Yafas who was an ancestor of the Mughals. Although it was the outcome of a factual investigation, the dominant power could not bear that the subdued rival be racially superior to them, and so termed the research as self-praise, which is like the writing on the stone, till now.[53]

Sayyad Bahadar Shah Zafar Kaka Khail states, as just mentioned, that the theory had been written after proper research and the investigation was conducted in Afghanistan. He further states that it was evident that Khan Jahan Ludi sent a delegation of his *umara* to Afghanistan to discover the Pukhtuns' race, and as a result of their research determined that the Pukhtuns were Bani Israel. But, subsequently, he raises the question that why the Pukhtuns mixed their race with the Bani Israel. In stating the reasons, he contends that the theory had been fabricated in India, and concludes that if it is evaluated in terms of national qualities and racial pride, each part was fabricated with great thought and consideration to corroborate with the Pukhtun environment. However, its fabricators were people who were born and grew up in India or who had spent a major portion of their lives in India. Their links and relationships with their original homeland had not remained intact. While they were still Pukhtun by nation and race, they were not totally conversant with the life, disposition, and language of the Pukhtuns. They did not know the Pukhtun nation (قام) by the name 'Pukhtun' nor did they consider it the real name of the nation. To them, Pukhtun was first 'Afghan' because the historians of the age had referred to it thus; later, it was Pathan because that was how the Pukhtuns were known in India. Arab historians, too, referred to the nation as 'Afghan', as did the Iranians (Persians). So, to them, the real name of this nation was Afghan. In their view, Pukhtun possessed a secondary status. Therefore, after establishing the racial link with Bani Israel, they were keen for such a base and fibre (root), from ancient history, with which they could link a relationship to 'Afghan'.

And this was the need to fabricate the story of Armya and Afghana in the family of Sawal (Saul). Had these writers known the Pukhtuns by the name 'Pukhtun' and written the history of the Pukhtuns, it is probable that this theory would not have sustained.[54]

A cursory glance at Bahadar Shah's contentions reveals the inconsistency. On the one hand, he terms the theory a result of a thorough investigation conducted in Afghanistan, in the Pukhtun land of his writing; on the other hand, he terms it a story fabricated in India by those who did not remain Pukhtun in manner or language. In another instance, he again contends that the theory had been composed by people who were born and grew up in India and were known as Afghans by the Mughals. But then, he promptly asserts that they called themselves Afghans as well. On the very next page he has given the names of some of the historians who had referred to the Pukhtuns as Afghans. We can note that the historians mentioned by Bahadar Shah belong to the pre-Mughal period; among them was Minhaj Siraj.[55]

Further, he refers to the marriage of Khalid bin Walid's (RA) daughter with Qays (Abdur Rashid), citing the *Makhzan-i Afghani*;[56] but, the *Makhzan-i Afghani* does not mention the marriage.[57] Similarly, in his book *Pukhtanah da Tarikh pah Ranra kay*, he asserts that the historians who invented the Bani Israelite Theory state that the Pukhtu language was introduced by Afghana,[58] but in his book *Pushtun: Apni Nasal kay Aayinay mayn* he states, on the authority of *Makhzan-i Afghani*, that the Pukhtu language, a changed form of Hebrew, was taught to Prophet Sulayman (AS) by the Jins (genies).[59] *Makhzan-i Afghani*, however, makes no such contention.

Bahadar Shah, with the aim of disproving and negating the Bani Israelite Theory, fell victim to clearly contradictory statements and inconsistencies, as mentioned above. While it is not necessary to evaluate all his inconsistent and contradictory statements, one more example will make the point clearer. Citing Sibte Hasan, he states that it was not only the twelve fishermen that believed in Jesus (Isa—AS), but (while the apostles were his most special students) thousands of Jews and Samri also believed in him and a number of them left their homes to accompany him in his missionary activities.[60] This suggests that the Jews adopted the new faith. But, in the very next paragraph, he asserts that, in light of the above historical evidence, it was patent that a Jew always remained a Jew and never changed his religion.[61]

Bahadar Shah, himself, partially proved the theory by providing evidence that the term Afghan was used at a time when the theory had not yet been written and by giving details which confirmed the settlement of the Bani Israel on modern-day Pukhtun land.[62]

Moreover, he contends that Pukhtuns continued to call themselves Pukhtanah and not Afghans.[63] Negating Olaf Caroe's assertion that 'A Yusufzai or a Khalil, for instance, if he is asked who he is, will always reply, "I am an Afghan." A man of these tribes will not say, "I am a Pakhtun." He speaks Pakhtu, but his stock he regards as Afghan',[64] he states that as far the Yusufzi, Khalil or other Pukhtuns are concerned, every Pukhtun who speaks the Pukhtu language and had Pukhtu as his mother tongue, would never call himself Afghan or Pathan, and that Olaf Caroe's statement is contrary to the facts.[65]

But, Caroe's statement is not contrary to the facts—at least to the extent of Swat where not only the Yusufzi call themselves Afghans but the Swat State record also reveals that besides the term 'Pukhtun', the term 'Afghan' has been written for the Yusufzi Pukhtuns.[66] The common use of Pukhtun (singular also Pukhtan) and Pukhtanah (plural) is a recent development and a result of the political developments of the twentieth century.

Sadullah Jan Barq supports the same argument for the invention of the Bani Israelite Theory, namely the exigency of the time,[67] and has tried to negate the theory consciously. But, to be precise, his contentions are also inconsistent and subject to contradictions. For instance, he states that it would be unjust not to admire those elders whose objective was to counter the reproach of the Mughals and who possessed great intelligence and imagination, and that their tale about the origin of the Pukhtuns was a masterpiece of a high calibre.[68] But, on the very next page, he asserts that the details of the story appears to be a figment of the imagination of a *mula* or another less-educated person who had neither any knowledge about the Arabs nor command over Arabic.[69]

Commenting on the need to fabricate the theory, Sadullah Jan Barq has given a version of *Tarikh Farishtah* (*Firishtah*), citing Preshan Khattak's book, *Pushtun Kaun? (Tarikh, Tahqiq, Tanqid)*, which also, according to Barq, contributed to the fabrication of the theory.[70] But, on the other hand, he concedes the view that the theory was brought by the delegation from Kabul.[71] Preshan Khattak, too, deems Nimatullah Harwi's *Tarikh Khan Jahani wa Makhzan-i Afghani* a reaction to Farishtah's and the other historians' assertions about the Pukhtuns.[72] Although Muhammad Qasim Farishtah visited the court of the Mughal Emperor Jahangir at Lahore in 1606 CE, when 'he was deputed on a mission' from the court of Bijapur and Jahangir was on his way to Kashmir, he was not a Mughal court writer. He was attached to the courts of the Deccani kingdoms,[73] and the real enmity between the Mughals and the Deccani rulers was no secret. Hence, bearing in mind Mughal-Deccan rivalries, linking Farishtah's assertion to Mughal court writings and a Mughal propaganda campaign is not justifiable. Barq's assertion does not withstand scrutiny.

Sadullah Jan Barq, moreover, completely refutes any relationship between Pukhtu and Hebrew (a language of the Bani Israel).[74] However, he did admit, rather unwillingly, that as far as the Pukhtu language is concerned, it is beyond doubt that its present form is of the Indo-European family of languages—but with some differences as, grammatically, Semitic marks are also found in Pukhtu. But, in an attempt to negate the Bani Israelite link, he adds that this does not mean that it is akin to the Bani Israel and their language Hebrew. These marks of Pukhtu are much older than the age of Bani Israel.[75]

Similarly, Olaf Caroe also observes the following, about the contents of the Bani Israelite Theory:

> This is all great fun. But it smells of the Delhi lamp, the lamp of the courtier of Afghan ancestry but now speaking and writing only Persian, trained to raise a titter at the expense of an uncouth Pathan soldiery to amuse the Mughal court. Even the Delhi courtier who had forgotten his Pakhtu, one would think, would only identify the racial appellation 'Pathan' with an obscure Mediterranean Arab seafarer's word to make a pun and to amuse. Even he must have known that no Afghan or speaker of Pakhtu or Pashtu ever referred to himself as a 'Pathan', and that the word was an Indian usage.[76]

It is noteworthy that unlike those Pukhtun writers who contend that the theory was a result of the Pukhtun response to the Mughal abuses, Caroe attributes this, too, to the Mughal's Afghan courtiers so as to raise 'a titter' and 'amuse the Mughal court'. It is probably because of this statement of Caroe that Sadullah Jan Barq, who believes that the story was fabricated by Indian Afghans, holds the opinion that it is also probable that this theory may have been formulated in Kabul for the benefit of the delegation sent by Khan Jahan Ludi, and that the Mughals or other enemies of the Pukhtuns may have been involved in it.[77]

After a lengthy discussion, Caroe concedes, contrary to his above-mentioned assertion, 'Under this interpretation even the Bani Israel story *may reflect some part of the truth, and at least indicate a cause for a belief which, however unreasonable, it is hard to shake* [italics mine].'[78]

In negation of the Bani Israelite Theory, Sadullah Jan Barq tries to compare some of the traits, nature, and way of life of the Jews with those of the Pukhtuns, and concludes that they prove that the Bani Israelite

Theory is absolutely wrong. It had only been founded in response to the accusations of the Mughals.[79] Some of Sadullah Jan Barq's findings may be regarded to be sound, but on the whole they do not stand up to the test, and on close comparison and observation most of the mentioned traits are found in the Pukhtuns. For instance, Sadullah Jan Barq contends that the Jews only participated in trade and never in agriculture, whereas the Pukhtuns are agriculturists and hate trade. But what about the Jews who engage in agriculture in present-day Israel, and also the Jewish tribes of Banu Nuzair and Banu Qurayzah as well as the Jews of Khyber and Fadak, and what about those Pukhtuns who are engaged in trade (particularly these days)?

It is pertinent to mention that Sadullah Jan Barq makes a great effort to untangle the puzzle of the origin of the Pukhtuns. He has done a tremendous job on his own which has been published in three volumes, in Pukhtu, titled: *Da Pukhtanu Asal Nasal*.[80] It is impossible, rather irrelevant or unnecessary, here in this chapter, to critically analyse all the contents of and contentions made in the book; for it needs a separate chapter or a book. However, some of the contentions he made in his articles and are also found in his aforesaid book are critically evaluated above; and hence it would suffice here to state that like his above analysed contentions, the book suffers from contradictory contentions and also such assertions that do not withstand scrutiny. His effort and labour, however, warrant appreciation.

Moreover, Bahadar Shah Zafar Kaka Khail argues that both the Pukhtuns and the Jews are proud of their race.[81] Also, in support of the Pukhtuns' Bani Israelite extraction theory, Mr Thorburn quotes 'some peculiar customs' that he discovered among Pukhtun tribes that are claimed to have intermarried the least—'for instance the Passover-like practice...of sacrificing an animal and smearing the doorway with its blood in order...to avert calamity, the offering up of sacrifices, the stoning to death of...blasphemers, [and] the periodical distribution of land'.[82] Qazi Ataullah states that the Pukhtuns' general habits, physique, features, and way of life is like the Bani Israel.[83] It is to be highlighted that the Bani Israel never imply to be from Jews or of Jewish extraction. Hence, while Pukhtuns are from Bani Israelite stock, their comparison with the Jews has no great force and relevance.

It is pertinent, here, to elaborate on some points in the light of Nimatullah Harwi, Akhun Darwizah, and Khushal Khan Khattak's versions. Nimatullah Harwi did not mention Qays' marriage with Khalid bin Walid's (RA) daughter, a delegation travelling to Kabul on Khan

Jahan's orders, or the investigation in Afghanistan and the subsequent writing of the theory based on the delegation's findings. He did mention when, where, and why he wrote the book, and who assisted him.[84] Having already refuted the argument that he was unaware of the viewpoint of Khalid bin Walid's (RA) Arab origin, as he had already referred to it, he stood by his own assertion.[85] He was also aware of the fact that the contention about Khalid bin Walid's (RA) invitation to the Ghaur's Bani Israelites, the consequent proceeding of the Afghan delegation under Qays, and so forth, although are not found in the books of *ahadith,* are found in a number of books of history and *sirat.*[86] Moreover, he neither mentions the contentions vis-à-vis the Pukhtu language, i.e., its institution by Afghana etc., nor about Prophet Muhammad's (S.A.W.) remarks that Pukhtu would be spoken in Hell.

The allegation—that the theory was written or fabricated by Indians (whether by adoption or birth) who referred to Afghan instead of Pukhtun, which was a misnomer and so led to an incorrect study into the origin of the Pukhtuns—needs to be evaluated in light of the writings of those who were Pukhtun by ethnicity, birth, abode, and language as well as those who were not Pukhtun by ethnicity but by birth, abode, and language, namely Khushal Khan Khattak, and Akhun Darwizah and his son Karimdad, respectively, who lived and wrote in the sixteenth and seventeenth centuries.

Akhun Darwizah, who was a contemporary of Nimatullah Harwi's, wrote about the origin of the Pukhtuns, around the same time as Harwi, in Pukhtunkhwa instead of in India. Although there are differences in details and some points, as is evident from the versions of the theory given above, Darwizah's version basically has the same theme. He has used the term Afghan, and not Pukhtun, throughout his book: *Tazkiratul Abrar-i wal Ashrar.* Moreover, in his book *Makhzan,* he has used both Afghan and Pukhtun for the same people, Pukhtunkhwa (Pukhtankhwa) for their homeland, and both Afghani and Pukhtu for their language, indiscriminately and alternately. He has specified the Afghans by referring to the territory of their abode, namely from Qandahar to Swat and Bunair.[87] It is also noteworthy that he uses the name Afghanistan once.[88] Akhun Darwizah's son Karimdad uses the name Pukhtu and Pukhtanah, but also uses Afghani for Pukhtu language.[89] It might be alleged, in some quarters, that Akhun Darwizah did so to serve the Mughals, playing a pro-Mughal role, but it does not make sense as he had also used the terms Pukhtanah, Pukhtu, and Pukhtunkhwa. (It is to be underlined that though the general or common use of 'Pukhtunkhwa' and 'Pukhtankhwa', for the Pukhtun/

Afghan land, is a later development, Pukhtunkhwa/Pukhtankhwa, as stated above, for the first time had been used by Akhun Darwizah in his book *Makhzan*, written in the sixteenth century and is the second first known book of Pukhtu prose. [The first known book of Pukhtu prose is Bayazid Ansari's *Khairul Bayan*; after this Akhun Darwizah wrote the *Makhzan*, hence it is the second of the first known books of Pukhtu written in prose.] After him, the term was used by Khushal Khan in the same meaning in the seventeenth century CE;[90] and in the eighteenth century by Ahmad Shah Abdali in his verse given hereinafter in this chapter.)

But, the most important evidence in this respect is found in the writings of Khushal Khan Khattak because, unlike Nimatullah Harwi, Akhun Darwizah, and the others, he is commonly regarded as a great opponent of the Mughals and the foremost champion of the Pukhtun cause and Pukhtu language. It is evident from his version of the theory that though he has given a different background for the names Afghan, *malak*, and Pathan, he concedes these names too. Moreover, although he uses the term Pukhtun and Pukhtanah in the *Dastar Namah* and elsewhere in his writings, he also uses the name Afghan for Pukhtuns,[91] and Afghani for the Pukhtu language.[92] Besides his other verses, in which he uses the term Afghan for the Pukhtuns, the one verse for which he received universal acclaim was written at a time when he had become—by self-claim—the enemy of the Mughals. Hence, this is to be considered the opinion of a person who neither sympathised with, nor felt an inclination towards, the Mughals but of a person who considered or claimed himself to be a champion of the Pukhtun cause against the Mughals: it is still regarded as so by many. The verse is:

دَ افغان په ننگ مے وتړله توره [93]

ننگیالے دَ زمانے خوشحال ختک یم

Meaning: I rose up my sword (against the Mughals) for the sake of the Afghan *nang* (honour). I, Khushal Khattak, am the esteemed of the age.

Not only have the Pukhtuns and Pukhtu-speaking writers of the sixteenth and seventeenth centuries, of the present-day Khyber Pukhtunkhwa, used the name Afghan for Pukhtun, but the writers of the succeeding centuries and even the recently passed writers have also used Afghan for Pukhtun. For instance, among others, the following verses of the famous Pukhtun poet of the twentieth century, Amir Hamzah Khan Shinwari, speak of how proud he is of his Pukhtu language and Pukhtun-hood.

وائی اغیار چه د دوزخ ژبه ده ⁹⁴

زۀ به جنت ته د پښتو سره ځم

Meaning: The rivals term Pukhtu as the language of Hell, but I assure them that I shall go to Paradise with my Pukhtu.

حمزه سفر که د حجاز وی نو هم ⁹⁵

زۀ د پښتون د قافلو سره ځم

Meaning: Hamzah! Even on the journey to Hijaz, viz. for pilgrimage to the holy places, I am to go (only) with the Pukhtun's caravans.

However, Amir Hamzah Khan Shinwari has also used the term Afghan for the Pukhtun in a number of places and contexts.[96] Among others, his famous verses are:

ما کوز ورته لیمۀ کړۀ ځما سر نۀ ټیټیده ⁹⁷

شاید چه په الفت کښې هم افغان پاتے کیدم

Meaning: I lowered my eyebrows to my beloved but could not bow my head. Perhaps in the matter of love too I was to remain an Afghan.

زۀ لکه مزرئ یمه پیشه ده شجاعت زما ⁹⁸

زۀ حمزه افغان یمه پیشه ده شجاعت زما

Meaning: I am like a lion, my profession is valour. I Hamzah am Afghan, my profession is valour.

Similarly, Ghani Khan, another renowned Pukhtun nationalist poet of the twentieth century, also used the name Afghan besides Pukhtun. A verse of his famous 'children's anthem' says:

سر به ښکته نه کړم که زرګونه کشالے لرم ⁹⁹

ربه ښکته مه کړے چا ته سر ته دَ افغان

Meaning: Despite thousands of problems, I will not bow down my head to any one. O Lord! Do not make Afghan's head bow before anyone.

زما ملک کښې دولت نشته خوشحالی ده [100]

دی زمزم زما شراب سر افغانے

Meaning: Happiness prevails in my country without wealth. Mere water of my country is as good as wine to my proud Afghani head.

Ghani Khan also uses *Afghani tahzib* (افغانی تهذیب Afghani civilisation) for the Pukhtun civilisation (culture).[101]

Talking of his visit to, and conversation with the students of, Habibiyah College in Kabul, during his stay in Kabul as a result of the *hijrat* movement in 1920, Abdul Ghaffar Khan has used 'Afghan' for 'Pukhtun' and 'Afghani' for 'Pukhtu' language. He also states about a banquet by Mahmud Tarzi, Foreign Minister of Afghanistan, for the migrants in which, during a discussion about language, a participant asked Mahmud Tarzi what a strange place Afghanistan is that there is no 'Afghani': meaning they do not speak Pukhtu language. Ghaffar Khan also states about his arguments with Mahmud Tarzi, and also with the Afghan Monarch Amanullah Khan, advocating them to speak and implement Pukhtu officially in Afghanistan. Thus, a staunch Pukhtun nationalist of the twentieth century hailing from the Pukhtunkhwa has also used 'Afghan' for 'Pukhtun' and 'Afghani' for 'Pukhtu' language.[102] Until this time Pukhtu was not the official language of Afghanistan. It was in 1930s that Pukhtu was declared the second official language of Afghanistan.

Similarly, to reform the evil customs and practices of the Pukhtuns, to encourage them to abstain from violence, and to infuse the spirit and love of nationalism in them, Abdul Ghaffar Khan and his associates founded an association with the name 'Anjuman Islah-ul-Afaghinah' (Association for reformation of the Afghans)[103]—not Anjuman Islah-ul-Pukhtuns. Moreover, Abdul Ghaffar Khan was later given the title of 'Fakhr-i Afghan' (Pride of the Afghans), and not Fakhr-i Pukhtun (Pride of the Pukhtuns), at a public meeting arranged by the Anjuman Islah-ul-Afaghinah.[104] This took place in the present-day Khyber Pukhtunkhwa in the 1920s, by the people of the province or the Pukhtuns, and not in India or Afghanistan nor by the Arabs, Persians, Indianised Pukhtuns, nor the inhabitants of the modern-day Afghanistan, nor in the remote past.

It is also pertinent to dispel the contention that the name Pukhtun has been used in verse only, and that Pukhtun was used for countering the term 'Pathan' after publication of Caroe's book, *The Pathans*.[105] The name Pukhtun has been used not only in verse but also in prose, even in the sixteenth and seventeenth centuries.[106] Moreover, Pukhtun has not been used for countering the term, 'Pathan', used by Caroe, but, as just mentioned, since at least the sixteenth century.

The term 'Pathan' has not only been used by Caroe, but also by those who had raised their voices for Pukhtuns' rights; staunch Pukhtun nationalists also used it for Pukhtuns much earlier. For instance, Qaiyum Khan titled his famous book, *Gold and Guns on the Pathan Frontier*, in 1945;[107] and Abdul Ghani Khan, commonly known as Ghani Khan, had his famous book, *The Pathans: A Sketch*, published in 1947. Olaf Caroe's book, *The Pathans*, was published in 1958—much later than the aforementioned books. This also dispels the contention that Pukhtun writers had not used the term Pathan.[108]

Showing his disagreement with the term 'Pathan', used by Olaf Caroe for the Pukhtuns in his book *The Pathans*, Abdul Qadir—commonly called Mawlana Abdul Qadir (Founding Director of Pukhtu Academy, University of Peshawar)—asserts that deeming the words Pathan, Afghan, and Pushtun as one, or using the name Pathan and Afghan for the Pushtun, is not only an error but a grave mistake.[109] If using the terms Pathan and Afghan for the Pukhtun is a grave mistake, then those Pukhtuns who are considered the champions of the Pukhtun cause also committed this mistake, both before and after Caroe's writing, as is clear from the evidences given above: from both prose and verse. Moreover, in light of the above discussion and also other evidence, Abdul Qadir's contention that the Pushtuns had used neither Pathan nor Afghan for themselves in the past nor do they do so now is incorrect.[110]

The versions of the Bani Israelite Theory about the origin, or race, or ethnicity, of the Pukhtuns/Afghans/Pathans, given by Nimatullah Harwi and others, no doubt, suffer from weaknesses and mistakes, and possess notions and fantasies, and hence cannot be accepted in their entirety or at face value. However, the theory, or viewpoint, also has elements of the truth and hence cannot be overruled or dismissed altogether.

THE ARYAN RACE THEORY

The advocates of the Aryan Race Theory are of the opinion that the Pukhtuns are not Bani Israel by origin, or race, or ethnicity, but are Aryans. According to their viewpoint, the Pukhtuns are a branch of those Aryans who are known in history as Indo-European Aryans. The Aryan Race Theory is based on the historical research and philological evaluation of the word Pukhtun and the Pukhtu language, as is claimed.

THE THEORY[111]

The exponents and advocates of the Aryan Race Theory argue that proving similarity and closeness between the languages of the Indo-Europeans nations, supported by scientific proofs provided by European scholars and philologists at the beginning of the nineteenth century, led to the conclusion that the speakers of these languages were (probably) one, racially; that, in the beginning, their forefathers inhabited the same place and spoke the same language; and that when, later, these people migrated to different parts of the world their languages became different due to environmental and geographical factors. The source of all these languages is the Arik (آریک) language that the Aryan nations spoke in their original homeland before migration—and is extinct now—and has been mentioned by a French researcher, Mr le Bon (موسیولیبان),[112] viz. Dr Gustav le Bon.

Western scholars have varying opinions about the original homeland of the Aryans. Some are of the opinion that their original homeland was Scandinavia, or Finland, or the Danube Valley, in Europe; some have claimed that they belonged to Mongolia and Chinese Turkistan; some have said that southern Russia was their original homeland; while others have stated that it was the Balkan Peninsula. Whereas some speak about the northern shores of the Black Sea (بحیره اسود), and others consider the area between Altai (الٹائی) and the Aral (رال) as their original homeland. But, the majority of the historians and scholars believe that their original homeland was in the heights of the Pamir hills and at the source of the Oxus River.[113]

Wherever the original homeland of the Aryans was, it has been proved that a branch of them inhabited Bectia (Bakhtar باختر). During their stay in Bectia (also Bactria), they lived simple lives, and their habits were similar to shepherds, but they were not nomads. They lived in small villages and sustained themselves on milk, curd, and vegetables. Their beliefs were simple. According to their beliefs, gods were superior to goddesses. In the beginning, they did not believe in idol worship.[114]

With the passage of time they grew in number, and the territory and resources of Bectia were not enough to meet their needs. Hence, they were compelled to migrate in different directions at different times. These Bectian (also Bectrian) Aryans were divided into three groups. One group, which later became famous as the Indo-Aryans, began to migrate first. They crossed the passes of the Hindu Kush mountains, and some of them settled in the valleys of the Kabul River and its tributaries in southern Afghanistan. In the course of their migrations, they settled in the territories of modern Afghanistan, and the Khyber Pukhtunkhwa and Baluchistan of present-day Pakistan. After some time, they migrated from these areas, crossed the Indus, and occupied the lands of Punjab and Sindh. As time went by, they continued their advance to meet their economic needs as well as because of the arrival of new tribes, and so slowly and gradually wrested the Ganges-Jumna Doab and all the north-western areas of the South Asian subcontinent from the old inhabitants, the Dravidians. The exact time of this migration of the Indian branch of the Bectian Aryans is not known, but some scholars are inclined to believe that it happened between 2000 and 800 BCE.[115]

The second group of Bectian Aryans migrated in a south-westerly direction via Herat and through Khurasan, occupying the land of Fars and creating modern Iran. The period of their migration is considered to be between 1900 and 1000 BCE. These tribes established their first kingdom in Iran—called the Medes (ماد)—about the seventh century BCE.[116]

With the migration of the two main branches of the Aryans from Bectia, i.e. the Indian and Iranian Aryan branches, their lands remained open to the remaining tribes. The tribes that remained behind in Bectia are known as the Central and Bectian Aryans. According to the supporters of the Aryan Race Theory, these remaining tribes were the forefathers of the present-day Pukhtuns, the historical evaluation of which will be dealt below. These settled people lived in scattered settlements along the northern and southern slopes of the Hindu Kush, up to the bank of the Indus. Bakhdi (باخدی), Bakhdi (بخدی), Balkh (بلخ), Tukharistan, Arya (Herat), Aracosia (Arakushiya), Kabul, Sakistana, and Gandhara etc. were among the central areas of the land of the different tribes of these people.[117]

When the Aryan tribes spread and settled on the northern and southern slopes of the Hindu Kush, the area became known as Aryana (also Ariana), meaning the land of the Aryans (namely the country of the nobles). The name Aryana had been used, for the first time, for the land of modern Afghanistan by a Greek historian Eratosthenes (276–194 BCE). Although his writings did not survive, another Greek historian, Strabo (70–19 BCE), has quoted the name Aryana based on Eratosthenes' work. Besides Strabo, Ptolemy (بطلیموس) and Plini had also mentioned the word Aryana. In the second century Hijrah (Islamic Calendar), Hamzah Isfahani mentions the country between India and Iran as Mumlikat al-Aryan; it is evident that this is Afghanistan.[118]

Moreover, the names of the regions, tribes, etc. of the Pukhtun area found in the *Reg Veda*, and other books written in languages with the same origins, have also been used as evidence to support the Aryan Race Theory. For instance, the mention of Gandhara, the Arghandab region, and the Sarasvati River (about which, although it had been commonly believed to be the Sarasvati River of the Punjab, or by some the Indus, Albanian orientalist Gilbrant was inclined towards the view that it meant the river of the Arghandab region) in the *Reg Veda*, which had also been mentioned in the *Avesta* as the Haravetu; moreover, Bahlika (Balkh) is mentioned in the *Atharva Veda*, although it is not found in the *Reg Veda*.[119]

According to the *Atharva Veda*, the Suma plant used to grow on the mountain Manjwan, or the mountain of Manjan, which is in the eastern series of the Hindu Kush. A pass with the same name also exists between Nuristan and Badakhshan. Moreover, a nation with the name of Manjwat has been mentioned in the *Atharva Veda*. Zafar Kaka Khail has quoted Macdonald who believed that it meant the tribe that resided in the vicinity of the Manjwan or mountain Mujawat; and was in the neighbourhood of the Gandhari tribe. As the Gandhari tribe resided in Gandhara, and in the wider context Gandhara means the region situated between Kabul and Peshawar, this appears to be proof that present-day Manjan is the old Manjwan and the Manjwat tribe would have resided in the north of Gandhara in some parts of Lamghanat and Nuristan.[120]

Over a period of time, the Aryans, who had migrated to India, composed their first-known sacred religious book, *Reg Veda*, which contains 1,028 verses and is divided into ten parts. The language of each part is somewhat different from the other, the reason being that the parts were narrated at different times and in different places by different poets and were later compiled and composed as a book. Although the date of the compilation of *Reg Veda* has not been agreed upon, most scholars, on the basis of evidence, are of the opinion that the *Reg Veda* was compiled in the mid-second millennium BCE, in 1500–1400 BCE. In the *Reg Veda*, too, the five main rivers related to the land of the Khyber Pukhtunkhwa are mentioned. These are the rivers Sindu (Indus), Kubha (Kabul), Suvastu (Swat), Krumu (Kurram), and Gomati (Gumati; Gumal).[121]

Similarly, the names of the rivers to the east of the Indus have been mentioned as the 'Vitasta (Jhelum), Asikni or Chandrabhaga (Chenab), Parushni or Iravati (Ravi), Vipasa (Vyasa), Sutudri (Satlaj), Sarasvati, and Drishadvati'. The names Ganga (Ganges) and Yamuna (Jamuna) are rarely mentioned in the *Reg Veda*.[122] The geographic region occupied by the Aryans of the Vedic Age is clearly evident from the aforementioned rivers. The mention of these rivers in the *Reg Veda* supports the theory that the Aryan tribes occupied the vast area from eastern Afghanistan to the upper valley of the Ganges, an area that is known in history as Sapta-Sindhu meaning seven rivers or the land of seven rivers. This has been referred to as Haptah-Hindu in the *Avesta*. Some scholars are of the opinion that this referred to the Punjab region.[123]

Like the names of the rivers and areas of Pukhtunkhwa (the Pukhtuns' land), names of some of the Aryan tribes, and some information regarding them, are also available in the *Reg Veda*. With the passage of time, the Indian Aryans separated into two rival groups. One group comprised the Bharata (بهارته) and its allied tribes; the other comprised five tribes, namely the Yadus (يادو), Turvasas (تورواشا), Druhyus (درهيو), Anus (انو), and Phrus/Puros (پورو). These five tribes were also known as the Pankah Jana (پنکه جانا), meaning group of five. These two groups were great rivals and fought each other. Two of their wars are related to the history of Pukhtuns. One was called the War of the Arghandab region, while the second was the War of the Ten Malaks. The War of the Ten Malaks is very important from the viewpoint of the historical research of the Pukhtuns because, in the description of this war, the names of all the tribes that took part in it are mentioned. The war was fought on the banks of the Ravi—between the Bharata tribe and their allies on the one side, and the Yadus group or the Pankah Jana and their allies on the other. In this war, the Aryans of the trans-Indus territory joined hands with the Yadus group (Pankah Jana) against the Bharata and their allies. Ten tribes—five of the Yadus group and five from the trans-Indus region's Aryans—fought to assist Vesumitra (ويسومترا) against the Sudas (سوداس), the king of the Bharata tribe, and their allies.[124]

The names of those five trans-Indus Aryan tribes or Paktha (پکتها)— who fought on the side of Vesumitra and the Yadus group—were Chivas also Sivas (شيوا), Pakthas (پکتها), Alinas (الينا), Bahalana (بهالانا) and Visanan (ويشانن). According to the advocates of the Aryan Race Theory, the Chivas were the inhabitants of the Kabul Valley; the Pakthas (Pukhtanah يبنتانة) were the residents of the Krumu (Kurram) and Gomati (Gomal, Gumal) valleys; the Alinas inhabited Kafiristan (presently both Nuristan in Afghanistan and Kafiristan in Pakistan); the Bahalanas were the residents of the Bulan (Bolan) Valley; and the Visanans resided in the Gandhara region. Among these, the Pakthas are believed to be the present-day Pukhtanah or Pukhtuns. This reference, in the *Reg Veda,* confirms that the Pukhtun people were present, and known by the same name, in this land before 1400 BCE. However, it is worth mentioning that in the *Reg Veda*, the name 'Paktha' has sometimes been used for the nation and sometimes for the king (head of the Paktha people).[125]

It is claimed that the clear and detailed mention of Paktha in the hymns (songs) of the *Reg Veda* mean that Paktha (Pukhtanah) was a renowned and influential tribe in the comity/council of the Aryan tribes. Besides Paktha, names of some other tribes are found in the *Reg Veda*. It seems that these Pukhtun tribes were present, and known by the same names, in their present areas. They participated in the war—King Devadasa (دیواداسا) of the Bharata tribes fought in the Arghandab region, to which reference has already been made. The names of these tribes were Dasa (داسا), Pani (پانی), Brisaya (بریسایا), and Paravata (پاراواتا). The war was fought on the bank of the Sarasvati River which, according to the orientalist Helerant, is the Arghandab River, as mentioned in the *Avesta* as Haraveti (Haravetu). Helerant has stated that the people of Arakuziya (اراکوزیا) (Arakozia; modern Qandahar) took part in this war. The Paravata tribe of the *Reg Veda* is believed to be the Paruiti (پاروئتی) tribe mentioned by the Greek writer Ptolemy in connection with the pastures of Arghandab. Similarly, some tribes such as the Dasa are part of the Pukhtuns; while the Dasu (داسو) tribe is also present among the Sulaiman Khail. Likewise, the Pani of the Vedic Age, whom genealogists include among the Kakars, are the present-day Panri (پنی) or Pini (پینی), residing in Sibi in the north of Dadar (ڈاور). Similarly, there is only a minor difference between Brisaya and Baris (بریخ). The present-day Baris were referred to as the Brisaya in the Vedic Age. These people live in the Shurawak (شوراوک) of Qandahar and are spread along the southern section of this region up to Hilmand. Likewise, the Vedic Paravata, and Ptolemy's Paruiti, are still a branch in the Alkuzi (الکوزی), known as the Prut (پروت). Like the Alkuzi are the residents of Arakuzi (اراکوزی), the old Paravata is considered to originate in the name Prut. Thus, in the *Reg Veda*, a renowned tribe named Pakht (پکهت) or Paktha (پکنها) is found among the Aryan tribes. The names of some other tribes in the Arghandab region have also been referred to, which conform to the names of some present-day Pukhtun tribes.[126]

After the migration of the two branches of the Aryans from Bectia, the language, beliefs, and way of life of the Bectian Aryans also changed with the passage of time and under various influences. A new language, called Zend (زند), came into being in the area; the *Avesta* (اوستا), the religious book of the Bectian Aryans, was written in this language. The exact dates for the compilation of the *Avesta* are not known but scholars are of the opinion that it was probably written during the period 1000–600 BCE. Although there is no clear account of the Pukhtuns in it, Balkh has been referred to in the *Avesta* as Bakhdi (بخدی). The majority of the scholars are of the opinion that the city Bakhdi (بخدی) has taken its name after its residents, the Bakhd (بخد). According to these scholars, Pakht (پکهت)

of the *Veda*, and Bakhd (بخد) of the *Avesta* are, in fact, one word, in the same way as 'pay' (پ) is changed to 'bay' (ب), 'kaf' (ک) to 'khay'(خ), and 'tay' (ت) to 'dal' (د). Hence, Pakht (پکهت) of the *Veda* has become Bakht (بخت) of the *Avesta*, in the same way as 'khay' (خ) changed to 'khin' (ښ) so Pakt (پکت) of the *Veda* became Bakht (بخت), Pakht (پخت), Pakht (پښت). This demonstrates that in the Bectian (باختری) accent (لهجه), the Pukhtuns were known as the Bakhd (بخد).[127]

The mention of Pukhtuns and their homeland can also be found in the writings of Greek historians and writers, which helps us solve the puzzle of the origin of the Pukhtuns. Herodotus, the Greek historian, has referred to the Pukhtuns as the Pactavis (پکتویس) and Pactyan (پکتوان), and to their homeland as Pactica (پکتیکا) and Pacticay (پکتیکی). According to him, these people resembled the Bectians in dress, way of life, and customs. Hence, the analogy and presumption that the Pukhtuns and the Bectians remained settled in one place for a long time, and that their culture and civilisation were the same. It is also evident, from Herodotus' writings, that four tribes resided in Pactica—the Gandarii (گندهاریان), Aparytai (اپاریتی), Sattagydai (ستاگیدی), and Dadicai (دادیکی). The Gandarii were assumed to be the inhabitants of Gandhara, and the Aparytai to be the Apridi (اپریدی); Afridi (افریدی). The Sattagydai have not been conclusively identified as yet. While the Elamis and Babylonians referred to them as the Stagui (ستاگوی) and the Satgusu (ست کوسو), Dr Bellew referred to them as the Khattak and Shitak.[128] Denzil Ibbetson believes the Dadicai are the Dadi (دادی).[129] However, Bahadar Shah Zafar Kaka Khail, citing Ahmad Ali Kuhzad, states that the Dadicai are the Tajaks (Tajeks), and Ptolemy mentioned the land of the Pukhtuns as the Paktin (پکتین).[130]

Advocates of the Aryan Race Theory contend that Paktha (پکتھا) and Phakt (پهکت) of the *Reg Veda*, and the Bakhdi (بخدی) and Bakhdi (باخدی) of the *Avesta* (the languages of both the books are the offshoots of Arik, the language of the Aryans in their original homeland) are the names of the people whom the Greeks have referred to as Pactyan (پکتوان) and Pactavis (پکتویس) and their homeland with the names of Pactica (پکتیکا), Pacticay (پکتیکی), and Pactin (پکتین). They were the Pukhtuns who the Greeks referred to, as above, in their own accent. Moreover, according to linguistic rules, Pactica (پکتیکا) becomes Pukhtunkhwa (پښتونخوا). As all these names are used for the Pukhtuns, it proves that the Pukhtuns are a branch of the Aryan tribes.[131]

As resemblance and closeness between languages are considered strong signs of nations' ethnic and racial oneness and unity, the advocates of the Aryan Race Theory have elaborated on this aspect. A number of linguists are of the opinion that Pukhtu belong to the Aryan group of languages, and great resemblance has been found between Zend and its offshoot, Sanskrit, and other languages that belong to the Aryan group of languages. Some renowned scholars, such as Professor Klaproth, Professor Dorn, H.G. Raverty, H.W. Bellew, G.A. Grierson, James Darmesteter, and Dr Trump, held the view that Pukhtu had no conformity or resemblance with Semitic languages, and that, based on the structure of its words and the form of the principles of its grammar, it is an Aryan language. Although there was some difference in details, these scholars were unanimous that Pukhtu is the offshoot of the language of the Aryans.[132]

Similarly, resemblance of words in the languages of the Aryans and of words in Pukhtu has also been observed. For example:[133]

Pukhtu	Zend/Pahlavi/ Persian	Sanskrit/ Hindi/Urdu	English	German
Plar پلار	Pidar, Bap پدر ، باپ	Pata, Patri, Pati پتا ، پاتری ، پاتی	Father فادر	Vater فاتر
Mur مور	Mam, Matu, Madar مام ، ماتو ، مادر	Mata, Matri ماتا ، ماتری	Mother مدر	Muter موتر
Khur خور	Hunhar, Khwahir خواہر ، ہونہار	Swasar, Susri سواسر ، سوسری	Sister سسٹر	Schwester شوستر
Wrur ورور	Biradar برادر	Bhratar, Bhayi بھراتر ، بھائی	Brother برودر	Bruder برودر
Sturay ستورے	Sitara, Sturya ستارا ، ستوریہ	Sitara ستارا	Star سٹار	Stern سٹرن
As, Aspah اس ، اسپہ	Asp, Aspah اسپ ، اسپہ	Ashu, Asva اشو ، اسو	Horse ہارس	Phered
Myasht میاشت	Mah ماہ	Mas, Mahinah ماس ، مہینہ	Month منتھ	Monat مونات
Num نوم	Nam نام	Nam نام	Name نیم	Name نوم
Nah, Na نہ ، نا	Nah, Na, Ney نہ ، نا ، نے	Na, Nahyn نا ، نہیں	No نو	Nein نائن
Naway نوے	Nau, Nawayn نو ، نویں	Naya نیا	New نیو	Neu نوئی

All these support the assumption and contention that the Pukhtu language belongs to the Indo-European group of languages, with their common origin in the language of the Aryans. Thus, the Pukhtuns are a branch of the Aryan tribes and their language, Pukhtu, is from the group of Aryan languages. Hence, they are Aryans by origin, or race, or ethnicity.

CRITICAL ANALYSIS

There is historical evidence and proof to support the statement that Aryan tribes settled in the present-day Pukhtun/Afghan/Pathan areas of Pakistan and Afghanistan, and that their progeny populated these areas. In addition to the linguistic and philological evidence, some similarities are also evident in the rituals, customs, way of life, and beliefs—in the past and even today—of the Pukhtuns and the Aryan groups which also support the Pukhtuns' Aryan-hood.[134]

Bahadar Shah Zafar Kaka Khail—a great exponent and advocate of the Aryan Race Theory, and on whose authority the contents of the theory are given above—has referred to the shortcomings in the Bani Israelite and other theories about the origin of the Pukhtuns. On the basis of these shortcomings, he challenges their authenticity and negates all other theories except the Aryan Race one. However, thorough study and in-depth analysis of the Aryan Race Theory as well as a cursory glance at the contents and discussion of the theory as given and advocated by Bahadar Shah, reveals similar shortcomings in the Aryan Race Theory, raising doubts about its authenticity. So, instead of blindly accepting what Bahadar Shah advocates, the theory needs a critical and objective evaluation as he himself states that human theories are not static but continue to change because, as long as the door of research is open, no theory is final.[135]

A weakness of the Aryan Race Theory is that it was propounded, for the first time, by European scholars and philologists in the nineteenth century. This suggests that, at least until the nineteenth century, the Pukhtuns/Afghans/Pathans themselves had no common belief or knowledge or tradition of their Aryan-hood. If the Pukhtuns were purely Aryan by origin, or race, or ethnicity, they would never have forgotten this, and would have referred to and written about their Aryan roots before the nineteenth century—as they did vis-à-vis the Bani Israelite Theory. But, we have come across no proof of the then Pukhtuns/Afghans/Pathans being aware of their Aryan origin. As pointed out by Abdul Qadir (Founding Director of the Pukhtu Academy, University of Peshawar), this does not conform to their national traditions and values.[136] Moreover, neither Akhun Darwizah nor Khushal Khan Khattak mentions or make a reference to the Aryan roots of the Pukhtuns.[137] Before the nineteenth century, therefore, there was no idea, or belief, or myth, among the Pukhtuns/Afghans/Pathans about their being from the Aryan race, or root, or stock.

Negating the Bani Israelite Theory, Bahadar Shah has referred to the gaps or the voids, in the theory, of about 400 years between Prophet Sulayman (AS) and Bukhtunasar's (Nebuchadnezzar) attack; and of about 1,200 years between Bukhtunasar's attack and the destruction of the Bani Israelites at his hands; and the advent of Islam in Arabia and the conversion of the Ghaurid Israelites (Ghauris) to Islam.[138] However, Bahadar Shah has ignored rather longer gaps in his own account of the Aryan Race Theory—more than 400 years between the accounts of the *Reg Veda* and the *Avesta*, about 1,200 years between the account of the *Reg Veda* and the Greek historians, and more than 2,000 years between the writings of the Greek historians and the European linguists and philologists of the nineteenth century, as has also been pointed out by Preshan Khattak.[139]

In his version of the theory, Bahadar Shah infers, based on an account of Herodotus', the similarities in dress, wares, and way of life of the Pukhtuns and the Bectians, and uses this to support the premise that the Pukhtuns and Bectians lived with each other for a long time, and had the same kind of culture and civilisation. Moreover, he states that, based on Herodotus' writings, four tribes, namely the Gandarii, Aparytai, Sattagydai, and Dadicai, resided in Pactica,[140] and that their offspring are still settled in Pactica (Pakhtikha, sic.) and are now called 'Pukhtanah' (Pukhtuns).[141] This contention, on the one hand, speaks of the similarity between the Bectians and Pacticans (or Pukhtuns) while, on the other hand, also speaks of difference between them, and, hence, is somewhat contrary to his argument.

While negating the commonly held belief that the Gandharans, or the residents of Gandhara—referred to by the Greek writers—were the forbearers of the present-day Pukhtun tribes—a view also subscribed to by Olaf Caroe—A.H. Dani states:

> In the last chapter [of the book] sufficient arguments have been given to show that Gandhara of Herodotus was entirely different from his Paktuike. It is on the older geographic scene that the Pakhtu tribes came to settle, and their emergence in history has to be traced on fresh lines, different from that narrated by Sir Olaf Caroe.[142]

Dani's contention also negates the view that the Gandharans were one of the tribes considered to be the forbearers of some of the Pukhtun tribes, especially the Yusufzi.[143]

Ghani Khan, too, was critical of the writings of the 'charming old humbug, Herodotus', and has contended that he 'believed all that he heard, and wrote all that he believed. he [He] refers to the Pathan's part of the world as Bectia, and says it is inhabited by a small dark people who deal in gold and spices.' After having given some details of Herodotus' account about the manner in which the gold was collected, Ghani Khan infers some points about the then-inhabitants of Herodotus' Bectia (and Bahadar Shah's Pactica or Pukhtunkhwa), on the basis of which he notes:

> It also proves that the people who now inhabit the vague Bectia of Herodotus (he is poor in geography—all gossips are and the old Greek is a delightful old gossip—with a solemnity that makes you laugh and a skin that makes you wonder) are neither small nor dark nor clever monopoly traders. On the contrary they are big and fair and straight and look upon murder as a much more respectable pastime than trade.[144]

In the light of Ghani Khan's argument, about the authenticity of Herodotus' writings and information about the inhabitants of Bectia, Herodotus' contentions about the Bectians, or Bahadar Shah's Pukhtuns, do not appear to be based on sound historical evidence.

Bahadar Shah Zafar Kaka Khail questions Roshan Khan's assertion that though the Pukhtuns/Afghans belonged to a number of Israelite tribes, they became famous as Pukhtuns because of Bani Pukht/Pakht, which was a prominent tribe of the exiled Israelite tribes of whom the Pukhtuns were the offspring.[145] Not only did he try to negate the argument, he also concludes his discussion and argument with the remark that all Israelite tribes are mentioned by their own names in the Jewish Scriptures, and, hence, he could not determine which of the Israelite tribes became Pukhtun because of the exalted name of Bani Pukht.[146] On the other hand, regarding the Aryan roots of the Pukhtuns, he states that present-day Pukhtuns are not the progeny of the Paktha tribe alone, but also of the (then) five trans-Indus Aryan tribes, namely the Paktha, Siva, Bahalana, Alina, and Visanan. However, as the Paktha and Siva were the prominent tribes of the trans-Indus Aryans, it was after Paktha that all the five tribes of the trans-Indus Aryans (Paktha group) became known as the Pukhtuns.[147] He also states that the Pakthas were the inhabitants of the Kurram and Gumal valleys.[148]

One may question that if, in the case of the Bani Israelite Theory, the contention that the name Pukhtun came into use because of the Bani Pukht/Pakht (the name of the prominent Israelite tribe which was one of the lost or exiled tribes of whom the Pukhtuns are considered to be the offshoot) is not sound, then, how and why has a similar argument been put forward about the offshoot of the five Aryan tribes—that they became known as Pukhtun because of the exalted position and prominence of the Paktha tribe (when the names of the other tribes are also known). Furthermore, Bahadar Shah did not mention which of the present-day Pukhtun tribes are the progeny, especially of the Paktha tribe. Moreover, he himself has stated that the name Paktha was sometimes used for a tribe and sometimes for a person, which further questions the validity of acknowledging the 'Paktha' as the Pukhtuns.

While dealing with Sultan Muhammad Khan Sabir's (Quetta, Baluchistan) contention that the Pukhtuns are Sythian by origin, and negating his viewpoint, Bahadar Shah argues that the learned historian's stand seems to be based on 'may be' (ہوسکتا ہے) and 'would be' (ہوگا) (i.e. uncertain hypotheses, analogies, and conjectures). Deriving and building the structure of one's theory on such uncertain grounds becomes difficult to accept.[149] But, on the other hand, Bahadar Shah's main arguments in support of his own contentions are based on the same sort of assertions and possibilities: namely 'I think' (زما خیال دا دے), 'in my opinion' (زما په خیال کښې), 'my analogy is this' (زما قیاس دا دے), 'according to my analogy' (زما په خیال کښې), 'in light of this analogy' (د دے قیاس په رڼا کښې), and so forth.[150] Even in critical evaluation of Sultan Muhammad Khan Sabir's theory, he has based his arguments on 'may be' (ہوے ہوگے), 'may have been' (ہوگے، ہوگی), and 'may be so' (ہوسکتا ہے).[151]

There are a large number of other inconsistencies in Bahadar Shah's statements and assertions. For instance, he says that the Aryans who settled in Bectia at first, were divided into three groups—those who migrated to and settled in India, and later became famous as Indo-Aryans; those who migrated towards Iran; and those who remained in Bectia, the Central or Bectian Aryans—and it was these Bectian Aryan tribes who were the forefathers of the present-day Pukhtuns.[152] Later, he states that the Indo-Aryans were divided into two major groups, one comprised the Bharata and its allied tribes, the second comprised the five tribes: Yadus, Turavasas, Druhyus, Anus, and Phrus.[153] But later he states, to the contrary, that the Indo-Aryans were divided into three groups which can, for convenience, be termed as the Bharata group, the Yadus group, and the Paktha group.[154] He also frequently mentions that the Paktha group comprised Bectian Aryans,[155] and, hence, they did not become Indo-Aryans because the Indo-Aryans were the Aryans who migrated to India. In the same account, he later states that the Pactians lived in areas that were generally hilly and, unlike the Indo-Aryans, their geographical environment was such that they always remained busy striving against natural forces for their necessities of life.[156] He considers the Pukhtuns and the Aryans to be different people in a sense, as is evident from his assertion that the above details prove that Pukhtuns and Aryans were from the same race,[157] mentioning the two as two separate identities: namely Pukhtuns and Aryans.

One of Bahadar Shah's arguments, to prove that Pukhtuns are Aryans, was that since the Yadus group and Paktha were allies—supported by the War of the Ten Malaks fought on the bank of the Ravi River—we can surmise that the Yadus group and the Paktha group had the same origin and had the same beliefs and language.[158] How could the Pukhtunkhwa's Aryans have participated in the War of the Indus Valley Aryans, if their languages were different? In that case, their position would have been like the Persian saying: زبان یارمن ترکی ومن ترکی نمی دانم 'My friend speaks Turkish and I do not understand Turkish.'[159] However, building one's case on this point—the need for the same ethnic group, beliefs, and language—is not very sound. After all, is it sound and justified to say that the allies of both sides in World War I (1914–1918 CE) and World War II (1939–1945 CE) belonged to the same group and had the same beliefs and language? Or, to term the world-wide allies in the twenty-first century's war between the US and her allies on the one side, and the Al-Qaida and Taliban on the other side as being from the same group or race and having the same beliefs and language, only on the grounds that they are allies in the war? And, if their language is not the same, how can they join hands, converse, and know the other says?

To support his view, one of Bahadar Shah's arguments was to point out the similarity between the social and communal institutions of the ancient Aryans and ancient Pukhtuns. He has noted the resemblance in appearance, and physical features of the ancient Aryans and Pukhtuns. Based on this, we should accept with open heart that the Pukhtuns are Aryan by race.[160] However, we see similar arguments, with supporting evidence, that the Pukhtuns are from Bani Israelite stock,[161] as we do for the Greek mixture theory[162] which Bahadar Shah is not ready to accept. We also see the similarities between the Pukhtuns and Arabs (if not among present-day Pukhtuns and Arabs, at least among those of the past), for example, bravery, hospitality, asylum, honour, resolving and deciding disputes by mediation, omens, charms, juggling, belief in spirits, enchantment and amulets, tribal practices, and war-like propensities. However, this is not sufficient to prove an ethnic relationship between Arabs and Pukhtuns.

If such similarities between the Pukhtuns and ancient Aryans, as Bahadar Shah Zafar Kaka Khail also mentions for the Bectians and Pacticans or Pukhtuns, can be accepted as proof to support the theory that Pukhtuns are linked to the Aryans or that they belonged to the Aryan race or origin, then such similarities can also be recognised as proof in support of the other theories.

Abdul Qadir (Founding Director of the Pukhtu Academy), who had advocated the ancient lineage of the Pukhtuns, attributes the similarities of the Pukhtun race to a number of other ethnic groups—such as the Greek, Huns, Sakas, Kushanas, Semitic, and other Aryan sects, among whom the Shinayi and Gujars are also included—to their coming and mixing with the existing inhabitants, i.e., the Pukhtuns, hence resulting in similarities among the Pactin nation with the other ethnic groups' physique, manners, customs, and usage.[163]

Allah Bakhsh Yusufi, on the other hand, contends that there is no similarity in physique, stature, customs, way of life, dress, worship, etc. between the Pukhtuns (or Afghans) and ancient Aryans.[164] Yusufi, moreover, deals with the question of the name Aryan and the basis of the origin of Aryans, and argues that Aryan is not the name of a permanent race or ethnicity but a specific belief. Every person who adopted that belief, irrespective of race or colour, was called Aryan. He concluds that, in this scenario, the Afghans or Pathans are not Aryans.[165]

Another inconsistency in Bahadar Shah Zafar Kaka Khail's assertion is that he, on the one hand, state that Major Raverty was the advocate of the Bani Israelite Theory[166] and, on the other, held that Raverty supported the Aryan Theory as he was of the opinion that the Pukhtu language bore no resemblance to the Semitic languages but is from the family of Aryan languages in its grammar and structure of words.[167] Olaf Caroe contends, on the authority of Raverty's *Pukhtu Grammar*, 'The last pleader for the Bani Israel tradition in English is the redoubtable Raverty.'[168] Preshan Khattak, too, refers to the inconsistencies and contradictions in the assertions and contentions of the orientalists in respect of the grammar and structure of the words in the Pukhtu language and also in respect to different groups of languages.[169]

While dealing with the origin and race of the Pukhtuns, Bahadar Shah frequently uses the word Pukhtun *qaam/qaum*[170] (قوم / قام nation) instead of *nasal* (نسل race/ethnicity) and ignores the evident difference in the meaning and usage of the words nation and race/ethnicity despite the fact that he himself has criticised Ghani Khan for the same. He asserts that by terming the Pukhtuns as Greek in origin, Ghani Khan did not distinguish between the meanings of *qaum* (nation), *nasal* (race), and *mulk* (country), whereas all the three are different scientific terms with different meanings.[171] Bahadar Shah also deals with the meanings of these three terms.[172] He even laments that a major reason for the complexity of the question of the origin/race of the Pukhtuns was that even in the scientifically advanced age of the twentieth century, attention was not being paid to the meaning and tenor of *nasal* (race).[173] While he himself frequently uses the words *nasal, mulk,* and *qaum* in different meanings and contexts,[174] he uses the term *qaum* for the Pukhtuns instead of *nasal*, calling them Aryan as well. His statement that no nation (قوم) is made up of one or two tribes nor of a single race[175] is, in itself, sufficient to negate his own contention that the present-day Pukhtuns are Aryans.

Elsewhere, he states that the outcome of the discussion was that the people who have lived in Pukhtunkhwa for generations, whose mother tongue is Pukhtu, and who follow Pukhtun traditions are Pukhtuns, irrespective of their fathers and predecessors' ethnicity (race). Because 'nation' is not born of the womb of a single race (*nasal*) or tribe, history plays a leading role in the making of a nation. Historical processes and forces unite people of different races and groups into mutual relationships. It is neither race nor tribe, but history, that makes nations. Therefore, all the people living in Pukhtunkhwa are members of one Pukhtun nation.[176] But, strangely enough, Bahadar Shah again connects this to his familiar contention that, racially, they are Aryans.[177] His argument, in support of his claim of the Aryan connection of the Pukhtun nation, is that Pukhtu is from the group of Aryan languages, and that of the nations who entered Pukhtunkhwa during the various periods of its history, some would have settled on the land (اس سرزمین پر آباد ہوئے ہوں گے) and those people would have mixed with the Pukhtuns (پشتونوں میں ان کی آمیزش ہوئی ہوگی). Most of them were Aryan or mixed Aryan by race.[178] In the light of the above discussion, and the one that follows, his claim regarding the Aryan origin of the Pukhtuns becomes doubtful.

It is mainly on the basis of the assertions and contentions of the European linguists and philologists that the Pukhtun/Afghan exponents of the Aryan Race Theory have based their arguments in support of the Aryan Race Theory. But can one call the present-day Americans Aryan by race or origin on the basis of the English language, which it is said is from the Indo-Aryan group of languages? Or when, after 2,000 years, Americans from different regions, origins, ethnic groups, and backgrounds become one community, having lived together for a very long time, and speak the same English language—when their descendants will not know their backgrounds and they will be one community—can they be called, or will they become, Aryans? If this does not sound logical, how can one justify taking the present-day Pukhtuns/Afghans/Pathans for Aryans merely on the basis of words that are in common with other languages of the Indo-Aryan group?

Preshan Khattak, too, critically evaluates this linking of people with races or ethnic groups on the basis of language. He has invalidated such contentions and assertions with sound arguments and examples, as well as the contentions of the Aryan Race Theory about the origin of the Pukhtuns. He has given the example of Mexico, the population of which is composed of varied origins and ethnic groups, but they all speak the Spanish language as they were ruled by Spain for a few centuries. Speaking Spanish does not mean that all Mexicans are of Spanish origin.[179]

Hence, 'rightly said', by Sayyad Abdul Jabbar Shah, 'language is no proof of ethnic origins'.[180] Mr le Bon (Dr Gustav le Bon) also contends that current research demonstrates that merely a common linguistic source is not evidence of a common origin of nations.[181] C.C. Davies, too, states that 'neither is affinity of race any criterion of language'.[182] Davies contends:

> If affinity of race is no criterion of language, the converse is still more true. Language is not by any means a test of race, for, in the mountain fastnesses to the north and north-east of Peshawar, Pashtu serves as a convenient *lingua franca* and is used in many cases by the supposed aboriginal population.[183]

While negating the Aryan link of the Pukhtuns, Allah Bakhsh Yusufi contends that language cannot be termed as the basis for the origin or ethnicity of a nation because there are a number of nations in the world whose pedigree is established without a doubt, but they have no acquaintance with their national languages.[184]

Bahadar Shah, moreover, argues that the word Aryan is a linguistic terminology. It is not the name of a specific person or a specific nation or of the forefather of a nation. Hence, any person who speaks any of the Aryan languages can be termed an Aryan.[185] This is a strange contention! Will a Jew or Arab, speaking an Aryan language, become Aryan? Certainly not. Allah Bakhsh Yusufi states that Max Muller considered the Aryans to be a cultural group,[186] which means they are not a specific race or ethnicity.

While acceding, to some extent, to the similarities of the Pukhtu language with other languages of the Indo-European group of languages, Abdul Qadir states, on the authority of the Afghan scholar Abdul Hai Habibi, that there is no proof of what the original Aryan language was or of how long it existed. Moreover, it is evident from the available Aryan inscriptions that the language of the *Vedas* is not the real Aryan language but that some other language existed before it.[187]

According to Abdul Qadir, Max Muller was the first to use the word Eryan (ايرين) for a group of languages that included the Indo-European languages as well as a number of other old languages of Aryana land. Max Muller used another word, Eryan (ايرين) race, which was adopted by the Germans with vigour. Although Max Muller, himself, later strongly opposed his aforesaid contention, it was too late.[188] Abdul Qadir is of the opinion that the idea of the Pukhtuns being of Aryan race may, if it still holds, exist in a few youths influenced by Nazism, but not otherwise. An ordinary Pukhtun will accept what has been commonly believed for centuries, i.e. the Bani Israelite link—if you tell an ordinary Pukhtun that his forefathers were Aryan, he might be ready to pick a fight.[189] He, moreover, considers the French scholar Mr Hegan's (موسيوهيگن) contention about the Aryan link of the Pukhtuns as absurd.[190] He assert that no one has the right to tie all the Pukhtuns to the skirts of some orientalists.[191]

Allah Bakhsh Yusufi states that it cannot be denied that many non-Afghan historians had tried to link the Afghan *millat* with Egyptian Qibtis, Asian Turanis, Aryans, and other ancient nations, but the Afghans attached no value to these views until the beginning of the twentieth century. Hence, the Afghans did not support or adopt these ideas. Yusufi attributes the significance and support given to these views later, and to the concept of Pukhtuns/Afghans Aryan origin, as an outcome or consequence of the political developments on the international scene and in Afghanistan. He states that during the reign of King Amanullah Khan, Sardar Faiz Muhammad Khan (who was probably the education minister at that time) tried to give the stamp of authority, through his writings, to the view that the Pathans were Aryans. However, neither did it strike a chord with the common man, nor the historians and scholars give it any special consideration, and even the Afghan government did not take on the task of imposing it on the people. Nevertheless, it is undeniable that the topic came under discussion, and the views of some orientalists were given consideration under the leadership of Sardar Faiz Muhammad Khan.[192]

Abdul Qadir has stated that while the Pukhtun nation may have had relations with other nations, attributing it to the Aryans or Indo-Aryans or to someone else is akin to erasing the origin of this race. It is enough that the Pukhtun nation is the Pukhtun race. We need not tie this race to the tail of another race; because of it being ancient and having folk traditions.[193] Although all of Abdul Qadir's contentions do not stand when critically evaluated, some of the views that he adopted in negating the Aryan Race Theory certainly carry some weight.

Contrary to terming or considering the Pukhtu language to be from the Indo-European group of languages, as has been done by some European scholars and exponents of the Aryan Race Theory, Grierson, quoting Darmesteter in *Linguistic Survey of India*, 'holds [that] it to be conclusively proved that this language [Pukhtu] belongs to the eastern group of the Iranian family. He admits that it has borrowed extensively from north-western India, but affirms that its parentage is the Avesta with its so-called Zend commentaries.'[194] Whereas, Morgenstierne, who, according to Olaf Caroe, is 'the most up-to-date authority, is better acquainted with the Pathans in the field than any who have written with authority on their language', says that 'Pakhtu is probably a Saka dialect [introduced] from the north, but it is not possible to define its relationship more closely'.[195] These contentions suggest that Pukhtu is not from the Indo-European group of languages but from the Indo-Iranian group and from Saka. An Afghan scholar, Dr Mujawar Ahmad Zyar, concurs in a recent study that Pukhtu is from the Saka.[196]

After dealing with the religious thoughts and beliefs of the ancient Aryans and Pukhtuns, Bahadar Shah Zafar Kaka Khail goes on to argue that the Pukhtuns, no matter what religion they followed till then, adopted Islam when the message of Islam reached them, because Islamic teachings were in harmony with their nature. They adopted Islam to such an extent that whoever be Pukhtun also be a Muslim; and this is a distinction of only the Pukhtun nation.[197] This raises the question: why did the other Aryans not embrace Islam in the manner in which their brethren-in-blood, the Pukhtun, did? If the Pukhtuns were Aryans, other Aryans would have had the same nature, so why was Islamic teachings not in harmony with their nature? Elsewhere, Bahadar Shah has contended that it took the Pukhtuns centuries to embrace Islam. Islam reached the Pukhtun land in the seventh century. In the eleventh century, when the Muslim Pukhtuns fought alongside Mahmud of Ghazna,[198] the non-Muslim Pukhtuns fought alongside the Hindu Shahi[199] rulers. In the twelfth century, Muslim Pukhtuns fought alongside Muhammad Ghauri[200] while the non-Muslim Pukhtuns fought alongside Prithviraj,[201] the Hindu ruler of Delhi and Ajmir.[202] So, if the Aryan Pukhtuns embraced Islam because it was in harmony and conformity with their previous way of life, why did it take centuries for them and the other Aryan groups to embrace the religion? Advocates of the Old Race Theory have also contended that Islamic teachings conformed to the Pukhtun code of life, and hence they embraced Islam *en masse*;[203] some advocates of the Bani Israelite Theory, too, have contended that they embraced Islam *en masse*.[204]

The concluding section of Bahadar Shah's contention, negating the viewpoint that the Pukhtuns are more ancient than even the Aryans and the Bani Israel, suggests that he believe in the racial superiority of the Pukhtuns which he was trying to prove.[205] This is in spite of the fact that he blames the advocates, or in his opinion the fabricators, of the Bani Israelite Theory for the same and has given this as a cause for the fabrication of the Bani Israelite Theory.[206]

Bahadar Shah has given an extract from Khushal Khan's *Dastar Namah* to support his argument, but at the same time has referred to Khushal Khan's Patan (پتان) as Batan (بطان). He did not negate his Patan/Pathan (پتهان/پتان) argument nor the assertion about how the name was given to the Pukhtuns by Mahmud of Ghazna,[207] although he vehemently refutes and negate Pathan as stated by other writers.[208] This downgrades his criteria of critical evaluation.

While dealing with the past history of the Peshawar Valley, A.H. Dani states: 'The earlier picture, remote in age, gets darker and is shrouded in the paucity of reliable evidence.' Regarding the Aryans, he has referred to 'their exploits on the banks of the rivers Suvastu, Kubha and Krumu' and has argued that 'but so far no archaeological remains have been traced to catch their monuments'. He then put the question, 'How then can we recognize and identify them?' and subsequently states: 'We hear of a few names like *Pakhthu*, *Siva* and *Yadu*, all busy in tribal feuds and mutual jealousies.' But then again, he questions the presence of the Aryans among the modern Pukhtuns by stating: 'But how far can we take them to survive in the modern Pakhtuns, or the people living around the village of *Siva* and Mardan district, or the Gaduns or Jaduns on either bank of river Indus, is difficult to say.'[209] Dani's assertion is a weighty question mark on the authenticity and historical worth of the argument of Pukhtuns' link with the Aryan, or at least on the acceptance of the Aryan Race Theory at face value and in its entirety.

Bahadar Shah restrict the Pukhtuns and Pukhtunkhwa to a specific and narrow piece of land, namely the present-day Khyber Pukhtunkhwa of Pakistan, and has ignored and excluded present-day Afghanistan and Baluchistan and the Pukhtuns living there from his Pukhtunkhwa and Pukhtun nation (*qaum/qaam*), as well as the Pukhtuns who had settled, in large numbers, in other parts of the subcontinent. Ahmad Shah Abdali,[210] who is regarded as the founder of modern Afghanistan, in his famous verse talks of Pukhtunkhwa (the Pukhtun land) as under:

$$\text{دَ دهلی تخت هیرومه چه را یاد کړم}^{211}$$

$$\text{څما دَ خپلی پښتونخوا دَ غره سرونه}$$

Meaning: I tend to forget the pleasures of the throne of Delhi, when I recall the hill-peaks of my Pukhtunkhwa.

So, Pukhtunkhwa, historically, is not restricted to only the Pukhtun land of the present-day Khyber Pukhtunkhwa, but encompasses the Pukhtun lands of the present-day Khyber Pukhtunkhwa, Baluchistan, and Afghanistan.

The above discussion and critical evaluation of the Aryan Race Theory reveals that there are a number of weaknesses in the theory about the origin, or race, or ethnicity, of the Pukhtuns. Although some scholars and authorities do not accept the authenticity of the theory—and the theory of the Aryan migration to India is now questioned seriously in some circles; it is asserted that it is no more maintainable—there is historical evidence that confirms the settlement of Aryan tribes in the present-day Pukhtun areas of both Pakistan and Afghanistan. The descendants of these tribes became part of the population in these areas over the course of time, and hence some of the present-day Pukhtuns have Aryan blood in their veins. Therefore, while the theory cannot be regarded as authentic in its entirety or accepted at face value, it cannot be discounted altogether either.

THE MIXED RACE THEORY

C. Collin Davies has observed: 'No ethnological problem is more complicated and intricate than that which is presented by the North-West Frontier of India.' And that: 'Hidden away in dark, inhospitable nullahs and still darker ravines, in lonely mountain passes and on barren, wind-swept plains, dwell a people, the human flotsam and jetsam of the past.'[212] After referring to the migrations and invasions that took place, to and over the land over the course of time, Davies states: 'All these migrations and invasions added to the heterogeneity of the existing population on the Indian borderland.'[213]

Bahadar Shah Zafar Kaka Khail claims that Ghani Khan is the chief exponent of the Greek Origin Theory.[214] While Ghani Khan states, 'I have been very curious about his [the Pukhtun] origin',[215] he also has contended, after talking about the resemblance between the Greeks and the Pukhtuns, that 'racially he is clearly Greek' but adds 'crossed with something. What that something was I do not know. Nor would I worry about it any further. What he was five thousand years ago does not matter.'[216] This suggests that Ghani Khan did not believe in the present-day Pukhtuns' pure Greek origin, which he made clear, when he state:

> He is perhaps a mixture of every race that came to India from the heart of Asia—the Persian, the Greek, the Mongol and the Turk.
>
> Each race has contributed something to his virtues and vices, looks and beliefs, religion and love-songs....
>
> The best course would be to forget how it all started and look upon what he really is today. Neither a Jew nor a Greek.[217]

The aforementioned contentions of C.C. Davies and Ghani Khan lead us to the point where instead of clinging to the previously mentioned theories and establishing our studies on who the Pukhtuns/Afghans/Pathans were millennia back, we need to research the matter of their origin objectively and try to untangle the issue of who they are today.

James W. Spain, too, states, 'Just who and what these people are has not yet been made completely clear. In a purely scientific sense, it is doubtful if it ever will be.'[218] He, however, continues:

> It is sufficient for our present purpose, however, to emphasize that the inhabitants of the Frontier are clearly of varying origin. They probably include among their ancestors some of the original Aryan occupiers of the region. Over the course of the centuries the Greek, Persian, Turkic, and Mongol invaders who passed through the Frontier also added their blood.[219]

THE THEORY

Since early times, population growth and an increase in the necessities of life, trade, and mercantile compelled nations and ethnic groups to interact with each other. The thirst for supremacy created acrimony between various ethnic groups and nations. The subsequent encroachments, invasions, and wars led to the phenomena of migration, which, in turn, resulted in the mixing of different ethnic groups.[220] Consequently, the pure races were diluted, especially in areas that were subjected to frequent migrations or invasions.

The area inhabited by the Pukhtuns/Afghans/Pathans is one of the world's significant and important regions because of its geostrategic location. It has remained a centre of great military activity and has been invaded, trampled on, and occupied by different invaders—remaining a battlefield throughout its known history. It has also had links with different nations and ethnic groups. Not only has there been migration to the land inhabited by the Pukhtuns/Afghans/Pathans, but the land and its people have, as stated earlier, also frequently been invaded throughout the course of their history. This has resulted in the settlement of a large number of people, who have either migrated to, or invaded, the area and have then become members of the local population, or Pukhtuns, over the course of time, adopting their language and customs as well as contributing to their vices and virtues (culture).

In light of the above, the Pukhtuns/Afghans/Pathans have not remained a pure race or ethnic group because of the mixing of the blood of a number of other races and ethnic groups, which has resulting in the Mixed Race Theory being put forth, to which C.C. Davies, Ghani Khan, and others refers to and which is worth considering.

Referring only to the areas of the North-West Frontier region of former India and now Pakistan, Davies states, 'Even folklore, traditions and legends are singularly silent about the races who inhabited the frontier prior to the Pathan invasions.'[221] After dealing with some of the tribes, Davies has contended, 'Thus a study of these legendary aborigines, though interesting, is barren of useful results and need not detain us. From traditional aborigines we turn to existing races.'[222]

Although the Bani Israelite Theory about the origin, or ethnicity, of the Pukhtuns has been questioned by a number of scholars and writers on different grounds, and a number of arguments have arisen against it, there is some evidence that cannot be ignored or ruled out altogether. Therefore, although personally not a believer of the Bani Israelite Theory, after a lengthy discussion about the pros and cons of the theory, Olaf Caroe contend, 'Under this interpretation even the Bani Israel story may reflect some part of the truth, and at least indicate a cause for a belief which, however unreasonable, it is hard to shake.'[223]

Bahadar Shah, although a strong opponent of the Bani Israelite Theory, maintains that evidence from the *Taurat* (*Tora* or the *Old Testament*) has confirmed the existence of Jewish, or Bani Israelite, tribes in all parts of the Achaemenian Empire of Persia, of which most of the Pukhtun areas were also a part. Archaeological excavations carried out in the present-day Khyber Pukhtunkhwa and Afghanistan unearthed evidence that revealed the settlement of Bani Israelites in the Pukhtun areas, and also that the Aramaic and Syriac languages were in vogue in the Pukhtun areas. For instance, old Syriac alphabets can be seen in their original form in two of the inscriptions preserved at the Lahore Museum. One of the inscriptions, No. 126, was excavated from the Mahabanr area from the ruins of an old settlement; the second, No. 134, was excavated from the ruins of a village in the Khudu Khail area of present-day Khyber Pukhtunkhwa. Both the areas are in the Mandanr branch of the Yusufzi tribe. Moreover, inscriptions in the Aramaic language were also found in the Laghman and Qandahar areas of Afghanistan. Keeping in view the evidence of Aster in the *Bible* or the *New Testament*, along with other evidence, it becomes clear that the Jews (the Bani Israelites) were one of the nations who came to the North-West region of the present-day Pakistan and the southern region of Afghanistan. It has been confirmed that the origin and source of the Kharushti (خروشتی) script, which was in vogue for about 800 years in Northern India and Gandhara, was an Aramaic script revealing that the language of the Jews (Bani Israelites) of these north-western areas was Aramaic and their script was Finiqi (فینقی), Sabai (سبائی), and Aramaic; and that Semitic nations have remained settled in these areas.[224]

He further contends that there are places in both the Pukhtun areas and the Bani Israelite areas in the Middle East that have similar names. For instance, the area near Mardan in the Yusufzi (Mandanr) area is named Sudam, while a city in the Bani Israelite country in which the *qaum* of the Prophet Lut (AS) resided also bears the same name. Similarly, Khyber is the name of a place near Peshawar (within present-day Khyber District of Khyber Pukhtunkhwa) and it also was the name of a Jewish settlement in Arabia. Advocates of the Bani Israelite Theory also contend that the Yusufzi resemble the Bani Israel in dressing, appearance, customs, and habits.[225]

Keeping in view the aforesaid, as well as other evidence, it appears that, in ancient times, the Semitic/Bani Israelite tribes largely settled in the present-day Pukhtun/Afghan/Pathan land. As the Aramaic language and script are associated with the Bani Israelites, and the Aramaic inscriptions have been found in the Gandhara, Laghman, and Qandahar areas of the Pukhtun land, this proves that the Bani Israelites migrated to, and settled in, these areas. Therefore, although the Bani Israelite Theory about the origin of the Pukhtuns cannot be accepted in its entirety, in as much as accepting that all Pukhtuns/Afghans/Pathans were Bani Israel by origin, or ethnicity, it cannot be rejected and ruled out altogether either.

Similarly, the Aryan Race Theory about the origin of the Pukhtuns cannot be accepted in its entirety, nor can it be ignored altogether. It is evident from the *Reg Veda* that some of the Aryan tribes, who settled in the trans-Indus area of the modern-day Pukhtun areas, included the tribes of Paktha (پكتها), Siva (شيوا), Bahalana (بهالانا), Alina (الينا), and Visanan (ويشانن).[226] It is evident from studying the contents of the Aryan Race Theory that Pukhtuns are the descendants of the Paktha tribe of the Ayrans only. However, since the descendants of other Aryan tribes also remained in the area, as there is no evidence of their migration elsewhere, their descendants are also a part of the population of the area.[227]

Greek historians have also referred to the land and people of modern-day Pukhtun areas. Scholars are not unanimous about the exact location of the Pactica (پكتيكا) and Gandhara areas, or the Gandarii (گندهاريان), Dadicai (داديكى), Aparytai (اباريتى), and Sattagydai (ستاگيدى) tribes who inhabited these areas. However, we can be quite certain that they correspond to modern-day Pukhtun areas as the names of the tribes bear a resemblance to the names of some modern-day Pukhtun tribes; or attempts have been made to establish the links.[228]

Bahadar Shah contends that the people who settled in the Arghandab, Kurram, Gumal, Kabul, Kunar, Gandhara, Talash, and Swat areas and valleys, up to the western bank of the Indus, in around 1400 BCE were Aryan by origin. They comprised five tribes, namely the Paktha, Siva, Visanan, Bahalana, and Alina. As the Paktha were the prominent and influential tribe, the language of these tribes later became known as Pakhtu (after Paktha) and the entire region where they lived became known as Paktika (Pactica)/Pakhtunkhwa. Later, Greek historians referred to these people as Pactavis (پكتويس), Pactyan (پكتوان), Pactin (پكتين), and Pristai (پرستائ), etc. all of which now mean Pukhtun/Pashtun. Bahadar Shah further asserts that during later times, the two major branches—the Aparytai and Sattagydai—were made famous by the genealogists (شجره نويسو) as the Wasli Afaghinah (allied or attached Afghans) and Karlanri (كرلانى) tribes.[229]

After dealing with the issue of the tribes residing mostly in the mountainous strip, now termed Karlanri or Wasli Afaghinah by genealogists, Olaf Caroe contends:

> At the least it illustrates a conviction that the Karlanris are not Afghans in the true line, and may be much older established.

However this may be, the Karlanri tribes of today, Wazirs, Bannuchis, Khataks, Bangash, Orakzais, Afridis and the rest, proudly own to the Pathan name; they, above all others, preserve the Pakhtunwali, the Pathan code. And this may be the reason why, unlike the Yusufzais, for instance, they prefer a Pathan to an Afghan nomenclature. Here then is support from tradition that Afghan and Pathan, while they speak variants of the same language and live mixed up together, represent widely different strains. The Afghan holds for the most part the fertile plains, Kandahar, Herat, Kabul (by conquest) and Peshawar; the Pathan is a hillman.[230]

The narration of the genealogists regarding the Karlanri tribes tells us that these people were different from the present-day inhabitants of the Gandhara region, namely the Khakhi/Khakhai (خبنی/خابئی) and Ghurya Khail (غوریاخیل) tribes. Moreover, names of some other Pukhtun tribes are also found in the *Reg Veda* with minor variations, e.g. Pani (پنی) (Panri [پنی]), Dasu (ڈاسو), Prut (پروت), and Baris (بریځ), all of whom were settled in the Arakuziya region—Ghazni and Qandahar regions including the modern-day Quetta region. All the aforesaid tribes still reside in the region, which means that they are the descendants of those Aryan tribes.[231]

Even proponents of the Aryan Race Theory have admitted that the Aryans were not the original inhabitants of the present-day Pukhtun/Afghan/Pathan land, but migrated from their original homeland elsewhere and, over the course of time, settled here; and that, after the migration of two of their groups from the Pukhtun land, only the third group established themselves in the land.[232] The Pukhtun homeland, however, was not devoid of humans before the arrival of the Aryans. Being a rich and fertile region, and having a number of rivers and plenty of water, the area must have been inhabited before the Aryans arrived. Although no clear information exists about those inhabitants and their potential migration from the area on the arrival of the Aryans, it can be inferred that, even if they did so, some would have remained in the land and absorbed by the Aryans into their fold, as has been the case in India.

Amidst this scenario, Abdul Qadir put forth the theory that the Pukhtuns are the original inhabitants of the present-day Pukhtun land, as they have also been mentioned by the Greek historians as Pact (پکت) and Pactin (پکتین); and the Pukhtuns' language, Pukhtu, can claim to be older than the languages that originated from the Prakrit (پراکرت). The Paktin (Pactin), or Paktya, or Pakhtu, or Pashtu, included the language, race, ethical code, and folk traditions of the original inhabitants of the region in a single term. From this, it is inferred that in the determination of the early stages of the (social) life of human beings, the ancient history and centrality (in terms of early human settlements) of the Pakt, Paktin, Pakhtun, or Pashtun (Pukhtun/Pushtun) race and tribe must be recognised.[233]

Abdul Qadir further contends that it is a fact that the Pukhtun race and language are ancient but, in spite of acknowledging this fact, historians have persisted to link them with different races, colours, and languages. However, if research is conducted seriously and scientifically, on the basis of this theory, researchers will certainly reach the conclusion, and will be justified in the assertion that the beginnings of the social life of human beings took place from the Pukhtun race and Pukhtu language.[234]

Moreover, he contends that attributing the Pukhtun nation to the Aryans, or Indo-Aryans, or someone else, is akin to erasing the origin of this race. The Pukhtun nation is the Pukhtun race. There is no need to associate this race with any other race as it has its own history and folk traditions.[235]

The pre-Aryan residents of the Pukhtun homeland may be referred to as aborigines, as has been mentioned by C.C. Davies[236] and as is the case with the original inhabitants of America and Australia. So, besides the Aryans and the Bani Israel, the aborigines, or the natives, or the indigenous people, have their progeny and blood in the Pukhtuns, or, rather, the Aryans and Bani Israels mixed with the aborigines, or the natives, or the indigenous people, (or the original inhabitants) of the Pukhtun land who, according to Abdul Qadir, were Pukhtun as their language was Pukhtu as was their code of conduct or way of life.[237] Allah Bakhsh Yusufi, too, is of the opinion that Pukhtu was the language of the ancient inhabitants of the land, which the newcomers had adopted.[238]

Being situated on the route of invaders going to or from India, the Pukhtuns mixed with the people who invaded the Pukhtun areas and India, and subsequently settled in the region. The first such recorded influence, beside the Aryans and Bani Israelites, is the Iranian (Persian) one. The Pukhtun land remained a part of the Achaemenian Empire for about 200 years from 550 BCE. Being a neighbouring and ruling power, Iranian (Persian) soldiers and administrators must have been posted in the area and so it was natural, in Bahadar Shah Zafar Kaka Khail's opinion, that the Pukhtun race, culture, civilisation, and language would have been influenced by that of the Iranians (Persians).[239]

With the fall of the Achaemenian Empire at the hands of Alexander of Macedonia, Alexander invaded the Pukhtun areas *en route* to India. He established military garrisons and cantonments in which he stationed Greek soldiers who later settled in those areas. Bahadar Shah Zafar Kaka Khail states that 200 years before the arrival of Alexander's Greek soldiers, the Achaemenian ruler had settled some Greek tribes in the Pukhtun land because of political considerations.[240] They were the Greeks who attended Alexander when he came to conquer their town, Nysa, and whose request Alexander honoured.[241]

The Nysans 'claimed to be descended from the soldiers of Dionysus, the divine conqueror of India'. They not only 'welcomed Alexander as a fellow Greek', but also 'provided a force of three hundred cavalry for his army'.[242] George Woodcock has contended that 'the story of Nysa....has the ring of truth' and 'there is little doubt that the people of Nysa were a group of islanded Greeks living among the Kafir tribesmen who then inhabited the region of Swat'.[243] The location of Nysa, however, has not been agreed upon by the sources.

In Thomas Holdich's words: 'Amongst the clans and tribal sections of Afghans and Pathans are to be found to this day names that are clearly indicative of this pre-historic Greek connection.'[244] Continuing his contention of the presence of the Greeks in the modern-day Afghanistan and the Pukhtun land of Pakistan, Thomas Holdich asserts:

> As this is nearly two centuries after the overthrow of Greek dominion in Afghanistan, it at least indicates that the Greek settlements established four centuries earlier must have continued to exist, and to be reinforced by Greek women (for children speak their mother's tongue) to a comparatively late period; and that the triumph of the Jat over the Greek did not by any means efface the influence of the Greek in India for centuries after it occurred. It is probable that when the importation of Greek women (who were often employed in households of Indian chiefs and nobles at a time when Greek ladies married Indian Princes) ceased, then the Greek language ceased to exist also. The retinue and followers of Alexander's expedition took the women of the country to wife, and it is not, as is so often supposed, to the results of that expedition so much as to the long existence of Greek colonies and settlements that we must attribute the undoubted influence of Greek art on the early art of India.[245]

It was because of the Greek settlement in the area that those Greeks became known as Indo-Greeks or Bactrian Greeks. They established their rule in the area, at the fall of the Mauryan Empire.[246] In the course of time, the Indo-Greek, too, lost their separate entity and their descendants became an integral part of the local population. Not only did they mix with the local population through marriage but also influenced their art and architecture. It is because of this influence of the Greeks, on the Pukhtuns, that we can see a resemblance of the Greeks in the Pukhtuns' appearance and indications of Greek culture in Pukhtun culture. This has provided the base for the Greek Origin Theory. Olaf Caroe states:

> It is often said now upon the Frontier that such-and-such a tribe, or even family, claims Grecian or Macedonian blood inherited from Alexander or his soldiers. The Afridis, for instance, have their tradition of an admixture of Greek blood. They point to the Grecian features, and indeed many a young Afridi might stand as a model for Apollo, while the Afridi elder can display the gravity of Zeus. There are young Pathan warriors, not only among the Afridis, whose strong classical profile and eagle eye recall the features of Alexander himself. It is said that Alexander's army in its passage through this country left behind deserters who mingled their blood with that of the people of Tirah and the Khaibar.[247]

Later, during the course of time, a number of other tribes came into the region from Central Asia, invaded the Pukhtun land, and established their rule in the area. The tribes included the Sakas, the Parthians, and the Kushanas. A large percentage of those nations settled in the Pukhtun land and, with the passage of time, were absorbed into the local population.[248]

At the beginning of the fifth century, another Sythian tribe called White Huns (also called Ephthalites), and Hayatilah in Muslim accounts, invaded the Pukhtun land and established their rule. With the passage of time, those White Huns who had settled in the Pukhtun areas became a part of the Pukhtun population. Some scholars are of the opinion that the Ghalji (Ghalzi, Khalji) tribes of the Pukhtuns are the descendants of the White Huns,[249] while others contend that they are Turks by origin.[250] However, tradition ascribe them to be the descendants of one Shah Husain, a refugee from Istakhar (the capital of Fars), from a Bitani woman Bibi Matu.[251] Denzil Ibbetson, on the one hand, wrote the traditional version about the origin of the Ghalzi[252] while, on the other hand, he stated that they were 'probably of mixed Turkish and Persian extraction';[253] and that they 'are a race probably of Turkish origin, their name being another form of Khilchi, the Turkish word for "swordsman," who early [earlier] settled, perhaps as mercenaries rather than as a corporate tribe, in the Siah-band range of the Ghor [Ghaur] mountains where they received a large admixture of Persian blood'.[254]

At the fall of the Hun rule, the Turki Shahis established their rule and occupied most Pukhtun areas.[255] According to the account by Hiuen Tsiang (now spelled and pronounced as Xuanzang, also Xuan Zang), the ethnicity of the Turki Shahis was Kshatriya.[256] In the ninth century, the Hindu Shahis replaced the Turki Shahis and established their own rule.

The ethnicity of the Hindu Shahis has not been agreed upon. According to Bahadar Shah Zafar Kaka Khail, they were a mixed race of the Kushana and Huns.[257] However, Muslim historians, with the exception of Albiruni, considered them to be Rajputs; but, it has also been maintained that, like the Turki Shahis, the Hindu Shahis were Kshatriyas or Rajputs as well. According to Albiruni, on the other hand, they were Brahmanas.[258] The Hindu Shahis were followed by the rule of the Ghaznavids who were Turks by origin. The Turki Shahis, the Hindu Shahis, and the Ghaznavid Turks became a part of Pukhtun population and society.

With the advance of the Muslim armies under the Umayyads, a large number of Arabs, who were Semitic by origin, settled in the Pukhtun land. They married among the local population and their descendants, with the passage of time, became part of the Pukhtun population.[259]

In the thirteenth century, the Mongols erupted from Mongolia, and invaded and occupied the Pukhtun areas. A number of them settled there, resulting in intermarriage among the local people in some areas of Afghanistan. Features of the Mongol race are clearly visible in the people of Hazarajat.[260] Similarly, the Turks, under Amir Timur (Timur Lane), came out of their homeland and occupied the Pukhtun land. A number of them settled there and, with the passage of time, became an integral part of the Pukhtun population.

These different ethnic groups and the locals intermarried and, over the course of time, lost their separate identities and were absorbed into the local population. One can say that the Pukhtuns are mainly Aryans and Bani Israel by origin/race/ethnicity, as is evident from the theory about Asli (real or original) and Wasli (allied or adopted) Afghans, but the blood of a large number of other races and ethnic groups has mixed with their blood and, over the course of time, they have emerged as a mixed race ethnicity.

Although the various ethnic groups lost their separate identities, inevitably they left their mark on the Pukhtun race or ethnicity—by way of physique, complexion, habits, rituals and customs, facial features, and so forth. Signs of the Aryans, Semitic races, Greeks, Huns, Mongols, Turks, and the other aforementioned races, or ethnicities, are found in the Pukhtuns in one way or another. Moreover, certain words in the Pukhtu language, as well as certain customs and habits, are found among the Pukhtuns/Afghans/Pathans that speak of their resemblance and deep relationship with the aforementioned races, or ethnicities, clearing the way for the different theories about the origin/ethnicity/race of the Pukhtuns/Afghans/Pathans.

It would not be amiss to reproduce excerpts from Ibbetson's account that, although we may not agree with in its entirety, illustrate and support the Mixed Race Theory:

> The origin and early history of the various tribes which compose the Afghan nation are much disputed by authorities of weight who hold very different views. I have in the following sketch followed the account given by Dr Bellew, as it affords a convenient framework on which to base a description of those tribes. But it is said to be doubtful whether the distinction which he so strongly insists upon between Pathan proper and Afghan proper really exists or is recognised by the people.... Meanwhile, about the 5th and 6th century of our era, an irruption [eruption] of Scythic tribes from beyond the Hindu Kush into the Indus Valley drove a colony of the Buddhist Gandhari, the Gandarii of Herodotus and one of the four great divisions of that Pactyan nation which is now represented by the Pathans proper, from their homes in the Peshawar valley north of the Kabul river and in the hills circling it to the north; and they emigrated *en masse* to a kindred people on the banks of the Helmand.[261]
>
> Thus the Afghan proper includes, firstly the original Afghans of Jewish race whose principal tribes are the Tarin, Abdali or Durrani and Shirani, and secondly the descendants of the fugitive Gandhari, who include the Yusufzai [Yusufzi], Mohmand [Muhmand], and other tribes of Peshawar.[262]
>
> I have said that the Gandhari were one of the four great divisions of the Pactiyae of Herodotus. The other three nations included under that name were the Aparytoe [Aparytai] or Afridi,[263] the Satragyddae [Sattagydai] or Khatak, and the Dadicae or Dadi, all alike of Indian origin... These three nations constitute the nucleus of the Pathans proper. But around this nucleus have collected many tribes of foreign origin, such as the Scythic Kakar, the Rajput Waziri, and the many tribes of Turk extraction included in the Karlanri section who came in with Sabuktagin and Taimur;[264] and these foreigners have so encroached upon the original territories of the Pactyan nation that the Khatak and Afridi now hold but a small portion of the countries which they once occupied, while the Dadi have been practically absorbed by their Kakar invaders. The whole have now become blended into one nation by long association and intermarriage, the invaders have adopted the Pakhto [Pukhtu] language, and all alike have accepted Islam and have invented traditions of common descent which express their present state of association.[265]
>
> The Ghilzai [Ghalzi] are a race probably of Turkish origin, their name being another form of Khilchi, the Turkish word for 'swordsman,' who early settled, perhaps as mercenaries rather than as a corporate tribe, in the Siah-band range of the Ghor [Ghaur] mountains where they received a large admixture of Persian blood.[266]
>
> I have included in my account of the Pathans a few allied races, who though not usually acknowledged as Pathans, have by long association become closely

assimilated with them in manners, customs, and character. They chiefly occupy Hazara, and are called Dilazak [Dalazak], Swati, Jodun [Jadun], Tanaoli [Tinawli], and Shilmani [Shalmani].[267]

Thus, the Pukhtuns/Afghans/Pathans residing in the present-day Pukhtun/ Afghan/Pathan land did not remain a pure breed but became of mixed race/ethnicity, having the blood of different ethnic groups in them; those who left the Pukhtun/Afghan/Pathan land, in one way or the other, over the course of time and settled in different parts of the subcontinent and the world, became further admixed due to intermarriages.

ANALYSIS OF SOME POINTS

Bahadar Shah Zafar Kaka Khail, while negating the Mixed Race Theory, contends that no nation in the world, such as the French, English, German, Italian, or Greek, has remained pure because of the mixing of the blood with other nations and races; hence, there is no justification in referring to the Pukhtun nation as a mixed race. To support his contention, Bahadar Shah gives the example of the Indus River which remains the Indus despite being joined by all its tributaries. He has concluded that all the inhabitants of Pukhtunkhwa who have resided here for generations, whose language is Pukhtu, and who follow Pukhtun traditions are Pukhtun, and so members of one Pukhtun nation; they are Aryan by origin because most of the nations, whose blood has been mixed in their veins, were also Aryan by race.[268]

Saying that if other nations are mixed races then the Pukhtuns cannot be called mixed race either is not a strong argument. Similarly, the example of the Indus River does not prove that the Indus carries only its own water. On the contrary, the example negates Bahadar Shah's own contention. If the example is to be accepted as valid then the Pukhtuns, whose veins carry the blood of a number of tribes, nations, ethnicities, and races should have been called 'Arya' (Aryans). Bahadar Shah, however, speaks of the Aryan race, and uses the terms Pukhtun and Pushtun, not as a race but as a nation,[269] ignoring the difference between nation and race—even though he criticises Ghani Khan for the same.[270] Also, if the name used by Bahadar Shah, viz. Pukhtun, and the example given by him, viz. the Indus River, are to be considered valid, then the Pukhtuns are Pukhtun by origin/race/ethnicity, as is the opinion of Abdul Qadir[271] and supported by Preshan Khattak,[272] being the original inhabitants of the land, and not Aryans by origin—the Aryans and the people from other ethnicities/races have only mixed with them over the course of time.

Bahadar Shah tries to oppose Abdul Qadir and Preshan Khattak's contentions and has concluded his discussion with the remarks that if the Pukhtuns are to be taken as the ancient nation of Central Asia and their language Pukhtu as the mother of other Central Asian languages on the basis of analogies and wishes rather than solid evidence, the result would be that the Pukhtuns would either be an unknown race or belong to the Dravidian race, which would be mischievousness to the nation by its own scholars.[273]

If this were so, one would like to ask: which race the Aryans belonged to? Were the Aryans not from an unknown race? If the Pukhtuns were really Dravidians, why referring to them thus would be an injustice to the Pukhtun nation? Facts have to be recognised as facts. Bahadar Shah's assertion demonstrates that he, too, believed in the racial superiority of the Pukhtuns and was determined to prove this—something that he had criticised in the advocates of the Bani Israelite Theory.

The mixed nature of other nations, quoted by Bahadar Shah, did not take place on a large scale nor over millennia, as was the case with the Pukhtuns. Moreover, he had not taken into account the mixing of the inhabitants of the Pukhtun land with the Aryans when they came and settled in this land. In addition, in the case of the Pukhtuns, its admixture of origin does not entirely resemble the nations mentioned by him, but present-day Americans.

The perspective put forth by Abdul Qadir—in response to the views and theories of Olaf Caroe and others—and supported by Preshan Khattak, is worthy to the extent that Pukhtun land had been inhabited by humans before migration and settlement there. Abdul Qadir contends that those people were Pukhtun, and their language and code of life was Pukhtu; that, in different periods of history, not only had people from the Paktin (Pactin) or Pukhtun race—those Pukhtuns who had previously migrated to other areas from the Pukhtun land—but also the Greeks, Sakas, Kushanas, Huns, Semitic, and other Aryan groups, that included the Shinayi and Gujars, had come and mixed with the local Pukhtuns. Therefore, as similarities are to be found in the features, physique, manners, and folk traditions of the Paktin nation with other nations, the Pukhtun nation resembles, to some extent, with most nations of the world.[274]

However, Abdul Qadir's claim that Pukhtuns are the oldest race in the world and Pukhtu the oldest language, is an exaggeration.[275] Preshan

Khattak has demonstrated his reservations about these assertions of Abdul Qadir by stating that one could not fully agree with the latter's claim that Pukhtu is the mother of all the languages in the world, nor that all the races of the world are from the Pukhtun race. Also, it is not easy to prove that the first settlement in the world was in the region where the Pukhtuns resided.[276] Also, Abdul Qadir's claim that the names 'Pathan', 'Afghan', and 'Pushtun' (Pukhtun) are not one and the use of the terms 'Pathan' and 'Afghan' for 'Pushtun' (Pukhtun) is not only an error but a grave mistake,[277] could not be fully agreed.

Although there is some substance in Abdul Qadir's argument that the Pukhtuns were the ancient inhabitants of the present-day Pukhtun land, there are a number of contradictory statements in his detailed discussion,[278] which cannot be critically evaluated and analysed here in detail. But, as stated above, he himself has acknowledged the mixing of other races and ethnic groups with the Pukhtuns due to which not only do his attempts to negate the Mixed Race Theory about the origin, or ethnicity, or race, of the Pukhtuns not stand, but his this assertion that the Pukhtun nation is Pukhtun race also do not stand. Abdul Qadir, moreover, asserts that this race does not need to be tied on to another race, because of its age and folk traditions; and, it does not matter whether historians and thinkers do or do not support this idea or oppose it—it makes no difference to the race of Pukhtuns, their being ancient, their exalted status, and their superior traditions.[279]

While Abdul Qadir's assertion demonstrates his good opinion, love, esteem, and well-wishes for the Pukhtuns and their way of life, it does not explain to nagate the mixed race status of the present-day Pukhtuns/ Afghans/Pathans. One's wishes cannot change the facts. Moreover, he himself states at another place that one can infer that Pukhtun is neither, solely, one race or another. In some aspects the Pukhtun's resemblance inclines towards the Greeks. In his tribal manners and spirits, the Semitic elements seem dominant, and in language that of the Aryans. Inter-tribal dominance seems a factor of the Semitic race, and Mughal admixture is equal to none.[280] Besides, in spite of being of mixed blood, all Pukhtuns follow Pukhtu, i.e. the Pukhtun code of life, and have the virtues that have prompted Abdul Qadir to view them as superior and different from others. Furthermore, it is not possible to separate the real or ancient Pukhtuns from those who mixed in them, over the course of time.

After dealing, in length, with the ethnological problem of the Pukhtuns, Syed Abdul Quddus is of the opinion, 'Therefore, it can be safely concluded that the present day *Pathans* are mostly, notwithstanding their claims, the descendants of Central Asian tribes of *Sakas*, *Kushans*, *Huns* and *Gujjars*.'[281] In spite of admitting to the settlement of the Bani Israel, Aryans, Greeks, and Persians in the Pukhtun land, and their submerging in the newly invading Sakas, Kushanas, Huns, and Gujars,[282] he ignores and omit the names of the aforesaid races and ethnic groups, i.e. Bani Israel, Aryans, Greeks, and Persians, and also of the aborigines, or the natives, or the indigenous people, from his conclusion. Hence, Abdul Quddus' contention and conclusion, or the word 'mostly', cannot be easily accepted.

It is evident from the contents and discussion on the preceding pages, and also from that of the Bani Israelite and Aryan Race theories, that there are a number of viewpoints and theories about the race/origin/ethnicity of the Pukhtuns/Afghans/Pathans. The advocates of each theory and viewpoint stand by their own assertions on the basis of their own evidence and arguments.

However, as Ghani Khan contends, 'The best course would be to forget how it all started and look upon what he [the Pukhtun] really is today.'[283] Today, the Pukhtuns are neither purely Bani Israel, nor Greeks, nor Aryans, but a mixture of the races and ethnicities who resided here before the migration of the Aryans, those who migrated 'from the heart of Central Asia', and the Bani Israel, the Aryans, the Greeks, the Persians, the Arabs, and the Mongols. Preshan Khattak, too, contends that this claim is not based on analogy but fact—that the present-day Pukhtuns are a mixed race, and all the new races (mentioned earlier) joined the original Pukhtun race who were settled in these hills from the prehistoric period, adopting their code of life: Pukhtu.[284] According to Charles Miller, 'Actually, they had been on the scene for centuries, a bubbling ethnic stew of Persian, Greek, Scythian, Turk and Mongol, to mention only a few of the invading and migrating peoples who contributed their racial ingredients to the Afghan stock.'[285]

The aforementioned historical evidence leads to the conclusion that the Pukhtuns/Afghans/Pathans have not remained a pure race, or ethnic group, and it is not prudent to claim that they are ethnically either purely Bani Israel, or Aryan, or Greek, or Saka, or any other race or ethnicity. They have the blood, and are the progeny, of all the aforementioned races and ethnic groups. Although individual tribes can be attributed to different races, ethnic groups, roots, and origins, on the whole they have not remained purely one race, or ethnicity, but are of mixed ethnicity.

Notes

1. C. Collin Davies, *The Problem of the North-West Frontier, 1890–1908: With a survey of policy since 1849*, 2nd edn., rev. and enlarged (London: CPL, 1975), 37.

2. See Sayyad Bahadar Shah Zafar Kaka Khail, *Pukhtanah da Tarikh pah Ranra kay* [henceforward Kaka Khail, *Pukhtanah*] (Pukhtu) (Pikhawar: UBA, n.d.), 51–4.

3. See Khushal Khan Khattak, *Dastar Namah* (Pukhtu), with *pishlafz* by Muhammad Nawaz Tair, *pijandgalu* by Purdal Khan Khattak (Pikhawar: PA, 1991), 153–7; Also see 'Khushal Khan's Version' below; and in Sultan-i-Rome, 'Origin of the Pukhtuns: The Bani Israelite Theory', *JPHS* (Karachi), vol. 54 (No. 4, October–December 2006), 73–104.

4. See Mujawar Ahmad Zyar, *Pukhtu aw Pukhtanah da Jabpuhanay pah Ranra kay (Lah Saki Makhinay Sarah)* (Pukhtu) (Pikhawar: Da Sapi Pukhtu Siranu aw Parakhtya Markaz, 2001).

5. The contents of the Bani Israelite Theory given here are, on the whole, based on the English translation of Khwajah Nimatullah Harwi's book *Tarikh Khan Jahani wa Makhzan-i Afghani* entitled *History of the Afghans: Translated from the Persian of Neamet Ullah*, trans. Bernhard Dorn, 3rd edn. (Karachi: IP, 2001). It is to be noted that there is variance between the accounts of Bernhard Dorn's English translation and Muhammad Bashir Husain's Urdu translation of Nimatullah Harwi's book *Tarikh Khan Jahani wa Makhzan-i Afghani*, sometimes on crucial points. This is either the result of a difference in the understanding of both the translators of the original Persian version, or due to a difference in the Persian copies from which the translations were done.

6. For more details about the point, see Kaka Khail, *Pukhtanah*, 15 n., 48; Sayyad Bahadar Shah Zafar Kaka Khail, *Pushtun: Apni Nasal kay Aayinay mayn* [henceforward Kaka Khail, *Pushtun*] (Urdu) (Peshawar: UBA, 1994), 15, 158–62; Preshan Khattak, *Pushtun Kaun? (Tarikh, Tahqiq, Tanqid)* (Urdu) (Peshawar: PA, 1984), 13–15; Sadullah Jan Barq, 'Da Pukhtanu Asal Nasal (Trikh Tarikh)', *Pukhtu* (Pikhawar), vol. 29 (Nos. 9–10, September–October 1997), 27–9.

7. Harwi, *History of the Afghans*, 2. Also see Khwajah Nimatullah Harwi, *Tarikh Khan Jahani wa Makhzan-i Afghani*, Urdu trans. Muhammad Bashir Husain [henceforward Harwi, *Tarikh Khan Jahani*] (Lahore: Markazi Urdu Board, 1978), 33–7, 324–5.

8. Harwi, *History of the Afghans*, 3. Also see Harwi, *Tarikh Khan Jahani*, 35–6.

9. Harwi, *History of the Afghans*, 3–4. Also see Harwi, *Tarikh Khan Jahani*, 36–7.

10. Harwi, *History of the Afghans*, 5–10. Also see Harwi, *Tarikh Khan Jahani*, 39–51.

11. Harwi, *History of the Afghans*, 10. Also see Harwi, *Tarikh Khan Jahani*, 51–2.

12. Harwi, *History of the Afghans*, 11–16. Also see Harwi, *Tarikh Khan Jahani*, 53–66.

13. Harwi, *History of the Afghans*, 16–18. Also see Harwi, *Tarikh Khan Jahani*, 67–9.

14. Harwi, *History of the Afghans*, 18. Also see Harwi, *Tarikh Khan Jahani*, 70–2.

15. Harwi, *History of the Afghans*, 18–19 cf. Harwi, *Tarikh Khan Jahani*, 72–6.

16. Harwi, *History of the Afghans*, 19–20. Also see Harwi, *Tarikh Khan Jahani*, 76–80.

17. Harwi, *History of the Afghans*, 20–3. Also see Harwi, *Tarikh Khan Jahani*, 80–5.

18. Harwi, *History of the Afghans*, 23. Also see Harwi, *Tarikh Khan Jahani*, 84–6.

19. Harwi, *History of the Afghans*, 24–5. Also see Harwi, *Tarikh Khan Jahani*, 87–90.

20. Harwi, *History of the Afghans*, 25 cf. Harwi, *Tarikh Khan Jahani*, 90–1.

21. Harwi, *History of the Afghans*, 26–38. Also see Harwi, *Tarikh Khan Jahani*, 92–117.

22. Harwi, *History of the Afghans*, 38. Also see Harwi, *Tarikh Khan Jahani*, 117–19.

23. Harwi, *History of the Afghans*, 38. Also see Harwi, *Tarikh Khan Jahani*, 119–20.

24. Akhun Darwizah, *Tazkiratul Abrar-i wal Ashrar* (Persian) (Peshawar: Islami Kutub Khanah, n.d.).

25. Ibid., 247.

26. Ibid., 79–81.

27. Ibid., 81–2.
28. Ibid., 82.
29. Ibid., 82–3.
30. Ibid., 83.
31. Ibid., 83–4.
32. Ibid., 84–5.
33. Sultan Muhammad Khan, *Pukhtunu ka Tarikhi Safar: Bani Israel kay Tanazur mayn* (Urdu) (Karachi: Pakistani Adab Publications, 1997), 105. Also see Kaka Khail, *Pukhtanah*, 19; Razia Sultana, 'Pukhtoons Settlement in the Peshawar Valley: An Appraisal', *JPHS* (Karachi), vol. 50 (No. 4, October–December 2002), 67; Denzil Ibbetson, *Punjab Castes*, repr. (Delhi: LPP, 1993), 62; Qazi Ataullah Khan, *Da Puhktanu Tarikh* (Pukhtu), 3rd impr. (Pikhawar: UBA, 2012), 11.
34. Khan, *Pukhtunu ka Tarikhi Safar*, 84; Kaka Khail, *Pukhtanah*, 20.
35. 'In the Zend and Pahlawi the term *daiv* is used for evil spirit while in Sanskrit, or earlier in the *Veda*, it is used for gods and deities. (See Platt's *Dictionary for Urdu Classical, Hindi and English*, OUP, 1960. pp. 558–559)', Sultan-i-Rome, 'Origin of the Pukhtuns: The Bani Israelite Theory', 83, editor's note.
36. Available sources on the Mughal period 'have no reference to any such episode'. Ibid., 84, editor's note.
37. For the contention, see Kaka Khail, *Pukhtanah*, 47–8; Barq, 'Da Pukhtanu Asal Nasal (Trikh Tarikh)', 27–8, 41.
38. See Barq, 'Da Pukhtanu Asal Nasal (Trikh Tarikh)', 27–8. It is to be noted that while Sadullah Jan Barq mention his source as *Tarikh Khurshid Jahan*, Preshan Khattak's reference to the devil-figured (*Diw surat*) and Satanic character (*Shaitan sirat*) man— instead of a demon—too is based on *Tarikh Khurshid Jahan*. See Khattak, *Pushtun Kaun?*, 23–4.
39. See Kaka Khail, *Pukhtanah*, 20.
40. Khattak, *Dastar Namah*, 153–4. It is worth mentioning that in *Kulyat-i Khushal Khan*, Khushal Khan has mentioned the Pukhtuns as offspring of Prophet Yaqub (AS), who was grandson of Prophet Ibrahim (AS) himself. See Khushal Khan Khattak, *Kulyat-i Khushal Khan Khattak: Ghazliyat* (Pukhtu), *muratabah* and with *da Khushal pah haqlah* by Sher Shah Tarkhawi, vol. 1 [henceforward Khattak, *Kulyat*, vol. 1] (Pikhawar: APH, n.d.), 341. At another place, he has stated this as well that by origin Pukhtun is the Sarabanay (Saraban), or the Ghurghustay (Ghurghust), or the Bitanay (Bitan). And allied with the Saraban is the Karlanray (Karlani). See Khushal Khan Khattak, *Kulyat-i Khushal Khan Khattak: Qasaid, Rubaiyat, Qitat aw Mutafariqat*, vol. 2 [henceforward Khattak, *Kulyat*, vol. 2] (Pikhawar: APH, n.d.), 197.
41. Khattak, *Dastar Namah.*, 154–5. It is to be mentioned that in a latter research study it has been contended that Khushal Khan Khattak was not a Pukhtun by ethnicity, which negates his being from his mentioned genealogical line or family tree of the Afghans/Pukhtuns. For detail about this new contention, see Khwajah Muhammad Sayal, *Khushalyat aw Haqayaq (Intiqadi Jaaj)* (Pukhtu) (n.p.: By the Author, 2006).
42. In this sentence, a portion of the line in the Pukhtu edition of the *Dastar Namah* is blank, and so some words of the account are missing. We have translated those words from the Urdu translation of the book and given them in brackets in the sentence. For the missing words in the Pukhtu version, see Khattak, *Dastar Namah*, 156; for the Urdu version, translated here, see Khushal Khan Khattak, *Dastar Namah*, Urdu trans. Khatir Ghaznawi, review by Purdal Khan Khattak, with *pishlafz* by Muhammad Nawaz Tair, and *dibachah* by Preshan Khattak (Urdu) (Peshawar: PA, 1980), 161.
43. Khattak, *Dastar Namah*, 155–6.
44. Ibid., 156–7.

45. See Kaka Khail, *Pushtun*, 9.
46. See Khattak, *Pushtun Kaun?*, 111 f.n.
47. For the details of these points, see Kaka Khail, *Pukhtanah*, 21–41. Also see Kaka Khail, *Pushtun*, 15–172.
48. For details, see Barq, 'Da Pukhtanu Asal Nasal (Trikh Tarikh)', 29–41.
49. For such contentions, see Kaka Khail, *Pukhtanah*, 41–51, 121; Olaf Caroe, *The Pathans: 550 B.C.–A.D. 1957*, repr. (Karachi: OUP, 1976), 7–9; Sadullah Jan Barq, 'Da Pukhtanu Asal Nasal: Da Qays Abdur Rashid Qisah', *Pukhtu* (Pikhawar), vol. 30 (Nos. 1–2, January–February 1998), 45–7; Barq, 'Da Pukhtanu Asal Nasal (Trikh Tarikh)', 33–7; Khattak, *Pushtun Kaun?*, 30–1.
50. Kaka Khail, *Pukhtanah*, 41–2; Caroe, *The Pathans*, 7.
51. Kaka Khail, *Pukhtanah*, 50.
52. See ibid., 45–8; Barq, 'Da Pukhtanu Asal Nasal (Trikh Tarikh)', 26–8, 41.
53. See Kaka Khail, *Pukhtanah*, 48. Also see Kaka Khail, *Pushtun*, 158–62.
54. See Kaka Khail, *Pukhtanah*, 48–50. Also see ibid., 82; Kaka Khail, *Pushtun*, 162–6.
55. See Kaka Khail, *Pukhtanah*, 82–3.
56. See Kaka Khail, *Pushtun*, 17.
57. For the absence of any reference to such a marriage in *Tarikh Khan Jahani*, also see the Editor's note to Razia Sultana, 'Pukhtoons Settlement in the Peshawar Valley: An Appraisal', 67.
58. See Kaka Khail, *Pukhtanah*, 20.
59. See Kaka Khail, *Pushtun*, 16.
60. See ibid., 123.
61. See ibid.
62. For detail, see Kaka Khail, *Pukhtanah*, 82–7, 109–17.
63. See ibid., 87.
64. Caroe, *The Pathans*, 14.
65. See Kaka Khail, *Pukhtanah*, 88 n.
66. See records of the Swat State, especially the *Dasturul Amal*s, in the District Record Room at Gulkadah, Swat.
67. See Barq, 'Da Pukhtanu Asal Nasal (Trikh Tarikh)', 26–9; Sadullah Jan Barq, 'Da Pukhtanu Asal Nasal: Da Jinnatu Masalah, Trikh Tarikh', *Pukhtu* (Pikhawar), vol. 30 (Nos. 5–6, May–June 1998), 7.
68. See Barq, 'Da Pukhtanu Asal Nasal: Da Qays Abdur Rashid Qisah', 45.
69. See ibid., 46.
70. See Barq, 'Da Pukhtanu Asal Nasal (Trikh Tarikh)', 26.
71. See ibid., 28.
72. See Khattak, *Pushtun Kaun?*, 14–15.
73. See 'The Life of the Author' in Mahomed Kasim [Muhammad Qasim] Ferishta's *History of the Rise of the Mahomedan Power in India, till the year A.D. 1612*, trans. from the original Persian of Mahomed Kasim Ferishta by John Briggs, vol. 1, repr. (Lahore: SMP, 1977), xxxix–xlvi.
74. See Barq, 'Da Pukhtanu Asal Nasal (Trikh Tarikh)', 33–7.
75. See Sadullah Jan Barq, 'Da Pukhtanu Asal Nasal: Pukhtanah Arya Di?; Trikh Tarikh', *Pukhtu* (Pikhawar), vol. 30 (Nos. 7–8, July–August 1998), 12.
76. Caroe, *The Pathans*, 8.
77. See Barq, 'Da Pukhtanu Asal Nasal (Trikh Tarikh)', 29.
78. Caroe, *The Pathans*, 10.
79. See Barq, 'Da Pukhtanu Asal Nasal (Trikh Tarikh)', 37–41.
80. See Sadullah Jan Barq, Da Pukhtanu Asal Nasal, vol. 1 (Pukhtu) (n.p.: By the Author, 2008), vol. 2 (Pukhtu) (Pikhawar: UBA, 2009), vol. 3 (Pukhtu) (Pikhawar: UBA, 2010).

81. Kaka Khail, *Pukhtanah*, 49; Kaka Khail, *Pushtun*, 162. Nevertheless, Dr Ansar Zahid Khan has pointed out: 'The Jews regard all other human beings as "gentiles" and look down upon them. The Pathans though proud as an ethnic entity do respect groups like the decendents [descendants] of the holy [Holy] Prophet [S.A.W.].' Sultan-i-Rome, 'Origin of the Pukhtuns: The Bani Israelite Theory', 95, editor's note.

82. Ibbetson, *Punjab Castes*, 59.

83. Khan, *Da Pukhtanu Tarikh*, vol. 1, 12.

84. See Harwi, *Tarikh Khan Jahani*, 33–7; Harwi, *History of the Afghans*, 2–4.

85. See Harwi, *Tarikh Khan Jahani*, 92–4; Harwi, *History of the Afghans*, 26.

86. See Harwi, *Tarikh Khan Jahani*, 119–20.

87. See Akhun Darwizah, *Makhzan* (Pukhtu/Persian), with *muqadimah* by Sayyad Muhammad Taqwim-ul-Haq Kaka Khail, 2nd impr. (Pikhawar: PA, 1987), 1–2, 31–2, 42, 61–2, 65, 75, 92, 96, 98, 102, 104, 119–37.

88. See ibid., 127.

89. See ibid., 140, 142, 145, 156, 183, 192, 195, 210.

90. See Khattak, *Kulyat*, vol. 2, 49, 311.

91. See Khattak, *Kulyat*, vol. 1, 42, 164, 173, 312, 376; Khattak, *Kulyat*, vol. 2, 37, 52, 62, 68, 70, 88, 177, 257, 269–70, 283, 321, 340, 345, 362; Khushal Khan Khattak, *Kulyat-i Khushal Khan Khattak: Sarah da Muqadimay aw Hashyay da Dost Muhammad Khan Kamil (Momand)* (Pukhtu), 2nd edn. (Pikhawar: IIS, 1960), 46, 58, 214, 226, 405, 492, 566, 579, 587, 589, 612, 713, 807, 823, 824, 842, 858, 892, 915, 920, 937. As mentioned in note 41, according to a latter research study Khushal Khan Khattak too was not Afghan/Pukhtun by ethnicity. For detail, see Sayal, *Khushalyat aw Haqayaq (Intiqadi Jaaj)*.

92. See Khattak, *Kulyat*, vol. 1, 42; Khattak, *Kulyat*, vol. 2, 102; Khattak, *Kulyat-i Khushal Khan Khattak: Sarah da Muqadimay aw Hashyay da Dost Muhammad Khan Kamil (Momand)*, 46, 628.

93. Khattak, *Kulyat*, vol. 2, 52. Khushal Khan's this claim has been questioned now and it do not stand scrutiny. For instance, see Sultan-i-Rome, 'Khushhal Khan Khattak: An Afghan Nationalist or a Mughal Loyalist?', *JPHS* (Karachi), vol. 64 (No. 3, July–September 2016), 61–94.

94. Amir Hamzah Khan Shinwari, *Ghazawanay* (Pukhtu), 14th edn. (n.p.: Hamzah Academy, 2010), 42.

95. Ibid.

96. For examples, see ibid., 91, 93, 115, 117, 192–5, 282, 292–3, 312, 332, 337, 376.

97. *Pishlafz*, to Shinwari, *Ghazawanay*, p. ﯾﺰ (*yaz*).

98. Shinwari, *Ghazawanay*, 195.

99. Khan Abdul Ghani Khan, *Da Ghani Kulyat: Da Panjray Chaghar, Palwashay aw Panus* (Pukhtu) (Afghanistan: Da Qaumunu aw Qabailu Wazarat, Da Nashratu Riyasat, 1985), 588.

100. Ibid., 163.

101. Liwanay Falsafi [Abdul Ghani Khan], *Gaday Waday* (Pukhtu), with *muqadimah, hashyah aw latun* by Sayyad Iftikhar Husain (Pikhawar: Pakistan Studies Centre, Pikhawar University, n.d.), 36.

102. See Abdul Ghaffar [Khan], *Zama Jwand aw Jidujahd* (Pukhtu) (Kabul: DM, 1983), 176-7; Khan Abdul Ghaffar Khan, *Ap Biti* (Urdu) (Lahore: FH, 2004), 44–5.

103. See Ghaffar, *Zama Jwand aw Jidujahd*, 183–4.

104. See ibid., 308.

105. The contention was made by Haroon Rashid in his speech at the launching ceremony of his book *History of the Pathans*, vol. 1, *The Sarabani Pathans* (Islamabad: By the Author, 2002) on 27 May 2003 at the Area Study Centre for Russia, Central Asia and China, University of Peshawar.

106. For instances, see Darwizah, *Makhzan*, passim; Khattak, *Dastar Namah*, passim.

107. It is noteworthy that Qaiyum Khan banned the book, himself, after becoming chief minister of the province—unique in terms of a book being banned by its own author.

108. This contention, that Pukhtun writers had not used the name Pathan, was made by Dr Sayed Wiqar Ali Shah, while voicing his disagreement with the name of Haroon Rashid's book, *History of the Pathans*, in his address at the launching ceremony of the latter's book *History of the Pathans*, vol. 1, *The Sarabani Pathan*, on 27 May 2003 at the Area Study Centre for Russia, Central Asia and China, University of Peshawar.

109. See Abdul Qadir, *Muqadimah* to Olaf Caroe, *Pathan*, Urdu trans. Sayyad Mahbub Ali, with *pishlafz* by Raj Wali Shah Khattak, and trans. *ikhtitamiyah* by Ashraf Adeel, 3rd edn. (Peshawar: PA, 2000), 16.

110. For his contention, see ibid., 8.

111. The contents of the Aryan Race Theory given here are based, on the whole, on Sayyad Bahadar Shah Zafar Kaka Khail's book: *Pukhtanah*. And most of his contents and contentions, it seems, are based on Ahmad Ali Kuhzad, *Tarikh Afghanistan*, vol. 1, *Az Adwar Qabal al-Tarikh ta Saqut Sulta [Sultanat] Mauriya, Hisah Awal Fasl-i Fanjum "Lashkar Kashi Hayi Iskandar": Az Safhah 364 ta 426* by Muhammad Usman Sadafi (Persian) (facts of publication torn out). Not only did Bahadar Shah Zafar believe in the theory, but he also has advocated it. Also see Kaka Khail, *Pushtun*, 222–316; Khattak, *Pushtun Kaun?*, 62–73.

112. Kaka Khail, *Pukhtanah*, 55. Also see Kaka Khail, *Pushtun*, 222–3, 266; Khattak, *Pushtun Kaun?*, 63. For Mr le Bon (Dr Gustav le Bon) contention, see Gustav le Bon, *Tamadun-i Hind*, Urdu trans. Sayyad Ali Bilgrami, with *muqadimah* by Rais Ahmad Jafri (Lahore: Maqbul Academy, n.d.), 209.

113. Kaka Khail, *Pukhtanah*, 55–6. Also see Khattak, *Pushtun Kaun?*, 63 cf. Kaka Khail, *Pushtun*, 223.

114. Kaka Khail, *Pukhtanah*, 56. Also see Kaka Khail, *Pushtun*, 223–4; Khattak, *Pushtun Kaun?*, 63–4.

115. Kaka Khail, *Pukhtanah*, 56–7. Also see Kaka Khail, *Pushtun*, 227; Khattak, *Pushtun Kaun?*, 64–5.

116. Kaka Khail, *Pukhtanah*, 57. Also see Kaka Khail, *Pushtun*, 227; Khattak, *Pushtun Kaun?*, 65.

117. Kaka Khail, *Pukhtanah*, 58. Also see Kaka Khail, *Pushtun*, 227–8; Khattak, *Pushtun Kaun?*, 65.

118. Kaka Khail, *Pukhtanah*, 58–9.

119. Ibid., 62–3.

120. See ibid., 63–4.

121. Ibid., 59–61 cf. Kaka Khail, *Pushtun*, 228, 232.

122. A.H. Dani, *Book One: Pre-Muslim Period* in I.H. Qureshi, ed., *A Short History of Pakistan: Books One to Four*, 2nd edn. (Karachi: UK, 1984), 48.

123. Kaka Khail, *Pukhtanah*, 62.

124. Ibid., 66–8. Also see Kaka Khail, *Pushtun*, 229–30.

125. Kaka Khail, *Pukhtanah*, 68–70. Also see Kaka Khail, *Pushtun*, 229–30.

126. Kaka Khail, *Pukhtanah*, 70–1.

127. Ibid., 71. Also see Kaka Khail, *Pushtun*, 233–4.

128. Kaka Khail, *Pukhtanah*, 71–3; H.W. Bellew, *An Inquiry into the Ethnography of Afghanistan*, repr. (Karachi: IP, 1977), 107, 110.

129. See Ibbetson, *Punjab Castes*, 63.

130. Kaka Khail, *Pukhtanah*, 74.

131. Ibid., 74–6, 81.

132. See ibid., 76–81.

133. Kaka Khail, *Pushtun*, 268. For other examples and similar words in Pukhtu and Sanskrit/Hindi, and Pukhtu and Zend/Pahlawi/Persian, see ibid., 268–79.

134. See ibid., 234–6, 257–65.

135. Ibid., 20. He, moreover, has quoted an Arabic saying: انظرالی ماقال ولاتنظر الی من قال (meaning: See to what was said and not to who said it) to support his critical analysis of the other theories. See ibid.; Kaka Khail, *Pukhtanah*, 15.

136. For Abdul Qadir's contention, see Abdul Qadir, *Da Fikar Yun: Da Mawlana Abdul Qadir da Mazmununu Majmua*, comp. Abdur Rahman Shabab (Pukhtu), 2nd edn. (Pikhawar: UBA, 1997), 105–6.

137. See Darwizah, *Tazkiratul Abrar-i wal Ashrar*, 79–86; Khattak, *Dastar Namah*, 153–7.

138. See Kaka Khail, *Pukhtanah*, 36, 41. For details, see ibid., 21–41. Also see Caroe, *The Pathans*, 7.

139. For Preshan Khattak's critical evaluation of the gap in the account of the Aryan Race Theory, see Khattak, *Pushtun Kaun?*, 72–4.

140. See Kaka Khail, *Pukhtanah*, 72–3.

141. See ibid., 76.

142. Ahmad Hasan Dani, *Peshawar: Historic City of the Frontier*, [2nd edn.] (Lahore: SMP, 1995), 77.

143. Also see ibid., 92–4.

144. Ghani Khan, *The Pathans: A Sketch*, repr. (Islamabad: PASR, 1990), 3–4.

145. For Roshan Khan's assertion, see Khan Roshan Khan, *Tazkirah (Pathanu ki Asliyyat aur un ki Tarikh)* (Urdu), 4th impr. (Karachi: Roshan Khan and Company, 1983), 61–2.

146. See Kaka Khail, *Pushtun*, 81–8.

147. See Kaka Khail, *Pukhtanah*, 95–6. Also see Kaka Khail, *Pushtun*, 256.

148. See Kaka Khail, *Pukhtanah*, 68.

149. See Kaka Khail, *Pushtun*, 185.

150. See Kaka Khail, *Pukhtanah*, 55–124 passim.

151. See Kaka Khail, *Pushtun*, 199.

152. See Kaka Khail, *Pukhtanah*, 56–8.

153. See ibid., 66.

154. See ibid., 94.

155. For instance, see ibid., 75.

156. See ibid., 97.

157. See Kaka Khail, *Pushtun*, 295.

158. See Kaka Khail, *Pukhtanah*, 95.

159. See Kaka Khail, *Pushtun*, 230–1.

160. See ibid., 292.

161. Also see Ibbetson, *Punjab Castes*, 59–60; Qadir, *Da Fikar Yun*, 112; Allah Bakhsh Yusufi, *Yusufzai* (Urdu) (Karachi: Muhammad Ali Educational Society, 1960), 644–5.

162. See Khan, *The Pathans*, 4.

163. See Qadir, *Muqadimah* to Caroe, *Pathan*, Urdu trans. Sayyad Mahbub Ali, 22–3.

164. See Yusufi, *Yusufzai*, 644–5.

165. See ibid., 645–55. Also see Khan, *Tazkirah*, 262–6.

166. See Kaka Khail, *Pukhtanah*, 16.

167. See ibid., 78, 80–1.

168. Caroe, *The Pathans*, 6.

169. See Khattak, *Pushtun Kaun?*, 92–3, 100.

170. See Kaka Khail, *Pukhtanah*, 14–125; Kaka Khail, *Pushtun*, passim.

171. See Kaka Khail, *Pushtun*, 173.

172. For details, see ibid., 10–14, 173, 251–4 for *nasal*, *mulk*, and *qaum* respectively.

173. See ibid., 207.

174. See ibid., passim.

175. Ibid., 199.

176. Ibid., 220.
177. Ibid., 220–1.
178. Ibid., 221.
179. For details, see Khattak, *Pushtun Kaun?*, 73–95.
180. Caroe, *The Pathans*, 10.
181. See Bon, *Tamadun-i Hind*, Urdu trans. Sayyad Ali Bilgrami, 210.
182. Davies, *The Problem of the North-West Frontier*, 41.
183. Ibid.
184. Yusufi, *Yusufzai*, 642.
185. See Kaka Khail, *Pushtun*, 222.
186. Yusufi, *Yusufzai*, 641. Also see Khattak, *Pushtun Kaun?*, 94–8.
187. See Qadir, *Muqadimah* to Cario, *Pathan*, Urdu trans. Sayyad Mahbub Ali, 23–4.
188. Qadir, *Da Fikar Yun*, 115.
189. See ibid., 110.
190. See ibid., 108–9.
191. See ibid., 114.
192. See Yusufi, *Yusufzai*, 636–8.
193. See Qadir, *Muqadimah* to Caroe, *Pathan*, Urdu trans. Sayyad Mahbub Ali, 29.
194. Caroe, *The Pathans*, 65. Also see Khattak, *Pushtun Kaun?*, 93.
195. Caroe, *The Pathans*, 66.
196. For details, see Zyar, *Pukhtu aw Pukhtanah da Jabpuhanay pah Ranra kay.*
197. See Kaka Khail, *Pushtun*, 259–65.
198. For Mahmud of Ghazna or Sultan Mahmud Ghaznavi, see Muhammad Nazim, *The Life and Times of Sultan Mahmud of Ghazna*, with foreword by Thomas Arnold (Cambridge: At the University Press, 1931); Mohammad Habib, *Sultan Mahmud of Ghaznin*, 2nd edn. (Delhi: SCC, n.d.).
199. For the Hindu Shahis, see Yogendra Mishra, *The Hindu Sahis of Afghanistan and the Punjab, A.D. 865–1026* (Patna: Vaishali Bhavan, 1972).
200. For Muhammad Ghauri and his exploits, see S.M. Ikram, *A History of Muslim Civilization in India and Pakistan: A Political and Cultural History*, 6th edn. (Lahore: IIC, 1994), chap. 3.
201. Prithviraj was the Hindu Raja (ruler) of Ajmir and Delhi who fought against the Afghan invader, Muhammad Ghauri, at the two famous battles of Tarain (modern Traori) in 1191 and 1192. He was successful in the first battle, exacting heavy losses on Muhammad Ghauri, but was defeated in the second battle and later executed for treason.
202. See Kaka Khail, *Pukhtanah*, 44. For a somewhat different version, see Kaka Khail, *Pushtun*, 263, 280–1. For the contention that the Pukhtuns embraced Islam gradually, during the time of Mahmud of Ghazna and Muhammad Ghauri, also see Caroe, *The Pathans*, 9–10, 121; Dani, *Peshawar*, 77, 266. Dr Ansar Zahid Khan, however, has contended: 'There is no evidence to show the presence of non-Muslim Pukhtuns or Afghans in the army of Prithviraj. It was basically a Rajput army comprising elephants and infantry. For details of the war see Minhaj Siraj; *Tabaqat-i Nasiri*, Habib edition, pp. 400–401, Urdu tr., Lahore, 1975, pp. 711–712 cf. Farishta, *Tarikh-i Farishtah*, Urdu tr. Karachi ed., 1962, Vol. 1, pp. 225–239'. Sultan-i-Rome, 'Origin of the Pukhtuns: The Aryan Race Theory', *JPHS* (Karachi), vol. 56 (No. 3, July–September 2008), 55, editor's note.
203. See Qadir, *Muqadimah* to Caroe, *Pathan*, Urdu trans. Sayyad Mahbub Ali, 27–9, 44; Khattak, *Pushtun Kaun?*, 134.
204. See Darwizah, *Tazkiratul Abrar-i wal Ashrar*, 83–4; Harwi, *Tarikh Khan Jahani*, 119; Khan, *Pukhtunu ka Tarikhi Safar*, 105; Syed Abdul Quddus, *The Pathans* (Lahore: Ferozsons (Pvt.) Ltd., 1987), 25.
205. See Kaka Khail, *Pushtun*, 213–14.
206. See Kaka Khail, *Pukhtanah*, 47–51

207. See Kaka Khail, *Pushtun*, 93, 280–1. For Khushal Khan's version, see Khattak, *Dastar Namah*, 157.

208. See Kaka Khail, *Pushtun*, 144–50; Kaka Khail, *Pukhtanah*, 42, 50.

209. Dani, *Peshawar*, 44–5.

210. For Ahmad Shah Abdali's rise to power and his successes, see *Caroe, The Pathans*, 249–61; R.C. Majumdar, H.C. Raychaudhuri, and Kalikinkar Datta, *An Advanced History of India*, repr. (Lahore: Famous Books, 1992), 534–6; Ganda Singh, *Ahmad Shah Durrani: Father of Modern Afghanistan* (Bombay: Asia Publishing House, 1959).

211. Abdul Hai Habibi, *Pukhtanah Shuara: Hisah Awal* (Pukhtu) (Pikhawar: IIS, n.d.), 310.

212. Davies, *The Problem of the North-West Frontier*, 37.

213. Ibid.

214. See Kaka Khail, *Pukhtanah*, 54; Kaka Khail, *Pushtun*, 173–8. Also see Khattak, *Pushtun Kaun?*, 61–2.

215. Khan, *The Pathans*, 3.

216. Ibid., 4.

217. Ibid., 5.

218. James W. Spain, *The Pathan Borderland*, repr. (Karachi: IP, 1985), 39.

219. Ibid.

220. Also see Kaka Khail, *Pukhtanah*, 93.

221. Davies, *The Problem of the North-West Frontier*, 38.

222. Ibid., 39.

223. Caroe, *The Pathans*, 10.

224. See Kaka Khail, *Pukhtanah*, 109–14.

225. See ibid., 115. Also see Ibbetson, *Punjab Castes*, 59; Davies, *The Problem of the North-West Frontier*, 43.

226. See Kaka Khail, *Pukhtanah*, 95–6.

227. Ibid.

228. For detail, see ibid., 71–6, 97–107.

229. See ibid., 107.

230. Caroe, *The Pathans*, 23–4.

231. Kaka Khail, *Pukhtanah*, 107–8.

232. See ibid., 55–9.

233. See Qadir, *Muqadimah* to Caroe, *Pathan*, Urdu trans. Sayyad Mahbub Ali, 21. Preshan Khattak and Sadullah Jan Barq have also referred to Abdul Qadir's contention that the Pukhtun lands were not devoid of humans prior to the migration of the Aryans. See Khattak, *Pushtun Kaun?*, 126–35, 193–4; Barq, 'Da Pukhtanu Asal Nasal: Pukhtanah Arya Di?'; Trikh Tarikh', 9–12.

234. Qadir, *Muqadimah* to Caroe, *Pathan*, Urdu trans. Sayyad Mahbub Ali, 22.

235. Ibid., 29.

236. See Davies, *The Problem of the North-West Frontier*, 39.

237. Qadir, *Muqadimah* to Caroe, *Pathan*, Urdu trans. Sayyad Mahbub Ali, 21.

238. Yusufi, *Yusufzai*, 623. Also see ibid., 665–8.

239. See Kaka Khail, *Pukhtanah*, 117.

240. See Kaka Khail, *Pushtun*, 176. Also see, Thomas Holdich, *The Gates of India: Being an Historical Narrative*, 1st edn. published in Pakistan (Quetta: GA, 1977), 20–1.

241. See Yusufi, *Yusufzai*, 167–9.

242. George Woodcock, *The Greeks in India* (London: FFL, 1966), 21.

243. Ibid.

244. Holdich, *The Gates of India*, 21.

245. Ibid., 21–2.

246. For details, see A.K. Narain, *The Indo-Greeks*, repr. (Oxford: At the Clarendon Press, 1962); Woodcock, *The Greeks in India*.
247. Caroe, *The Pathans*, 44–5.
248. See Kaka Khail, *Pukhtanah*, 118. Also see Caroe, *The Pathans*, 70–80.
249. Kaka Khail, *Pukhtanah*, 118–19, 347–61. Also see Caroe, *The Pathans*, 81–90.
250. See Kishori Saran Lal, *History of the Khaljis: A.D. 1290–1320* (Karachi: Union Book Stall, n.d.), 9–13.
251. For details, see Bellew, *An Inquiry into the Ethnography of Afghanistan*, 11–15.
252. See Ibbetson, *Punjab Castes*, 65.
253. Ibid., 60.
254. Ibid., 64.
255. For the Turki Shahi rule, see Abdur Rehman, *The Last Two Dynasties of the Sahis (An analysis of their history, archaeology, coinage and palaeography)* (Islamabad: Director, Centre for the Study of the Civilizations of Central Asia, 1979).
256. Mishra, *The Hindu Sahis of Afghanistan and the Punjab*, 5.
257. See Kaka Khail, *Pukhtanah*, 119.
258. See Mishra, *The Hindu Sahis of Afghanistan and the Punjab*, 3–5.
259. Also see Kaka Khail, *Pukhtanah*, 119–20.
260. Ibid., 120.
261. Ibbetson, *Punjab Castes*, 62–3.
262. Ibid., 63.
263. Note 1, given by Ibbetson, states: 'The Afridi still call themselves Aparide. There is no *f* in Pashto proper.'
264. Note 2, given by Ibbetson, states: 'The various accounts given of Karlan's origin all recognise the fact that he was not a Pathan by birth; and even the affiliation of the Karlanri is doubtful, some classing them as Sarbani and not Ghurghushti.'
265. Ibbetson, *Punjab Castes*, 63.
266. Ibid., 64.
267. Ibid.
268. See Kaka Khail, *Pushtun*, 217–18, 220–1.
269. See ibid., 220.
270. See ibid., 173.
271. See Qadir, *Muqadimah* to Caroe, *Pathan*, Urdu trans. Sayyad Mahbub Ali, 22, 43.
272. See Khattak, *Pushtun Kaun?*, 201.
273. See Kaka Khail, *Pushtun*, 201–14.
274. See Qadir, *Muqadimah* to Caroe, *Pathan*, Urdu trans. Sayyad Mahbub Ali, 21–3.
275. For Abdul Qadir's claim, see ibid., 22.
276. See Khattak, *Pushtun Kaun?*, 126–7.
277. See Qadir, *Muqadimah* to Caroe, *Pathan*, Urdu trans. Sayyad Mahbub Ali, 16. For the author's comments about this claim of Abdul Qadir's, see the Bani Israelite Theory above.
278. See Qadir, *Muqadimah* to Caroe, *Pathan*, Urdu trans. Sayyad Mahbub Ali, 6–44.
279. See ibid., 29.
280. See Qadir, *Da Fikar Yun*, 113.
281. Quddus, *The Pathans*, 28.
282. See ibid., 27.
283. Khan, *The Pathans*, 5.
284. See Khattak, *Pushtun Kaun?*, 200–1.
285. Charles Miller, *Khyber: British India's North West Frontier; The Story of an Imperial Migraine* (London: Macdonald and Jane's Publishers Limited, 1977), 8.

3 Pukhtu: The Pukhtun Code of Life

Pukhtu is not only a language but also the code
that governs the lives of those who speak it.

THE MAJORITY of the inhabitants of Khyber Pukhtunkhwa are ethnically Pukhtuns (as stated in Chapter 1) and are now a mixed ethnic group (evaluated in Chapter 2). For most of their history, most parts of the land they have occupied has remained independent, and without a centralised government of its own, because of the geographical nature of the land as well as the nature of the people. This chapter deals with what regulated and ruled the lives and actions of the people, maintained peace, and ensured security in their tribal and semi-acephalous society, in the absence of advanced means of communication, a centralised authority, or a government and governmental machinery, particularly in earlier times.

Despite the fact that Pukhtun society has remained tribal, the lives and actions of the people have been regulated and ruled by unwritten but well-defined and well-known customs, norms, codes, and rules. This explains why, although it might have appeared disorderly to an outsider and a casual observer of the society, it has undoubtedly been an organised and regulated society. These unwritten but well-defined and well-known customs, codes, rules, and norms are called Pukhtu (also written as Pashtu, Pashto, Pashtoo, Pukhtoo, and Pakhtu), which is the name of the language of the people as well. That is why, it is said that Pukhtu is not only a language but also the code that governs the lives of those who speak it. The term 'Pukhtunwali' is also used, in this sense, for 'Pukhtu' which is technically unsound. Pukhtu is the most appropriate and technically sound term. Pukhtu also means enmity, obstinacy, and firmly standing by one's stance, viewpoint, or decision.

Dr Salma Shaheen (a renowned Pukhtu scholar and poet) cites a scholar who observes that Pukhtu is not only a language but also the constitution and way of life of the Pukhtuns. Pukhtu or Pukhtunwali is the name of a specific culture and civilisation, and represents a code of ethics and behaviour. Even slight deviation from them leads to expulsion from Pukhtu. If observed keenly, throughout the life of a Pukhtun, emphasis is laid on دا پښتونه (it is Pukhtu) and دا پښتونه ده (it is not Pukhtu). Laying a misplaced step between ده (is) and نه ده (is not) carries the risk of falling out of the net of the constitutions of Pukhtu and Pukhtunwali.[1] Muhammad Nawaz Tair has contended that Pukhtunwali is the name of the code of conduct and national customs that the Pukhtuns have adopted since a long time and under which they still live today.[2] According to Ashruf Altaf Husain:

> As a matter of fact, among Pathans 'Pakhto' (Plural of 'Pakhtoon' [sic]) is the name given to the valour, sense of honour and *Lex non scripta* of the nation…. The word 'Pakhto' stands for hospitality, generosity, bravery, truthfulness, straightforwardness, keeping of a promise, patronage of the weak, giving of shelter to all including enemies, moral courage in claiming one's rights, sacrificing one's life for personal as well as national honour, dying in the name of religion, and a number of other desirable attributes and worthy traditions. To say that one is not a true 'Pakhtoon' implies that one is devoid of all these virtues and is, therefore, regarded a term of abuse.[3]

A Pukhtu *tapah* (ټپه)[4] says:

په پښتو ټينگ پښتون ولاړ دے

بې پښتو نه مني پښتون مېړه پښتونه

Meaning: The Pukhtun holds on fast to Pukhtu. The Pukhtun woman does not accept a Pukhtun husband who holds on not fast to Pukhtu.

Pukhtu 'embraces all the activities from the cradle to the grave'.[5] Its main elements and commandments are known to every Pukhtun, including children. Ghani Khan says:

> When a law is bred into the very fibre of a race it becomes a custom and persists long after the need is gone and the occasion forgotten. For man gives to his children not only the shape of his nose and the cranks in his character, he also teaches them his fears and forebodings, his songs and curses. He moulds his child as nearly as he can to his own shape.[6]

Addressing the Britons, and comparing British law made for the Pukhtuns with Pukhtun codes or Pukhtu, Ghani Khan states: 'There is absolutely no difference between your law and his custom in object and purpose.' But, 'Your laws are as stupid to him as his customs are to you.'[7] The codes and rules of Pukhtu are transferred and transmitted from parents to their children, and from one generation to the next. Addressing the Britons, Ghani Khan elaborates:

> You call it law and keep it in big books. He calls it custom and keeps it in his wife's treasure chest. You have to be either a judge or a criminal to know your law. He knows his customs before he knows how to eat. It is bred in him. It is mixed in his bones and works in his liver. He does not have to go to a learned man in a wig to know the law against which he sinned. He knows it as soon as he does it. He is his own judge and jailer. His ancestors have seen to it that it is so.[8]

The components of Pukhtu are simple and well-defined principles, which not only guide but also regulate and govern the lives and actions of the Pukhtuns: male and female, adults and children, alike. James W. Spain observes:

> Nonetheless, there are important traditional and social factors which guide community life and in many cases influence or even determine the actions of individuals. These mores vary considerably in different parts of the Pathan area, and codification of them is virtually impossible. However, certain of them are almost universal, and some knowledge of these is essential to an understanding of what the Pathan is and how he got that way.[9]

The major components and commandments of Pukhtu—termed in English as The Pukhtun Code of Life, The Way of the Pathans, and the Unwritten Constitution of the Pukhtuns[10]—are given below.

BADAL (بدل)

Badal is one of the main commandments of Pukhtu. Although *badal* means revenge, as stated by Denzil Ibbetson[11] and others,[12] it has other meanings and uses as well. *Badal* is the term used for reciprocating assistance rendered in any kind of work, as with deeds committed or favours received, but preferably in a manner that is even better than the one they were received. In Pukhtu, *badal* is regarded as the foremost obligation for one person, and greatest liability for the other, in all senses of its meaning and use; the person who does not care for, or does not observe it, is not considered a true Pukhtun.

In the case of revenge, *badal* is considered an obligation for all forms of criminal acts, and is carried out without any thought of potential consequences or costs. Not only the aggrieved person, but other family members and sometimes the subtribe and the tribe, too, are involved in *badal*; similarly, not only are the culprit(s) or aggressor(s) implicated but his/their family members and sometimes the subtribe and tribe, too. The decision on how to react—take revenge, or accept compensation, or to forgive—depends on the nature of the crime as well as the aggrieved. Generally, in cases of murder, the most influential and worthy person in the offender's family (called *da sar saray* د سرسرے: the leading figure) is murdered, creating a greater loss to the offender's family. Usually, *badal* is not time- or space-barred. A famous Pukhtu saying (پښتون چې سل کاله پس بدل اخلي نو هم تادي کوي) meaning 'When the Pukhtun takes revenge after hundred years, then too he does hurry' explains it well.

In cases of revenge, *badal* may have negative consequences as it leads to bloodshed, which may continue for generations, and in which innocents may also suffer. However, its positive effects cannot be underestimated. *Badal* is the restraining force and pillar responsible for maintaining and ensuring peace, order, and respect for human life and honour in the Pukhtun tribal and semi-acephalous areas, in the absence of law-enforcing agencies and courts. It compels a person to think about the potential consequences—not only for himself but also for his other family members, tribe, and descendants—before committing any crime. Even if the crime is not detected at the time, *badal* would be obligatory if it is detected later. Hence, *badal* is a restraining force, a tool of checks and balances, and a surety bond that a crime will not go unpunished. Moreover, *badal* is considered a right; the person who does not take *badal* is looked down upon, and is liable to *pighur* (پيغور taunt) if forgiveness has not already been granted or conciliation has not been reached.

In its other forms and uses, such as providing assistance in some work, granting a favour, or passing something on, *badal* has great significance socially. It results in cooperation and unity among the people, and makes communal life easier through contribution and assistance which leads to development. In this way, reciprocating *badal* is also obligatory; one who does not reciprocate is not honoured or esteemed. *Badal* is reciprocated in an even better way than the one in which it was received. While *badal* has been demonised and regarded as a curse in general literature and by the media, its positive aspect, impact, and contribution dominates the negative—something that is ignored and underestimated in general.[13]

MILMASTYA (میلمستیا)

The second main component of Pukhtu is *milmastya* (also spelled as *melmastia*), meaning hospitality. This is not only offered to relatives, friends, and those known to the host, but also to strangers and those who ask for it. In *milmastya*, guests are served food and offered boarding and lodging when required or asked for. James W. Spain has observed that *milmastya*

> is exercised…to a degree frequently embarrassing to the guest—whether he be foreigner who knows he will never be in a position to return it, or fellow-tribesman who may fear that he will not be in a position to return it adequately when the occasion demands.[14]

A point to note in Spain's statement is regarding the return of *milmastya*. It is expected that today's guest shall be a host tomorrow. There is a Pukhtu saying: پښتون خپله ووړی د بل پۀ کور خوري meaning: 'Pukhtun eats his own food at other's home.' A person who lacks a desired minimum of hospitality (*milmastya*) is not regarded as a true Pukhtun, and is looked down upon. Guests are mainly of two types: those who may be expected to, one day, be the hosts and reciprocate the entertainment they received (preferably in a better way), and those who would be unlikely to be the hosts in turn. The stranger or poor wayfarer is called *Khudayi milmah* (خدائي مېلمه), meaning the guest to be served for the Almighty's sake.

James W. Spain states, 'The lavishness of the hospitality varies according to the circumstances of the host. A poor villager will offer tea and stew up a few pieces of goat-meat. A wealthy chief will place his house and retainers at the guest's disposal and feast him with a whole sheep.'[15] He, however, contends that *milmastya*, 'it must be confessed, is more a matter of personal prestige and self-aggrandisement than of charity or brotherly love'.[16] The significant aspect of value in *milmastya* is the warmth with which the guest is received and the manner in which he or she is served, not the food itself. A number of Pukhtu proverbs and sayings support this, such as ووړی ته مۀ ګوره خو زما رووڼ تندي ته ګوره which means: 'Do not look at the foodstuff but into the warmness in my eyes (with which I serve you)' and کۀ د غوړو ګوټ وي خوچي تندي بوټ وي پۀ هغې به څۀ کوې which means: 'To hell with a lavish food which is served with wrinkles on the host's fore-head.'

Another aspect of *milmastya* is protection of the guest. If the guest has an enmity, or needs protection because of some other reason, his protection is regarded the responsibility of the host as long as the guest remains within his house or territorial limits. This aspect of *milmastya* is considered to be obligatory by the Pukhtuns. Even a British administrator, who was no fan of the Pukhtuns, stated in his report: 'For gold, they will do almost anything except betray a guest.'[17]

> On occasion, protection may be extended into a wider sphere by proclaiming the visitor the guest of a particular chieftain or clan as long as he remains within the Pathan community. This is traditionally symbolized by the giving of a possession of the sponsoring chieftain, perhaps a dagger or a garment, which the guest wears as a symbol of the protection he is under.... Violence or hurt of any kind is almost never offered to a bonafide guest, regardless of how poor or distasteful he may be—both because of the high regard in which the obligation of *melmastia* is held and because of the obligation to take *badal* which would automatically be placed upon the host.[18]

It was because of *milmastya* that the Pukhtuns, even in the absence of modern means of communication and hotels, did not have to worry about food or boarding while travelling. They had only to go to a nearby settlement at meal times or at night, for food and a place to stay, without concern about their safety or protection.

BADRAGAH/JALAB (جلب/بدرگه)

Another commandment of Pukhtu, mainly related to *milmastya*, is *badragah* or *jalab*, meaning an escort. James W. Spain states: 'A formal escort or guarantee of safe conduct to a stranger, emissary, or even enemy, is called *badragga*.'[19] However, *badragah* is not restricted to the safe conduct of the concerned people, but also to escorting friends or other guests so as to give them honour and respect. The following *tapah* illustrates the first purpose of *badragah*, i.e. guarantee of safe conduct or passage:

په گودر څه بلا لګېږي

چې کشر وروریې بدرگه ورسره ځینه

Meaning: What catastrophe descends on the *gudar*[20] that her younger brother escorts her in *badragah*!

Raising a tribal force from the community to enforce a decision of the *jargah*, if the situation so requires, is also termed *badragah*.[21] This sort of force, however, is generally called *lakhkar* (*lashkar*).

JARGAH (جرگه)

Jargah (also spelled as *jirga*, *jirgah*, and *jarga*) means consultative assembly, forum, council, or the council of tribal chiefs. *Jargah* is the forum and assembly where issues of common interest and communal affairs are discussed and decided but, unlike a modern Western democracy, not by majority votes but by consensus or unanimity after deliberations.

When there is a problem or issue of common interest, or a communal affair, the stakeholders assemble and discuss it. The attendants are free to express their point of view and put their opinions forward openly. Decisions are not majority-imposed, but are reached by consensus or unanimity after deliberations. Among other authorities,[22] the statement of the official *Report on the Administration of the Border of the North-West Frontier Province for the year 1938–39* has endorsed that in the *jargah*s a mere majority is not sufficient for decision making, but consensus and unanimity is required. The report titled 'The Tribal Constitution', states:

> Each tribe has a tribal 'jirga', or representative body of persons with an acknowledged position in the tribe...where every man considers himself a member of the tribal jirga and where the political officer's task is not completed until he has convinced the last man of a 'jirga' numbering anything up to three thousand.... In Waziristan...almost every head of a household considers himself a member of the tribal jirga and has no intention of obeying the jirga's decision unless he happens to agree with it.[23]

Attendance depends on the nature of the problem and the issue being discussed but, generally, not everybody participates in the proceedings of the *jargah*s (in Pukhtu *jargay*). Only the elders or representatives of the families, members of religious families, religious figures of note and influence, and people having some degree of influence, participate in *jargah*s at the ward and village levels; and, select representatives from among them to represent them in the *jargah*s at the segment and tribe levels. McMahon and Ramsay's observation, regarding the tribes of Dir, Swat, and Bajawar, together with the Utman Khail and Sam Ranizi, tends to apply to other Pukhtun tribes and localities as well:

> The power is entirely in the hands of the land (*daftar*) owning Pathans (*Pukhtana*). The *fakir* or artisan classes, cultivating tenants (*kashtkars*), soldiery (*mallatars* [*mlatar*]), musicians (*doms*), etc., are without the franchise, their position being practically that of serfs.... The management of all matters relating to a village rested with the village council or Jirga. Each village was

represented in the Jirga of its Khel [Khail], each Khel in that of the sub-division, and each sub-division in the Jirga of the whole tribe.[24]

In addition, each tribe and subtribe has its chief called *malak* (plural: *malakan* and *malakanan*) and *khan* (plural: *khanan*). They act as chiefs for the tribe and subtribes, or section and subsections, but have no ruling authority over them, and usually play the role of their leaders in war and act as their agents 'in dealings with others'. They 'possesses influence, rather than power'; 'the real' power 'rests with the' *jargahs*.[25]

Jargah has other meanings, functions, composition, and uses in different contexts. These include having to conciliate opposing and inimical parties, cool down tempers, strive for amity, effect settlements, mediate between parties, and bring normalcy in cases of tension and disputes. In such situations, the meaning, formation, composition, and function of a *jargah* is based on a case-to-case basis.

Writing about the composition, powers, functions, etc. of *jargah*s, in the 1950s, James W. Spain states that, 'in its simplest form', a *jargah* 'is merely an assembly'. All 'community business, both public and private, is subject to its jurisdiction'. It has exercised 'executive, judicial, and legislative functions', and frequently acted as 'an instrument for arbitration or conciliation'. Mughal 'ambassadors, Sikh generals, British administrators, unrepentant tribesmen, Pakistani politicians, and American celebrities have stood before' *jargah*s over 'the years'. The *jargah* has essentially been 'a round-table conference', having 'no chairman or presiding officer'. Anyone, whose interest is likely to be affected, has the 'right to speak. Decisions must be unanimous and solemnized by a prayer.' In case of failure in achieving a unanimous decision, the *jargah* has to break up. 'Any outstanding problems' are to be settled by a sagacious 'leading *malik*', seated at the fore of the gathering, who has to applaud all views but speak only to facilitate matters or to bring about a compromise. 'There is seldom any voting in a' *jargah*. Because 'of the volatile nature' of the Pukhtuns and the heavy armament that they carry, armed members of the *jargah* are assigned to control the *jargah*, in case it breaks up in a fight; however, it is rarely that such a need arises and it is a testimony to the 'triumph of tradition over instinct'. 'The traditional penalty for defiance' of a *jargah* has been 'the burning of the culprit's house'. 'The body's function is to settle peacefully an existing situation', rather 'than to judge right from wrong, determine guilt, or pass sentence'. In working out a proper settlement, *jargah* members take 'the requirements' of Pukhtu, 'the circumstances' of 'the particular situation', 'and the character of the individuals concerned' into account. Their 'decisions are usually very simple'. Where 'complex disputes over property or intertribal feuds are involved, settlement' becomes 'more complicated' and the *shariat* is usually turned to for recourse.[26]

The institution and system of the *jargah* provides a forum for solving and deciding common, communal, tribal, and inter-tribal problems, issues, and disputes, as well as personal and domestic problems, and problems between families.

NANG (ننگ)

Nang means honour, although the English word 'honour' does not have the same meaning and sense. *Nang* is an important component of Pukhtu and plays a vital role in the Pukhtun social system. Its primary importance, however, is in preserving national honour and independence. *Nang* has compelled the Pukhtuns to take-up arms in defence of the homeland and the protection of national honour when the occasion demanded it, while also retaining personal esteem as well as that of the family, one's beloved, friends, the subtribe, and the tribe. The Pukhtun is required to be *nangyalay* (ننگيالی): the one who has *nang*, and to behave in the required manner in different circumstances and on different occasions. Khushal Khan Khattak says:

$$په جهان د ننگيالى دى دا دوه كاره^{27}$$
$$يا به وخورى ككرئ يا به كامران شى$$

Meaning: A *nangyalay* faces two ends in life: either he will lose his life or will emerge successful.

A *nangyalay* is honoured and esteemed. Ignoring and keeping aside the *nang* is called *biynangi* (بي ننگي), and is looked down upon. One devoid of *nang* is considered worthless. Although not having a son is considered a misfortune and bad luck in Pukhtun society, a *tapah* says:

$$بي ننگه ځوے مې پکار نۀ دے$$
$$كۀ پۀ ديدن پسې بې رنده پۀ سترګو شمه$$

Meaning: I need no son who would have no *nang*; even if I may lose my eyesight in pining away to see him.

Another similar *tapah* says:

خدایه بې ننگه خُوے را مهٔ کړې

کهٔ پهٔ دیدن پسې یې رِنده پهٔ سترګو شمه

Meaning: O! My God! Do not give me a son, who would have no *nang*; even if I may lose my eyesight in pining away to see him.

And still another *tapah* says:

پهٔ هندوستان دې ثْلے جوړ شه

د بې ننگیٔ آوازدې را مهٔ شه مئینه

Meaning: O! My beloved! I will prefer you dead and buried far away in India than you living dishonoured and ignominious.

Riwaj (رواج)

Riwaj means custom, tradition, and customary law. It governs the conduct, lives, and behaviour of the Pukhtuns to a large extent, and is followed more than the Islamic law. For instance: common law marriage (court marriage) is not recognised; the eldest son receives a greater share of a father's inheritance, called '*da masharai hisah*' (د مشری حصه) and '*mashari*' (مشري); daughters do not receive an inheritance; a widow is entitled to support only until her death or remarriage.

It is necessary to abide by *riwaj*: to observe the norms and practices of the society. In other words, 'While in Rome, do what the Romans do.' While *riwaj* varies from tribe to tribe and from locality to locality, regarding various matters, abiding by *riwaj* is considered obligatory. Hence, the Pukhtu proverb which means 'Leave the village if you are not happy with the prevalence but do not disobey it' (د کلي اوخه خو د نرخه یې مهٔ اوخه.).

Tur (تور)

Tur literally means 'black', but in this context it means adultery and illicit relations that do not remain secret. The male is called '*tur shaway*' (تور شوی), and the female '*turah shaway*' (توره شوې); both mean 'smutted' or 'blackened'. *Tur* is considered a major crime in Pukhtun society; those who commit it are liable to be murdered by the family of the female involved. Under *tur*, death is prescribed for both adultery and elopement (called 'matiz takhtidal' متيز تختبدل, 'matizah tlal' متيزه تلل, 'matizah takhtidal' متيزه تختبدل, 'matizah kawal' متيزه كول). While stating that 'this ancient principle' of death for adultery and elopement 'is active and living in the blood of the Pathan even today', Ghani Khan gives the reason for it in the following words:

> The Pathan is short of girls and generous of emotions. He must breed well if he is to breed fighters. The potential mother of the man of tomorrow is the greatest treasure of the tribe and is guarded jealously. This primitive custom is also useful for weeding out the over-sexed. It is a subtle system of selective breeding. But does the Pathan realise any of these things when he lifts his rifle to shoot the culprit? He does not. He is mad with anger. He must shoot, there is no alternative. If he does not, his neighbours will look down upon him, his father will sneer at him, his sister will avoid his eyes, his wife will be insolent and his friends will cut him dead. It is easier to be misunderstood by a judge who does not speak his language and be hanged by a law that does not understand his life. He does his duty by [to] his people. He will play true to his blood even if he breaks his heart and neck in the bargain. He will walk to the gallows with proud steps with his hands covered with the blood of his wife or sister. And the admiring eyes of his people will follow him as they always do those who pay with their life for a principle.[28]

The effects of the consequent killing of an adulterer, and of *badal* in the case of murder, cannot be underestimated. Ghani Khan notes:

> This very custom when given a chance to act alone works perfectly. In the tribal area where nearly four million people live [in 1940s] without law courts, policemen, judges and hangmen, you seldom hear of adultery or murder. Elopements are rare. For the risk is great and the price heavy for rare lips and beautiful eyes.[29]

Nevertheless, in Pukhtu too, there is the possibility and provision for averting the consequent murder in case of *tur*, by the marriage of the involved individuals, provided the involved woman/girl's family members agree. Although the hunt slackens in this way, the man/boy often has 'to pay damages in the form of giving away two or three girls to the family from which he stole one'.[30] Protection to the woman/girl married to the man/boy, both involved in the affair and married under this provision, has been provided to the extent that she must be retained as the wife. 'If he deceives her or deserts her', 'he won't live long' because not only will 'the whole tribe of the girl...hunt him down' but 'his own will refuse to protect him'. As 'Custom does not allow protection to the breakers of custom. He stands alone and must pay the price. Even his friends will avoid the funeral.' Although 'It is hard and brutal, but it works.' Because 'After all you cannot use a dog leash to tame a wolf.'[31]

Tui (توئے)

Tui (also spelled as *toi*) literally means 'spilled'. However, in Pukhtu, *tui* is related to *badal* and *tur*. The above discussion has demonstrated that the main settlement in the case of a dispute over a murder is *badal*. Not only does Pukhtu recognise *badal* as a right, but as an obligation as well. A seemingly negative aspect of *badal* is that it may compromise the weak who may not be in a position to take *badal*, because of the possibility of reprisal or fear that they may not be able to protect themselves against a powerful and influential wrongdoer. While it, seemingly, gives a free hand to the powerful and ill-tempered person and restrains the weak from protecting his interest, honour, and life, Pukhtu actually has a clause, or regulation, of *tui* to resolve this aspect of *badal*.

Under this clause, the blood of the person who loses his life because of an unlawful or unrecognised act is considered *tui*, and hence, is not avenged. In such a case, the act of the person who has been murdered is recognised as being unlawful while that of the murderer lawful. For instance, the murder of an adulterer is the right and duty of the involved female's family; the blood of the adulterer is considered *tui*, and hence will not be avenged provided the charge of adultery is established. In case it is revealed that it was simply an accusation to justify a murder, then the blood will not be considered *tui*. Similarly, the blood of a person who is shot when caught red-handed while committing a crime—for example, during a dacoity, burglary, or theft—is considered *tui*, irrespective of his influence or power.

The heinous crimes, for which death is the punishment and is recognised as *tui,* are known to all, and so *tui* plays a significant role in minimising unwanted, immoral, and unacceptable acts and behaviour. In case the situation is unclear, the concerned *jargah* declares whether the blood was *tui*, and, hence, the taking of *badal* will be justified or not.

Panah (پناه)

Panah, meaning 'asylum' or 'sanctuary', is an important commandment of Pukhtu. Any Pukhtun from whom *panah* is sought, must provide it.

It cannot be denied, even to an arch-enemy. The person in *panah* is protected and defended at all costs, as long as he remains in the *panah* of the concerned person, tribe, etc. Seeking *panah* is the right of those who need it, and providing it is the obligation of those from whom it is sought. Olaf Caroe rightly observes that 'the denial of sanctuary is impossible for one who would observe Pakhtu'.[32]

James W. Spain states: 'The concepts of asylum and sanctuary are known and accepted as part of *melmastia*.'[33] Although both *milmastya*, and sanctuary or asylum have the same obligations, both are different. For sanctuary and asylum, the phrases *panah ghukhtal* (پناه غوختل asking for asylum and sanctuary) and *panah warkawal* (پناه ورکول providing sanctuary and asylum) are used, but *milmastya* has its own phrases, such as becoming guest (مېلمه کېدل), making guest (مېلمه کول) and providing hospitality (مېلمستيا ورکول ، مېلمستيا کول). One would not ask an enemy to become a guest (*milmah*), but one is obliged to provide *panah* (asylum) to an enemy, if so required. The terms *panah* and *milmastya*, therefore, are used in different senses.

An attempt on the life of the person in *panah* is regarded as an act against the provider of *panah*, and, hence, he has to fight those who do not respect his *panah*. There have been instances where, in the absence of male members of a household, the female(s) have defended and protected the person(s) who sought *panah*. Even enemies have been entertained and protected when they have sought *panah*.

Westerners fail to understand the obligation of *panah*. Like the other rules, regulations, codes, and commandments of Pukhtu, failure to understand this concept created difficulties and losses for the British, in the North-West Frontier, during the British rule in India. This failure to understand also became the overt cause of the Americans and their allies' invasion of Afghanistan in 2001, when the Taliban refused to hand Usama bin Laden (who was in their *panah*) over to them. As a consequence, Taliban rule was toppled, and army operations and fighting took place, which continued till August 2021 in Afghanistan and is still continued in October 2021, in the erstwhile tribal areas of Pakistan. It is such challenges faced, while abiding by Pukhtu, that has given rise to the Pukhtu proverb which means: 'If you abide by Pukhtu, you may get broken ribs' (پۀ پښتو کښې پښتۍ ماتېږي). The following *tapah* clarifies it:

پښتو آسانه نۀ ده خلقه

څوک چي پښتوکړي پښتی ماتي گرځوينه

Meaning: Listen! O people! Pukhtu is not easy to observe. Those who abide by Pukhtu get around with broken ribs.

NANAWATAY (ننواتے)

Badal is the Pukhtu commandment in which wrong-doing is avenged. The negative aspect of this commandment is that it leads to unending bloodshed. However, there are certain codes under which conciliation can be effected and the potential bloodshed avoided. One of these codes is *nanawatay*.

When the guilty party wishes to bring an end to the bloodshed and dispute, in a peaceful manner, before *badal* is taken, it goes to its adversary, admits its guilt, expresses shame, and throws itself at the adversary's mercy seeking pardon. This is called *nanawatay*, which is a type of repentance, and expression of regret of the wrong doing, and to give great esteem to the aggrieved party. The party that resorts to *nanawatay* may send, or take with them, their women who are sometimes unveiled/bareheaded; the custom of going unveiled/bareheaded is known as *sartur* (also spelled as *sartor*) *sar tlal* (سرتور سرتلل). They may also take the Holy Quran, and have a rope around their necks, known as '*paray pah gharah tlal*' (پرے پۀ غاړه تلل going with rope in the neck). The repentant party may also send members of religious families as *nanawatay*.

If the aggrieved party accepts the repentance and agrees to renounce the right of *badal*, *nanawatay* is honoured, a *jargah* is held, conciliation effected, and the matter is settled amicably and peacefully. Although *nanawatay* 'is surrender rather than sanctuary', as stated by James W. Spain,[34] the aggrieved party is required to honour it. Spain has asserted: 'It is a "going in" or a "giving in" to an enemy, carrying with it a connotation of great shame for the one who undertakes it and no obligation to accept it on the part of the one to whom it is offered.'[35] Although, no doubt, 'it is "a going in" or a "giving in" to an enemy', it never carries a 'connotation of great shame for the one who undertakes it'. And, it is considered an obligation, 'on the part of the one to whom it is offered', to honour the *nanawatay*. There is no doubt that 'the honour of the party solicited... incur a stain'[36] if it fails to honour it. *Nanawatay* is sometimes referred to as 'the granting of asylum',[37] 'the right of asylum',[38] and 'sanctuary',[39] but that is giving *panah* which is different from *nanawatay*.

SWARAH (سوره)

In cases of *badal* and *tur*, there are other rules in Pukhtu, besides murder or revenge to settle scores and protect and maintain honour, to solve the issues peacefully and amicably, preventing further bloodshed. Under one of these rules, if the aggrieved party agrees to settle the issue amicably, the party that has committed the crime gives a girl in marriage to a male member of the aggrieved party. At times, the aggrieved party may ask for a girl. The girl, from the family of the guilty party, who is married to a male member of the aggrieved party in this manner is called *swarah* (also written as *swara*).

As generally, in the Pukhtun society, marriages of both the males and females take place in the early years of their life, or when they have yet not reached puberty or just reached adolescence, the word girl is used. Hence, this may not be taken, as is generally misunderstood and misrepresented, that in *swarah* the marriage of a girl or girls were sought and arranged. It was the general practice that at the marriage time the females were yet in girlhood, mostly early teenagers.

Although *swarah* is rarely practised, and may be misused in some cases, it is, nowadays, generally misunderstood and misinterpreted. A girl married in this way is now termed—by those who fail to understand the practice properly—the price of blood, a scapegoat,[40] 'a penalty for being a woman',[41] and so forth. These are incorrect views. *Swarah* literally means the female who is riding. In the absence of modern means of communication, although the people generally travelled on foot, the females of well-off families were taken to and from their father and husband's houses on horse-back. If a bride showed lethargy and laziness, or did not carry out the domestic chores, she was often asked, '*swarah raghalay yay sah*' (سوره راغلې يې څه؟) meaning have you come *swarah* (so nobly as on horse-back)[42] due to which you do not do any work? This suggests that *swarah* is not a derogative or insulting term but honourable and prestigious; the practice was instituted in good faith and females thus married have been honoured and respected.

In Pukhtun society it is an established fact, and a commonly recognised rule, that decisions, not only in the case of *swarah*, but also about betrothal and marriage, are made by the girl's parents or other family members. Although, generally, the girl's consent is sought in some way, the final decision rests with the family members. There is no difference in the manner in which marriages are arranged both in the cases of *swarah* as well as common marriages.

The significance of the marriage, arranged as *swarah*, is that both the families cement their relationship through matrimony. The marriage becomes a bond ensuring that both sides will not resort to bloodshed in the future, and the arrival of the couple's children further strengthens the relationship. The marriage minimises the chances of future bloodshed between the two families because, in Pukhtun society, matrimonial relations are mostly respected and maintained—which, in turn, restrains the aggrieved family from resorting to *badal*. Besides, 'the affinal tie creates opportunities', between the two families or sides, 'for frequent social interaction through joint participation in associations for *rites de passage*'.[43]

Marriage between family members of erstwhile enemies serves as a guarantee of peace, as planning to take revenge within a family becomes nearly impossible as the girl may oppose it or leak the secret out. This aspect is also evident from the contents of the Bani Israelite Theory, about the origin of the Pukhtuns (see Chapter 2), that when Jalut planned the murder of Dawud (AS) and visited his sleeping apartment for this purpose, it was his daughter—now wife of Dawud (AS)—who leaked her father's plan to her husband; as a result of which Dawud (AS) escaped the murder. Also, the sister of Malak Ahmad—the Yusufzi's chief at the time of their leaving Afghanistan in the fifteenth century and the conquest of Swat in the sixteenth century—married to Sultan Awais (Uwais, Wais), one of the then rulers of Swat, was killed as it was suspected that she was spying for the Yusufzi.[44]

Such marriages, therefore, have not only played a vital role in bringing bloodshed to an end but have also turned enemies into relatives, thus remaining an important code of Pukhtu. It has also been a practice in the course of the settlement of a blood feud that, to further cement the peace, both parties give their girls in marriage to each other. Hassan M. Yousufzai and Ali Gohar notes:

> The tradition of Swara is a hot issue with international advocacy and women's rights groups. To locals, giving a girl in marriage should serve two purposes: it provides a replacement for the life lost and binds the two families in a marital alliance that should act as a barrier against further hostilities.[45]

The most important point, which is generally ignored while criticising *swarah*, is that the girl's betrothal and marriage is decided by her family members, with her having no say in the affair, but the same is also the case for the boy, from whom consent is not sought either; it is his parents or family who make the decision. Moreover, arranged marriages are common practice in Pukhtun society, and not only in cases of *swarah*. In Pukhtun society, while the consent of the male and the female is sought to some extent, or they are at least informed about the decision, the final decision is made by the parents or elders of the families concerned; hence, almost all marriages are arranged.

If it is unfair and unjust to say that a female has no say, or is denied the power, to make a decision about her marriage, the same is the case for a male as well. However, it is observed that the male's view is generally ignored and voices are only raised on behalf of the females. Those who are raising their voices for the women, fail to examine the issue in perspective, and also suffer from prejudice and fall prey to gender imbalance in favour of the women. Dr Sher Zaman Taizai states that the woman married as *swarah* 'is mistreated all her life. She is never regarded as an equal. She is persecuted.'[46] This is a sweeping generalisation. There may be such cases but it depends on the nature and behaviour of the family to whom the lady is married. If they mistreat the lady married as *swarah*, they probably mistreat the other married ladies in their family as well. Like other societies, Pukhtun society is not devoid of families and individuals who do not give due regard to their women, and mistreat and persecute them, but this behaviour is not specific to *swarah* cases.

Pighur (پیغور)

Pighur (taunt) is also a component of Pukhtu. This is generally considered to be negative, but it has positive repercussions as well. Although *pighur* or 'sarcastic remark by peers' or others 'can drive a person blindly to follow the tenants of Pukhtoonwali, leading to violence and bloodshed',[47] it also works as a restraining force. Because apprehensions of possible *pighur* 'generate internal social controls on people limiting their actions and forcing them to conform to the ethics' of Pukhtu.[48] This also refrains a strong and powerful person from oppressing and mistreating the weak.

Pighur even 'can come from one's own relative, like a father or mother, or even a friend'. It 'helps people maintain a character worthy of a good Pukhtoon'[49]—the renowned Pukhtu poet Amir Hamzah Khan Shinwari says:

دا څنګه بے وفا شوے پښتنے پس له وعدے [50]

پیغور هم تیتی نکړلے انګریزے سترګے ستا

Meaning: How could you turn faithless after making promises O! Pukhtun lady that even taunt could not make you sheepish.

Tigah (تیگه)

Tigah literally means 'stone', but in the context of Pukhtu it has a different meaning and use. When a truce is effected in a feud by a *jargah*, or mediators, but a formal settlement and peace has not yet been achieved, a stone is laid, called '*tigah kaykhawdal*', as a mark of the endeavour/truce so that people may know about it; also, that the concerned parties do not resort to fighting or violations. *Tigah* represents a temporary peace that may eventually lead to permanent settlement.[51]

Mirat/Miratah (میراته/میرات)

Mirat/miratah, although un-Islamic in essence, has been a recognised code of Pukhtu. The man who has no male child is called *mirat* and the woman *miratah*; and when there is no child at all it is called '*pah nakhas mirat/miratah*' (په نخاس میرات/میراته). The female child of *mirat* holds no right to inherit the property left by her deceased father; and the nearest male agnates of the man concerned inherit the property. Not only both movable and immovable property of *mirat* is considered the right of the nearest male agnates but the widow and the female unmarried children as well: in the sense that they are to be married by the nearest male agnates of the deceased, if they wish so, generally not giving weight to or seeking the will or consent of the females concerned.

Ghag (غږ)

Ghag is related to marital affairs. If a man/boy wishes to marry a particular women/girl, but he or his family have not yet negotiated for her, and in the meantime a third person/family starts negotiating for the betrothal of that women/girl, he can declare his wish, which is called *ghag* or *tak kawal* (ټک کول) and *tapus kawal* (تپوس کول). In this way, he at 'least gets... involved in the negotiations for the lady's hand in one way or another, even if it doesn't always get him the lady'.[52] No other party usually enters negotiations until the claimant and the lady's family fail to conclude their negotiations. This can, sometimes, lead to murder and bloodshed if the lady's family refuses to honour the claim or if another party does not pay regard to the claim and resolves to marry the lady despite the previous claim.

SHARMALAH (شرمله)

Sharmalah is a kind of *jargah*, usually called by the offender or his representatives, to seek a negotiated settlement of a quarrel or feud. Such a *jargah* has to negotiate between the parties and effect a settlement, in which the offender may have to agree to a compensation in some form or agree to give a daughter in marriage[53] (*swarah*).

KALAY KALWIGHI (کلے کلویغي)

Kalay kalwighi is related to communal life. It lays down the guidelines for a number of circumstances: participation in betrothals, weddings, and other affairs relating to happiness and joy; going to the house of a deceased to express sorrow, grief, and sympathy; visiting a sick person; providing the needed assistance to fellow villagers. *Ashar ghubal* (اشرغوبل) or cooperating with and assisting each other while harvesting, threshing, cutting grass, and such other jobs that cannot possibly be done individually, or by one family, are also part of *kalay kalwighi*. As the society is tribal, and the people mainly live in villages, *kalay kalwighi* is an important code and commandment of Pukhtu.

PAT (پت)

Maintaining friendships, relationships, and positive links is called *pat*. Pukhtu requires that friendships and relationships are not broken unless there is a justifiable reason. The significance of *pat* can be judged, from Pukhtu folklore, and from a *tapah* that says:

پښتون پهٔ پت باندې پښتون دے

د پت نشان تل به اوچت پهٔ جهان وينه

Meaning: *Pat* is part and parcel of Pukhtu. The signatories of *pat* will have highest regard in the world.

SHARIAT (شریعت)

Shariat, or Islamic law, is among the codes and rules of Pukhtu. Being Muslims, following and observing *shariat* is a must for Pukhtuns. Although the Pukhtuns abide by and follow *shariat* in some aspects, they ignore and violate it in others; that is to say, they have tailored *shariat* to their Pukhtu codes (*riwaj*). For instance, Pukhtuns fast in Ramazan with great zeal, and those who do not fast are looked down upon; but *shariat* is violated in matters of inheritance, in which *riwaj* is followed. Similarly, *shariat* is not followed in its spirit in cases of revenge, adultery, and so forth. While *shariat* is part of Pukhtu, there are other features that are contrary to *shariat*. That is why some people consider Pukhtu to be purely Islamic,[54] while others see it as the opposite.

It is evident, from critical analysis, that Pukhtu has both Islamic and un-Islamic customs, codes, rules, regulations, and commandments and, on the whole, people follow them as they are. A few Pukhtu sayings and idioms are narrated which give an idea of how little *shariat* is respected when its injunctions go against the whims and interests of a Pukhtun: One saying is پښتون يو وخت زبرګ وي او بل وخت شيطان which means: 'A Pukhtun may be saint at one time and devil at another'; another Pukhtu saying means 'Although I acknowledge *shariat* (according to which the ass is of the plaintiff) but I state on oath that I will not hand over the ass' (شريعت خو منم خو خر خو قسم دے که ورکړم); Yet another Pukhtu saying (ملا ګرمولم خو زه نۀ ګرميدم) means 'The *mula* (priest) reproved me but I could not be reproved'; a proverb states د پښتون يوه ښپه پۀ جنت کښې بی او بله پۀ دوزخ کښې which means 'The Pukhtun has his one foot in Heaven and the other in Hell.' Still another proverb (پښتونيم کفر دے) means 'Pukhtu is half infidelity'; and still another one پښتون نيم قرآن مني او نيم نۀ means 'Pukhtun believe in only half of the Quran.'

Although *shariat* is dominated by *riwaj* in many situations, it is not only a commandment of Pukhtu but plays a vital role on many counts; hence, its significance cannot be underestimated.

AMR-I BIL MARUF WA NAHI ANIL MUNKAR
(امر بالمعروف و نهى عن المنكر)

Islamic injunctions '*Amr-i bil maruf*' (meaning calling to righteousness), and '*nahi anil munkar*' (meaning prohibiting from wrong), have their place in Pukhtu. Through this, the people, being Muslims, are induced to abstain from unwanted acts and activities, to follow Islamic teachings, and to behave in a righteous manner. Religious segments and religious figures are required to direct the people towards righteousness, and to persuade them to give up evil ways and unwanted acts both in their personal and communal lives. On occasion, this code plays a vital role.

BUNGAH, BRAMATAH, BUTAH (بونگه/برامته/بوته)

According to Pukhtu conventions, *bungah* (also spelled as *bongah*, *bonga*), *bramatah*, and *butah* are recognised, which are forms of 'tit-for-tat'. If a person's property—'usually an animal'—is stolen, he has the right to resort to *bramatah*, i.e. to gain possession of a similar or relatively more valuable property of the thief or of his clan, so compelling him to negotiate and return the property in exchange. If the aggrieved party is unable to recover the loss, either by force or through the *bramatah* system, it has to pay a cash ransom to the possessor, worth one-fifth of the value of the property.[55] The property, thus hijacked or possessed for ransom, is called *bungah*; the sum received as ransom by the thief or the hijacker is *butah*.

TARBURWALI (تربورولي)

Tarbur (تربور) is used for both paternal 'cousin'[56] and 'enemy', and *tarburwali* for paternal 'cousinhood' and 'enmity'. In Pukhtun society, paternal cousins depend on and protect each other, and seek revenge in case of any kind of loss or dishonour incurred on a *tarbur*. On the other hand, they consider each other enemies, being immediate rivals for family power and influence, and equal and match. Various proverbs explain it well; for example the proverb تربورچي دي ورکے وي نو لويه وه يې اوچي لوئے شي نو دشمن دے جنگه وه يې :meaning 'When a cousin is little, rear him, but when he grows up he is an enemy, make him fight with others'; or another proverb دتربورغاښ پۀ تربورماتيري which means 'A cousin starts biting his cousin first'; and still another one تربورخوار ساته خو استعمالوه يې says: 'Keep the cousin poor but use him against others'. Whereas another one refers to the lack of trust among cousins by stating تربور که دي خر شي هم لتی پرې مۀ اړوه ارتاؤ به دې کري meaning: 'If the cousin becomes your ass still do not ride him, he may throw you down.' Thus, *tarburwali* has a recognised and established role in both its aspects in Pukhtu.

HUJRAH (حجره)

In a traditional society, a *hujrah* is not personal property, but is the communal property of all the Pukhtuns of the corresponding block of the village or of the whole village. They hold the proprietorial rights jointly, and are collectively responsible for its maintenance. *Hujrah*s (in Pukhtu *hujray*) have played a vital role in the Pukhtuns' lives not merely as men's houses, but they have also served numerous roles including guest houses, focal points for community action and opinions, and as places for unmarried males to sleep. *Hujrah*s are multi-purpose community centres; 'It was from here that the marriage processions started and the bier was carried to the grave.'[57]

The above are only some of the predominant norms, commandments, codes, rules, regulations, and components of Pukhtu. Although the term Pukhtun is applied to a specific group or segment within Pukhtun society, it is expected and required of all the people, whether or not they belong to the particular group or segment, to abide by the norms, values, rules, regulations, codes, and components of Pukhtu; those who do not abide by them, or do not observe them, are looked down upon and are not regarded as true Pukhtuns.[58]

Preshan Khattak comments that the four alphabets (*pay* پ, *khin* ښ [*shin* ش], *tay* ت, and *wau* و) of which Pukhtu (Pushtu) is comprised, stand for *pat*, *khigarah/shigarah* (ښېگړه / ښبگړه) meaning welfare of others and serving them in need, *turah* (توره) meaning bravery, valour, and firmly opposing the enemy, and *wafa* (وفا) meaning loyalty, standing by relationships, respectively. Adding the fifth alphabet, *nun* (ن), to Pukhtu/Pushtu (پشتو/پښتو) makes Pukhtun/Pushtun (پشتون/پښتون); *nun* stands for *nang*, which has already been discussed.[59] Interestingly, in this interpretation, there is nothing about *badal*, *milmastya*, *jargah*, *panah*, and *hujrah*—particularly about *badal* and *milmastya* which are the cardinal components and codes of Pukhtu.

As also stated earlier, some people consider Pukhtu, the Pukhtun code of life, to be in conformity with Islamic teachings and codes, and, hence, consider it their other form; while some have the opposite view. There is a Pukhtu saying پښتو پينځم مذهب دے, which means 'Pukhtu is the fifth of the Muslim schools of *fiqah*' (the first four being the Maliki, Hanafi, Shafi'i, and Hanbali *fiqah*s, or schools of thought, or Islamic jurisprudence). This implies that Pukhtu is different from the recognised Islamic codes, but it is considered equally sacred.

Those who have written on the subject in English have ignored the term 'Pukhtu' altogether, and have only used Pukhtunwali. But the basic and commonly used, and as stated earlier the most appropriate and technically sound, term is Pukhtu, both for the language and for the code of life of the people. Also, they have dealt with, and described, Pukhtu in the context of the erstwhile FATA only, and have mentioned only a few of the codes. Pukhtu does not comprise purely legal rules and regulations but is a combination of customs, values, norms, codes, rules, regulations, and commandments. 'This…is a doctrine, a law, rule, system and a way of life', and 'thus is repeated, trusted, and sustained by old and young a like [alike]'.[60] McMahon and Ramsay notes at the beginning of the twentieth century that 'being an unwritten law' Pukhtu or Pukhtunwali 'is capable of extensive interpretation. It can be made to necessitate, justify or excuse most actions. It is regulated, however, by established local and tribal custom.'[61] It covers all aspects of life, from the cradle to the grave. Although Pukhtu includes *shariat* within its fold, in practice, it is subservient to *riwaj*. However, over the course of time, and with the spread of both modern and Islamic education, some changes have taken place: the effect of government and its authority, and of modern laws, is visible.

Notes

1. Salma Shaheen (collector, comp., and researcher), *Ruhi Sandaray (Tapay)* (Pukhtu), vol. 2, with *pishlafz* by Muhammad Nawaz Tair (Pikhawar: PA, 1994), 21.
2. Muhammad Nawaz Tair, *Tapah aw Jwand* (Pukhtu) (Pikhawar: PA, 1980), 41.
3. Muhammad Asif Khan, *The Story of Swat as told by the Founder Miangul Abdul Wadud Badshah Sahib to Muhammad Asif Khan*, with preface, introduction, and appendices by Muhammad Asif Khan, trans. preface and trans. by Ashruf Altaf Husain (Printed by: Ferozsons Ltd., Peshawar, 1962), 27 f.n. It is to be noted that Pakhto or Pukhtu has never been the plural of 'Pukhtun' or 'Pakhtoon', as stated by Ashruf Altaf Husain. Moreover, 'to say that one is not a true Pakhtoon' is applied not only to the person who is devoid of all the virtues mentioned by Ashruf Altaf but, on occasion, to those who are devoid of any or some of the virtues dictated by Pukhtu. Besides, instead of mentioning 'Pakhto' as given by Ashruf Altaf Husain, James W. Spain has used the word *Pukhtunwali*. Moreover, he has attributed the mentioned statement about Pukhtu to Miangul Abdul Wadud, the ruler of Swat State (1917–1949), but it is Ashruf Altaf Husain's statement and footnote. For James W. Spain's assertion, see James W. Spain, *Pathans of the Latter Day* (Karachi: OUP, 1995), 40–1.
4. *Tapah* is a genre of Pukhtu folk verse. Its formation is not attributed to anyone; it is believed that, in general, it originates from females: but not necessarily.
5. Hassan M. Yousufzai and Ali Gohar, *Towards Understanding Pukhtoon Jirga: An indigenous way of peacebuilding and more…* (Peshawar: Just Peace International, 2005), 31.
6. Ghani Khan, *The Pathans: A Sketch*, repr. (Islamabad: PASR, 1990), 24.
7. Ibid., 24–5.
8. Ibid., 25.
9. James W. Spain, *The Pathan Borderland*, repr. (Karachi: IP, 1985), 63.
10. Hassan M. Yousufzai and Ali Gohar have termed Pukhtunwali (Pukhtu) in English as 'a code of honor' and 'the Pukhtoon code of honor' (Yousufzai and Ali Gohar, *Towards Understanding Pukhtoon Jirga*, 30–1) which is erroneous and not holistic.
11. See Denzil Ibbetson, *Punjab Castes*, repr. (Delhi: LPP, 1993), 58.

12. For instances, see James W. Spain, *The Way of the Pathans*, 7th impr. (Karachi: OUP, 1994), 46; Spain, *The Pathan Borderland*, 64; Syed Abdul Quddus, *The Pathans* (Lahore: Ferozsons (Pvt.) Ltd., 1987), 67.

13. For instances, see Spain, *The Pathan Borderland*, p. 64 and C. Collin Davies, *The Problem of the North-West Frontier, 1890–1908: With a survey of policy since 1849*, 2nd edn. rev. and enlarged (London: CPL, 1975), p. 49 in which only the revenge aspect of *badal* and, at that, only the negative aspect, has been discussed. Also see Ibbetson, *Punjab Castes*, 58.

14. Spain, *The Pathan Borderland*, 64.

15. Spain, *The Way of the Pathans*, 47.

16. Ibid., 52.

17. Quoted in Spain, *The Pathan Borderland*, 65.

18. Ibid.

19. Ibid.

20. *Gudar*, in this context, means the part of a river, stream, fountain etc. from which water is manually brought for domestic use.

21. Yousufzai and Ali Gohar, *Towards Understanding Pukhtoon Jirga*, 50, 76.

22. For instances, see ibid., 21, 31, 47, 50, 63.

23. *Report on the Administration of the Border of the North-West Frontier Province for the year 1938–39* (Delhi: The Manager of Publications, 1940), 11–13.

24. A.H. McMahon and A.D.G. Ramsay, *Report on the Tribes of Dir, Swat, and Bajour together with the Utman-Khel and Sam Ranizai*, repr., ed. with introduction by R.O. Christensen (Peshawar: SBB, 1981), 33; A.H. McMahon and A.D.G. Ramsay, *Report on the Tribes of the Malakand Political Agency (Exclusive of Chitral)*, rev. R.L. Kennion (Peshawar: Government Press, North-West Frontier Province, 1916), 67.

25. Ibbetson, *Punjab Castes*, 61.

26. Spain, *The Pathan Borderland*, 69–72.

27. Khushal Khan Khattak, *Kulyat-i Khushal Khan Khattak: Qasaid, Rubayat, Qitat aw Mutafariqat* (Pukhtu) (Pikhawar: APH, n.d.), 89.

28. Khan, *The Pathans*, 25–6.

29. Ibid., 26.

30. Ibid.

31. Ibid.

32. Olaf Caroe, *The Pathans: 550 B.C.–A.D. 1957*, repr. (Karachi: OUP, 1976), 351.

33. Spain, *The Pathan Borderland*, 66.

34. Ibid., 67.

35. Ibid., 66.

36. Caroe, *The Pathans*, 351.

37. Yousufzai and Ali Gohar, *Towards Understanding Pukhtoon Jirga*, 32.

38. Davies, *The Problem of the North-West Frontier*, 49.

39. Caroe, *The Pathans*, 351.

40. For an example, see Idrees Asar, *Pakhtoonwalee: Code of Love & Peace* (Peshawar: Printed at Danish Book Store, 2005), 159–60.

41. Quoted in Gul Ayaz, '*Swara*: Stigma on Pukhtun Social Code', in *Statesman* (English Daily), Peshawar, 6 May 2002.

42. While dealing with the point, Fredrik Barth also states: 'These would normally not include compensation, but almost invariably include a woman in marriage (*swara*='one coming on horse', fem.) from the defeated to the victors.' Fredrik Barth, *Political Leadership among Swat Pathans* (London: The Athlone Press, 1959), 96. Although, the last portion of Barth's statement is incorrect as it is the vice versa, viz. *swarah* comes from the victors to the defeated, or from the oppressors or those on the wrong, to the oppressed or those who have sustained the loss, he has clarified the meaning of *swarah*.

43. Ibid., 107.
44. See Pir Muazam Shah, *Tawarikh Hafiz Rahmat Khani*, with *dibachah* by Muhammad Nawaz Tair, 2nd impr. (Pukhtu/Persian) (Pikhawar: PA, 1987), 63–5.
45. Yousufzai and Ali Gohar, *Towards Understanding Pukhtoon Jirga*, 37, f.n. 27.
46. Quoted in Ayaz, '*Swara*: Stigma on Pukhtun Social Code', in *Statesman* (English Daily), Peshawar, 6 May 2002. For a similar contention, see Asar, *Pakhtoonwalee: Code of Love & Peace*, 160.
47. Yousufzai and Ali Gohar, *Towards Understanding Pukhtoon Jirga*, 34.
48. Ibid.
49. Ibid.
50. Amir Hamzah Khan Shinwari, *Ghazawanay* (Pukhtu), 14th edn. (n.p.: Hamzah Academy, 2010), 7.
51. Also see Spain, *The Pathan Borderland*, 67.
52. Ibid.
53. Ibid.
54. For instance regarding the contention of Abdul Qadir (Founding Director of Pukhtu Academy, University of Peshawar) that Pukhtu is the second name of Islam, see Preshan Khattak, *Pushtun Kaun? (Tarikh, Tahqiq, Tanqid)* (Urdu) (Peshawar: PA, 1984), 135–6. Also see Tair, *Tapah aw Jwand*, 42.
55. Spain, *The Pathan Borderland*, 73.
56. Among the Pukhtuns, only a cousin from the father's side is called *tarbur*; hence, cousinhood in this context refers to brothers' sons or paternal cousins.
57. Makhdum Tasadduq Ahmad, *Social Organization of Yusufzai Swat: A Study in Social Change* (Lahore: Panjab University Press, 1962), 27. For the significance and function of *hujrah*s (in Pukhtu: *hujray*), also see Abdul Qaiyum, *Gold and Guns on the Pathan Frontier* (Bombay: HK, 1945), 25–6.
58. Also see Khattak, *Pushtun Kaun?*, 176–91.
59. For details about Preshan Khattak's contention in this respect, see ibid., 135–75.
60. Yousufzai and Ali Gohar, *Towards Understanding Pukhtoon Jirga*, 43.
61. McMahon and A.D.G. Ramsay, *Report on the Tribes of the Malakand Political Agency (Exclusive of Chitral)*, rev. R.L. Kennion, 11.

4 British Occupation

> The first colossal mistake [of the Britons] on the Panjab frontier was
> the initial step, the taking over of the frontier districts from the Sikhs,
> and the acceptance of an ill-defined administrative boundary.
> – *The Cambridge History of India*

THE SUBCONTINENT was famous for its fabulous wealth. It was a rich
area of agricultural and industrial products, and enjoyed a trading
relationship with European countries for a long time. The trade was
mainly carried by the Arabs. The merchandise was transported by sea to
the Arabian Peninsula, from where it was taken to the Syrian markets,
and then onwards to the Western countries. This flourishing trade between
Europe and the East continued after the advent of Islam. As the Muslims
studied and explored navigation, their merchant navy excelled, facilitating
and enhancing trade between the East and the West.

COMING OF THE EUROPEANS

The fall of Constantinople, to the Ottoman Turks in 1453 CE,[1] made those
European powers that were involved 'in the Eastern trade anxious to
discover a new route' to the east that would be 'beyond the control of
the Turks'. Because of their favourable position, and because of state
patronage, 'Portugal and Spain took the lead' in searching for a direct
sea-route to the east. It was during one such attempt that Columbus ended
up going west, discovering America, instead of the east.[2] Interestingly,
a retired British naval officer has claimed, in a book, that it was a
Chinese admiral, General Jing, who discovered America seventy years
before Columbus.[3]

Finally, the Portuguese sailor Vasco de Gama succeeded in discovering
a sea route to the east. With the help of an experienced Arab sailor, Abdul
Maajid of Zanzibar, he crossed the ocean and landed at the port of Calicut,
on the coast of the subcontinent, in May 1498.[4] About Vasco de Gama's
finding the new sea route to India, it has been noted that 'Perhaps no
event during the Middle Ages had such far-reaching repercussions on the
civilised world as the opening of the sea-route to India.'[5] To help put the

time-frame into context, it may be noted that at this time the Mughals had not yet established their rule in the subcontinent.

The Portuguese were followed by other European nations—the Dutch, Britons,[6] Danes, French, and Germans. The Portuguese established their position along the coasts of India, maintaining an upper hand and monopoly for quite a long time. But, over time, the Britons and the French became more powerful and the Portuguese hold lessened. As the other European nations did not maintain their positions in India, the French and the Britons wrestled for supremacy and established their own monopoly on trade.[7] Finally, following the three Karnatak (Carnatic) wars,[8] the Britons emerged as the victors of this rivalry and struggle for supremacy in the subcontinent.

THE MUGHALS AND THE BRITONS

In the meantime, Babur invaded the subcontinent and established Mughal rule after defeating Ibrahim Ludi (Lodi) at the First Battle of Panipat in 1526; the Britons had not, as yet, established their trading company to trade in the subcontinent. His son, Humayun, succeeded Babur in 1530, but was defeated and expelled from India by Sher Shah Suri in 1540. However, after Sher Shah's death, Humayun succeeded in regaining the throne in 1555. His son, Akbar, succeeded Humayun, on the latter's death in 1556, and ruled until 1605.[9]

It was during the reign of Akbar that the Britons formed a company to trade in the East Indies. Queen Elizabeth I, granted it a charter, 'after much hesitation', on 31 December 1600, under the title of 'Governor and Company of Merchants of London trading into the East Indies', 'which later became the East India Company'. 'The Charter authorised the London Company to traffic and trade freely "into and from the East Indies, in the countries, and parts of Asia and Africa, and into and from all Islands, ports, havens, cities, creeks, towns and places of Asia and Africa and America, or any of them beyond the Cape of Bona Esperanza to the Streights [sic] of Magellan".'[10]

Akbar was succeeded by Jahangir (1605–1627 CE), whose court was visited by three British envoys in succession, two with letters from the British King James I, to gain permission and concessions for trade for the Britons company. Early in 1613, Jahangir issued a permit for trade, and also for a factory (trading centre) at Surat. This permit is vital to the history of the subcontinent as it provided a legal base for the Britons trade, and the establishment of factories (trading centres) in India. Jahangir's successor, Shah Jahan (1628–1658 CE), granted permits to the Britons for factories in Hugli and Qasim Bazar. The Governor of Bengal, Shah Shuja, in 1651, granted the East India Company trading privileges on payment of 3,000 rupees as a fixed annual duty. In 1656, Shuja granted further concessions to the company.[11]

Shah Jahan was succeeded by Aurangzeb, who ruled from 1658 to 1707 CE. His Governor of Bengal, Shaista Khan, granted, in 1672, 'exemption from the payment of duties'. In 1680, Aurangzeb himself ordered that neither should the company's trade be obstructed nor its people be maltreated for custom duties. However, hostilities between the Mughals and the Britons led to an armed struggle, resulting in the Britons feeling compelled to sue for pardon. Aurangzeb granted both the pardon and a new permit, conditionally. The company got further concessions during the reign of Aurangzeb: in 1690, a new factory was established at Sutanuti, 'the future capital of British-India'. In 1696, the Britons were permitted to fortify the factory; in 1698, they received the *zamindari* (right of realisation of revenue) of the villages of Sutanuti, Kalikata (Calcutta/Kulkata), and Govindapur on the payment of 1,200 rupees to the proprietors; and a new fortified settlement, Fort William, was established in Bengal.[12]

POST-AURANGZEB PERIOD

The disintegration of the Mughal Empire started after the death of Aurangzeb. While the Britons were strengthening their position and increasing their power, the Indians were wrestling each other for power. Making use of the opportunity to increase their influence and hold, the Britons began to interfere in local politics and wars. At the same time, they became more powerful and headstrong, and tried to misuse the privileges already granted to them. This was one of the factors that led to the Battle of Plassey in 1757 which resulted in Britons victory over the Nawab of Bengal, Sirajudaulah. The result of the Battle of Plassey 'was more important than that of many of the greatest battles of the world. It paved the way for the British conquest of Bengal and eventually of the whole of India.'[13]

The Britons' victory at Plassey was a significant one. Nevertheless, the turning point in the history of the subcontinent, and the struggle between the Indians and the Britons, proved to be the Battle of Buxer. It was fought in 1764 between the Britons on the one side and the Nawab of Bengal (Mir Qasim), the Nawab of Awadh (Shujaudaulah), and the Mughal

Emperor (Shah Alam II) on the other. While only the Nawab of Bengal was defeated at the Battle of Plassey, the greater confederacy of the two Nawabs and the Mughal Emperor was defeated at the Battle of Buxer. As a result, the Britons ensured their supremacy in Bengal, Bihar, and Orissa, and the East India Company practically emerged as a sovereign power in the subcontinent.[14]

THE MARATHAS AND AHMAD SHAH ABDALI

The Britons were gaining strength and emerging as a strong force in India. The Marathas, who were indigenous Indians, were flexing their muscles as well. Taking advantage of the inefficient Mughal rule at the centre, and of the other weak local rulers, the Marathas rapidly continued their advance towards the north, reaching Delhi and occupying Punjab.

In the meantime, Ahmad Shah Abdali, also known as Ahmad Shah Durrani, was installed as the ruler in Afghanistan in 1747.[15] After securing his position in Afghanistan, Ahmad Shah attacked the cis-Indus territories several times, taking Punjab from the Marathas. The Marathas, however, remained a strong force, determined to occupy all of northern India. Some Indian Muslims—Najibudaulah (a leader of the Ruhilahs: the Indian Afghans) and Shujaudaulah (Nawab of Awadh)—allied with Ahmad Shah Abdali to get rid of the Marathas. And so, Ahmad Shah Abdali, with a large force under his command, came to India once again. He and his allies defeated the Marathas at the historic Third Battle of Panipat on 14 January 1761.[16] An Indian scholar of the time, Shah Waliullah, also worked towards creating the alliance against the Marathas, and the resultant Third Battle of Panipat.[17]

Having crushed the powerful Marathas, Ahmad Shah Abdali did not stay in Delhi but went back to Afghanistan. Thus, not only did he leave a power vacuum, but also made it easier for the Britons to further occupy India as the strong Maratha power had been weakened—the Marathas could have faced and stood up to the Britons. It has been aptly observed:

> But none the less the third battle of Panipat 'decided the fate of India'. 'The Marathas and the Muhammadans weakened each other in that deadly conflict, facilitating the aims of the British for Indian supremacy.' The rising British power got thereby the opportunity it needed so much to strengthen and consolidate its authority in India. 'If Plassey had sown the seeds of British supremacy in India, Panipat afforded time for their maturing and striking roots.'[18]

Taking advantage of the situation, the Britons wasted no time in extending their direct and indirect occupation. The Mughal emperors remained nominal sovereigns while the Britons became the paramount power in India. During the course of the expansion of their occupation, the Britons established their suzerainty and dominance up to the borders of Punjab.

RISE OF SIKH POWER

In the aforementioned political scenario and developments, the Sikhs had already started a struggle to gain political power in Punjab. Taking advantage of the political conditions in India, they occupied various territories.

The invasions of Ahmad Shah Abdali also helped the rise of the Sikh power to a great extent. Though they met with some reverses after 1752, they ultimately gained complete victory. Especially after the third battle of Panipat, they took advantage of the disturbed political condition of the country to organise and strengthen themselves sufficiently, and greatly harassed the Abdali on his return march. They opposed the Abdali in his subsequent invasions, and after his invasion in 1767 reoccupied the entire open country.[19]

As mentioned earlier, Ahmad Shah Abdali became the ruler, in 1747 CE, and established the modern state of Afghanistan. He crossed the Indus a few times, ravaged the country, and occupied Punjab. Having defeated the Marathas at the Third Battle of Panipat and weakened their power, he did not occupy the seat at Delhi but departed, leaving India in chaos and anarchy. After his return to Afghanistan, the open land of the Punjab was lost to the Sikhs. Between 1793–1798, his grandson, Zaman Shah, invaded India and made Punjab a part of the dominion of Afghanistan. He appointed Ranjit Singh as the Governor of Lahore in 1798, bestowing the title of Raja on him for the services rendered.[20] Ranjit Singh (who was the leader of a chief Sikh *misl*) took possession of Amritsar, the holy city of the Sikhs, and declared his independence from Afghanistan in 1801.

Ranjit Singh organised the Sikh *misl*s (fraternities) into a strong state, and absorbed the territories of the trans-Sutlej Sikh chiefs into his kingdom, following which he tried to incorporate the cis-Sutlej Sikh areas into his dominion as well. Some of the cis-Sutlej Sikh chiefs were alarmed by his cis-Sutlej expeditions and occupation of Ludhiyana, and sought the assistance of the Britons. Using diplomatic means, the Briton Governor-General, Lord Minto, sent Charles Metcalfe to the court of

Ranjit Singh—a treaty of 'Perpetual Amity' was signed by the Britons and Ranjit Singh at Amritsar in 1809. The treaty barred Ranjit Singh from expanding into the cis-Sutlej area, but no restriction was placed on his expansion towards the north and northwest. In 1813, he captured Attak (Attock) after defeating the Afghans at Hazru. He occupied Multan in 1818, and Kashmir in 1819. In 1823, he took Peshawar. By 1824, he held sway, even if it was nominal, over most of the plains of the present-day Khyber Pukhtunkhwa.[21]

THE SIKH KINGDOM AND THE BRITONS

Ranjit Singh maintained friendly relations with the Britons until his death in 1839. Following his death, confusion, disorder, and anarchy prevailed in the Sikh kingdom. Deplorable conditions at the court, and weak rulers, led to the Khalsa army (the Sikh army or the army of the Sikh kingdom) becoming more powerful and headstrong—virtually the ruling force. To get rid of the Khalsa army, the Lahore Darbar encouraged it to attack the territory under the Britons' protection and control, with the design of crushing its power. Hence, in December 1845, Khalsa forces crossed the Sutlej—also encouraged to do so because of Britons' advances towards Punjab—but the Britons were quick to oppose them. Although somewhat successful at first, the Sikhs were defeated and the Britons occupied Lahore in February 1846.[22]

After the defeat of the Sikhs, the Briton Governor-General, Lord Hardinge, dictated the Treaty of Lahore to them in March 1846, which was revised in December 1846. Under the treaty, the Sikhs *inter alia* agreed that Dilip Singh, as the Raja, and Lal Singh, as his minister, would conduct the affairs of the state under the supervision of the Briton Resident stationed in Lahore. A Briton force was to be stationed in Lahore until the Raja came of age, and all the expenses were to be borne by the Sikh government. Briton officers were stationed at other key locations in the kingdom to look after the affairs of the state. Thus, as a result of the First Anglo-Sikh War (1845–1846 CE), the Britons assumed complete control in directing and controlling matters in every sphere of the Sikh state; the Khalsa army, too, was disbanded.[23]

The Sikhs were unhappy with the Treaty of Lahore—at the presence of the Briton army, the power of the Briton officers, and the disbanding of the Khalsa army. Diwan Mulraj, the governor who had to resign earlier, led a revolt that started in Multan. Two Briton officers—'Vans Agnew of the Civil Service and Lieutenant Anderson of the Bombay European

Regiment'—who had come to Multan to install the new governor, Sardar Khan Singh, were murdered in April 1848 at Mulraj's instigation. The situation then took a turn; the Sikhs started to rally around the rebel leaders. Finally, in October 1848, Lord Dalhousie, the Briton governor-general, declared war on the Sikhs, which in turn led to an uprising by Sikh troops.[24]

In spite of their initial successes, the Sikhs suffered a great setback at the hands of the Briton forces; their commanders, Chattar Singh and Sher Singh, had to surrender to the Britons in March 1849. Lord Dalhousie, the Briton governor-general, of his own accord,[25] read out a proclamation on 29 March 1849 under which, inter alia, the East India Company, on 30 March 1849, took control of 'the Punjab and all the properties of the Sikh state "in part payment of the debt due by the State of Lahore to the British Government [East India Company's government], and of the expenses of the war".'[26]

THE OCCUPATION

Being part of the Sikh kingdom, the settled areas of the (prospective) North-West Frontier Province (present-day Khyber Pukhtunkhwa) of British India came under the supervision and indirect control of the Britons as a result of the First Anglo-Sikh War and the Treaty of Lahore. However, as a result of the Second Anglo-Sikh War (1848–1849 CE), the Afghan Amir, Dost Muhammad Khan, made a bid to take advantage of the situation. He reached Peshawar in December 1848 and tried to reoccupy the territories lost to the Sikhs. Having reoccupied the trans-Indus areas from the Sikhs, he proceeded to join up with the Sikh General, Chattar Singh, who had revolted against the Britons. Further, he sent 'a strong force of cavalry which fought on the Sikh side at the battle of Gujrat, at which Sikh resistance was finally broken'.[27]

Following their success over the Sikhs, the Britons pursued Dost Muhammad and his cavalry; in the words of Olaf Caroe, 'over the Salt Range hills, past Margalla and Hasan Abdal, over the Indus and across the Peshawar plain, into the very mouth of the Khaibar Pass, up which they galloped, losing a few stragglers'.[28] After the defeat of the Sikhs and the pursuit of the Afghan Amir, the Briton forces marched into the trans-Indus areas of Peshawar, Kuhat, Bannu, and Dirah Ismail Khan—previously held, albeit loosely, by the Sikhs and reoccupied by the Afghan Amir during the Second Anglo-Sikh War—and also into the cis-Indus Hazarah.[29]

The formal annexation of Punjab, on 30 March 1849, under the proclamation of 29 March 1849[30] was, therefore, the result of the Second Anglo-Sikh War. As a result of that annexation, the territories of the Frontier plains—the prospective districts of Hazarah, Peshawar, Kuhat, Bannu, and Dirah Ismail Khan—fell to the Britons 'as the successors of the Sikhs',[31] and became part of the Britons' dominion of India. In this way, the Britons 'took over the old Sikh boundary running along the edge of the tribal lands, though from the experience of the previous years they had some idea of the troubles in store for them'.[32] A commentary on this annexation was:

> The first colossal mistake [of the Britons] on the Panjab frontier was the initial step, the taking over of the frontier districts from the Sikhs, and the acceptance of an ill-defined administrative boundary. Indeed, it was extremely unfortunate for the British that the Sikhs had been their immediate predecessors in the Panjab, for Sikh frontier administration had been of the loosest type. They possessed but little influence in the trans-Indus tracts, and what little authority they had was confined to the plains. Even here they were obeyed only in the immediate vicinity of their forts which studded the country.[33]

Thus, the frontier districts or settled areas of the (prospective) Frontier Province were annexed—having been part of the Sikh kingdom of Punjab, although loosely and mostly nominally—by the proclamation of 29 March 1849, to the Indian territories ruled by the Britons.

'For a short time', the territories comprising 'the districts of Peshawar, Kohat [Kuhat] and Hazara [Hazarah] were under the direct control of the Board of Administration at Lahore'. However, 'they were formed into a regular division under a Commissioner' in 'about 1850'. The territories of the then Bannu and Dirah Ismail Khan districts were put under one deputy commissioner, forming 'part of the Leiah [Layah] Division till 1861, when two Deputy Commissioners were appointed and both districts were included in the Derajat Division'. This arrangement continued 'until the formation of the North-West Frontier Province'.[34]

'There was no serious suggestion' after the occupation of the Sikh state 'that the Peshawar plain should be abandoned, though John Lawrence was said to be in favour of this course'. But, 'there was no suggestion either of pushing forward' as 'the disasters of the First Afghan War still burned deep in the mind of every soldier and administrator'.[35] Therefore, the territories of the later-declared tribal areas, or political agencies, being no part of the Sikh state, did not fall under the Britons' domain with the occupation and annexation of the territories previously held by the Sikhs nor were attempts made in the succeeding years. However, as a result of the Second Anglo-Afghan War (1878–80 CE), the British forces entered and passed through the Khyber Pass area; and the Treaty of Gandamak of 1879, concluded between Yaqub Khan and the British, 'left the Khyber tribes for the future under British control'. The Khyber political agency, created in 1879, included the territories of the Mulaguri, Afridi of Tirah, and the 'country on both sides of the Khyber Pass'; none of these, however, was 'administered' by the British.[36]

The years 1890 to 1897 were remarkable for the extension of political control, although not firm occupation, over various tracts beyond the border of the settled districts. The Durand Line Agreement of 1893 put these areas on the Indian side of the border with Afghanistan, and brought them under the British sphere of influence.[37]

During the Second Anglo-Afghan War, the British extracted the Kurram Valley out of Afghanistan. Although it was subsequently evacuated in 1880, it led to a Shia-Sunni tussle. According to a British official report, the Afghan Amir 'suggested the occupation of the country'. 'In 1892, troops' were mobilised, 'the valley was reoccupied', and, 'since then', 'though not considered a part of British India', 'the whole valley' was 'ruled by the Political Officer on a rough, but effective, system'.[38]

In 1891, the Samana crest was 'declared the *de facto* British boundary' and was occupied in the same year. In 1889, it was decided to open 'the Gomal Pass'. Finally, in 1890, 'levy posts were established' within the Shirani limits in the South Waziristan area, and 'the routes by the Zao and Chuhar Khel [Khail] passes through the Sherani [Shirani] country to Fort Sandeman opened and maintained'. In spite of the opening of the Gumal Pass, the situation in Waziristan was disturbing for the British interests; so, it was decided to extend British 'control over Waziristan'. In 1894, the Waziristan Field Force overran 'the Mahsud country'; in 1895, 'a column from Bannu entered' the Tuchi Valley and the Dawar 'formally petitioned for British occupation'. 'The whole of Waziristan was', thus, 'taken under [British] political control'. The control was 'exercised by two' political officers posted in Wana and Miranshah—for which, the political agencies of North and South Waziristan were created in 1895 and 1896, respectively—where garrisons were also established.[39]

'The importance of exercising some control over the external relations' of Dir, Swat, and Chitral 'had long been recognized by the [colonial British] Government of India'. Relations with the Mehtar (Mihtar: ruler) of Chitral State had been friendly since 1885, and were put under the sphere of the British political agent in Gilgit. The death of Mehtar Amanul Mulk, in 1892, and the subsequent wrangle for power in Chitral created problems for the British. As a result of the siege of the British garrison in Chitral, in 1895, by the forces of Umara Khan of Jandul (also spelled as Jandol) and Sher Afzal, brother of Amanul Mulk and claimant to the seat of Chitral, the British forces were mobilised—as the Chitral Relief Force from Gilgit under Colonel Kelley, and from Peshawar under General Sir Robert Low, via Swat and Dir. The garrison at Chitral was relieved; garrisons were stationed at Malakand and Chakdarah, to keep the road open between the British-held territory, north of Peshawar and Chitral, via Swat and Dir. The Political Agency of Dir and Swat was created in 1895. The Swat River's left-bank area of Lower Swat, up to the border of Landakay, was brought under loose British control, as was the case in the Kurram Valley. This Agency, however, was placed under the direct orders of the Government of India, instead of the Punjab government; its political agent was to maintain a relationship with, and deal with, the affairs of, the chiefs and tribes of Bajawar, Dir, and Swat—which were not under British political control. Chitral, formerly under Gilgit Agency, was added to this Agency in 1897; hence, its name was changed from the Agency of Dir and Swat to the Agency of Dir, Swat and Chitral.[40] The territories of Swat, Dir, Bajawar, Sam Ranizi, Utman Khail, and Chitral were linked to this agency. In 1901, at the creation of the North-West Frontier Province, it 'was transferred from the Foreign Department of the Government of India to the Chief Commissioner of the North-West Frontier Province'.[41]

By the end of 1896, both by the demarcation of the boundary between British India and Afghanistan and by the extension of British influence to Khyber area, Shirani country, the Samana, the Kurram Valley, Waziristan, a portion of Swat and the Chitral road, via Swat and Dir, and the creation of the five political agencies—Khyber Agency (created in 1879), Kurram Agency (created in 1892), Dir, Swat and Chitral Agency (created in 1895), North Waziristan Agency (created in 1895) and South Waziristan Agency (created in 1896)—brought the now-former or the erstwhile tribal areas under the political control, although not under direct occupation and rule, of the British. The special status of the tribal areas, since then, remained intact until May 2018, when it was brought to an end through the 25th Amendment in the Pakistan Constitution of 1973.

Notes

1. The dynasty of the Turks, who established their rule in 1299 CE, is known as the Usmani Turk Dynasty, after the founder of the dynasty, Usman (Uthman). They are also referred to as Ottomans and Ottoman Turks. They ruled until 1924, when the Grand National Assembly of Turkey formally brought an end to the Usmani Khilafat. For some details about the rule of the Ottoman Turks, see Lane-Poole, *Farmanrawayan-i Islam*, Urdu trans. Ghulam Jilani Barq (Lahore: Shaikh Ghulam Ali and Sons, 1968), 204–14; Sarwat Saulat, *Millat-i Islamiyah ki Mukhtasar Tarikh* (Urdu), Part 2, 4th edn. (Lahore: Islamic Publications (Private), Limited, 1988), 200–46, 443–78.

2. Hakim Mohammed Said, S. Moinul Haq, Shariful Mujahid, and Ansar Zahid Khan, eds., *Road to Pakistan: A comprehensive history of the Pakistan Movemennt–1947*, vol. 1, *712–1858* (Karachi: Hamdard Foundation Pakistan, and Pakistan Historical Society, 1990), 485.

3. See Max Hastings, 'Did Chinese discover America?', *The Guardian*, Urdu trans. '*Amrica Chiniyu nay Daryaft kiya?*', trans. Muhammad Sharif Shakib in *Roznamah Aaj Peshawar* (Urdu, daily), 7 May 2005, 3.

4. Said, S. Moinul Haq, Shariful Mujahid, and Ansar Zahid Khan, eds., *Road to Pakistan*, vol. 1, 485.

5. Quoted in R.C. Majumdar, H.C. Raychaudhuri, and Kalikinkar Datta, *An Advanced History of India*, repr. (Lahore: Famous Books, 1992), 631.

6. In this book, the term or the word 'Britons' has neither been used in racist sense nor is it referring to the primitive ethnicity. The term or the word 'Briton' also means and is used for the native or citizen of Great Britain, person from Britain, and British person. In her rare televised address to the nation, on 5 April 2020, in connection with the coronavirus (Covid 19) pandemic, Queen Elizabeth II also used the word 'Britons', which testified that this is neither racist nor unsound. It was the East India Company not the British Government or British Crown that came to India and gradually occupied territories and emerged a ruling power. The Government of India Act of 1858 and the Queen Proclamation of 1858 divested the Company of its ruling power in India and took over control of its occupied territories. This is why, to differentiate between the Imperial British Government or British Crown and the East India Company, 'Britons' has been used for those from Great Britain who were working in India under the East India Company until the Government of India Act of 1858 and the Queen Proclamation of 1858. Used in the given context and sense, the term or word 'Britons' is more correct and relevant than the commonly used term or word 'English'.

7. For details, see Said, S. Moin-ul-Haq, Shariful Mujahid, and Ansar Zahid Khan, eds., *Road to Pakistan*, vol. 1, 486–92; Majumdar, H.C. Raychaudhuri, and Kalikinkar Datta, *An Advanced History of India*, 631–44.

8. For details, see Majumdar, H.C. Raychaudhuri, and Kalikinkar Datta, *An Advanced History of India*, 645–69.

9. For details, see Sh. A. Rashid, *Book Three: The Mughal Empire* in I.H. Qureshi, ed., *A Short History of Pakistan*, 2nd edn. (Karachi: UK, 1984), 17–75.

10. Said, Moin-ul-Haq, Shariful Mujahid, and Ansar Zahid Khan, eds., *Road to Pakistan*, vol. 1, 486; Vidya Dhar Mahajan, *Constitutional History of India (including the National Movement)*, 5th edn., thoroughly rev. and enlarged (Delhi: SCC, 1962), 1.

11. For details, see Majumdar, H.C. Raychaudhuri, and Kalikinkar Datta., *An Advanced History of India*, 636–9.

12. Ibid., 639–40.

13. Ibid., 665.

14. For details, see M.A. Rahim, M.D. Chughtai, W. Zaman, and A. Hamid, *Book Four: Alien Rule and the Rise of Muslim Nationalism* in Qureshi, ed., *A Short History of Pakistan*, 64–8; Majumdar, H.C. Raychaudhuri, and Kalikinkar Datta, *An Advanced History of India*, 669–74.

15. For Ahmad Shah Abdali's rise to power and his successes, see *Olaf Caroe, The Pathans: 550 B.C.–A.D. 1957*, repr. (Karachi: OUP, 1976), 249–61; Majumdar, H.C. Raychaudhuri, and Kalikinkar Datta, *An Advanced History of India*, 534–6; Ganda Singh, *Ahmad Shah Durrani: Father of Modern Afghanistan* (Bombay: Asia Publishing House, 1959).

16. For details about the rise of Maratha power, their successes, advances into the north, and defeat at the hands of Ahmad Shah Abdali, see Majumdar, H.C. Raychaudhuri, and Kalikinkar Datta, *An Advanced History of India*, 543–53; Said, S. Moin-ul-Haq, Shariful Mujahid, and Ansar Zahid Khan, eds., *Road to Pakistan*, vol. 1, 476–7.

17. S. Moinul Haq, *Islamic Thought and Movements in the Subcontinent (711–1947)* (Karachi: Pakistan Historical Society, 1979), 407–8.

18. Majumdar, H.C. Raychaudhuri, and Kalikinkar Datta, *An Advanced History of India*, 553.

19. Ibid., 542.

20. Ibid., 736.

21. For details, see Caroe, *The Pathans*, 286–306; Majumdar, H.C. Raychaudhuri, and Kalikinkar Datta, *An Advanced History of India*, 736–9; Diwan Chand Obhrai, *The Evolution of North-West Frontier Province: Being a Survey of the History and Constitutional Development of N.-W. F. Province, in India*, repr. (Peshawar: SBB, n.d.), 26–7.

22. Majumdar, H.C. Raychaudhuri, and Kalikinkar Datta, *An Advanced History of India*, 739–44. Also see Obhrai, *The Evolution of North-West Frontier Province*, 32–3.

23. Majumdar, H.C. Raychaudhuri, and Kalikinkar Datta, *An Advanced History of India*, 744–5; Rahim, M.D. Chughtai, W. Zaman, and A. Hamid, *Book Four: Alien Rule and the Rise of Muslim Nationalism* in Qureshi, ed., *A Short History of Pakistan*, 106; Obhrai, *The Evolution of North-West Frontier Province*, 33–5.

24. Majumdar, H.C. Raychaudhuri, and Kalikinkar Datta, *An Advanced History of India*, 745–6; Rahim, M.D. Chughtai, W. Zaman, and A. Hamid, *Book Four: Alien Rule and the Rise of Muslim Nationalism* in Qureshi, ed., *A Short History of Pakistan*, 106; Obhrai, *The Evolution of North-West Frontier Province*, 38.

25. Majumdar, H.C. Raychaudhuri, and Kalikinkar Datta, *An Advanced History of India*, 746–7; Obhrai, *The Evolution of North-West Frontier Province*, 38; Rahim, M.D. Chughtai, W. Zaman, and A. Hamid, *Book Four: Alien Rule and the Rise of Muslim Nationalism* in Qureshi, ed., *A Short History of Pakistan*, 106.

26. Arthur Swinson, *North-West Frontier: People and Events, 1839–1947* (London: Hutchinson & Co (Publishers) Ltd, 1967), 97–8.

27. Caroe, *The Pathans*, 323–4. Also see Andre Singer, *Lords of the Khyber: The Story of the North-West Frontier* (London: FFL, 1984), 100.

28. Caroe, *The Pathans*, 324.

29. Obhrai, *The Evolution of North-West Frontier Province*, 39.

30. *Administration Report on the North-West Frontier Province from 9th November 1901 to 31st March 1903* [henceforward *Administration Report NWFP from 9th November 1901 to 31st March 1903*] (Peshawar: Printed at the North-West Frontier Province Government Press, 1903), 6.

31. Caroe, *The Pathans*, 324.

32. Swinson, *North-West Frontier*, 98.

33. *The Cambridge History of India*, Vol. 6, *The Indian Empire, 1858–1918, With chapters on the development of Administration 1818–1858*, ed. H.H. Dodwell, *and the Last Phase 1919–1947*, by R.R. Sethi (Delhi: SCC, 1964), 449–50.

34. *Administration Report NWFP from 9th November 1901 to 31st March 1903*, 6.

35. Swinson, *North-West Frontier*, 98.

36. *Imperial Gazetteer of India: Provincial Series; North-West Frontier Province* [henceforward *Imperial Gazetteer of India, NWFP*], repr. (Lahore: SMP, 1991), 230–1.

37. For the Durand Line Agreement, 1893, see Sultan-i-Rome, 'The Durand Line Agreement (1893):– Its Pros and Cons', *Journal of the Research Society of Pakistan* (Lahore) vol. 41 (No. 1, July 2004), 1–25; chap. 5 of this book.

38. *Administration Report NWFP from 9th November 1901 to 31st March 1903*, 9. The report gives 1800 as the year of the evacuation, which is erroneous. Also see *Imperial Gazetteer of India, NWFP*, 239–40.

39. *Administration Report NWFP from 9th November 1901 to 31st March 1903*, 8–9. Also see *Imperial Gazetteer of India, NWFP*, 243–4. The *Administration Report* also gave 1895 as the year of the creation of the South Waziristan Agency, but the *Imperial Gazetteer of India, NWFP* has stated the year as 1896 (see *Imperial Gazetteer of India, NWFP*, 251).

40. *Administration Report NWFP from 9th November 1901 to 31st March 1903*, 9. The *Imperial Gazetteer of India, NWFP*, and also Dr Lal Baha—citing C. Collin Davies—wrote of the formation of the agency in 1896, but it was actually created in 1895. (See *Imperial Gazetteer of India, NWFP*, 210; Lal Baha, *N.-W.F.P. Administration under British Rule, 1901–1919* (Islamabad: NCHCR, 1978), 7. cf. Caroe, *The Pathans*, 383, 414. In *Files of the Commissioner Office Peshawar*, in the Record Section of the Provincial Archives at Peshawar, Bundle No. 33, Serial No. 947, there are diaries of the Political Officer, Dir and Swat, relating to the year 1895—testimony to the creation of the agency in 1895.

41. *Imperial Gazetteer of India, NWFP*, 210.

5 Durand Line Agreement

> The essential function of any frontier is that of separation. But a good frontier, while serving this useful purpose, should at the same time constitute a line of resistance following, as far as possible, easily recognisable natural features, and avoiding sharp salients and re-entrants. If possible, it should also be based upon ethnic considerations.
> – *The Cambridge History of India*

A S IS EVIDENT from the previous chapter, the Britons came to India to trade, but with the passage of time strengthened their position enough to be able to play a prominent role in the political affairs and governance of India. Furthermore, they used their position in India to counter Russian advances towards India and the warm waters of the Persian Gulf and Indian Ocean. Although, at the time, they had no common border with Afghanistan, their attempts to protect India, and the British position in Asia, from the Russians resulted in 'The Great Game'[1] in Central Asia.

BRITISH AND RUSSIAN INTERESTS IN AFGHANISTAN AND CENTRAL ASIA

On 15 November 1814, Britain and Persia signed the Treaty of Tehran. The terms of the treaty clearly reflected British fears and apprehensions about Russian advance towards India. One of the clauses of the treaty stated that the Persians would assist Britain in case of war. However, after the attempts to possess Herat, the British became apprehensive of Persia's intentions and possible relationship with Russia. To protect Britain's interests, the governor-general in India, Lord Auckland, tried to establish friendly relations with the Afghan Amir, Dost Muhammad Khan. In September 1836, he sent Alexander Burnes as his envoy to Afghanistan. At the same time, the Russians sent an emissary to Afghanistan and to Persia, which caused a stir in London. Consequently, a clear warning against interference, or any advance, in Afghanistan was communicated to Russia.[2]

The Persian siege of Herat in 1837, with the instigation of the Russian envoy, had created a very tense situation. Britain despatched a naval force to the Persian Gulf, and warned the Persians against the use of force. Alexander Burnes, who was in Kabul, urged the Afghan Amir to take action against the Persians in Herat, and to establish his authority in western Afghanistan. Although Dost Muhammad—the Afghan Amir— wanted to take possession of Herat, he demanded assurance of the restoration of the trans-Indus areas from the Sikhs, as a price 'for making common cause with the British'. But, Lord Auckland was not ready to appease the Afghan Amir at the cost of the Sikhs, whom he considered his strongest ally. The Britons' refusal to meet Dost Muhammad's demands; and because of Russian overtures and promises towards him, formed a tripartite alliance of Lord Auckland (Briton Governor-General of India), Ranjit Singh (the Sikh ruler of Punjab), and Shah Shuja (the deposed Amir of Afghanistan) in 1838. Although the Persians retreated from Herat, Lord Auckland decided to replace the hostile Dost Muhammad with the friendly Shah Shuja,[3] which in turn resulted in the First Anglo-Afghan War (1838–42 CE).

The British army was despatched to Afghanistan, through the Bulan (Bolan) Pass, in considerable numbers. Qandahar, Ghazni, and Kabul were occupied in April, July, and August 1839, respectively. As Dost Muhammad had already left Afghanistan, Shah Shuja was returned to the throne, an army was stationed in Kabul to support him, and a Briton mission was established at his court. The Afghans, however, were not pleased with these arrangements. Consequently, rebellion, coordinated by Dost Muhammad's son, Akbar Khan, took place all over Afghanistan. This was a disaster for the Briton forces in Afghanistan. A flying column was sent to Afghanistan to avenge the disaster, and Kabul was ransacked. However, the forces were withdrawn hastily, without achieving their objectives, because of frequent attacks. The First Anglo-Afghan War created a hatred for the British in Dost Muhammad and among the Afghan masses. In January 1843, Dost Muhammad returned and resumed charge of affairs.[4]

Although Dost Muhammad 'reluctantly accepted a peace with the British, agreeing to be "friends [friend] of its friends, and the enemies [enemy] of its enemies",'[5] he did not establish genuinely friendly relations with the Britons. He did not allow a Briton envoy in Kabul until the end, nor did he cooperate with the Britons in order to relieve the pressure they were facing from 'the tribes on the Frontier'.[6] However, while he did throw his lot in with the Sikhs in the Second Anglo-Sikh War (1848–49 CE), he 'refused to take advantage of British vulnerability and restrained his followers from declaring *jihad* (holy war)'[7] against the Britons during the Indian War of Independence in 1857.

After Dost Muhammad's death in 1863, his son Sher Ali struggled to ascend to the throne of Kabul, succeeding in 1870. In the meantime, Britons victory in the Second Anglo-Sikh War had brought about the end of the Sikh kingdom of Punjab. The Britons had occupied Punjab and made it a province of the Britons' domain in India. The annexation of Punjab brought the plains of the present-day Khyber Pukhtunkhwa under the control of the Britons—as the area had been part of the former Sikh kingdom, however loosely held. The Britons, therefore, became the immediate neighbours of the Afghan kingdom. As a result of the 1857 War of Independence, the British Crown brought about the end of the East India Company's rule and took direct control of the Company's Indian possessions. The Russian 'bugbear' proved to be the key factor in formulating British policy regarding Central Asia, Afghanistan, and the trans-Indus area. In this respect, two schools of thought emerged among the British: one advocated a 'close border policy',[8] while the other a 'forward policy'.[9]

An understanding was arrived at, between the Russians and the British, about Central Asia: it was agreed, in principle, that there would be a neutral zone in Central Asia, and that Afghanistan would be ideal for this. However, instead, in the actual agreement of 1873, as stated by James W. Spain,

> the Oxus was accepted as the basis of the yet undemarcated northern boundary of Afghanistan,... The main results were: (1) establishment of the Oxus as the dividing line between Afghan and Russian territory, (2) Russia's formal exclusion of Afghanistan from its sphere of influence, and (3) acceptance by the British of eventual absorption by Russia of all of the khanates north of the Oxus, including areas once under the suzerainty of the Amir of Kabul. [Interestingly,] Neither the British nor the Russians consulted the Amir in making the arrangement.[10]

The Russian rise in Central Asia alarmed Amir Sher Ali Khan and made him apprehensive of the impending danger. He, therefore, apprised, 'more than once', the British envoy in Kabul 'of his fears of the approach of Russia'. He 'wanted a guarantee and security' from the British 'against Russian invasion of Afghanistan', but the authorities in Britain did not pay serious heed to his fears and apprehensions. This caused Sher Ali to be annoyed at, and feel bitter towards, the British and led him to turn towards the Russians.[11] However, the situation changed in 1874 when the Conservatives, with Benjamin Disraeli as prime minister, formed the government in Britain. Lord Lytton became the new governor-general in India. As both Disraeli and Lytton 'were advocates of [a] more direct involvement in Afghanistan', they tried to bring Sher Ali to the table. Although Sher Ali attended a conference in Peshawar in 1876, and 'Lord Lytton's policy of friendship and active support for the Afghan Amir was being actively pursued', even then the Amir was more inclined towards the Russians and 'was suspicious of the sudden volte-face' of the British towards him. He not only refused to discontinue communication with the Russians, but also welcomed them 'under General Nicholai Grigorevich Stolietoff', while refusing to receive a British mission in Kabul.[12] 'Lytton decided to send' the mission, in spite of the Amir's refusal 'to welcome it'. So, a mission under Neville Chamberlain left for Afghanistan; but on 25 August 1878 it was denied entry into Afghanistan at the Khyber Pass.[13]

The Governor-General, Lord Lytton, and the Secretary of State for India, Lord Cranbrook, thought it prudent to teach Amir Sher Ali Khan a lesson for his insolence. On 2 November 1878, the Afghan Amir was asked to tender an apology for the treatment meted out to the British mission, by the Afghan soldiers, at the Khyber Pass, and to accept a British mission—otherwise he would be considered an enemy. The ultimatum expired on 20 November and, in spite of Sher Ali Khan's endeavours to amend and avert a war, war was proclaimed against Afghanistan. Afghanistan was invaded through the Khyber Pass, Kurram Valley, and Bulan Pass. Sher Ali fled to the north, dying on 21 February 1879. His son, Yaqub Khan, having entered into negotiations with the British, concluded the Treaty of Gandamak. He accepted all the British demands and ceded the territories of Kurram Valley, Pashin, Sibi, and the Khyber Pass to them. A British mission was stationed in Kabul; Qandahar and Jalalabad were evacuated, and a handful of forces were left behind in Kabul.[14]

Everything seemed to be normal, but the situation changed suddenly. A rebellion broke out, and the mission's members were killed on 3 September 1879. British forces were quickly re-mobilised. Afghanistan was reoccupied, and Yaqub Khan exiled to India. A tribal uprising followed, which spread quickly. To come out of the quagmire, the British decided to appoint, as the Amir of Afghanistan, someone who would be acceptable to both the British and the Afghans. At last, Abdur Rahman, a nephew of the former Amir Sher Ali Khan, was proclaimed the new Amir on 22 July 1880. Abdur Rahman restored order in Afghanistan and established his authority with great success. The British did not achieve all their objectives; the Treaty of Gandamak was considered dead.[15] However, the Second Anglo-Afghan War (1878–1880 CE) left its mark, at least in terms of the cession of the territories of Sibi, Chaman, Kurram Valley, and the Khyber area, due to which the important passes—Khyber, Kurram, and Bulan—were now held by the British.

Afghanistan became a buffer state between Russia and British India. However, its boundaries were not yet clearly demarcated, which created problems on several occasions.

The Russians advanced towards Afghanistan, and occupied Merv in its north-western corner, in 1884. They had their eyes on Panjdeh which, under the terms of the Treaty of 1873, was the territory of Afghanistan. Attempts at a peaceful settlement of the dispute bore no fruits, and the Russian troops occupied Panjdeh on 30 March 1885. Amir Abdur Rahman, who was in Rawalpindi at the time, averted a war for the possession of Panjdeh by suggesting that the Russians retain Panjdeh but the Zulfiqar Pass would remain in Afghans' hands. The Russians accepted the suggestion and, in July 1886, a boundary commission was set up to demarcate the boundary between Russia and Afghanistan in light of the protocol signed on 10 September 1885. The commission completed its work in June 1888, and the final boundaries between Afghanistan and Russia were confirmed on 12 June 1888.[16]

NEGOTIATIONS FOR THE AGREEMENT

Afghanistan's boundary with Russia was thus defined and demarcated, but its boundary with British India was still undefined. There were areas that both the sides either laid claim to, or coveted, or wanted under their control or sphere of influence. Amir Abdur Rahman was not unmindful of the dangers from Russia to the north, but at the same time he was apprehensive about British intentions towards his southern and eastern lands. His remark, 'though England does not want any piece of Afghanistan, still she never loses a chance of getting one—and this friend has taken more than Russia has!',[17] speak of his apprehensions. An Indian army officer hinted at the ground situation when he stated:

> What a wonderful power of absorption the British possess... We, of course, on our side, have always repudiated any idea of advance or annexation...but circumstances have often been in the past, and will be no doubt in the future, too strong for us.... By whatever name we may describe them, the result is the same: we advance, we absorb, we dominate, we destroy independence.[18]

Consequently, the Amir was cautious and heedful in his dealings with the British. On occasion, he not only showed his displeasure at the forward moves by the British, but also tried to assert his claim over the tribal areas and create trouble for the British there.[19] That was why the Viceroy, Lord Dufferin, told him in a letter, dated 20 July 1887, that he

> will merely observe that on many occasions Your Highness has shown a jealousy of our officers, a distrust of our intentions and an unwillingness to comply with our suggestions which was hardly consistent either with the kindness we have shown you or the friendship you profess towards us.[20]

T.H. Holdich states: 'To put the situation into political language, "relations had been strained" with the Amir for some time before actual aggression led to the consideration that a boundary was necessary between Afghanistan and these independent tribes.'[21] Moreover, he asserts:

> Indeed it is not too much to say that when the question of a boundary to eastern Afghanistan was pressed on the Council of India it was a question either of a boundary or of war with Afghanistan. Nothing short of this could have justified a measure which was so likely to raise a frontier hornets' nest about our ears.[22]

However, it 'was the second Afghan War, 1878–80, and the consequent occupation of Afghan territory, that impressed upon [the British] statesmen the necessity for a scientific frontier'[23] with Afghanistan.

One viewpoint is that Amir Abdur Rahman wanted to settle his eastern and southern boundaries with British India as well. Hence, in October 1888, he asked that a British mission be sent to Kabul; but the mission did not come. Again, in 1893, he suggested a mission be sent to 'Kabul to settle the boundary question'. The Government of India agreed and formed a mission headed by the then Foreign Secretary of the Government of India, Sir Mortimer Durand.[24]

In this respect, Amir Abdur Rahman himself states: 'Having settled my boundaries with all my other neighbours, I thought it necessary to set out the boundaries between my country and India, so that the boundary line should be definitely marked out around my dominions, as a strong wall for protection.' He, therefore, asked the viceroy in India, Lord Dufferin, and later Lord Ripon, to send a mission to Kabul to discuss certain matters. He also 'thought it better to exploit' the 'question of the boundary with such a Mission'. The proposed mission, however, did not proceed to Afghanistan for the time-being due to other developments.[25]

In 1890, Amir Abdur Rahman sent a letter to the Secretary of State for India, Salisbury, who, in response, asked the Amir to first settle the misunderstandings that existed between the governments of Afghanistan and India. At that time, the Viceroy, Lord Lansdowne, wrote to the Amir telling him that 'he had appointed Lord Roberts to be the head of the Mission'. However, due to his preoccupation with the Hazarah War, and his apprehensions about potential problems and the formation of the mission under Lord Roberts, who had fought against the Afghans in Afghanistan during the Second Anglo-Afghan War, the Amir 'thought it an unwise and unsuitable time for the Mission to assemble, and accordingly postponed it'.[26]

The British were not happy with the Amir's delaying tactics. According to the Amir's own statement: 'The Viceroy was so insistent on this matter that he addressed a letter to me, which was practically an ultimatum, to the effect that "the Indian Government cannot wait for your indefinite promises of uncertain date, and therefore after such-and-such a time, will draw its own conclusions".' The viceroy's ultimatum made Abdur Rahman apprehensive, and he took prompt steps to cool the situation down lest 'the matter should not become serious and irremediable'.[27] The Amir states:

> I immediately posted a letter to the Viceroy on this subject, saying that 'Mr Pyne [a Briton in the Amir's service] is going to see your Excellency, taking with him my letter, to make all the necessary arrangements about the Mission.' This message was intended to satisfy the authorities in India, and to prevent their taking any serious steps in the matter. After posting this letter I gave Mr Pyne one letter for the Viceroy and another addressed to Sir Mortimer Durand, the then Foreign Secretary; and bade him, Mr Pyne, go to India, with instructions to travel slowly, and if possible to postpone or delay the Mission for a few days, so that Lord Roberts, whose time for leaving India was very near, should leave for England. I requested the Viceroy to send me a map, having marked out the boundary lines as they proposed to decide them approximately, to show me which parts of Yaghistan (the land of the unruly) they proposed to take under their influence and sphere. I succeeded in this plan; Lord Roberts left India after writing a letter to me…and I at once invited the Mission to visit Kabul.[28]

The view that Amir Abdur Rahman consented to the Durand Line Agreement under duress and pressure appears to be supported by the facts that the Secretary of State for India had asked the Amir to settle disputed issues with the Government of India, the Amir was employing delaying tactics, and the ultimatum issued by the viceroy. James W. Spain states: 'In 1893, Amir Abd-ur-Rahman of Kabul reluctantly agreed to delimitation of his eastern boundary.'[29] The *Imperial Gazetteer of India: Provincial Series; North-West Frontier Province*, states the same in the following words: 'In 1893[,] the Amir consented to a precise fixing of boundaries, and a mission, under Sir Mortimer Durand, proceeded to Kabul to discuss the question.'[30] According to Vartan Gregorian: 'In 1893, caught between Russian pressure, British intransigence, and his own unwillingness and unpreparedness to start a war with the government in India, Abdur Rahman signed the Durand Agreement.'[31] While discussing 'the next series of important developments' that 'took place in the 1890's [1890s]', F.A.K. Harrison states that the occupation of the Kurram Valley by British forces during the Second Anglo-Afghan War, and their subsequent withdrawal, left a vacuum. Therefore, 'In 1892 it was decided to fill the vacumm [vacuum] by moving forward from Thal [Tal] to Parachinar.' Harrison contends: 'Worried by this move and also the moves forward in Baluchistan up to Chaman, the Amir Abdurrahman [Abdur Rahman] agreed to accept a British Mission to Kabul to put an end to further disputes and misunderstandings.'[32] T.H. Holdich also states: 'It requires no great strain of the imagination, and not much reading between the lines of official correspondence, to conceive that the Amir disliked the boundary exceedingly. There was indeed no reason why he [the Amir] should do otherwise. The independent tribes interfered very little with him. And they might at any time be brought under his sovereign control.'[33]

The Amir was not happy with the map sent to him, wherein 'all the countries of the Waziri, New Chaman, and the railway station there, Chageh, Bulund Khel, the whole of Mohmand, Asmar, and Chitral, and other countries lying in between, were marked as belonging to India'. He apprised the viceroy of his reservations and the potential consequences of taking away, from him, the areas shown on the map as belonging to India. He wrote to the viceroy:

But if you should cut them out of my dominions, they will neither be of any use to you nor to me: you will always be engaged in fighting and troubles with them, and they will always go on plundering. As long as your Government is strong and in peace, you will be able to keep them quiet by a strong hand, but if at any time a foreign enemy appear on the borders of India, these frontier tribes will be your worst enemies.... In your cutting away from me these frontier tribes who are people of my nationality and my religion, you will injure my prestige in the eyes of my subjects, and will make me weak, and my weakness is injurious to your Government.[34]

The British government, however, was adamant on absorbing these tribal areas. Instead of heeding Abdur Rahman's advice, they expelled his 'officials from Bulund Khel and Wana Zhob by force and threat of arms'.[35] It was in such circumstances that the mission under Mortimer Durand left Peshawar on 19 September 1893 and reached Kabul on 2 October. A magnificent reception was 'accorded to the mission at Kabul' and perfect 'arrangements made for its safety'.[36] Negotiations were held in a peaceful and friendly atmosphere,[37] and proved to be a success. The outcome was an agreement between the two sides, signed on 12 November 1893 by Amir Abdur Rahman and Henry Mortimer Durand; the agreement is commonly known as the Durand Line Agreement. In Charles Miller's words: 'The treaty formalized the emergence of the British Empire's longest land frontier next to the United States-Canadian border. It was a concession on a grand scale.'[38] The success of Durand's mission, however, 'was in no small measure due to his decision to enter Afghanistan without any escort and as the guest of the Amir'.[39]

TEXT OF THE AGREEMENT

The text of the agreement, signed by Amir Abdur Rahman Khan (Amir of Afghanistan) and Henry Mortimer Durand (British envoy), is as follows:

Whereas certain questions have arisen regarding the frontier of Afghanistan on the side of India, and whereas both His Highness the Amir and the Government of India are desirous of settling these questions by a friendly understanding, and of fixing the limits of their respective spheres of influence, so that for the future there may be no difference of opinion on the subject between the allied Governments, it is hereby agreed as follows:—

1) The eastern and southern frontier of His Highness's dominions, from Wakhan to the Persian border, shall follow the line shown in the map attached to this agreement.

2) The Government of India will at no time exercise interference in the territories lying beyond this line on the side of Afghanistan, and His Highness the Amir will at no time exercise interference in the territories lying beyond this line on the side of India.

3) The British Government thus agrees to His Highness the Amir retaining Asmar and the valley above it, as far as Chanak. His Highness agrees, on the other hand, that he will at no time exercise interference in Swat, Bajaur, or Chitral, including the Arnawai or Bashgal valley. The British Government also agrees to leave to His Highness the Birmal tract as shown in the detailed map already given to His Highness, who relinquishes his claim to the rest of

the Waziri country and Dawar. His Highness also relinquishes his claim to Chageh [Chaghi].

4) The frontier line will hereafter be laid down in detail and demarcated whereever [wherever] this may be practicable and desirable, by Joint British and Afghan Commissioners, whose object will be to arrive by mutual understanding at a boundary which shall adhere with the greatest possible exactness to the line shown in the map attached to this agreement, having due regard to the existing local rights of villages adjoining the frontier.

5) With reference to the question of Chaman, the Amir withdraws his objection to the new British Cantonment and concedes to the British Government the rights purchased by him in the Sirkai Tilerai water. At this part of the frontier the line will be drawn as follows:—

From the crest of the Khwaja Amran range near the Peha[40] Kotal, which remains in British territory, the line will run in such a direction as to leave Murgha Chaman and the Sharobo spring to Afghanistan, and to pass half-way between the New Chaman Fort and the Afghan outpost known locally as Lashkar Dand. The line will then pass half-way between the railway station and the hill known as the Mian Baldak, and, turning southwards, will rejoin the Khwaja Amran range, leaving the Gwasha Post in British territory, and the road to Shorawak to the west and south of Gwasha in Afghanistan. The British Government will not exercise any interference within half-a-mile of the road.

6) The above articles of agreement are regarded by the Government of India and His Highness the Amir of Afghanistan as a full and satisfactory settlement of all the principal differences of opinion which have arisen between them in regard to the frontier; and both the Government of India and His Highness the Amir undertake that any differences of detail, such as those which will have to be considered hereafter by the officers appointed to demarcate the boundary line, shall be settled in a friendly spirit, so as to remove for the future as far as possible all causes of doubt and misunderstanding between the two Governments.

7) Being fully satisfied of His Highness's goodwill to the British Government, and wishing to see Afghanistan independent and strong, the Government of India will raise no objection to the purchase and import by His Highness of munitions of war, and they will themselves grant him some help in this respect. Further, in order to mark their sense of the friendly spirit in which His Highness the Amir has entered into these negotiations, the Government of India undertake to increase by the sum of six lakhs of rupees a year the subsidy of twelve lakhs now granted to His Highness.[41]

Interestingly, instead of referring to the governments or states on both the sides, in the text of the agreement, one side is mentioned as His Highness the Amir, or His Highness, and the other side is referred to as the British government, or the Government of India. But, at the end of article (6), instead of 'His Highness the Amir', or 'His Highness', and 'the British government', or the 'Government of India', reference is made to 'the two Governments'.

On 13 November, the Amir held a public *darbar* at the Salam Khanah Hall, which was also attended by his 'two eldest sons', the leading chiefs of various tribes, and both 'the civil and military officers of Kabul'. He presented, before the audience, an outline of the understanding that 'had been agreed upon', and the terms signed by the two sides: for the information of those present and for the nation as a whole. He 'also thanked Sir Mortimer Durand and the other members of the Mission for their wise way of settling the disputes'. Mr Durand also made a speech in which he spoke of the Viceroy and Secretary of State for India's 'great pleasure and satisfaction' at the friendly understanding of the agreement. The representatives and officials of Afghanistan, present on the occasion, 'expressed their satisfaction and consent to the agreements and understandings, and their great pleasure and rejoicing at the friendship between the kingdoms of Great Britain and Afghanistan'. The Amir rose 'a second time' and read the 'paper to the members of the Mission' and the audience.[42] On 14 November 1893, the mission left Kabul and 'returned to Peshawar with great rejoicing and was accorded honours such as no mission has received before or since'.[43] The viceroy, in his letter to the Secretary of State for India, termed the agreement 'most satisfactory' and 'hoped that it would lead to the termination of the state of unrest that had disturbed the peace of the frontier'.[44]

Thus, the Amir 'surrendered', to the British, 'nearly all of the land in which the British presence had been stirring his anxieties and fury for years'.[45] The two sides formed joint commissions, in accordance with the agreement, which worked for two years: 1894 and 1895. In demarcating the boundary line from Chitral to the Persian border, however, they only set up pillars in the sections where both sides agreed upon the line and its demarcation was possible. The boundary line, thus demarcated, is known as Durand Line, which also forms the present Pak-Afghan border.[46]

PROS AND CONS OF THE AGREEMENT

The Durand Line Agreement was signed, and the boundary demarcated at the most feasible and agreed-upon places. It remains the international boundary between Afghanistan and Pakistan to this day. As a result of the Durand Line Agreement, and the demarcation of the line, Afghanistan's boundaries with its two powerful and ambitious neighbours—Russia and

British India—became fixed and established. Afghanistan now did not have to fear further encroachment on its territory by the British from the Indian side. Amir Abdur Rahman himself states:

> The province of Wakhan, which had come under my dominion, I arranged to be left under the British for protection, as it was too far from Kabul, and cut off from the rest of my country, and therefore very difficult to be properly fortified.
>
> The boundary line was agreed upon from Chitral and Baroghil Pass up to Peshawar, and thence up to Koh Malik Siyah in this way that Wakhan, Kafiristan, Asmar, Mohmand of Lalpura, and one portion of Waziristan came under my rule, and I renounced my claims from the railway station of New Chaman, Chageh [Chaghi], the rest of Waziri, Bulund Khel [Khail], Kuram, Afridi, Bajaur [Bajawar], Swat, Buner [Bunair], Dir, Chilas, and Chitral.[47]

The Amir further states:

> The misunderstandings and disputes which were arising about these frontier matters were put to an end, and after the boundary lines had been marked out according to the above-mentioned agreements by the Commissioners of both Governments, a general peace and harmony reigned between the two Governments, which I pray God may continue for ever.[48]

This, however, did not prove to be the end to Afghanistan's claims over the areas lost to the Sikhs, and later to the British as a result of the Second Anglo-Afghan War and the Durand Line Agreement. Nor did the Durand Line abolish British desire to squeeze further land from Afghanistan. James W. Spain points out: 'The Durand Line, as the boundary came to be called, has been a source of dissension between Afghanistan and British India (later Pakistan) ever since.'[49] Referring to Amir Abdur Rahman's 'reluctance' and opposition 'to the conclusion of the agreement', and to the tribesmen's apprehensions and opposition as well, H.L. Nevill states:

> After some show of reluctance, the Boundary Agreement was at length signed by the Amir Abdur Rahman, and the actual demarcation of the frontier by pillars began. In all probability the Amir was opposed to the conclusion of the agreement, because he feared that the formal recognition of a sphere of British influence among the frontier tribes would be only a prelude to permanent annexation, and ultimately cause the removal of the only buffer between his country and India. The tribesmen, also considering the matter from their own point of view, foresaw no result from the agreement but the eventual loss of their jealously guarded independence, and opposed the demarcation of the boundary-line from the very beginning.[50]

The British government disregarded Afghanistan's apprehensions and demands. To force the British to return the tribal areas that had been taken from Afghanistan's sphere of influence, Amir Abdur Rahman—although he denied it—attempted to create anti-British sentiments and stir up a *jihad* in the tribal areas on the Indian side of the Durand Line. His endeavours and machinations[51] proved a stimulating factor in the famous uprising of 1897, which turned the year of the British Queen's 'Diamond Jubilee',[52] and the fortieth anniversary of the successful emergence of the Britons' from the Indian War of Independence of 1857, into 'surely one of the most troublous years in all Indian history'.[53] It has aptly been stated:

> The new boundary line was not based upon sound topographical data, for, during the process of demarcation, it was discovered that certain places, marked on the Durand map, did not exist on the actual ground. Many ethnic absurdities were perpetrated, such as the handing over to the amir [Amir] of the Birmal tract of Waziristan, peopled by Darwesh Khel Waziris, the majority of whom were included within the British sphere of influence. The worst blunder of all was the arrangement by which the boundary cut the Mohmand tribal area into two separate parts. It seems certain that this could not have been a tripartite agreement, for there is no evidence that the tribesmen were consulted before 1893. To give but one example: it was not until the year 1896 that the Halimzai [Halimzi], Kamali, Dawezai [Dawizi], Utmanzai [Utmanzi], and Tarakzai Mohmands [Tarakzi Muhmands], afterwards known as the eastern or 'assured' clans, accepted the political control of the Government of India... In all probability the political issues at stake occasioned this sacrifice of ethnological requirements. If the amir [Amir] had not been promised the Birmal tract, it is quite likely that he would have refused his consent to the inclusion of Wana within the British sphere of influence. In the light of subsequent events it is difficult to understand the reasons which prompted the amir [Amir] to sign this agreement. It may have been that the increase of his subsidy to eighteen lakhs of rupees, and the recognition of his right to import munitions of war, bribed him into acquiescence.[54]

In Charles Miller's words:

> It hardly needs saying that the treaty created more problems than it solved. Although the 1893 boundary—commonly known as the Durand Line—has not changed to this day, it has come under continual and often severe criticism for its flaws. Fraser-Tytler calls it 'illogical from the point of view of ethnography, of strategy and of geography,' noting particularly that 'it splits a nation in two, and it even divides tribes.' This arbitrary amputation could barely be justified, even on grounds of geopolitical expediency. Despite the cantankerous

independence of the Frontier Pathans, they were by history, tradition, race, language and temperament Afghans. If their allegiance to the Amir was spotty at best, they were even less suited to becoming subjects of the Queen; trying to absorb them and their lands into British India was like trying to graft a cactus spine to the trunk of an oak tree.[55]

According to another writer:

The Durand Boundary was not [on] the whole a conventional line separating the Baluch from the Afghan and the Afghan from frontier tribes who, however much affiliated to the Afghan, had never been under their domination. Though it was a concrete symbol of compromise it was the manifestation of a policy which, whatever its merits, was not carried to its logical conclusion. The British in refusing to obey the law of political and strategic development by a physical occupation of the natural frontiers of India had to take the consequences of such a refusal. They solved the major problem but in such a way that they set up for themselves minor problems which have defied solution ever since.[56]

The issue of the Durand Line Agreement again came to the surface after the accession of Amir Habibullah Khan, son and successor of Amir Abdur Rahman, when the British refused to pay the subsidy to the new Amir without the 'renewal of the previous agreement'. According to L.W. Adamec, the Amir asked the viceroy, among other points, 'If the previous agreements were no longer valid, was not also the Durand Agreement no longer valid? This was indeed a difficult question for the government of India to answer.'[57] The Government of India discussed the issue and deemed the agreement of 1880 to be a personal one. However, it was difficult to agree with the view that the Durand Line Agreement of 1893 was also a 'personal' one. Because if it, too, was to be acknowledged 'personal, then the articles dealing with the boundary question could not be considered perpetual and would have to be renegotiated'.[58]

The issue was discussed at length between England and India, and between India and Afghanistan. Finally, the previous agreements were endorsed in a new agreement, signed by both the sides on 21 March 1905. Having signed the agreement, Amir Habibullah Khan sent a letter to Mr Dane, Foreign Secretary of the Government of India and head of the Indian mission to Afghanistan, in which, among other matters, he reaffirmed that 'with regard to the frontier tribes', he 'would "not go beyond his father's principles".'[59] However, none of this solved the matter of the demarcation of the still-disputed sections of the Durand Line during his reign. L.W. Adamec states:

The question of demarcation of the Indo-Afghan boundary also did not find its solution under Habibullah. The Durand Agreement of 1893 laid down the border, but when demarcation was taken up in 1895 Abdur Rahman claimed that he was to receive the entire Mohmand territory and not merely a section of it. In 1896 the Amir protested discrepancies on the map attached to the Durand Agreement, but Lord Elgin told him that the frontier drawn on the map must be followed. The Viceroy made some minor concessions to the Amir, coupled with an ultimatum that these concessions would be withdrawn if the Amir failed to begin demarcation of the boundary. Abdur Rahman permitted British and Afghan commissions to be set up for demarcation of the boundaries, but demarcation was never accomplished because the Amir failed to arrange for the protection of the British commissioners (protection from tribes on the British side of the border). During the frontier disturbances of 1897, British troops overran the Mohmand territory including Bohai Dag which was previously given to the Amir in exchange for an early demarcation. Habibullah defended his full rights to Bohai Dag, and the government of India began to regret having permitted this valley to remain in the possession of the Amir.... Habibullah asserted his right to Smatzai in 1905; a request from Lord Curzon for demarcation of parts of the boundary did not lead to any solution.[60]

When Amanullah Khan succeeded in acquiring power in April 1919, after his father 'Habibullah was assassinated in Kalla Gush in the Laghman district', on the night between 19 and 20 February 1919, he declared Afghanistan 'entirely free, autonomous and independent both internally and externally'. Moreover, he informed the Viceroy of India about the Afghan government's readiness to 'conclude...such arrangements and treaties with the mighty Government of England' as 'may be useful and serviceable' to both the governments. This put the Government of India in an awkward situation because, 'After maintaining for so long that Anglo-Afghan agreements were made personally with the amirs [Amirs], it was difficult to deny that Amanullah had a right to demand a new treaty for Afghanistan.'[61]

The uneasiness between Afghanistan and British India resulted in the Third Anglo-Afghan War of 1919, which 'was an attempt at reestablishing Afghanistan's former borders with India, of redressing what the Afghans felt was a great injustice to them'.[62] One of the outcomes of the War was the negotiation of a settlement regarding territorial claims caused by the Durand Line Agreement of 1893. While the British had their own territorial concerns—'acceptance of the old border, except where Britain defines adjustments'[63]—'The Afghans intended to propose an "astounding" readjustment of the border whereby they would receive Waziristan and other tribal areas.'[64] However, under article V of the

Treaty of Peace, concluded at Rawalpindi on 8 August 1919, the Afghan government accepted 'the Indo-Afghan frontier accepted by the late Amir [Habibullah]'. The Afghan government, moreover, acceded 'to the early demarcation by a British Commission of the undemarcated portion of the line west of the Khyber, where the recent Afghan aggression took place, and to accept such boundary as the British Commission may lay down'.[65]

The British 'completed the demarcation' of the requisite undemarcated Durand Line before the evacuation of Spin Boldak and Dakka. Accompanied by 'the Afghan General, Ghulam Nabi Khan', the demarcation was carried out by John Maffey, defining the border on the spot 'as he went along'. The Afghan general did not take part in the demarcation but only 'watched the proceedings'. The British 'postponed the "rectification" in' her 'favor of the Durand Line, over and above [the] assertions of previously disputed claims, for future discussions and negotiations when the treaty of friendship was concluded'.[66] While accepting the Afghan frontier as accepted under article V of the Treaty of Peace, the British ceded some more areas to Afghanistan under article II of the Treaty, signed by Britain and Afghanistan in Kabul on 22 November 1921.[67] Although Amanullah Khan attained Afghan independence, 'he was forced to recognize the Durand Line'.[68]

A significant feature of the agreements, concluded during Amanullah Khan's reign, was that they were concluded and signed by the Afghan and British governments, whereas the previous ones had been concluded between the Afghan Amirs, instead of the Afghan government, and, hence, were considered to be personal by the British—even if not so by the Afghans.

The disappointment of the successive Afghan Amirs, from Abdur Rahman till Amanullah Khan, with the Durand Line Agreement is also evident from the fact that 'the Asmar Commission (1894) demarcated' the boundary 'from the Bashgal valley on the border of Kafiristan to Nawa Kotal', at the juncture of the Bajawar and Mohmand territories; demarcation 'south of the Nawa Kotal' was not carried out 'owing to disagreement' between the British and the Afghan Amir. The Amir was not willing 'to admit the boundary framed by the Durand agreement in the Mohmand territory'.[69] Moreover, the demarcation of the boundary line between the Kabul River and Sikaram (Safaid Kuh) was not attempted because of disagreement on both the sides; 'and it was not until 1919, after the conclusion of the Third Afghan War, that this demarcation was defined'.[70]

According to Pakistan's point of view, King Nadir Shah—who came into power in Afghanistan after Bacha Saqau's removal from the scene (who had come to power following his coup against Amir Amanullah Khan)—reaffirmed the agreement of 1893 in 'the letters exchanged between the new Afghan Government and Great Britain', respectively, by reaffirming 'the 1921 Treaty which...had accepted the Durand Line as the legal Indo-Afghan frontier'.[71] His successor, Zahir Shah, at first made no attempt to recover the lost territories, but when the British announced, in 1946, the transfer of power in India to its people, the Afghan government, under Zahir Shah, made 'a formal representation' to the then Government of India 'demanding the restoration of a large area' on the grounds that the Durand Line Agreement of 1893 would automatically lapse 'with the withdrawal of the British'.[72]

The Department of External Affairs, Government of India, 'rejected the validity' of Afghanistan's claim to the 'territory east of the Durand Line'. 'The British Government informed the Afghan Government on July 1, 1947', in reply to its representations, that

> 'the Afghan representation relates to an area which forms an integral part of India and is recognised as such by the Afghan Government in the Anglo-Afghan Treaty of 1921', that they cannot 'admit the right of any foreign Government to intervene in matters which are the sole concern of the inhabitants of the territory in question', and that any such interference would be 'incompatible with the undertakings exchanged by the British and Afghan Governments in Article 1 of the Treaty of 1921.[73]

The British did not recognise the Afghan government's plea, nor did the Afghan government withdraw its demand and claim.

At the end of British rule in the subcontinent, the area demanded and claimed by the Afghan government came under the Government of Pakistan, as the successor of the British Indian government in the area. Consequently, the issue of the validity of the Durand Line, as well as that of the Afghan demand and claim, fell to Pakistan. The Pakistan government contended:

> The Government of Pakistan as a successor to the British Indian Government for areas which comprise Pakistan succeeded to all the rights and obligations arising under international agreement vide Indian Independence (International Arrangements) Order, 1947 passed under Independence Act, 1947.
>
> Further, the Government of the United Kingdom which exercised, through the Government of India, full control, and was in actual possession of the

territories up to the Durand Line prior to the Independence of Pakistan, have repeatedly confirmed the legality of the Durand Line as international frontier between Afghanistan and Pakistan.[74]

The Pakistan government further contended:

The Afghan demand for the right of self-determination for the Pathans is equally untenable. The future of the...North West Frontier Province, where the Pathans live, was in fact decided through a referendum held on July 6, 1947 [between 6 and 18 July 1947] and therein 99% of the votes cast were in favour of accession to Pakistan....

Further, the tribesmen living in the tribal belt willingly expressed their consent to be a part and parcel of Pakistan through separate agreements concluded between the Government of Pakistan as successor to the British Indian Government and notable Maliks and representative heads of various tribes living on the Pakistan side of the Durand Line.[75]

The Afghans, on the other hand, claimed the opposite and were of the opinion that the referendum, held in July 1947, did not offer a third option: an independent Pukhtun country.[76] The option to join Afghanistan was not offered either. As a consequence, Afghanistan voted against Pakistan's entry into the United Nations and, in 1949, the Afghan National Assembly 'passed a resolution repudiating all treaties, conventions and agreements concluded between the Afghan government and the British India government, thus, formally rejecting the Durand Line'.[77] In 1955, the *Luyah* (*Loya*) *Jargah* (Grand National Assembly) of Afghanistan 'adopted a resolution...stipulating the non-recognition of Pukhtun territories as part of Pakistan'.[78] Strained relations persisted between the two countries over this issue, until Afghanistan broke off diplomatic relations with Pakistan in September 1961. This, however, did not prove to be the end of the opposing viewpoints and contentions about the nature and validity of the Durand Line Agreement, and of the consequent delimited line.

Thus, the opposing viewpoints of both the sides—first Afghanistan and Britain, and later Afghanistan and Pakistan—about the status of the Durand Line, and Afghanistan's endeavours for its lost territories created discord on both sides. Afghanistan's views on the validity of the Durand Line Agreement at the end of British rule in the subcontinent, and their consequent demand and claim, as well as their support and propagation of the Pukhtunistan slogan became the bone of contention and strained relations between Afghanistan and Pakistan ever since the inception of

Pakistan. Successive Afghan governments—including the interim Afghan President, Burhanuddin Rabbani, and later the Taliban—held the same views. 'President Daud once remarked that the "British did a wrong many years ago and we have been fighting to rectify it. Until that is done the struggle will continue".'[79]

Mula Muhammad Zaif, the Taliban government's ambassador to Pakistan, stated in an interview that Pakistan had tried to raise the Durand Line issue a number of times but he had declined to enter into deliberation on the subject on the basis that it was not the Taliban's, but the Afghan people's, issue. His reply was that the Taliban even did not think of talking on the subject until their government had become sufficiently strong and had been recognised by the United Nations. When asked, in case the situation was according to their desire, whether the Taliban would have accepted Pakistan's plea to recognise the Durand Line as a permanent international border, Mula Zaif replied: No, we would never have accepted this. Because only the people across the border have the right to decide: for their language, religion, custom and usage, and traditions are common. This is a line drawn on the heart of a nation.[80] Afghan President, Hamid Karzai, also abstained from giving clear and frank responses to questions about the Durand Line in a programme arranged by the BBC's Urdu programme, *Sairbin*. In the backdrop of the accusations, from both Afghanistan and Pakistan, about militants crossing the Durand Line into both the countries and their militant activities on both the sides of the border, Pakistan embarked on closing the border by erecting barbed fence. This, too, was objected by Afghanistan; in a special interview with BBC's correspondent, Khudai Nur Nasir, the Afghan ambassador to Pakistan, Dr Hazrat Umar Zakhailwal, termed the fencing of the border one-sided action. He said that according to the agreement, in case of any construction or fencing the Afghan government should be taken into confidence but they have not been taken into confidence. Terming the merger of the tribal areas into Khyber Pukhtunkhwa a sensitive issue, the Afghan ambassador said that they have a historical stance on the Durand Line and no change in that stance has taken place so far. He contended that the right of negotiation over this is beyond the sphere of power of the government. This power solely and surely lies with the masses along the Durand Line.[81] Pakistan, however, continues to deny and negate the Afghan arguments.

The 'dispute about', and the unstable nature of, the Durand Line in places also became 'the root-cause of the divergent stand[s] of the Pakistan and US governments' in the post-Taliban period, when the Americans bombarded 'a Pakistani border village'. Pakistan acknowledged that 'one bomb dropped by a US jet fighter fell in Pakistani territory'. However, 'the US military authorities' maintained that 'the bombs fell in Afghanistan about 300 metres from the Pakistan[i] border'. 'The Americans pointed out that the Pakistanis' had, in fact, 'set up checkposts in the Afghan territory'.[82] Commenting on this scenario, Rahimullah Yusufzai, a senior journalist and expert on Afghan issues, states:

> Islamabad has all along claimed that it had set up checkpoints on its side of the Durand Line that divides Pakistan and Afghanistan. But [the] Afghan authorities, whether mujahideen, Taliban or the new pro-US rulers, felt Pakistan had exploited the unstable situation in Afghanistan to extend its border beyond the Durand Line. Afghan military commanders and tribal elders in Paktika province, which borders Pakistan's South Waziristan tribal agency, have been particularly vocal in accusing Pakistani militiamen belonging to the Frontier Corps of encroaching upon Afghanistan's territory.[83]

In addition, 'by insisting that the bombs…fell in Afghanistan', and that Pakistan had 'established checkposts on the Afghan side of [the] Durand Line, the Americans are making it clear that they accept the Afghan claim to the chunk of territory which Islamabad claims'. Moreover, the 'Pakistani tribesmen in the Angoor Adda some years ago complained that they were subject to two kinds of law, that of Pakistan and the Taliban'.[84]

Commenting on this state of affairs, Muhammad Mushtaq Jadoon, Deputy Secretary, Home and Tribal Affairs Department, NWFP (now Khyber Pukhtunkhwa), states:

> There are certain myths about Durand line. Some of these area [are]:-
>   i) That Durand Line Agreement was for 100 years only.
> ii) That Durand Line Agreement was made with the British Government and not with Pakistan so it is null and void now.
> iii) That the Amir accepted the Durand line Agreement with 'Heavy heart' so, now, they are justified to re-agitate it.
> iv) That Durand Line passing through Mohmand Agency is disputed since it was not demarcated on ground and thus Afghan Government has every right to have claim over Khawazai.[85]

Mushtaq Jadoon has tried to examine these points 'one by one', and to clarify the position from Pakistan's viewpoint. Besides other contentions and arguments, he asserts:

Thus it is clear from the Agreement that no area was shown, either in the draft of agreement, or attested map as 'disputed'. There is lot of difference between 'un-demarcated' on the ground and 'disputed'.

As far as question of perpetual validity of this agreement is concerned suffice to state that the Northern and Western Frontiers of Afghanistan with Russia and Persia were also demarcated by the Britishers. Russia has disintegrated but states of Turkistan [Turkmenistan?] and Uzbekistan are successor-in-interest of Russia. Neither Afghanistan nor the Central Asian States have ever raised any objections to these agreements. Similarly Boundary with Sistan (Iran) was also demarcated by the Britishers. Pakistan is also successor-in-interest of Great Britain and bound to honour all those agreements related to its geographic territory and so is Afghanistan.[86]

Moreover:

It is amply clear from the above discussion and reference of various Treaties that Durand Line Agreement was ratified, affirmed and re-affirmed under various Treaties in 1894, 1895, 1905, 1919, 1921 and 1930.[87]

Interestingly, not only do the governments on both sides of the border hold different stands and viewpoints about the Durand Line, and its Agreement and validity, but historians, too, maintain different and divergent viewpoints. Vartan Gregorian has briefly summarised them as:

Afghan historians contend that the line of demarcation, the Durand Line, was imposed on Afghanistan under the threat of war and economic blockade. Muhammad Ali asserts that it deprived the country of 'a quarter of a million Pathans of military age' (*The Mohammedzai Period*, pp. 140–41). British historians, for their part, maintain that the Durand Line was a negotiated settlement and cite as evidence both the Amir's public adherence to the agreement and his positive references to it in his autobiography (see Munshi, *Life of Abdur Rahman*, II, 166). As noted, the Afghans question the authenticity of these portions of the autobiography. An interesting idea has been advanced by Fraser-Tytler (*Afghanistan*, p. 189). He suggests that Abdur Rahman, unfamiliar with reading maps, did not understand all the implications when the line was drawn on a map before him, but was too conceited to say so. According to Singhal (pp. 152f), there were considerable differences between the map the Amir supplied his representative and the one on which the Durand Line was marked at Kabul. Says Singhal: 'For the Amir it can properly be argued that the map drawn in 1893 had been prepared in a hurry and was not without inaccuracies.' Rastogi also suggests that the maps varied (p. 180). According to Forrest (*Lord Roberts*, p. 172), 'The Amir signed the treaty, but he did not sign the official maps indicating the boundary. He disliked the boundary because he considered it damaged his authority and prestige, and he determined by all the indirect means in his power to prevent its demarcation.'[88]

Notes

1. For some details about the Great Game in Central Asia, see W.K. Fraser-Tytler, *Afghanistan: A Study of Political Developments in Central and Southern Asia*, 2nd edn. (London: OUP, 1953), 75–180; Munawwar Khan, *Anglo-Afghan Relations, 1798–1878: A Chapter in the Great Game in Central Asia* (Peshawar: UBA, n.d.).

2. James W. Spain, *The Pathan Borderland*, repr. (Karachi: IP, 1985), 123–5. Also see J.G. Elliott, *The Frontier, 1839–1947: The Story of the North-West Frontier of India*, with preface by Olaf Caroe (London: Cassell & Company Ltd, 1968), 13; Azmat Hayat Khan, *The Durand Line—Its Geo-Strategic Importance*, ed. M.Y. Effendi, 3rd edn. (Peshawar: Area Study Centre, University of Peshawar, 2005), 57–8.

3. Spain, *The Pathan Borderland*, 125–8. Also see Andre Singer, *Lords of the Khyber: The Story of the North-West Frontier* (London: FFL, 1984), 94–8; Elliott, *The Frontier*, 14–16; Khan, *The Durand Line*, 59–62.

4. Spain, *The Pathan Borderland*, 128–9. Also see Singer, *Lords of the Khyber*, 98–9; Elliott, *The Frontier*, 16–28; Khan, *The Durand Line*, 62–4; Arthur Swinson, *North-West Frontier: People and Events, 1839–1947* (London: Hutchinson & Co (Publishers) Ltd, 1967), 26–84.

5. Singer, *Lords of the Khyber*, 100. Also see Khan, *The Durand Line*, 67.

6. Spain, *The Pathan Borderland*, 131.

7. Singer, *Lords of the Khyber*, 100.

8. Advocates of the 'close border policy' were of the opinion that, in Churchill's words, 'nothing should have lured the Government of India beyond their natural frontier line'. They maintained: 'Over all the plains of India will we cast our rule… But that region, where the land rises like the waves of a sea, shall serve us as a channel of stormy waters to divide us from our foes and rivals' in Central Asia. Winston S. Churchill, *The Story of the Malakand Field Force: An Episode of Frontier War*, repr. (London: Leo Cooper, 2002), 213. For the 'close border policy', also see Olaf Caroe, *The Pathans: 550 B.C.–A.D. 1957*, repr. (Karachi: OUP, 1976), 346–59; Spain, *The Pathan Borderland*, 115–19; *The Cambridge History of India*, vol. 6, *The Indian Empire, 1858–1918, With chapters on the development of Administration 1818–1858*, ed. H.H. Dodwell, *and the Last Phase 1919–1947*, by R.R. Sethi (Delhi: SCC, 1964), 456–60; Khan, *The Durand Line*, 68–82.

9. The 'forward policy' aimed, in Churchill's words, 'at obtaining the frontier—Gilgit, Chitral, Jelalabad, Kandahar [Qandahar]'. Churchill, *The Story of the Malakand Field Force*, 212. For details about the forward policy, see ibid., 209–16; Spain, *The Pathan Borderland*, 116–19; C. Collin Davies, *The Problem of the North-West Frontier, 1890–1908: With a survey of policy since 1849*, 2nd edn., rev. and enlarged (London: CPL, 1975), 71–98; *The Cambridge History of India*, vol. 6, 456–60; Richard Isaac Bruce, *The Forward Policy and its Results or Thirty-Five Years work amongst the Tribes on Our North-Western Frontier of India*, with illustrations and a map, 2nd edn. in Pakistan (Quetta: NT, 1979); Khan, *The Durand Line*, 70–8.

10. Spain, *The Pathan Borderland*, 133.

11. Mohammad Anwar Khan, *England, Russia and Central Asia (A Study in Diplomacy), 1857–1878* (Peshawar: UBA, n.d.), 252–4.

12. Singer, *Lords of the Khyber*, 113. Also see Khan, *England, Russia and Central Asia*, 254–9; Khan, *The Durand Line*, 92–103.

13. Spain, *The Pathan Borderland*, 133. Also see Elliott, *The Frontier*, 31–3.

14. Spain, *The Pathan Borderland*, 134–5. Also see Singer, *Lords of the Khyber*, 114–17; Swinson, *North-West Frontier*, 153–67; Khan, *The Durand Line*, 103–23.

15. Spain, *The Pathan Borderland*, 135–6. Also see Singer, *Lords of the Khyber*, 117–19, 148–55; Elliott, *The Frontier*, 36–45; Khan, *The Durand Line*, 123–5.

16. Spain, *The Pathan Borderland*, 137–9. For details about the Russo-Afghan boundary issues, see T. Hungerford Holdich, *The Indian Borderland, 1880–1900*, 1st repr. in India (Delhi: Gian Publishing House, 1987), 94–179.

17. Charles Miller, *Khyber: British India's North West Frontier; The Story of an Imperial Migraine* (London: Macdonald and Jane's Publishers Limited, 1977), 239.

18. Quoted in ibid., 259.

19. See ibid., 239–40.

20. Quoted in Ludwig W. Adamec, *Afghanistan, 1900–1923: A Diplomatic History* (Berkeley: University of California Press, 1967), 22.

21. Holdich, *The Indian Borderland*, 228. Also see *The Cambridge History of India*, vol. 6, 461–2.

22. Holdich, *The Indian Borderland*, 228.

23. *The Cambridge History of India*, vol. 6, 456–7.

24. See *Durand Line* (n.p., n.d.), 4–5.

25. Sultan Mahomed Khan, ed., *The Life of Abdur Rahman: Amir of Afghanistan*, with new introduction by M.E. Yapp, vol. 2, repr. in Pakistan (Karachi: OUP, 1980), 154–5.

26. Ibid., 155–6.

27. Ibid., 156.

28. Ibid., 156–7.

29. Spain, *The Pathan Borderland*, 117.

30. *Imperial Gazetteer of India: Provincial Series; North-West Frontier Province* [henceforward *Imperial Gazetteer of India, NWFP*], repr. (Lahore: SMP, 1991), 25.

31. Vartan Gregorian, *The Emergence of Modern Afghanistan: Politics of Reforms and Modernization, 1880–1946* (California: Stanford University Press, 1969), 158.

32. F.A.K. Harrison, 'The British Interest in the North West Frontier', *Peshawar University Review* (Peshawar), vol. 1 (No. 1, 1974–75), 50–1.

33. Holdich, *The Indian Borderland*, 230.

34. Khan, *The Life of Abdur Rahman*, vol. 2, 157–8.

35. Ibid., 158.

36. Holdich, *The Indian Borderland*, 230.

37. Also see Khan, *The Durand Line*, 142–3.

38. Miller, *Khyber*, 241.

39. Adamec, *Afghanistan*, 23.

40. Ludwig W. Adamec gives it as 'Peha Kotal' (Adamec, *Afghanistan*, 177), M. Hasan Kakar as 'Psha Kotal' (M. Hasan Kakar, *Afghanistan: A Study in International Political Developments, 1880–1896* (Kabul, 1971), 287), and Azmat Hayat Khan as 'Pasha Kotal' (Khan, *The Durand Line*, 258).

41. Adamec, *Afghanistan*, 176–7; Kakar, *Afghanistan*, 286–8.

42. Khan, *The Life of Abdur Rahman*, vol. 2, 162–3.

43. Holdich, *The Indian Borderland*, 230.

44. Khan, *The Durand Line*, 148.

45. Miller, *Khyber*, 241.

46. For details about the Durand Line Agreement and demarcation of the boundary, see Holdich, *The Indian Borderland*, 225–313; Khan, *The Durand Line*, 144–69.

47. Khan, *The Life of Abdur Rahman*, vol. 2, 161.

48. Ibid., 164.

49. Spain, *The Pathan Borderland*, 117 f.n. 26.

50. H.L. Nevill, *Campaigns on the North-West Frontier*, repr. (Lahore: SMP, 2003), 209.

51. For Amir Abdur Rahman's role in inciting the tribesmen against the British in 1897, see chap. 6 of this book. Also see Sultan-i-Rome, 'The Malakand Jihad (1897): An Unsuccessful Attempt to Oust the British from Malakand and Chakdara', *JPHS* (Karachi), vol. 43 (No. 2, April 1995), 178–9.

52. Eknath Easwaran, *A Man to Match His Mountains: Badshah Khan, Nonviolent Soldier of Islam*, with afterword by Timothy Flinders, 2nd print (California: Nilgiri Press, 1985), 25.

53. Holdich, *The Indian Borderland*, 338.

54. *The Cambridge History of India*, vol. 6, 462–3.

55. Miller, *Khyber*, 241.

56. Khan, *The Durand Line*, 149.

57. Adamec, *Afghanistan*, 37.

58. Ibid., 39.

59. Ibid., 49–62.

60. Ibid., 79.

61. Ibid., 107, 110.

62. Ibid., 167.

63. Ibid., 120.

64. Ibid., 128.

65. 'Treaty of Peace between the Illustrious British Government and the Independent Afghan Government, concluded at Rawalpindi on August 8, 1919...', in Adamec, *Afghanistan*, 183.

66. Adamec, *Afghanistan*, 131.

67. Treaty between Great Britain and Afghanistan Establishing Friendly and Commercial Relations, Signed at Kabul, November 22, 1921... Ratifications Exchanged at Kabul, February 6, 1922, in Adamec, *Afghanistan*, 184.

68. Gregorian, *The Emergence of Modern Afghanistan*, 231.

69. *Imperial Gazetteer of India, NWFP*, 25–6.

70. Lal Baha, *N.-W.F.P. Administration under British Rule, 1901–1919* (Islamabad: NCHCR, 1978), 7.

71. *Durand Line*, 9–10.

72. Ibid., 10.

73. Ibid., 10–12.

74. Ibid., 12.

75. Ibid., 14–15. Also see Khan, *The Durand Line*, 196–200.

76. For instance, see Abdul Ghaffar (Khan), *Zama Jwand aw Jidujahd* (Pukhtu) (Kabul: DM, 1983), 735; Khan Abdul Ghaffar Khan, *Ap Biti* (Urdu), repr. (Lahore: FH, 2004), 199–200; Abdul Wali Khan, *Facts are Sacred*, English trans. by Aziz Siddiqui (Peshawar: Jaun Publishers, n.d.), 111–12; *A Journal*, with *sarizah* by Muhammad Gul (Jahangiri) (Pukhtu) (facts of publication have been thorn but it was published in Afghanistan), 209–15; Khan, *The Durand Line*, 186.

77. Khan, *The Durand Line*, 188.

78. Ibid., 189.

79. Ibid., 186.

80. BBCURDU.com, Wednesday, 07 February 2007, 11:57 GMT 16:57 PST, http://www.bbc.co.uk/urdu/pakistan/story/2007/02/printable/070207_mullah_zaeef_part2_rs, accessed: 14 November 2007.

81. Khudai Nur Nasir, 'Durand Line par baat karnay ka Ikhtiyar sirf aur sirf Durand Line kay Aas paas Awam kay paas hayn: Afghan Safir', 11 June 2018, https://www.bbc.com/urdu/regional-44440204, accessed: 13 June 2018.

82. Rahimullah Yusufzai, 'It's Durand Line again', *The News International* (daily), Islamabad/ Rawalpindi, 4 January 2003.
83. Ibid.
84. Ibid.
85. Muhammad Mushtaq Jadoon, 'Note on Durand Line Issues' (Unpublished, June 2003), *Tribal Affairs Research Cell, Home & Tribal Affairs Department, North-West Frontier Province, Peshawar*, Book No. 988.
86. Ibid.
87. Ibid.
88. Gregorian, *The Emergence of Modern Afghanistan*, 158 f.n.*

6 Uprising

The history of the North-West Frontier of India is one long record of strife with the wild [sic] and war-like tribes that inhabit the difficult mountainous region which is the Borderland between British India and Afghanistan.
– F.M. Roberts

The year 1897 witnessed the most serious conflagration which has ever disturbed the North-West Frontier.
– *Administration Report on the North-West Frontier Province from 9th November 1901 to 31st March 1903*

S INCE THEIR OCCUPATION of the trans-Indus Pukhtun area in 1849, the Britons faced stiff and persistent opposition and resistance from the tribesmen of the neighbouring tribal areas from the Black Mountain to the border of Baluchistan. Not only did the tribal belt become a refuge and rendezvous for outlaws and discontented elements, but also a base of operations and raids on Britons occupied territory. The annexation of the trans-Indus Pukhtun area was, therefore, 'followed by a series of encounters with almost every tribe along the whole of the North-West Frontier'.[1] James W. Spain is of the opinion:

> The military and political history of the Pathans is more than anything else a story of revolt. They revolted against Moguls [Mughals], against dynasties of their own race, and against the Sikhs. Most of all they revolted against British India. Revolt, the theory, practice, and fruits of it, was the Pathans' principal contribution to the history of British rule in the north-western corner of India.[2]

The *Imperial Gazetteer of India: Provincial Series; North-West Frontier Province* has listed forty-eight expeditions against various tribes, from one end of the tribal area to the other, from 1849 till 1896.[3] Before 1890, the tribesmen were armed 'very indifferently' and so depended 'on the *arme blanche*' instead of firearms for their success. However, by 1890 they had improved their weapons and adopted the relatively new techniques of warfare.[4] During the struggle and protracted war between the Britons and the Pukhtun tribesmen, 'In 1897 occurred the most formidable outbreak

155

the British arms have ever been called upon to suppress on the North-West Frontier of India.'[5]

THE CAUSES

James W. Spain, under the title 'Motivation of the 1897 Rising', writes:

> Contemporary British opinion was divided on the causes of the 1897 rising. Some officials were convinced that the outbreaks all over the Frontier had been coordinated and planned as a major effort to drive the British from the area. Others believed that the incidents were spontaneous and unconnected. Some ascribed them to a spirit of religious fanaticism. The more far-sighted saw them as a reaction to the British forward movement into Tribal Territory in the 1890's [1890s].[6]

The following are the various factors that contributed to, and caused, the uprising.

VISIT OF DURAND MISSION AND DEMARCATION OF FRONTIER

The root cause of the uprising can be attributed to the visit to Afghanistan, in 1893, by the Durand Mission, the conclusion of the Durand Line Agreement, and the consequent demarcation of the Durand Line which divided the tribal areas and the tribesmen. Not only did the agreement, and the consequent boundary line between British India and Afghanistan, divide the Frontier tribesmen but it also brought the majority of them under the British sphere of influence. This generated a fear of the loss of their independence, at the hands of the British, and hence caused resentment throughout the Frontier.

H.L. Nevill admits that, 'considering the matter from their own point of view', the tribesmen 'foresaw no result from the agreement but the eventual loss of their jealously guarded independence, and opposed the demarcation of the boundary-line from the very beginning'.[7]

TURKO-GREEK WAR AND ROLE OF TURKEY

The Turko-Greek war—although fought outside India, in Europe, with no direct relationship with the tribesmen—contributed to the uprising. A Turkish agent (then 'at war with Greece') 'reached Kabul' in early May 1897, and under his influence, the Afghan Amir instructed the leading *mula*s (in Pukhtu: *mulan/mulyan*) to 'preach a holy war'.[8] The fever of religious war was in the air; not only had 'Turkish emissaries... left Constantinople for India', but correspondence had also taken place between the *mula*s of the Frontier and of Delhi.[9]

Turkey emerged victorious in the war. As it was the success of a Muslim power over a Christian one, it was taken as a good omen for similar Muslim successes in the tribal area against Christian British power. Religious figures, who were trying to raise a revolt against the British, attempted to use the success of the Turks to their own ends. 'They made capital out of the result of the Turco-Greek War',[10] which is how the Turko-Greek war contributed to the uprising.[11] *Jihad* and fighting against the Christian powers was first preached to assist the Turks, but the 'fervour of that preaching lost nothing subsequently by the success of Turkey against Greece',[12] as there was an attempt to exploit the success for a war against the British.

FORWARD POLICY

Britain's Forward Policy has been implicated by many as an important cause of the 1897 uprising. Elaborating the Forward Policy point, Davies has written that 'from the distant north, where the snows of Rakapushi keep watch over Hunza and Nagar, to the confines of Baluchistan', the British extended their 'authority in many directions over the debatable area, known as independent territory'. Therefore,

> To the border Pathan there appeared the vision of a great mailed fist, the fingers of which, in the 'nineties, seemed to be closing around him. Isolated forts garrisoned by British troops commanded the trade routes running through his territory, or frowned down upon his native hamlet or terraced fields. Dazzling white roads wound their way like serpents towards his fastnesses in the mountains. In the wake of demarcation commissions had sprung up long lines of white boundary pillars, enclosing his country and threatening that independence which was his proudest boast. It is therefore my considered opinion, after sifting all the available evidence, that the 1897 disturbances were mainly the result of the advances which had taken place in the 'nineties. Although many of these advances were justified from a military point of view, they nevertheless were looked upon as encroachments into tribal territory.[13]

The *Administration Report on the North-West Frontier Province* also testifies to the Forward Policy being a cause of the uprising by stating that 'there can be no doubt that the suspicions of the tribes' were 'excited by the extension of British influence and the establishment of British garrisons in what' was 'formerly independent territory. The demarcation of the Durand Line was regarded as a step to annexation.'[14]

SUCCESSFUL OPERATION OF AFGHANS IN KAFIRISTAN

The Afghans, under Amir Abdur Rahman, invaded Kafiristan. The operation was a success; most of Kafiristan was occupied and the area was named Nuristan, as a separate province. A section of the senior members of the colonial authority in India believed that this success of Muslims over non-Muslims inspired the tribes, and induced them to obey the calls for *jihad*, issued by the *mula*s, aimed at expelling the British government from India.[15]

ROLE OF THE AFGHAN AMIR AND *SIPAH SALAR*

As discussed in Chapter 5, the Afghan Amir had tried to convince the British that the tribal area should not be taken away from him.[16] He had informed the viceroy of his apprehensions about the potential consequences of the Frontier tribal area being taken away from him, and the benefits of the tribesmen being under him. As the British authorities did not agree, the Amir encouraged the tribesmen to create trouble for the British in the Frontier, in the hope that the British would feel compelled to return the tribesmen to his sphere of influence; or, at least, they would accept that his viewpoint and stance were correct and justified.

'Inspired by the Amir himself and written to his command',[17] the Amir published a pamphlet/book titled *Taqwim-ud-Din*, which stressed the need for *jihad* and the defence of the frontier of Muslim territories.[18] The Amir also 'increased rather than diminished' the 'uneasy feeling, and, to give topical significance to the book', conferred, at his court, with the influential religious men from all over his country.[19] H. Woosnam Mills asserts that 'These religious men—*mullahs* [*mula*s] as they are known in India—are the levers by which the fanaticism of a frontier tribe is set in motion, as the British Government has over and over again found to its cost.' Mills further writes: 'Why did Abdur Rahman hold a conference of these men? If it was to enjoin them to preserve peace on the frontier, where was the necessity? Was not the frontier in peace? These were the pertinent questions asked.'[20] Moreover, the Amir, 'for years', had been 'a personal friend of the Hadda Mullah [Hadah Mula], one of the chief apostles of [the] insurrection',[21] who he described 'as a "light of Islam",' and who he 'directed his officials to cherish and honour'.[22]

Further, the Afghan *sipah salar* at Asmar, Ghulam Haidar Khan, had a relationship with anti-British elements who he assured of assistance in case they rose against the British. As A.H. McMahon and A.D.G. Ramsay asserts, it was certain that the unrest 'received the active support of the Afghan Sipah Salar Ghulam Haider and other Afghan officials'.[23] T.H. Holdich contends: 'Those who say that Ghulam Haidar (the "Red Prince" of the Kunar) was acting in direct hostility to the Amir's good intentions towards us [the British] are strangely ignorant of the length of the Amir's arm and the weight of his blow.' He, however, added: 'Ghulam Haidar went, perhaps, a little too far—and paid for his temerity.'[24] And, in J.G. Elliott's words:

> Two months later Ghulam Haidar Khan, the Afghan Army Commander, died. It is not possible to say just how much he always acted on the exact orders of his master but for many years, from the Dorah Pass to the Kabul river, he was behind much of the unrest that occurred among the tribes living on the British side of the Durand Line.[25]

Hence, while the Amir did, at 'a strong remonstrance from the Government of India', deny 'sympathy with the revolting tribesmen' and ordered 'that his subjects should give neither assistance of any kind' to the tribesmen who revolted against the British nor 'asylum to any armed refugees',[26] and though he denied and disavowed responsibility for 'the tribesmen and their actions',[27] his and his *sipah salar*'s role in causing the uprising cannot be overruled. Even some Afghan soldiers fought on the tribesmen's side at Shabqadar and Bedmani.[28] Thus, not only were the Afghan Amir and *sipah salar* involved—although indirectly and secretly, if not directly and openly—but they had also further ignited the situation by inciting the sentiments of the tribesmen and promising them help.

FACTORS AND EVENTS OF A LOCAL NATURE

Some local factors also contributed to the uprising. For instance, the colonial[29] government raised the tax on rock salt exported from Kuhat District 'from eight annas to two rupees a *maund*'.[30] As the salt was one of the principal sources of income for the tribesmen, the increase aggrieved them and this was exploited by the *mula*s.[31] Similarly, the colonial authorities annoyed the tribesmen when they refused 'to return to the Afridis some captive women who had fled from the tribesmen to take refuge in the settled districts'.[32] Being a matter of honour for the Afridi, the refusal not only generated resentment but also added to the gravity of the situation. In H. Woosnam Mills' words:

> The explanation or local causes put forward for the rising of the Afridis were three in number, *viz.*, the increase in the salt tax, the fact that their women who ran away to Peshawar were not sent back by our Government, and their objection to our presence as far as the tomb of Akhund in Swat. To these might be added a fourth, the fear that a military road would be built along the Khyber Pass which they themselves would have to construct.[33]

The first incident in the uprising, at Maizar, was local in nature, i.e. the non-payment of a fine by the tribesmen for the murder of a Hindu, a year earlier, and the arrival of British personnel in the area in this backdrop.[34] Besides, 'the tribesmen doubtless believed that if they could kill the British officers at once the sepoys would be demoralised, and they could be cut off to a man. Success would mean the capture of two mountain guns, 300 rifles and a large quantity of ammunition, not to mention the baggage animals and camp equipage.'[35] The Urakzi's discontent at the establishment of forts along the Samana Range was another local cause,[36] besides it being part of the Forward Policy.

Retaining Malakand and Chakdarah, and the Road to Chitral

Amanul Mulk, Mehtar (Mihtar) of Chitral, had friendly relations with the British, who established a garrison at Chitral. After his death in 1892, a war of succession began between his sons. Taking opportunity of the prevailing situation, Amanul Mulk's brother, Sher Afzal, invaded Chitral with the assistance of Umara Khan of Jandul (Jandol); resulting in the siege of the British garrison at Chitral. As the request, to Umara Khan, of the British authorities to relieve the garrison was not heeded, they decided to march towards Chitral from two sides: from Peshawar and from Gilgit.[37]

The relief force from Peshawar was to proceed through Swat and Dir. So, a proclamation was issued to the people of Swat and Bajawar informing them of the purpose of the relief force, and assuring them that their country would not be occupied if they did not attack the British forces passing through their territories.[38] Disregarding the proclamation, the people of Swat blocked the passage of the British forces and fought them in Malakand. The British forces, however, were victorious and entered Swat for the first time, going on to relieve their garrison at Chitral.[39] However, on 8 May 1895, the colonial government 'decided to retain a garrison in Chitral..., and, to ensure its safety, proposed the construction of a road from Peshawar through Swat'.[40]

'The Liberals', in England, 'considered the construction of the new road to be contrary to the spirit of the proclamation of March, 1895' and that 'it not only constituted a deliberate breach of faith with the tribes, but, in their opinion, it was also likely to lead to the annexation of tribal territory, the very thing' they had avowed 'not to do'.[41] But the Conservatives did not pay heed to these apprehensions. They decided to construct the road, and to ensure its safety and the safe passage of relief forces to Chitral, Malakand and Chakdarah were retained and garrisons were stationed there. The British government did not consider this a breach of the proclamation as the tribes had disregarded the proclamation and resisted the British advance. Moreover, the viceroy telegraphed the Secretary of State for India on 24 September 1895, informing him that the tribes did not regard the 'occupation of Malakand...as infringement of the proclamation', and that they had petitioned that British troops should be retained 'to protect them, to help them in protecting road, and to maintain internal peace'.[42] However, with the passage of time, these steps were resented by the people who saw them as a prelude to further annexation and expansion. This resentment and fear, generated by the construction of the road to Chitral through Lower Swat, and the retaining of Malakand and Chakdarah—factors both of a local nature and of Forward Policy—contributed to the uprising in Swat.[43]

LINKS WITH INDIA AND AFGHANISTAN

Those who were at the forefront of the uprising had links with anti-British elements in both India and Afghanistan.

The Sartur (Sartor) Faqir's links to India and Afghanistan are evident from his travels to both the countries, and his long stays there.[44] The presence of the Faqir's companion during the fighting—allegedly, 'a Mulla from India' who 'was killed at his side'[45] during the course of the fighting—suggests an Indian link. The Faqir, being assured of help by the Afghan *sipah salar* at Asmar, as mentioned above, is testimony to the Afghan factor. Moreover, it was Najmuddin, the Hadah (Hadda) Mula—

originally from Hadah in Afghanistan, but who had later moved to the independent Muhmand territory—who led the Muhmand and attacked the British at Shabqadar. Interestingly, the Hadah Mula was known to be a friend of both the Afghan Amir and the *sipah salar*.[46]

It has been suggested that the uprising 'was a scheme preconcerted from both Kabul and India', and that it 'was intended to be a simultaneous one along the border'.[47] Winston Churchill, too, has mentioned the Indian and Afghan factor: 'Secret encouragement came from the South— from India itself. Actual support and assistance was given from Cabul [Kabul].'[48] Davies has contended that, although it is difficult to ascertain with any degree of certainty the extent to which discontent in India affected the Frontier tribesmen, 'correspondence did take place between frontier mullahs [*mula*s] and those of Delhi'.[49] At the start of his march for Malakand and Chakdarah, the Sartur Faqir 'had with him a young boy of about thirteen years of age whom he represented [presented] as the sole surviving heir to the throne of Delhi'[50] and 'whom he proclaimed king of Delhi',[51]—further testament to the links with India.

ROLE OF THE *MULAS*, RELIGIOUS FERVOUR, AND FANATICISM

The *mula*s, and religious fervour, were the main forces that helped induce and entice the tribesmen to take up arms against the infidel alien power. In the previous sections, we have examined the roles played by the Afghan Amir's publication of a book on *jihad* and his call for a council of the religious *ulama*, the impact of the Turko-Greek war, and the Afghans' successes in Kafiristan and the local religious figures' calls for *jihad*. We can now conclude that religion appears to have been the main trigger. In McMahon and Ramsay's words: 'The information gleaned slowly, but surely placed it beyond doubt that the rising was a purely religious affair, and that it was a scheme preconcerted from both Kabul and India.'[52]

The religious leaders also propagated the view that the subsidies paid to the various tribes by the colonial government had been 'the price of that peace which force of arms was powerless to insure [ensure]' in the tribal belt.[53] It were religious leaders such as Sartur Faqir, Hadah Mula, and Aka Khail Mula (Mula Sayyad Akbar) who were not only behind the uprising, but leading it. These religious leaders were held in such esteem by the people (or else, they were so powerless before them) that when William Lockhart told the Chamkani the terms for a treaty, their reply included: 'Friendship and enmity are not in our choice; whatever orders we may receive from the *Fakir Sahib* of Swat, the *Mulla Sahib* of Hadda or the Aka Khel Mulla, and from all Islam, we cannot refuse to obey them; if we lose our lives, no matter.'[54]

When during the course of the punitive campaign, Robert Warburton asked the Afridi 'What made you come down?', the reply was: 'The Mullahs [*mulas*] brought us down.' To his query, 'Why did you obey the Mullahs [*mulas*], and why did you not turn them out of your country?', the Afridi's response was: 'They were too powerful for us.' To his subsequent question, 'Then why did you attack the posts?', their reply was: 'The Mullahs [*mulas*] forced us.'[55] These exchanges speak of the *mulas*' power and role in the uprising.

While concluding his chapter dealing with the causes of the uprising, Davies states: 'The chief part played by fanaticism was the way in which the frontier mullahs [*mulas*] used it to stir up the latent passions of the turbulent tribesmen. Without the force of fanaticism and the sinister influence of Afghan intrigues, the risings would hardly have been so widespread, so united, or so simultaneous.'[56] To that effect, fanaticism, or religious fervour and zeal, certainly played a major role. It, however, has rightly been said, 'Contemporary opinion, especially that of officers and officials in the war zone, favoured fanaticism as the chief cause of the outbreak, but they have ever been ready *to confuse fanaticism with the natural desire of the tribesmen for independence* [italics mine]'.[57] Dr Munawwar Khan, too, refers to 'the chivalry and bravery' of the tribesmen being perceived as 'fanaticism to the British historians'.[58] H.G. Raverty pointed out, in a sardonic tone, that 'all are "fanatics," "rebels["]", or "dacoits," who fight against us [the British] according to some people'.[59]

THE EVENTS

In spite of the fact that there were no evident signs of discontent and disturbance, the situation on the North-West Frontier of British India did not normalise because of the aforementioned causes and factors. 'By the summer of 1897...the whole north-west frontier from the Gomul [Gumal] river to the hills south of Chitral was in a condition of seething irritation.'[60] In the outwardly contented and calm, but inwardly discontented and volatile, situation 'only a spark was needed to set the whole Frontier in a blaze'; 'the train was lit at Maizar'[61] by way of an attack on the party of the Political Officer, Mr Gee, and his camp.

THE WAZIR'S UPRISING AT MAIZAR

On 10 June 1897, H.A. Gee, Political Officer in the Tuchi Valley, accompanied by an unusually large military escort, came to Maizar (above Datta Khail in the Madda Khail Wazir country). The purpose of Gee's visit to the area 'was to fix on a site for the most westerly levy post in the valley, and also to meet, by arrangement, the Madda Khel Maliks there and discuss the question of the distribution of a fine which was outstanding against the tribes'.[62] The fine, of 2,000 rupees, had been imposed on the tribes 'for the murder of a Hindu writer attached to the levy post at Sheranni'. But, 'the inhabitants of the group of villages known as Maizar objected to the payment of their share of the fine, on the ground that the whole burden should be borne by the guilty parties'.[63]

Originally, the visit had been arranged for 9 June, but was delayed by a day because of rains; it provided the tribesmen the time to plan an attack on Gee's party. Gee's party, having selected a suitable place to camp, did not notice any unusual moves by the tribesmen nor were their suspicions raised. Yet, they took 'all the usual precautions' required 'when camping in a hostile country' by ordering their men 'to keep their arms with them and not to pile them, and guards, pickets and sentries placed where considered necessary'. After this, Gee, accompanied by an escort and some of the *malaks* (in Pukhtu: *malakan/malakanan*), visited Dotoi. On his return, Gee was told that 'the question of the fine' had been settled amicably by the tribesmen themselves. The tribesmen provided food for the escort's Muslim sepoys and 'there was not the slightest suspicion of [the] unfriendliness on the part of the tribesmen'.[64]

'Colonel Bunny ordered the pipers', 'after *tiffin*', 'to play for the villagers to listen to, and they played one tune'. 'Just as they began another', a man waved 'a drawn sword on a tower in the Drepilare *kot*'. 'The villagers' quickly 'cleared off towards the village. A single shot was fired, apparently as a signal, and a fusillade at once commenced, directed at the British officers, who were together under a tree, and the Sikhs. This was taken up on all sides, the sepoys in the meantime falling in at once and taking up positions.' Disaster 'quickly befell' Gee's party. 'Lieutenant Seton Browne was hit in the leg at the second or third shot, and Colonel Bunny, the commander, was mortally wounded.' The British guns, however, opened fire 'almost immediately' and 'did great execution among a party of men who attempted to rush them'. The 'officers stood to their posts, but as they were in an exposed position the two British officers afforded an easy mark for the men in the *bagh*. Captain Browne was hit at about the fifth shot and Lieutenant Cruikshank shot dead almost directly after.'[65]

All this happened 'within five minutes of the first shot'. As the tribesmen's fire did not slacken, and the colonial guns had expended their ammunition, the British forces made a movement 'back towards the *kotal*, the guns limbering up and going first up the lane'. At this withdrawal by the infantry, the tribesmen came out from all sides in great numbers. Although 'a stand was made round the corner of the *bagh* to allow the wounded men to retire', 'further disasters befell the little force'. As the tribesmen directed fire 'at the British officers Lieutenant Higginson was shot through the arm and Surgeon-Captain Cassidy in the knee'. The tribesmen 'were, however, successfully held in check by a mixed party of 1st Sikhs and 1st Punjab Infantry, and the latter retired up to the *kotal* when everything was over'. The retreating forces successively took up positions 'on the six ridges which stretch from Maizar to the plain above Sheranna, a distance of about two miles, and though the Waziris followed up in a most determined fashion and occupied all availing positions on the hills around, the retirement was perfect'. However, 'Lieutenant Higginson was shot in the arm a second time while crossing the hills'. Although 'all the British military officers were now wounded, two of them mortally, yet they all continued to carry out their duties and lead their men'.[66]

The survivors of the British party started to withdraw, with the tribesmen 'constantly enveloping the flanks'.[67] 'The tribesmen made the most determined attempts', throughout, 'to get to close quarters and annihilate' the men of the British party. The tribesmen's number, estimated at 500 at the onset, subsequently grew 'to probably much over 1000'.[68] Once the British had reached the reinforcement force in the evening, the tribesmen withdrew. Hence, the rest of the British force was able to withdraw unharmed, with the rear-guard reaching camp at 12:30 a.m.[69]

Interestingly, the Khiddar Khail helped the British by bringing 'water for the wounded during the retreat', and 'during the following two days' bringing the 'bodies of all killed'.[70] Thus ended the first of a series of uprisings, leaving about '100 killed and many wounded' on the tribesmen's side, and 26 killed (including three British officers) and 35 wounded (including three British officers) on the British side.[71]

While dealing with the 'explanations of the Maizar disaster', H. Woosnam Mills asserts that 'there is ample evidence to show that the whole business was carefully planned beforehand, and that the headmen were parties to the treacherous attack on Colonel Bunny's party', that 'probably the wires were pulled by men who knew when the Political

Officer meant to visit Maizar, what the strength of his escort would be, and the probable time of its arrival at the village'.[72] James W. Spain contends that, 'for one of the few times on record, the tribesmen grossly violated their own code of honor' as they attacked the party after welcoming and feeding them as guests.[73] The Maizar incident, however, proved the spark that lit the fire which soon spread to other parts of the tribal area and became a blaze.

THE SWAT UPRISING

The Sartur Faqir[74] appeared in Upper Swat the next month, July 1897, and established himself at Landakay. Besides proclaiming that 'his mission was to turn the British off the Malakand and out of Peshawar',[75] he also claimed to have magical powers and unseen support. In spite of the prevailing mood and developments, the colonial authorities and their local allies regarded him as a mad man, and so paid little importance to his movements at first.[76] But later, towards the end of the month, 'the gravity of the situation' could not be ignored any longer; troops stationed in Malakand were alerted and told to be ready 'for action at the shortest notice'. On 26 July 1897, the situation became so grave that the authorities at Malakand summoned the Guides force from Mardan.[77]

On 26 July, Sartur Faqir started his march down from Landakay. He announced that 'he would sweep' the British forces out of Malakand and Chakdarah 'in eight days'.[78] At first, 'only a few boys' followed him, 'one of whom he proclaimed king of Delhi',[79] but then people began to respond to his appeals and join him in droves as he proceeded towards Malakand. Most of the people 'were carried away by the popular enthusiasm and by nightfall a resolute body of tribesmen' was 'on the move to attack' Malakand, 'while another party turned' its attention towards Chakdarah.[80]

At 9:15 p.m., Major Deane, the political agent in Malakand, was informed about the tribesmen's approach. Before the tribesmen could commence their attack, 'the alarm was sounded' and a detachment of the 45th Sikhs was sent to stop their advance.[81] The tribesmen, however, pushed the British force back and, in 'a determined attack' on the northern and central camps, over-ran 'a detached post at the serai', 'without resistance'. They also 'succeeded in entering the camp occupied by the sappers and miners, and carrying off a considerable quantity of ammunition before they could be ejected'. On 27 July, the Guides arrived from Mardan, but by then the tribesmen were attacking 'all along the line'. The tribesmen 'were repulsed everywhere except at the serai', which they 'succeeded in setting' on fire, compelling the garrison to retreat to its main position. On 28 July, the 24th Punjab Infantry made a successful counter-attack.[82] By then, the mobilisation of troops in India had also been ordered.[83] The tribesmen, however, again made attacking forays, mainly against the centre, and the troops 'were practically besieged'. The tribesmen occupied 'all the heights' and continued firing, mostly at the camp, all day. At the night, they again commenced fighting, and 'displayed their usual energy on the centre'.[84]

The Sartur Faqir's standard 'became the rallying point for thousands of fighting-men from the Upper Swat, Buner [Bunair], the Utman Khel [Khail] country, and even more distant parts'.[85] The force of tribesmen, who 'barely exceeded 1,000' men on the first night, had grown to 12,000 or more at Malakand, and more than 8,000 men at Chakdarah.[86]

During the night of 29 July, the tribesmen attacked the flanks, especially the left. On the morning of 29 July, they began to trouble the colonial forces on all sides, and by the afternoon had renewed their attacks 'all along the line'. On the night between 29 and 30, the night of the new moon and a Friday, they 'rushed up to the *sangars*' (parapets of rock and stones, thrown up as a barricade or fortification) at various points as they 'evidently meant to fulfil their promise of making their biggest effort on that night'.[87] On 30 July, while relief did arrive in the form of the 35th Sikhs and 38th Dogra regiments, 'the wire between Malakand and Dargai was cut, and the levy posts burnt'.[88] On the night of 31 July, the tribesmen made another forceful all-night attack and 'time after time charged right up to the *sangars*'.[89]

Early in the morning of 31 July, the tribesmen concentrated their men and firepower on the right flank of the British forces, and sent a detachment to cut-off the approach of relief for British troops.[90] As more British troops arrived on 31 July, the Bunairwal came to the tribesmen's assistance.[91] During the night of 1 August, the tribesmen once again attacked the right and left of the British positions vigorously. However, the British forces were able to relieve Malakand, and a relief column was ordered 'to move out to Chakdara'. But, when the relief forces entered the valley, the tribesmen 'swarmed down from the heights' and in the most reckless manner 'rushed to certain death'.[92] The relief forces were resisted strongly along the way, especially at Batkhilah (Batkhela) and Amandarah.

The attack on Chakdarah was carried out simultaneously as on Malakand—on the night of 27 July. At 10:15 p.m., the alarm had sounded and the garrison manned their posts. The tribesmen attacked from the west, but gave up due to incessant firing from the post, and after a short while resumed their attack from the northeast. Although they tried to scale the walls with ladders, they were repulsed. Their next attempt was on the eastern side, but it could not be sustained for long as they had to withdraw before daylight. The same night, they cut the telegraph wires, preventing communication with Malakand. On 27 July, they began their most determined attack and 'time after time standard-bearers, backed up by swordsmen, would charge straight up to the walls of the fort, only to fall riddled with bullets'.[93]

On the night of 28 July, the tribesmen surrounded the fort on all sides, intent on scaling its walls. Having been repulsed once, they returned with ladders after some hours and attacked the northeast corner of the fort. However, having failed again, they returned to the hills before daybreak. On the evening of that day, they again advanced to the attack with 200 standard bearers. While they were able to work their way to the base of the fort's walls, their attack was repelled by steady fire. On 29 July, they made a concerted attack against the signal tower and, in spite of very heavy fire from the tower and the fort, 'succeeded in reaching the doorway' which they attempted to set alight.[94]

The tribesmen launched more attacks from 30 July to 1 August. They 'loopholed the walls of the hospital, which was situated between the fort and the signal tower', and so were able 'to command the interior of the fort'. On 2 August, when they made one more 'bid for victory', the situation became critical for the hard-pressed British garrison. However, relief forces from Malakand came to the rescue, and it was saved.[95]

Heavy fighting continued at Malakand and Chakdarah (relieved simultaneously on 1 and 2 August); the tribesmen engaged the mighty British for a full week, fighting 'against untold odds'.[96] However, discouraged by their failed attempts to turn the British out of Malakand and Chakdarah, the tribesmen 'disappeared as quickly and as strangely as they had come, leaving behind them several hundred of their own and British dead'.[97]

Rajmohan Gandhi refers to attacks by the Afridi on the forts of Malakand and Chakdarah in 1897,[98] which is erroneous. The Afridi live far away, in the Khyber Agency (now Khyber District); it was the people of Swat who launched the attacks, and were later joined by people from the neighbouring areas.

THE MUHMAND'S UPRISING

While the dust of the fighting at Malakand and Chakdarah was yet to settle and the colonial authorities were planning punitive expeditions against the tribes involved, a series of uprisings spread down to the Peshawar border. In early August 1897, the colonial authorities received news that the Muhmand, under Najmuddin aka Hadah Mula (who was more than 80 years old now), were preparing for an attack on British-controlled territory. Army officers wanted to take precautionary measures, but they were over-ruled by the civilian authorities who gave no importance to the news. However, on the afternoon of 7 August 1897, 4,000 to 5,000 Muhmand, under the command of Hadah Mula, entered the territory under British control in the Peshawar District, some 18 miles from the city of Peshawar. H. Woosnam Mills observes:

> Never before in the annals of the British in India has such a daring move been made by the tribesmen. The public mind which had been deeply concerned over the disturbances in the Tochi and Swat Valleys, became distinctly apprehensive when the disorder spread to Peshawar.[99]

On entering the British-controlled territory, the tribesmen attacked and destroyed the village of Shankargarh, an old Sikh cantonment bazaar that was inhabited by Hindus and Sikhs. Having received information about the impending attack, and sensing danger, the inhabitants of Shankargarh had already left the village—except for two or three people who elected to stay behind and consequently lost their lives in the attack. After destroying the village and burning its bazaar, the tribesmen attacked Shabqadar, making a determined attempt to capture the fort.[100] But, as it stood 'on a mound' and was surrounded by 50 feet high walls, the fort was 'practically impregnable to any force without artillery'. So, the 'garrison of forty Border Police', manning the fort, was able to hold 'out for twelve hours' until the next morning when a relief force arrived from Peshawar—at which the tribesmen withdrew,[101] having lost forty to fifty people in the action. Further fighting and casualties took place as the British forces pursued the tribesmen.

THE AFRIDI'S AND URAKZI'S UPRISING

Next came the turn of the Afridi and Urakzi (Orakzi), who were encouraged by the call for a similar uprising by Aka Khail Mula, namely Mula Sayyad Akbar.[102] 'In the middle of August, 1897', the British authorities received reports about negotiations that were taking place between the Afridi and the Urakzi about the British posts in the Khyber Pass, Kurram Valley, and Samana Ridge. The difficulties and delays in arranging a simultaneous uprising of the Urakzi and Afridi provided sufficient time and opportunity to the colonial authorities to take defensive and precautionary measures. They strengthened their garrisons (in the forts of Jamrud and Barah), reinforced their troops in Kuhat, and sent Brigadier-General A.G. Yeatman-Biggs 'to command the troops in Kohat District'. The tribesmen, however, finally struck the first blow on 23 August, with 'an overwhelming attack...on Ali Masjid and Fort Maude'. 'Ali Masjid was abandoned' by the British garrison 'without a struggle', but the 'garrison of about forty men at Fort Maude held' their position 'for a time till they, too, fell back on a force sent out from Jamrud to the mouth of the Khaibar Pass' and both the 'forts were burnt to the ground'.[103] Thus, on 23 August the whole of the Khyber Pass, from Ali Masjid to Landi Khanah, passed into 'the possession of the Afridis'.[104]

'Flushed with their initial success, the tribesmen then retraced their steps up the [Khyber] pass and appeared before Landi Kotal [Kutal] at noon the next day.' In spite of some defections, the garrison 'of 370 men' of the Khyber Rifles at Landi Kutal defended the position till about 10 a.m. on 25 August, 'when the gate of the fort was treacherously opened and the assailants rushed in'. At this point, some of the men at the garrison deserted, and 'some were allowed to escape after giving up their arms, but others succeeded in fighting their way through, and reached Jamrud in safety, bringing their rifles with them'. After looting the fort and setting the troops' quarters on fire, 'the tribesmen dispersed to their homes'.[105] Although some of the Khyber Militiamen of the garrison at the Pass had defected, 'others held out until overwhelmed'. But, ironically, the British officers withdrew 'at an early stage' which 'did little to increase tribal respect for British standards of behavior'.[106] H. Woosnam Mills admits that 'the fall of such impregnable fortresses as Ali Musjid [Masjid] and Landi Kotal [Kutal], and the securing of the [Khyber] Pass was universally held to be the worst blow' that British 'prestige could suffer on the north-west frontier'.[107]

On 26 August, the day after the dispersal 'of the Afridis from Landi Kotal', the Urakzi resumed the offensive. They not only 'seized the Ublan Pass, some six miles north-west of Kohat', but also 'threatened the British post of Muhammadzai, situated near the foot'. At dawn, on 27 August, a force under General Yeatman-Biggs moved out of Kuhat and, in spite of heavy firing from the tribesmen, succeeded in gaining the summit at about

8:00 a.m. While the majority of the tribesmen 'fled down the northern slopes of the pass', their snipers, 'concealed among the rocks', harassed the British forces as they withdrew, causing several casualties. As the Urakzi pushed on hard towards the police posts at Lakha and Saifaldarah, the force at Hangu led an expedition to the Samana Ridge to relieve them. The task 'was accomplished without much fighting', although the withdrawal of the troops was marked by persistent harassment by the tribesmen.[108]

On 30 August, a force started for Sadah (Sadda), under Colonel Richardson, to rescue the Kurram Valley post that was being threatened by the tribesmen. However, on 5 September, before the troops reached there 'a force of some 3,000 Afridis and Orakzais was in the neighbourhood, more were expected to arrive'.[109] On 1 September 1897, 'the post of Balish Khel, three miles north-west of Sadda, was attacked as a preliminary to an assault on the latter'. The garrison at the post was in a critical situation as the Afridi pressed on hard with their assault. However, it was saved as the Afridi backed off when fifty men of Malik Khail, of the Turi tribe of the Kurram Valley, arrived from Sadah. On the night between 16 and 17 September, the tribesmen attacked Sadah; although the attack led to some casualties, it ultimately failed because of the 'discipline of the troops, and their allotment to the defensive perimeter'.[110]

On the Samana Range front, on 26 August news arrived at Fort Lokhart that a large Urakzi force was planning an attack on 'the Shenowri border police post' below Fort Gulistan. In spite of night-long heavy firing from Gulistan Fort, aimed at the invading tribesmen, at dawn on 27 August, the tribesmen held the big hills above Gulistan. However, British reinforcements arrived from Hangu and the situation was saved. On 29 August, the tribesmen 'raided and burnt' 'the Kahi police post'. Since 27 August, the tribesmen had practically besieged Fort Gulistan, and on 3 September, at 2:00 p.m., 'they made a determined attack on the horn work', succeeding in reaching close to the fort. Although 'the attack continued with slight intermission till noon next day', the defence was gallant. The colonial authorities issued orders to the commander of the troops at Hangu, General Yeatman-Biggs, to send 'supplies to Fort Lockhart' and to clear the Samana Range of the tribesmen. The relief force, therefore, left Hangu on 7 September.[111]

According to H.L. Nevill, on 11 September General Yeatman-Biggs marched out to intercept the movement of a large force of the Afridi and Urakzi 'marching down the Khanki Valley towards the eastern end of the Samana Ridge'. Although he 'succeeded in turning the tribesmen back', he had 'to return to Hangu for want of water'. Taking advantage of the situation, on 12 September the tribesmen succeeded in capturing the small post of Saragarhi, situated on the Samana Ridge between Lockhart and Gulistan Forts. Although the garrison of twenty-one men held out their position 'from nine o'clock in the morning till' 4:30 p.m. 'in the afternoon against odds which from the first were clearly overwhelming', the tribesmen at last succeeded in scaling 'the walls and all was over'; eventually, the entire garrison lost their lives. Twenty tribesmen were killed by one soldier from the guard-room, who lost his own life when the room was set on fire.[112] While the entire attack on Saragarhi was visible to the garrisons at Lockhart and Gulistan forts, they could do nothing to save the situation as the tribesmen 'were in such force that it was quite impossible to do anything to save the situation'.[113]

At the same time, tribesmen had already attacked Fort Gulistan. So, at the fall of Saragarhi, they 'pressed forward with great daring' to Fort Gulistan. The garrison was again saved by the gallant acts of some of its members who came out of the fort and fought the tribesmen. Not only did this raise 'the spirits of the garrison', but also a large number of tribesmen 'at once returned to their homes'. The confrontation, however, continued. On 13 September, the garrison asked for reinforcements but, by evening, the tribesmen had surrounded the post and continued firing on the garrison throughout the night. On 15 September, the besieged garrison 'heard the welcome sound' of firing from the relief column; the tribesmen 'then made a supreme bid for victory, but at noon Saragarhi was recaptured by General Yeatman-Biggs, and the tribesmen round Gulistan melted away'.[114] After the relief of Fort Gulistan, the tribesmen 'evacuated the neighbourhood of the Samana Forts' and the colonial authorities seized the opportunity to improve 'the defences and communications'.[115]

THE MAHSUDS

James W. Spain notes: 'Strangely, the Mahsuds, usually ready to fight at the slightest provocation, played little part in the 1897 rising.'[116] Olaf Caroe, however, has explained this when he states: 'The southward spread of the conflagration was checked by the fact that the first outbreak had occurred—prematurely from the point of view of the tribes—in the Tochi.' Because of this, 'controlling operations were well under way there before Tirah rose', due to which 'the troops in Tochi were able to interpose a screen between Tirah and the Mahsuds, who indeed were in chastened mood after an expedition in 1894, three years before'.[117] They, however, rose the next year, in 1898, under the leadership of Mula Powindah (Pawindah), and remained active against the British for three years.

CAUSES OF FAILURE

As is evident from the above-mentioned events, most of the tribesmen on the North-West Frontier of India took up arms and participated in attacks against the British forces, posts, and positions during the summer of 1897. Nevertheless, their attempts failed and they did not succeed in ousting the British from the tribal area. While dealing with, and describing, the events and fighting, British writers such as H. Woosnam Mills and Winston S. Churchill[118] have repeatedly mentioned the gallantry, courage, and bravery of the colonial forces. They were justified in making such statements because, as Zia Gokalp points out: 'To be biased in favour of our own community or the communities which are of the same religion or race, or which are allied with us against our enemies, is not something that is within our own will. It is especially difficult to rid ourselves of all bias in our feelings for our own people.'[119] And as Ghani Khan states, the stone 'is the only thing that may be described truthfully as unbiased'.[120]

However, the tribesmen—each of whom, in Ghani Khan words, 'will wash his face and oil his beard and perfume his locks and put on his best pair of clothes when he goes out to fight and die'[121]—also possessed and demonstrated the same, if not more, gallantry, courage, and bravery. This is evident from Mills and Churchill's own writings as well as from other British writers' accounts. H.L. Nevill's comments seem to be more relevant to the situation:

> At Malakand and Chakdara, and in a minor degree at Nawagai, the same reckless impulse is to be seen which hurled the Mahdists against the British squares at Abu Klea, El Teb, and Omdurman, for the sake of a martyr's crown. To some extent the North-West Frontier tribes of India present an anomaly to the world in their methods of warfare. At times they show all the characteristics of well-armed but unorganized adversaries, at others the latent fire of the untamed barbarian blazes forth, and no epithet but savage can be applied to the class of warfare which is the result. The desperate and repeated attacks on the garrisons of Malakand and Chakdara are conspicuous examples of the savage side of the methods of war practised by the Muhammadan tribes inhabiting the north-western borderland of India.... Before Malakand and Chakdara the tribesmen were religious maniacs for eight days, and advanced to the attack with a bravery which fully entitled those that fell to any reward that such a death may bring.[122]

Similarly, T.H. Holdich states: 'So fierce was the fanatical fervour of that half-armed mob that General Meiklejohn has told me that he saw unarmed boys and men actually turning on the cavalry and attacking them with sticks and stones.'[123] He also observes:

> It would not be difficult to quote writers who brand our transfrontier neighbours—Swatis [people of Swat], Mohmands, Afridis, and Waziris alike—as cowards. They must know now that in calling them cowards they erred. It is perhaps one of the most useful lessons that we learnt from this boundary war—the lesson of respect for the people who fought well for their independence.[124]

Keeping these facts and observations in mind, it is apparent that the tribesmen failed to achieve their goals not because of lack of courage, bravery, or manliness but because of a combination of other factors, which are discussed below.

LACK OF PLANNING FOR, AND NON-ACQUAINTANCE WITH, LONG-DRAWN WAR

The tribesmen took up arms to attack British positions, on the whole, at the instigation of their religious leaders. However, contrary to their expectations, they failed to achieve their objectives during their first assaults or within a few days. Moreover, they were neither acquainted with, nor trained for, long-drawn-out wars. On the one hand, they took to the field without planning for a long-drawn war, while, on the other hand, the colonial forces either provided stubborn resistance or their reinforcements came to their rescue; hence, the tribesmen were destined to fail.

NO DISCIPLINE AND ORGANISATION

There was no proper discipline and organisation in the rank and file of the tribesmen. They took to the field as tribal *lakhkar*s (in Pukhtu: *lakhkaray*). The 'lake of organization has always been the keynote of those guerrilla tactics which have baffled again and again the armies of civilized nations'.[125] The tribesmen, although they knew the tactics, lacked 'the higher branches of the art of war—the domain of strategy'.[126] Napoleon had said that 'in war men are nothing—the man is everything'. Discipline and working in unison 'have always been the foundation of the success of civilized armies against irregular foes, and both require the presence of a master-hand'.[127] J.G. Elliott asserts that 'the tribesman was by civilized standards reckless of human life' but at the same time 'he lacked collective discipline and would not stand against a determined charge, particularly if made by cavalry'.[128] As the tribesmen lacked both discipline and strategy of a force led by a skilled leader, their zeal, courage, and bravery proved to be futile.

THE FAQIR'S FALSE CLAIMS

When the Sartur Faqir appeared in Landakay in July 1897, to raise the people in revolt against the British, he made strange claims, such as having 'an invisible army from heaven at his side to assist him', and 'the power of making himself invisible and feeding multitudes with a few grains of rice'.[129] 'Besides supernatural and unseen support', he also 'claimed to have been visited by all' the deceased *faqirs* (in Pukhtu: *faqiran*) 'who told him' that 'the mouths' of the British 'guns and rifles would be closed' and that their 'bullets would be turned to water'; and 'that he had only to throw stones into' the Swat River for each one of them to have 'the effect of a gun' on the British forces.[130] The Faqir's claims and exhortations impressed the tribesmen to a great extent and they were deluded by the images of magnificent cavalry, artillery, and infantry concealed in the hills, at the Faqir disposal, and of sweeping away the British by the time of the sighting of the new moon.[131] However, as no such thing occurred during the course of the fighting, the tribesmen became apprehensive and desperate, resulting in their dispersal from the war front.

FALSE PROMISES OF AFGHAN AMIR AND *SIPAH SALAR*

Despite his denial of any role in the affair, the Afghan Amir, Abdur Rahman, played a significant role in causing the uprising. In addition, Ghulam Haidar Khan, his *sipah salar* at Asmar, played an important role in causing the uprising, at least by instigating the tribesmen, and in particular the religious leaders who led the uprising. He wrote to the Sartur Faqir, on 20 July 1897, to commence a *jihad* and 'promised to afford him help'.[132] The tribesmen, therefore, expected the Afghan Amir and his *sipah salar*'s moral and material support. But the Amir did a *volte-face* at the critical juncture and denounced and disavowed the tribesmen and their actions, asking his subjects to neither assist, nor give a refuge to, the tribesmen involved in the uprising.[133] Moreover, he abhorred the role of the *sipah salar* and ensured that he was impotent to deliver the promised help to the tribesmen.

No Arrangements for Provision and Supply of Food and Ammunition

The tribesmen took to the field without making arrangements for the supply of food and ammunition in case the fighting took the shape of a war instead of a lone battle. Contrary to the tribesmen's expectations, the British forces put up a strong resistance and the colonial government organised prompt reinforcements. On the other hand, although fresh contingents from both neighbouring and remote areas joined the tribesmen, especially at Malakand and Chakdarah, most of them were unarmed; those who possessed arms exhausted their ammunition very soon. In such a situation, i.e. a total lack of arrangements for the provision and supply of ammunition and food, the tribesmen could not continue fighting the mighty British for long.

The Faqir's Precipitation of Matters and Non-Simultaneous Uprising

While discussing whether or not the uprising of 1897 was a coordinated effort that was planned to be simultaneous all along the Frontier, Robert Warburton state:

> It was not difficult or impossible from Jellalabad and Asmar to be in touch with Sayad Akbar in Tirah, the 'Hadda Mullah' at Jarobi, and the 'Mad Fakir' in Swat; so that if a combined move in all three quarters was required, it might, under favourable circumstances, have been executed nearly simultaneously within a period of seven days.[134]

Referring to the non-simultaneous uprising, he asserts:

> It may be accepted, therefore, that there is no proof of any attempt having been made to raise the border from Maizar round northwards to the Swat Valley in one combined movement against us. The 'Mad Mullah' made his attack, and when he found that he could not succeed he applied to the priest of Hadda for help, and that gentleman in his turn sent messengers to Sayad Akbar, asking him to co-operate and make a diversion with a joint lashkar of Afridis and Orakzais.[135]

Nevertheless, A.H. McMahon and A.D.G. Ramsay asserts:

> The information gleaned slowly, but surely placed it beyond doubt that the rising was a purely religious affair, and that it was a scheme preconcerted from both Kabul and India to raise the Muhammadan tribes on our border; that agitators had been sedulously working on the feelings of the tribesmen on the Peshawar border, in Buner [Bunair], Bajaur [Bajawar], Swat and the Afridi and Mohmand [Muhmand] country; that the *fakir* [Sartur Faqir] so far from being mad was a man of some acuteness, and on first starting was well supplied with funds. It further came to light that the rising…was intended to be a simultaneous one along the border, but that the *fakir* precipitated matters.[136]

McMahon and Ramsay's assertion not only negates Warburton's, but also hints to another dimension. Had the uprising been simultaneous throughout the tribal area, the situation would have been more critical for the British government as they would have had to arrange for reinforcements on all the fronts at the same time. This would have divided their forces and attention, and would have worked to the benefit of the tribesmen. But Sartur Faqir's haste foiled the plan of a simultaneous uprising along the tribal area, and indirectly contributed to the failure of the tribesmen's goal.

As all the attempts—from the Wazir at Maizar to Swat, and from Swat down to the Muhmand, Afridi, and Urakzi—were not made simultaneously, it made the task of the British easier. This was also pointed out in a report published in *The Pioneer* about the attempt of the Muhmand headed by Hadah Mula:

> The raid was doubtless designed to effect a diversion in favour of the Swatis [people of Swat], still suffering from their failure to capture the Malakand or Chakdara. If the Hadda Mullah [Hadah Mula] had timed his effort so that Shabkadr [Shabqadar] should be attacked on the same day as the Malakand, he would have done a clever stroke of business, and widespread uneasiness would have been caused all along our Peshawar frontier. As it was, our troops (as already shown) had swept the Lower Swat clear of tribesmen, and two full brigades in the Malakand were now ready to operate in any direction, while a reserve brigade had been formed at Mardan which could move at a few hours' notice into the Peshawar Valley.[137]

Lack of proper coordination and non-simultaneous uprising by the tribesmen are the reasons cited while explaining the non-participation of the Mahsuds in the uprising of 1897, as discussed earlier.

LACK OF PROPER COORDINATION AMONG THE TRIBESMEN AND THEIR LEADERS

There was some degree of coordination, communication, and linkage among the leaders of the uprising and their supporters abroad. While simultaneous uprising had been planned all along the Indian border, the uprising did not start as per the plan—the Maizar attack and fighting, and then the Sartur Faqir, expedited matters. This adversely affected coordination and communication among the tribesmen, as well as among the leaders of the uprising. No arrangements had been made to establish communication links between them during the course of the uprising, unlike the British. This lack of effective coordination and communication resulted in an unplanned, uncoordinated, and non-simultaneous uprising, which divided their force, and, hence, led to failure.

BRITISH SUPREMACY IN ARMS, AMMUNITIONS, AND COMMUNICATION SYSTEM

Britain, a continental and global power, had a large well-trained and well-equipped army. Despite their bravery and courage, the tribesmen were no match for the British in arms, ammunitions, and communication systems, which is always required while fighting a formidable enemy. Thus, British supremacy in arms, ammunitions, and communication systems was a vital factor in the tribesmen's failure.

REGULAR, TRAINED, AND DISCIPLINED FORCES OF THE BRITISH

In spite of their war-like nature, and fighting on their home-ground in large numbers, the tribesmen possessed neither the modern training of regular armed forces nor the artillery required to assault the British garrisons stationed and posted in forts and pickets, mostly on hills and hill-tops. While the tribesmen were full of fervour, zeal, and determination, and were in large numbers, they were divided and a huge unorganised mob. H.L. Nevill acknowledges their skill in carrying out nocturnal operations when he states:

> It is a well-known fact that night operations are not generally popular among irregular warriors, probably because this class of warfare requires a high standard of discipline and combination, which is the prerogative of well-trained troops. Nevertheless, the record of events in 1897, in or near the Swat

Valley, affords numerous instances in which night attacks on a considerable scale were planned and carried out by men possessing neither organization nor recognized leader.[138]

He, however, subsequently points out: 'At the same time the results of these same night attacks are instructive, for without exception they are all examples of the reward for vigilance and discipline on the part of regular troops in face of superior numbers.'[139] Britain's regular, trained, and disciplined forces were able to counter the tribesmen's superiority in numbers, in spite of the tribesmen fighting, to a great extent, in a manner that would not have been expected of irregular forces and tribesmen. Thus, for the British, it was a 'victory of organization over sheer mass power'.[140]

THE CONSEQUENCES, RESULTS, AND EFFECTS

Although the tribesmen failed in achieving their goal, the consequences of the uprising were of no less significance and should not be underestimated.

THE YEAR OF DIAMOND JUBILEE TURNED INTO A TROUBLESOME ONE

The year 1897 was a year of celebration as it marked the 'Diamond Jubilee' of the then British Queen, Queen Victoria, acceding the throne. On 22 June 1897, the Queen 'touched her fingers to the brass transmitting key in the telegraph room at Buckingham Palace and started to click out a message to the 372 million subjects of the British Empire. It was the morning of her Diamond Jubilee—sixty years on the British throne.'[141] It was also the fortieth year of the Britons success against the Indians—in the Indian War of Independence of 1857—and the 49th year of direct British occupation of the Frontier's settled areas. However, the Frontier tribesmen, by conducting their uprising in the summer of the same year, turned this year of celebrations into 'surely one of the most troublous years in all Indian history',[142] shaking the foundation of the mighty British Empire.

PUNITIVE EXPEDITIONS

The uprising came to an end in September 1897. But, skirmishes and troubles continued between the colonial authorities and the tribesmen, as the former deemed it necessary to send punitive expeditions against the tribes that fought against them—to pacify them and to take them to task. These expeditions were sent in spite of their condemnation earlier by 'Lord Lytton in his memorable minute of 22 April, 1877,...as "a system of semi-barbarous reprisals," which had not always proved successful, even in the most limited sense'.[143]

On receiving news of the Maizar outrage, the Government of India decided to despatch a force of two brigades—as the Tochi [Tuchi] Field Force—under the command of Major-General G. Corrie Bird, 'with as little delay as possible into the Tochi Valley, to exact punishment from the...tribesmen'.[144] Despite some initial difficulties, 'at length all preparations were made, and the concentration of the force at Datta Khel was completed by July 19'. The next day, the brigade occupied Shirani and the attached cavalry proceeded to Maizar. The tribesmen, however, had already deserted both the places—although their snipers continued to shoot at the soldiers at night, while others attacked convoys. The forces spent 'the next sixteen days...destroying the towers and hamlets in the neighbourhood'. Although news of the uprising in Swat boosted the tribesmen's aggression, the forces accomplished their task, albeit with difficulties, and the Madda Khail accepted the terms on 15 November 1897. The Tuchi Field Force was dissolved in January 1898.[145]

Realising the serious nature of the outbreak in Swat, the Government of India lost no time. On 30 July 1897, the governor-general sanctioned the formation of the Malakand Field Force under the command of Sir Bindon Blood—to hold Malakand and its adjacent posts, and to punish the involved tribes.[146] Early in August, it was decided to immediately form a reserve brigade to support the field force. Although both Malakand and Chakdarah were relieved and saved by 2 August, 'the task of punishment and prevention of further combination [of the tribes] was taken in hand at once'.[147] The Field Force under Major General Sir Bindon Blood led the first punitive expedition in the Swat Valley. In spite of facing stiff resistance while moving up the valley, and suffering heavy losses—especially the death of H.L. MacLean and Lieutenant R.T. Greaves near Kutah and Naway Kalay above Landakay[148]—the Force reached Mingawarah on 19 August. From here, reconnoitring parties were sent to Manglawar, Charbagh, and Gulibagh. After staying at Mingawarah for four days and accomplishing their task, the Force returned to Malakand.[149] Similar punitive expeditions were sent against all the tribes that took part in the fighting at Malakand and Chakdarah.

After the punitive expedition into Swat, Sir Bindon Blood wanted to 'advance into' Bunair 'before turning his attention to the north and west'. However, in view of the situation in the Peshawar environs, the Government of India preferred moving forward 'in a westerly rather that an easterly direction'. Therefore, he was ordered to proceed to Bajawar, to assist 'the Mohmand [Muhmand] Field Force under General Elles' against the tribes that had followed the Hadah Mula during the attack on Shankargarh and Shabqadar.[150]

The task of conducting the punitive expedition into Bajawar was assigned to Sir Bindon Blood. The Muhmand Field Force under General Elles was also formed for the same purpose. Proceeding from Swat, the Force led by Bindon Blood made the first move in that direction. On 8 September 1897, the vanguard arrived at Panjkurah River; and on 13 September, Bindon Blood was at Khar. As the tribesmen were doing their best to obstruct the advance and operations of the British Forces, the latter faced resistance and difficulties—not only was their progress very slow but they also sustained considerable casualties. Interestingly, while the Muhmand submitted peacefully, the Mamund gallantly opposed and fought the British Forces. The Forces' operations, and the tribesmen's resistance, continued until a settlement was finally reached on 18 October 1897 after which the troops were withdrawn.[151]

After the punitive measures in Bajawar, an expedition was led against the Utman Khail for taking part in the Malakand uprising. The expedition lasted from 23 November until 6 December 1897 when the Utman Khail submitted peacefully. The colonial authorities now turned their attention to the tribes inhabiting Bunair (Buner, Bunir), and those between Bunair and the Indus, for which the Bunair Field Force was organised. Before the punitive expedition began, the concerned tribesmen were asked to comply with the terms of the colonial authorities and to surrender peacefully. Although the tribes inhabiting the tract between Bunair and the Indus submitted forthwith, the Bunairwal refused to comply with the terms of the British. So, on 1 January 1898, the British concentrated their forces at Kunda; their eastward march began the next day. The Bunairwal, who held all the passes leading to their country, did their best to ward off the British. However, the submission of Bunairwal and the Chamlawal was achieved by 17 January 1898, and the British forces returned to the British territory on 19 January.[152]

After relieving Gulistan, preparations were made for the despatch of the Tirah Field Force against the Urakzi and Afridi tribes. Although the punitive operation was delayed since the British forces waited for the arrival of troops from the Malakand and Muhmand Field Forces and because of the difficulties they faced in arranging for the provision of transport and supplies, the march into Shinawari started on 11 October 1897. On 18 October, the British Force had its first success—the taking of Dargai. They did not occupy it but moved forward into the Khanki Valley. However, it was soon realised that they need to occupy Dargai to be able to secure the road to the Khanki Valley. Hence, after some fierce fighting, it was again captured on 20 October. To prevent night-time sniping on the camps, strong pickets were successfully established on the nearby peaks, within range of the camps. On 28 October, the advance towards Sampagha Pass began. Although the tribes put up resistance, the British troops continued on. After taking the Sampagha Pass on 29 October, and leaving the 1st Brigade at the camp at Mastura, the Force resumed its advance, on 31 October, from the Urakzai country into Tirah Maidan, over the Arhanga Pass.[153]

On occupying the deserted Tirah Maidan, reconnoitring parties were sent up the valley to Bagh, and surveying operations were undertaken for eight days. However, the Zakha Khail frequently attacked, and fired intermittently on, the camp. On 9 November, a reconnoitring party was sent to Saran Sar—which commanded the eastern end of the Tirah Maidan. On its way back to the camp, it met with fighting and incurred heavy casualties. Nevertheless, on 11 November, another reconnaissance was carried out to the Saran Sar. On 13 November, a reconnoitring party to the Tseri Pass in the Waran Valley was greatly harassed by the tribesmen. They returned to camp on 16 November, and the camp was moved to Bagh on 18 November. On 22 November, the next important series of operations commenced. A reconnoitring party sent to Dwatoi in the Barah (Bara) Valley was also fired upon by the tribesmen, time and again, until they returned to Bagh on 24 November. On 26 November, a combined move was made, with the Kurram Column, against the tribes to the extreme west of Afridi country, in the course of which fighting took place on various occasions. This operation came to an end on 6 December and the British troops returned to Bagh. On accomplishing the task, and with winter approaching, the British forces evacuated Tirah—their withdrawal started on 7 December and was completed on 14 December 1897. The retreat, however, was not completely safe as the Afridi made frequent sniping and direct attacks; the British forces sustained heavy losses—164 people were killed and wounded—during the retreat.[154]

After their return from the Urakzai area and Afridi valleys, preparations were made to send punitive expeditions into the Zakha Khail Valley of Bazar, and up the Khyber Pass. On 22 December 1897, the British forces advanced in both directions, as per their plan. The British forces marched unopposed and unharmed but trouble overtook them later as fierce attacks and heavy fighting, including hand-to-hand fighting, took place resulting in heavy casualties on the British side—among others four officers including the eminent Colonel Haughton lost their lives. The Zakha Khail, however, also at last came to terms with the British.[155] With this, the consequent punitive measures of the 1897 uprising came to end. About the punitive expeditions, H. Woosnam Mills is of the opinion:

> With the successful pacification of the Swat Valley, the peaceful submission of the Mohmands [Muhmands] and the final success of Sir Bindon Blood among the stubborn Mamunds the first act in the frontier war drama of 1897 ended, and the curtain was rung down preparatory to the second act, when Sir William Lockhart with the flower of the British and Indian army marches on the plateau of Tirah, and in their own fastnesses proves to the truculent Afridis and Orakzais [Urakzis] that though the patience of the *Sirkar* [*sarkar*] is as enduring as a summer's day yet his arm when put forth against his foes is long as a winter's night.[156]

The mighty British arm 'took more than three years'—including pacification of the Mahsud, who rose in 1898—to accomplish the task, in the process employing 'a total of more than 75,000 troops'.[157]

FINES LEVIED, PROPERTIES DESTROYED, AND AGREEMENTS EXTRACTED

H.L. Nevill states: 'To compel the surrender of guerrillas, such as the frontier tribes of India, by the usual process of breaking down the means of defence would entail operations so prolonged and costly as to be out of all proportion to the interests at stake.' Hence, he contends: 'Other means, therefore, must be found to achieve the same result, such as the destruction of villages and personal property, which has always been the only effective way of dealing with the elusive tribesmen beyond the North-West Frontier of India.' He, however, asserts: 'At the same time this is only the last resource when other means fail, and even then must be resorted to with caution, or exasperation rather than submission may be the result.'[158] That was why, besides employing other means and tactics, the colonial authorities resorted to destroying the properties of the involved tribes[159]—to punish them and compel them to agree to their terms. So, 'to keep the peace', they extracted agreements 'from such *jirga*s [*jargahs/jargay*] as could be coerced into assembling'. Moreover, they levied huge fines on the tribes and, where they could, confiscated 'large numbers of rifles'.[160]

PICKETS BUILT

To protect their garrisons and strategic positions in the future, the colonial government built pickets around the garrisons and 'along the lines of march'.[161] Because, as H.L. Nevill points out: 'The Pathan has a strong dislike to having an enemy above him, so, by holding the commanding points in the vicinity of a camp, he is not only prevented from using them as positions for his sharpshooters, but the best posts of observation—the necessary preliminary to accurate sniping—are denied to him.'[162] And, as J.G. Elliott points out, the three things the tribesmen disliked are 'an enemy on high ground above him, having his line of retreat threatened, and artillery fire which, as he had no guns of his own, he always thought to be slightly unfair'.[163]

RECALLING OF BRITISH FORCES TO SETTLED AREAS

To pacify the tribesmen, and remove their fears about further British expansion into the tribal area and their resentment against the forward policy and move, Lord Curzon, the new viceroy, withdrew the 'forces behind the administrative border, which was completed by 1902'. This 'reduced tension considerably, and an unusually long period of relative quiet followed'.[164]

DEATH OF FORWARD POLICY

As the Forward Policy was a major cause of the uprising, a hue and cry was raised against it in British circles, which compelled the policy makers to rethink their policy. Consequently, 'wiser counsels prevailed under Lord Curzon, whose policy can be described as one of withdrawal and concentration. In other words, the policy pursued in the 'nineties was to be replaced by one of non-interference resembling in many respects the old "close border" system.'[165]

Therefore, although the uprising seemingly failed, it ultimately resulted in 'the quiet death of the "Forward Policy" on the north-western marches of the British Indian Empire'.[166] In Arthur Swinson's words, the uprising 'triggered off another round in the political controversy over the "Forward Policy", and perhaps the most ferocious of all. This time not only the strategic and military problems of the Frontier were examined but the basic structure of the administrative system'[167] as well.

James W. Spain rightly observes that 'the result of it all', namely the punitive expeditions, fines levied, properties destroyed, agreements extracted, pickets built, withdrawal of armed forces to the settled areas, and death of the Forward Policy, however, 'was a return to the *status quo*'.[168]

EXTENSION OF RAILWAY LINES AND ROADS

During the course of the uprising, the colonial authorities felt the need to extend railway lines and roads to different parts of the Frontier tribal area, and to improve the communication system for strategic reasons: to enable the forces to reach the war-front in as short a span of time as possible, and also to transport arms, ammunition, and baggage easily. Therefore, railway lines and roads were stretched and extended where it was feasible and could be managed, either to the borders of the tribal area or even within the tribal area.[169] This facilitated the colonial government in achieving the above-mentioned objectives, but at the same time provided the tribesmen with an easy means of transport and communication, and also boosted trade by facilitating export from, and import to, the tribal area.

FORMATION OF NWFP

Separation of the trans-Indus areas from Punjab, and making it a separate province, was not a new phenomenon as 'for at least a quarter of a century, viceroys, administrators and generals had, tentatively or otherwise, put forward proposals for the creation of a new administrative unit, which', according to Collin Davies, 'they hoped would usher in an era of peace on the blood-stained border and prove a panacea for most of the evils to which it was subject'.[170] The idea, however, had not been finalised for one reason or another. The uprising of 1897 gave a fresh impetus to the Frontier problem, and stimulus to the issue of the creation of a separate Frontier administrative unit. Hence, one of the 'direct and far-reaching' consequences of the uprising proved to be 'the creation of a separate North-West Frontier Province, under the viceroyalty of Lord Curzon, in 1901'.[171]

It is evident, from the available sources, that the North-West Frontier had remained a constant source of trouble for the British since their occupation of Punjab and the trans-Indus Frontier plains. Lord Curzon emphasises: 'No man who has read a page of Indian history will ever prophesy about the Frontier.'[172] Frequent attacks and inroads were made, from the tribal area, into the areas under colonial control: the colonial authorities had faced constant troubles and fighting at the hands of the tribesmen since 1849. However, 'the year 1897' not only 'witnessed the most serious conflagration which has ever disturbed the North-West Frontier'[173] but it was also the year when 'the British in India were facing their gravest crisis since the Mutiny [the War of Independence of 1857]'.[174] Although caused by a combination of factors, each one important in its own way, the religious element and the concept of *jihad* proved to be the key factor and the trigger, and the *mulas* and *faqirs*—the religious men—the leading figures of the 1897 uprising.

Akbar S. Ahmed states: 'The "jihads" in the colonial encounters of the nineteenth century were a last grand and futile gesture of the "traditionalist" forces of Islam tilting against the most powerful nations on earth.' He, however, rightly observes: 'The inevitability of the outcome merely underlines the conceptualization of the rationale contained in the "jihad" by its participants: the struggle is more important than victory; the principle more important than the objective.'[175]

Notwithstanding the failure of the tribesmen to attain their immediate objective in 1897, they fought the 'struggle' with zeal and fervour and stood by their 'principle'. The uprising, moreover, brought about far-reaching consequences, especially in the administrative set-up of the region and in the formulation of a policy of containment on the side of the British. It also demonstrated that religious sentiments could overcome tribal jealousies and unite people to make huge sacrifices, even in the most divisive tribal-cum-feudal society, a fact that still holds true. The state of affairs in the post-11 September 2001 scenario in the erstwhile tribal area, in both the FATA and PATA, is also testimony to it. As stated earlier, the tribal status of both FATA and PATA was brought to an end in May 2018 through the 25th Amendment in the Constitution of Pakistan, 1973.

While going through the reports and writings about the 1897 uprising, we can find ample evidence of the strategy and course adopted by the tribesmen in 1897 that applies to the situation in the twenty-first century as well. The difficulties faced, and course adopted, by the then-British forces and by the present-day Pakistani forces also bears great similarity.

Notes

1. H.L. Nevill, *Campaigns on the North-West Frontier*, repr. (Lahore: SMP, 2003), 14.

2. James W. Spain, *The Pathan Borderland*, repr. (Karachi: IP, 1985), 174.

3. See *Imperial Gazetteer of India; Provincial Series; North-West Frontier Province* [henceforward *Imperial Gazetteer of India, NWFP*], repr. (Lahore: SMP, 1991), 80–2.

4. Nevill, *Campaigns on the North-West Frontier*, 11–12.

5. Ibid., 209.

6. Spain, *The Pathan Borderland*, 179.

7. Nevill, *Campaigns on the North-West Frontier*, 209.

8. F.A.K. Harrison, 'The British Interest in the North West Frontier', *Peshawar University Review* (Peshawar), vol. 1 (No. 1, 1974–75), 52. Also see Robert Warburton, *Eighteen Years in the Khyber, 1879–1898*, repr., 3rd impr. (Karachi: OUP, 1975), 290–1; Charles Miller, *Khyber: British India's North West Frontier; The Story of an Imperial Migraine* (London: Macdonald and Jane's Publishers Limited, 1977), 260.

9. T. Hungerford Holdich, *The Indian Borderland, 1880–1900*, 1st repr. in India (Delhi: Gian Publishing House, 1987), 340. Also see Arthur Swinson, *North-West Frontier: People and Events, 1839–1947* (London: Hutchinson & Co (Publishers) Ltd, 1967), 233.

10. Nevill, *Campaigns on the North-West Frontier*, 210.

11. Also see H. Woosnam Mills, *The Pathan Revolt in North West India*, repr. (Lahore: SMP, 1996), 5; Winston S. Churchill, *The Story of the Malakand Field Force: An Episode of Frontier War*, repr. (London: Leo Cooper, 2002), 26; H.C. Wylly, *The Borderland: The Country of the Pathans*, repr. (Karachi: IP, 1998), 312; *Frontier and Overseas Expeditions from India*, vol. 2, *North-West Frontier Tribes between the Kabul and Gumal Rivers*, 2nd edn. published in Pakistan (Quetta: NT, 1982), 63–4.

12. Holdich, *The Indian Borderland*, 340.

13. C. Collin Davies, *The Problem of the North-West Frontier, 1890–1908: With a survey of policy since 1849*, 2nd edn., rev. and enlarged (London: CPL, 1975), 97–8. Also see *The Cambridge History of India*, vol. 6, *The Indian Empire, 1858–1918, With chapters on the development of Administration 1818–1858*, ed. H.H. Dodwell, *and the Last Phase 1919–1947*, by R.R. Sethi (Delhi: SCC, 1964), 461; Miller, *Khyber*, 259.

14. *Administration Report of the North-West Frontier Province from 9th November 1901 to 31st March 1903* [henceforward *Administration Report NWFP from 9th November 1901 to 31st March 1903*] (Peshawar: Printed at the North-West Frontier Province Government Press, 1903), 10; *Administration Report of the North-West Frontier Province for 1921–22* (Peshawar: North-West Frontier Province Government Press, 1923), 10. Also see Lal Baha, *N.-W.F.P. Administration under British Rule, 1901–1919* (Islamabad: NCHCR, 1978), 5–8; Churchill, *The Story of the Malakand Field Force*, 24–5; Wylly, *The Borderland*, 311–12; J.G. Elliott, *The Frontier, 1839–1947: The Story of the North-West Frontier of India*, with preface by Olaf Caroe (London: Cassell & Company Ltd, 1968), 153; *The Cambridge History of India*, vol. 6, 465; *Frontier and Overseas Expeditions from India*, vol. 2, 64.

15. See Mills, *The Pathan Revolt in North West India*, 5.

16. Also see Sultan Mahomed Khan, ed., *The Life of Abdur Rahman: Amir of Afghanistan*, with new introduction by M.E. Yapp, vol. 2, repr. in Pakistan (Karachi: OUP, 1980), 158–60; Sultan-i-Rome, 'The Durand Line Agreement (1893):- Its Pros and Cons', *Journal of the Research Society of Pakistan* (Lahore), vol. 41 (No. 1, July 2004), 8–9.

17. Mills, *The Pathan Revolt in North West India*, 2.

18. See Nevill, *Campaigns on the North-West Frontier*, 212; Mills, *The Pathan Revolt in North West India*, 2; Holdich, *The Indian Borderland*, 339; Wylly, *The Borderland*, 312; Swinson, *North-West Frontier*, 233. Also see *The Cambridge History of India*, vol. 6,

465; Miller, *Khyber*, 260; *Frontier and Overseas Expeditions from India*, vol. 2, 65. The name of the book has also been given as *Targhib-ul-Jihad* in A.H. McMahon and A.D.G. Ramsay, *Report on the Tribes of the Malakand Political Agency (Exclusive of Chitral)*, rev. R.L. Kennion [henceforward McMahon and A.D.G. Ramsay, *Report on the Tribes of the Malakand Political Agency*] (Peshawar: Government Press, North-West Frontier Province, 1916), 49; A.H. McMahon and A.D.G. Ramsay, *Report on the Tribes of Dir, Swat and Bajour* [Bajawar] *together with the Utman-Khel and Sam Ranizai* [henceforward *Report on the Tribes of Dir, Swat and Bajour*], repr., ed. with introduction by R.O. Christensen (Peshawar: SBB, 1981), 108–9.

19. Mills, *The Pathan Revolt in North West India*, 2. Also see Swinson, *North-West Frontier*, 233; Miller, *Khyber*, 260.

20. Mills, *The Pathan Revolt in North West India*, 2.

21. Wylly, *The Borderland*, 313.

22. Churchill, *The Story of the Malakand Field Force*, 89.

23. McMahon and A.D.G. Ramsay, *Report on the Tribes of the Malakand Political Agency*, 49; McMahon and A.D.G. Ramsay, *Report on the Tribes of Dir, Swat and Bajour*, 108. Also see Warburton, *Eighteen Years in the Khyber*, 291–6; Elliott, *The Frontier*, 195; *The Risings on the North-West Frontier (Compiled from the Special War Correspondence of the "Pioneer")* (Allahabad: Printed and Published at the Pioneer Press, 1898), 66, 150, 157.

24. Holdich, *The Indian Borderland*, 339.

25. Elliott, *The Frontier*, 161.

26. Nevill, *Campaigns on the North-West Frontier*, 212.

27. Mills, *The Pathan Revolt in North West India*, 3. Also see *The Risings on the North-West Frontier*, 150–7; Elliott, *The Frontier*, 170.

28. Mills, *The Pathan Revolt in North West India*, 3. Also see *The Risings on the North-West Frontier*, 150–1; Elliott, *The Frontier*, 170.

29. With the Government of India Act of 1858 and the Queen's Proclamation in 1858, the entire subcontinent was not taken over to become British India or part of the British Empire or Imperial British. It was only the territory occupied by the colonialist East India Company that was taken over and became British India or part of British Empire. As the Indian or Princely states and the tribal areas were not taken over they were not part of British India or British Empire or Imperial British. That was why the British government executed agreements and entered into treaty relations with the Indian states and the tribes of the tribal areas. Besides, the Pukhtun land occupied by the colonialists as part of the then Sikh kingdom, later separated from the province of Punjab as the North-West Frontier Province in 1901, was denied, till 1932, the reforms granted to and the laws introduced in British India. Even when granting the status of a full-fledged province in 1932 and extending the reforms introduced under the Government of India Act, 1919, and later the Government of India Act, 1935, the repressive and infamous Frontier Crimes Regulation, 1901, was not repealed. This still operated even in the settled districts of the Province. Therefore, the Pukhtun land made part of British India was neither brought on a par with the British territory in Europe nor with other areas of British India, and was ruled on colonial lines. The Pukhtun tribal areas were neither part of British India nor were they ruled under the laws in vogue in Britain or British India. Moreover, although the head of British India was now called 'Viceroy', being representative of the British Crown, the title and the post of 'Governor-General' was not abolished. The Viceroy also acted and governed British India in the capacity of governor-general, which testifies to the colonial tinge of the British rule in India. The post of governor-general was retained till the last day of the British rule in India. In this backdrop, the adjective 'colonial' or the term 'colonialists' used for the British in this book at the time of their campaigns or communications, etc., in the Pukhtun lands are historically correct and appropriate.

30. Spain, *The Pathan Borderland*, 176–7. Also see Davies, *The Problem of the North-West Frontier*, 95.

31. See Davies, *The Problem of the North-West Frontier*, 94–6; Warburton, *Eighteen Years in the Khyber*, 289, 297–8.

32. Spain, *The Pathan Borderland*, 177. Also see Davies, *The Problem of the North-West Frontier*, 94–5; Warburton, *Eighteen Years in the Khyber*, 289, 297–8.

33. Mills, *The Pathan Revolt in North West India*, 8–9.

34. Spain, *The Pathan Borderland*, 177.

35. Mills, *The Pathan Revolt in North West India*, 20.

36. Ibid., 9.

37. For details, see G.J. Younghusband and Francis Younghusband, *The Relief of Chitral*, with map and illustrations, repr. (Rawalpindi: English Book House, 1976), 1–29.

38. See Nevill, *Campaigns on the North-West Frontier*, 166–7; Davies, *The Problem of the North-West Frontier*, 85–6; Mills, *The Pathan Revolt in North West India*, 4; Younghusband and Francis Younghusband. *The Relief of Chitral*, 26; *The Cambridge History of India*, vol. 6, 464.

39. For details, see Younghusband and Francis Younghusband. *The Relief of Chitral*, 83–128; *Frontier and Overseas Expeditions from India*, vol. 1, *Tribes North of the Kabul River*, 2nd edn. published in Pakistan (Quetta: NT, 1982), 42–78, 521–48; Nevill, *Campaigns on the North-West Frontier*, 164–96.

40. Davies, *The Problem of the North-West Frontier*, 86.

41. Ibid.

42. Ibid., 87. Also see Mills, *The Pathan Revolt in North West India*, 4; Churchill, *The Story of the Malakand Field Force*, 22–3; *The Cambridge History of India*, vol. 6, 464.

43. Also see Churchill, *The Story of the Malakand Field Force*, 22–5.

44. See McMahon and A.D.G. Ramsay, *Report on the Tribes of the Malakand Political Agency*, 49; McMahon and A.D.G. Ramsay, *Report on the Tribes of Dir, Swat and Bajour*, 109; Mills, *The Pathan Revolt in North West India*, 34; Swinson, *North-West Frontier*, 233.

45. McMahon and A.D.G. Ramsay, *Report on the Tribes of the Malakand Political Agency*, 50; McMahon and A.D.G. Ramsay, *Report on the Tribes of Dir, Swat and Bajour*, 111.

46. See Wylly, *The Borderland*, 313; Churchill, *The Story of the Malakand Field Force*, 89.

47. McMahon and A.D.G. Ramsay, *Report on the Tribes of the Malakand Political Agency*, 50; McMahon and A.D.G. Ramsay, *Report on the Tribes of Dir, Swat and Bajour*, 112.

48. Churchill, *The Story of the Malakand Field Force*, 25.

49. Davies, *The Problem of the North-West Frontier*, 94.

50. Ibid., 97; Eknath Easwaran, *A Man to Match His Mountains: Badshah Khan, Nonviolent Soldier of Islam*, with afterword by Timothy Flinders, 2nd print (California: Nilgiri Press, 1985), 49; Miller, *Khyber*, 266.

51. *Imperial Gazetteer of India, NWFP*, 23.

52. McMahon and A.D.G. Ramsay, *Report on the Tribes of the Malakand Political Agency*, 50; McMahon and A.D.G. Ramsay, *Report on the Tribes of Dir, Swat and Bajour*, 112.

53. Nevill, *Campaigns on the North-West Frontier*, 210.

54. *Frontier and Overseas Expeditions from India*, vol. 2, 67.

55. Warburton, *Eighteen Years in the Khyber*, 298. For further details on the degree of the *mulas'* influence in the tribal area, see ibid., 299; T.L. Pennell, *Among the Wild Tribes of the Afghan Frontier: A Record of Sixteen years Close Intercourse with the Natives of the Indian Marches*, with introduction by Earl Roberts, and with 37 illustrations & 2 maps (London: George Bell & Sons, 1909), 114–25; Andre Singer, *Lords of the Khyber: The Story of the North-West Frontier* (London: FFL, 1984), 158–73.

56. Davies, *The Problem of the North-West Frontier*, 98. Also see Churchill, *The Story of the Malakand Field Force*, 25–7.

57. *The Cambridge History of India*, vol. 6, 466.
58. Munawwar Khan, 'Swat: Second Instalment', *Peshawar University Review* (Peshawar), vol. 1, (No. 1, 1974–75), 67.
59. Henry George Raverty, *Notes on Afghanistan and Baluchistan*, vol. 1, 2nd edn., published in Pakistan (Quetta: NT, 1982), 251 n.
60. Holdich, *The Indian Borderland*, 338.
61. Olaf Caroe, *The Pathans: 550 B.C.–A.D. 1957*, repr. (Karachi: OUP, 1976), 387. Also see Akbar S. Ahmed, *Millennium and Charisma among Pathans: A Critical Essay in Social Anthropology* (London: Routledge & Kegan Paul Ltd, 1976), 105.
62. Mills, *The Pathan Revolt in North West India*, 10–11. Also see Wylly, *The Borderland*, 466.
63. Nevill, *Campaigns on the North-West Frontier*, 214. Also see Wylly, *The Borderland*, 466.
64. Mills, *The Pathan Revolt in North West India*, 11–12. Also see Nevill, *Campaigns on the North-West Frontier*, 215.
65. Mills, *The Pathan Revolt in North West India*, 12.
66. Ibid., 12–13. Also see Nevill, *Campaigns on the North-West Frontier*, 216–17.
67. Mills, *The Pathan Revolt in North West India*, 13.
68. Ibid., 14. Also see Nevill, *Campaigns on the North-West Frontier*, 218.
69. Nevill, *Campaigns on the North-West Frontier*, 217–18; Wylly, *The Borderland*, 467–8.
70. Mills, *The Pathan Revolt in North West India*, 14.
71. Ibid., 14–15, 19. For details about the Maizar outrage, see ibid. 10–23; *The Risings on the North-West Frontier*, 1–17; George Macmunn, *The Romance of the Indian Frontiers*, 1st edn. published in Pakistan (Quetta: NT, 1978), 188–93; Nevill, *Campaigns on the North-West Frontier*, 213–18; Wylly, *The Borderland*, 466–68; *Frontier and Overseas Expeditions from India*, vol. 2, 431–3.
72. Mills, *The Pathan Revolt in North West India*, 19–20.
73. Spain, *The Pathan Borderland*, 177. Also see Elliott, *The Frontier*, 240.
74. For details about the Sartur Faqir, see Sultan-i-Rome, 'The Sartor Faqir: Life and Struggle against British Imperialism', *JPHS* (Karachi), vol. 42 (Part 1, January 1994), 93–105.
75. PP Encl. 28, 8 August 1897, quoted in Ahmed, *Millennium and Charisma among Pathans*, 108.
76. See McMahon and A.D.G. Ramsay, *Report on the Tribes of the Malakand Political Agency*, 49; McMahon and A.D.G. Ramsay, *Report on the Tribes of Dir, Swat and Bajour*, 109–10.
77. Nevill, *Campaigns on the North-West Frontier*, 223, 225.
78. Mills, *The Pathan Revolt in North West India*, 35.
79. *Imperial Gazetteer of India, NWFP*, 23.
80. Mills, *The Pathan Revolt in North West India*, 35.
81. McMahon and A.D.G. Ramsay, *Report on the Tribes of the Malakand Political Agency*, 50; McMahon and A.D.G. Ramsay, *Report on the Tribes of Dir, Swat and Bajour*, 110–11.
82. Nevill, *Campaigns on the North-West Frontier*, 225–7.
83. McMahon and A.D.G. Ramsay, *Report on the Tribes of the Malakand Political Agency*, 50; McMahon and A.D.G. Ramsay, *Report on the Tribes of Dir, Swat and Bajour*, 111.
84. Mills, *The Pathan Revolt in North West India*, 47.
85. Ibid., 35.
86. McMahon and A.D.G. Ramsay, *Report on the Tribes of the Malakand Political Agency*, 50; McMahon and A.D.G. Ramsay, *Report on the Tribes of Dir, Swat and Bajour*, 111; *Imperial Gazetteer of India, NWFP*, 23.
87. Mills, *The Pathan Revolt in North West India*, 48–9.
88. McMahon and A.D.G. Ramsay, *Report on the Tribes of the Malakand Political Agency*, 50; McMahon and A.D.G. Ramsay, *Report on the Tribes of Dir, Swat and Bajour*, 111.
89. Mills, *The Pathan Revolt in North West India*, 51.
90. Ibid.

91. McMahon and A.D.G. Ramsay, *Report on the Tribes of the Malakand Political Agency*, 50; McMahon and A.D.G. Ramsay, *Report on the Tribes of Dir, Swat and Bajour*, 111.
92. Mills, *The Pathan Revolt in North West India*, 52.
93. Ibid., 56–8.
94. Ibid., 58–9.
95. Nevill, *Campaigns on the North-West Frontier*, 230.
96. Mills, *The Pathan Revolt in North West India*, 35. For details about the fighting at Malakand and Chakdarah, see ibid., 36–63; Wylly, *The Borderland*, 132–7; Churchill, *The Story of the Malakand Field Force*, 33–72; Macmunn, *The Romance of the Indian Frontiers*, 193–203; *The Risings on the North-West Frontier*, 29–51; *Frontier and Overseas Expeditions from India*, vol. 1, 366–81; Swinson, *North-West Frontier*, 234–40.
97. James W. Spain, *The Way of the Pathans*, 7th impr. (Karachi: OUP, 1994), 67.
98. See Rajmohan Gandhi, *Ghaffar Khan: Nonviolent Badshah of the Pakhtuns* (New Delhi: Penguin Books India (Pvt.) Ltd, 2008), 36, 38.
99. Mills, *The Pathan Revolt in North West India*, 87.
100. Ibid., 87–8.
101. Nevill, *Campaigns on the North-West Frontier*, 255. For details about the Muhmand Rising, see ibid., 255–6; Mills, *The Pathan Revolt in North West India*, 87–103; Wylly, *The Borderland*, 244–7; *The Risings on the North-West Frontier*, 65–74; Churchill, *The Story of the Malakand Field Force*, 88–91; Macmunn, *The Romance of the Indian Frontiers*, 206–10; *Frontier and Overseas Expeditions from India*, vol. 1, 472–8; Elliott, *The Frontier*, 166–70.
102. See Mills, *The Pathan Revolt in North West India*, 106–7, 125; Spain, *The Pathan Borderland*, 178.
103. Nevill, *Campaigns on the North-West Frontier*, 261–2.
104. Mills, *The Pathan Revolt in North West India*, 107.
105. Nevill, *Campaigns on the North-West Frontier*, 262.
106. Spain, *The Pathan Borderland*, 178.
107. Mills, *The Pathan Revolt in North West India*, 108.
108. Nevill, *Campaigns on the North-West Frontier*, 263–4.
109. Ibid., 264.
110. Ibid., 264–5.
111. Mills, *The Pathan Revolt in North West India*, 123–4.
112. Nevill, *Campaigns on the North-West Frontier*, 267–8.
113. Ibid., 269.
114. Ibid., 270–1.
115. Ibid., 273. For details about the Afridi and Urakzi risings, see ibid., 261–73; Mills, *The Pathan Revolt in North West India*, 103–44; Wylly, *The Borderland*, 313–18, 380–8; *The Risings on the North-West Frontier*, 107–42; Macmunn, *The Romance of the Indian Frontiers*, 215–24; Holdich, *The Indian Borderland*, 345–50; Swinson, *North-West Frontier*, 242–4; *Frontier and Overseas Expeditions from India*, vol. 2, 68–74, 248–64.
116. Spain, *The Pathan Borderland*, 178.
117. Caroe, *The Pathans*, 387–8.
118. Interestingly, it has been stated and believed that Winston Churchill—later the renowned British prime minister—was present in the Malakand war. However, at the time of the Malakand war, Mr Churchill was not in India but in England. He came to India later to join the Malakand Field Force, but not as a member of the Force. Because there was no vacancy on the staff of Sir Bindon Blood, commander of the Malakand Field Force, he was advised by Bindon to come to the Frontier as a correspondent. Consequently, Churchill approached the editor of the *Allahabad Pioneer* who showed a willingness to use his articles about the Malakand Field Force and 'would pay for them, too, though not a princely sum'.

He also asked his mother, Lady Randolph Churchill, to make arrangements with a London newspaper, upon which she 'arranged with the editor of the *Daily Telegraph* to use his work and to pay for it at the rate of £5 a column' (John Marsh, *The Young Winston Churchill* (London: World Distributors, 1962), 47–8. For details, see ibid., 44–50. Also see Elliott, *The Frontier*, 159; Miller, *Khyber*, 268). He, thus, came to India and accompanied the Malakand Field Force later as a war correspondent. He was not with the Malakand Field Force at the time of the punitive expedition to Swat, even as a correspondent of the *Daily Telegraph* or the *Pioneer*. He only accompanied the Malakand Field Force in its operation in Bajawar and against the Utman Khail. His account of the Malakand war, and the punitive expedition to Swat, was not an eye-witness account but one written on the basis of what he later heard from others. His account and narration, moreover, consisted of fancies and fantasies and suffered from factual errors and absurdities. For instance, about the Pukhtuns, he wrote: 'Their wives and their womankind generally have no position but that of animals. They are freely bought and sold and are not infrequently bartered for rifles' (Churchill, *The Story of the Malakand Field Force*, 6). And, about the men hailing from the religious segment or group, besides other things he has stated that 'no man's wife or daughter is safe from them' (Ibid., 7). These assertions are far from facts and ground reality.

119. Zia Gokalp, *Turkish Nationalism and Western Civilization: Selected Essays of Zia Gokalp*, trans. and ed. with introduction by Niyazi Berkes (London: George Allen and Unwin Ltd, 1959), 113–14.
120. Ghani Khan, *The Pathans: A Sketch*, repr. (Islamabad: PASR, 1990), 50.
121. Ibid., 51.
122. Nevill, *Campaigns on the North-West Frontier*, 249–50.
123. Holdich, *The Indian Borderland*, 344.
124. Ibid., 350.
125. Nevill, *Campaigns on the North-West Frontier*, 276.
126. Ibid.
127. Ibid.
128. Elliott, *The Frontier*, 110.
129. McMahon and A.D.G. Ramsay, *Report on the Tribes of the Malakand Political Agency*, 49; McMahon and A.D.G. Ramsay, *Report on the Tribes of Dir, Swat and Bajour*, 109. Also see Swinson, *North-West Frontier*, 232.
130. PP Encl. 28, 8 August 1897, quoted in Ahmed, *Millennium and Charisma among Pathans*, 108. Also see Mills, *The Pathan Revolt in North West India*, 36; McMahon and A.D.G. Ramsay, *Report on the Tribes of the Malakand Political Agency*, 49; McMahon and A.D.G. Ramsay, *Report on the Tribes of Dir, Swat and Bajour*, 109; Miller, *Khyber*, 266.
131. Churchill, *The Story of the Malakand Field Force*, 29; Mills, *The Pathan Revolt in North West India*, 36.
132. McMahon and A.D.G. Ramsay, *Report on the Tribes of the Malakand Political Agency*, 50; McMahon and A.D.G. Ramsay, *Report on the Tribes of Dir, Swat and Bajour*, 112.
133. Also see Mills, *The Pathan Revolt in North West India*, 3; *The Risings on the North-West Frontier*, 150–7.
134. Warburton, *Eighteen Years in the Khyber*, 295.
135. Ibid., 296.
136. McMahon and A.D.G. Ramsay, *Report on the Tribes of the Malakand Political Agency*, 50; McMahon and A.D.G. Ramsay, *Report on the Tribes of Dir, Swat and Bajour*, 112.
137. *The Risings on the North-West Frontier*, 66–7.
138. Nevill, *Campaigns on the North-West Frontier*, 250.
139. Ibid.
140. Joseph Hell has used the quoted words for the victory of the Muslims over the non-Muslim confederates at the Battle of Ditch or *Ahzab*, fought in 5 AH/627 CE, which also applies

to the success of the British against the Frontier tribesmen in the uprising of 1897. See Joseph Hell, *The Arab Civilization*, English trans. by S. Khuda Bakhsh, repr. (Lahore: Sh. Muhammad Ashraf, 1969), 29.

141. Easwaran, *A Man to Match His Mountains*, 25. For some details about the Jubilee and its importance, and the prowess and strength of the British Empire, see ibid., 25–7.

142. Holdich, *The Indian Borderland*, 338.

143. *The Cambridge History of India*, vol. 6, 452.

144. Nevill, *Campaigns on the North-West Frontier*, 218.

145. Ibid., 219. For details about the punitive measures in the Tuchi Valley, see ibid., 218–19; Mills, *The Pathan Revolt in North West India*, 23–32; *The Risings on the North-West Frontier*, 18–27, iii–vii; *Frontier and Overseas Expeditions from India*, vol. 2, 434–6.

146. See Mills, *The Pathan Revolt in North West India*, 64–5; Nevill, *Campaigns on the North-West Frontier*, 231.

147. *Imperial Gazetteer of India, NWFP*, 23.

148. Lieutenant-Colonel Adams and Viscount Fincastle were awarded the Victoria Cross for gallantry displayed during an encounter with the tribesmen near Kutah and Naway Kalay, above Landakay. But, Lieutenant MacLean was to be deprived of the award because of his death during the fighting (*Frontier and Overseas Expeditions from India*, vol. 1, 386; Churchill, *The Story of the Malakand Field Force*, 81; Macmunn, *The Romance of the Indian Frontiers*, 205). A later 'announcement (1907) in the *London Gazette*', however, stated 'that Lieutenant Maclean would also have received the Victoria Cross had he survived, and the decoration' was 'handed to his relatives' (*Frontier and Overseas Expeditions from India*, vol. 1, 386 n. 1].

149. For details about the punitive expedition in Swat, see Mills, *The Pathan Revolt in North West India*, 64–86; *The Risings on the North-West Frontier*, 45–7, 52–63, viii–xvi; Churchill, *The Story of the Malakand Field Force*, 73–86; Wylly, *The Borderland*, 137–42; *Frontier and Overseas Expeditions from India*, vol. 1, 381–8.

150. Nevill, *Campaigns on the North-West Frontier*, 233.

151. For details, see ibid., 233–43; 256–61; Mills, *The Pathan Revolt in North West India*, 144–85; Churchill, *The Story of the Malakand Field Force*, 91–195; Wylly, *The Borderland*, 175–82, 247–54; *The Risings on the North-West Frontier*, 75–106, xvii–xxvi; Macmunn, *The Romance of the Indian Frontiers*, 210–14; *Frontier and Overseas Expeditions from India*, vol. 1, 478–91, 567–87; Elliott, *The Frontier*, 170–4. It was for their fighting against the Mamund at Shah Tangi, in one of the battles, that Lieutenants T.C. Watson, J.M.C. Colvin, and Corporal Smith were awarded the Victoria Cross (Nevill, *Campaigns on the North-West Frontier*, 236 n.*; Macmunn, *The Romance of the Indian Frontiers*, 214).

152. For details about the punitive measures against the Utman Khail, Bunairwal, and Chamlawal, see Nevill, *Campaigns on the North-West Frontier*, 243–7; *The Risings on the North-West Frontier*, 239–50; Wylly, *The Borderland*, 102–5, 152–4; *Frontier and Overseas Expeditions from India*, vol. 1, 311–19, 413–16.

153. Nevill, *Campaigns on the North-West Frontier*, 276–87.

154. Ibid., 287–301.

155. Ibid., 301–5. For details about the punitive expedition against the Afridi and Urakzi, see ibid., 276–306; Wylly, *The Borderland*, 318–37, 407–10; *The Risings on the North-West Frontier*, 143–9, 158–238, xxvii–lxiii; Macmunn, *The Romance of the Indian Frontiers*, 224–40; Holdich, *The Indian Borderland*, 351–64; Swinson, *North-West Frontier*, 244, 246–51; *Frontier and Overseas Expeditions from India*, vol. 2, 74–117, 264–73.

156. Mills, *The Pathan Revolt in North West India*, 10.

157. Spain, *The Pathan Borderland*, 178.

158. Nevill, *Campaigns on the North-West Frontier*, 322.

159. For instances, see Nevill, *Campaigns on the North-West Frontier*, 297, 299–300, 303; *Frontier and Overseas Expeditions from India*, vol. 1, 581; McMahon and A.D.G. Ramsay, *Report on the Tribes of the Malakand Political Agency*, 52; McMahon and A.D.G. Ramsay, *Report on the Tribes of Dir, Swat and Bajour*, 115–16; *The Risings on the North-West Frontier*, 24.

160. Spain, *The Pathan Borderland*, 178. For instances, also see McMahon and A.D.G. Ramsay, *Report on the Tribes of the Malakand Political Agency*, 51–2; McMahon and A.D.G. Ramsay, *Report on the Tribes of Dir, Swat and Bajour*, 113–17; *The Risings on the North-West Frontier*, 23–6; *Frontier and Overseas Expeditions from India*, vol. 1, 587; *Frontier and Overseas Expeditions from India*, vol. 2, 113–16, 435; Elliott, *The Frontier*, 207.

161. Spain, *The Pathan Borderland*, 178.

162. Nevill, *Campaigns on the North-West Frontier*, 317.

163. Elliott, *The Frontier*, 110–11.

164. Spain, *The Pathan Borderland*, 179. For details about the withdrawal of the regular British forces from the advanced positions in the tribal areas, see Baha, *N.-W.F.P. Administration under British Rule*, 12–14; *The Cambridge History of India*, vol. 6, 466–7.

165. *The Cambridge History of India*, vol. 6, 466.

166. Ahmed, *Millennium and Charisma among Pathans*, 111.

167. Swinson, *North-West Frontier*, 251.

168. Spain, *The Pathan Borderland*, 178.

169. For details, see Baha, *N.-W.F.P. Administration under British Rule*, chap. 4: titled 'strategic railways and roads', 107–31; *The Cambridge History of India*, vol. 6, 467.

170. Davies, *The Problem of the North-West Frontier*, 104.

171. Ahmed, *Millennium and Charisma among Pathans*, 111. Also see Caroe, *The Pathans*, 388; Arnold Keppel, *Gun-Running and the Indian North-West Frontier*, repr. (Lahore: SMP, 2004), 1–2.

172. Swinson, *North-West Frontier*, 267.

173. *Administration Report NWFP from 9th November 1901 to 31st March 1903*, 10; *Administration Report on the North-West Frontier Province for 1921–22*, 10.

174. Miller, *Khyber*, 250.

175. Ahmed, *Millennium and Charisma among Pathans*, 93.

7 Formation

The political history of the Frontier under British rule hangs
more on milestones of suppression than on those of reform.
– James W. Spain

THE FRONTIER DISTRICTS, or settled areas, of North-West Frontier
Province, which were part of the Sikh kingdom of Punjab—although
loosely and mostly nominally held—were annexed to the Indian
territories ruled by the Britons through the proclamation of 29 March
1849. For a short while after that, the territories comprised 'the districts
of Peshawar, Kohat [Kuhat] and Hazara [Hazarah] were under the direct
control of the Board of Administration at Lahore'. However, they were
formed into a regular division, under a commissioner, in about 1850.
The territories of the then-districts of Bannu and Dirah Ismail Khan
were put under one deputy commissioner, forming part of the Layah
Division. It remained so till 1861 when two deputy commissioners 'were
appointed and both districts were included in the Derajat Division'.
This arrangement continued till 'the formation of the North-West
Frontier Province.'[1]

Since their direct occupation in March 1849 and making the trans-
Indus Pukhtun areas part of the Punjab province, separation of the
trans-Indus areas was proposed from time to time for various reasons.
Most of the experts on Frontier matters—Bartle Frere, Henry Durand,
Lord Roberts, James Browne, Roberts Warburton, Robert Sandeman,
William Lockhart, Lord Lytton, Charles Aitchison, George Chesney,
and Lord Lansdowne—agreed that there was a need for a separate
Frontier administrative unit, which, according to C.C. Davies, they
'hoped would usher in an era of peace on the blood-stained border
and prove a panacea for most of the evils to which it was subject'.[2]
The issue, however, became more important in the last quarter of the
nineteenth century, especially due to developments in Central Asia
because of the Russian advance as well as the strategic importance of
the trans-Indus areas.

EARLIER SCHEMES FOR SEPARATE FRONTIER ADMINISTRATIVE UNIT

Different schemes were put forward for the formation of a separate Frontier administrative unit after the uprising of 1857. Proposals for the separation of Sindh from Bombay, and its amalgamation with Punjab for 'co-ordinating the Frontier policies of the two administrations', remained the central point of the Frontier question, for which schemes were submitted but to no avail. The Viceroy, Lord Northbrook, submitted a scheme along the same lines: the separation of Sindh from Bombay and its amalgamation with the province of Punjab—which was accepted in principle by Secretary of State for India, Salisbury, in 1876. However, the scheme failed partly because of the potential cost but more so because of opposition by the Bombay Presidency which demanded compensation for giving up its jurisdiction over Sindh.[3]

A 'vigilantly precautionary Frontier policy' was strongly felt to be the need of the day during the viceroyalty of Lytton (1876–80), because of the Russian advance into Central Asia. Salisbury, therefore, thought it wise to bring the western and north-western frontiers of India 'under the direct control of the Government of India' for a unitary action by the government. Accepting his suggestion, in April 1877, Lytton submitted a scheme for the creation of a trans-Indus province. He proposed that the new province should comprise six districts of Punjab, namely Hazarah, Peshawar, Kuhat, Bannu, Dirah Ismail Khan, and Dirah Ghazi Khan (excluding the cis-Indus areas of Bannu and Dirah Ismail Khan) and the trans-Indus Sindh (excluding Karachi). It was also proposed that the province should be headed by a chief commissioner and agent to the governor-general; and there should be two commissioners under him: one each for the Pukhtun and Baluch areas.[4]

Salisbury, however, rejected Lytton's scheme as it involved major changes and a huge financial burden, and proposed an alternative scheme instead. Salisbury proposed that there would be one commissioner each for the trans-Indus Punjab and Sindh, who would be directly appointed by the viceroy; and that the commissioners would be under the Punjab government for their internal administration, but would correspond directly with the viceroy for matters related to external affairs.[5] Nevertheless, the foreign secretary of the Government of India and the Lieutenant-Governor of Punjab condemned Salisbury's scheme and termed 'it as "full of the seeds of future misunderstanding, confusion...divided responsibility", and certain to cause "the worst effect upon the internal administration of the frontier districts".'[6] 'Lytton, however, accepted' Salisbury's scheme and nominated 'Frederick (afterwards Lord) Roberts as the first northern commissioner' for the trans-Indus districts of Punjab. However, further progress was halted by the Second Anglo-Afghan War (1878–80). At the end of the war, Lytton tried to materialise his plan once again, but events did not cooperate and he was replaced by Lord Ripon, who abandoned the scheme because of his objection to the separation of the trans-Indus districts from Punjab and the transfer of Sindh; hence, the scheme fell apart.[7]

During the viceroyalty of Lansdowne (1888–94), 'the Baluchistan Agency was created'—Sindh was no more a Frontier province. Lansdowne, however, wanted the creation of a separate Frontier administrative unit, managed by its own officer, under the direct control of the Government of India. The need to separate the trans-Indus areas from Punjab and to bring them 'under the direct control of the Government of India' was keenly felt—to allow better management and more effective control after 'the tribal uprising of 1897–98'.[8] The uprising had 'triggered off another round in the political controversy over the "Forward Policy", and perhaps the most ferocious of all. This time not only the strategic and military problems of the Frontier were examined but the basic structure of the administrative system'[9] as well. The cardinal point was: 'If the military situation was unsatisfactory, so was the administrative situation.'[10]

A solution was needed to address the situation effectively. So, deliberations took place between the Secretary of State for India, George Hamilton, and Lord Elgin, the viceroy (1894–99). Expressing his dissatisfaction over the existing arrangements, Hamilton suggested to Elgin 'that "the conduct of external relations with the tribes on the Punjab frontier should be brought more directly than heretofore under the control and supervision of the Government of India".' Disagreeing with, and having reservations about, Hamilton's contentions, Elgin noted 'that "very little is said of the grounds on which this opinion is based".'[11] Hamilton, however, later proposed a scheme which was simply a replica of Salisbury's proposal of 1877,[12] but in respect of the trans-Indus areas of the Punjab province only.

Lord Curzon and Formation of the New Province

The Indian government had yet to come to terms with the lessons of the 1897 uprising when the secretary of state for India's despatch of 5 August 1898 was received. The scheme envisaged in the despatch was, as stated above, a mere replica of Salisbury's proposal of 1877. The viceroy consulted his officials of the Punjab government about the proposed scheme and 'the majority of them objected to any dismemberment of the Panjab'. But, 'many of them', however, 'confessed that an entirely new province was the only alternative to the existing system'.[13]

In this backdrop and state of affairs, Lord Curzon became viceroy of India (1899–1905) in January 1899. He belonged to neither of the particular schools of the Frontier policy. Curzon was keenly interested in the affairs of India and agreed with the assessment of the India Office, London. He was determined to take the decision regarding 'who should control the Frontier in the future', and believed that the decision 'should be taken as swiftly as possible',[14] because it seemed to him 'obvious that the management of the difficult frontier areas where both foreign policy and defence were involved should not be divided' between the Punjab and the central governments.[15]

He discussed the matter with his predecessor before the former left India, and with the Lieutenant-Governor of Punjab and other concerned officers of the Frontier. The four possible solutions suggested by him were: (1) to maintain the status quo; (2) to create a Frontier province and commission; (3) to adopt Hamilton's plan; (4) to divide the trans-Indus districts into five or six administrative units under separate political officers.[16]

Curzon was unhappy with the way in which the Punjab government was handling the Frontier's affairs. He expressed his utter disgust with the Punjab government officials' knowledge and lack of interest in the Frontier affairs, and also with the chain of subordinate officials dealing with, and responsible for, the Frontier affairs under the viceroy—who was directly responsible for the Frontier administration but had no authority over appointments, transfers, and removal. Therefore, he had no time for the status quo and urged the creation of a new province comprising the trans-Indus Pukhtun majority areas of the four trans-Indus Frontier districts (Peshawar, Kuhat, Bannu, and Dirah Ismail Khan) and the five political agencies (Agency of Dir, Swat and Chitral, Khyber, Kurram, North Waziristan, and South Waziristan).[17]

Curzon, however, 'developed his case in characteristic fashion', Olaf Caroe asserts. 'First came a siting shot, followed by sharp single shots on the bull's-eye, culminating in a salvo of concentrated rapid fire.' On 5 April 1899, he wrote:

The Viceroy is responsible for the frontier policy, yet he has to conduct it not through the agency of officials directly under him, but through the elaborate machinery of a provincial government, to which the Frontier and its problems are necessarily something in the nature of side-shows, acting as an intermediary. The result is that in ordinary times the Panjab government does the Frontier work and dictates the policy without any interference from the supreme government at all, but that in extraordinary times the whole control is taken over by the Government of India acting through agents who are not its own; while the Panjab government, dispossessed and sulky, stands on one side, criticizing everything that is done.[18]

HAMILTON'S FOUR POSSIBLE OBJECTIONS

The Secretary of State for India, Hamilton, in his despatch of 5 August 1898 had already 'raised four possible objections' to the creation of a new Frontier province: (1) that the scheme would break up the existing 'administrative units of Punjab', would disturb the revenue system in the districts of Peshawar, Kuhat, and Bannu, and that the required trained officers for the revenue system were not available in the political department; (2) that territorial compensation and rectification would be required; (3) that the Punjab government would be deprived of the opportunity to train officers for the Frontier service, and to acquire knowledge about the tribesmen; (4) that it would cause a 'forward and aggressive policy' by the government.[19]

CURZON DEFENDS HIS SCHEME

Curzon, however, successfully defended his scheme in his minute of 27 August 1900, successfully dismissing the objections of the Secretary of State for India, one by one. His proposed solution for the first objection was that experienced officials would be taken from Punjab, as before, to run the revenue system of the new province, leaving the system undisturbed. He considered Hamilton's second objection as invalid because, in his opinion, the change needed no compensation to Punjab as the new province would deprive Punjab of only one-fourteenth of its area, one-fifteenth of its revenue, and less than one-eighteenth of its population. In addition, the area to be separated from Punjab, was not part of Punjab 'geographically, historically, or ethnologically'; and, despite being a part of the province of Punjab, the area was ruled under special rules and regulations that differed from the rest of Punjab. Moreover, the situation on the Frontier had changed greatly due to administrative and territorial changes, and adjustments effected in the preceding years through the creation of the Baluchistan Agency, the Durand Line Agreement, and the bringing of Chitral and Dir under the British sphere of influence and Waziristan under political protectorate. Moreover, these changes had made administration of the Frontier mostly a political affair and had brought it within the supreme government's sphere. Curzon augmented his plea, against any compensation to the Punjab, by citing the opinion of F.D. Cunningham, Commissioner of Peshawar, which he expressed in 1898.[20]

Regarding Hamilton's third objection, Curzon maintained that a separate Frontier province would provide greater opportunities for training the officers of the Frontier service as the officials would now belong to the political department of the Government of India. Officers who were working well with the tribes would not have to fear transfer unless their services were required in Baluchistan or in the political department 'for a more responsible post of a similar nature'; and the transfer, to another posting in the foreign department, of an officer who was not performing well with the tribes would be easily effected. The new Frontier province, moreover, would attract the most able men in both the civil and military services. The opportunity to train the officers would be enhanced, not diminished. Curzon termed Hamilton's fourth objection an 'entire illusion', and rejected it by referring to the history of the preceding fifty years when neither the intervention of the Punjab government proved to be a barrier for 'a forward policy' nor did it save the Government of India from the Frontier wars or forty military expeditions.[21]

In the same minute of 27 August 1900, Curzon sketched out his plan for the separation of the trans-Indus areas from Punjab and for the creation of a separate province, because not only was the area the 'most critical, most anxious and most explosive section of the entire frontier', but was also inhabited, in his opinion, by the 'most numerous, fanatical and turbulent of the Pathan tribes'. However, the Foreign Minister of India, i.e. the Viceroy, did not have the authority to issue orders or appoint subordinate officials but had to do it through the Punjab government.[22] In his opinion, the existing 'long official chain of reference' made quick decisions and swift action impossible, despite their being essential on such 'an exposed frontier'.[23] He further stated about such a system:

> I venture to affirm that there is not another country or Government in the world which adopts a system so irrational in theory, so bizarre in practice, as to interpose between its Foreign Minister and his most important sphere of activity, the barrier, not of a subordinate official, but a subordinate Government, on the mere geographical plea that the latter resides in closer proximity to the scene of action—a plea which itself breaks down when it is remembered that

for five months in the year the Supreme and the Local Governments are both located at the same spot, Simla.[24]

Moreover, Curzon stated that the Frontier's existing system of administration,

> attenuates without diminishing the ultimate responsibility of the Government of India. It protracts without strengthening their action. It interposes between the Foreign Minister of India and his subordinate agents, not an Ambassador, or a Minister, or a Consul, but the elaborate mechanism of a Local Government, and the necessarily exalted personality of a Lieutenant-Governor…. Worked as the system has been with unfailing loyalty and with profound devotion to duty, it has yet been the source of friction, of divided counsels, of vacillation, of exaggerated centralization, of interminable delay.[25]

Therefore, in Curzon's opinion, as stated earlier, the remedy was the creation of a new province comprising the trans-Indus Pukhtun majority areas of the four trans-Indus Frontier districts—the districts of Peshawar, Kuhat, Bannu, and Dirah Ismail Khan—and of the five political agencies of Dir, Swat and Chitral (commonly referred to as the Malakand Agency), Khyber, Kurram, North Waziristan, and South Waziristan. The new province would be headed by a chief commissioner and agent to the governor-general who would not only be 'directly subordinate to the Government of India' but would also be appointed by the said government. Curzon, moreover, elaborated about other senior officials, subordinate staff, the headquarter of the province, the provincial public service commission, the position of the officers belonging to Punjab government and serving in the Frontier at the formation of the new province, how and from where the needed staff would be taken, and so forth.[26] Political charge of Dir, Swat, and Chitral, and their political agent, was not subordinate to the Punjab government but directly to the Government of India, from the inception of the agency.[27] Therefore, it was a question of the separation, from Punjab, of only the four trans-Indus settled districts and the other four political agencies; the Agency of Dir, Swat and Chitral had never been under the Punjab government.

After working on the various aspects of the future Frontier province, and dismissing the objections previously raised by Hamilton, the Secretary of State for India, Curzon's next step was to convince members of the Viceroy's Council. 'At the end of August 1900', copies of his minute were sent to the Council members, and 'a special meeting of the Council' was called 'on 10 September 1900 for [the] final discussion'. The Council agreed, unanimously, with the main provisions of Curzon's minute and it was sent, on 13 September, to the British government for approval.[28]

THE NEW PROVINCE'S SCHEME AND THE PUNJAB GOVERNMENT

Interestingly, Curzon did not consult the Lieutenant-Governor of Punjab—despite describing him as 'one of the most honourable and high-minded of men, possessed of a high sense of duty and gifted with admirable manners'[29]—before sending his proposals to the Secretary of State for India and the approval of the British government. However, after sending the minute, he informed the governor privately, assuring him of consultations and his regard for the interests of the Punjab government if his scheme was approved by the British government.[30]

Mackworth Young, Lieutenant-Governor Punjab, however, resented the behaviour of the viceroy in this matter. He complained that the viceroy had ignored him and shown a lack of confidence in him. However, by November, Curzon asserted:

> I cannot expend hours in wordy argument with my Lieutenant-Governors as to the exact meaning, purport, scope, object, character, possible limitations, conceivable results, of each petty aspect of my Frontier policy. If they deliberately refuse to understand it, and haggle and boggle about carrying it out, I must get some fairly intelligent officer who will understand what I mean and do as I say.[31]

He, later on, also expressed the view: 'The Government of India…has placed between itself and the Frontier the Punjab Government which often knows less and which for twenty years has been an instrument of procrastination and obstruction and weakness.'[32]

Although the Government of India informed the Punjab government in January 1901, after receiving sanction from Britain, and asked for its cooperation in the execution of the scheme, relations between the governor and the viceroy were 'extremely strained' over the issue. Other issues relating to the new province also contributed to their bitter relations. The subordinate staff of the Punjab government resented the way the viceroy had proceeded in the issue, ignoring and bypassing the Punjab government. Herbert Fanshawe, Commissioner Delhi and an ex-Chief Secretary of Punjab, resigned in protest as he felt that 'a great public indignity had been thrust upon the [Punjab] administration as unmerited as it was ungenerous'.[33]

This, however, did not affect the validity of Curzon's case because, 'as some officers pointed out at the time, civil servants are not paid to create policy, but to carry it out'.[34] In Davies' words, 'Fanshawe was obviously in the wrong, for officials in his position were not colleagues of the Viceroy but executive agents, permitted to advise, even with great freedom, but bound, when a decision had been arrived at, to carry it out loyally to the best of their ability.'[35] And Caroe asserts: 'There is little doubt that in the circumstances then ruling Curzon was right.'[36]

FORMATION OF THE PROVINCE

The British government 'yielded gracefully and sanctioned the creation of the new Frontier Province' as they 'could not stand up to convictions pronounced' with Curzon's eloquence.[37] After receiving the approval from the British government, Curzon proceeded with his plan and appointed H.A. Deane, the then political agent of the Agency of Dir, Swat and Chitral, as the first chief commissioner and agent to the governor-general in the new province. He 'asked Deane to work out a plan' that would 'make the new province "independent, self-contained and self-supporting".' Although not included in Curzon's original plan, Deane suggested that the *tahsil*s of Haripur, Abbottabad, and Mansihrah (Mansehra) should also be included in the new province. In Deane's opinion, with the exception of the Abbottabad *tahsil*, Hazarah was a Frontier district and part of the Peshawar Division; it had 'the same Border Military Police System and the Frontier Crimes Regulations'; and a fair number of its inhabitants were of Pathan origin. Making Hazarah part of the new province, moreover, 'would bring the whole of the Punjab Frontier Force' within the limits of a single civil administration, with its headquarter at Abbottabad; it would furnish as a summer health resort for the head of the province and the officers; and would provide a base for the control of 'the cis-Indus Black Mountain tribes'.[38]

Curzon incorporated Deane's suggestion, dismissing Mackworth Young's views and criticisms of the scheme for the separation of areas from the Punjab and for the formation of the new province. He did not even accept Young's request to delay the scheme until his retirement in March 1902. He was too eager to inaugurate the new province at the earliest because, according to him:

The unfortunate attitude of M. Young is known everywhere in the Province, the idea had been widely disseminated that the Local and Supreme Governments are at loggerheads with each other; that the Lieutenant-Governor has successfully defied the Viceroy; and that it is possible that the new scheme may still fall to the ground.[39]

Therefore, the new province, named North-West Frontier Province, was formed on 9 November 1901—the British king's birthday—and formally inaugurated on 26 April 1902, five and half months later, by Curzon at a big *darbar* in Shahi Bagh, Peshawar, attended by 3,000 dignitaries of the province.[40] The province comprised the cis-Indus district of Hazarah and the trans-Indus districts of Peshawar, Kuhat, Bannu, and Dirah Ismail Khan. The trans-border tribal tract comprised the five tribal agencies— namely the Agency of Dir, Swat and Chitral with its headquarter at Malakand, Khyber Agency with its headquarter at Khyber, Kurram Agency with its headquarter at Parachinar, North Waziristan Agency with its headquarter at Miranshah, and South Waziristan Agency with its headquarter at Wana—were also linked or tied with the province for some sort of administrative purposes. In addition to the trans-border area of the five political agencies, the trans-border area 'also contained tribal tracts under the political control of the deputy-commissioners of the adjoining settled districts'.[41] With this, the Government of India assumed direct control in its dealings with the tribal area.

The creation of the new province, beside other things, provided recognition of the Pukhtun concept of oneness, as in Olaf Caroe's opinion, 'it did something to draw together the districts and the tribal territory'.

> Further, the very fact that the administration was subordinate to the Central Government stimulated in those early days a consciousness in the Pathan mind that his concerns and ambitions were of greater than provincial interest, so reviving a tendency, dating from Mughal times, to look to the east rather than to the west. Finally, in Peshawar he had once more a natural centre, one that was dear and familiar to him; no need now, except for pleasure, to travel to Lahore. Not entirely consciously, Curzon had provided a focus for Pathan self-esteem, and so done much to consolidate a firm frontier.[42]

And in J.G. Elliot's words:

> There is no trace in Curzon's dispatches that he was influenced by any motives other than those arising from his pre-occupation in foreign affairs, but he built better than he knew for he gave the Pathan the feeling, after fifty years of playing second fiddle, that he was once again of first importance in the land in which he lived.[43]

CURZON'S ADDRESS

Curzon addressed the *darbar*, held on 26 April 1902, at the formal inauguration of the new province. According to Dr Lal Baha, his 'address to the assembly was a full statement of his Frontier policy', in which he claimed 'sympathy with the new administration' and termed his presence 'proof of his interest in the new Province'. He expressed hope that the formation of the new province 'would lead to "the peace and tranquillity and contentment of the Frontier";' and that its direct 'control by the Government of India' would benefit both the government and people of the province.[44] He, moreover, stated:

> Business will be better done and more quickly done; and there will not be long and vexatious delays. The system of rule will not be altered, but it will be more efficiently worked. Every man in the Frontier districts ought to look upon it as a direct gain to himself that he has a local government on the spot, and that there is nobody above that local Government but the Government of India… Merit will be better known under the new system, service will be more quickly rewarded, abuses will be more promptly checked, responsibility will be more strictly enforced and punishment, when punishment is needed, will be more swift.[45]

Curzon asked the leaders to cooperate with the administration, with special stress on 'the detection and punishment of violent crimes' and in helping the government achieve its objective of 'peace and order in the Province'. He assured them that he would be watching 'the new administration "with a fond and parental eye",' jealously guarding 'local pride and local patriotism', and watching the province show 'itself "ever more and more deserving of the interest that has secured for it a separate existence and an independent name".'[46]

Although 'the idea of forming a new province across the Indus' was not Curzon's brainchild, its creation 'was the consummation of all his frontier policy', which in 'his own words…was "The Keystone of the Frontier Arch".'[47]

ADMINISTRATION AND OFFICIALS OF THE NEW PROVINCE

The head of the new province was designated as the chief commissioner and agent to the governor-general, who was not only appointed by, but was also directly responsible to, the Government of India. He 'combined in his person the administrative charge of the districts with the political control of the tribal belt'.[48] In his capacity as chief commissioner of the province, he had two commissioners under him: judicial and revenue.

The judicial commissioner was the head of the judicial administration of the province. His court was the highest appellate tribunal of the province, both in civil and criminal matters. Two divisional and session judges were subordinate to the judicial commissioner. They decided appeals in civil suits in the capacity of divisional judges, while in the capacity of session judges, they tried session cases and heard appeals in criminal cases.[49]

The revenue commissioner was both 'the controlling and final appellate revenue authority in the Province' in respect of revenue, and also the revenue and financial (finance) secretary to the chief commissioner. Moreover, he was the director of land records and agriculture, commissioner of excise, superintendent of stamps, registrar-general, inspector-general of registration, and registrar of joint-stock companies. For the courts of wards, he undertook the responsibilities of the financial (finance) commissioner and commissioner in the Punjab. Each of the five districts was under one deputy commissioner. The districts were divided into two to five sub-collectorates, called *tahsil*s (in Pukhtu: *tahsilunah*), whereas, the Yusufzi, Mardan, and Nawshirah *tahsil*s in Peshawar, and the *tahsil*s of Tal in Kuhat and Tank in Dirah Ismail Khan districts, formed subdivisions, each headed by an assistant or extra-assistant commissioner under the deputy commissioner.[50] However, it was 'impossible to separate the administration of the five settled districts from the political control of the adjoining unadministered areas'.[51]

As Agent to the governor-general, the head of the province (the chief commissioner and agent to the governor-general) 'controlled political relations' with the tribes of the political agencies in direct communication with the local political agents. A political agent headed each of the five political agencies, and was responsible for the control of the agencies and relations with the tribes. The political agents of the Kurram, North Waziristan, and South Waziristan agencies also wielded the power of district magistrates and courts of session for criminal cases.[52] The political agent of the Agency of Dir, Swat and Chitral also had to act as Agent to the government in affairs with the Indian States/Princely States situated in the agency, namely the states of Dir, and Chitral, and later also Swat.

Line departments, such as health, education, public works, forestry, and jails, were managed by officers who were specially recruited for these departments. The officers of the administrative, judicial, and political departments belonged to the Indian civil service, political department of the Government of India, and the Punjab commission. The posts of chief commissioner and his secretary, assistant secretary, and personal assistants, revenue commissioner and the revenue secretary, deputy commissioners and political agents, judicial commissioner, and the division, session, and district judges were exclusively reserved for persons belonging to the Indian civil service and political department of the Government of India.[53]

SPECIAL FEATURES OF THE PROVINCE

Two Types of Administrative Areas

The Frontier Province was essentially composed of the settled areas that comprised the five districts of Hazarah, Peshawar, Kuhat, Bannu, and Dirah Ismail Khan with their headquarters at Abbottabad, Peshawar, Kuhat, Bannu, and Dirah Ismail Khan, respectively. The tribal area, however—consisting of the five tribal/political agencies: the Agency of Dir, Swat and Chitral (also containing the states of Chitral and Dir, and later Swat as well), Khyber Agency, Kurram Agency, North Waziristan Agency, and South Waziristan Agency, with their headquarters at Malakand, Khyber, Parachinar, Miranshah, and Wana, respectively—was also linked to the province. Each of the districts was administratively headed by a deputy commissioner, and the agencies by a political agent. There was another type of tribal area, linked to the province, called the Frontier Regions. The Frontier Regions were tribal areas in essence, governed on the pattern of the political agencies, with special status and rules but administratively connected to the districts and under the charge of the concerned deputy commissioners.[54] The administrative system and the laws applied to these administrative units—the settled districts and tribal areas—were mostly different from each other.

Chief Commissioner Province

The province was not a full-fledged province, headed by a governor, like the other provinces of British India, but was a chief commissioner province, headed by a chief commissioner and agent to the governor-general. The laws and constitutional rights introduced in, and the reforms granted to, the other provinces of British India—via various acts and reforms—were not extended to the Frontier province. The province, and, to that effect, its inhabitants, therefore, remained deprived of the constitutional rights granted to the other provinces of British India and their inhabitants. It was not until 1932 that the province received the status of a full-fledged province, headed by a governor and agent to the governor-general, and a government with ministers. In 1935, the Government of India Act, 1935, was extended to the province, bringing its settled area and its inhabitants on a par, to some degree or from some counts, with the other provinces of British India and their inhabitants. However, both the types of tribal area: the political agencies and the Frontier Regions, and their inhabitants, were still denied the same rights and status.[55]

Dual Status of Its Head

Unlike the heads of other provinces of British India, the head of the Frontier Province had a dual status. He was called the chief commissioner and agent to the governor-general, and later the governor and agent to the governor-general. He was chief commissioner, and later governor, for the settled area, and Agent to the governor-general for the tribal area, and, had to perform dual duties. For the settled districts, he had the same power, authority, functions, and obligations as the governors of other provinces. For affairs relating to the tribal area, he had to act as Agent to the Governor-General of India and control political relations with the tribes of the political agencies; he had special powers, authority, functions, and obligations that were directly under the supervision and directives of the governor-general.[56]

Simplified Administration

The new system in the province considerably simplified its administration as the authority and power in the settled and tribal areas, was vested in one man: the chief commissioner and agent to the governor-general.[57]

Under Foreign and Political Department and Manned by Political Department's Personnel

Not only was the province under the Foreign and Political Department of the Government of India, but the officers of the Political Department also manned its higher posts, such as the posts of the chief commissioner/ governor, commissioners, deputy commissioners, and political agents.[58]

High Ratio of Staff from Military

Compared to the other provinces, a relatively greater number of officers posted to the province were military men. This was because of the nature of the province which, according to Curzon, 'provided an excellent training ground', and also because of the martial nature of its inhabitants.[59]

Deficit Budget

The province's budget had always been in deficit. As the motive behind, and primary purpose for, the creation of the province was to safeguard British interests along the border and in the region, both the revenue and expenditures of the province were entirely imperial until 1910. Later, a policy of decentralisation was adopted and revenue, under major heads—such as land revenue, stamps, excise, forests, registration, education, health, police, and jails—was transferred to the provincial administration. As regards 'the assigned revenue and expenditures', the chief commissioner had the authority to exercise powers like those exercised by 'the heads of other local governments'.[60] However, 'in general, budget figures indicate that even in good years the provincial administrators were unable to make ends meet'.[61]

To maintain the status quo in the tribal areas, and to safeguard British interests, expenditures were mainly incurred under the political and police heads. These expenditures rose rapidly and included, amongst others, enhanced tribal allowances, remunerations to the tribes in lieu of agreements with them, and the maintenance of increased tribal levies, and Border Military Police. Although 'revenue increased steadily', it did not keep pace with the increase in expenses, because of the 'geographical position and political importance of the Province, considerations of Imperial policy calling for special outlay under political...police, general administration and civil public works'. Therefore, the Government of India shared the responsibility of providing a budget for 'expenditures under' the heads: 'political subsidies', 'refugees and state prisoners', and 'salaries of officers borne on the cadre of the Political Department'.[62] And, as the 'expenditures for security dominated the budget throughout [the] British rule in the twentieth century', the central government provided, by the end of 1930s, 'more than half of the total receipts'[63] for this. It has aptly been observed that the 'critics often fail to realise that expenditure on frontier defence is not merely for the protection of the inhabitants of the settled districts from the marauding incursions of the turbulent tribesmen, but is also for the defence of India as a whole'.[64]

Different Kind of Judicial Administration

The province had a peculiar system of judicial administration. Although there was a judicial commissioner, with a subordinate hierarchy of judicial officials, the applicable laws mostly differed—both in the settled districts and the tribal agencies—from those in the other provinces of British India. The well-known repressive Frontier Crimes Regulation was enacted in the area in 1872 by the Punjab government. Some revisions were made to it in 1887; in 1901, after the creation of the province, the regulation was changed further, but its primitive, repressive, and tyrannical nature remained the same.

Under the Frontier Crimes Regulation, the deputy commissioner held the power 'to refer both civil and criminal cases' to *jargah*s (also written as *jirga, jarga*: plural in Pukhtu: *jargay*) comprising at least three members. He had the discretion to nominate and appoint the members of the *jargah*. The *jargah* members had to investigate a matter on the spot, in light of the ground realities, and submit their report to the deputy commissioner. In case the deputy commissioner was not satisfied with the report of the *jargah*, he had the option to ask the *jargah* for a fresh investigation and report, or to appoint a new *jargah*. The deputy commissioner had to give his decision and verdict based on the *jargah*'s report. However, endorsement by at least three-fourths of the *jargah* members was necessary before the deputy commissioner could issue his decree and verdict. In criminal cases, his powers were restricted to the extent that the accused had the right to object to a member(s) of the *jargah* nominated and appointed by the deputy commissioner. Moreover, in criminal cases 'the maximum penalty' 'was fourteen years rigorous imprisonment' or deportation for life.[65]

The *jargah* adjudicated disputes relating to local customs, matrimonial infidelity, debt, and so forth, without recourse to the ordinary law courts. The final decision of the deputy commissioner could not be challenged in a higher court of law; however, appeal to the chief commissioner, to review the deputy commissioner's decision, was common. Blockade of an unfriendly or hostile tribe was also authorised under the Frontier Crimes Regulation.[66]

In the tribal areas, the traditional methods of deciding disputes were kept intact. However, the political agents of the agencies of Kurram, North Waziristan, and South Waziristan wielded the power of district magistrates and courts of session in criminal cases only.[67]

Dr Lal Baha observes: 'The *jirga* [*jargah*] was a traditional indigenous institution for administering justice, which was recognized and resorted to by the tribesmen themselves. The Government preserved this institution in a modified form, and made use of it in the settled districts as well as in the administered tracts of the Political Agencies.'[68] Although the *jargah* system was an indigenous institution, and decisions of the *jargah*s in disputes forwarded to them, to administer justice, were recognised and resorted to by the people since earlier times as part of *Pukhtu*[69]— also referred to as *Pukhtunwali*, i.e., the Pukhtuns' code of conduct—the system introduced by the colonial government was quite different, as pointed out by James W. Spain who states: 'While the *jirga* [*jargah*] was beyond doubt a Pathan institution, the form it took under the Frontier Crimes Regulations was a far cry from its natural state.'[70] In Qaiyum Khan's words:

> While in theory the Jirga [*jargah*] was to give a finding on facts, which a Deputy Commissioner had to accept if unanimous, in practice, a Jirga was told what opinion or finding was expected of it. Woe to the member of a Jirga who dared flout the wishes of the Deputy Commissioner. His name would be instantly removed from the list of members and he would cease to sit on the Jirga. Sometimes very important civil cases were tried by Jirgas, in utter disregard of the principles of law or natural justice. While in theory the Jirgas were supposed to administer Afghan customary law, in practice all such Jirgas became engines of oppression.[71]

The *jargah*s (in Pukhtu: *jargay*) did not operate in the same way as the traditional system with regards to the power of the deputy commissioner: to nominate and appoint the members of the *jargah*; to term the findings of the *jargah* unsatisfactory; to nominate and appoint another *jargah*; and to give the final verdict himself. Although the decision and verdict of the deputy commissioner had to be endorsed by three-fourths of the *jargah* members for it to be implemented, it was difficult for the *jargah* members to be at loggerheads with the deputy commissioner because of the other powers he wielded in the system. Moreover, as the deputy commissioner had the power to term the investigation and finding of the *jargah* unsatisfactory, and appoint another *jargah* of his own choice, if three-fourths of the *jargah* members did not endorse his verdict, it was an open secret that this peculiar system was mostly used to safeguard the interests of the colonial government and also of the favourites of the administration.[72]

Visible Change Compared to Punjab

There was a visible change in the province's mode of ruling, as compared to the time it was part of the province of Punjab. The separate Frontier Province had a chief commissioner and agent to the governor-general and five deputy commissioners instead of a lieutenant governor and council; a judicial and a revenue commissioner instead of the chief court of Punjab; and ruling by executive regulations, issued by the governor-general or the chief commissioner, instead of the legislative acts passed by the Punjab legislative council.[73]

Security the Main Concern

The main factor responsible for the creation of the province was security, both external and internal. In F.A.K. Harrison's words:

> It should be noted that the main reason why the North West Frontier Province was created was administrative rather than political, with particular emphasis being laid on the importance of the area from the point of view of foreign relations—i.e. developments in the tribal areas having their repercussions in relations with Afghanistan, which itself was unreliable buffer against an expansionist Russian Empire.[74]

Therefore, unlike other provinces of British India, where the political history mostly became a story of the enactment of periodic reforms by the government, the story of the Frontier Province, according to James W. Spain, remained 'one of a struggle for control—a control which was never completely established and a struggle which ended only when the British departed in 1947'.[75]

The province was created solely to serve the cause of the imperial government, mainly in relation to the Russian bugbear. 'But at the same time, and probably unconsciously in intent', as pointed out by F.A.K. Harrison, 'it provided a framework for the development of political consciousness of a very largely Pathan region of which Peshawar and not Lahore was the focal point'.[76]

Notes

1. *Administration Report of the North-West Frontier Province from 9th November 1901 to 31st March 1903* [henceforward *Administration Report of the NWFP from 9th November 1901*

to 31st March 1903] (Peshawar: Printed at the North-West Frontier Province Government Press, 1903), 6.

2. C. Collin Davies, *The Problem of the North-West Frontier, 1890–1908: With a survey of policy since 1849*, 2nd edn. rev. and enlarged (London: CPL, 1975), 104.

3. Curzon's Minute, 27 August 1900, C.C. vol. 319, p. 3 quoted in Lal Baha, *N.W.F.P. Administration under British Rule, 1901–1919* (Islamabad: NCHCR, 1978), 15–16.

4. Lytton's Minute, 'Reorganization of the Frontier, 22 April 1877', L.P., vol. 8 quoted in Baha, *N.-W.F.P. Administration under British Rule*, 16.

5. Curzon's Minute, 27 August 1900, C.C. vol. 319, p. 3 quoted in Baha, *N.-W.F.P. Administration under British Rule*, 16.

6. Ibid.

7. Davies, *The Problem of the North-West Frontier*, 106–7.

8. Baha, *N.-W.F.P. Administration under British Rule*, 17.

9. Arthur Swinson, *North-West Frontier: People and Events, 1839–1947* (London: Hutchinson & Co (Publishers) Ltd, 1967), 251.

10. Ibid., 257.

11. Ibid.

12. See Baha, *N.-W.F.P. Administration under British Rule*, 17.

13. Davies, *The Problem of the North-West Frontier*, 107.

14. Swinson, *North-West Frontier*, 257–8.

15. F.A.K. Harrison, 'The British Interest in the North West Frontier', *Peshawar University Review* (Peshawar), vol. 1 (No. 1, 1974–75), 53.

16. Baha, *N.-W.F.P. Administration under British Rule*, 17.

17. For details, see ibid., 17–20.

18. Olaf Caroe, *The Pathans: 550 B.C.–A.D. 1957*, repr. (Karachi: OUP, 1976), 415.

19. Baha, *N.-W.F.P. Administration under British Rule*, 20–2; Davies, *The Problem of the North-West Frontier*, 113.

20. Curzon's Minute, 27 August 1900, quoted in Baha, *N.-W.F.P. Administration under British Rule*, 20–1. Also see Davies, *The Problem of the North-West Frontier*, 113–14.

21. Baha, *N.-W.F.P. Administration under British Rule*, 22. Also see Davies, *The Problem of the North-West Frontier*, 108–9, 114.

22. Baha, *N.-W.F.P. Administration under British Rule*, 18.

23. Davies, *The Problem of the North-West Frontier*, 108

24. Ibid.; Baha, *N.-W.F.P. Administration under British Rule*, 18–19; Caroe, *The Pathans*, 415–16.

25. Baha, *N.-W.F.P. Administration under British Rule*, 19–20; Caroe, *The Pathans*, 416.

26. See Baha, *N.-W.F.P. Administration under British Rule*, 20; Davies, *The Problem of the North-West Frontier*, 111–12.

27. *Imperial Gazetteer of India: Provincial Series; North-West Frontier Province* [henceforward *Imperial Gazetteer of India, NWFP*], repr. (Lahore: SMP, 1991), 26, 210; *Administration Report of the NWFP from 9th November 1901 to 31st March 1903*, 9.

28. See Baha, *N.-W.F.P. Administration under British Rule*, 20–3.

29. Caroe, *The Pathans*, 416.

30. See Baha, *N.-W.F.P. Administration under British Rule*, 23.

31. Swinson, *North-West Frontier*, 258; Caroe, *The Pathans*, 415.

32. Swinson, *North-West Frontier*, 258; Caroe, *The Pathans*, 415.

33. Baha, *N.-W.F.P. Administration under British Rule*, 23–4; Davies, *The Problem of the North-West Frontier*, 109; Caroe, *The Pathans*, 416–17.

34. Swinson, *North-West Frontier*, 260.

35. Davies, *The Problem of the North-West Frontier*, 109–10.

36. Caroe, *The Pathans*, 418.

37. Ibid., 416.

38. Baha, *N.-W.F.P. Administration under British Rule*, 24–5.
39. Curzon to Hamilton, 17 July 1901, C.C., vol. 161, quoted in Baha, *N.-W.F.P. Administration under British Rule*, 25.
40. Baha, *N.-W.F.P. Administration under British Rule*, 25.
41. *The Cambridge History of India*, vol. 6, *The Indian Empire, 1858–1918, With chapters on the development of Administration 1818–1858*, ed. H.H. Dodwell, *and the Last Phase 1919–1947*, by R.R. Sethi (Delhi: SCC, 1964), 468–9.
42. Caroe, *The Pathans*, 420.
43. J.G. Elliot, *The Frontier, 1839–1947: The Story of the North-West Frontier of India*, with preface by Olaf Caroe (London: Cassell & Company Ltd, 1968), 97–8.
44. Baha, *N.-W.F.P. Administration under British Rule*, 25–6.
45. Quoted in ibid., 26.
46. Ibid.
47. Davies, *The Problem of the North-West Frontier*, 104. Also see *The Cambridge History of India*, vol. 6, 467.
48. Caroe, *The Pathans*, 414.
49. Baha, *N.-W.F.P. Administration under British Rule*, 27; *Imperial Gazetteer of India, NWFP*, 60.
50. Baha, *N.-W.F.P. Administration under British Rule*, 27; *Imperial Gazetteer of India, NWFP*, 58.
51. *The Cambridge History of India*, vol. 6, 469.
52. Baha, *N.-W.F.P. Administration under British Rule*, 26–7.
53. James W. Spain, *The Pathan Borderland*, repr. (Karachi: IP, 1985), 143; Baha, *N.-W.F.P. Administration under British Rule*, 26–7.
54. Also see Davies, *The Problem of the North-West Frontier*, 111–12; *The Cambridge History of India*, vol. 6, 468–9.
55. For details, see Sultan-i-Rome, 'Constitutional Developments Relating to the North-West Frontier Province', *Journal of Law and Society* (Peshawar), vol. 30 (No. 43, January 2004), 79–100; chap. 8 of this book.
56. See Baha, *N.-W.F.P. Administration under British Rule*, 26–7; *Imperial Gazetteer of India, NWFP*, 57–9; Spain, *The Pathan Borderland*, 142; Davies, *The Problem of the North-West Frontier*, 112.
57. Spain, *The Pathan Borderland*, 142.
58. Baha, *N.-W.F.P. Administration under British Rule*, 27.
59. Spain, *The Pathan Borderland*, 143.
60. Baha, *N.-W.F.P. Administration under British Rule*, 28–9.
61. Spain, *The Pathan Borderland*, 148.
62. Baha, *N.-W.F.P. Administration under British Rule*, 29. Also see Spain, *The Pathan Borderland*, 147–8.
63. Spain, *The Pathan Borderland*, 148.
64. *The Cambridge History of India*, vol. 6, 473.
65. Baha, *N.-W.F.P. Administration under British Rule*, 30–1. Also see Spain, *The Pathan Borderland*, 145–6; *The Cambridge History of India*, vol. 6, 471–2.
66. Baha, *N.-W.F.P. Administration under British Rule*, 30–1; Spain, *The Pathan Borderland*, 145–6.
67. See Baha, *N.-W.F.P. Administration under British Rule*, 27; *Imperial Gazetteer of India, NWFP*, 61.
68. Baha, *N.W.F.P. Administration under British Rule*, 30.
69. For some details about Pukhtu, see Sultan-i-Rome, '*Pukhtu*: The *Pukhtun* Code of Life', *Pakistan Vision* (Lahore), vol. 7 (No. 2, December 2006), 1–30; chap. 3 of this book.

70. Spain, *The Pathan Borderland*, 145–6. Also see Abdul Ghaffar [Khan], *Zama Jwand aw Jidujahd* (Pukhtu) (Kabul: DM, 1983), 22–3.
71. Abdul Qaiyum, *Gold and Guns on the Pathan Frontier* (Bombay: HK, 1945), 15.
72. Also see ibid., 15–16,
73. Spain, *The Pathan Borderland*, 144.
74. Harrison, 'The British Interest in the North West Frontier', 53.
75. Spain, *The Pathan Borderland*, 145.
76. Harrison, 'The British Interest in the North West Frontier', 53. Also see Caroe, *The Pathans*, 420.

8 Constitutional Developments

> For reasons of strategy the personal administration of the Chief
> Commissioner should continue and no principle of responsibility
> should be introduced.
> – Montford Report, 1918

WHILE THE AREAS comprising the North-West Frontier Province
(NWFP) formed part of British India, the law, or constitution, of
British India provided a special status to these areas. They were governed
by special laws and regulations formulated by the executive authority
of British India. Initial constitutional development was that the settled
districts of NWFP were annexed by the Britons, making them part of
the province of Punjab (following the annexation of the Sikh kingdom).

These areas 'became regular parts of the Punjab province in 1850
when Peshawar, Kohat [Kuhat] and Hazara [Hazarah] formed a Division
under a Commissioner and Dera [Dirah] Ismail Khan and Bannu, under
one Deputy Commissioner, joined the Leiah [Layah] Division'.[1] Being a
part of Punjab province, these areas had the same constitutional rights as
other parts of the province. However, a special regulation known as the
Frontier Crimes Regulation (FCR) was enacted in 1872, to deal with some
aspects of the affairs of the area, to which some modifications were made
in 1887. The Indian States/Princely States, and the tribal areas adjoining
the province, also held special status.

The next constitutional development was the separation of the then
five districts—Hazarah, Peshawar, Kuhat, Bannu, and Dirah Ismail
Khan—from Punjab, on 9 November 1901, and the formation of the
North-West Frontier Province with the constitutional status of a province,
after which the affairs of the then five tribal/political agencies of Dir, Swat
and Chitral, Khyber, Kurram, North Waziristan, and South Waziristan
were to be conducted through the head of the new province. The new
province, however, was not a full-fledged province but one headed by a
chief commissioner under the direct control of the Governor-General of
India. The chief commissioner also acted as an Agent to the governor-
general, with respect to the affairs of the tribal areas. The Frontier Crimes
Regulation (FCR) was modified and re-promulgated, as FCR, 1901, after

the creation of the Frontier Province. It, however, was still 'notoriously repressive in nature and contrary to all tenets of civil liberty'.[2] Unlike the other provinces of British India, NWFP had no legislative authority, and was deprived of the constitutional provisions already extended to the other provinces as well as those previously extended to the area; when it was part of Punjab province.

In Qaiyum Khan's words: 'The Frontier was [later] likened to a gunpowder magazine, and to introduce reforms in such a land as this, it was asserted, was like holding a match to the gunpowder—an explosion was, of course, inevitable.'[3] The province was, therefore, ruled by the executive regulations issued by the Governor-General of India, or the chief commissioner of the province. Muhammad Ali Jauhar, later, aptly termed the province the land without law (سرزمین بے آئین).[4]

With the change in the political climate in the rest of India, the winds of change were also felt in the Frontier Province. Reform after reform was advocated for, proposed, recommended, and introduced, to develop the constitutional status of the province. The story of all these developments, after the formation of the province, is given below.

MORLEY-MINTO REFORMS, 1909

John Morley, the Secretary of State for India, and Lord Minto, the Viceroy and Governor-General of India, were behind the reforms that were introduced in India in 1909 and commonly known as the Morley-Minto Reforms.[5] The reforms admitted the Indians to limited consultation and involvement in local matters. They also introduced a separate electorate for the Muslims in India. The principles of election, along with nomination of the members of the councils, were also introduced. Members of the councils were given the right to discuss the budget and to 'ask questions and move resolutions' related to 'matters of public interest'. 'The scope of discussion' in the councils was also enlarged.[6] The Frontier Province, however, was kept outside the orbit of the constitutional reforms, and the Morley-Minto Reforms of 1909 were not extended to it. Thus, representative institutions of any type were also denied to the province. According to Diwan Chand Obhrai:

Perhaps these reforms, which were a concession to advanced public opinion in India, and were deemed 'the natural correlative to the repression of violence' in Bengal, were considered unnecessary here as the Province was seemingly satisfied with the existing political conditions, and there was no pressure of popular opinion to support the aspirations of any advanced party then existing in this corner of the country, for the establishment of real representative Government by the Legislative Council, or the inauguration of elective methods in municipalities or district boards. Even the idea of an Advisory Council, of hereditary leaders of the people was never put in the front.[7]

MONTAGU-CHELMSFORD REFORMS, 1919

The Montagu-Chelmsford Reforms of 1919, named after Montagu, the Secretary of State for India, and Lord Chelmsford, the Viceroy and Governor-General of India, were introduced in India after their passage through the House of Commons and their approval by the British Crown. The reforms, which formed the basis of the Government of India Act, 1919, brought vital changes to the structure of both 'the central and provincial governments' in India.[8] The Frontier Province, however, remained deprived of the benefits of the Montagu-Chelmsford Reforms, for these were not extended here.[9]

Interestingly, the Montagu-Chelmsford Report of 1918 had only 'suggested some sort of advisory council' for the Frontier Province and had recommended that 'the province must remain entirely in the hands of the Government of India' because of expediency. However, the suggestion of the advisory council was not honoured and 'the Government of India Act of 1919' brought about no change to the existing constitutional position in the province.[10]

THE BRAY COMMITTEE RECOMMENDATIONS, 1924

The Montagu-Chelmsford Reforms, or the Government of India Act of 1919, which marked 'the introduction of democracy in local bodies investing them with real responsibility in all matters of purely local or Provincial interest', was denied to the NWFP. However, 'a demand for "full-fledged reforms" for' the province came from a section of the population after the Third Anglo-Afghan War of 1919.[11] However, 'the Hindus, not only of the affected areas, but also of other parts of India... opposed' the separation of the Frontier from Punjab, and its creation as a separate province from the very beginning. They continuously struggled 'for its re-amalgamation with the Punjab'.[12] In this connection:

In September 1921, Sir Sivaswami Aiyer moved a resolution in the Central Legislative Assembly urging that judiciary in N.-W.F.P. should be placed under the Punjab High Court (of which Sir Shadi Lal was the all-powerful Chief Justice) and an Inquiry Committee be appointed to examine and report whether the purpose underlying the creation of the separate province of N.-W.F.P. had been fulfilled, and if not why the area should not be re-amalgamated with the Punjab. The resolution was passed and a Committee headed by (Sir) Denys Bray, Foreign Secretary of the Government of India, was appointed to undertake this survey.[13]

The committee was appointed, in April 1922, primarily to look into the administration of the NWFP, and also to examine the working of the province since its inception as a separate province, the question of its re-amalgamation with Punjab, and the possibility of the extension of the Montagu-Chelmsford Reforms to the province. The committee was known as the Bray Committee after its head, Sir Dennys Bray, the Foreign Secretary.[14]

The committee, which consisted of eight members—three Europeans, three Muslims, and two Hindus—submitted its report after touring the province. The report was published in March 1924. The committee, beside other observations, justly noted that when the Frontier Province was separated from Punjab in 1901, the legislative council—created for Punjab in May 1897 with jurisdiction over the settled districts of the North-West Frontier—was withdrawn. If these districts had not been separated, the Morley-Minto Reforms of 1909 and the Montagu-Chelmsford Reforms of 1919 would automatically have applied to them, but did not because of the separation.[15] The committee argued:

> If liberal institutions are now granted to the Frontier districts and the foundations of a Frontier Province are well and truly laid, it is not wholly visionary to hope that with the gradual march of civilization into the tribal tracts these two will eventually join the kindred of the districts in forming a strong and contended community at the danger-point of India's frontiers, a barrier against all possible enemies from the west.[16]

The 'Committee did not see its way to recommend, "full-fledged reforms" for the North-West Frontier Province' or to raise the status of the chief commissioner to governor. It stated that the chief commissioner must remain an agent to the governor-general in matters related to the affairs of the tribal areas, and should remain under the 'wider power' and 'closer supervision' of the governor-general—contrary to the practice in a governor's province. Regarding the 'skeleton constitution' that was recommended by the committee, it was claimed that 'It sets up a

Legislative Council with an elective majority; it includes a Minister, and an Executive Council, and it makes full provision for the introduction of adequate safeguards for the interests of the small non-Muslim minority and for the paramount interest of all India.'[17] However, the majority of the committee recommended:

> The Frontier inhabitants are assuredly not behind the rest of India either in intelligence or capacity to manage their own affairs; their aspirations for reforms have been awakened into full consciousness, and will not be satisfied by anything short of the essentials of the reforms enjoyed elsewhere. Whatever the form of the Council introduced in the Province it must be something live and vigorous. The day for an Advisory Council is past. A Legislative Council is essential.[18]

Since the Hindus were against the separation of the North-West Frontier from Punjab, as they regarded it a danger to their own interests and also 'a political danger for the rest of India', they not only struggled for the re-amalgamation of NWFP with Punjab, but also opposed the extension of reforms to it. The Hindu members of the committee, therefore, opposed the recommendations of its majority members, i.e., the European and Muslim members.[19] 'Sensing an air of communal frenzy' in 'the recommendations of the Committee', the government shelved them for the time-being, considering them to be harmful to the country. Although the government 'officially gave its verdict' in 1925, on the recommendations 'against the re-amalgamation' of the province with Punjab,[20] it paid no heed to the committee's other recommendations. Hence, the report did not lead to the granting of any reforms in the province. Interestingly, Dennys Bray, chairman of the Bray Committee, when appointed head of the Frontier Province, 'declared himself against reforms [in the province] on the ground that they would hurt the Hindu minority'.[21] The Bray Committee recommendations, nevertheless, 'greatly helped' the task of those who were striving for the extension of reforms to the Frontier.[22]

RESOLUTION IN THE CENTRAL LEGISLATURE OF INDIA, 1926

The Frontier Province remained deprived of constitutional reforms and advancement, compared to the rest of the provinces of British India, in spite of proposals and demands from various quarters. But it did not dishearten those who advocated the introduction of reforms in the province; they even raised their voices in the central legislature.

Sahibzadah Abdul Qayyum and Nawab Akbar Khan Huti—nominated non-official members in the central legislature representing the Frontier—particularly the former, 'often advocated in the legislature the cause of the extension of constitutional reforms'[23] to the province. In one such attempt, Sayyad Murtaza Bahadur, a member from Madras, tabled a resolution in the central legislature of India on behalf of the All India Muslim League on 16 February 1926. The resolution stated that the assembly proposes, to the governor-general in council, that those articles of the Indian constitution which were related to the formation of the legislative councils and appointment of ministers may be extended to the NWFP, and the reforms of 1919 may be introduced in the province without delay.[24] The resolution was put up for discussion before the assembly. Sahibzadah Abdul Qayyum, M.A. Jinnah, and others spoke in its favour and pleaded the case of the province. Interestingly, the majority of the Hindu members were against the resolution.[25] Although 'the resolution was passed', 'after a lucid speech' by the mover, nothing positive came out of it as 'no action was taken' for its implementation.[26]

DELHI PROPOSALS, 1927

In December 1926, after its meeting in Guhati, the All India National Congress initiated efforts for a Hindu-Muslim settlement of the outstanding issues. As a result of the initiative, some of the Muslim leaders held a meeting in Delhi which was headed by Muhammad Ali Jinnah. The proposals put forward by the meeting for Hindu-Muslim settlement are known as the 'Delhi Proposals' of 1927. One of the proposals was related to the constitutional position of NWFP, in which it was demanded that reforms should be introduced in NWFP on the same footing as in the other provinces of British India.[27]

NEHRU REPORT, 1928

In 1927, the British government appointed a seven-member commission, comprising members of the British parliament, to meet representatives of all the stakeholders in India and to submit a report so that the Indian viewpoint could be accommodated in the future constitution of India and in the reforms that were due in 1929. The commission was named the Simon Commission, after its head John Simon.

The non-inclusion of Indian members in the commission, was greatly resented in India; all the major parties announced a boycott of, and non-cooperation with, the commission. At this, the Secretary of State for India, Birkenhead, during an India debate in the House of Lords, asserted that 'India's inter-communal wrangles were eternal' and that Indians were unable to agree among themselves on the constitutional issues of India. The All India National Congress took this assertion up 'as a challenge' that had to be faced and answered boldly. Hence, an all-parties conference was convened to draw up a draft constitution in consultation with other parties. As a result of the conference's proceedings (1928), a committee was formed, under the chairmanship of Motilal Nehru, to study the Indian problem and draft a constitution. The memorandum of the committee, known as Nehru Report, 1928, also proposed raising the status of NWFP to that of the other provinces of British India, as recommended by the Muslim League in its Delhi Proposals of March 1927.[28]

JINNAH'S FOURTEEN POINTS, 1929

The Nehru Report was approved at the plenary session of the all-parties conference, held at Lucknow in August 1928, which was not attended by both the wings of the Muslim League. The League and some other Muslim leaders were disappointed with the Nehru Report. At the Calcutta session of the all-parties conference, they pleaded for amendments to the Nehru Report—to bring it into conformity with the Delhi Proposals of March 1927, but to no avail.[29]

Therefore, Muhammad Ali Jinnah, leader of the All India Muslim League, presented his historic demands in 1929—known as Jinnah's fourteen points—to safeguard Muslim interests in the future constitution of India. In this, he also demanded the introduction of reforms in the North-West Frontier Province 'on the same footing as in other provinces' of British India.[30] Interestingly, instead of 'fourteen' points, Sharif al-Mujahid has given 'fifteen' points.[31]

SIMON COMMISSION REPORT, 1930

As mentioned above, the British government appointed a seven-member commission to meet the representatives of all the stakeholders in India and to submit a report so that the Indian viewpoint could be accommodated in the future constitution of India and in the reforms that were due in 1929. Resenting the non-inclusion of Indian members in the commission, all the major parties in India boycotted the commission when its members reached India in February 1928. The commission, however, attempted to seek the cooperation of some groups and individuals.

Two committees of the commission—the Indian Central Committee and the Statutory Commission—went to the NWFP, and received a deputation from the province in Peshawar in November 1928. Although a section of the population of the province demonstrated against the commission's visit to the province, shouting 'Simon go back', groups from all the communities and classes of people, both Muslim and non-Muslim, welcomed the commission to the province as they were anxious to impress their own viewpoint 'on the members of the two Committees sitting in joint conference'.[32] While dealing with the problems of the province, the Indian Central Committee observed, among other points:

> As regards the main question at issue, it appears clear to us that the time has arrived when a beginning should be made of the introduction into the North-West Frontier Province of a system of representative Government. We accordingly recommend that reforms should be introduced into the N.-W. F. Province on the lines of the MORLEY-MINTO REFORMS. After a constitution on these lines has been in operation for a period of ten years, we consider that the question should be further examined, with a view to seeing what advance can then be made.[33]

The Simon Commission submitted its report, which was published in May 1930. The commission stated about the people of the province, that 'their geographical position ought not to deprive them of a share in India's political advance'. It, however, also added that 'it is not possible to change the plain facts of the situation. *The inherent right of a man to smoke a cigarette must necessarily be curtailed if he lives in a powder magazine.*' One of the recommendations of the Simon Commission was 'that steps should' promptly be taken to frame and enact 'proposals for the constitutional advance for N.-W. F. Province by setting up suitable representative institutions'. It, however, also stated that the 'broad principles of policy forbid us to recommend the establishment of the same measure of responsible Government in the N.-W. F. Province as we have proposed for the Governor's Province'. Further, the commission recommended a 'Legislative Council' for the province, consisting of forty members 'with powers of legislation, interpellation and discussion of resolutions and with power of imposing certain taxes and voting supplies in respect of those services which are maintained out of Provincial revenues; but executive responsibilities should, as at present, rest with the Chief Commissioner'.[34] About the composition and powers of the proposed legislative council for the province, the commission recommended that it

> should consist of an elected and a nominated element in about equal proportions. The former element should be composed of representatives of the Khans elected from a special constituency, of members elected by municipalities, and district boards (which as time goes on will acquire a more representative character as the method of composing them by election becomes more general) and of ex-soldiers.[35]

Moreover:

> The nominated element should be selected by the Chief Commissioner and would consist partly of officials and partly of non-officials. One of the former would be the Financial [Finance] Secretary. The latter would be chosen either to give representation to important elements not otherwise provided for, or to bring to the Council persons of weight and experience. Due provision should be made for the representation of minorities, including Hindus and Sikhs.[36]

About the central Indian legislature, the committee recommended that three Muslim and one Hindu members from the province 'should strengthen the Central Legislature', and that they should take part in discussions on all-India questions 'on the same footing' as members from the governor's provinces.[37]

CHIEF COMMISSIONER'S SCHEME OF REFORMS, 1930

Referring to the recommendations of the Indian Statutory Commission, the chief commissioner of the province while expressing his views, in August 1930, stated that 'the grant of reforms to the Frontier Province will lead to disturbances of the peace'. He, however, outlined a more liberal scheme of reforms for the province, than those 'recommended by the Statutory Commission', but with some safeguards. He suggested 'a slight majority' for the elected members in the council, i.e. 51 per cent of the total seats; 'the possible introduction of entirely direct election'; and two ministers in the executive: 'one official and the other non official'.[38]

GOVERNMENT OF INDIA'S PROPOSALS, 1930

The Government of India expressed its views about the Chief Commissioner's Scheme of Reforms in a despatch dated 20 September 1930. The authorities 'were careful to emphasize what the Chief Commissioner had said'.[39] They favoured a more liberal form of government for the province 'than that proposed by the Simon Commission'. Also, they recognised the great changes that had taken place during the years between the formation of the province and the Simon Commission's proceedings and proposals. Hence, they considered that any form of reforms granted to the province that would fall 'short of [the] Provincial expectations would not satisfy the political aspirations of the Province and would thus fail to enlist popular co-operation'. Therefore, like the chief commissioner, they 'recommended the adoption of a Unitary Scheme approximating to the form of Government in other Provinces, but with adequate power secured to the Head of the Province suitable to the particular local circumstances'.[40]

MASS UPSURGE, 1930

Although nothing concrete had come out of the struggles, schemes, and proposals for the extension and granting of constitutional reforms to the Frontier Province, 'the prospects...suddenly brightened up following the mass upsurge of 1930' in the province.

> The British authorities were anxious to restore normalcy in the Frontier and the constitutionalist moderates tried to utilise this psychological factor to their advantage. They and their friends beyond the Frontier attempted to make out that the unrest in the province was due to frustration among people 'over the manner in which their legitimate political aspirations have been consistently ignored by the Government for the last 20 years'... They endeavoured to impress upon the British authorities that unless the province was placed on an equal footing with other provinces and accorded constitutional rights, the unrest would perhaps linger on. Simultaneously they wanted the nationalist agitation in the Frontier to continue and pressurise the Government thereby to their advantage. Sir Abdul Qaiyum Khan [Sahibzadah Abdul Qayyum] was reported to have implored the newly released Abdul Ghaffar Khan to resume in 1931 the Congress-*Khudai Khidmatgar* agitation and thus facilitate the introduction of reforms... Subsequent to the stormy days of 1930, Indian opinion also became generally more sympathetic to the Frontier's demand for constitutional rights.[41]

FIRST ROUND TABLE CONFERENCE AND THE NORTH-WEST FRONTIER PROVINCE SUB-COMMITTEE, 1930–1931

In this backdrop, round table conferences were arranged in Britain in 1930–1931, 1931, and 1932, to examine the issue of reforms and constitutional modifications in India. Although there was intense lobbying against the introduction of reforms in the North-West Frontier Province, Sahibzadah Abdul Qayyum—'an ardent advocate of reforms' for the province and also the sole representative of the province at the round table conferences—not only lobbied intensively in London in favour of the extension of the reforms but also pleaded the province's case successfully at the conference table.[42] Therefore, one of the nine sub-committees—Sub-Committee No. 5—was set up at the First Round Table Conference 'to consider what modifications, if any, are to be made in the General Provincial Constitution to meet the special circumstances of the North-West Frontier Province'.[43] The North-West Frontier Province Sub-Committee, headed by Arthur Henderson, recommended, in principle, that the status of a governor's province should be granted to the NWFP, and that the Montagu-Chelmsford Reforms of 1919 be introduced in the province.[44]

Other recommendations of the Sub-Committee included: provincial subjects in the NWFP should be classified as they were in the governor's provinces; the executive should consist of the governor, assisted by two ministers selected from among the non-official members of the legislature, out of whom at least one should be elected; the governor would also act as Agent to the governor-general as regards the tribal areas and for the administration of the central subjects in the province; ministers would have no concern with the central subjects; there should be a single-chamber legislative council for the settled districts with legislative powers in respect of all provincial subjects; the legislature should comprise both elected and nominated members—in which, the nominated members should not exceed fourteen in a house of forty, and the number of official members among the nominated members should not exceed six or eight.[45]

The All India Muslim League expressed its disappointment over the outcome of the First Round Table Conference by adopting a resolution, on 5 March 1931, which stated:

> The Council of the All India Muslim League while approving of the decision of the Round Table Conference that the North West Frontier Province should be constituted into a separate Province, expresses its regret that the constitution

outlined at the Round Table Conference for the five settled districts of the North West Frontier Province fall short of the Muslim demands and does not give the same legislative and administrative responsibility as is proposed for the other provinces of British India, and considers that this defect should be removed.[46]

HAIG COMMITTEE, 1931

Continuing the work of the North-West Frontier Province Sub-Committee of the First Round Table Conference, the Government of India constituted a Subjects Committee for NWFP, through a resolution of the Government of India in the reforms office in May 1931. It was chaired by Henry Graham Haig (home member of the viceroy's executive council)—hence, named the Haig Committee. 'With reference to the report of Sub-Committee No. 5 of the Round Table Conference', the Haig Committee had

> to make recommendations as to the CLASSIFICATION OF SUBJECTS IN THE N.-W. F. PROVINCE as provincial or central; and on the basis of the classification proposed to examine the allocation of expenditure between the central and provincial heads, and to report the extent to which it would be necessary to supplement the provincial revenues in order to meet the charges under the Provincial head.[47]

The Haig Committee submitted its report and recommendations on 23 June 1931. The committee accepted the principle set by the Sub-Committee No. 5, or the committee for the NWFP, of the First Round Table Conference that the settled districts of the province should constitute the new governor's province and that the tribal areas should continue to be the concern of the centre. The committee also stated, among its recommendations, that the 'subjects which are Central throughout India must be Central also in the N.-W. F. Province'. The principle behind the non-inclusion of items covered by the existing central list was stated to be 'that matters which primarily concern the five settled districts should be provincial; and those which primarily concern tribal territories should be Central'.[48] About the gap between the revenue and expenditure of the province, the committee was of the opinion that the gap could be reduced via 'a central subvention' as the province was not created as a 'result of any popular demand' but 'for the reasons of general Frontier Policy for which the Central Government was responsible'.[49]

SECOND ROUND TABLE CONFERENCE AND CONSTITUTIONAL STATUS OF THE PROVINCE, 1931

In pursuance of the findings of the First Round Table Conference, of the special Sub-Committee of the First Round Table Conference on NWFP, and of the North-West Frontier Province Subjects Committee, the question of the province was discussed at the Second Round Table Conference. Consequently, it was decided to raise the status of the province to a governor's province and to introduce the reforms of 1919. The British Prime Minister, Ramsay MacDonald, declared, on 1 December 1931, at the Round Table Conference:

> We contemplate as one feature of the new order that the North West Frontier Province should be constituted a Governor's provinces [Province], but with due regard to the necessary requirements of the frontier and that, as in all other Governor's [Governors'] provinces, the powers entrusted to the Governor to safeguard the safety and tranquillity of the province shall be real and effective.[50]

WHITE PAPER, 1931

'A White Paper was issued' in December 1931, 'in consultation with [the] Indian representatives', containing 'detailed proposals for consideration by a Joint Select Committee' of the British parliament. The committee was required to submit its report on the proposals. The proposals, in respect of NWFP, were: the province would have a legislative assembly with a total of fifty seats: thirty-six Muslims, three Sikhs, nine general, and two land-holders special; the allocation of seats and the method of election for the provincial legislature would be in accordance with the 'Communal Award'; modifications to the communal elected arrangements were to 'be made after ten years' and with the assent of the affected communities for which suitable means were to be devised.[51]

RAISING THE STATUS OF THE PROVINCE, 1932

After a hard struggle by both the local and national organisations, as well as individuals, and also due to Sahibzadah Abdul Qayyum's struggle and role at the Round Table Conference, the British considered it appropriate to redress the grievance of the status and constitutional position of the NWFP. Hence, the Viceroy, Lord Wellington, declared in his opening address to the central legislative assembly on 25 January 1932:

In the new Constitution, the N.-W. F. Province will find a place, as Governor's Province of the same status as other Governor's Provinces, with due regard to the necessary requirements of the Frontier; but in the meantime, my Government and the Chief Commissioner have been earnestly engaged in preparing a constitution which will forthwith place the Frontier Province on the basis of a Governor's Province under the present Act.[52]

On 18 April 1932, Lord Wellington installed Sir Ralph Griffith, the then chief commissioner of the province, as the Governor of NWFP. The province was thus given the status of a governor's province, and the Montagu-Chelmsford Reforms of 1919 were extended to it. A legislative council was set up consisting of 40 members: 28 elected and 12 nominated. Of the 28 elected members, 22 were Muslim, 5 Hindu, and 1 Sikh. Among the 12 nominated members, 5 were European, 1 Muslim, and 1 Sikh were official while 4 Muslim and 1 Sikh were non-official members. Sahibzadah Abdul Qayyum became the sole appointed minister of the Transferred Subjects—education, public health, and local self-government—and Abdul Ghaffur Khan of Zaidah[53] was nominated as the first president/speaker of the council. The viceroy inaugurated the Frontier Legislative Council; its oath-taking ceremony was held at the Victoria Memorial Hall in Peshawar—currently, the Peshawar Museum Hall—on 29 April 1932. The viceroy addressed the council and read out the message of the British Crown. He also announced the suspension of the Frontier Crimes Regulation for one year, to demonstrate the positive spirit of the colonial government.[54]

Thus, 'at long last, after exactly thirty[-]one years of existence', the province 'received its first instalment of constitutional government. The development was significant, particularly in the light of the British belief in the Frontier's strategic importance and their policy to keep it "closed" from other parts of India.'[55] However, according to Amit Kumar Gupta, it 'was primarily meant to placate the agitated Frontier people. It was not an act of instantaneous magnanimity but a retreat under duress—a concession to quieten the popular discontent.'[56]

Nevertheless, the tribal areas were denied the rights and reforms introduced in the settled districts. They neither had representation in, nor were they under the jurisdiction of, the legislative council. Therefore, the new constitutional development and the raising of the status of the province, from chief commissioner-ship to governor's province, did not bring any change to the tribal areas.

GOVERNMENT OF INDIA ACT, 1935

As the status of the province had been raised to that of a governor's province in 1932, the Government of India Act, 1935—passed on 2 August 1935, to make further provision for the Government of India—was also extended to the NWFP. The province was a governor's province under section 46 of the Act. Thus, more constitutional reforms were introduced in the province on the same footing as the rest of the governor's provinces in India.[57]

The status of the legislative council was raised to that of the legislative assembly; the number of its members was raised to 50 from 40. Nomination of members was abolished; all members were now to be elected. The allocation of seats was: 36 Muslims, 9 General, 3 Sikhs, and 2 landlords—as mentioned in the proposals for Indian Constitutional Reforms and published in the 'white paper' of December 1931.[58] 'The Act and the Instrument of Instructions', moreover, stated:

> that, under Provincial autonomy, in all matters falling within the ministerial field, including the position of the minorities, the services, etc., the Governor will ordinarily be guided in the exercise of his powers by the advice of his ministers, and that those ministers will be responsible not to Parliament but to the Provincial legislature.[59]

THE PROVINCE AS PART OF PAKISTAN, 1947

Under section 2, subsection (2), paragraph (c), of the Indian Independence Act of 1947, as a result of the referendum held in the province in July 1947, territories of the NWFP became an integral part of the new dominion of Pakistan that came into being on 15 August 1947 under section 1 (1) of the Indian Independence Act, 1947.[60]

Keeping in view the common perception and the queries in this respect, it needs to be highlighted that on 14 August 1947 neither did India gain freedom and get divided into the two dominions of India and Pakistan, nor did Pakistan come into being on that day. The British gave up their power, and the two dominions of India and Pakistan came into being, simultaneously at zero hour or the midnight of 14–15 August 1947—as 14 August ended and 15 August began—under the above-mentioned section 1 (1) of the Indian Independence Act of 1947.

On 14 August 1947, only 'the formal ceremony of the transfer of power to the Government of Pakistan was to take place'[61] and 'the last ritual of the termination of the British Raj and the birth of Pakistan was to take place', in the Assembly building of Pakistan at Karachi;[62] 'Because Mountbatten was scheduled to hold the same type of function in New Delhi on August 15 and thus was not available on the actual transfer date. He could not even make it on August 16 because according to Indian Independence Act Pakistan areas would pass out of the British control on August 15.'[63] On 15 August 1947, 'the oath taking ceremony of Jinnah as the first Governor-General of Pakistan' took place in Karachi in the Governor-General House and 'Justice Mian Abdur Rashid, the Chief Justice of Lahore High Court, administered the oath to Jinnah.'[64] The point has further been clarified by Dr Farooq Ahmad Dar, in a note, as follow:

According to the Indian Independence Act, both Pakistan and India were to get independence on August 15, 1947. The Transfer of Power ceremony only took place in Karachi on August 14 because Mountbatten had to be there in Delhi on August 15. Otherwise in his speech at the Constituent Assembly of Pakistan on August 14, Mountbatten clearly declared that "Tomorrow the Government of the new Dominion of Pakistan will rest in your hands." See Mountbatten's Address in CAP [Constituent Assembly of Pakistan], August 14, 1947, in *Constituent Assembly of Pakistan Debates*, vol. I. No. 4, p. 49. Jinnah also in his broadcast address to the nation said, "August 15 is the birthday of the independent and sovereign State of Pakistan." See Broadcast by M.A. Jinnah, August 15, 1947 in Zaidi, ed. *Quaid-i-Azam Mohammad Ali Jinnah Papers*, vol. V, pp. 1–2. Independence Day used to be celebrated on August 15 between 1947 and 1953.[65]

It, too, should be noted that though Aqeel Abbas Jafri has proved—through the Hijrah calendar, the Indian Independence Act, 1947, other official correspondence, communiqué, Mountbatten's message and declaration of independence, announcements of Radio Pakistan from Lahore, Peshawar, and Dhaka radio stations, M.A. Jinnah's recorded message (broadcasted from Radio Pakistan on 8:30 a.m. on 15 August 1947), *Daily Dawn*'s first issue from Karachi, Pakistan's postal tickets, and so forth—the date of the emergence of Pakistan to be 15 August, he has contended, on the basis of official documents available in the National Documentation Centre Islamabad, that in the cabinet meeting, held in Karachi, chaired by Prime Minister Liaquat Ali Khan, on 29 June 1948, it was decided that the independence day should be celebrated on 14 August rather than 15 August. However, per the statement of the Prime Minister, Liaquat Ali Khan, this decision was not final as he would bring this into the notice of the Governor-General (M.A. Jinnah) and the final decision would be made after his approval. The official minute of the proceedings carry at the end in parenthesis: '(Quaid-i-Azam has approved the suggestions).' Hence, it was conveyed to all concerned that Pakistan's Independence Day celebrations would be held on 14 August. In pursuance of what has been said above, functions to celebrate Pakistan's first Independence Day were held on 14 August 1948. Although since then the Independence Day is celebrated on 14 August, rather than 15 August, this fact could not be changed or falsified that Pakistan's Independence Day is 15 August.[66]

NWFP General Elections Bill, 1951

In March 1951, the Constituent Assembly of Pakistan passed the North-West Frontier Province General Elections Bill, which paved 'the way for general elections on the basis of universal adult franchise' and raised the number of provincial assembly members from 50 to 85, of which only three were reserved.[67]

Report of the Basic Principles Committee, 1954

The Constituent Assembly of Pakistan appointed a committee, by a resolution dated 12 March 1949, to submit a report, in accordance with the Objectives Resolution, 'on the main principles on which the future Constitution of Pakistan should be framed'.[68] This committee, called the Basic Principles Committee, carried out its assigned tasks and submitted its report—Report of the Basic Principles Committee—in 1954.

In its report, the committee replaced the word 'province' with 'unit'. The report also recommended, in addition to the existing provinces of West Pakistan, the status of units for the tribal areas, Bahawalpur, Baluchistan states, Khairpur state, and the capital of the federation—for allocation of seats in the federal legislature, within the total 60 seats allocated for the West Pakistan.[69] Hence, the NWFP was treated as one unit and the tribal areas as a separate unit. Moreover, paragraph 98 (1) stated: 'For each Unit there should be a unicameral Legislature composed of members chosen by direct election.'[70] Also, under paragraph 98 (2) the number of the members of a unit's legislature 'should not be less than 75 and not more than 350'. However, the total number of seats for each of the units' legislature could be determined by the federal legislature, subject to the specified limits and 'the actual number of seats to be reserved for various communities on the basis of population as far as practicable'.[71] The title 'Governor' would be replaced by 'the Head of the Unit', while 'Chief Minister' was preserved for the head of the council of ministers of the unit.[72] Special provision was mentioned for the tribal areas under part V, chapter II.[73]

Nevertheless, in the report of the Basic Principles Committee, as adopted by the Constituent Assembly of Pakistan on 6 October 1954, the country was divided into two zones: eastern and western. The former comprised East Bengal, while the latter comprised all the areas of West Pakistan, divided into four constituent parts with NWFP, Frontier States, and the tribal areas being one of its parts.[74] Although paragraph 106, subparagraph (1) maintained that 'for each Unit there should be a unicameral Legislature composed of members chosen by direct election', in the subsequent subparagraph (2), in respect of the number of seats for the units legislature it stated:

> The Federal Legislature may by law determine–
>
>   (*i*)   the total number of seats for the Legislature of a Unit;
>   (*ii*) the actual number of seats to be reserved for various communities on the basis of population, as far as practicable; and
>   (*iii*) the number of seats to be reserved for women for a period of ten years from the commencement of the present constitution.[75]

The terms 'Head of the Unit' was used for the 'Governor', and 'Unit' for 'province'. It also stipulated, 'The life of the Legislature of a Unit should be five years unless sooner dissolved.'[76]

ONE UNIT AND LOSS OF PROVINCIAL STATUS, 1955

The Government of Pakistan resolved to do away with the separate provinces and other units of the then western wing of Pakistan, and to integrate them into One Unit or the Province of West Pakistan. So, the Establishment of West Pakistan Act, 1955, was passed by the Constituent Assembly of Pakistan on 30 September 1955, which received the assent of the Governor-General of Pakistan on 3 October 1955. In section 2, titled '*Integration of the Provinces and States into West Pakistan*', subsection (1) stated:

> The Governor-General shall declare by public notification that as from the date specified in such notification, hereinafter referred to as the 'appointed day', the territories which, before the appointed day, were the territories of–
>
>   (*i*) the Governors' Provinces of the Punjab, the North-West Frontier and Sind,

(*ii*) the Chief Commissioner's Province of Baluchistan and the Capital of the Federation.

(*iii*) the States of Bahawalpur and Khairpur, and the Baluchistan States Union.

(*iv*) the Tribal Areas of Baluchistan, the Punjab and the North-West Frontier, and the States of Amb, Chitral, Dir and Swat (hereinafter referred to as the 'specified territories'), shall be incorporated into the Province of West Pakistan.[77]

On 5 October 1955, the Establishment of West Pakistan Act, 1955 (*Order under section 2*) was issued, as Gazette, Extraordinary. It stated:

In exercise of the powers conferred by subsection (1) of section 2 of the Establishment of West Pakistan Act, 1955, the Governor-General is pleased to declare that on and from the 14th day of October 1955 the territories immediately before that day included in–

(*i*) the Governors' Provinces of the Punjab, the North-West Frontier and Sind;

(*ii*) the Chief Commissioner's Province of Baluchistan and the Capital of the Federation;

(*iii*) the States of Bahawalpur and Khairpur, and the Baluchistan States Union; and

(*iv*) the Tribal Areas of Baluchistan, the Punjab and the North-West Frontier, and the States of Amb, Chitral, Dir and Swat shall be incorporated into the Province of West Pakistan.[78]

Thus, the North-West Frontier Province lost its separate entity in spite of opposition by some political circles.

The tribal areas of Baluchistan, the North-West Frontier, and the states of Amb, Chitral, Dir, and Swat were made into, and referred to, as 'special areas' under section 2, subsection (3); and it was stated that 'nothing in this Act shall authorise any change in the internal administration' of the special areas 'except in accordance with this subsection'. The special provisions (*a*), (*b*), (*c*), and (*d*) that would apply to the special areas were given under this subsection (3).[79]

CONSTITUTION OF 1956

After its merger in the One Unit of West Pakistan, under the Establishment of West Pakistan Act of 1955, the former North-West Frontier Province became part of the province of West Pakistan under article 1 (2) of

'The Constitution of the Islamic Republic of Pakistan (1956)' adopted on 2 March 1956.[80] Here, too, the word 'provinces' was used instead of 'units'.

However, along with the tribal areas of Baluchistan and Punjab, the Frontier States of Amb, Chitral, Dir, and Swat and the North-West Frontier tribal areas were defined as 'Special Areas' and special status was given to them under article 104, which made the areas constitutionally different from the rest of the province of West Pakistan.[81]

CONSTITUTION OF 1962

'Report of the Constitution Commission appointed by President Ayub Khan' suggested the continuation of the One Unit.[82] It was maintained under article 1 (2) of the Constitution of the Republic of Pakistan (1962), enacted by the then President of Pakistan, Muhammad Ayub Khan, on 1 March 1962.[83] Hence, the former North-West Frontier Province remained a part of the province of West Pakistan.

However, along with the tribal areas of Baluchistan and Punjab, the tribal areas of the North-West Frontier—as they were on 13 October 1955—and the states of Amb, Chitral, Dir, and Swat were defined as 'Tribal Areas' and special status was given to them under article 223, which made the areas constitutionally different from the rest of the province of West Pakistan.[84]

PROVISIONAL CONSTITUTION ORDER, 1969

With the abdication of Ayub Khan, and the proclamation of martial law on 25 March 1969, the previous status of the province of West Pakistan and the special status of the Frontier States and the North-West Frontier tribal areas, known as the 'Tribal Areas', was retained under article 3 (1) of the Provisional Constitution Order which stated:

Notwithstanding the abrogation of the Constitution of the Islamic Republic of Pakistan brought into force on the 8th day of June 1962, hereinafter referred to as the said Constitution, by the Proclamation and subject to any Regulation or Order made, from time to time, by the Chief Martial Law Administrator, the State of Pakistan shall, except as otherwise provided in this Order, be governed as nearly as may be in accordance with the said Constitution.[85]

RESTORATION OF THE PROVINCIAL STATUS, 1970

After about fifteen years of the creation of One Unit, it was decided to restore the former provinces of West Pakistan, NWFP being one of them, under President's Order No. 1 of 1970. The order, among other points, stated—as declared by the president and chief martial law administrator in his address to the nation on 28 November 1969—that 'the Province of West Pakistan would be dissolved and in its place new Provinces would come into being'. Hence, it was stated that 'in pursuance of the Proclamation of the 25th day of March 1969, and in exercise of all powers enabling him in that behalf, the President and Chief Martial Law Administrator is pleased to make and promulgate the following Order'. Article 4 of this order entitled '*Constitution of new Provinces, etc.*' stated:

(1) As from the appointed day, the Province of West Pakistan, as it existed immediately before that day, shall cease to exist and there shall be constituted in its place four Provinces to be known respectively as (*a*) Baluchistan, (*b*) the North-West Frontier Province, (*c*) the Punjab and (*d*) Sind, and the following Centrally Administered Areas, namely:—

(*a*)   the Islamabad Capital Territory; and
(*b*)   the Centrally Administered Tribal Areas.

(2) The territories of the new Provinces and the Centrally Administered Areas shall be as set out in the Schedule.[86]

The areas that would be included in the North-West Frontier Province, under this order and referred to in article 4 (2), were given in the schedule as under:

Territories of–

(*a*)   Peshawar Division including former Amb State and Tribal Areas adjoining Hazara [Hazarah] District but excluding other Tribal Areas;
(*b*)   Dera [Dirah] Ismail Khan Division;
(*c*)   Malakand Division including the former States of Dir, Swat and Chitral and the Malakand Protected Area, but excluding other Tribal Areas.[87]

It is noteworthy that the Centrally Administered Tribal Areas were not made a part of NWFP under article 4 (2) of the Province of West Pakistan (Dissolution) Order, 1970. These areas were dealt with separately under their own heading, 'Centrally Administered Tribal Areas', about which it was stated: 'Such of the Tribal Areas as defined in the Constitution of 1962 as have not been shown in this Schedule as included in any of the new Provinces'.[88] However, the territories of the former states of Amb, Dir, Swat, and Chitral, the Malakand Protected Area, and the tribal areas adjoining Hazarah District were made part and parcel of the North-West Frontier Province.

This order, however, was only published. A later gazette notification, of 16 June 1970, stated: 'In exercise of the powers conferred by clause (2) of Article 1 of the Province of West Pakistan (Dissolution) Order, 1970 (P.O. No. 1 of 1970) the President is pleased to appoint the 1st day of July 1970, to be the date on which Articles 3 to 17 (both inclusive) and Article 21 of the said Order shall come into force.'[89] Thus, after about fifteen years, NWFP was restored, on 1 July 1970, as a governor's province.

LEGAL FRAMEWORK ORDER, 1970

The word 'province' was retained under the Legal Framework Order, 1970; under article 3 (2), it stated, about the provinces, that 'references to a Province and a Provincial Assembly shall be construed as references respectively to a new Province provided for in the Province of West Pakistan (Dissolution) Order, 1970, and the Provincial Assembly for such Province'. In article 5, reference was made to the number of members of the provincial assemblies to schedule II of this Legal Framework Order, wherein the number of members for NWFP was 42 out of which 40 were general seats and 2 were for women.[90]

INTERIM CONSTITUTION, 1972

'The Interim Constitution of the Islamic Republic of Pakistan' of 1972 stated that the Islamic Republic of Pakistan would comprise *inter alia* 'the Provinces as they existed immediately before the commencing day', i.e., 21 April 1972.[91] Details about the provincial governors, administration of provincial affairs, the provincial legislature, provisions regarding members of provincial assemblies, legislative procedure, procedure in financial matters, general procedure, legislative powers of the governor, and provisions in case of failure of the constitutional machinery were given in Part IV of the Interim Constitution.[92]

Under article 260 (*c*) of the Interim Constitution of 1972, the Centrally Administered Tribal Areas adjoining NWFP (now Khyber Pukhtunkhwa) were mentioned separately from the province—as were previously under article 4 of the Province of West Pakistan (Dissolution) Order, 1970. Moreover, under article 260 clause (*a*) ii 'the former States of Amb, Chitral, Dir and Swat' were also mentioned as tribal areas. But under clause (*b*) of the same article it was stated about the 'Provincially Administered Tribal Areas' that it 'means– (*i*) the districts of Chitral, Dir and Swat (which includes Kalam), Malakand Protected Area, the Tribal Area adjoining Hazara [Hazarah] district and the former State of Amb;…'.[93] It is to be emphasised that these areas held special status before the emergence of Pakistan, which continued after as well—as is evident from the preceding pages. Although they were made part of the Frontier Province under the Province of West Pakistan (Dissolution) Order, 1970, their special status was not done away with.

Thus, not only were the Provincially Administered Tribal Areas (PATA) created, but specified as well, for the first time. Article 261 stated that '(1) Subject to the provisions of this Constitution, the executive authority of the Federation shall extend to the Centrally Administered Tribal Areas, and the executive authority of the Province shall extend to the Provincially Administered Tribal Areas therein'. In the succeeding clauses, (3) to (5), details of the procedures that would be adopted for the extension of any law, ordinance, etc. to the tribal areas and of making regulations for these areas, and in clause (7) status of the jurisdiction of the Supreme Court and High Court in respect of these areas were given.[94]

In spite of the special status, the PATA were given representation in the provincial legislature as they were part of the province, but the Centrally Administered Tribal Areas were not granted representation in the provincial legislature because they were not part of the province.

CONSTITUTION OF 1973

In the *Constitution of the Islamic Republic of Pakistan, 1973*, NWFP was one of the four provinces mentioned under article 1 (2) (a), along with the other areas to which the constitution will apply. In Part IV of the Constitution, major issues relating to the provinces—the governors, provincial assemblies, financial procedure, ordinances, provincial governments—were stated,[95] which also applied to NWFP as one of the provinces of Pakistan.

Moreover, not only was the PATA retained, but the areas of the Centrally Administered Tribal Areas and PATA and the procedures that would be adopted for the extension of any law, ordinance, etc. to both the types of the tribal areas, were also retained as they were in the Interim

Constitution of 1972. However, in the Constitution of 1973, the title 'Centrally Administered Tribal Areas' was replaced with 'Federally Administered Tribal Areas' (FATA) under article 246.[96]

A significant aspect of the Constitution of 1973 was that the number of provincial assembly (of NWFP) members was increased to eighty. Three additional seats were reserved for the non-Muslim minorities; 5 per cent (on top of the total number of 80 members) additional seats were reserved for women until the expiration of a period of ten years from the commencing day of the constitution or the holding of a second general election to the assembly of the province, whichever occurred later.[97] Thus, the total number of Assembly members became 87: i.e. two more than the number that existed at the time of the establishment of the West Pakistan province in 1955, and sanctioned under the NWFP General Elections Bill of 1951.

PRESIDENT'S STATEMENT, 1973

The President of Pakistan, in his statement about provincial autonomy in the Constitution of 1973, which was also applicable to NWFP, stated:

> The subject which has most agitated the minds of the people concerns the relations between the Centre and the Provinces and the extent of provincial autonomy. The Constitution attempts to provide maximum provincial autonomy consistent with integrity and unity of the country. Consequently, it provides the Centre with responsibility in specified fields while all the residuary powers are with the Provinces.
>
> Financial autonomy is an essential element in any scheme of provincial autonomy. Provinces should have command over their financial resources. The present position where the elastic sources of revenue were mostly with the Centre giving little scope to the Provinces to mobilise resources for their development has been radically changed under the new Constitution.... I feel that this Constitution is a bold measure in favour of decentralisation and provincial autonomy.[98]

MARTIAL LAW OF 1977

On 5 July 1977, the Army Chief, General Muhammad Ziaul Haq, imposed martial law in the country and proclaimed that the constitution 'shall remain in abeyance'.[99] However, the Chief Martial Law Administrator's Order 1 of 1977 proclaimed under article 2 (1):

Notwithstanding the abeyance of the provisions of the Constitution of the Islamic Republic of Pakistan, hereinafter referred to as the Constitution, Pakistan shall, subject to this Order and any Order made by the President and any Regulation made by the Chief Martial Law Administrator be governed as nearly as may be, in accordance with the Constitution.[100]

The previous constitutional status of NWFP, and the number of provincial assembly seats, were thus retained.

REVIVAL OF THE CONSTITUTION OF 1973, 1985

On 2 March 1985, President's Order regarding the revival of the Constitution of 1973 was issued and enforced with immediate effect.[101] Under this order, the previous status of the province continued as before.

PROVISIONAL CONSTITUTION ORDER, 1999

On 14 October 1999, the Army Chief, General Pervez Musharraf, declared emergency in the country. Taking power into his own hands, as the Chief Executive, he kept the constitution in abeyance. The Provisional Constitution Order, 1999, however, stated under article 2 (1):

Notwithstanding the abeyance of the provisions of the Constitution of the Islamic Republic of Pakistan, hereinafter referred to as the Constitution, Pakistan shall, subject to this Order and any other Orders made by the Chief Executive, be governed, as nearly as may be, in accordance with the Constitution.[102]

Article 5 of the order further stated: 'Notwithstanding the abeyance of the provisions of the Constitution, but subject to the Orders of the Chief Executive all laws other than the Constitution shall continue in force until altered, amended or repealed by the Chief Executive or any authority designated by him.'[103] Thus, the previous constitutional status of NWFP remained intact.

It is to be underlined that though the army toppled Nawaz Sharif's elected government on 12 October 1999, and General Pervez Musharraf assumed power on the night between 12 and 13 October, the official proclamation was issued on 14 October 1999—under which emergency was declared in Pakistan and General Musharraf assumed the powers of the Chief Executive.

LEGAL FRAMEWORK ORDER, 2002

Under the Legal Framework Order of 2002, the Constitution of 1973 was revived but 'with the amendments made herein'.[104] The Legal Framework Order of 2002 retained the constitutional status of NWFP. The significant aspect of, and change brought about by, the Legal Framework Order of 2002 was the increase in the total number of provincial assembly seats to 124: out of which 99 were general seats, 22 were reserved for women and three for non-Muslims.[105]

CONSTITUTION 18TH AMENDMENT ACT, 2010

In 2010, the Pakistan legislative organs (National Assembly and Senate) passed 'The Constitution (Eighteenth Amendment) Act, 2010'. When President Asif Ali Zardari approved it, it became part of the Constitution. A significant aspect of this is the amendment in article 1 of the Constitution, under which the words 'North West Frontier' were changed to 'Khyber Pakhtunkhwa',[106] and thereby the name of the province changed from the North West Frontier to Khyber Pukhtunkhwa. In addition, a number of subjects were devolved to the provinces—a step towards provincial autonomy.

THE CONSTITUTION (25TH AMENDMENT) ACT, 2018

In May 2018, the Constitution (25th Amendment) Act, 2018 (Act No. 37 of 2018), brought a sea change regarding the Khyber Pukhtunkhwa province, as the existing special constitutional status of the so far Federally Administered Tribal Areas (commonly known as FATA), adjacent to the province, was brought to an end and the areas were made integral part of the province. Moreover, the existing constitutional status of the Provincially Administered Tribal Areas of the province (commonly known as PATA) was also brought to an end. Another significant aspect of, and the change brought about by, this amendment is increase in the number of the provincial assembly seats from 124 to 145: 115 general seats, 26 reserved for women and 4 for non-Muslims.[107] Although the amendment also speaks of the merger of the PATA into the province, it is technically unsound as the areas were part of the province since 1970, under article 4 (2) of the President's Order No. 1 of 1970, as stated earlier, and the succeeding constitutional documents and hence representation in the provincial assembly.

It is worth-noting that the manner in which the 25th Amendment in the Constitution was made and the special status of FATA and PATA was brought to an end suggests that something is wrong at the bottom. There was an inbuilt and clear mechanism for bringing an end to the special constitutional status of FATA and PATA in article 247 (6) of the Constitution, under which seeking the consent of the people concerned was required or obligatory for such a change. Disregarding the existing mechanism in the Constitution and seeking the consent of the people concerned, the change was brought about by making an amendment in the Constitution. This amendment was first approved in a hurriedly called meeting of the National Security Council, and then in other such hurriedly called meetings of the cabinet, National Assembly, Senate and the Khyber Pukhtunkhwa Provincial Assembly. The draft of the Amendment was not provided to the members of the cabinet, federal and provincial assemblies and the Senate per procedure well in time for reading, consultation and debate over it. It was provided to them moments before their meetings and they were not given the chance and time for an open debate. Besides, till its passage by the National Assembly, no hint or indication of bringing an end to the special status of PATA was given to the public, because of the expected opposition of the people of PATA to such a change. Prior approval of this amendment from the National Security Council, and completing the process of its passage and approval from five different forums in five days (only in one day from one forum), rather collectively in a few hours from five different forums, has neither justification nor a precedent in history. All this shows that the motive behind the change of the special status of FATA and PATA, assured and guaranteed by M.A. Jinnah (as the President of All India Muslim League; and later as Governor-General of Pakistan) and the successive constitutional documents (for the origin and continuation of the special constitutional status of the tribal areas, see also Chapter 12 of this book), was not the interest of the people concerned but something else.

Interestingly, following the Pakistani footstep of effecting changes, in the manner mentioned above, in some articles of the Constitution, especially in article 246, and omitting article 247 altogether, India, after fourteen months of the 25th Constitutional Amendment, revoked the special constitutional status of Jammu and Kashmir by bringing an end to article 370 of its constitution. India also used mainly the same logic to justify its act regarding Kashmir, as was used by Pakistan in case of the tribal areas, namely mainstreaming the area, bringing it on a par with other areas of the country, and eliminating militancy and backwardness of the area; and that the step will usher prosperity and development of the area and its inhabitants.

Moreover, Pakistan brought an end to the special status of FATA and PATA at a time when it had a huge presence of its armed forces in the area—possessing special powers under Actions (in Aid of Civil Power) Regulations of 2011: there were two regulations with the same title, one each for FATA and PATA—and in the wake of the strains from which the population of these areas was passing after years' long militancy and military operations. India, here too, followed Pakistan's footstep and deployed large contingents of troops in Kashmir before taking the step. The voices raised and the agitation started in PATA, against the change of its special status, was covertly silenced and suppressed by the army officials posted in the area.

The change in the special constitutional status of FATA and PATA was made in the wake of increasing pressure from the Financial Action Task Force (FATF) of blacklisting Pakistan as well as from America; and due to the interests of the security establishment of Pakistan. In 2014, Rustam Shah Mohmand, veteran civil servant and Pakistan's former ambassador to Afghanistan, told in an interview, published in the 'Sunday Magazine' of the Urdu daily *Aaj*, Peshawar, that America wish to bring an end to the special constitutional status of the tribal areas, for its own interest, and, hence, soon this status will end and the areas will be made integral part of the province; and that the Army Chief and President of Pakistan General Pervez Musharraf was in line with America[108]

THE CONSTITUTION (26TH AMENDMENT) ACT, 2019

Presented in the National Assembly by Muhsin Dawar, a member of the Assembly from North Waziristan, the National Assembly of Pakistan passed the Constitution (26th Amendment) Bill, 2019, on 13 May 2019, to increase the number of seats for the erstwhile FATA in both the national and provincial assemblies. This Bill has yet not been passed by the Senate. After its passage from the Senate, and getting assent of the President, it was to be applicable from the year 2020. As a result of this amendment, the number of provincial assembly seats in Khyber Pukhtunkhwa will increase to 153/155.[109] The passage of the Bill from the Senate and its operation from the year 2020 did not materialise till now, viz. October 2021.

Sum Up

Including the areas of the settled districts of the present-day Khyber Pukhtunkhwa in the province of Punjab in 1849, with the annexation of the Sikh kingdom, was a landmark development in the history of the province. This initial constitutional development brought the areas of the settled districts on a par with the other parts of Punjab regarding their constitutional status and development. The status, however, did not remain intact when a special regulation, the Frontier Crimes Regulation of 1872, was enacted to deal with some aspects in the area; the tribal belt bounding the area was also given special status. This gave a distinctive status to these areas.

Separating the areas of the North-West Frontier Province from Punjab, in 1901, and giving them the status of a province did not benefit the province much, for it was not given the status of a full-fledged province with a constitutional status on a par with the other provinces of British India. The province was made a chief commissioner province, was deprived of the constitutional advances it had enjoyed when part of the province of Punjab, was denied legislative authority on the same footing as the other provinces of British India, and was ruled by executive regulations.

In spite of further constitutional advancement by the other provinces of British India and the struggles and pleading from various quarters, and at various fora, to bring the province on a par with the other provinces of British India regarding its constitutional development, the position remained unchanged until 1932. It was in 1932 that the province was at last raised to the status of a governor province, and the constitutional provisions granted to the other provinces of British India were extended to the North-West Frontier Province as well. The settled districts of the province were now also subject to the regular law and had a legislative council. The province was entitled to all the constitutional advancements, and, hence, received them subsequently. The tribal areas adjoining the province, however, remained deprived of the constitutional advancements made in British India: their constitutional status remained unchanged.

As a result of the Indian Independence Act of 1947, the province became an integral part of Pakistan on 15 August 1947. Being a full-fledged province of the Federation of Pakistan, it had the same constitutional status as the other full-fledged provinces of the country. However, its status as a separate province was brought to an end on 14 October 1955 when it was made a part of the new province of West

Pakistan. Nevertheless, after about fifteen years, its separate provincial status was restored on 1 July 1970. In the subsequent constitutional developments, the province received its due share.

The North-West Frontier Province, thus, passed through ups and downs in respect of the constitutional developments related to it. It remained deprived of its due status and rights for quite a long time, depriving the inhabitants of their genuine rights. The Constitution of 1973 granted provincial autonomy to a greater extent; the then President of Pakistan, as well as a later Chief Executive and President, General Pervez Musharraf, also talked of granting the said autonomy to the provinces, NWFP being one of them. However, practically nothing came out of it. But then, under 'The Constitution (Eighteenth Amendment) Act, 2010', a number of subjects were transferred to the provinces—a sea-change towards provincial autonomy was in the offing for which concrete steps were imperative.

It needs to be underlined that so far (till October of the year 2021) no practical and visible change has been observed towards the provincial autonomy envisaged in and granted by the Constitution. Rather lobbying has been started, after Pakistan Tehreek-e-Insaf come to power at the federal level, in 2018, for undoing 'The Constitution (Eighteenth Amendment) Act, 2010' and, hence, to revert the process and deprive the provinces of the intended or would-be provincial autonomy.

Notes

1. Amit Kumar Gupta, *North West Frontier Province: Legislature and Freedom Struggle, 1932–47* (New Delhi: ICHR, 1976), 2; *Administration Report of the North-West Frontier Province from 9th November 1901 to 31st March 1903* (Peshawar: Printed at the North-West Frontier Province Government Press, 1903), 6.

2. Gupta, *North West Frontier Province*, 8.

3. Abdul Qaiyum, *Gold and Guns on the Pathan Frontier* (Bombay: HK, 1945), 26.

4. Allah Bakhsh Yusufi, *Sarhad aur Jidujahd-i Azadi, tarmim wa izafah shudah edn.* (Urdu) (Karachi: Nafees Academy, 1989), 96–7; Aziz Javaid, *Sarhad ka Ayini Irtiqa* (Urdu) (Peshawar: Idarah Tahqiq wa Tasnif, 1975), 63, 221. However, according to S.M. Ikram: 'Maulana Zafar Ali Khan, an important Khilafat leader and editor of *Zamindar*, who had a number of co-workers in the area, wrote a series of articles entitled *Sarzamin-i be-A'in*—"The Land Without Law"—dealing with the hardships of the people of N.-W.F.P.' [S.M. Ikram, *Modern Muslim India and the Birth of Pakistan*, repr. (Lahore: IIC, 2016), 349.]

5. Muhammad Nasir Khan has erroneously called it 'Minto-Morely Reforms'. See Muhammad Nasir Khan, 'History of Constitutional Development in N-W.F.P. (1901–1932)' (MPhil Thesis, Department of History, University of Peshawar, [1999]), 51–3.

6. M.A. Rahim, M.D. Chughtai, W. Zaman, and A. Hamid, *Book Four: Alien Rule and the Rise of Muslim Nationalism* in I.H. Qureshi, ed., *A Short History of Pakistan*, 2nd edn. (Karachi: UK, 1984), 175.

7. Diwan Chand Obhrai, *The Evolution of North-West Frontier Province: Being a Survey of the History and Constitutional Development of N.-W. F. Province, in India,* repr. (Peshawar: SBB, n.d.), 121. Also see Muhammad Anwar Khan, *The Role of N.W.F.P. in the Freedom Struggle* (Lahore: RSP, 2000), 43.

8. Rahim, M.D. Chughtai, W. Zaman, and A. Hamid, *Book Four: Alien Rule and the Rise of Muslim Nationalism* in Qureshi, ed., *A Short History of Pakistan*, 190–1.

9. Abdul Hamid, *Muslim Separatism in India* (n.p., n.d.), 189.

10. *The Administration Report of North-West Frontier Province, 1932–33* quoted in Obhrai, *The Evolution of North-West Frontier Province*, 255.

11. Obhrai, *The Evolution of North-West Frontier Province*, 122.

12. Ikram, *Modern Muslim India and the Birth of Pakistan*, 345. Also see Sayed Wiqar Ali Shah, *North-West Frontier Province: History and Politics* (Islamabad: NIHCR, 2007), 13–14; Yusufi, *Sarhad aur Jidujahd-i Azadi*, 106–7, 459–60.

13. Ikram, *Modern Muslim India and the Birth of Pakistan*, 345 cf. Shah, *North-West Frontier Province*, 14.

14. Syed Waqar Ali Shah, *Muslim League in N.W.F.P.* (Karachi: RBC, 1992), 9.

15. Obhrai, *The Evolution of North-West Frontier Province*, 92, 110.

16. Quoted in ibid., 104.

17. Ibid., 113–14.

18. Quoted in ibid., 112.

19. See ibid., 111–12, 124–8; Yusufi, *Sarhad aur Jidujahd-i Azadi*, 463; Muhammad Shafi Sabir, *Tarikh Khyber Pukhtunkhwa (Sabiqah Subah Sarhad)*, 2nd edn. (Peshawar: UBA, 2019), 893; Shah, *Muslim League in N.W.F.P.*, 9–12.

20. Shah, *North-West Frontier Province*, 14–15.

21. Hamid, *Muslim Separatism in India*, 189.

22. Ikram, *Modern Muslim India and the Birth of Pakistan*, 346.

23. Gupta, *North-West Frontier Province*, 20.

24. See Sabir, *Tarikh Khyber Pukhtunkhwa*, 894–5; Javaid, *Sarhad ka Ayini Irtiqa*, 89–122; Ikram, *Modern Muslim India and the Birth of Pakistan*, 346; Himayatullah, 'Jinnah, Muslim League and Constitutional Reforms in the N.W.F.P.', *JPHS* (Karachi), vol. 55 (Nos. 1–2, January–June 2007), 'All India Muslim League Centenary Special Number, Part I', 149. According to Sayyad Murtaza Bahadur's statement in the assembly, while speaking on the resolution, he was a member of the Swaraj Party (Congress) as well as a member of the All India Muslim League and its Council (see Javaid, *Sarhad ka Ayini Irtiqa*, 105–7). Allah Bakhsh Yusufi, however, has stated that he was president of the Central Khilafat Committee and a member of the Swaraj Party, from which he resigned due to differences with Congress on the issue of his resolution—which they wanted withdrawn, but he refused (see Yusufi, *Sarhad aur Jidujahd-i Azadi*, 467–73). S.M. Ikram has spoken of the pressure of the Swarajist Party on Sayyad Murtaza Bahadur to not move the resolution, his resisting the party pressure, and then resigning from the party and taking 'part in the discussions as an independent member' [Ikram, *Modern Muslim India and the Birth of Pakistan*, 346]. Also see Yusufi, *Sarhad aur Jidujahd-i Azadi*, 472–3.

25. See Himayatullah, 'Jinnah, Muslim League and Constitutional Reforms in the N.W.F.P', 149–50; Shah, *North-West Frontier Province*, 17–20; Ikram, *Modern Muslim India and the Birth of Pakistan*, 346.

26. Ikram, *Modern Muslim India and the Birth of Pakistan*, 346.

27. Sayyad Tufail Ahmad Mangluri, *Musalmanu ka Rushan Mustaqbil* (Urdu), [repr.] (Lahore: Himadul Kutba, n.d.), 426. Also see Sabir, *Tarikh Khyber Pukhtunkhwa*, 896–7.

28. Hamid, *Muslim Separatism in India*, 197. Also see Mangluri, *Musalmanu ka Rushan Mustaqbil*, 423–9.

29. Hamid, *Muslim Separatism in India*, 199–200; Uma Kaura, *Muslims and Indian Nationalism: The Emergence of the Demand for India's Partition, 1928–40* (Lahore: BT, n.d.), 42–6.

30. Sharif al-Mujahid, *Quaid-i-Azam Jinnah: Studies in Interpretation*, 2nd rev. edn. (Karachi: Quaid-i-Azam Academy, 1981), 480; B.R. Ambedkar, *Pakistan or the Partition of India*, 1st Pakistani edn. (Lahore: BT, 1976), 247. Also see Sabir, *Tarikh Khyber Pukhtunkhwa*, 898. For M.A. Jinnah and All India Muslim League's role for extension of the reforms to the Frontier Province and bringing the province on a par with the other provinces of British India, see Himayatullah, 'Jinnah, Muslim League and Constitutional Reforms in the N.W.F.P.', 141–57. Whereas, for the role in this respect—in the shape of resolutions and addresses—of The All India Muslim Conference, see K.K. Aziz, ed. & comp., *The All India Muslim Conference, 1928–1935: A Documentary Record* (Karachi: National Publishing House Ltd, 1972), 55, 59, 62, 66, 71, 73–4, 81, 83, 92–3, 105, 111.

31. See al-Mujahid, *Quaid-i-Azam Jinnah*, 479–81.

32. Obhrai, *The Evolution of North-West Frontier Province*, 123–4. For a summary of the views and demands of the different groups and stakeholders, put to the commission, see ibid., 124–31.

33. Quoted in ibid., 132.

34. Obhrai, *The Evolution of North-West Frontier Province*, 137–8.

35. Ibid., 138.

36. Ibid.

37. Ibid., 138–9.

38. Ibid., 139–40.

39. Ibid., 140.

40. Ibid., 256.

41. Gupta, *North-West Frontier Province*, 21. Also see Shah, *North-West Frontier Province*, 28–30; Abdul Khaliq Khaleeq, *Da Azadai Jang: Sah Lidali aw sah Awridali* (Pukhtu), 2nd edn. (Pikhawar: IIS, 1972), 110.

42. Gupta, *North-West Frontier Province*, 22; Shah, *Muslim League in N.W.F.P.*, 14.

43. Obhrai, *The Evolution of North-West Frontier Province*, 179, 184.

44. Ibid., 184; Shah, *Muslim League in N.W.F.P.*, 14.

45. Obhrai, *The Evolution of North-West Frontier Province*, 184–5.

46. Shah, *Muslim League in N.W.F.P.*, 14–15.

47. Obhrai, *The Evolution of North-West Frontier Province*, 192.

48. Ibid., 192–4.

49. Ibid., 199.

50. Quoted in Shah, *Muslim League in N.W.F.P.*, 15.

51. Obhrai, *The Evolution of North-West Frontier Province*, 272, 274.

52. Quoted in ibid., 257.

53. Diwan Chand Obhrai has given the name of the first speaker/president of the council as Khan Bahadur Abdul Ghaffar Khan, which seems to be a typographical error. The book itself, too, has given the name as Abdul Ghaffur Khan on page 209, and in the subject-index on page 331 where reference has been made to pages 209 and 259.

54. Obhrai, *The Evolution of North-West Frontier Province*, 258–9.

55. Gupta, *North-West Frontier Province*, 23.

56. Ibid., 25. For the official Indian viewpoint, now in favour of extension of the reforms and the benefit to the colonial government in the changed scenario, see ibid. 25–6.

57. Obhrai, *The Evolution of North-West Frontier Province*, 293.

58. Ibid., 272, 274; Javaid, *Sarhad ka Ayini Irtiqa*, 222, 240.

59. Quoted in Obhrai, *The Evolution of North-West Frontier Province*, 295.
60. 'Indian Independence Act, 1947', in Safdar Mahmood, *Constitutional Foundations of Pakistan (Enlarged and Revised)* (Lahore: Jang Publishers, 1997), 31.
61. Farooq Ahmad Dar, 'Jinnah and Pakistan's Independence Ceremonies', *JPHS* (Karachi), vol. 62 (No. 2, April–June 2014), 64.
62. Ibid., 67.
63. Ibid., 64.
64. Ibid., 69.
65. Ibid., 75 n. 76.
66. Aqeel Abbas Jafri, '14 August: Yaum-i Azadi Pakistan India kay Yaum-i Azadi say aik din pihlay kyau manaya jata hay?', 22 July 2020, https://www.bbc.com/urdu/pakistan-53482078, accessed: 29 July 2020.
67. Syed Minhaj ul Hassan, 'NWFP Administration under Abdul Qaiyum Khan, 1947–53' (Unpublished PhD Dissertation, Department of History, University of Peshawar, 2003), 100; Syed Minhajul Hassan, *The Dawn of New Era in Khyber Pakhtunkhwa: Abdul Qaiyum Khan Chief Ministership, 1947–53* (Islamabad: NIHCR, 2016), 73. Also see Safdar Mahmood, *Pakistan: Muslim League ka Daur-i Hukumat, 1947–1954* (Urdu) (Lahore: SMP, 1986), 215.
68. Mahmood, *Constitutional Foundations of Pakistan (Enlarged and Revised)*, 84.
69. 'Report of the Basic Principles Committee', in Mahmood, *Constitutional Foundations of Pakistan (Enlarged and Revised)*, 95.
70. Ibid., 109.
71. Ibid.
72. For details, see ibid., 107–8.
73. See ibid., 118–19.
74. 'Report of the Basic Principles Committee (As Adopted by the Constituent Assembly of Pakistan on the 6th October, 1954)', in Mahmood, *Constitutional Foundations of Pakistan (Enlarged and Revised)*, 162.
75. Ibid., 183.
76. Ibid., 181, 187. For details about the Units' legislature, functionaries, procedures, etc., see ibid., 181–92.
77. *The All Pakistan Legal Decisions (P.L.D.)* [henceforward *PLD*], 1955, vol. 7, Central Acts and Notifications, 273.
78. Ibid., 295–6.
79. Ibid., 273–4.
80. 'The Constitution of the Islamic Republic of Pakistan (1956)' in Mahmood, *Constitutional Foundations of Pakistan (Enlarged and Revised)*, 248.
81. See ibid., 275, 307–8.
82. 'Report of the Constitution Commission appointed by President Ayub Khan' in Mahmood, *Constitutional Foundations of Pakistan (Enlarged and Revised)*, 442.
83. 'Constitution of the Second [sic] Republic (1962)' in Mahmood, *Constitutional Foundations of Pakistan (Enlarged and Revised)*, 536. Also see *PLD*, vol. 14 (1962), Central Statutes, 150.
84. See 'Constitution of the Second [sic] Republic (1962)' in Mahmood, *Constitutional Foundations of Pakistan (Enlarged and Revised)*, 608, 620. Also see *PLD*, vol. 14 (1962), Central Statutes, 206, 215.
85. 'Provisional Constitution Order', *PLD*, vol. 21 (1969), Central Statutes, 41.
86. 'President's Order No. 1 of 1970, Province of West Pakistan (Dissolution) Order, 1970', *PLD*, vol. 22 (1970), Central Statutes, 218–19.
87. Ibid., 228.
88. Ibid., 229.

89. 'Province of West Pakistan (Dissolution) Order, 1970 (*Date of enforcement*)', *PLD*, vol. 23 (1971), Central Statutes, 48.

90. 'Legal Framework Order, 1970, (President's Order No. 2 of 1970)', *PLD*, vol. 22 (1970), Central Statutes, 230, 236. Also in Mahmood, *Constitutional Foundations of Pakistan (Enlarged and Revised)*, 656, 664.

91. 'The Interim Constitution of the Islamic Republic of Pakistan' in Mahmood, *Constitutional Foundations of Pakistan (Enlarged and Revised)*, 678.

92. See ibid., 702–17.

93. Ibid., 752.

94. Ibid., 753–4; 'The Interim Constitution of the Islamic Republic of Pakistan [1972]' in *PLD*, vol. 24 (1972), Central Statutes, 579–80.

95. 'The Constitution of the Islamic Republic of Pakistan [Passed by the National Assembly of Pakistan on the 10th April, 1973 and Authenticated by the President of the National Assembly on the 12th April, 1973]' in Mahmood, *Constitutional Foundations of Pakistan (Enlarged and Revised)*, 841, 889–908.

96. See ibid., 969–71.

97. See article 106 (1), (3) and (4) in ibid., 892–3.

98. Appendix A, 'Salient Features of New Constitution President's Statement', in Safdar Mahmood, *Constitutional Foundations of Pakistan* (Lahore: Publishers United Ltd., n.d.), 924–7.

99. 'Proclamation of Martial Law', Gazette of Pakistan, Extraordinary, Part I, 5th July 1977, *PLD*, vol. 29 (1977), Central Statutes, 326.

100. 'Chief Martial Law Administrator's Order 1 of 1977, Laws (Continuance in Force) Order, 1977', Gazette of Pakistan, Extraordinary, Part I, 5th July 1977, ibid., 327.

101. See 'President's Order 14 of 1985', Revival of the Constitution of 1973 Order, 1985, Gazette of Pakistan, Extraordinary, Part I, 2nd March 1985, *PLD*, vol. 37 (1985), Central Statutes, 456.

102. 'Provisional Constitution Order 1 of 1999', No. 2–10/99-Min.I, Islamabad, 14th October 1999, *PLD*, vol. 51 (1999), Central Statutes, 446.

103. Ibid., 447.

104. 'Chief Executive's Order 24 of 2002', Legal Framework Order, 2002, Gazette of Pakistan, Extraordinary, Part-I, 21st August 2002, *PLD*, vol. 54 (2002), Central Statutes, 1604.

105. Ibid., 1613.

106. See Munir Ahmad Mughal, Muhammad Khurram, and Muhammad Hammad Munir, *The Constitution (Eighteenth Amendment) Act, 2010* (Lahore: Muneeb Book House, 2010), 11.

107. See the 'Constitution (Twenty-fifth Amendment) Act, 2018', Registered No. M – 302/L.-7646, The Gazette of Pakistan, Extraordinary, Published by Authority, Islamabad, Tuesday, June 5, 2018.

108. See 'Sunday Magazine', *Roznamah Aaj* (Peshawar), Sunday, 6 July 2014, 7.

109. *Roznamah Aaj* (Peshawar), Tuesday, 14 May 2019, 1, 10; Shuja Mulk, 'PTI Hukumat kaa Aik Saal: Assembly kay Pihlay Baras mayn kiyaa Qanunsazi ki gayi?', https://www.bbc.com/urdu/pakistan-48866470, accessed: 17 August 2019.

9 Khudayi Khidmatgar Movement

> The Almighty does not need any service, serving His creatures
> is service to Him.
> – Abdul Ghaffar Khan

THE KHUDAYI (commonly spelled as Khudai) Khidmatgar movement
was one of the movements that brought about significant changes in
the outlook, manners, and behaviour of the people. It had the distinction
of bringing about changes in an area that had been termed 'the savage
frontier', likened to a gun-powder magazine by the British, and denied
constitutional reforms and rights on the same footing as the other
provinces of British India. These changes were brought about among
people who were considered treacherous, uncivilised, barbarian, savage,
and brutal. As the leading light of the Khudayi Khidmatgar movement
was Abdul Ghaffar Khan, it is imperative to give a biographical sketch
of his early life, mainly based on his own autobiography,[1] to know and
understand the movement in its true historical perspective.

ABDUL GHAFFAR KHAN'S EARLY LIFE

Abdul Ghaffar (also known as Abdul Ghaffar Khan, Khan Abdul Ghaffar
Khan, Ghaffar Khan, Bacha Khan, Badshah Khan, Sarhadi Gandhi, and
the Frontier Gandhi) was born in the village of Utmanzi in the Ashnaghar
(also Hashnaghar) area, in 1890, in the house of his father, Bahram Khan,
one of the *khan*s (in Pukhtu: *khanan*) of the area. He belonged to the
Muhammadzi tribe. He received his early traditional Islamic education
along traditional lines in the village. Then, he was admitted to the
Municipal Board High School in Peshawar, where he received modern
education, up to the primary level; subsequently, he joined the Edwardes
Memorial Mission High School in Peshawar in class VI. While the school
was situated in Peshawar city, its boarders stayed in the cantonment.
The selfless services of the headmaster of the school, E.F.E. Wigram,
and his brother, Dr Wigram—who was in-charge of a mission hospital
in Peshawar—greatly impressed Ghaffar Khan. During the course of his
class X examination, he was directly commissioned into the army, which

meant that he was unable to appear in the remaining papers, and, hence, failed the examination and had a break in his education.[2]

However, due to the racial discrimination policy and rude behaviour of the British officers in the army, towards the Indians, he left the army. He decided to re-start his education, and, after failing to get admission at Campbellpur and Qadyan, proceeded to Aligarh. His brother, Dr Khan Sahib (Sayb; Saib), suggested he go to England to study for an engineering degree, but his mother did not allow it. He then decided to give up on formal education and instead serve his homeland and nation.[3] Ghaffar Khan has noted that E.F.E. Wigram, headmaster at Edwardes Memorial Mission High School, played a great role in inculcating in him the spirit of humanitarianism, nationalism, brotherhood, fraternity, patriotism, and service to the creatures of the Almighty.[4]

During this time, Ghaffar Khan developed an association with the learned in the Frontier, such as Fazal Mahmud Makhfi of Charsadah, Mawlwi Abdul Aziz of Utmanzi, Mawlwi Fazl-i Rabi of Pakhlai, and Mawlwi Taj Muhammad who was the head of the Darul Ulum of Gadar. He also developed a close friendship with Fazl-i Wahid, also known as the Haji Sahib of Turangzi.[5] All these were educated, religious, and anti-British figures who had links and relations with the anti-British Muslim elements in India.

To achieve his objectives, Ghaffar Khan deemed it vital to educate the Pukhtuns. Hence, the first Azad School was opened, in association with Mawlwi Abdul Aziz, in Utmanzi in 1910 to impart both religious and modern education. More schools, which were called *madaris* (singular *madrasah*; plural in Pukhtu: *madrasay*), were opened in other areas as well. Due to his interaction with the above-mentioned religious figures, Ghaffar Khan developed a relationship and links with the *ulama* (in Pukhtu: *aliman*) at Deoband, like Mahmud-ul-Hasan and Ubaidullah Sindhi. As mentioned earlier, his teacher at the mission school had made an impression on Ghaffar Khan and influenced his ideas. Association with the nationalist *ulama* further strengthened his spirit of nationalism. He used to read the weekly *Al-Hilal* of Abul Kalam Azad, the daily *Zamindar* of Zafar Ali Khan, *Madinah* (published from Bijnur), and the *Civil and Military Gazette*. As the editors were nationalists and anti-British, the colonial[6] British government's attitude towards *Al-Hilal* and *Zamindar*, and their readers, was repressive. Articles in *Al-Hilal* and *Zamindar*, and the writings of Abul Kalam Azad and Zafar Ali Khan, impacted Abdul Ghaffar Khan's thinking.[7]

In 1913, the All India Muslim League's annual meeting was held in Agra. Ghaffar Khan attended the meeting, which lasted for three days. In January 1914, he visited Deoband and met the leaders of the Deoband school of thought. They decided to find a suitable place, in the independent tribal area adjoining the Frontier Province of British India, from which to carry out the struggle for the liberation of India. Ghaffar Khan visited the prospective suitable locations, and selected one, but the plan did not materialise because of new developments as a result of the outbreak of World War I. During the course of the war, anti-British activities were carried out in the tribal area; Ghaffar Khan toured the various tribal areas encouraging this activity.[8]

'At the end of 1917', the Government of India constituted a committee to 'probe into [the] revolutionary' crimes and to suggest measures for the suppression of anti-British 'seditious activities'. The committee, headed by Justice S.A. Rowlatt, submitted its report on the basis of which the colonial government promulgated the repressive 'The Anarchical and Revolutionary Crimes Act', commonly referred to as the Rowlatt Act, in 1919.[9] All-India agitation took place against the Act, which also spread to the Frontier Province. A public meeting, against the Act, was organised in the mosque of the Haji Sahib of Turangzi. Ghaffar Khan, who had by now gained political experience through his participation in political meetings, suggested that as such meetings needed a person to preside over them an elder be nominated as the president of the meeting. He was asked to become the president of the meeting. As some of the people could not differentiate between a president and a king, and the president of a state and that of a public meeting, they believed that he had been made the *bacha* (king) of the Pukhtuns, and so got to be popularly known as Bacha Khan: the title by which he is still referred to by his adherents and well-wishers. Ghaffar Khan and his associates continued agitating against the Rowlatt Act, for which they were finally imprisoned. He, however, was released after six months on a bond of 30,000 rupees. He achieved a lot of prominence during the course of this agitation.[10]

As a result of World War I, fear of unjust treatment towards Turkey and of the abolition of the *khilafat* prevailed. So, to save Turkey from division and loss of territory and to ensure the preservation of the *khilafat* which was the highest theoretical religious institution of the Muslims, the *khilafat* movement and its attendant agitation emerged in India.[11] Ghaffar Khan, inspired by the movement, joined the fold of agitators. He participated in the meeting of the *khilafat* committee, held in Delhi in the middle of 1920, when it was announced that only those who were prepared for martyrdom could participate in the meeting. Although he was not in favour of the unplanned *hijrat* (migration) to Afghanistan that took place during the course of the *khilafat* movement, compelled by circumstances, he too participated in it. He was appointed as one of the members of the committee formed in Afghanistan to look after the affairs of the *muhajirin* (migrants) to that land. On the failure of the *hijrat* movement, Ghaffar Khan returned from Afghanistan, but with the intention to educate the Pukhtuns.[12]

TOWARDS THE KHUDAYI KHIDMATGAR MOVEMENT

Abdul Ghaffar Khan was now firmly convinced that the desired change and revolution would take time; and that, it needed education and wisdom as well as learned persons and scholars. Hence, soon after his return from Aligarh—where he had gone with Qazi Ataullah to participate in a function at the Aligarh Muslim University in the last months of 1920—the Azad School Utmanzi was founded or, in other words, reopened (because, as stated earlier, it was first opened in 1910 but closed by the colonial government in the course of World War I) in 1921. Moreover, an association named 'Anjuman Islah-ul-Afaghinah' was also formed, with the objective to reform the evil customs and practices of the Pukhtuns, to dissuade them from violence, and to infuse the spirit and love of nationhood in them. Initially, only thirty-one people took membership of the association.[13] The aims and objectives of the association 'were economic and social. It was non-political and purely missionary.'[14]

In the meantime, Ghaffar Khan became president of the Peshawar Khilafat Committee, as a result of a rift among the *khilafat* activists. He was jailed for five years for his activities and participation in the non-cooperation non-violent movement. On his release from jail in 1924, a large public meeting was organised in his honour by Anjuman Islah-ul-Afaghinah where, besides an address in his honour, a medal, and a robe, he was given the title of 'Fakhr-i Afghan' (Pride of the Afghans). In his address to this public meeting, he urged the participants to endeavour and strive for their liberation and independence. The colonial government was not unmindful of the activities of Ghaffar Khan and his associates, and the consequent potential changes and their impact on it. Hence, it had to recourse to machinations to create dissension in the rank and file of the Anjuman, with some success.[15]

Another development, in 1929, was that students of Peshawar's Islamia College were also enthused; Mian Akbar Shah of Badrashu suggested the foundation of an association of Pukhtun youth. He discussed the idea with Abdul Ghaffar Khan; and a meeting of the youth and some members of the Anjuman Islah-ul-Afaghinah was arranged in Utmanzi to discuss the foundation of the 'Youth League'. Some suggested that instead of the 'Youth League', the new organisation should be named 'Frontier Province's Youths' Jargah'.[16] Abdul Akbar Khan and Khadim Muhammad Akbar, president and secretary of Anjuman Islah-ul-Afaghinah, respectively, opposed the foundation of the new organisation on the grounds that as the objectives of those who wanted to found the new organisation and those of the Anjuman Islah-ul-Afaghinah were the same; therefore, instead of a new organisation, the existing one should be strengthened. The youth, however, did not agree and founded a new organisation, called the 'Youth League', in December 1929.[17] According to other versions, it was called the 'Afghan Youth League'[18] and 'Da Subah Sarhad da Zalmu Jargah' (Frontier Province's Youths' Jargah), and the date of its foundation was 1 September 1929.[19]

FOUNDATION OF THE MOVEMENT

December 1929 brought about another event—the annual meeting of the All India National Congress in Lahore—which proved to be a milestone in the foundation of the Khudayi Khidmatgar movement. As Lahore was near the Frontier Province, Abdul Ghaffar Khan, Amir Mumtaz Khan (headmaster of Azad School Utmanzi), and others proceeded to Lahore as observers at the meeting. They were associated with the *khilafat* committee and Anjuman Islah-ul-Afaghinah and had no connection with the Congress. They were not only impressed by the meeting, but also by the national enthusiasm and spirit of the female volunteers of the Congress. Ghaffar Khan and his associates, from the Frontier, held a meeting in Lahore and discussed the awareness and endeavours, displayed by the Hindu women, for the national cause. They returned with a changed outlook.[20]

On their return, they organised a large public meeting in Utmanzi. In his speech, Ghaffar Khan talked about the changes that were taking place in India. He apprised the audience of the potential consequences of their deep slumber and lack of concern for Indian affairs, and asked them to become conscious and alert, and make the homeland their own in the true sense. The speech greatly impressed the audience and touched their hearts.[21]

At night, Muhammad Akbar Khan, Sarfaraz Khan, Hijab Gul, and some others youths went to Ghaffar Khan's *hujrah*[22], and discussed the formation of an organisation with him. Ghaffar Khan apprised them of the difficulties involved and asked them to rethink the issue. They came again the next night for the same reason, but he once more apprised them of the difficulties involved and sacrifices required in such a task and asked them to think the matter over. The third night, they came again and told him that they had thought the matter over and were prepared for all kinds of difficulties, hardships, and sacrifices for the sake of the nation (Pukhtuns) and the homeland. The name of the new organisation was now to be decided. According to Ghaffar Khan, the Pukhtuns had no idea of service (to fellow beings), so the organisation needed to be named in such a way that it would imbed the idea of service for the sake of the Almighty in the minds of the Pukhtuns. Various names were proposed but no agreement was reached. During the night, Ghaffar Khan came up the name Khudayi Khidmatgar, which he discussed with his associates the next day. They agreed, and thus the organisation was named Khudayi Khidmatgar.[23]

Abdul Ghaffar Khan, in his autobiography in Pukhtu, *Zama Jwand aw Jidujahd*, has written about the foundation of the organisation in December 1929, but Dr Sayed Wiqar Ali Shah states that it was founded in November 1929,[24] which corroborates with Ghaffar Khan's own autobiographical narrative in Urdu titled *Ap Biti*.[25] The narrative in Tendulkar's work gives 'September 1929'[26] as the date of its foundation, while Wali Khan's narrative speaks of the foundation of the organisation after Congress' Lahore session in 'October 1929'.[27] According to another version, it was Qazi Ataullah who proposed the name Khudayi Khidmatgar.[28] *Khudayi khidmat* means the work and services done and rendered solely for the sake of the Almighty, without any personal motive, gain, expectation, or reward; and *Khudayi khidmatgar* means the person who serves others only for the sake of the Almighty without any personal motive, gain, expectation, or reward. Accordingly, the Khudayi Khidmatgar Movement means the movement whose members serve others only for the sake of the Almighty, without any personal motive, gain, expectation, or reward. Hence, referring to the Khudayi Khidmatgars as the 'Servants of God', as stated by Qaiyum Khan, Dr Sayed Wiqar Ali Shah and others,[29] seems unsound. The 'Servants of God' would have been sound if the name was 'Da Khuday Khidmatgar'.

About Abdul Ghaffar Khan, or in other words the Khudayi Khidmatgars', notion of service, M. Banerjee is of the opinion:

The meaning of this notion of service was a complex and subtle one, but at its heart was the notion that Pathans should be willing to put aside the egocentricism of personal feuding in order to give up their time and energy, and even their lives, in the struggle to secure improved living conditions and political freedom for their brethren. Thus he [Ghaffar Khan] envisaged the KK [Khudayi Khidmatgar] movement as a vehicle for embarking on a far more committed and intensive programme of social activism and directly confrontational political protest.[30]

INITIAL STEPS AND ADDRESS

At the foundation of the Movement, Ghaffar Khan and his associates embarked upon visits to the nearby villages to awaken the people and apprise them of the impending danger. Although the *mulas* (in Pukhtu: *mulan/mulyan*) had banned the playing of drums and other musical instruments, Ghaffar Khan asked the musicians to take their instruments up again. They happily joined the Khudayi Khidmatgars, accompanying Ghaffar Khan and his associates on their tours and facilitating the task of assembling the people by beating the drums on reaching the villages. Collecting the people—males and females, the children and the old— in this way, Ghaffar Khan would then deliver a brief speech along the lines: Pukhtun brothers! We are your brothers, your servers, and have come to serve you. Look! We have come to bring order to our disorderly motherland. If you are illiterate, you have eyes; look at the world. Other people and nations are at the apogee, but we have remained backward. They are human beings like us but we ask grain and cash of them. The Almighty has bestowed on us a Paradise-like land, which is full of wealth and blessings, but what is our position? We do not even find sufficient coarse food. Why are the other people and nations developed and prosperous while we are backward? The reason is that they have brotherhood, nationhood, and unity whereas we have factions, groups, differences, hatred, and animosities. Today's world is the world of nationhood; if you become a nation you will be successful in this world and in the hereafter as well.[31]

BASIC PRINCIPLES AND PLEDGE

These local tours, and Ghaffar Khan's addresses, worked well and people started joining the movement. It is noteworthy that prospective members were apprised of the obstacles and hardships. They also had to understand that the Almighty does not need any service but serving His creatures for His sake is service to Him. The intending members had, moreover, to pledge to the effect that they would:

- give up factions, groupings, and enmities because these had ruined their homeland.
- not avenge highhandedness and would remain patient.
- abstain from violence, because the Pukhtuns' homeland was ruined due to the violence that they practised against their own brothers.
- serve their nation and homeland for the sake of the Almighty, without any other objectives.
- give up evil customs and practices.
- work daily, for at least two hours, with their own-hands.

A person's name was registered in the list of the Khudayi Khidmatgars only after he had pledged that he would abide by the aforementioned terms.[32]

UNIFORM

The Khudayi Khidmatgars had a uniform; there was a separate trained body of uniformed Khudayi Khidmatgars. At first the uniform was of white *khadar* (local, coarse, cloth made on handlooms); later, deep red was adopted as their uniform's colour. According to Abdul Ghaffar Khan, the white uniform used to soon get dirty, as the Khudayi Khidmatgars went on long tours and could not wash their uniform frequently. They complained to him about this, suggesting their uniform be dyed. A deep red colour was unanimously agreed on and adopted by all the Khudayi Khidmatgars, becoming the permanent colour of the uniform.[33] Ghani Khan states that during the course of the visits, Ghaffar Khan's

> companions found that their white clothes got easily dirty. So they decided to colour them. One of them took his to the local tannery and dipped them in the solution of pine bark prepared for the skins. The result was a dark browny red. The rest did the same.... Badshah Khan [Ghaffar Khan] adopted the colour for his new workers.[34]

It has also been stated that 'one day a Khudai Khidmatgar dipped his white' uniform 'in a local tannery of pine bark' which was 'prepared for [the] hides'; this attracted the other Khudayi Khidmatgars and soon the colour was adopted for the uniform on 'the advice of Qazi Attaullah

Khan'.[35] According to another version, the Khudayi Khidmatgars kept carrying out various experiments, using various colours. However, finally when they were injured and martyred by the British forces, and their clothes had taken on the red stains of their blood, they decided that if they dyed their clothes red then, on the one hand, they would be a memorial to the martyred and injured, and on the other, the blood-stains would not be visible in case they were beaten.[36] On the other hand, Dr Sayed Wiqar Ali Shah states: 'Because of the poverty of the people, any special uniform for the volunteers was not possible; therefore, they were advised to have their ordinary clothes dipped in brown or chocolate colour, which was cheap and easily available.'[37]

Whatever the reason may have been for adopting the deep red colour, it was because of this colour that the Khudayi Khidmatgars were also called *surkhpush* (literally red-dressed, but the term Red Shirts was used) and the movement as '*surkhpush tahrik*' or Red Shirts' Movement. However, because of the red of their uniforms, the Khudayi Khidmatgars were lumped together with the Bolsheviks and adherents of Bolshevism by the British.

TOURS AND PROGRESS

After touring through Ashnaghar and Duwawa (Duabah; Doaba), Abdul Ghaffar Khan and Mian Ahmad Shah toured the villages of Swabi, Peshawar, Khalsah, Dawudzi, Mardan, Baizi, Sudam, and Rustam, as well as the area from Amazu Gharai to Naranji. Afterwards, they held public meetings at the *milah*s (in Pukhtu: *milay*) in Nasru and Akbar Purah, and toured Taru, Nawkhar (Nowshera, Nawshihrah), Khwishkay, and Nisti. Public meetings were addressed during the tours; the response was marvellous. *Jargah*s (in Pukhtu *jargay*) were formed at the village levels. People started joining the movement, and membership increased in a short span of time. With the increase in the number of members of the *jargah*s and of the Khudayi Khidmatgars, a central office was established in Utmanzi, with Sarfaraz Khan as the commander-in-chief of the uniformed Khudayi Khidmatgars. District organisations were also formed in Peshawar, Mardan, Kuhat, Bannu, Dirah Ismail Khan, and Hazarah with *salar*s (commanders; in Pukhtu: *salaran*) Inzar Gul, Munir Khan, Aslam Khattak, Yaqub Khan, Maula Dad, and Dawud Khan, respectively. Kanwar Bhan Narang was also made a *salar*.[38]

Progress in the Swabi *tahsil* was very good. In March 1930, the organisation heads of the village Marghuz, in the then Swabi *tahsil*, arranged a public meeting. The meeting was successful in all its respects. The most significant aspect of the meeting was the decision that neither tea nor food would be consumed in the village where a public meeting was being held nor would they spend the night there, to avoid any hardships to the residents of the village or competition among the hosts in serving the guests; that the participants would go back to their homes but, if they could not reach their homes, a large number of them would not go to one village nor would they all become the guests of a single Khudayi Khidmatgar; that special arrangements would not be made but that all the Khudayi Khidmatgars of the village would bring ordinary food from their homes and everyone would eat collectively; in the case of tea, no more than two cups would be consumed.[39]

A public meeting, at provincial level, was organised at Utmanzi for 21–22 April 1930. A *mushairah* (meeting at which poets recite their poetry) was also organised with the verse set: 'جنگ د آزادي له هميشه محلمى وتلى دي' (the youth have always marched out for the war of independence). The colonial government did not want the meeting to take place and tried their best, using all the means at their disposal, to make the meeting a failure, but to no avail. The meeting was a success, attended by thousands of men and women, and the parade, rally, and salute of the Khudayi Khidmatgars impressed the crowd.[40]

In Qaiyum Khan's words: 'The movement spread like wild fire throughout the province. Soon great numbers of young men joined up, pledged to the sacred cause of the freedom of their country, and eager to lay down their lives for it.'[41] It is noteworthy that not only the men but women also participated in the public meetings of the Khudayi Khidmatgars,[42] which hinted at political awareness and a process of social change as a result of the activities of the movement.

ORGANIZATIONAL STRUCTURE

The basic organisational unit was a *jargah* on the village basis, comprising members of the movement; the leaders of a number of villages formed the *jargah* of a *tapah* (ټپه); representatives of the *jargah*s (in Pukhtu: *jargay*) of the *tapah*s (in Pukhtu: *tapay*) formed a *jargah* of a *halqah/ tahsil*; representatives of the *jargah*s of the *halqah*s/*tahsil*s (in Pukhtu: *halqay/tahsilunah*) formed a district *jargah*; and representatives of the districts *jargah*s formed the provincial *jargah*. Each *jargah* had its own working body, president, and secretary.[43]

The branch of the Khudayi Khidmatgars known as the Red Shirts had an officer at the branch (village) level called a *karnail* (colonel). He had, under his command, certain *liftinan* (lieutenants). There was a *jarnail* (general) at the *tapah* level, a *tahsil jarnail* over all the *tapah*s, the *tahsil* level *jarnail*s (in Pukhtu: *jarnilan*) were under the district *naib salar* (deputy commandant), and the *naib salar*s (in Pukhtu: *naib salaran*) were under a provincial *salar-i azam* (chief commander). Both the provincial president of the Khudayi Khidmatgars and the *salar-i azam* of the Red Shirts were subject to the orders of Ghaffar Khan.[44]

The village, *tapah*, *tahsil*, district, and provincial *jargah*s, or committees, 'were all elected bodies', but 'the volunteer' or uniformed branch of the movement, called the Red Shirts, 'was built up on a different footing'. Here, it was selection rather than election—for the sake of discipline. And, 'to avoid faction-feeling', Ghaffar Khan nominated the *salar-i azam*, who in turn nominated and appointed the officers who were 'placed in charge of the different units'.[45] 'All such officers and men', however, rendered 'free service' and accepted 'no remuneration whatsoever'. These volunteers were 'the greatest source of strength to the organization'. They formed 'the spearhead of the movement' and carried out 'its decrees'.[46] Juma Khan Sufi, however, opines, 'The organisation of the *Khudai Khidmatgars* was a fascist-type paramilitary association, loyal to its leader. The very oath of the organisation negated its democratic credentials.'[47] And, 'The participants in the movement are genuine; the leaders not untainted by selfish motives.'[48]

During the course of the tours by the leaders of the Khudayi Khidmatgar movement in 1941, besides the addresses to the public meetings by the leaders, Amir Muhammad Khan used to deliver a lecture after each *isha* prayer (the fifth and last prayer of the day) covering the points: for the success of any movement, it is a must for all the members of the movement to firmly believe in their leader; each member of the movement must consider sacrifice for the leader as his duty; the leader's orders must be obeyed without hesitation; all the members of the movement must firmly accept that the movement's leader and founder would know the working of the movement better than its other members, as he had run through each stage of the movement in his thoughts.[49] These utterances somewhat endorses Juma Khan Sufi's opinion, quoted above, about the organisation's fascist type loyalty to the leader and its democratic credentials. According to Rittenberg:

Patterns of dominance and subordinance in Pakhtun society carried over to the nationalist movement. Leadership at all levels came mainly from the Pakhtun elite, and *parajamba* determined that it consisted mostly of men from the junior branches of Khani lineages. The rank-and-file consisted predominantly of small Pakhtun landholders and members of lower classes.[50]

CIVIL DISOBEDIENCE: ARRESTS AND BRUTALITIES

At the conclusion of the public meeting, held at Utmanzi on 21–22 April 1930, the Congress members from Peshawar, who attended the meeting, asked Abdul Ghaffar Khan (still not in the Congress) to visit their civil disobedience the next day, when they would produce salt at Pabu (Pabi). On 23 April, not only was Ghaffar Khan arrested, while on his way to participate in the civil disobedience movement, but a number of other Khudayi Khidmatgars as well. This created great resentment among the Khudayi Khidmatgars, but disturbance and violence was averted by the timely arrival of Dr Khan Sahib (Dr Khan Sayb: Ghaffar Khan's elder brother) and because of Ghaffar Khan's request to the people not to resort to violence. He pleaded that their movement adhered to non-violence and that they had pledged not to revert to violence; instead, they should strive to strengthen the Khudayi Khidmatgari (Khudayi Khidmatgar-ship). On their refusal to submit bonds, they were sentenced to three years' rigorous imprisonment under section 40 of the Frontier Crimes Regulation.[51]

In the colonial government's move to arrest those who had resorted to non-cooperation and *satyagraha*, Allah Bakhsh Barqi, secretary of the Congress committee in Peshawar, was also arrested and brought to the Kabuli police station. At the news of the arrest, people proceeded to the police station in a public procession. They were asked to disperse; and on their refusal, the armed forces were called and asked to fire on the mob. The Indian soldiers refused to fire at the unarmed non-violent crowd and so were removed from their posts and British forces were called, who opened indiscriminate fire on the crowd resulting in a considerable number of injuries and deaths.[52]

The government resorted to violence and atrocities to suppress the Khudayi Khidmatgar movement. Blockades of the villages were ordered; force and all kinds of brutal measures were employed to suppress the people and eradicate the movement. Incidents of firing took place. *Hujrah*s (in Pukhtu: *hujray*) were burnt down. But all these measures proved to be futile; in fact, they worked to the benefit of the Khudayi Khidmatgar movement which spread even further. Attacks, originating from the tribal areas, were carried out on British positions and forces. Fighting continued for three months, during which the British dropped bombs on the Muhmand and Bajawar areas. Tribesmen, from the Muhmand in the north to the Mahsud area in the south, took up arms in support of the Khudayi Khidmatgars, and the terms of agreement with the government were made conditional on the release of Ghaffar Khan and Gandhi. In spite of the government's atrocities and use of force, the number of Khudayi Khidmatgars increased and were now in their thousands. The movement gained further popularity as the colonial government tried to suppress it.[53] Resultantly, 'government and village officials resigned...; revenue collections stopped; regular police activity ceased; and courts were supplanted by nationalist *jirgas* [*jargahs*]'.[54] For nearly a year, the colonial authorities 'were perpetually under the threat of a complete breakdown of their authority and administrative system'.[55] An official report stated: 'Probably at no time since British influence was first extended to the Frontier have conditions given cause for such acute anxiety.'[56] Jawaharlal Nehru admits:

> The North-West Frontier Province, which is an almost entirely Moslem province (95 per cent Moslems [Muslims]) played a leading and remarkable part in this movement. This was largely due to the work and personality of Khan Abdul Ghaffar Khan, the unquestioned and beloved leader of the Pathans in this province.[57]

However, according to Rittenberg, 'Support from the Khani elite was the key to the success of the movement.'[58] Referring to the results of the agitation and civil disobedience movement of the Khudayi Khidmatgars, Arthur Swinson asserts:

> It should be conceded, however, that its efforts had not been without some results. That year [viz. 1932] the North-West Frontier Province was raised from a Chief Commissonerate to a Governor's Province, and from now on its political rights and institutions were equal to those in the rest of India.[59]

KHUDAYI KHIDMATGARS AND CONGRESS

The atrocities of the colonial government did not come to an end. Besides other steps, the Khudayi Khidmatgar movement and the 'Zalmu Jargah' were banned, and martial law was declared in the province on 16 August 1930. A blockade of the whole province was carried out. Entry to and exit—

from the province were not allowed and communications were strictly censored. The government composed proclamations, dropping them by aeroplanes and distributing them among the Khans, Chiefs, and other leading pro-government men in the Frontier through the *tehsildars* and *patwaris*, asking them to help the government, and in reward it 'will consider your demands and remedy your evils'.[60]

Moreover, special *jargah*s were constituted under the Frontier Crimes Regulation 'to try those who' took part in the anti-government activities and 'a concerted effort was made to break up the Khudai Khitmatgar organization'.[61]

Not only was the Frontier Province cut off from the rest of the world, but its situation was also not known to the outside world. Mian Jafar Shah Kaka Khail and Mian Akbar Shah of Qazi Khail, Charsadah, succeeded in travelling from the province to Gujrat jail, where they apprised the jailed Khudayi Khidmatgar leaders about the prevailing situation in the province. The leaders asked them to contact the leaders of the All India Muslim League for help and to inform the outside world about the British atrocities in the province. On failing to receive a positive response from the Muslim League's leaders, the Khudayi Khidmatgars turned to the other political parties in India. Only the All India National Congress agreed to help them at this critical juncture, because both the organisations held the same view about their status—slavery under the British; had the same aim—freedom from British rule; had the same tool of war—non-violence; and had a common enemy—the British. When the delegation apprised the jailed leaders of the willingness of the Congress, the leaders asked them to put the issue before the provincial *jargah* for the final decision about association with the Congress which they would accept unconditionally. The provincial *jargah* not only approved the affiliation with the Congress, it also enacted it immediately. The Congress sent a committee for inquiry, headed by the speaker of the central assembly. As the colonial government did not allow the committee to enter the province, it held its inquiry at Rawalpindi and then published a 350-page report. The government confiscated the report as soon as it was published, but the Congress somehow managed to send it to the USA and Europe. The government, realising its blunder, asked the jailed leaders to enter into negotiations, promising an extension of the reforms of 1919 and the introduction of other reforms to the province. But the offer came with a condition: to part ways with the Congress. The Khudayi Khidmatgar leaders refused, and did not accept the government's offer. Finally, Ghaffar Khan and the others were released as a result of the Irwin-Gandhi Pact in March 1931.[62]

Juma Khan Sufi and M.S. Korejo, however, have questioned Ghaffar Khan's version of the Muslim League's ineptitude in the matter and the Khudayi Khidmatgars' consequent alliance with the Congress.[63] Besides, Dr Ansar Zahid Khan points out that the Muslim League, at that time, was itself paralysed and virtually inactive. Not only had M.A. Jinnah suffered a 'family tragedy', but he 'was also facing opposition from other Muslim leaders', who had 'formed the All Parties Muslim Conference and kept him away from [the] R.T.C. [Round Table Conference] delegation'. Jinnah, therefore, attended the Round Table Conferences as a government nominee and later proceeded to 'self-exile in England'.[64]

Interestingly, Abdul Khaliq Khaleeq has stated that it was Sahibzadah Abdul Qayyum who contacted Mian Jafar Shah and Mian Abdullah Shah and told them that the colonial government was in no mood to tolerate the Khudayi Khidmatgar organisation and, hence, asked them to merge their party with the Congress, as the Congress was a recognised party of India. They were told that, to crush the Khudayi Khidmatgars, the government was searching for an excuse to prove that the movement was working at the behest of the Russian government. Having apprised Bacha Khan of the issue, and having consulted and deliberated with their colleagues, they joined the Congress.[65]

Mukulika Banerjee has given an interesting account of the resolution that was passed by the Congress Working Committee in Bombay in August 1931, which refers to the Congress' wish to absorb the Khudayi Khidmatgar movement within its fold. Amongst its other points, the resolution stressed that the Khudayi Khidmatgar movement should follow the 'constitution, rules and programme' of the Congress and 'should become a Congress Volunteer organization'.[66] Ghaffar Khan's account has referred to the Khudayi Khidmatgars' affiliation with the Congress in 1930, but James W. Spain has placed the formal affiliation in August 1931.[67] It, however, can be inferred that the movement was affiliated with the Congress in 1930, but the Congress Working Committee gave formal approval to the affiliation in its meeting in August 1931 because of their desire to absorb the movement into the fold of the Congress.

A delegation of the Khudayi Khidmatgars participated in a public meeting that the Congress held in Karachi. The participation and behaviour of the delegation impressed the Congress delegates, washed certain misconceptions about them away, and led to a regard for the

Pukhtuns. They also participated in the annual session of the Jamiat-ul-Ulamay-i Hind, held in Karachi at the same time. A delegation of the Khudayi Khidmatgars visited India after the Congress meeting in Karachi—another fruitful expedition.[68] This, in turn, removed misgivings about the Pukhtuns, cemented links and bonds between Congress' leaders and the Khudayi Khidmatgars, and brought the Khudayi Khidmatgars—and so the Pukhtuns—to the front in Indian politics.

The significance of the association of Khudayi Khidmatgar movement with the Congress can also be judged from the following event: when it was propagated that Ghaffar Khan was parting ways with the Congress, Sahibzadah Abdul Qayyum—a well-known loyalist to the British, who had a great love for the Frontier too—sent an envoy to Lahore asking him to not do so because in that case the British would give nothing to the Frontier Province.[69]

The Khudayi Khidmatgars' close association and affiliation with the Congress and Gandhi created dissension in the rank and file of the movement, too. Juma Khan Sufi writes:

In August Bacha Khan went to Bombay to strike a formal deal with the Congress Committee. *Khudai Khidmatgars* were formally inducted as the Congress Volunteer Organization. Their black flag was changed into the tricolour of Congress. The Frontier Afghan *Jirga* was renamed as the Frontier Congress Committee. This decision on the part of Bacha Khan outraged his erstwhile colleagues in the Afghan Youth League. Both the President and the Secretary opposed it. They had been in favour of alliance with the Congress, but the organization's total merger or subordination to Congress violated their prior understanding. There were allegations and counter allegations. Abdul Akbar Khan and Barrister Mian Ahmad Shah on the one hand and Bacha Khan on the other, made their positions clear through publishing pamphlets.[70]

However, elsewhere, he has contradicted his contention by stating: 'In July 1939 Gandhi again visited the Province and repeatedly stressed "… the desirability for the Red Shirts to become part of the Congress Party".'[71]

Some of those who had been the founding members, or associated with the movement from its inception and were among the top leadership, developed grudges against Ghaffar Khan because of his, and the movement's, affiliation and intimate relationship with the Congress and Gandhi. Among these were Mian Ahmad Shah, Abdul Akbar Khan Akbar, Khadim Muhammad Akbar, Haji Abdul Ghaffar, Sarfaraz Khan, Rab Nawaz Khan, Mian Abdullah Shah, Shah Nawaz Khan, Taj Muhammad

Khan, Pir Lal Badshah, Mian Abdul Maruf, and Ghulam Muhammad Khan of Lundkhwar. Khadim Muhammad Akbar referred to the reason for his parting in the following *tapah* (ټپه):

باچا   امام   زهٔ   مقتدی   وم 72

ګاندهی امام شو ځکه ځان له نیت ترمه

Meaning: Bacha (Abdul Ghaffar Khan) was the leader and I the follower, but as Gandhi became the leader I am going to follow my own way.

Although Rittenberg has denied any significant effect on the movement because of Abdul Akbar Khan and Mian Akbar Shah's parting ways with the organisation,[73] they later became the leaders of the opposition to Ghaffar Khan and the Khudayi Khidmatgar movement, joining hands with the movement's opponents and creating difficulties for both Ghaffar Khan and the movement.

Adopting the tricolour flag of the Congress, and following its policies in a number of issues, the Khudayi Khidmatgars testified their closeness to, and the extent to which the movement and its leaders were associated with, the Indian body, even though they continued the use of a separate name, uniform, programme, and organisational structure—proving that they were determined to maintain their separate identity as well.

PROVINCIAL *JARGAH*

The Khudayi Khidmatgars were not an integral part of the Congress but an affiliated body which used to be opposed by the Frontier Congressmen on various occasions. To cement the bond between the Congress and the Khudayi Khidmatgars, it was decided to change the name of the 'Congress Committee' of the province to '*jargah*'. Accordingly, the name was changed and a *jargah* instituted with its own office bearers.[74] Despite the opposition of the Congressmen of the province, the Congress Working Committee endorsed the decision during its annual meeting in Bombay, naming it the 'grand *jargah*' of the Frontier. This joint *jargah* of the Congress and the Khudayi Khidmatgars was opposed not only by the Congressmen of the province but also by some of the Khudayi Khidmatgars[75]—thus giving an indication of the resentment of some of the Khudayi Khidmatgars and their opposition to the movement's closeness to the Congress.

GOVERNMENT'S APPREHENSIONS AND STEPS

The most striking feature of the Khudayi Khidmatgar movement was its adherence to non-violence—among a people who, traditionally, were both militant and violent. To curb the violent temper of the Pukhtuns, Abdul Ghaffar Khan told them that 'bravery does not consist in beating others; rather it consists in developing the power to bear and to berate beating'. Claiming non-violence as 'a matter of faith' for himself, and expressing happiness at the result of non-violence among the followers of the Khudayi Khidmatgar movement, he further stressed the need to follow non-violence by asserting: 'We know only too well the bitter results of violence from the blood feuds which spoil our fair name. We have an abundance of violence in our nature. It is good in our own interests to take a training in non-violence.' Moreover, he questioned, 'Is not the Pathan amenable only to love and reason?'[76]

Ghaffar Khan claims that the Pukhtuns' adherence to non-violence created great difficulties for the British. They tried hard to encourage them to revert to violence, so that they would have the justification to crush them brutally, but they did not succeed because the spirit of non-violence had been inculcated in them by the Khudayi Khidmatgar movement. The British would state that they had the means to crush the violence, but not to crush non-violence, and so would often say: '*The non violent* [non-violent] *Pathan is more dangerous than the violent Pathan.*'[77]

Besides their other apprehensions and fears, the British also saw, in the programme and tactics of the Khudayi Khidmatgars, 'a dangerous and politically inflammable element that could easily be ignited and manipulated either by the Soviets or by the Afghans, the one in pursuit of revolutionary goals, the other seeking recovery of the Peshawar region and some degree of authority over the transfrontier tribes'.[78] Interestingly, Ghaffar Khan contends that, until that time, they did not know that the Bolsheviks had red uniform and that they had adopted the red uniform accidentally; also, till then, neither had he read a book by Marx, Lenin, or Gandhi, nor did he know about them.[79]

The Soviets, at first, deemed the Khudayi Khidmatgar movement 'a revolutionary organization' with 'an emblem that included a hammer and sickle', and saw in it 'the potential of a revolutionary peasant movement'. But their hopes were soon dashed; and 'by the end of 1931 the Soviets' had attacked the Khudayi Khidmatgar movement and termed the Khudayi Khidmatgars the 'Servants of Imperialism' and betrayers of the Pukhtun peasantry. The Soviets, moreover, 'charged that the organization listened more and more to its religious and mystical elements, who had drowned out the objective revolutionary demands of the peasant masses against the dominant classes'.[80]

Despite the Soviets' terming the Khudayi Khidmatgars the 'Servants of Imperialism' and propagating against them, the British still feared them and suggested that though they called themselves Khudayi Khidmatgars, 'in reality they are the servants of Gandhi. They wear the dress of Bolsheviks. They will create the same atmosphere' as had been 'heard in the Bolshevik dominion'. The movement was termed a subversive organisation with the objective of driving 'the British out of India by force'.[81]

Not unmindful of the activities of the Khudayi Khidmatgars, the spread of the movement by leaps and bounds, the awareness of the people, and the potential consequences for the colonial government, ever since its inception the government did its best to arrest the progress of the movement. All ways and means were used and adopted, even the use of brutal force, but to no avail. Brutalities of the colonial government, such as the castration of some Khudayi Khidmatgars and the insults and degradation they had to endure did not work either, and the movement progressed.[82] The colonial authorities were not only disturbed by 'the clear expression of nationalist solidarity among the Frontier people', but also 'surprised at the success of the *Khudai Khidmatgar* agitation and by "the degree of unity achieved by Muslims, Hindus and Sikhs".'[83]

The unity and solidarity, however, did not last long. Dissension came to the surface, among the leaders of the Khudayi Khidmatgars, at the time of the Round Table Conference of 1931. While it appeared that the disagreement—which was overtly caused on the issue of parting ways with the Congress, although that was not the real reason—was over, all attempts at remaining united failed. At this stage, Mian Akbar Shah and Abdul Akbar Khan declined to be content with the decision of the *luyah* (commonly spelled as *loya*) *jargah* (grand *jargah*) and parted ways with the movement. Later, some other prominent figures also expressed their differences and parted ways with the movement, joining other organisations and opposing the Khudayi Khidmatgars, as has been stated earlier.[84]

Although 'denounced as betrayers of the revolution by the Soviets and as subversives by the British', the Khudayi Khidmatgars 'did not receive any encouragement' from the Afghan monarch or 'the Afghan government either'. Instead of supporting and encouraging them, the Afghan monarch, Nadir Shah, and his government opposed and worked against the Khudayi

Khidmatgars for a number of reasons which included, among others, the following: Ghaffar Khan's close ties with, and endeavours for the cause and support of, Amanullah Khan; due to Nadir Shah's fear and apprehensions lest 'the movement might be used against' the monarchy and 'Afghan interests'; and to avoid conflict with the British. So, Nadir Shah's government tried its best 'to discourage the activities' of the Khudayi Khidmatgars and 'disassociate itself from them'.[85]

TOURS

After his release from jail in 1931, Abdul Ghaffar Khan started his tours along with Mian Jafar Shah and Abdullah Shah. During the course of these tours, the Khudayi Khidmatgars in Nawkhar (Nawshihrah) presented a red *jubah* (*joba;* robe of honour) to Abdul Ghaffar Khan with the message that the robe was red with their blood, so that he might not forget their persecuted fellows. During these tours the people were apprised of the aims and objectives of the meetings and of the Khudayi Khidmatgars.[86]

Taking advantage of the occasion, Ghaffar Khan started to visit other parts of the province. He travelled to Dirah Ismail Khan, Bannu, and Hazarah, and even the Chach area of Punjab, successfully, in spite of the government's endeavours to make it a failure. He also went on a tour to the Khalil and Mumand,[87] as well as the *tahsils* of Nawkhar and Swabi, and the Mardan area. He asked the people to be patient; not to take revenge; to leave themselves' to the mercy of the Almighty; to do away with dissension and self-interest; to be well-behaved and have good morals; and not to fear the British but only keep the fear of the Almighty in their hearts. At the failure of the Round Table Conference, Ghaffar Khan and his brother were arrested, once again, on the night of 24 December 1931, followed by the arrests of other Khudayi Khidmatgars in their thousands. Atrocities were committed against the Khudayi Khidmatgars. The imprisoned were released after three years. Although released from jail, Ghaffar Khan was banned from entering the Frontier and Punjab provinces.[88]

The endeavours of the Khudayi Khidmatgar leaders to change the outlook of the people of the Frontier, to encourage them to abstain from violence, and to instil the spirit of non-violence in them proved to be of great success in a short span of time. This is evident from the behaviour of the Khudayi Khidmatgars during the course of the civil disobedience movement of 1930–1934, when they never resorted to violence or the use of force despite the brutalities and inhuman treatment that they were subjected to by the province's authorities. This was 'confirmed by the members of the India League who visited India to collect correct information "about the state of affairs" there'. They stated:

> The severity of the repression [in the NWFP] has produced something like a state of war in the Frontier. Yet, though the display of force on the British side is overwhelming, no British official claimed that the movement had been crushed. That non-violence against the persons of British officials still remains the rigidly observed rule of the national movement in an area where arms are so readily obtainable, and in fact are openly, and usually, owned by the villagers, is a tribute to the sincerity with which the creed has been embraced.[89]

ELECTIONS OF 1932

On raising the status of NWFP to that of a full-fledged province, and extending the reforms of 1919, elections to the provincial legislative council were scheduled for April 1932. The Khudayi Khidmatgars had already rejected the 1919 reforms, and were stressing for complete independence. They were, therefore, not interested in participating in the elections. However, they could not have participated in the elections, even if they had wanted to, as their organisation was already banned. Even then, they 'focussed on the elections. Their object, however, was to frustrate the polls rather than to take part in them or win them.'[90] They led anti-election demonstrations and even picketed the polling stations, which resulted in a very low turnout.[91]

ELECTIONS OF 1937 AND MINISTRY

After his release from jail in 1934, Abdul Ghaffar Khan's entry into the province was banned 'under the Public Tranquility Act and the Khudai Khitmatgars remained banned'. Yet, 'the movement continued to grow underground' and Ghaffar Khan's popularity increased. The Khudayi Khidmatgars, therefore, 'emerged...stronger...than ever when a new constitution for India was promulgated in the Government of India Act of August 2, 1935'.[92]

The Khudayi Khidmatgars participated in the elections, held in the province in February 1937, in collaboration with the Congress, and won 19 out of the 50 seats of the provincial assembly. Interestingly, 'Among the party's [Khudayi Khidmatgars-Congress] Muslim nominees, even those with strong nationalist credentials tended to be distinguished as well by belonging to the Pakhtun landed elite.'[93] Although the movement was only affiliated with the Congress, it became so intimately linked with it that it was deemed to be part of the Congress—so much so that though victory in the elections of 1937 was due to the movement, it was considered Congress' victory and the ministry was referred to as the Congress ministry. Even Ghaffar Khan states that the Frontier Muslim majority province went with the Congress, and speaks of Congress ministries in 8 out of the 11 provinces of British India. He, however, also speaks of the success of 19 Khudayi Khidmatgar members, out of 50, and of the formation of the Khudayi Khidmatgars' government.[94] The Congress had no hold in the other Muslim-majority provinces, and had no significant successes in those provinces in the elections of 1937 and 1946. It was because of the Khudayi Khidmatgars that a significant success was achieved in the Frontier Province in the elections of 1937 and 1946.

With the success of the no-confidence motion against Sahibzadah Abdul Qayyum's ministry (1937), Ghaffar Khan's brother, Dr Khan Sahib, became the new, or the second, chief minister, of the province. But, instead of strengthening the movement and moving it forwards, the Congress-Khudayi Khidmatgars' ministry produced a poor impression with far reaching consequences. The ministry re-promulgated the repressive and infamous Frontier Crimes Regulation which proved detrimental to the interests, aims, and progress of the movement; and, its members, once more, fell prey to the atrocities and persecutions under the regulation. Also, Dr Khan Sahib, who had blind faith in the British and played along with the Governor, Cunningham, proved a stumbling blow for the movement. Ghaffar Khan admitted that the rule of the Congress/Khudayi Khidmatgars ministry greatly damaged the movement. Therefore, not only did he want the resignation of the ministry, but the Khudayi Khidmatgars' *jargah* also decided in its favour because the non-cooperation on the part of the government was damaging the movement instead of strengthening it.[95]

REVISED PLEDGE AND PRINCIPLES

There was an attempt to expand the movement beyond the Frontier Province to other parts of India—the Punjab, Saharanpur, Sindh, Baluchistan, etc. On Ghaffar Khan's return to the Frontier in 1937, the people reverted to the red uniform and violated the ban. The government resorted to punitive measures but failed to suppress the movement in spite of employing various means. Instead, the movement flourished by leaps and bounds as the people became politically aware. Finally, the government lifted all restrictions on the Khudayi Khidmatgars,[96] interestingly under Sahibzadah Abdul Qayyum's ministry.

The pledge and principles of the Khudayi Khidmatgar movement were revised, composed in Pukhtu, in 1937, and were as follows:

I acknowledge the Almighty omnipresent and omniscient and believe in Him, and declare on oath that I will strictly abide by it.

1. I sincerely and faithfully offer my name to be a Khudayi Khidmatgar.
2. I will sacrifice my life, property, rest and comfort faithfully for the freedom of my nation and the homeland (*qaam aw hiwad*).
3. I will refrain from making such factions and fractions in the organisation of the Khudayi Khidmatgars that will bring loss or weakness to the organisation.
4. I will not become a member of any other organisation or party and, in the war of independence, I will neither tender apology nor submit any security.
5. I will be ready, at all times, to obey any lawful order of my leader.
6. I will always strictly abide by the principles of non-violence.
7. I will serve all creatures of the Almighty alike. My aim will be the independence of the homeland.
8. I will always strictly stand by doing good and pious deeds.
9. I will never keep expectations, or expect rewards, of anything for my service.
10. All my endeavours will be for the sake of the Almighty; and will not be for showing off or affectation.[97] [translation mine]

According to Fazl-ur-Rahim Saqi, Abdul Ghaffar Khan repeated the pledge of the Khudayi Khidmatgars at a public meeting in Sardhiru, on 25 March 1946, to the effect:

1. I will serve all the creatures of the Almighty.
2. All my services will be for the sake of the Almighty. I will not ask for a reward from anyone.
3. I will oppose all oppressors and assist the oppressed.
4. I will never abstain from sacrificing my life, property, and progeny in the way of the Almighty; and I will not tender an apology in the struggle against the oppressor; will not submit any security bond.

5. I will consider all Pukhtuns, equally, my brothers, and will not involve myself in racial discrimination.
6. I will strive to do pious deeds and will abstain from bad acts.
7. I will not resort to violence, fighting, or quarrelling.
8. I will strive for winning freedom for my homeland and maintaining its independence.
9. I will obey every lawful order of my officer.
10. I will not be part of factions and fractions.
11. All my services will be for the sake of the Almighty and not for getting any rank or for showing off.
12. I will use locally-made articles.[98] [translation mine]

Dr Sayed Wiqar Ali Shah, on the other hand, has given a translation of the terms of the pledge and principles, from the record of the Special Branch Police, as follows:

I call on God as a witness, and solemnly declare on oath that I will abide by the following principles:

1. With sincerity and faith, I offer my name for Khudai Khidmatgarship.
2. I will sacrifice my wealth, comfort and self in the service of my nation and for the liberation of my country.
3. I will never have 'para jamba' (party feeling), enmity with or wilfully oppose anybody; and I shall help the oppressed against the oppressor.
4. I will not become a member of any other rival party nor will I give security or apologize during the fight.
5. I will always obey every lawful order of every officer of mine.
6. I will always abide by the principle of non-violence.
7. I will serve all human beings alike, and my goal will be the attainment of the freedom of my country and my religion.
8. I will always perform good and noble deeds.
9. All my efforts will be directed to seeking the will of God and not towards mere show or becoming an office-holder.[99]

CIVIL DISOBEDIENCE AND QUIT INDIA MOVEMENT

After the resignation of the Congress ministries in 1939, the Congress Working Committee passed a resolution for civil disobedience. It was decided that only the All India Congress Committee members and the members of the central and provincial assemblies would observe the civil disobedience, and further details regarding how it would be carried out were to be chalked out. But most of those to whom it applied did not comply. Ghaffar Khan has, especially, despised the behaviour and role played by the lawyers associated with the Khudayi Khidmatgar movement. Only a few people, out of those on whom it applied, behaved in the required manner.[100]

When, after Japan joined World War II, the Congress decided to rescind its policy and principle of non-violence, in spite of Gandhi and Ghaffar Khan's opposition, Ghaffar Khan resigned from the Congress and its working committee and became more involved in the work of the Khudayi Khidmatgars. He decided to resume his tours of the province, especially the tribal areas, to counter British machinations. The permission of the colonial government, for travelling to the tribal areas, was sought but the government wanted his attempts to fail. The political agents, in the tribal political agencies, did their best, through the *malak*s (in Pukhtu: *malakan/malakanan*) and others, to not allow the delegates to enter the tribal areas. The tours, however, produced favourable results for the movement, even though the British as well as the Afghan government were involved in this anti-Khudayi Khidmatgar drive.[101]

During the Quit India movement, in 1942, the provincial *jargah* and the Khudayi Khidmatgars held a meeting to chalk out a course of action for the new scenario. It was decided to send delegations to ask the government's native servants to resign from their jobs. Moreover, British courts were to be raided, British officers removed from their chairs, and people to be asked to adjudicate their disputes and cases themselves rather than taking them to the British officers. As the delegations proved ineffective, the Khudayi Khidmatgars started raiding the district courts in Peshawar, Mardan, Kuhat, and Bannu. At first, the Khudayi Khidmatgars were not imprisoned for the raids but were beaten by the police and their accomplices. Some lost their lives because of the severity of the beatings. The native officers, and even those who had been recruited by the Congress ministry and the scions of the Khudayi Khidmatgars, were strict and brutal in their use of force so as to prove their loyalty and adherence to the British cause. The government abstained from arresting the Khudayi Khidmatgars and used other means to make the movement fail. But when Ghaffar Khan started his tours and meetings, the government resorted to arrests. Ghaffar Khan, and a large number of the Khudayi Khidmatgars, were put behind bars, and remained there for three years.[102]

CENTRE—MARKAZ-I AALIYAH-I KHUDAYI KHIDMATGARAN

The need for a centre for the movement was perceived, and so a site was selected on the western side of the Sardaryab Bridge on the Peshawar-Charsadah Road, and the land was endowed by the concerned landowners. Work on its construction was started on 5 August 1942. A great plan was prepared for the centre—to be named the Markaz-i Aaliyah-i Khudayi Khidmatgaran—but before its construction could be completed Pakistan came into being, the Congress ministry was dissolved, and the Muslim League ministry, headed by Qaiyum Khan, was formed. Qaiyum Khan put the Khudayi Khidmatgars behind bars and confiscated and sold the centre. As he did not want any trace of the centre to remain, it was blown up with explosives in 1948.[103] Although Abdul Wali Khan has given the year as 1949,[104] quoting the order of the chief secretary of the province, Dr Syed Minhaj ul Hassan has stated that it was 'on 15 September 1948' that the 'headquarter of the *Khudai Khudmatgars*, along with the attached lands at Sardaryab, were confiscated'.[105]

ZALMAY PUKHTUN

Abdul Ghaffar Khan has asserted that the Muslim League sent Major Khurshid—who had been dismissed from the army—from Punjab to the Frontier at the time of the elections (of 1946) to create civil war among the Pukhtuns. Major Khurshid instigated the people to murder the Khudayi Khidmatgar leaders. To foil his nefarious designs, an organisation of Pukhtun youth, named Zalmay Pukhtun, was founded—probably in December 1946 but it came to prominence in May 1947—headed by Ghaffar Khan's eldest son Ghani Khan.[106] Only those youth who did not believe in non-violence joined the organisation. The members of the new organisation announced that their sole aim was the protection of the Khudayi Khidmatgars, to foil any attempted violence against them as they themselves believed in non-violence. The League founded a counter organisation in the Frontier, named Ghazi Pukhtun, but clashes were averted because of a fear of retribution.[107]

Ghaffar Khan tries to disown any connection of Zalmay Pukhtun with the Khudayi Khidmatgars by stating that it 'has no connection with [the] Red Shirt movement... It is quite a separate body. I still believe in non-violence, as it is my firm conviction that the country in general and the Frontier Province in particular should stick to non-violence. Violence spreads hatred, while non-violence spreads love.' He, moreover, terms its foundation a 'direct reaction on Pathans of the violent movement pursued by the Muslim League in the Frontier Province'.[108] He, however, tacitly approves it and its activities by appreciating its role.

Interestingly, the Zalmay Pukhtun 'laid even more stress on Pakhtun nationalism than the Khudai Khidmatgars and were much more vociferously Muslim'. They, moreover, 'disclaimed any connection' with the Congress and 'were openly scornful of its Hindu-tainted ideology'.[109] Ghani Khan mocked the non-violence in the Pukhtuns, and 'in a fiery manifesto, published in May 1947', declared that the Zalmay Pukhtun 'was a movement of the youth, "meant for the Pakhtun nation alone".' The organisation

> had nothing to do with any central Hindu organisation. The goal was 'Freedom and Prosperity'. On its flag there were two swords and the words 'Allah-o-Akbar'. Its only message was *Pakhtunwali*. The members wore smart red uniforms, but their real uniforms were their Darra-made guns and fearless eyes; a pistol on a Pakhtun was as beautiful as bangles on a girl from Delhi. The handloom, on the other hand, was nothing for a man. As for *ahimsa* (the Hindu doctrine of non-violence) it would be understood by the Pathans only when the offspring of lions learnt to bleat like sheep.[110]

Although Ghani Khan mocked the ideology of non-violence and *ahimsa*, and disowned any connection with the Congress, and Ghaffar Khan tried to disown the Zalmay Pukhtun and its ideology, the latter organisation proved a great asset and strength to the Khudayi Khidmatgar movement at the critical juncture of its life. However, it was disbanded after Independence because of differences with Ghaffar Khan about the proposed course of action and policy in the new scenario; and Ghani Khan retired permanently from armed struggle and politics.

PROGRAMME AND PLAN OF WOULD-BE RULE

The Khudayi Khidmatgar movement's programme and plan of the ruling can be ascertained from what Ghaffar Khan said during the course of his speeches at public meetings. At the time of his visits to the Khalil-Muhmand, where he was referred to as the king, he asked the people not to talk of making him a king. He told them that their movement is not for his kingship. If they make him a king: firstly, there is no kingship in Islam, and secondly, he would be rolling in luxury but they would perish. They could not make him or any other person their king. We neither wish to make kings nor have need for kings. We would have a head (elder, leader) who would be nominated through consultation, and the will and consent of the nation (*qaum*). The head would be the servant of the nation. There would be no discrimination on the basis of birth and status, but personal virtues would be valued. The organisation would not be under the government, but the government would be under the organisation. No one person would be made the *khan*, but would try to make all the people *khan*s. It was their endeavour to constitute a government that would benefit all alike. Food would be taken collectively, whether tasteless or delicious. Peace and justice would be ensured. There would be a common *jargah*, and a president would be appointed with the consent of the *jargah*.[111]

During the course of the Quit India movement, while addressing a public meeting at Chawk Yadgar in Peshawar, Ghaffar Khan told the audience that in case they succeeded and got independence, they should remember that the homeland belongs to the nation and all Pukhtuns collectively. They would eat their food collectively, whether maize or wheat. It would not be that one person would be hungry while the other would have delicious food to eat. Their priority would be to cater to the needs of the poor first. They would not make a person *khan* or king, and would not empower one person because, in doing so, others would perish while the empowered one and his relatives and friends would flourish. Hence, power would be in the hands of the nation and the national *jargah*.[112] These words spoke of the future designs and plans of the movement, and the structure, form, duties, and obligations of a future government of the Khudayi Khidmatgars. How far their plans were feasible or practical is open to discussion.

FINANCES

Running an organisation or movement without finances is impossible. The same was applicable to the Khudayi Khidmatgar movement and its organisation. The Khudayi Khidmatgars, however, refused to accept any financial assistance or support from other organisations, including from its ally, the Congress—something the Congress' leaders did not appreciate.[113] Its financial needs were met by donations from the people to whom their appeals were always made.

After the establishment of the centre at Sardaryab, a *bait-ul-mal*, or national exchequer, was established for the organisation, and for the assistance of the movement's needy members, orphans, and family members. Appeals were made to the wealthy for financial support.[114]

Supporters were also asked to give five per cent of their incomes as a donation to the organisation. The response was quite encouraging.[115] With the establishment of the *bait-ul-mal*, some of the financial needs of the movement were met and the will of the Khudayi Khidmatgars increased.

While speaking of the mistakes of Dr Khan Sahib and Ghaffar Khan that benefited the opposition, Abul Kalam Azad talks about their miserliness and states: 'Their miserliness extended even to public funds spent under their direction. During the General Elections, Congress placed large amounts at their disposal, but the Khan brothers spent as little as possible out of these funds.'[116] Azad's statement creates the impression that the Khudayi Khidmatgars received funds from the Congress. Ghaffar Khan, however, repudiates Azad's contentions, and contends that the Khudayi Khidmatgars had never taken a single *paisah* (*paisa*) from the Congress, and that even Jawaharlal Nehru had become annoyed at his refusal to accept financial support from the Congress (in 1931) and termed him proud; had they given something to the Congress Parliamentary Board (in 1946) that, too, would have been taken by them and hence not by the Khudayi Khidmatgars.[117]

Dr Ansar Zahid Khan, however, asserts: 'The statement of Abul Kalam Azad cannot be totally ignored as he was incharge [in charge] of elections for the provinces in northern India together with Rajendra Prasad.'[118] M.S. Korejo and Juma Khan Sufi, too, have expressed their reservations and observations in this respect. Juma Khan Sufi tries to prove that funds were received from the Congress and has alleged that money also went into Ghaffar Khan's family members' pockets—that they benefited materially, in different ways, from the movement and the struggle, and that they amassed wealth both in the pre- and post-partition days:[119] a contention open to further investigation.

AT THE THRESHOLD

When the politics of India took a turn after the failure of the Cabinet Mission Plan, and the division of India was ultimately decided, the situation became grave for the Khudayi Khidmatgars because of their long-standing association with the Congress and also because of the Congress' *volte face*. The Khudayi Khidmatgar leaders participated in the combined meeting of the Provincial Jargah, members of the assembly, Khudayi Khidmatgars, and Zalmay Pukhtun held on 21 June 1947 in Bannu, where the decision was taken for an independent Pukhtun state and where it was resolved that the Pukhtuns wanted to join neither India nor Pakistan.[120]

The Khudayi Khidmatgars demanded that the option of an independent Pukhtun state should also be included with the previously-given two options of joining India or Pakistan. As the British, Congress, and Muslim League did not accede to the demand, they decided to boycott the referendum, to be held in the province, on the question of whether the people of the province wanted to join India or Pakistan.[121] The League, however, pursued the referendum campaign vigorously, tirelessly, and zealously.

In the backdrop of the boycott by the Khudayi Khidmatgars and the zealous campaigning by the League, the referendum was held in July 1947 in the settled districts of the province. 50.99% of the total registered votes of 572,798 were cast, out of which 289,244 were in favour of joining Pakistan and 2,874 were in favour of joining India.[122] The Khudayi Khidmatgars, however, alleged that rigging and casting of spurious votes in favour of Pakistan had taken place.[123]

Qaiyum Khan asserted, in 1945, that 'throughout the vicissitudes of time'—after the affiliation of the Khudayi Khidmatgars with Congress—Ghaffar Khan 'has never had occasion to regret' the decision of the affiliation.[124] The situation, however, changes somewhat subsequently and Ghaffar Khan laments Congress' policy and the course adopted by them at the end—agreeing to the division of India and the referendum in the Frontier Province—and terms it a conspiracy of Mountbatten's and Sardar Patel's. He contends that non-violence was the policy of the Congress but the belief of the Khudayi Khidmatgars. Moreover, he expresses grief over the consequent dismemberment and disillusionment of the arrangements of the Khudayi Khidmatgar movement, which was created with great labour, hardships, difficulties, and sacrifices. He concludes his autobiography with the *tapah*:

د زړه په باغ می بلئ وشوه [125]

بویه چه بیا پسرلی راځی سپږی ګلونه

Meaning: The hailstorm nipped the flowers of my heart's garden. There is no telling when spring will come again and the garden blossom.

POST-INDEPENDENCE SCENARIO

The Khudayi Khidmatgars were not in favour of the partition of India in the manner in which it took place. They demanded the inclusion of a third option, of an independent Pukhtun state, in the referendum to be held on whether the people of the Frontier Province wanted to join India or Pakistan. At the non-acceptance of their demand, they resolved to boycott the referendum. The result of the referendum was in favour of joining Pakistan, and, hence, the province became an integral part of Pakistan when it came into being on '15 August 1947' under the 'Indian Independence Act, 1947'.[126] Afterwards, on the instruction of the Governor-General of Pakistan, M.A. Jinnah, the governor dissolved the Congress-Khudayi Khidmatgars ministry in the province, headed by Dr Khan Sahib, and replaced it with a League ministry headed by Abdul Qaiyum Khan. Qaiyum Khan was determined to take the Khudayi Khidmatgars to task.

The Khudayi Khidmatgars, however, expressed their allegiance to Pakistan shortly after its formation. They held a large gathering at Sardaryab on 3–4 September 1947, attended by Khudayi Khidmatgars, the Provincial Jargah, the Parliamentary Party, the Zalmay Pukhtun, and representatives from the tribal areas. They resolved that they 'regard Pakistan as their own country' and pledged that they would do their best 'to strengthen and safeguard its interest, and [will] make every sacrifice for the cause'.[127] They further resolved that though 'dismissal of Dr Khan Sahib's ministry and the setting up of Abdul Qaiyum's ministry is undemocratic, but as our country is passing through a critical stage, the Khudai Khidmatgars shall take no step which might create difficulties in the way of either the Provincial or Central Government'. They, moreover, resolved: 'After the division of the country the Khudai Khidmatgars sever their connection with the All-India Congress organisation and, therefore, instead of the Tricolour adopt the Red Flag as the symbol of their party.'[128]

Ghaffar Khan also solemnly took the oath of allegiance to the Constitution of Pakistan, being a member of the Pakistan parliament. He, however, demanded a united Pukhtun province within Pakistan and started touring the province for this purpose. He was arrested, on 15 June 1948, and sentenced to three years' 'rigorous imprisonment' which, after a few months, was extended to an indefinite period by the central government 'under Bengal State Prisoners Regulation 111 of India 1818'.[129] In his bid to eradicate the Khudayi Khidmatgar movement, Qaiyum Khan arrested and tortured a large number of the Khudayi Khidmatgars and, on 15

September 1948, the governor banned the movement under the North-West Frontier Province Public Safety Ordinance.[130]

The Khudayi Khidmatgars organised demonstrations against the steps and actions of the government. On 12 August 1948, they organised a peaceful demonstration and march in Charsadah, which was also meant 'to press the government for the acceptance of their demand to impose Shariat Law in the country'.[131] The government, however, imposed section 144 of the Criminal Procedure Code in the Charsadah area to stop the meeting. In spite of the government's endeavours, a number of the Khudayi Khidmatgars succeeded in reaching the venue, and leading a procession. The police opened indiscriminate fire on the peaceful and non-violent agitators, causing a dreadful toll of lives and injuries. Although the actual number of dead and injured is not known, the number of the dead was estimated at 'more than 600'. Whereas one official source claimed '15 killed and 50 wounded', another stated '20 killed and 25 wounded'.[132] As the incident took place near the village of Babara (Babarah), it is known as the 'Babara incident' or 'Babara massacre'. Qaiyum Khan, during his rule, even had his self-authored book, titled *Gold and Guns on the Pathan Frontier,* confiscated[133]—what a unique act of confiscating one's own book![134] The book had been written at a time when Qaiyum Khan was in the Congress and it contained pro-Khudayi Khidmatgars, pro-Ghaffar Khan, and pro-Dr Khan contents, and was dedicated to Dr Khan Sahib.

Abul Kalam Azad also has spoken of Qaiyum Khan's machinations, mischief, and highhandedness against the Khudayi Khidmatgars. He states:

Khan Abdul Qayyum Khan, who had formed the Ministry in the Frontier, was naturally opposed to any reconciliation between Mr Jinnah and the Khan brothers [Abdul Ghaffar Khan and Dr Khan Sahib]. He therefore behaved in a way which made any understanding impossible. In fact his Government acted without any sense of decency or justice and harassed the Khudai Khidmatgars by adopting all kinds of illegal and unfair measures. Democracy was crushed and force became the order of the day. Khan Abdul Ghaffar Khan, Dr Khan Saheb [Sahib] and all other leaders of the Khudai Khidmatgars were sent to jail where they languished for almost six years without any legal charge or trial. Khan Abdul Qayyum Khan's vendetta became so bitter that even a section of the Muslim League was disgusted and said that either the Khan brothers should be prosecuted or released. All such efforts were however of no avail. Lawless oppression was perpetrated in the name of the law.[135]

James W. Spain states that 'the unnatural alliance' between the Khudayi
Khidmatgars and the Congress 'lasted until the end of British rule, with
the bulk of the Khudai Khitmatgars refusing even to vote in favor of
Pakistan over India in the referendum of 1947. However, once the die
was cast and the Frontier opted for Pakistan, the Khudai Khitmatgars
disintegrated rapidly.'[136] He, moreover, contends that 'the Khudai
Khitmatgars, after less than twenty years of violent [sic] and sometime
spectacularly successful political activity, ceased [in 1948] to exist, and
with this, the crisis of Partition on the Frontier ended'.[137] Although the
Partition proved a set-back for, and a turning point in the life and struggle
of, the Khudayi Khidmatgar movement, and many parted ways with it in
light of the changed circumstances, the new scenario after the creation
of Pakistan, and the ban on it by the government, the movement still
adhered to by its exponents and adherents and Ghaffar Khan was regarded
as its leader.

Out of prison in 1953, after six years, Ghaffar Khan bitterly criticised
the dissolution of the first constituent assembly of Pakistan by Ghulam
Muhammad in 1954. The Khudayi Khidmatgars also opposed the
creation of one-unit—through the merging of all the then-West Pakistan
provinces—but to no avail. They did their best to block the scheme—
demanding that if the government was determined to proceed with
the scheme, public opinion should be sought through a referendum;
alternatively, a general election should be held after which the opinions
of the elected representatives should be sought. Ghaffar Khan was
arrested in 1956 for his opposition to the one-unit plan; he was released
on 25 January 1957.[138] A new political party, the National Awami
Party (NAP), was formed by some Pakistani politicians in 1956, while
Ghaffar Khan was in jail. On 27 January 1957, after his release from jail
on 25 January, Ghaffar Khan announced an affiliation of the Khudayi
Khidmatgar movement with the National Awami Party.[139] According to
another version, he 'announced his decision to join Pakistan National
Party' (PNP) on 27 January 1957, and in July 1957 he, along with Abdul
Hamid Khan Bashani, G.M. Sayyad, and Mian Iftikhar-ud-Din, 'formed
the National Awami Party' (NAP) in Dhaka.[140]

Although Ghaffar Khan joined the NAP and affiliated the Khudayi
Khidmatgar movement with it, the step was not of much use because the
NAP was a political party with aims and objectives on an all-Pakistan
level. Moreover, by joining the NAP, the main concern of some of the
Khudayi Khidmatgars, like Ghaffar Khan's son Abdul Wali Khan, shifted
from the Khudayi Khidmatgars to the NAP and Pakistani politics. Besides,

Ghaffar Khan himself mostly remained in jail, followed by self-exile. Moreover, although Dr Khan Sahib was not a Khudayi Khidmatgar, his favouring the One Unit and becoming the chief minister of the province of West Pakistan proved to be neither good nor favourable for the movement—because he was Ghaffar Khan's brother and he had thrice been the chief minister of the former Frontier Province on behalf of the Khudayi Khidmatgars-Congress.

> It was quite fascinating that in the 1950,s [1950s] when Abdul Ghaffar Khan was at daggers drawn with the government, Dr Khan Sahib enjoyed enormous political standing. In 1954, he was inducted as central Minister of Communications and Railway in the Muhammad Ali Bogra ministry... When the One-Unit was formed in 1955 Dr Khan exploited the infighting of the Muslim League and was elected as the first Chief Minister of the West Pakistan on 14th [14th] October 1955... At times when Abdul Ghaffar Khan was exerting for provincial autonomy and annulment of One Unit, Dr Khan was limning rosy picture of the new set up.[141]

Dr Khan Sahib went to the extent of forming his own party, the Republican Party, for his own ends. The strained relations between Dr Khan Sahib and the Khudayi Khidmatgars can be judged from the fact that the National Awami Party, which Ghaffar Khan and his son Wali Khan had joined and with which the Khudayi Khidmatgar movement was affiliated, entered into an alliance with their former arch-enemy, the Muslim League, against Dr Khan Sahib.[142]

Dr Khan Sahib's rule and role proved detrimental to the cause, aims, and progress of the Khudayi Khidmatgar movement, both in the pre- and post-partition days.

REFORMULATION OF THE PRINCIPLES AND PLEDGE

Although Ghaffar Khan went into self-exile, in Afghanistan from Pakistan, in 1964 and remained so till 1972, it has been stated that he reformulated the basic principles of the Khudayi Khidmatgars in 1967, to the effect that:

1. Every Khudayi Khidmatgar will not harm the creatures of the Almighty either through tongue or hands, and the work that he does not like for himself will also not like for others.
2. Every Khudayi Khidmatgar will not backbite and degrade any person and will not tell lies.

3. Every Khudayi Khidmatgar will be patient, and combat high-handedness and oppression with good disposition, and will correct the wrong-doers with love and affection.
4. Every Khudayi Khidmatgar will not side with the oppressor but will assist the oppressed.
5. Every Khudayi Khidmatgar will not get involved in faction politics, fraction making, or enmity.
6. Every Khudayi Khidmatgar will give up bad customs and practices that bring losses to the nation and the homeland, and will preach and endeavour for the elimination of the evil customs.
7. Every Khudayi Khidmatgar will adopt a simple life.
8. Every Khudayi Khidmatgar will do his lawful profession and work, and will not like the life of idleness and dependence.
9. Every Khudayi Khidmatgar will have love for the nation and homeland, and will serve them honestly; will not bargain the nation and the homeland away for wealth and office; will not abstain from any kind of sacrifice for the nation and the homeland.
10. Every Khudayi Khidmatgar will accept and abide by the majority and the agreed decision and resolution of his party.

Pledge of the Khudayi Khidmatgars:

I acknowledge the Almighty omnipresent and omniscient and pledge that I will remain faithful to my party and will abide by the abovementioned ten principles.[143] [translation mine]

ACHIEVEMENTS

Addressing a query about what the Khudayi Khidmatgars and the non-violent movement achieved, Ghaffar Khan says that the Khudayi Khidmatgari had two objectives: independence of the homeland and inculcation of a sense of nationhood, brotherhood, love, affection, unity, and a sense of oneness in the Pukhtuns. He contends that the sense was inculcated and the homeland got independence, and all this was achieved not through violence but through non-violent means. The Khudayi Khidmatgari created such a sense of love and affection, and awakened the spirit of brotherhood among the Muslims, Hindus, and Sikhs alike, that those Hindus and Sikhs who were compelled to leave the Frontier continued to refer to themselves as Khudayi Khidmatgars, and their love and affection was still palpable in their hearts. The Khudayi Khidmatgars faced great hardships in protecting their Sikh and Hindu members, whose lives and properties they had protected because they had adopted non-violence as a belief whereas the Congress took it only as policy.[144]

The great achievement of the movement was that it was not simply a showpiece of the upper classes, but reached the grassroots level of the society. Not only did it create political awareness and wisdom among all sections and classes of the Pukhtun society, but it also had its adherents in all the sections and classes. It infused a sense of equality and brotherhood, and enthused a spirit of public service and sacrifice in its adherents. It was due to the Khudayi Khidmatgar movement and its ideals that the common people and laymen of the province became politically aware and enjoyed a sense of equality, as compared to the other provinces of Pakistan. Moreover, politics in the province did not remain the domain of the landlords and upper class only, as was the case in the other provinces.

About the Khudayi Khidmatgars, Ghani Khan states, 'Their aim was freedom: their motto service.'[145] Although the aim was achieved, the motto gradually melted away in the heat of the struggle for the aim, and also because of the association with the Congress: an all-India party that had little concern for the Frontier's affairs—and no special or great interest in the amelioration of its social and educational problems, backward conditions, or the distress of the people—due to its broader range of activities and interests on an all-India basis.

Largely being a socio-economic reform movement, the Khudayi Khidmatgar movement aimed at ameliorating the social and economic as well as political conditions of all segments and classes of Pukhtun society, which is evident from the objectives and principles set forth and modified from time to time, and the pledges required of and taken from the Khudayi Khidmatgars. Although the movement took on a dominantly political shape with the passage of time, because of the factors suggested above and because its leadership focussed on political issues, there is no doubt that it greatly lessened the inter-tribal, and particularly the inter-family, violent conflicts. It also resolved socio-economic problems, at least of its members. The Khudayi Khidmatgars, for instance, were compulsorily required to work with their own hands every day; also, they could not resort to violence, had to abstain from factional fighting and oppression, and had to side with the oppressed, could not backbite or take revenge.

In this way, it changed the outlook and behaviour of the people. Old rivalries and enmities were turned into friendships and cordial relations. The sense of shame and the feeling of inferiority at working with one's own hands—found especially in the landlord and elite circles of the society—came to an end. The Pukhtuns, especially the wealthy and landlord segment, started to trade—which had, till then, been considered the occupation of the Hindus and Parachas—and undertake agriculture— which had been considered the occupation of the landless gentry and the poor Pukhtuns who possessed small land holdings.

DOWNFALL

There is no doubt that the Khudayi Khidmatgar movement progressed tremendously. A large number of people joined it in its early phase and pre-Partition days, and its membership increased by leaps and bounds. The main reason for its progress, according to Dr Sayed Wiqar Ali Shah, was that its programme was interpreted by various sections of the Pukhtun society—

> in their own way. To the Pashtoon intelligentsia, it was a movement for the revival of Pashtoon culture with its distinct identity. To the smaller Khans, it was a movement that demanded political reforms for the province that would enfranchise them and give them a greater role in governance. Its anti-colonial stand suited the majority of the anti-establishment ulema, who always regarded British rule in the subcontinent as a 'curse'. For the peasants and other poor classes it was against their economic oppressors, British imperialism and its agents—the pro-British Nawabs, Khan Bahadurs and the big Khans.[146]

Whereas, according to James W. Spain:

> A large part of the Khudai Khitmatgars' success lay in the organization's conformity to traditional Pathan methods and outlook. It served as a vehicle for the expression of discontent growing out of the absolute and rigid British administration of the N-WFP and the stern implementation of the Razmak Policy. In a sense, it probably contributed to the peace of the Frontier by providing the means for political action where previously violent action had been the exclusive mode. Added to this were some rudimentary new ideas of economic and social improvement. It was above all, however, a Pathan party, and at this early stage fairly remote from Congress control.[147]

The movement was basically socio-economic reform movement; its 'most remarkable feature...was the adoption of non-violence' as its creed and its 'strict adherence to it. The volunteers were taught not to resort to violence; they bore no arms and carried no weapons.'[148] It took a political turn because of the policies of the colonial government, its affiliation with the Congress, and the changed circumstances. Ghaffar Khan 'always tried to maintain' the 'blending of idealistic and ethical points of view' of the movement but 'with a strong anti-imperialist outlook'.[149] When the editor of the *Civil and Military Gazette* told Ghaffar Khan, in Simla after the Irwin-Gandhi Pact of 1931, that as peace had been made with the government what is the need of the Khudayi Khidmatgar movement? You are to dissolve the movement immediately. Ghaffar Khan replied that it was possible, provided the government met a single condition. When asked about the condition, he said that if the British gave independence to the Indians, the movement would automatically come to an end.[150]

This statement and prophecy proved true on the independence of India. It is not strange that the movement dwindled and went into oblivion after the departure of the British because it had already evolved from a socio-economic reform movement into one with a dominant political shape. With the changed scenario and ground realities, and the movement's political stand, its dissolution and sinking into the realm of insignificance—despite Ghaffar Khan's claim, 'Our movement has never waned and never will'[151]—although may seem surprising at first, was not unnatural.

In the post-Partition days, the situation changed greatly both politically and socially. In the changed political scenario, the interest, outlook, and challenges also changed when compared to the time when the movement was formed and the succeeding years. Adhered to by a number of its exponents and adherents, the principles of the Khudayi Khidmatgari were reformulated in the new and changed scenario. Although the Khudayi Khidmatgars endeavoured to reactivate it as a social reform movement, they met with little success. Not only was it too late, but their leader was also out of the homeland. The process of its disintegration had already started. Therefore, endeavours for its reactivation and revitalisation with the reformulation of its principles and objectives brought about no significant progress or achievement. The process of its decay— already started due to a number of factors—continued and the movement ultimately went into oblivion.

Nevertheless, most Pukhtun nationalists claim their lineage from the movement and call themselves followers of Ghaffar Khan. Therefore, the impact of the Khudayi Khidmatgar movement still persists, even if not in its true and original form or with a mass following. The leaders of the now Awami National Party still carry out their politics in Ghaffar Khan's name, and do their best to cash in on his and the Khudayi Khidmatgar movement's names and services in spite of a great difference between the two organisations and their leaders.

Notes

1. Abdul Ghaffar [Khan], *Zama Jwand aw Jidujahd* (Pukhtu) (Kabul: DM, 1983).
2. Ibid., 1–57. Also see Khan Abdul Ghaffar Khan, *Ap Biti* (Urdu), repr. (Lahore: FH, 2004), 8–11, 15, 23–4; D.G. Tendulkar, *Abdul Ghaffar Khan: faith is a battle* (Bombay: PP, 1967), 13–19.
3. Ghaffar, *Zama Jwand aw Jidujahd*, 57–61. Also see Tendulkar, *Abdul Ghaffar Khan*, 19–20; Khan, *Ap Biti*, 16–18, 24; K.B. Narag, *My Life and Struggle: Autobiography of Badshah Khan as narrated to K.B. Narag*, with foreword by Jayaprakash Narayan, repr. (n.p.: DAT, 2008), 11–14.
4. Ghaffar, *Zama Jwand aw Jidujahd*, 30–1. Also see Tendulkar, *Abdul Ghaffar Khan*, 20–1; Narag, *My Life and Struggle*, 18–20.
5. Ghaffar, *Zama Jwand aw Jidujahd*, 64–5. Also see Tendulkar, *Abdul Ghaffar Khan*, 22; Narag, *My Life and Struggle*, 20.
6. For the 'colonial' and 'colonialist', see note 29 in chap. 6.
7. Ghaffar, *Zama Jwand aw Jidujahd*, 66–77. Also see Tendulkar, *Abdul Ghaffar Khan*, 22–3; Khan, *Ap Biti*, 24–5; Narag, *My Life and Struggle*, 20–1.
8. Ghaffar, *Zama Jwand aw Jidujahd*, 84–113. Also see Tendulkar, *Abdul Ghaffar Khan*, 24–5; Khan, *Ap Biti*, 26–31; Narag, *My Life and Struggle*, 24–30. For anti-British activities in the tribal areas during the course of the World War I, also see Sultan-i-Rome, 'Swat State under the Walis (1917–69)' (Unpublished PhD Dissertation, Department of History, University of Peshawar, 2000), 73–6; Sultan-i-Rome, *Swat State (1915–1969): From Genesis to Merger; An Analysis of Political, Administrative, Socio-Political, and Economic Developments* (Karachi: OUP, 2008), 76–9; Lal Baha, *N.-W.F.P. Administration under British Rule, 1901–1919* (Islamabad: NCHCR, 1978), 81–100.
9. M.A. Rahim, M.D. Chughtai, W. Zaman, and A. Hamid, *Book Four: Alien Rule and the Rise of Muslim Nationalism* in I.H. Qureshi, ed., *A Short History of Pakistan*, 2nd edn. (Karachi: UK, 1984), 185.
10. Ghaffar, *Zama Jwand aw Jidujahd*, 135–60. For a different version of why and how the epithet Bacha Khan was given to Ghaffar Khan, see Tendulkar, *Abdul Ghaffar Khan*, 26; Eknath Easwaran, *A Man to Match His Mountains: Badshah Khan, Nonviolent Soldier of Islam*, with afterword by Timothy Flinders, 2nd print (California: Nilgiri Press, 1985), 79.
11. For some details about the *khilafat* and *hijrat* movements and the role of the province, see Sultan-i-Rome, 'The Role of the North-West Frontier Province in the Khilafat and Hijrat Movements', *Islamic Studies* (Islamabad), vol. 43 (No. 1, Spring 2004), 51–78.
12. Ghaffar, *Zama Jwand aw Jidujahd*, 170–80. Also see Tendulkar, *Abdul Ghaffar Khan*, 32–3; Khan, *Ap Biti*, 43–4; Narag, *My Life and Struggle*, 41–4.
13. Ghaffar, *Zama Jwand aw Jidujahd*, 182–4. Also see Khan, *Ap Biti*, 47–8; Narag, *My Life and Struggle*, 44–6; Abdul Khaliq Khaleeq, *Da Azadai Jang: Sah Lidali aw sah Awridali* (Pukhtu), 2nd edn. (Pikhawar: IIS, 1972), 23–4.
14. Tendulkar, *Abdul Ghaffar Khan*, 36.
15. For details, see Ghaffar, *Zama Jwand aw Jidujahd*, 186–319. Also see Khan, *Ap Biti*, 49–79; Narag, *My Life and Struggle*, 48–75.
16. For *jargah*'s meaning, kinds, and functions, see chap. 3 of this book.
17. Ghaffar, *Zama Jwand aw Jidujahd*, 350–2.

18. *A Journal* (Pukhtu) with *sarizah* by Muhammad Gul (Jahangiri) (facts of publication have been torn but it was published in Afghanistan), 130.

19. See Khaleeq, *Da Azadai Jang*, 54–5 cf. Abdul Khaliq Khaleeq, *Zah aw Zama Zamanah* (Pukhtu) (Pikhawar: IIS, 1968), 59.

20. Ghaffar, *Zama Jwand aw Jidujahd*, 354; Khan, *Ap Biti*, 97; Narag, *My Life and Struggle*, 92. Also see Khaleeq, *Da Azadai Jang*, 57–8; Khaleeq, *Zah aw Zama Zamanah*, 61–2.

21. Ghaffar, *Zama Jwand aw Jidujahd*, 354–5.

22. For *hujrah,* and its functions and significance, see chap. 3 of this book.

23. Ghaffar, *Zama Jwand aw Jidujahd*, 355–6. Also see Khaleeq, *Da Azadai Jang*, 60–1. Interestingly, in Ghaffar Khan's narrative told to K.B. Narag a somewhat different version of the foundation of the movement is given. See Narag, *My Life and Struggle*, 85–8, 92. Also Khan, *Ap Biti*, 91–4, 97.

24. Sayed Wiqar Ali Shah, *Ethnicity, Islam, and Nationalism: Muslim Politics in the North-West Frontier Province, 1937–1947* (Karachi: OUP, 1999), 26–7.

25. See Khan, *Ap Biti*, 91–4. Also Narag, *My Life and Struggle*, 85–8.

26. Tendulkar, *Abdul Ghaffar Khan*, 58–9.

27. See Khan Abdul Wali Khan, *Bacha Khan aw Khudayi Khidmatgari* (Pukhtu), vol. 1 (Charsadah: WB, 1993), 92–3.

28. *A Journal*, 130.

29. For instance, see Abdul Qaiyum, *Gold and Guns on the Pathan Frontier* (Bombay: HK, 1945), 29; Shah, *Ethnicity, Islam, and Nationalism*, 26–7; Mukulika Banerjee, *The Pathan Unarmed* (Karachi: OUP, 2000), 56.

30. Banerjee, *The Pathan Unarmed*, 56.

31. Ghaffar, *Zama Jwand aw Jidujahd*, 356–7.

32. Ibid., 357–8. Also see Khan, *Ap Biti*, 94; Narag, *My Life and Struggle*, 89.

33. Ghaffar, *Zama Jwand aw Jidujahd*, 360–1.

34. Ghani Khan, *The Pathans: A Sketch*, repr. (Islamabad: PASR, 1990), 48.

35. Interview of Mahdi Shah Bacha by Munir Khan, Nowshera, 6 April 1994, quoted in Munir Khan 'The Khudai Khidmatgar Movement', (A term paper submitted to the Department of History, University of Peshawar, 2 May 1994), 5.

36. *A Journal*, 131.

37. Shah, *Ethnicity, Islam, and Nationalism*, 28.

38. Ghaffar, *Zama Jwand aw Jidujahd*, 359–62.

39. See ibid., 366–8, 536.

40. Ibid., 368–9. Also see Khaleeq, *Da Azadai Jang*, 63–5. Abdul Khaliq Khaleeq, however, has stated the dates of the meeting as 19–20 April 1930. See ibid., 63.

41. Qaiyum, *Gold and Guns on the Pathan Frontier*, 29.

42. See Ghaffar, *Zama Jwand aw Jidujahd*, 356–7, 416–18, 454–7, and passim; Tendulkar, *Abdul Ghaffar Khan*, 101–2, 134, and passim.

43. Fazl-ur-Rahim Saqi, *Da Khudayi Khidmatgarai pah Tahrik kay Zama Jwandun* (Pukhtu) (n.p.: Yusuf Lodi, n.d.), 33.

44. Ibid., 34.

45. Qaiyum, *Gold and Guns on the Pathan Frontier*, 43.

46. Ibid.

47. Juma Khan Sufi, *Bacha Khan, Congress and Nationalist Politics in NWFP* [henceforward Sufi, *Bacha Khan*] (Lahore: VB, 2005), 21.

48. Ibid., 7. Also see Chaudhri Muhammad Ali, *The Emergence of Pakistan*, 5th impr. (Lahore: RSP, 1985), 146.

49. See Saqi, *Da Khudayi Khidmatgarai pah Tahrik kay Zama Jwandun*, 45.

50. Stephen Alan Rittenberg, *Ethnicity, Nationalism, and the Pakhtuns: The Independence Movement in India's North-West Frontier Province* (Durham: CAP, 1988), 81.

51. Ghaffar, *Zama Jwand aw Jidujahd*, 370–4. Also see Khaleeq, *Da Azadai Jang*, 69.

52. Ghaffar, *Zama Jwand aw Jidujahd*, 376. For details of the incident, also see Allah Bukhsh Yusufi, *The Frontier Tragedy*, 2nd edn., Karachi: Mohammed Ali Education Society, 1986; Khaleeq, *Da Azadai Jang*, 67–8.

53. Ghaffar, *Zama Jwand aw Jidujahd*, 377–86. Also see Khaleeq, *Da Azadai Jang*, 70–86. For details about attacks on British-held areas and posts emanating from the tribal areas, about the colonial authorities' use of force, and about Gandhi's release being included as part of the tribesmen's demands for a settlement with the colonial government, see James W. Spain, *The Pathan Borderland*, repr. (Karachi: IP, 1985), 166–7, 169; Arthur Swinson, *North-West Frontier: People and Events, 1839–1947* (London: Hutchinson & Co (Publishers) Ltd, 1967), 313–18.

54. Rittenberg, *Ethnicity, Nationalism, and the Pakhtuns*, 80.

55. Amit Kumar Gupta, *North West Frontier Province: Legislature and Freedom Struggle, 1932–47* (New Delhi: ICHR, 1976), 16.

56. *India in 1930–31* (Calcutta: Government of India, 1932), p. 129 quoted in Gupta, *North West Frontier Province*, 16–17.

57. Jawaharlal Nehru, *The Discovery of India*, 12th impr. (New Delhi: JNMF, 1992), 381.

58. Rittenberg, *Ethnicity, Nationalism, and the Pakhtuns*, 81.

59. Swinson, *North-West Frontier*, 319.

60. Shah, *Ethnicity, Islam, and Nationalism*, 33.

61. Spain, *The Pathan Borderland*, 166.

62. See Ghaffar, *Zama Jwand aw Jidujahd*, 386–408. Also see Khan, *Ap Biti*, 103–20; Narag, *My Life and Struggle*, 99–118; Shah, *Ethnicity, Islam, and Nationalism*, 34; Easwaran, *A Man to Match His Mountains*, 120–9.

63. For details, see Sufi, *Bacha Khan*, 52–9; MS Korejo, *The Frontier Gandhi: His Place in History*, 2nd edn. (Karachi: OUP, 1994), 22–6. Also see Rittenberg, *Ethnicity, Nationalism, and the Pakhtuns*, 82–3.

64. See *JPHS* (Karachi), vol. 55 (Nos. 1–2, January–June 2007), 154, editor's note.

65. Khaleeq, *Da Azadai Jang*, 89–90. Also see Khaleeq, *Zah aw Zama Zamanah*, 77 n. 1.

66. Banerjee, *The Pathan Unarmed*, 69–70. Also see Gupta, *North West Frontier Province*, 18.

67. See Spain, *The Pathan Borderland*, 169.

68. Ghaffar, *Zama Jwand aw Jidujahd*, 418–30. Also see Khan, *Ap Biti*, 123–4; Narag, *My Life and Struggle*, 119–20.

69. Ghaffar, *Zama Jwand aw Jadujahd*, 486; Khan, *Ap Biti*, 133; Narag, *My Life and Struggle*, 130. Also see Khaleeq, *Da Azadai Jang*, 111.

70. Sufi, *Bacha Khan*, 33–4. For Abdul Akbar Khan and Mian Akbar Shah's contention, countering Ghaffar Khan's, also see Rittenberg, *Ethnicity, Nationalism, and the Pakhtuns*, 112–14.

71. Sufi, *Bacha Khan*, 74.

72. Farkhanda Liaqat, 'Da Abdul Akbar Khan Akbar da Jwand Halat', *Quarterly Tatara* (Pukhtu) (Pikhawar), vol. 10 (No. 1, January–March 2006), 71.

73. See Rittenberg, *Ethnicity, Nationalism, and the Pakhtuns*, 113–14.

74. Ghaffar, *Zama Jwand aw Jidujahd*, 441.

75. Ibid., 469–73, 496–500. Also see Khaleeq, *Da Azadai Jang*, 106–8.

76. Vartan Gregorian, *The Emergence of Modern Afghanistan: Politics of Reforms and Modernization, 1880–1946* (California: Stanford University Press, 1969), 324–5.

77. Ghaffar, *Zama Jwand aw Jidujahd*, 460. Also see Khan, *Ap Biti*, 139–40; Narag, *My Life and Struggle*, 134–5.

78. Gregorian, *The Emergence of Modern Afghanistan*, 326.

79. See Ghaffar, *Zama Jwand aw Jidujahd*, 361–2.

80. Gregorian, *The Emergence of Modern Afghanistan*, 327.

81. Ibid. Also see Qaiyum, *Gold and Guns on the Pathan Frontier*, 29, 32.

82. See Ghaffar, *Zama Jwand aw Jidujahd*, 458–69, 532–3, passim; Khan, *Ap Biti*, 140–1; Qaiyum, *Gold and Guns on the Pathan Frontier*, 31–4.

83. Gupta, *North West Frontier Province*, 24.

84. See Ghaffar, *Zama Jwand aw Jidujahd*, 472–5, 490–4, passim.

85. Gregorian, *The Emergence of Modern Afghanistan*, 328–9. Also see Ghaffar, *Zama Jwand aw Jidujahd*, 660–4.

86. See Ghaffar, *Zama Jwand aw Jidujahd*, 416–18, 431–5.

87. See ibid., 488–528. Also see Khan, *Ap Biti*, 120–21, 125–7.

88. Ghaffar, *Zama Jwand aw Jidujahd*, 535–78.

89. Shah, *Ethnicity, Islam, and Nationalism*, 37–8.

90. Gupta, *North West Frontier Province*, 29.

91. See ibid., 29–30. Also see Khaleeq, *Da Azadai Jang*, 115–16.

92. Spain, *The Pathan Borderland*, 171.

93. Rittenberg, *Ethnicity, Nationalism, and the Pakhtuns*, 136. For the composition and background of the party's candidates, see ibid., 135–6.

94. See Ghaffar, *Zama Jwand aw Jidujahd*, 589–95. Also see Saqi, *Da Khudayi Khidmatgarai pah Tahrik kay Zama Jwandun*, 22, 158.

95. See Ghaffar, *Zama Jwand aw Jidujahd*, 621–44. Also see Khan, *Ap Biti*, 155–6; Qaiyum, *Gold and Guns on the Pathan Frontier*, 38.

96. Ghaffar, *Zama Jwand aw Jidujahd*, 612.

97. *A Journal*, 132–3.

98. Saqi, *Da Khudayi Khidmatgarai pah Tahrik kay Zama Jwandun*, 145.

99. Shah, *Ethnicity, Islam, and Nationalism*, 44, n. 38.

100. See Ghaffar, *Zama Jwand aw Jidujahd*, 646–7.

101. See ibid., 654–64; *A Journal*, 181–4; Narag, *My Life and Struggle*, 150–8.

102. See Ghaffar, *Zama Jwand aw Jidujahd*, 666–84; Khan, *Ap Biti*, 157–66; *A Journal*, 194–8; Tendulkar, *Abdul Ghaffar Khan*, 353–8. Also see Nehru, *The Discovery of India*, 486.

103. See Ghaffar, *Zama Jwand aw Jidujahd*, 664–6, 715–16; Tendulkar, *Abdul Ghaffar Khan*, 349; *A Journal*, 186–90; Narag, *My Life and Struggle*, 150–1. Also see Khaleeq, *Da Azadai Jang*, 151–2; Khan Abdul Wali Khan, *Bacha Khan aw Khudayi Khidmatgari* (Pukhtu), vol. 2 (Charsadah: WB, 1994), 177.

104. See Khan, *Bacha Khan aw Khudayi Khidmatgari*, vol. 2, 177.

105. Syed Minhaj ul Hassan, 'NWFP Administration under Abdul Qaiyum Khan, 1947–53' (Unpublished PhD Dissertation, Department of History, University of Peshawar, 2003), 72; Syed Minhajul Hassan, *The Dawn of New Era in Khyber Pakhtunkhwa: Abdul Qaiyum Khan Chief Ministership, 1947–53* (Islamabad: NIHCR, 2016), 49.

106. Abdul Ghani (1913–1997) aka Ghani or Ghani Khan remained an active and vocal member of the central legislature of India before Partition. He was also known as the *liwanay falsafi* (insane philosopher). He was a renowned poet in Pukhtu as well as a prose writer in Pukhtu, Urdu, and English. Also see Rittenberg, *Ethnicity, Nationalism, and the Pakhtuns*, 232; Erland Jansson, *India, Pakistan or Pakhtunistan: The Nationalist Movements in the North-West Frontier Province, 1937–1947* (Stockholm: AWI, 1981), 208.

107. See Ghaffar, *Zama Jwand aw Jidujahd*, 687–8. Also see Narag, *My Life and Struggle*, 190–1.

108. Tendulkar, *Abdul Ghaffar Khan*, 418.

109. Jansson, *India, Pakistan or Pakhtunistan*, 208–9.

110. Ibid., 209.

111. See Ghaffar, *Zama Jwand aw Jidujahd*, 527–8.

112. See ibid., 669–70 cf. Tendulkar, *Abdul Ghaffar Khan*, 130.

113. See Ghaffar, *Zama Jwand aw Jidujahd*, 718.

114. *A Journal*, 190–1.
115. See Saqi, *Da Khudayi Khidmatgarai pah Tahrik kay Zama Jwandun*, 146–9. Also see Khaleeq, *Da Azadai Jang*, 152.
116. Abul Kalam Azad, *India Wins Freedom: An Autobiographical Narrative*, repr. (Bombay: OLL, 1964), 170.
117. See Ghaffar, *Zama Jwand aw Jidujahd*, 718. Also see Khan, *Ap Biti*, 124, 201–2; Tendulkar, *Abdul Ghaffar Khan*, 125, 448; Narag, *My Life and Struggle*, 198–200.
118. *Hamdard Islamicus* (Karachi), vol. 30 (No. 1, January–March 2007), 48, editor's note.
119. See Sufi, *Bacha Khan*, 343–7, passim. For M.S. Korejo's observations, see Korejo, *The Frontier Gandhi*, 40–2. Also see Ali, *The Emergence of Pakistan*, 146; Rittenberg, *Ethnicity, Nationalism, and the Pakhtuns*, 150.
120. See *A Journal*, 213–14; Tendulkar, *Abdul Ghaffar Khan*, 439.
121. *A Journal*, 209–15. Also see Ghaffar, *Zama Jwand aw Jidujahd*, 732–9; Khan, *Ap Biti*, 175–6; Tendulkar, *Abdul Ghaffar Khan*, 439–46.
122. Syed Waqar Ali Shah, *Muslim League in N.W.F.P.* (Karachi: RBC, 1992), 159. Also see Abdul Wali Khan, *Facts are Sacred*, trans. Aziz Siddiqui (Peshawar: Jaun Publishers, n.d.), 113; Abdul Wali Khan, *Rikhtya, Rikhtya di (Pirangay–Muslim League aw Mung)* (Pukhtu) (Kabul: Da Qaumunu aw Qabailu Wazarat, Da Nashratu Riyasat, 1987), 278; Wali Khan, *Facts are Facts: The Untold Story of India's Partition*, trans. Syeda Saiyidain Hameed, repr. (Peshawar: Publication Cell, Baacha Khan Trust, 2006), 166.
123. See Khan, *Facts are Sacred*, 112–13; Khan, *Rikhtya, Rikhtya di*, 276–8; Khan, *Facts are Facts*, 166; Tendulkar, *Abdul Ghaffar Khan*, 446–8; Khan, *Ap Biti*, 176–7; Narag, *My Life and Struggle*, 168.
124. Qaiyum, *Gold and Guns on the Pathan Frontier*, 44.
125. See Ghaffar, *Zama Jwand aw Jidujahd*, 732–40; Khan, *Ap Biti*, 175–6, 199–200.
126. See 'Indian Independence Act, 1947' in Safdar Mahmood, *Constitutional Foundation of Pakistan (Enlarged and Revised)* (Lahore: Jang Publishers, 1997), 31.
127. Tendulkar, *Abdul Ghaffar Khan*, 450. Also see Easwaran, *A Man to Match His Mountains*, 185; Hassan, 'NWFP Administration under Abdul Qaiyum Khan, 1947–53', 36, 55; Hassan, *The Dawn of New Era in Khyber Pakhtunkhwa*, 18–19, 33–4.
128. Tendulkar, *Abdul Ghaffar Khan*, 451.
129. Hassan, 'NWFP Administration under Abdul Qaiyum Khan', 61–2; Hassan, *The Dawn of New Era in Khyber Pakhtunkhwa*, 39–40.
130. Hassan, 'NWFP Administration under Abdul Qaiyum Khan', 71–2; Hassan, *The Dawn of New Era in Khyber Pakhtunkhwa*, 48–9. For details of Qaiyum Khan's policy and the steps to suppress the Khudayi Khidmatgars, see ibid., 33–54.
131. Hassan, 'NWFP Administration under Abdul Qaiyum Khan', 66; Hassan, *The Dawn of New Era in Khyber Pakhtunkhwa*, 44.
132. See Hassan, 'NWFP Administration under Abdul Qaiyum Khan', 67–9; Hassan, *The Dawn of New Era in Khyber Pakhtunkhwa*, 44–5. Also see Tendulkar, *Abdul Ghaffar Khan*, 466–7.
133. Abdul Qaiyum, *Gold and Guns on the Pathan Frontier* (Bombay: HK, 1945).
134. Abdul Wali Khan's interview by Adeeb Javidani, Editor, *Moon Digest*, in Javaid Ahmad Sidiqi, *Wali Khan Aaj aur Kal* (Urdu) (Karachi: Shibal Publications Limited, 1986), 180.
135. Azad, *India Wins Freedom*, 196. For Qaiyum Khan's policy and machinations to suppress not only the Khudayi Khidmatgars but also his other opponents, would-be rivals, and threats, even in the Muslim League, see Hassan, 'NWFP Administration under Abdul Qaiyum Khan', chap. 2; Hassan, *The Dawn of New Era in Khyber Pakhtunkhwa*, chap. 2.
136. Spain, *The Pathan Borderland*, 173.
137. Ibid., 202.
138. See *A Journal*, 227–45. Also Saqi, *Da Khudayi Khidmatgarai pah Tahrik kay Zama Jwandun*, 165.

139. Also see *A Journal*, 246–7 cf. Easwaran, *A Man to Match His Mountains*, 186.
140. Sayed Wiqar Ali Shah, 'Abdul Ghaffar Khan' in Parvez Khan Toru and Fazal-ur-Rahim Marwat, eds., *Celebrities of NWFP*, vol[s]. 1–2 (Peshawar: Pakistan Study Centre, University of Peshawar, 2005), 121. Also see Sayed Wiqar Ali Shah, *North-West Frontier Province: History and Politics* (Islamabad: NIHCR, 2007), 82; Khan, *Bacha Khan aw Khudayi Khidmatgari*, vol. 2, 312.
141. Fakhr-ul-Islam, 'Doctor Khan Sahib' in Toru and Fazal-ur-Rahim Marwat, eds., *Celebrities of NWFP*, vol[s]. 1–2, 65.
142. Ibid., 66.
143. *A Journal*, 133–4.
144. Ghaffar, *Zama Jwand aw Jidujahd*, 739–40.
145. Khan, *The Pathans*, 48.
146. Shah, *Ethnicity, Islam, and Nationalism*, 27–8.
147. Spain, *The Pathan Borderland*, 169.
148. Shah, *Ethnicity, Islam, and Nationalism*, 28. Also see Qaiyum, *Gold and Guns on the Pathan Frontier*, 30.
149. Gupta, *North West Frontier Province*, 15.
150. Ghaffar, *Zama Jwand aw Jidujahd*, 480.
151. Tendulkar, *Abdul Ghaffar Khan*, 448.

10 Muslim League

Muslim League in the Frontier emerged its own away [way], as it had
no model to emulate. None of the Muslim majority provinces of India
had any League organization.
– Dr Muhammad Anwar Khan

The growth of the Frontier League, in short, was not an independent
phenomenon but a response to its more powerful rival [the Frontier
Congress-Khudayi Khidmatgars].
– Stephen Alan Rittenberg

T HE NORTH-WEST FRONTIER PROVINCE was not only 'north-westerly
and not south-easterly in its outlook', as stated by Roos-Keppel,[1] but
also by nature and location. In Dr Muhammad Anwar Khan's opinion,
the 'Frontier…was slow in picking up with the political development of
India',[2] but it was the British government's discriminative treatment of
the Frontier land and its people that was responsible for this. The Frontier
was kept backward and cut off from the developments that were taking
place in India and abroad. However, those from the Frontier who got a
modern education, although few in number, broke the chain. They took
an interest in events that were taking place on the Indian and global scene,
and lifted the curtain on the Frontier's seclusion.

One significant event of this kind was the initial inclusion of Raja
Jahandad Khan of Hazarah in the Muslim delegation, led by the Agha
Khan, that called on the Viceroy, Lord Minto, in Simla in October 1906—
commonly referred to as the Simla Deputation of 1906—to persuade 'him
to treat' the Indian Muslims as 'separate from the Hindus'.[3] According to
a correspondent of the *Indian Daily Telegraph*: 'The following gentlemen
intended to have attended the presentation of the address to the Viceroy,
but were prevented by illness or other causes'. They included 'Khan
Bahadur Raja Jahandad of Hazara'.[4] After the Simla Deputation, the All
India Muslim League was founded in Dhaka in December 1906. And, it
was the Muslim League that proved to be the first political party in India
to enter the Frontier.

Although there was no branch of the League in the Frontier until 1912, and Raja Jahandad Khan was not among those who actually visited the viceroy with the Simla Deputation, despite being included in the delegation, the Frontier had representation in the All India Muslim League since its inception. Barrister Mufti Fida Muhammad Khan and Barrister Abdul Aziz of Peshawar were among 'those 35 members who were entrusted with the task of framing the Rules and Regulations under Resolution No. 2 of the Dacca session held on 30 December 1906'. They were in the second group of the All India Muslim League's members. Ten members were allocated for the Frontier Province, out of a maximum of 400 members of the All India Muslim League.[5] Barrister Abdul Aziz was also among '*the Members Present and Elected at the Meeting held on the 18–19 March 1908*'.[6]

FIRST PHASE

In the words of Sayed Wiqar Ali Shah:

> A commonly believed view about the Frontier League is that of all the political parties in the Province, it was the last to take a start. Some feel that by the time it emerged on the scene the fight for freedom was over and that it reaped the harvest sowed by others. True, the growing strength of the Muslim League in the Frontier is a late phenomenon, but it was the first political party to be established in the Frontier, it having been founded first in 1912.[7]

Dr Muhammad Anwar Khan, however, states that 'both governmental records and Allah Bakhsh Yussafi, a veteran freedom fighter report, [the] foundation of a local chapter of the Muslim League in 1913'.[8] Allah Bakhsh Yusufi, however, has spoken of the foundation of the League in the Frontier in 1912,[9] to which Dr Anwar Khan also refers in a note: 'Yussafi dates the foundation of [the] league [League] in 1912'.[10]

The driving force behind the foundation of the Muslim League in NWFP, it is said, was a youth from Peshawar, Sayyad Ali Abbas Bokhari [Bukhari]. Imbued with a pan-Islamic spirit and a passion for the liberation of India, he took a lawyer from Peshawar, Qazi Mir Ahmad, and a copyist at the session court in Peshawar, Sultan Jan, into confidence. An initial meeting was held at the chamber of Qazi Mir Ahmad, also attended by Barrister Aziz Ahmad. Wazir Jan, a student of the Municipal Board School, was engaged as the private secretary, and a larger political meeting was planned. As per the official diary entry dated 15 February 1913, the provincial Muslim League was founded with the following office bearers: Barrister Aziz Ahmad: president; Sayyad Ali Abbas Bokhari: secretary; Qazi Mir Ahmad and Qazi Akbar Jan: assistant secretaries; and the chamber of Qazi Mir Ahmad was made its office.[11]

Sayed Wiqar Ali Shah, however, states that 'the organizers of the Frontier League were Mian Abdul Aziz, Qazi Abdul Wali Khan, Sayyid Ali Abbas Bokhari, Qazi Mir Ahmad, and Hakim Mohammad Amin'. And, 'The office bearers were Mian Abdul Aziz, Bar-at-Law (President), Qazi Abdul Wali Khan (Vice President), Sayyid Ali Abbas Bokhari (General Secretary), Qazi Mir Ahmad (Joint Secretary), and Hakim Mohammad Amin (Treasurer).'[12]

The organisers of the Frontier League tried to establish links with the All India Muslim League. Sayyad Ali Abbas Bokhari and Mian Abdul Aziz—general secretary and president, respectively, of the Frontier League—were delegates to the Agra session of the All India Muslim League, held in December 1913.[13] 'Ali Abbas Bokhari wrote a lengthy letter' to Sayyad Wazir Hassan, general secretary of the All India Muslim League, apprising him of 'the conditions in which the Frontier Muslim League was working'.[14] In Dr Muhammad Anwar Khan's words:

> Police intelligence report for 1914 talks of the provincial Muslim League initiated by Abbas Bokhari in 1913, had twenty members on its roll. Barrister Abdul Aziz was still placed at the head of the organization with Bokhari as the secretary. The 'troublesome' figure in the organization says the dairy [diary], was Qazi Wali, who since his visit from abroad (Egypt and Tripoli) was running the affairs of the party and was the cause of friction with the government.
>
> Nothing further we have in records, governmental or private on the working of the Muslim League.[15]

Sayyad Ali Abbas Bokhari was also a delegate at the All India Muslim League's session held in Bombay on 31 December 1915.[16] However, 'Unlike its parent organization at the all-India level, this nascent branch was anti-British. The provincial Leaguers', therefore, 'approached the Muslims of the NWFP urging them to fight the anti-Muslim forces in the Balkan wars'.[17] The outbreak of World War I greatly changed the situation and 'the three major actors'—Sayyad Ali Abbas Bokhari, Qazi Abdul Wali, and Barrister Abdul Aziz—in the Frontier League gradually disappeared from the scene. The first two left the country because of the treatment they had received from the colonial government due to their anti-British activities as well as their own tempers, while the third left for Bombay. The other members and supporters of the organisation were also silenced.[18]

With this, the League in the Frontier virtually came to an end, despite the fact that Mian Abdul Aziz had 'grown in political stature at national level and was placed on the Central Committee of the Muslim League in 1926, holding number three position in the fourteen members committee'.[19] But, as stated earlier, Mian Abdul Aziz's political stature in the League was high since its inception. At the December 1906 meeting, he was among the thirty-four members entrusted with framing the rules and regulations for the League. Government records speak of the participation of the men from the Frontier in the League's sessions, held in other parts of India, but nothing of their gatherings within the province.[20] Thus, the first Frontier Muslim League 'remained in existence for only four years. After the expatriation of its first organizers it ceased to function in the NWFP.'[21]

SECOND PHASE

In 1934, 'some local elites' made a bid to organise the League in the province so as 'to foil the political offensives of Hindu Sabha which was organizing meetings and rallies in support of Hinduism in [the] Frontier'.[22]

When 'elections to the provincial assemblies were announced for the winter of 1936–37', the All India Muslim League not only 'resolved to contest' the elections but 'authorized Jinnah to organize election boards at the Central and Provincial levels'.[23] Jinnah wanted to know 'about the general conditions in the Frontier' and, hence, made overtures to Allah Bakhsh Yusufi and Pir Bakhsh. Sahibzadah Abdul Qayyum informed Jinnah about his Muslim Independent Party, and invited him to visit the party in Peshawar. A reception committee was formed by the Peshawarites, with Agha Sayyad Lal Badshah as president and Pir Bakhsh as general secretary, but differences 'soon emerged among the leaders'. Abdur Rab Nishtar tried his level-best to convince 'Jinnah to postpone his visit', but to no avail.[24] Allah Bakhsh Yusufi also proceeded to Lahore to ask Jinnah to postpone his visit, but also in vain.[25] Jinnah reached Peshawar on the morning of 18 October 1936, and stayed with Sahibzadah Abdul Qayyum until 24 October. While in Peshawar, he held and addressed meetings.[26] 'As a result of Jinnah's visit a consultative board was set up to prepare the ground for the formation of a provincial Muslim League'[27] in the Frontier. Allah Bakhsh Yusufi has asserted that Jinnah's visit was unsuccessful and that he received the wrong invitation.[28] According to Abdul Khaliq Khaleeq, although Sahibzadah Abdul Qayyum outwardly facilitated Jinnah, he was instrumental in making his visit a failure.[29] Jinnah 'did not succeed in getting a single nomination from the Frontier Muslims on the League's ticket'[30] but, as reported by the *Khyber Mail*, he 'cherished strong hopes of a bright future'.[31] Quoting the official reports, Dr Sayed Wiqar Ali Shah states: 'On Jinnah's advice', during his visit, 'a local branch of AIML [All India Muslim League] was formed with Malik Khuda Bakhsh as President, Pir Bakhsh as General Secretary, and Hakim Abdul Jalil Nadvi, Lal Badshah, Rahim Bakhsh, Syed Ali Shah, and Abdul Latif as members of the executive council'.[32] Although his visit to the Frontier proved to be of no benefit as far the forthcoming election was concerned, it cannot be underestimated as far as the future organisation and growth of the League in the province is concerned.

In February 1937, Muzaffar Ali, of Peshawar Cantonment, made an attempt 'to start a branch' of the Muslim League in the Frontier, for which he also contacted the League leaders of the Punjab and sought their cooperation. However, 'the first organized attempt to start a branch of the Muslim League' in the Frontier 'was made in May 1937 by a few educated Muslims of Nowshera'. The 'moving spirit' behind the formation 'of this branch of the League' was Abdul Wahid, 'a former Congress activist'. The office-bearers were Tila Muhammad (president), Abdul Wahid (secretary), and Ali Ahmad Khan (treasurer). The organisers urged the Frontier Muslims to lend their support to, and join, the All India Muslim League.[33] On 25 August 1937, some anti-Congress Muslims from Peshawar discussed, at their meeting, the formation of another branch of the League—'to "safeguard the rights" of the [Frontier] Muslims' and to counter the Khudayi Khidmatgars' propaganda. The opening of League branches in Peshawar, Bannu, and Abbottabad was proposed and, on '29 August, another meeting was convened at Abbottabad for the same purpose'. 'About one thousand' delegates 'from Rawalpindi, Mardan, Peshawar, Nowshera, and Abbottabad' attended the conference, in Abbottabad, chaired by Mawlana Muhammad Ishaq. In addition to passing several resolutions, the conference expressed 'full confidence in the leadership' of the League central president, Jinnah.[34]

As a result of the election for the provincial assembly, held in February 1937, although the Congress-Khudayi Khidmatgars were the largest party in the assembly holding 19 out of the 50 seats, Sahibzadah Abdul Qayyum formed the government in April 1937 because of a deadlock between the Congress and the British over some points. Although he himself 'did not publicly embrace the League while he was Chief Minister', Sahibzadah Abdul Qayyum 'covertly encouraged its development in hopes that it would help to stem the Congress' rising popularity'. Hence, 'partly in response to his request, a small group of *ulema* and urban politicians from Hazara gathered in Abbottabad on September 3, 1937, to form a "Frontier Muslim League." They chose Maulana Muhammad Shuaib as their president, and Qazi Abdul Hakim as General Secretary'.[35] In Erland Jansson's words: '*Maulvis* played a prominent part in the formation of this Muslim League branch.'[36]

The same day, the Sahibzadah's ministry collapsed because of the passage of a no-confidence vote. 'The collapse' of Sahibzadah's ministry, Dr Muhammad Anwar Khan contends, 'was [a] rude shock to most of the Frontier political elite averse to Congress'. Sahibzadah Abdul Qayyum 'also took it seriously'. He endeavoured to organise the League in the Frontier, because 'fighting an all India organization [i.e. Congress] single handed from [the] Frontier was well nigh impossible'. Therefore, a meeting was arranged in Abbottabad.[37]

The no-confidence move, and foundation of the League at Abbottabad, received attention in other parts of the Frontier; 'efforts surged all along the province in lining up with the League'. Secret diaries of the police department speak of 'hectic efforts...in Peshawar and elsewhere to counter-act painful influence of the Khudai Khidmatgars in the body politics of the Frontier'.[38]

Some of the *khans* (in Pukhtu: *khanan*) in the United Muslim Nationalist Party—formed by Sahibzadah Abdul Qayyum in the assembly—'independently gravitated to the League', but 'were unprepared to accept' the leadership of those who founded the party at Abbottabad. They, therefore, 'in cooperation with some urban professionals and businessmen in Peshawar city, formed only a District Muslim League at a meeting on October 23, 1937. Mirza Salim Khan was elected President and Muhammad Ismail Ghaznavi General-Secretary.'[39] Thus, in 1937, the League again emerged onto the political scene of the Frontier. At first, its progress was slow but, in January 1938, the provincial governor, George Cunningham, reported that it had 'made some headway lately, particularly among the Khans and big landowners, who are becoming more and more conscious of the attack which is being made on them by [the] Congress'.[40] Stephen Rittenberg asserts that it was the Frontier Congress' policies that

spawned the Frontier League and defined the pool of its potential members—the groups which were alienated or simply ignored by the Congress. They also determined the issues it espoused and the tactics it adopted. The growth of the Frontier League, in short, was not an independent phenomenon but a response to its more powerful rival.[41]

Commenting on the situation that then arose, Erland Jansson states:

> There existed a party—the Muslim League—which needed a following, and a class—the big khans—in need of a party. Although the big khans were not greatly interested in the programme of the AIML there was nothing in it which they were particularly opposed to either, and so they joined the League.[42]

'After the death' of Sahibzadah Abdul Qayyum on 4 December 1937, 'most of the members of his party [United Muslims Nationalist Party] joined the newly formed Muslim League, electing Sardar Aurangzeb Khan as its party leader in the assembly'.[43] In 1938, the 'Abbottabad League' was completely eclipsed. 'The new Provincial Muslim League quickly evolved into an umbrella organization for the non-Congress Khans who found their old, contentious brand of political individualism a liability once their rivals assumed control of the government.'[44] And, in Cunningham's words:

> The Congress attitude toward[s] the Khans was also largely the cause of the revival of the Muslim League, at the expense of [the] Congress. . . . when some of the anti-Khan measures were taking shape, it was clear that the Muslim League was becoming popular among the Khanate, even among those old-fashioned Khans who had hitherto hardly known the name of the League. They saw in it their main bulwark against the attacks of the Congress.[45]

ORGANISATION AND CONSTITUTION

As its provincial-level body was still lacking, on 10 March 1938, the Leaguers arranged a meeting at Islamia High School, Nowshera, and 'executive bodies of the party at all levels' were elected. The provincial working committee comprised Mawlana Muhammad Shuaib (president), Muhammad Ismail Ghaznavi (secretary), Sajjad Ahmad Jan and Abdul Wahid Khan (joint secretaries), Qazi Abdul Hakim (propaganda secretary), and Arbab Shamsuddin (treasurer). The twenty-one-member provincial council comprised Mawlana Muhammad Shuaib, Ismail Ghaznavi, Saadullah Khan, Sardar Aurangzeb Khan, Abdul Wahid Khan, Mian Ghulam Hussain, Allah Bakhsh Yusufi, Bahram Khan, Fida Muhammad Khan, Hamidullah Khan, Ali Quli Khan, Sajjad Ahmad Jan,

Baseerudin Qureshi, Abdul Hamid Khan, Haq Nawaz Khan, Mouladad Khan, Pir Saeed Shah, Ghulam Hyder Akhtar, Ghulam Hyder Khan, Nasrullah Khan, and Faqira Khan. In the same session, 'affiliation with the central League' was applied for.[46]

The constitution of the Frontier Muslim League was framed in 1938. Among the objectives of the Frontier League, the foremost was 'the establishment in India [of] full independence in the form of a federation of free democratic States in which the rights and interests of the Mussalmans and other minorities are adequately and effectively safeguarded in the Constitution'. Every Muslim resident of British India, who was at least eighteen years old, was qualified to become a member, subject to the payment of an annual subscription—paid in advance—of two *anna*s (*anah*s) and a declaration 'in writing that the candidate will adhere to the objects and rules of the League mentioned' in the constitution. The office bearers were (one) president, (one) vice president, (one) honorary secretary, (one) honorary treasurer, and (two) honorary joint secretaries. There would be a provincial council of the party, comprising 110 members. The council members would be elected by 'the District Leagues' as per each district's quota, for one year, one month before the League's annual session. However, they would be eligible for re-election. In addition, the League's members of the provincial legislature (subject to conditions) and the secretaries of the District Leagues would be considered ex-officio members of the council. The constitution also laid out details about the meetings and functions of the council, the sessions of the League, the working committee and their meetings and functions, the powers and duties of the executive, the funds of the League, and general provisions.[47] The Frontier League was formally affiliated with the All India Muslim League during its Calcutta session on 17 April 1938.[48]

Progress

While many in the 'League circles' welcomed its 'joining by the big Khans in large numbers' and took 'it as the best course for counteracting the Congressite activities, some felt alienated'.[49] The big *khan*s and landlords joining the League proved to be a great boost to its progress in the province, especially when it was joined by Khan Bahadar Saadullah Khan and Sardar Aurangzeb Khan. The Muslim League, which was so far practically restricted to district and local organisations only,[50] became a provincial organisation; with prominent *khan*s from all parts of the province joined it. Some of the policies and acts of the Congress government also proved to be a blessing to the League's progress in the Frontier. Allah Bakhsh Yusufi states that, due to participation of the *khans* in the League's meetings, large numbers of motor cars were seen at the meeting venues—owing to which the 'Muslim League' was referred to as the 'Motor League' by its opponents.[51] And, 'a visitor to the province described' the party as the 'Calling League' as 'the work of the leaders consisted only in "travelling by car to the places where the meetings are convened, taking tea, and returning to their houses".'[52] Erland Jansson observes: 'Another consequence of the way in which the League was organised was that right from the beginning its work was bedevilled by traditional rivalries and factionalism.'[53]

Although the organisation was 'a patch-work of alliances among Khans', and the *khans* were persuading 'other Khans to build the party in their respective regions through kin ties, factional associations, and social contacts',[54] the League now became a provincial organisation in real terms. Besides, 'the League tried its best to get support from the masses'.[55] Stephen Rittenberg has asserted that 'the leaders of the All-India Muslim League did little' to assist the Frontier League, which forced it 'to rely for funding on membership dues and the generosity of local donors, neither of which proved substantial'.[56] The high command, however, increased its interest later. Sayed Wiqar Ali Shah contends that 'the Muslim League high command took personal interest in the Frontier affairs' and, in August 1938, Jinnah wrote to Mian Ziauddin that 'he was looking forward to the day when the NWFP will be a Muslim League Government. "I feel confident that, it will come, perhaps sooner than many people imagine".'[57]

The Frontier League received an invitation from the central body of the League to participate in its meeting scheduled for April 1938 in Calcutta. Consequently, a fourteen-member delegation, from the Frontier League, 'attended the meeting'. It proved fruitful as the Frontier delegates deliberated with leaders such as Jinnah, Liaquat Ali Khan, and Fazlul Haq. Affairs of the Frontier League were discussed, and the factors responsible for its slow growth were identified. The Frontier delegates stressed that the Muslim leaders should visit the Frontier for public meetings and addresses the public so as to 'negate' the impact of Nehru and Gandhi's visits and 'also [to] expose the Congress high handedness outside the Frontier', which Jinnah agreed to.[58] Therefore, in May 1938, Mian Jamal Farangimahal and Mawlana Shaukat Ali, accompanied by Mawlana Hamid Ali Badayuni, visited the province and held public meetings and addressed gatherings. In September, a League delegation comprising some of its leaders, namely Chaudhary Khaliq-uz-Zaman, Mawlana Zafar Ali

Khan, Mawlana Abdul Hamid Badayuni, Mehdi Hussain Raja of Pirpur, and Jamal Mian visited the province, as did Abdul Majid Sindhi.[59] The visits and public meetings addressed by these leaders popularised the League in the province. In Dr Muhammad Anwar Khan's words:

> Muslim League, all records agree, was getting public attention in the Frontier. Its membership was slowly swelling. Milad, Palestine day, Shaheed Ganj mosque, Mustafa Kamal and Maulana Muhammad Ali days and such like events brought greater public participation in its gatherings. Its workers and volunteers, it was reported at places were demonstrating their strength.[60]

The League was taking ground in the Frontier and asserting its presence, but at the same time there was—

> bickering and leg pulling. The Khan group within the League was in bulldozing mood. Aurangzeb hated Ghulam Hussain and the Charsadah-Mardan groups of Khans were harassing Shuaib. Western democracy enshrines in capitalism, advocates self imposition and imperitates western knowledge and mechanism. Both Ghulam Hussain and Shuaib misfitted the requirement.[61]

Consequently, the leaders of the Frontier League met at a meeting in Peshawar on 20 November 1938 and elected the following new office-bearers for the provincial organisation: Saadullah Khan (president), Mian Ziauddin (vice president), Ismail Ghaznavi (secretary); and Mir Alam Khan, Fateh Muhammad Khan, Arbab Madad Khan, Allah Bakhsh Yusufi, Hamidullah Khan, Bahram Khan, Fida Muhammad Khan, Faqira Khan, Abdul Rashid Tahirkhili, Abdul Majid Khan, Pir Jalal Shah, and Ghulam Hyder Khan (members of the provincial council). Consequently, Mawlana Muhammad Shuaib 'left the office [provincial president-ship] and the party under "toady pressure".'[62] In addition, 'some of the recently elected office-bearers and members of the Muslim League council, including Ghulam Hussain, Yusufi, and Rahim Bakhsh, all from Peshawar' also, shortly after their elections, 'tendered their resignations, protesting against "the capture of the Muslim League by the Khans".'[63]

Although 'the League drew its adherents from the province's non-Pakhtuns and senior Khans whose past connections with the British made them suspect in Pakhtun eyes',[64] the progress of the League could be gauged from the fact that there was no League-nominated candidate in the 1937 elections; however, they won seats in the Haripur area—although not in the Razar and Amazi seats—in the by-elections of 1938.[65] Despite internal wrangling, some policies and acts of the Congress ministries—

both in the Frontier and outside—were exploited for the League's cause, it became a strong and active party both in the assembly and with the public. The League's senior members, from other parts of India, regularly visited the province. On 29 October 1939, the Frontier League was reorganised. The elected office-bearers were: Saadullah Khan (president), Agha Sayyad Lal Badshah (vice-president), Mian Ziauddin (secretary), Malik Shad Muhammad (joint secretary), and Mian Ghulam Hussain (treasurer). Also, twenty-one people were elected as members of the council.[66] 'The year 1939' proved to be the year of the 'League's consolidation and of mass contact in the Frontier';[67] by the end of the year, it had established roots in the masses, especially in the urban areas, and was also represented in the provincial assembly.

The Frontier League delegation and its volunteers played a remarkable role in the historic session of the All India Muslim League in Lahore in March 1940. The Frontier League leaders intended to use the occasion, and their mass participation, to counter the Congress in the Frontier and so resolved to send 'at least five hundred persons' to the session. Failing to arrange a special train for the leaders and volunteers, they left for Lahore on a routine passenger train and reached on 'the morning of 22 March'. The situation seemed grave as the Khaksars were planning a demonstration at the session, and there were rumours that they would attack Jinnah and destroy the camp. However, responsibility for controlling the situation was accepted by the leaders of the Frontier contingent, and although the situation became grave on occasions, the Frontier contingent performed their duty courageously and successfully. The historic Lahore Resolution—later called the Pakistan Resolution—demanding the creation of independent Muslim states in the north-western and eastern zones, was presented before the audience on 23 March. From the Frontier, Sardar Aurangzeb Khan spoke in its favour.[68] It needs to be emphasised that though the resolution was presented in the session on 23 March 1940, it was passed the next day, i.e., 24 March 1940, after completing deliberations over it.

The huge participation and active role of the Frontier League at the Lahore session strengthened and enthused the organisation and the Leaguers in the province. They started touring the province, addressing public meetings, to popularise the Pakistan cause.[69] April 1940 marked the establishment of a women's branch of the Frontier League in Peshawar. Its meeting was held in Shahi Bagh and was presided over by Begum Qazi Aslam; tributes were paid to Begum Mir Ahmad Khan, 'the pioneer in women awakening in the Frontier'.[70]

New elections for the Frontier League were held in November 1940; the office-bearers elected were: Bakht Jamal Khan (president), Khan Bahadar Saadullah Khan (vice president), Mian Ziauddin (general secretary), Malik Shad Muhammad (joint secretary), Muhammad Zaman Khan (assistant secretary), and Mian Ghulam Hussain (treasurer). Twenty-two people were nominated as members of the All India Muslim League council.[71] There, however, were complaints against the way the League was organised and about the men who maintained a hold over the body, but it did not bear any results and 'the Peshawar leaders, the trio of Aurangzeb, Zia [Mian Ziauddin] and later Bakht Jamal managed the League office their way'.[72]

Nevertheless, the League faced difficulties in the province because of the popularity of the Khudayi Khidmatgars as well as the fact that none of the leaders of national repute had visited the province in the last one and a half year. The *Khyber Mail* complained that there was 'not a single popular and capable leaders [leader] at its back', and that there were 'no primary Leaguers outside the towns'. In February 1941, All India Muslim League leaders—Nawab Bahadur Yar Jang, Qazi Muhammad Isa, Mawlana Abdul Hamid Badayuni, and Mawlana Karam Ellahi Malihabadi—went to Peshawar and successfully toured the province and addressed huge public meetings.[73] In June 1942, another weighty delegation from the central League, comprising Nawab Muhammad Ismail, Khwaja Nazimuddin, Chaudhary Khaliq-uz-Zaman, and Qazi Muhammad Isa went to the Frontier. They visited different parts of the province, and attended and addressed public and private meetings. In September, Amir Ahmad Khan—the Raja Sahib of Mahmudabad—visited Peshawar 'to judge' the 'League's strength in the Frontier and possibility of power assumption'. He was also taken 'to Shabqadar to meet the Mohmand Maliks', where he was 'warmly treated' and 'assured possible support to the League cause'.[74]

MUSLIM LEAGUE MINISTRY

In 1939, when the Viceroy, Lord Linlithgow, declared that India had joined Britain against Germany in World War II, without consulting the Indians or taking them into confidence, Congress resented the decision and decided to resign from their ministries in protest. Consequently, when on 7 November 1939, the Khudayi Khidmatgar-Congress ministry in the Frontier, headed by Dr Khan Sahib (Sayb; Saib), resigned, Jinnah stressed on Sardar Aurangzeb Khan—the League's Frontier leader—to 'form [the] Ministry [at] any cost', to show that the Frontier was with the League. As Aurangzeb Khan was not in a position to do so, he 'informed Jinnah in somewhat euphemistic terms that "local league [League] and party opinion" was not in favour of accepting [the] office'. On Aurangzeb's failure to form a government, the governor took power into his own hands under section 93 of the Government of India Act, 1935.[75]

However, as both the British and the League were anxious to form ministries to counter Congress' influence and propaganda, in 1943 Sardar Aurangzeb Khan, in collaboration with the governor, succeeded in creating a coalition with the Akali Party, some independents and some members of the Congress. Then, assuring the governor of what he wanted from him, Aurangzeb Khan formed a ministry, headed by himself as the chief minister and Samin Jan Khan, Abdur Rab Nishtar, Raja Abdur Rahman Khan, and Ajit Singh as education, finance, information, and public works ministers, respectively, which took office on 25 May 1943.[76] Ayesha Jalal contends:

> The Governor, not Jinnah, was Aurangzeb's real master, and it was the Governor who protected the ministry from Dr Khan Sahib... The price of this protection was to keep Jinnah at arm's length; the Governor had 'warned Aurangzeb at the outset to keep Pakistan in the background as much as possible'.[77]

In July 1943, elections were held for the vacant seats in the assembly; all four Muslim seats were won by the League, indicating the improvement in the League's position in the province.[78] However, according to the Frontier Governor, Cunningham, the 'Muslim League successes in these by-elections are generally accepted as being a victory for the British Government over the subversive elements in the country'; 'Certainly, the League had no "organisation for the polling", indeed it had little organisation at all.'[79]

The ministry's first and last legislative action was a manifold raise in the salaries of the chief minister, ministers, speaker, and deputy speaker.[80] 'In a small province' which existed 'mainly on a subvention from the Centre, the number of Ministers was raised to five'. 'Seven more' members 'got jobs as Speaker, Deputy Speaker, and Parliamentary Secretaries'. Thus, out of a house of forty—of which the ministry claimed the support of twenty-one members, and ten of the Congress members were in jail—'jobs were found for twelve'.[81]

The manner in which the ministers were running their affairs, and misusing their powers, was not approved of by the governor or by a significant segment of the Frontier League. In November 1944, Saadullah Khan, in a long letter, apprised Jinnah of his grievances; Taj Ali Khan—Aurangzeb Khan's supporter—also wrote to Jinnah about the manner in which the Frontier League ministry was working. The ministry's esteem fell in the eyes of the governor as well as the British. On 12 March 1945, during the budget session of the assembly, a no-confidence motion—moved by Dr Khan Sahib—was passed and the ministry resigned. Even five League members—Saadullah Khan, Khan Bahadar Faizullah Khan, Muhammad Afzal Khan, Abdur Rashid Khan, and Raja Manuchehr—voted against Aurangzeb's ministry. Saadullah Khan, when questioned by the convenor of the All India Muslim League Committee of Action, justified his action of voting against the League ministry.[82]

EFFORTS FOR REORGANISATION

The League ministry not only made the governor feel resentful because of the manner in which the ministers were running their affairs and misusing their powers, but also brought differences among the Frontier League's leaders to the surface. Some of the party's officials were unhappy with Aurangzeb Khan's refusal to consult them about governmental affairs; others, with his previous record in office. Factional feuds within the party leaders, and 'complaints against Aurangzeb in the central League office... panicked the League office in Delhi and in early 1944 it decided to send an Action Committee under Nawab Muhammad Ismail Khan to visit the Frontier and apprise itself of the situation'.[83] A relatively larger committee, comprising Liaquat Ali Khan, the Nawab of Mamdot, Qazi Muhammad Isa, Nawab Ismail Khan, Haji Sattar Essack Sait, and G.M. Sayyad went to Peshawar in June 1944. They toured most of the province and gathered various complaints.[84] Another source states the names of the committee members as 'Liaqat Ali Khan, Qazi Muhammad Isa, Nawab Ismail Khan, Chaudhary Khaliquzzaman and G.M. Syed'.[85]

The Committee of Action deputed Qazi Muhammad Isa 'to take charge of the work' of 'a thorough overhauling' of the Frontier League, to 're-organise the League strictly in accordance with the model constitution for the Provincial Muslim Leagues' which was 'drawn up by the Committee'. Qazi Isa, it was stated, 'will exercise all necessary powers in connection with the discharge of his responsibilities and proceed on the following lines...'. It was further stated: 'The present office-bearers and the Council will continue to do the ordinary routine work apart from the work relating to reorganization, election etc. entrusted to Qazi Mohammad Isa Sahib till the new office-bearers and the Council are elected.'[86] Factional feuds within the provincial leaders, however, continued and 'Aurangzeb Khan's group' replaced Bakht Jamal Khan by electing 'Taj Ali Khan of Bannu' as the new provincial president in 'the organizational elections' held 'in August 1944'.[87]

Qazi Isa started his work in October, cancelling membership of all the Frontier League members, followed by a tour of the province and re-enlistment of members and the establishment of primary League branches.[88] He, however, did not proceed in the required manner and fell short of expectations. In Dr Muhammad Anwar Khan's words: 'Isa unfortunately played [the role of a] bull in [a] china shop. The Frontier League on his advice was dissolved in April 1945. Thus, the lone League working body in the future land of Pakistan was done away with by a rude stroke of a pen.'[89]

Not only was the Frontier League dissolved on Qazi Isa's advice in April 1945, but, in the summer of the same year, new organisational elections were postponed indefinitely—to enable the party to concentrate on the campaign for the forthcoming elections to the provincial assembly. And, 'What was left of Qazi Isa's reorganization was an *ad hoc* structure which was only a cosmetic change from the old jerry-built, faction-ridden organization.'[90]

FURTHER PROGRESS

The League ministry fell in 1945 and negative effects were created, because of the internal wrangling among the Frontier League's stalwarts, as well as the steps taken by Qazi Isa and the way in which the Frontier League had been dealt with. However, the Frontier League was strengthened in 1945 because, in the backdrop of the failure of the Simla Conference, communal feelings, as Cunningham has observed, were worsening and 'well-educated Muslims [were] becoming anti-Hindus and pro-Muslim League'.[91] In Dr Muhammad Anwar Khan's words:

And, coincidentally when Khanna [Mehar Chand Khanna] and his band were heralding the end of the League in [the] Frontier some most notable individuals were entering the portals of the Frontier Muslim League. They included amongst them some of the front line leaders of the Khudai Khidmatgar party like Arbab Abdul Ghafoor and Abdul Qayyum Khan besides others like Arbab

Noor Muhammad of Landi, Ghulam Muhammad Lundkhwar, Muhammad Ali Hoti, Amin-ul-Hassanat Pir of Manki and with reassertion Abdul Latif Pir of Zakorri. They all held eminent socio-political status in the province. Their entry infused new determination in the party lines.[92]

Qaiyum Khan, who succeeded Dr Khan Sahib in the central legislative assembly in 1938 and became deputy leader of the Congress Parliamentary Party—which he remained until 1945[93]—joined the League in self interest in the wake of the failure of the Simla Conference.[94] Interestingly enough, Qaiyum Khan himself remarked about the League's progress in the Frontier, in his book published the same year, 1945:

> The League began to win increasing support amongst the vested class-interests in the N.-W.F.P. The honorary magistrates, 'Zaildares' [Ziladars], 'Muafidars', the landed aristocracy which had a monopoly of the public services, and all other reactionary elements joined the League. These people thought there was an admirable opportunity for them—by raising the cry of 'Islam in danger' they could seize power and secure their class-interests which had been rudely assailed by the Congress. Persistent attempts were made to form a Ministry, but all to no purpose.[95]

Jinnah visited the province for the second time from 19 to 27 November 1945 and explained the cause of Pakistan. He stressed that 'jockeying for positions in ministries' should be stopped for the sake of the supreme cause—the interest of the then 100 million Indian Muslims. During his week-long stay in the province, Jinnah 'met with various professionals, students and businessmen' and 'visited Landi Kotal, Torkham-(Pak Afghan border)[,] Manki Sharif, Nowshera and Mardan'. The visit produced 'far reaching effects' and 'to some extent…cleared the way' for the League's success in 'the forthcoming general elections of January, 1946'.[96]

ELECTIONS OF 1946 AND AFTERMATH

In August 1945, the viceroy announced the holding of elections in India in the winter of 1945–46. The elections 'were important for all parts of India, but it was particularly so for N.W.F.P.'. Here, the elections were 'expected to result in a keen contest between the Congress and the Muslim League as much for the right to form a ministry as to demonstrate before the outside world their respective claims to speak for the Frontiermen [people of the Frontier]'.[97] As the elections were a trial for the Muslim League, the Frontier Leaguers started preparing for them. The League's central command set up the Muslim League Selection Board, Muslim League Election Board, and Muslim League Finance Board, with the powers and responsibilities of selecting candidates, 'organizing and making all necessary arrangements' to contest the elections, and collecting funds and maintaining 'regular and proper accounts' of the funds, respectively.[98]

In nominating candidates, factional feelings came to the fore. Abdul Qaiyum Khan, the Congressite-turned-Leaguer and convenor of the Selection Board, prevailed, while the president of the Selection Board, Nawab Mamdot, was busy in Punjab. Hence, although Abdur Rab Nishtar succeeded in getting a ticket, some of the older, prominent Leaguers including Sardar Aurangzeb Khan, Saadullah Khan, Samin Jan Khan, Bakht Jamal, and Mian Ziauddin did not. Mian Ziauddin, however, succeeded in getting a ticket 'after appealing to the Central Selection Board'.[99]

In addition, there was a rift between Qaiyum Khan and Nishtar. All this created disunity among the workers and alienated those whose support was indispensable for the League's success, even if they held no party portfolios. Many either contested as independent candidates or else supported non-League candidates. Complaints were made to Jinnah about this state of affairs but to no avail.[100]

The League's election slogan was Pakistan, and that the League alone represented Indian Muslims. The League decided to contest the elections for 38 seats: 36 seats were Muslim and two were landholders' seats. Of the League's nominees for the 38 seats, 'there were 5 big *Nawabs*, 1 Knight, 7 *Khan Bahadurs*, 3 rich military contractors, 2 army recruiting officers and atleast [at least] 1 person known to have participated in the communal riots in Dera Ismail Khan'.[101] In the elections held between 26 January and 14 February 1946, the League bagged only 17 out of the 38 seats, while Congress took 19. Most of the seats the League won were non-Pukhtun Muslim seats. 'By contesting 38 seats (11 more than the Congress) it secured 1,47,880 Muslim votes or 41.46 percent [per cent] of the total number of Muslim votes polled (3,56,776). The Congress, in its turn, received 1,39,975 or 39.24 percent [per cent] of the total Muslim votes polled.' However, the total anti-League Muslim votes, 'including those polled in favour of *Jamiat-ul-Ulema*, Ahrars, Khaksars and independents, amounted to 2,08,896 or 58.75 percent [per cent] of the total Muslim votes registered'.[102]

The 'League failure in the provincial election brought hue and cry from all quarters' of the League. Its 'workers were dismayed and partymen disgusted'. Whether the unexpected result of the elections was due to

'Aurangzeb's presence [absence] from the League scene' as he was not granted a party ticket for the election, or the 'Machiavellian tactics of Mehrchand Khanna', or 'Qazi Isa's psychopathy',[103] or all of these, it resulted in a new Congress ministry in the Frontier. Having a majority in the provincial assembly—30 out of the 50 seats—the Congress-Khudayi Khidmatgars formed a government headed by Dr Khan Sahib. But, being the second largest party in the assembly, some of the League members held a meeting in Kafur Dheri (Dhirai)—some leaders from outside the province also participated—and at last selected Abdul Qaiyum Khan and the Nawab of Tank as the leader and deputy leader of the opposition, respectively.[104] The League's local organisational meetings 'were convened in all districts of the Frontier following the election debacle'. The government reports indicate that 'a sense of hope and optimism prevailed'.[105] Despite its failure in the elections of 1945–46, the League, for the first time, entered the field in the Frontier as a political party.[106]

In April 1946, consultations were held, convened by the League's Committee of Action, by a select group of provincial leaders on the future of the Frontier League. On 19 April, the secretary of the Committee of Action of the All India Muslim League appointed a League organising committee for the Frontier Province, with Samin Jan Khan as president, Muhammad Ali Khan Huti as secretary, and Arbab Noor Muhammad Khan of Landi as treasurer. The committee was to comprise the members elected by the districts' Leagues. The committee's responsibilities included enrolling primary members, setting up primary and district Leagues in the province, conducting and controlling elections of office-bearers of the Leagues. The new forty-member organising committee superseded ad-hoc committee formed by Qazi Isa, and was asked to accomplish the assigned task by the end of September. Mian Ziauddin displayed resentment at the way the committee was formed and also at its membership.[107]

To accomplish the assigned task, the organising committee for the Frontier met on 1 and 16 May in Peshawar and Kuhat, respectively, allotting responsibility among its members and forming two three-member sub-committees to assist them in their respective districts. The Pir of Manki toured the province and tribal areas, and was later made chairman of the Frontier Committee of Action. The organising committee also appointed Rab Nawaz Khan—formerly Khudayi Khidmatgars' Salar-i Azam—to mould the party volunteers—the National Guards—'into a single cohesive body' to act as the League's 'volunteer wing', as the Khudayi Khidmatgars were acting for the Frontier Congress.[108] 'The Organizing Committee never completed its assigned task' due to other developments, but 'the Frontier Committee of Action, chaired by the *Pir* of Manki, confirmed the officers of the Organizing Committee in equivalent ranks in the provincial party and appointed officers for subordinate party branches' with which 'the reorganization of the Frontier Muslim League ended'. In spite of not completely reorganising the League in the required manner or up to the required mark, and having deficiencies, 'the organizational efforts of 1946 adequately met the requirements of the Frontier Muslim League' as 'the deterioration of Hindu-Muslim relations in the rest of India' made its task easy.[109]

To solve the Indian problem, Britain sent a mission to India comprising some cabinet members, hence called the Cabinet Mission. The mission, after its deliberations in India, presented a plan in 1946 called the Cabinet Mission Plan. The Frontier League 'seemed to avoid discussions on the Cabinet Mission scheme, particularly on the grouping arrangements. It preferred to concentrate all its energies on the anti-Congress propaganda'.[110] As the long-term proposals of the plan resulted in a deadlock between Congress and the League, to press its demands, the central League, in its council meeting in July 1946, decided on Direct Action and asked the Muslims to renounce the titles conferred upon them by Britain. From the Frontier, Khan Bahadur Jalaluddin, Mian Musharaf Shah, Malikur Rahman Kiyani, Dr Muhammad Rahim Khan, and Quli Khan were among those who 'renounced their titles'. The League also fixed 16 August 1946 as Direct Action Day, which resulted in great loss of life in Bengal and Bihar. In the Frontier, the League observed the day peacefully but resented the atrocities meted out to the Muslims of Bihar.[111]

When, in October 1946, Nehru resolved to visit the Frontier, the League did its best to benefit from his visit. The Frontier Leaguers were divided on the issue of staging demonstrations on the eve of Nehru's visit, but the Provincial League had already passed a resolution to do so and had formed a committee for that purpose.[112] They 'seized the opportunity... to intensify their propaganda, especially among the tribesmen'. For this purpose, the Pir of Manki 'was sent on a tour of tribal territory, so timed as just to precede Pandit Nehru's visit'.[113] Nehru's visit provided the League with a golden opportunity 'for effective publicity' and, in Qaiyum Khan's words, what they 'could not hope to achieve in several years, was in fact achieved within about a week'.[114] Interestingly, Nehru made the trip, despite the opposition of Olaf Caroe (the Frontier Governor), Abul Kalam Azad, Gandhi, and Sardar Patel,[115] 'hoping to add strength to [Dr] Khan Sahib's government and to convince the Pathans of the wisdom of loyalty to the Congress',[116] but 'the Governor's considered judgement, long afterwards, was that this visit of Nehru's to the Frontier, more than anything else, made partition inevitable'.[117]

As 'the League's communal propaganda was flourishing in the Frontier with the news of riots in Eastern India, particularly in Bihar', communal riots broke out in Hazarah in January 1947, 'apparently on the slogan of avenging the massacre of Muslims in Bihar'.[118] This, coupled with the shortage of 'food and other consumable articles' in the Congress-governed Frontier, benefited the League in the province. Not only did the League's leaders and workers talk about these and condemn the 'Congress government's complacency in this regard', but on 20 February 1947 a provincial 'League meeting was held in Peshawar', presided over by Pir of Manki. Attended 'by all other party leaders', it was decided to launch a civil disobedience movement in the province and to march to freedom. The 'movement started the following day'.[119]

Although 'the party made it clear to its workers that the movement did not aim' to harm 'any ethnic or religious group in the province and was purely directed against the provincial government',[120] it took on a communal shape not only because of what had happened to the Muslims in Bihar and UP (United Provinces) but also because of Basanti's[121] issue. The League's 'civil disobedience movement initially remained confined to processions, assemblies, demonstrations, mostly chanting slogans, picketing of the offices and courts and blocking of the railway service'. As 'life was getting paralyzed in the provincial capital on account of mass participation in the League led agitations', Dr Khan Sahib got 'panicky' and hence 'ordered the arrest of League leaders', which 'intensified the movement' and it spread to the districts.[122] The Frontier League Council also constituted a 'war council' to continue 'the struggle...forced upon them'.[123]

The Committee of Action, All-India Muslim League deputed Abdur Rab Nishtar, member [of the] Committee of Action, and Siddiq Ali Khan, 'Salar-i-Ala' [of the] All-India Muslim League National Guards, to visit Peshawar, in order to study the situation in the NWFP...

From then on, violence became an integral part of [the] civil dis-obedience. League leaders continued to issue appeal[s] to keep the agitation non-violent. By their own admissions, party officials from the War Council, down to the local level helped in organizing the disturbances which followed March 10.[124]

'Major Khurshid Anwar, "the Naib Salar-i-Ala" of the All-India Muslim League National Guards' also came to the Frontier and worked there from 28 February till 24 April 1947.[125] Besides the Leaguers, the Sarhad

Muslim Students Federation and the women Muslim Leaguers also played a remarkable role in the agitation.[126] In the course of time, 'these developments produced a spate of communal riots in March and April 1947'. These 'riots became serious in Peshawar, spread to Kohat, Mardan and Hazara and finally reached Bannu and Dera Ismail Khan'.[127]

As, in the meantime, the British Prime Minister, Mr Attlee, had announced the transfer of power to Indians by June 1948, the scenario in the Frontier Province 'presented a high complexed constitutional tangle in the framework of India's partition plan'. Because 'geographically, ethnically and ideologically it ought to form part of the proposed Muslim state of future India, but constitutionally the elected government in power', Dr Muhammad Anwar Khan has contended, 'was pro-Hindu'. Mountbatten, the viceroy, 'decided to ascertain the situation for himself' and hence 'visited the province for two days, April 28 and 29, 1947'.[128]

The Leaguers arranged a mass demonstration in Peshawar on the eve of Mountbatten's visit, to demonstrate their strength in the Frontier; men from all parts of the province participated in the demonstration. The League's agitation and civil disobedience movement took a serious turn as violence became an integral part of it. A large number of Leaguers, including the leadership, were put behind bars by Dr Khan Sahib's government, but the agitation and disturbances did not subside. Keeping in view this state of affairs and observing the situation personally, while in Peshawar, the viceroy hinted at the possibility of holding a referendum in the Frontier. The Congress leaders, the Muslim League, and the British government later agreed to this. As a result, 'The League called off its 105-day-old civil disobedience campaign as soon as the referendum was announced and began a full-scale campaign for Pakistan.'[129] The League concentrated on the referendum campaign, aimed at making the Frontier an integral part of the future Pakistan. In the wake of the boycott by Khudayi Khidmatgars and Frontier Congress, the result of the referendum was in favour of joining Pakistan (for details see Chapter 11). The Frontier's decision to join Pakistan was a great success and decisive victory for the Frontier Muslim League—closing one chapter of the Frontier League's career but opening another.

POST-INDEPENDENCE SCENARIO

The referendum in the Frontier Province went in favour of Pakistan and was construed as a vote for the Muslim League and against the Khudayi Khidmatgars and Congress. 'But the complexion of the parliamentary parties did not reflect the changes which had occurred at the public level'[130] after the elections of 1946. The British government refused to dismiss Dr Khan Sahib's (Sayb's, Saib's) ministry after the result of the referendum 'on the plea of constitutional impropriety';[131] Dr Khan Sahib's ministry refused to resign as they had the majority in the assembly.[132] However, on 22 August 1947, the governor dismissed the ministry on the directives of the Governor-General, M.A. Jinnah, and 'Qayyum Khan, leader of the Muslim League parliamentary party, formed the' Muslim League ministry in the province.[133]

In the pre-Partition days, Qaiyum Khan faced 'discontent and opposition amongst his own Muslim League fellows'. Hence, 'when the rumours of his appointment as Chief Minister of NWFP reached the province' some of the Frontier League old guards sent telegrams to Jinnah and Liaquat Ali Khan against his 'appointment as the future Chief Minister'. They, however, 'set aside their differences and rallied round him' once appointed.[134] As the League was in the minority in the assembly, Qaiyum Khan's ministry continued to work 'as the Assembly was not to meet till March 1948'. 'The Governor was considering the dissolution of the' assembly 'before its budget session', but Qaiyum Khan successfully persuaded 'seven Congress members' of the assembly 'to join the Muslim League parliamentary party'.[135]

'However, Qaiyum Khan and [the] old guards of the' Frontier League could not work together for long as he 'was averse to all sorts of criticism and opposition' both from within and outside the party. His policies led to disputes within the party and 'many stalwarts formed an opposition to him'. Khan Saifullah Khan, member of the Provincial League Council, 'strongly criticized' his 'style of politics'.[136] The Pir of Manki was Qaiyum Khan's main rival in the Frontier League; various sources have given differing reasons for the rivalry.[137] In April 1948, at the time of Jinnah's visit to Peshawar, 'a delegation of disgruntled' old Leaguers of the province, including Samin Jan Khan, the Pir of Manki, Khan Bahadar Saadullah Khan, and Mian Ziauddin 'called upon him and lodged many complaints against the arbitrary policies of Qaiyum Khan' but in vain.[138]

When the reorganisation of the Frontier League began in 1948, both Qaiyum Khan and the Pir of Manki tried to enlist a large number of their personal supporters. However, the organising committee had Qaiyum Khan's blessings and hence it started organising the League in a manner that would ensure the hold of Qaiyum Khan's supporters over the party. The Pir of Manki's endeavours to counter Qaiyum Khan's machinations were nullified; the League's central president, Chaudhary Khaliq-uz-

Zaman, abstained from forming an enquiry committee to probe into the matter.[139] On 12 August 1948, the Frontier League organising committee reorganised the party, electing the following office bearers: Badshah Gul (president), Muhammad Yusuf Khattak (general secretary), and Mir Dad (treasurer). Also, 'a rule-framing committee was…appointed', and it was decided to request the Pakistan Muslim League president, Khaliq-uz-Zaman, to extend the members' enrolment date from September to October. This, however, did not bring an end to the grouping and wrangling in the party; resentment against Qaiyum Khan's machinations and policies continued. There was a plan to move a no-confidence motion in the assembly against him but, as the plan got disclosed, not only was Qaiyum Khan able to foil it but he also arranged for strong disciplinary action to be taken against eight prominent Leaguers, including six members of the assembly.[140]

In July 1949, a delegation of the Frontier League including Samin Jan Khan, the Pir of Manki, and Ghulam Muhammad Lundkhwar, called on Liaquat Ali Khan in Karachi to apprise him of the grievances against Qaiyum Khan, but to no avail. The Pir of Manki, along with Ghulam Muhammad Lundkhwar, therefore, left the party and in September 1949 formed a new party, the Awami Muslim League.[141] The party was later re-named the Jinnah Awami League, after entering into a coalition with Huseyn Shaheed Suhrawardy and Nawab Iftikhar Hussain Mamdot.[142]

In the manoeuvred party elections held on 29 April 1951, during the meeting of the Frontier League's councillors, presided over by Liaquat Ali Khan, Abdul Qaiyum Khan (president), Jalaluddin Khan (vice president), Malikur Rahman Kiyani (general secretary), Yusuf Shah and Amin Jan (joint secretaries), and Muhammad Ali Khan (treasurer) were elected as provincial office-bearers. This, however, did not stop factionalism and infighting in the party. Qaiyum Khan tried to take the dissenters to task and to eliminate them from the League, mostly employing unfair and foul means. Although he succeeded in taking 'full control of the provincial Muslim League', his machinations weakened the party and split it into factions. Interestingly, although the rival group appealed to the party leaders, apprising them of Qaiyum Khan's machinations and foul play, the leaders turned a deaf ear to them, for their own reasons and because they had confidence in Qaiyum Khan.[143]

During the general elections of 1951, Qaiyum Khan 'did not accept all the nominees of the Muslim League Board. He gave tickets to those of his favourites whom the Board hadn't nominated despite his recommendation.'[144] 'He even encouraged aspirants to contest as independents against those Muslim Leaguers who were granted tickets against his recommendations, and made sure that they won the elections.'[145] Some prominent Leaguers were denied party tickets while some independent candidates were supported; the elections were allegedly rigged.[146] As 'Muslim League success was ensured by various tactics' by Qaiyum Khan, 'it won sixty-seven out of a total of eighty-five seats'. Four seats went to the Jinnah Awami League, thirteen to independents, and one to the non-Muslims.[147] 'The Muslim League Parliamentary Party', in its meeting on 14 December 1951, 'chose Qaiyum Khan' as its leader in the house. Therefore, his interim ministry resigned, the governor asked him to form a new ministry, and on 17 December 1951 he announced his new cabinet.[148] In M. Rafique Afzal's words:

> A few days after the elections, the thirteen independents and the one non-Muslim pledged their support to the Muslim League. Having once secured such a constitutional majority, Qayyum Khan knew how to preserve it. The complaints of the aggrieved group of the party went unheard in the ensuing controversies over finding an agreed formula for the country's constitution.[149]

In April 1953, the central government moved Qaiyum Khan to the centre. He nominated the then-provincial inspector-general of the police, Sardar Abdur Rashid Khan, as his successor as the head of the government in the province, but retained the presidentship of the Frontier League. The situation in the party, however, soon changed and 'in August 1953, the working committee of the party laid down the condition that every office-holder in the party should have permanent residence in the province'. Qaiyum Khan made 'frantic efforts to save his' party office but failed. Consequently, on 29 October 1953, 'he resigned his office as president' and 'a week later, the party council elected Chief Minister Sardar Abdur Rashid as president'.[150] Sardar Abdur Rashid remained in power until 18 July 1955; he was succeeded by Sardar Bahadar Khan on 29 July 1955, who remained in power until 14 October 1955.[151] On 14 October 1955, all the provinces of the then-west wing of the country were merged into One Unit and a new province, West Pakistan, was created. Consequently, the Frontier Province and the Frontier Muslim League came to an end.

In 1970, the Chief Martial Law Administrator and President, General Yahya Khan, brought an end to the One Unit and restored the old provinces, the Frontier being one of them. During this period, the Muslim League had split into factions; Qaiyum Khan headed one of them, called the Qaiyum Muslim League. Other groups included the

Convention Muslim League and the Council Muslim League. During the general elections of 1970, the Qaiyum Muslim League contested forty seats for the Frontier provincial assembly, and won eleven (from Hazarah, Dirah Ismail Khan, Swat, and Dir). Qaiyum Khan was defeated by Hayat Muhammad Khan Sherpau for the provincial assembly seat, but was successful for three National Assembly seats. His party won nine National Assembly seats in the province. The Council Muslim League contested fourteen seats, winning only one, while the Convention Muslim League contested five seats and also won one.[152] On 15 February 1973, when the Jamiatul Ulama-e-Islam (Jamiat-ul Ulamay-i Islam) and National Awami Party's (NAP) coalition ministry resigned as a protest against Zulfiqar Ali Bhutto's central government policies, the Mutahida Mahaz in the Frontier legislature formed the ministry, in which the Qaiyum Muslim League received a notable share.[153]

The Muslim League continued to play a role in the Frontier's politics. On 5 July 1977, General Ziaul Haq imposed martial law in the country, and political activities were banned. In 1985, elections were held on a non-party basis, but later parliamentary parties were formed in the assemblies. And so, the Muslim League was revived and a large number of assembly members joined it. In the Frontier Province, too, the Muslim League became the ruling party, with Arbab Muhammad Jahangir Khan as the chief minister of the province. In 1988, General Zia dissolved the National Assembly—using his powers under article 58 (2) B of the constitution—and the governors dissolved the provincial assemblies. The League contested the next general elections in 1988 but did not come into power in the province.

However, after the general elections of 1990, the League formed a coalition government with the ANP (Awami National Party) in the Frontier, headed by Pir Sabir Shah of the League. After the 1993 elections, it formed the opposition in the provincial assembly; after the 1997 elections, it came into power once again, forming a government headed by Sardar Mehtab Khan Abbasi. On 12 October 1999, following the army coup, not only did the League's government came to an end, but the party later split into the Muslim League (Quaid-i-Azam)—the group supporting army rule under General Pervez Musharraf—and the Muslim League (Nawaz)—the group opposing General Pervez Musharraf. Both groups contested the general elections of 2002 but were unsuccessful in the province and, hence, remained in the opposition in the provincial assembly. The party remained split into two groups in the province: Muslim League (Quaid-i-Azam)—headed by Engineer Amir Muqam—

which was General Musharraf's favourite and Muslim League (Nawaz)—headed by Pir Sabir Shah. Both the factions failed to make a noteworthy mark in the province during the general elections of 2008 as well.

In the meantime, Amir Muqam gravitated and turned to Muslim League (Nawaz) before the general elections of 2013; the move gave Muslim League (Quaid-i-Azam) a set-back and it virtually became a non-entity in the province. This, however, did not strengthen Muslim League (Nawaz) either, as it annoyed a segment of the old guards of the party in the province. Moreover, as Amir Muqam influenced and manipulated the granting of the party tickets for the general elections of 2013, it created grudges and dissensions in the rank and file of the party, dividing it between the old guards—who stood with Nawaz Sharif through thick and thin after General Musharraf's taking over power in 1999—and the new Muslim League (Quaid-i-Azam) lot—who left Nawaz Sharif in the wake of trials and tribulations after General Musharraf's taking over power in 1999. This not only resulted in some of the old guards leaving the party but also in the party's failure to show progress and good result in the elections. The central president of the party, Nawaz Sharif, later selected Amir Muqam as head or president of the provincial wing of the party.

As Amir Muqam retained the provincial presidentship of Muslim League (Nawaz), it proved to be a continued source of dissension in the rank and file of the party. At the time of the 2018 general elections, too, the manipulation and faction politics in granting tickets to the party candidates for the elections, proved to be one of the causes of the party's failure in showing remarkable progress and bagging considerable seats from the province, for both the central and provincial assemblies.

Notes

1. Muhammad Anwar Khan, *The Role of N.W.F.P. in the Freedom Struggle* (Lahore: RSP, 2000), 43.
2. Ibid., 47.
3. Ibid., 39. For the number and names of the members of the deputation who called upon the viceroy, and for the address presented to him, see *JPHS* (Karachi), vol. 55 (Nos. 3–4, July–December 2007), 'All India Muslim League Centenary Special Number, Part II', 32–8.
4. B.R. Ambedkar, *Pakistan or the Partition of India*, 1st Pakistani edn. (Lahore: BT, 1976), 430 n.
5. *JPHS* (Nos. 3–4, July–December 2007), 'All India Muslim League Centenary Special Number, Part II', 136–9.
6. Ibid., 152.

7. Syed Waqar Ali Shah, *Muslim League in N.W.F.P.* (Karachi: RBC, 1992), 20. Also Sayed Wiqar Ali Shah, *Ethnicity, Islam, and Nationalism: Muslim Politics in the North-West Frontier Province, 1937–1947* (Karachi: OUP, 1999), 17.

8. Khan, *The Role of N.W.F.P. in the Freedom Struggle*, 48.

9. See Allah Bakhsh Yusufi, *Sarhad aur Jidujahd-i Azadi, tarmim wa izafah shudah edn.* (Urdu) (Karachi: Nafees Academy, 1989), 699–700.

10. Khan, *The Role of N.W.F.P. in the Freedom Struggle*, 77 n. 17.

11. Ibid., 48–9.

12. Shah, *Muslim League in N.W.F.P.*, 20.

13. Muhammad Shafi Sabir, *Quaid-i Azam aur Subah Sarhad* (Urdu) (Peshawar: UBA, n.d.), 36.

14. Shah, *Muslim League in N.W.F.P.*, 20–1.

15. Khan, *The Role of N.W.F.P. in the Freedom Struggle*, 49.

16. Sabir, *Quaid-i Azam aur Subah Sarhad*, 36.

17. Shah, *Ethnicity, Islam, and Nationalism*, 17.

18. See Khan, *The Role of N.W.F.P. in the Freedom Struggle*, 49–50; Shah, *Muslim League in N.W.F.P.*, 21–2; Shah, *Ethnicity, Islam, and Nationalism*, 17–18; Stephen Alan Rittenberg, *Ethnicity, Nationalism, and the Pakhtuns: The Independence Movement in India's North-West Frontier Province* (Durham: CAP, 1988), 66.

19. Khan, *The Role of N.W.F.P. in the Freedom Struggle*, 57.

20. Ibid., 83.

21. Shah, *Ethnicity, Islam, and Nationalism*, 17–18.

22. Khan, *The Role of N.W.F.P. in the Freedom Struggle*, 84–5.

23. Shah, *Muslim League in N.W.F.P.*, 26.

24. Ibid. Also see Shah, *Ethnicity, Islam, and Nationalism*, 96–7; Sayed Wiqar Ali Shah, *North-West Frontier Province: History and Politics* (Islamabad: NIHCR, 2007), 150.

25. Yusufi, *Sarhad aur Jidujahd-i Azadi*, 708.

26. See Shah, *Muslim League in N.W.F.P.*, 27–8; Shah, *Ethnicity, Islam, and Nationalism*, 97–9; Shah, *North-West Frontier Province*, 150–2 cf. Sabir, *Quaid-i Azam aur Subah Sarhad*, 63–6.

27. Erland Jansson, *India, Pakistan or Pakhtunistan: The Nationalist Movements in the North-West Frontier Province, 1937–47* (Stockholm: AWI, 1981), 108. Also see Sabir, *Quaid-i Azam aur Subah Sarhad*, 67.

28. See Yusufi, *Sarhad aur Jidujahd-i Azadi*, 708.

29. See Abdul Khaliq Khaleeq, *Da Azadai Jang: Sah Lidali aw sah Awridali* (Pukhtu), 2nd edn. (Pikhawar: IIS, 1972), 119–20.

30. Shah, *Ethnicity, Islam, and Nationalism*, 57. Also see ibid., 95, 99–100; Shah, *North-West Frontier Province*, 153.

31. Quoted in Shah, *Muslim League in N.W.F.P.*, 28.

32. CID Diaries, F.No. 30, SBP, p. 382 quoted in Shah, *North-West Frontier Province*, 152.

33. Shah, *Ethnicity, Islam, and Nationalism*, 100. Dr Sayed Wiqar Ali Shah states: 'Before the "discovery" of this two-page handwritten letter of Abdul Wahid Khan, addressed to the president AIML in the QAP [Quaid-i-Azam Papers], and the CID Diaries dated 7 June 1937, all previous writings on the area including Rittenberg, "Independence Movement", p. 255, Jansson, *Pakhtunistan*, p. 108 and Talbot, *Provincial Politics*, p. 10, seems to be misinformed on the matter. All of them are of the opinion that the first branch of the FPML [Frontier Provincial Muslim League] was started in Abbottabad in September 1937. But as is evident from these documents the first branch of the NWFP Muslim League was the one started in Nowshera on 16 May 1937. Abdul Wahid to President AIML, 16 May 1937, F. No. 865, QAP, pp. 64–5.' Ibid., 115–16 n. 31. But, Dr Sayed Wiqar Ali Shah himself has

stated, on the authority of the CID diaries, of the foundation of a local branch of the All India Muslim League at the time of Jinnah's visit to Peshawar in October 1936, as quoted above.

34. Ibid., 100–1.
35. Rittenberg, *Ethnicity, Nationalism, and the Pakhtuns*, 154 cf. Khan, *The Role of N.W.F.P. in the Freedom Struggle*, 97. Also see Khaleeq, *Da Azadai Jang*, 131–2.
36. Jansson, *India, Pakistan or Pakhtunistan*, 108.
37. Khan, *The Role of N.W.F.P. in the Freedom Struggle*, 94.
38. Ibid., 98.
39. Rittenberg, *Ethnicity, Nationalism, and the Pakhtuns*, 154.
40. Jansson, *India, Pakistan or Pakhtunistan*, 109.
41. Rittenberg, *Ethnicity, Nationalism, and the Pakhtuns*, 153–4.
42. Jansson, *India, Pakistan or Pakhtunistan*, 109.
43. Shah, *Ethnicity, Islam, and Nationalism*, 61.
44. Rittenberg, *Ethnicity, Nationalism, and the Pakhtuns*, 155.
45. Ibid.
46. Khan, *The Role of N.W.F.P. in the Freedom Struggle*, 113–15.
47. See *The Constitution and Rules of the Frontier Muslim League (Provincial Muslim League N.W.F.P.)* (Published for the League by: Mohammad Ismail Khan Ghaznavi, L.L.M. (London), Barrister-at-Law, Honorary Secretary, n.d.); Khan, *The Role of N.W.F.P. in the Freedom Struggle*, 115; ibid., 'Appendix V', 406–18.
48. Shah, *Ethnicity, Islam, and Nationalism*, 106.
49. Ibid., 103–4.
50. For the foundation and existence of the local Muslim League organizations, also see Khan, *The Role of N.W.F.P. in the Freedom Struggle*, 98–102, 111–13; Shah, *Ethnicity, Islam, and Nationalism*, 101.
51. See Yusufi, *Sarhad aur Jidujahd-i Azadi*, 715–16. Also see Rittenberg, *Ethnicity, Nationalism, and the Pakhtuns*, 156; Sabir, *Quaid-i Azam aur Subah Sarhad*, 62–3; Shah, *Ethnicity, Islam, and Nationalism*, 104.
52. Jansson, *India, Pakistan or Pakhtunistan*, 110–11. Also see Rittenberg, *Ethnicity, Nationalism, and the Pakhtuns*, 156.
53. Jansson, *India, Pakistan or Pakhtunistan*, 111.
54. Rittenberg, *Ethnicity, Nationalism, and the Pakhtuns*, 155.
55. Shah, *Muslim League in N.W.F.P.*, 36. For the names of those 'who struggled to popularise' the League in the Frontier, see ibid., 36–7.
56. Rittenberg, *Ethnicity, Nationalism, and the Pakhtuns*, 157.
57. Shah, *Muslim League in N.W.F.P.*, 37.
58. See Khan, *The Role of N.W.F.P. in the Freedom Struggle*, 116–18. Also see Shah, *Ethnicity, Islam, and Nationalism*, 109.
59. Khan, *The Role of N.W.F.P. in the Freedom Struggle*, 118–20. Also see Shah, *Ethnicity, Islam, and Nationalism*, 109–12.
60. Khan, *The Role of N.W.F.P. in the Freedom Struggle*, 120–1.
61. Ibid., 121.
62. Ibid., 122. Also see Shah, *Ethnicity, Islam, and Nationalism*, 104–5.
63. Shah, *Ethnicity, Islam, and Nationalism*, 105–6.
64. Rittenberg, *Ethnicity, Nationalism, and the Pakhtuns*, 160.
65. See Shah, *Muslim League in N.W.F.P.*, 39–40; Shah, *Ethnicity, Islam, and Nationalism*, 113.
66. See Khan, *The Role of N.W.F.P. in the Freedom Struggle*, 123–30.
67. Shah, *Muslim League in N.W.F.P.*, 41.
68. For details, see ibid., 48–55; Khan, *The Role of N.W.F.P. in the Freedom Struggle*, 133–7. Also see Syed Sharifuddin Pirzada, 'The Lahore Resolution (1940)' in S. Moinul Haq, ed.,

A History of the Freedom Movement, vol. 4, *1936–1947*, Parts I and II (Karachi: Pakistan Historical Society, 1970), 98.

69. See Khan, *The Role of N.W.F.P. in the Freedom Struggle*, 137–9.

70. Ibid., 139.

71. Shah, *Muslim League in N.W.F.P.*, 57. Also see Khan, *The Role of N.W.F.P. in the Freedom Struggle*, 140.

72. Khan, *The Role of N.W.F.P. in the Freedom Struggle*, 161–2.

73. Shah, *Muslim League in N.W.F.P.*, 58.

74. Khan, *The Role of N.W.F.P. in the Freedom Struggle*, 167–8.

75. Jansson, *India, Pakistan or Pakhtunistan*, 115. Also see Shah, *Ethnicity, Islam, and Nationalism*, 139–40.

76. See Amit Kumar Gupta, *North West Frontier Province: Legislature and Freedom Struggle, 1932–47* (New Delhi: ICHR, 1976), 132–4.

77. Ayesha Jalal, *The Sole Spokesman: Jinnah, the Muslim League and the Demand for Pakistan* (Cambridge: Cambridge University Press, 1985), 115–16.

78. See Shah, *Muslim League in N.W.F.P.*, 67.

79. Cunningham to Linlithgow, 24 August 1943, L/P&J/5/220, I.O.L., p. 56 quoted in Jalal, *The Sole Spokesman*, 116.

80. See Shah, *Muslim League in N.W.F.P.*, 67–8; Abdul Qaiyum, *Gold and Guns on the Pathan Frontier* (Bombay: HK, 1945), 40.

81. Qaiyum, *Gold and Guns on the Pathan Frontier*, 40. Also see Jawaharlal Nehru, *The Discovery of India*, 12th impr. (New Delhi: JNMF, 1992), 432.

82. See Shah, *Muslim League in N.W.F.P.*, 69–71; Jalal, *The Sole Spokesman*, 116–18; Shah, *Ethnicity, Islam, and Nationalism*, 144–7; Rittenberg, *Ethnicity, Nationalism, and the Pakhtuns*, 183.

83. *Jinnah Papers*, A.F.M. 342, 31 March 1994 [1944], pp. 70–1 quoted in Khan, *The Role of N.W.F.P. in the Freedom Struggle*, 175. Also see Rittenberg, *Ethnicity, Nationalism, and the Pakhtuns*, 183.

84. See Shah, *Muslim League in N.W.F.P.*, 73–7.

85. See Khan, *The Role of N.W.F.P. in the Freedom Struggle*, 175.

86. Mohammad Zafar Ahmad Ansari's statement to the Press, 26 July 1944, *AFM*, F. 344 quoted in Shah, *Muslim League in N.W.F.P.*, 77–8.

87. Rittenberg, *Ethnicity, Nationalism, and the Pakhtuns*, 183.

88. Ibid., 184.

89. Khan, *The Role of N.W.F.P. in the Freedom Struggle*, 176.

90. Rittenberg, *Ethnicity, Nationalism, and the Pakhtuns*, 185.

91. Cunningham to Wavell, 9 October 1945, *TP*, VI, pp. 318–19 quoted in Shah, *Muslim League in N.W.F.P.*, 82.

92. Khan, *The Role of N.W.F.P. in the Freedom Struggle*, 199. Also see Sabir, *Quaid-i Azam aur Subah Sarhad*, 105–7; Shah, *Ethnicity, Islam, and Nationalism*, 192–3, 231 n. 6.

93. Rittenberg, *Ethnicity, Nationalism, and the Pakhtuns*, 190. Also see Khaleeq, *Da Azadai Jang*, 140–1.

94. Also see Khaleeq, *Da Azadai Jang*, 161.

95. Qaiyum, *Gold and Guns on the Pathan Frontier*, 39.

96. Shah, *Muslim League in N.W.F.P.*, 84–5. For details, also see Sabir, *Quaid-i Azam aur Subah Sarhad*, 108–35; Shah, *North-West Frontier Province*, 153–62.

97. Gupta, *North West Frontier Province*, 172.

98. Shah, *Muslim League in N.W.F.P.*, 94.

99. See ibid., 96, 123 n. 14; Khan, *The Role of N.W.F.P. in the Freedom Struggle*, 204; Gupta, *North West Frontier Province*, 173–4; Shah, *Ethnicity, Islam, and Nationalism*, 161.

100. See Shah, *Muslim League in N.W.F.P.*, 97–9; Jalal, *The Sole Spokesman*, 169–70; Sabir, *Quaid-i Azam aur Subah Sarhad*, 279–80.

101. Gupta, *North West Frontier Province*, 174.

102. Ibid., 179. For the alleged Congress machinations against the League in the elections, and for other causes for Congress' victory, see Sabir, *Quaid-i Azam aur Subah Sarhad*, 141–2; Shah, *Ethnicity, Islam, and Nationalism*, 166.

103. Khan, *The Role of N.W.F.P. in the Freedom Struggle*, 207.

104. Shah, *Muslim League in N.W.F.P.*, 103.

105. Khan, *The Role of N.W.F.P. in the Freedom Struggle*, 214.

106. Sabir, *Quaid-i Azam aur Subah Sarhad*, 144.

107. Shah, *Muslim League in N.W.F.P.*, 111–12. Also see Khan, *The Role of N.W.F.P. in the Freedom Struggle*, 214–17.

108. Shah, *Muslim League in N.W.F.P.*, 112–13; Rittenberg, *Ethnicity, Nationalism, and the Pakhtuns*, 207–9.

109. Rittenberg, *Ethnicity, Nationalism, and the Pakhtuns*, 209.

110. Gupta, *North West Frontier Province*, 192.

111. Shah, *Muslim League in N.W.F.P.*, 107–10.

112. See ibid., 114–21; Khan, *The Role of N.W.F.P. in the Freedom Struggle*, 223–6.

113. H.V. Hodson, *The Great Divide: Britain–India–Pakistan*, with epilogue written in 1985 which sums up the events since partition, and with new introduction, 7th impr. of the Jubilee Series edn., 1997 (Karachi: OUP, 2005), 279–80.

114. Shah, *Muslim League in N.W.F.P.*, 121; Shah, *Ethnicity, Islam, and Nationalism*, 181–2. Also see Shah, *North-West Frontier Province*, 141.

115. See Hodson, *The Great Divide*, 279; Shah, *Ethnicity, Islam, and Nationalism*, 176–7; Shah, *North-West Frontier Province*, 140; Rittenberg, *Ethnicity, Nationalism, and the Pakhtuns*, 212–13; Latif Ahmed Sherwani, *The Partition of India and Mountbatten* (Karachi: Council for Pakistan Studies, 1986), 147; Abul Kalam Azad, *India Wins Freedom: An Autobiographical Narrative*, repr. (Bombay: OLL, 1964), 169–70.

116. James W. Spain, *The Pathan Borderland*, repr. (Karachi: IP, 1985), 194.

117. Hodson, *The Great Divide*, 282.

118. Gupta, *North West Frontier Province*, 193.

119. Khan, *The Role of N.W.F.P. in the Freedom Struggle*, 227–9. Also see Shah, *Ethnicity, Islam, and Nationalism*, 199; Shah, *North-West Frontier Province*, 141–2.

120. Khan, *The Role of N.W.F.P. in the Freedom Struggle*, 229.

121. Basanti, a Sikh woman whose husband was murdered in the Hazarah communal riots, was then married by a Muslim, Muhammad Zaman, in spite of her being pregnant. Muslims claimed that she had become Muslim and had married Muhammad Zaman by her own choice, but her community claimed otherwise. She was brought to and kept in the Chief Minister, Dr Khan Sahib's, house, so that she could be questioned in a free atmosphere. Subsequently, she was returned to the Sikhs according to her will, as the government claimed, while the Muslim League claimed that she was returned to the Sikhs under the pressure of the non-Muslims. The League exploited this matter against Dr Khan Sahib's ministry [see Shah, *Muslim League in N.W.F.P.*, 134; Khan, *The Role of N.W.F.P. in the Freedom Struggle*, 229–30; Rittenberg, *Ethnicity, Nationalism, and the Pakhtuns*, 218–19; Gupta, *North West Frontier Province*, 194; Jansson, *India, Pakistan or Pakhtunistan*, 191–2]. Abdul Khaliq Khaleeq, however, has stated that she fled with the Muslim [see Khaleeq, *Da Azadai Jang*, 167].

122. Khan, *The Role of N.W.F.P. in the Freedom Struggle*, 230–1.

123. Shah, *Muslim League in N.W.F.P.*, 134; Shah, *Ethnicity, Islam, and Nationalism*, 199; Shah, *North-West Frontier Province*, 142; Rittenberg, *Ethnicity, Nationalism, and the Pakhtuns*, 218; Jansson, *India, Pakistan or Pakhtunistan*, 192.

124. Shah, *Muslim League in N.W.F.P.*, 138. Also see Shah, *Ethnicity, Islam, and Nationalism*, 201; Rittenberg, *Ethnicity, Nationalism, and the Pakhtuns*, 225.

125. Shah, *Muslim League in N.W.F.P.*, 135. Also see Shah, *Ethnicity, Islam, and Nationalism*, 201; Rittenberg, *Ethnicity, Nationalism, and the Pakhtuns*, 220, 225.

126. See Shah, *Muslim League in N.W.F.P.*, 140–4. Also see Shah, *Ethnicity, Islam, and Nationalism*, 209–10; Rittenberg, *Ethnicity, Nationalism, and the Pakhtuns*, 220, 222–5.

127. Gupta, *North West Frontier Province*, 194. Also see Rittenberg, *Ethnicity, Nationalism, and the Pakhtuns*, 218–29.

128. Khan, *The Role of N.W.F.P. in the Freedom Struggle*, 232. Also see Chaudhri Muhammad Ali, *The Emergence of Pakistan*, 5th impr. (Lahore: RSP, 1985), 130.

129. Spain, *The Pathan Borderland*, 198. Also see Sabir, *Quaid-i Azam aur Subah Sarhad*, 251–2.

130. M. Rafique Afzal, *Political Parties in Pakistan, 1947–1958*, vol. 1, 9th edn. (Islamabad: NIHCR, 2013), 107.

131. Ibid.

132. Also see Shah, *Ethnicity, Islam, and Nationalism*, 228–30.

133. Afzal, *Political Parties in Pakistan*, vol. 1, 107. Also Shah, *Ethnicity, Islam, and Nationalism*, 230.

134. Syed Minhaj ul Hassan, 'NWFP Administration under Abdul Qaiyum Khan, 1947–53' (Unpublished PhD Dissertation, Department of History, University of Peshawar, 2003), 78; Syed Minhajul Hassan, *The Dawn of New Era in Khyber Pakhtunkhwa: Abdul Qaiyum Khan Chief Ministership, 1947–53* (Islamabad: NIHCR, 2016), 54.

135. Afzal, *Political Parties in Pakistan*, vol. 1, 107–8. The ones who defected were: Mian Jafar Shah Kaka Khail, Arbab Abdur Rahman Khan (Guli Garhi), Pir Shahinshah (Kuhat), Salar Aslam Khan (Kuhat), Sahib Gul (Bugaray), Yaqub Khan (Bannu), and Abdullah Khan (Putah) (Sabir, *Quaid-i Azam aur Subah Sarhad*, 269).

136. Hassan, 'NWFP Administration under Abdul Qaiyum Khan', 79–80; Hassan, *The Dawn of New Era in Khyber Pakhtunkhwa*, 56. Also see Ali, *The Emergence of Pakistan*, 368.

137. See Hassan, 'NWFP Administration under Abdul Qaiyum Khan', 81–4; Hassan, *The Dawn of New Era in Khyber Pakhtunkhwa*, 57–9.

138. Hassan, 'NWFP Administration under Abdul Qaiyum Khan', 82; Hassan, *The Dawn of New Era in Khyber Pakhtunkhwa*, 58. Also see Sabir, *Quaid-i Azam aur Subah Sarhad*, 279–80.

139. Safdar Mahmood, *Pakistan: Muslim League ka Daur-i Hukumat, 1947–1954* [henceforward Mahmood, *Pakistan*] (Urdu) (Lahore: SMP, 1986), 83–4, 211–12. Also see Ali, *The Emergence of Pakistan*, 373–4.

140. For details, see Hassan, 'NWFP Administration under Abdul Qaiyum Khan', 83–5; Hassan, *The Dawn of New Era in Khyber Pakhtunkhwa*, 58–61.

141. For details, see Hassan, 'NWFP Administration under Abdul Qaiyum Khan', 90–1; Hassan, *The Dawn of New Era in Khyber Pakhtunkhwa*, 64–5. Also see Abdul Khaliq Khaleeq, *Zah aw Zama Zamanah* (Pukhtu) (Pikhawar: IIS, 1968), 113.

142. Mahmood, *Pakistan*, 215.

143. For details, see Hassan, 'NWFP Administration under Abdul Qaiyum Khan', 93–8; Hassan, *The Dawn of New Era in Khyber Pakhtunkhwa*, 67–71; Afzal, *Political Parties in Pakistan*, vol. 1, 108–9; Mahmood, *Pakistan*, 215–22.

144. Hassan, 'NWFP Administration under Abdul Qaiyum Khan', 105; Hassan, *The Dawn of New Era in Khyber Pakhtunkhwa*, 77.

145. Hassan, 'NWFP Administration under Abdul Qaiyum Khan', 111; Hassan, *The Dawn of New Era in Khyber Pakhtunkhwa*, 83.

146. See Hassan, 'NWFP Administration under Abdul Qaiyum Khan', 111–20; Hassan, *The Dawn of New Era in Khyber Pakhtunkhwa*, 83–9. Also see Khaleeq, *Zah aw Zama Zamanah*, 114–15.

147. Afzal, *Political Parties in Pakistan*, vol. 1, 111–12.

148. See Hassan, 'NWFP Administration under Abdul Qaiyum Khan', 121–2; Hassan, *The Dawn of New Era in Khyber Pakhtunkhwa*, 91–3. Also see Mahmood, *Pakistan*, 224.
149. Afzal, *Political Parties in Pakistan*, vol. 1, 112.
150. Ibid., 112–13. Also see Mahmood, *Pakistan*, 225–7.
151. Aziz Javaid, *Sarhad ka Ayini Irtiqa* (Urdu) (Peshawar: Idarah Tahqiq wa Tasnif, 1975), 289.
152. See ibid., 311–18, 327.
153. See ibid., 319–20.

11 Referendum

The Congress-Muslim League battle, which was being fought
out all over India, was waged more intensely in the N-WFP than
in any other province.
– James W. Spain

The Viceroy was looking for ways and means to ascertain the
views of the people. The Congress as a whole under the leadership
of Nehru and Patel was on line and NWFP had become a joint
problem for the British and the Congress.
– Juma Khan Sufi

L IKE OTHER EUROPEANS, the Britons came to the subcontinent
as traders. Initially, they struggled and fought against the other
Europeans in India, but slowly and gradually entered the power game,
and over time emerged as a power to be reckoned with. Taking advantage
of the political instability in the subcontinent, and the power struggle
between the different groups, ethnicities, and individuals, the East India
Company strengthened its position by playing on the vanity of the locals
and siding with the different contenders to serve its own interests. It
was not a sovereign power in itself; even its charter needed to be
renewed by the British Crown for the purpose of trade. But, it occupied
territories, emerged as a paramount power, occupied a major portion of the
subcontinent, and continued to expand its dominion by occupying more
areas. In this way, the Britons in the East India Company did not keep
their activities limited to trade but also became a ruling power.

The situation remained so for quite a long time, but certain policies
of the Britons, including that of expansion, generated resentment and
discontent in various circles and segments of the subcontinent, culminating
in the uprising of 1857—termed 'mutiny' by the Britons and 'war of
independence' by the Indians. As 'the Charter of 1853 was not renewed for
20 years as was the case with the earlier Charters', 'it left the door open
for the' British government to 'take over the administration' of the Indian
territories occupied by the East India Company.[1] (The Charter of 1853
empowered the East India Company to retain the territories and revenues

in India in trust for the crown not for any specified period as preceding Charter Acts had provided but only until Parliament should otherwise direct.) A significant outcome of the uprising was that it 'gave an impetus to the demand that a trading company should not be allowed to continue to exercise political power', and so the British 'government decided to put an end to the political functions of the Company'.[2] Therefore, under the Government of India Act of 1858, 'the Government of India passed from the hands of the English East India Company to the [British] Crown' and 'the Governor-General came to be known as the Viceroy'. Besides, 'the Military and Naval forces of the Company were transferred to the Crown', and the company's 'Board of Control and the Court of Directors were abolished and their powers were transferred to the Secretary of State for India and his India Council'.[3] In this way, the East India Company was divested of its powers and the territories held by it were placed under the direct control of the British Crown and government.

With this, not only further expansion of British India—the Indian territories under Britons control and rule—came to a halt but the British government started introducing reforms in the sphere of governance and, although slowly and gradually, also introduced a representative form of governance, even though it was in a rudimentary form and in the local bodies only at first. Over the course of time, and with the spread of modern education, a need was perceived for a body that could put Indian aspirations before the colonial government, using peaceful means. An ex-English civil servant, Allan Octavian Hume (commonly written as A.O. Hume), strived for, and succeeded in founding, the All India National Congress in 1885.[4] Slowly and gradually, other associations and parties were also founded, with different aims and objectives. One of them was the All India Muslim League, founded in 1906—some twenty-one years after than the Congress.

The colonial government granted reforms periodically. Gradually, more rights and participation were granted to the Indians in the ruling sphere. The Indians also demanded more and more rights, powers, and a greater share in governance. This led to a demand for self-rule, and then for complete independence from the British yoke. On the other side, in its annual session held in Lahore in March 1940, the Muslim League demanded the division of India into Muslim and Hindu majority areas; a resolution was accordingly passed on 24 March 1940, called the Lahore Resolution or Pakistan Resolution. (As stated in the previous chapter, the resolution was presented in the session on 23 March and was passed on 24 March, after completing the deliberations over it.) Due to internal and external pressures, the British government endeavoured to settle the Indian issue amicably. A mission, known as the Cripps Mission, was sent to India but it failed in its task. To end the deadlock between Congress and the Muslim League on India's future, a conference was arranged at Simla, known as the Simla Conference, but it too was unsuccessful. The next attempt was made by the Cabinet Mission, which comprised members of the British parliament, but the Cabinet Mission Plan also failed to satisfy the aspirations of both the parties (Congress and the Muslim League) and the deadlock continued.

On the provincial political scene, the settled districts of the North-West Frontier Province (now Khyber Pukhtunkhwa) were brought under the Britons rule in 1849, but were kept at a distance from the politics of the rest of India. This changed with the province's participation, and active role, in the *khilafat* and *hijrat* movements of the early 1920s.[5] Political awareness and political activities began in the province—demand for the introduction of reforms, and raising the status of the province to that of a full-fledged province, also received momentum.

In 1929, the Khudayi Khidmatgar movement was founded which, in spite of having a local agenda and local objectives, brought the province into the broader fore of Indian politics within a year because of its association and alliance with the All India National Congress.[6] Other factors that tied the province and the future course of its events to the politics and developments on an all-India basis were: raising the status of the province to that of a full-fledged province in 1932; the extension of reforms, on the same footing as in the other provinces of British India; the Government of India Act, 1935;[7] M.A. Jinnah's visit; the election of 1937; and the re-organisation of the provincial Muslim League.

Although it talked about the rights and liberty of *qaam* and *watan*—(قام او وطن) nation and homeland, implied only the Pukhtuns and their homeland—the Khudayi Khidmatgars and their movement seemingly became a part of the Congress rather than an ally; their leader, Abdul Ghaffar Khan also known as Bacha Khan, became a member of the Congress Working Committee. The Khudayi Khidmatgars followed and endorsed the policies and programmes of the Congress in the province, whether it was the civil disobedience movement of the early 1930s, the formation of a ministry after the election of 1937, the resignation of the ministry in 1939, the civil disobedience and Quit India movements, and all other such issues and concerns. They even adopted the tricolour flag of the Congress.

At the same time, the All India Muslim League also dragged the province into the fore of all-India politics by its re-organisation and activities in the province and also by the Lahore and Pakistan resolution, passed on 24 March 1940 in Lahore, when it was demanded that the province be part of a state comprising the north-western Muslim majority areas of the subcontinent.

Thus, during the course of trying to solve the Indian problem—the Cripps Mission Plan, the Simla Conference, and the Cabinet Mission Plan—the province was not treated or dealt with separately but as part of British India. The Khudayi Khidmatgar leaders, although continually repeated the old rhetoric of *qaam* and *watan* (meaning the Pukhtun nation and homeland), did not plead the case of the province separately—as a separate entity and geographical and political unit that was only incorporated into, and made part of British India, by the colonial authorities. The Khudayi Khidmatgar leaders, while conducting negotiations and meetings from the Congress platform, tied the province to India and did their best for the province to remain so in the case of departure of the British.

In this scenario, the British Prime Minister, Mr Attlee, announced the transfer of power to the Indians by June 1948. To materialise the plan, Lord Mountbatten was sent to India as the new viceroy, with the task of chalking-out a programme for the transfer of power. Immediately after his arrival in India on 22 March 1947, Mountbatten

> initiated a period of intensive political discussions which culminated on June 3rd with the announcement of a plan to partition India and advance the date of independence from June 1948 to August 15, 1947. *The North-West Frontier Province formed an important topic in those negotiations, one which complicated his attempts to reach a settlement to India's political crisis* [italics mine].[8]

Interestingly, 'of the various areas which were expected to become part of Pakistan, the position of the Frontier Province was unique in several aspects'. The province 'was ruled by a Congress Ministry' with a strong majority, two of its three representatives in the central legislature 'were Congress nominees', and 'the most outstanding leader of the Province, Ghaffar Khan, was also one of the most respected leaders of the Congress'. On the other hand, it 'had an overwhelming Muslim majority (92%)' and 'had no land or sea link with non-Muslim parts of India'.[9]

Having an overwhelming majority in the provincial legislature, the Khudayi Khidmatgars-Congress had formed the government in the province with Dr Khan Sahib—Dr Khan Sayb: Ghaffar Khan's elder brother—as the chief minister, but the Muslim League resorted to agitation and civil disobedience to achieve its goal and objectives in the province. The League's agitation (although it started over the issue of a Sikh woman, Basanti [see Chapter 10, n. 121], and the demand for the removal of the ministry) resulted in a serious situation in the province. Mountbatten, 'at one point', termed the Frontier 'the greatest danger spot in India and the bone of contention between Congress and Muslim League'.[10] To assess the situation personally, the viceroy, in spite of the governor's opposition, visited the province on 28–29 April 1947. Consequently, he was convinced that the mandate of the 1946 election should not be considered valid for deciding the province's future—in the event of the division of India. As holding fresh elections at this stage in the province would have had its own associated problems and technicalities, the viceroy decided to seek a fresh mandate of the people of the province, instead of the legislature, on the question of whether the province should be made part of the new dominion of India or Pakistan on 15 August 1947. Hence, the 3rd June Plan, also known as the Mountbatten Plan, stated that the position of the Frontier Province 'is exceptional'. Although,

> Two of the three representatives of this Province are already participating in the existing Constituent Assembly. But it is clear, in view of its geographical situation, and other considerations, that if the whole or any part of the Punjab decides not to join the existing Constituent Assembly, it will be necessary to give the North West Frontier Province an opportunity to reconsider its position. Accordingly[,] in such an event, a referendum will be made to the electors of the present Legislative Assembly in the North West Frontier Province to choose which of the alternatives mentioned in paragraph 4 above they wish to adopt. The referendum will be held under the aegis of the Governor-General and in consultation with the Provincial Government.[11]

The viceroy, even at the time of his visit to the province (on 28–29 April 1947) and during the course of his meeting with the governor and the chief minister—when both alleged that the other was not cooperating but creating troubles—said: 'I am out here to do a job with no axe to grind. I want to transfer power in terms of the will of the people. *Ideally I would have a plebiscite here, but there is no time* [italics mine].'[12] This suggests that the idea of a referendum was not new. In Dr Sayed Wiqar Ali Shah's words:

Some writers have rightly termed the Viceroy's visit of the NWFP a 'turning point'...in the history of the province, as it was during this visit that the Viceroy was convinced of the Muslim League's popularity and decided on a referendum on the issue of Hindustan and Pakistan.[13]

Even before this, during the governors' conference held on 15–16 April 1947, Mountbatten called Jawaharlal Nehru, Liaquat Ali Khan, Baldev Singh, Field Marshal Auchinleck, and Olaf Caroe—governor of the Frontier Province—together. During the deliberations, the viceroy proposed his plan of a general election in the province 'before the transfer [of power] had been effected'. Nehru 'strongly objected' to the procedures proposed by the viceroy and, hence, 'no agreement could be reached'. However, he accepted, 'in principle', the desirability of obtaining 'the views of the people' of the province before taking 'a final decision'. 'The idea of a plebiscite, which eventually prevailed', H.V. Hodson asserts, 'can be traced to this occasion'.[14]

REFERENDUM AND THE CONGRESS

Before announcing the 3rd June Plan and envisaging a referendum in the province about its joining either India or Pakistan, Mountbatten had to decide the best way to seek the views of the respective areas regarding which of the prospective dominions they wanted to join. In this backdrop, he told Liaquat Ali Khan, the League leader, that one of the proposals 'under examination' was to leave the provinces 'to choose their own future', but the number of the provincial legislatures is too small in the case of NWFP 'to leave the decision in their hands'.[15]

For this reason, during the course of his visit to the province (on 28–29 April), the viceroy mentioned a referendum but did not elaborate on how it would be conducted. However, the plan the viceroy put before the governors' conference on 15–16 April 1947, which he sent to London as well, spoke of fresh elections in the province. This, however, was opposed by both the provincial Congress and its chief minister, who called it a 'conspiracy' and by Congress leaders and the working committee.[16] Instead of elections, Mountbatten, therefore, recommended 'a referendum on the basis of the provincial electoral rolls'.[17] According to Parshotam Mehra:

It would thus appear that as between 3 and 10 May, Mountbatten's thinking on the Frontier had taken a U-turn: *from* dismissal of the Ministry and holding of fresh elections proceeded by a 2–3 month interregnum of governor's rule *to* no elections and no Section 93 rule. What was being advocated in their place was a referendum under the viceroy's aegis: neither under the control of the incumbent Khan Sahib ministry nor yet that of the governor and his civil officers. Regulated in fact, by military officers appointed by the governor-general and responsible to him.[18]

Interestingly, Mountbatten's original 'plan for the transfer of power', sent to London 'in the first week of May', was revealed to Nehru in confidence. Under the original plan, the provinces would be granted the right to self-determination; hence, the Frontier would also have been free, if it so chose, to join neither India nor Pakistan. It was on the Congress and Nehru's reaction that the viceroy 'redrafted' the plan which 'sealed', beside others, 'the fate of the Frontier outside the orbit of Pakistan'.[19]

The viceroy wrote to Lord Ismay in a telegram: 'You will have seen my telegram No. 235-GT to the Secretary of State containing the principal news item on the front page of the *Hindustan Times* of today.' He expressed his opinion on Congress leaking the secret about the planned referendum in NWFP: 'I consider that this deliberate leakage of secret information by [the] Congress, coupled with such blatant blackmail, indicates that [the] Congress realise that they have a really weak case in the N.W.F.P.'[20]

Although he opposed it at first, the governor of the province, Olaf Caroe, later lent 'his support to the idea of a referendum' in the province. By 6 May 1947, the viceroy was 'absolutely convinced' about holding the referendum. Even Jawaharlal Nehru 'accepted the idea', in view of Mountbatten's assurance that he (Mountbatten) did not 'intend to dissolve the Ministry or go into Section 93'. But the British government was cautious and 'very doubtful' as it feared this would lead to a 'further delay' in transferring power, as a verdict in Pakistan's favour would entail general elections.[21]

Despite opposition by Gandhi, and having informed the viceroy on 10 May about his 'very strong opinion' about the referendum both in the Congress Working Committee and the provincial government, 'Nehru was in agreement with the idea that the will of the Frontier people should be consulted *before* a final decision in regard to the province was taken'. Nehru's position 'briefly was: (*a*) that "an election or referendum, except in the all-India context", would cause trouble; (*b*) that it "would result" in similar demands from hundreds of places in India; and (*c*) that he (Nehru) was "intellectually" in favour of a referendum if it could be held "in a calmer atmosphere".[22] On Mountbatten's countering his objections, Nehru agreed to the referendum, but then the question arose about when it should be held.[23] The Congress Working Committee 'members were reconciled to partition' and the holding of a referendum in the Frontier Province. 'They considered Mountbatten's proposals the best available under the circumstances and were not prepared to press the question of the Frontier to the point of jeopardizing the entire plan.'[24] The Congress, thus, 'agreed in the end to a compromise which was acceptable to the British and Muslim League but not to their Pakhtun allies'.[25] In Juma Khan Sufi's words: 'Gandhi and his Hindu followers knew which direction they' were 'heading in, but Gandhi's Pathan disciple [Ghaffar Khan] was just a camp follower knowing nothing about the real intentions of the Congress'.[26]

In his books, Wali Khan ignores the role played by Nehru, Patel, and the Congress in the holding of the referendum in the Frontier Province— by their agreeing to the decision, and also by excluding the option of an independent Pukhtun state from the available options. Even, Ghaffar Khan, Wali Khan's father, laments the role and volte-face of Sardar Patel, Rajagopal Acharia (Rajagopalachri), Nehru, and Gandhi, and of the Congress as a whole, at this critical juncture.[27] It is a pitiable and sad commentary on his subjectivity that Wali Khan only took the Muslim League and the British to task.[28] The contents of his book justify Juma Khan Sufi's remarks in which he terms his attempt: 'a poor defence of a poor case by an average lawyer'.[29]

Interestingly, 'there was only a token protest from J. Kripalani, the Congress president, who protested over the holding of referendum without the Frontier Congressmen being given the choice of the inclusion of a third option, i.e. an autonomous Pashtoonistan'. But it was mere whitewash and crocodile tears as, 'on the Viceroy's refusal, the Congress withdrew its suggestions without the slightest protest and dropped the issue forever'.[30] Juma Khan Sufi, therefore, is justified, to an extent, in contending:

> The Province was unwisely knotted with Congress. There was no understanding whatsoever with Delhi about the ultimate destiny of the people and their province in the event of British withdrawal. The Khan brothers considered the Province part and parcel of Congress-led India. No more, no less. It was a tail of Congress in all respects, even sharing in Congress' opposition to the federal scheme of the united but federal India of the Cabinet Mission, and adhering to their policies and strategies in every sphere. Far from giving it autonomy, there was no plan even to rename it.[31]

REFERENDUM AND MUSLIM LEAGUE

The All India Muslim League continued with its civil disobedience campaign to topple Dr Khan's government and started extensive propaganda in favour of Pakistan. The League was demanding the resignation of Dr Khan Sahib's ministry and the holding of fresh elections at the same time as claiming that the province was to be part of Pakistan. M.A. Jinnah 'demanded imposition of Section 93 rule and holding of fresh elections' and his 'reaction to the referendum plan was not exactly enthusiastic'—for his own reasons.[32] However, when the viceroy told him about the abolition of the weightage (the Hindu-Sikh minority held twelve seats out of the province's fifty seats) in case of a referendum, 'he also preferred referendum to an election'.[33]

Therefore, announcement, in the 3rd June Plan, of the referendum in the province led to the formal ceasing of League's agitation on 5 June amid jubilation.[34] In a radio broadcast on All-India Radio, Jinnah outlined the alternatives open to the province's people and enjoined: 'I call upon all the leaders of the Muslim League and all Musalmans generally to organise our people to face this referendum with hope and courage.' He expressed his confidence that the people of the province would join Pakistan 'by a solid vote'.[35]

Jinnah's broadcast led to protest from the Congress and from the Frontier ministry, as well as rebuke of the League's agitation in the Frontier and its legitimacy and consequences.[36] The 3rd June Plan, however, divided the Congress and its stand, especially the All India National Congress and the Frontier Congress-Khudayi Khidmatgars, on the referendum issue in the province. On the other hand, the 3rd June Plan, although accepted 'as a compromise'[37] greatly strengthened the League's position.

The League's central president, M.A. Jinnah, 'appointed some prominent Leaguers to visit' the province 'to persuade the people to join' Pakistan. He sent I.I. Chundrigar, Ghazanfar Ali Khan, and Syed Wajid Ali to assist the local League leaders in the 'referendum campaign'.[38] On 17 June, Jinnah announced the constitution of a four-member committee comprising I.I. Chundrigar, Ghazanfar Ali Khan, the Pir of Manki, and Syed Wajid Ali—interestingly, only one of the four was from the province. The committee's task was 'to supervise and control the Muslim League organization' in the province 'and to make arrangements' for facing 'the referendum'. The committee was to 'remain in close contact and touch' with Jinnah and was to be 'guided' by him 'in making all the arrangements that will be necessary' for the League to effectively participate 'in the referendum'.[39]

The League worked towards the referendum campaign with great fervour and zeal. Students, women, and workers, as well as the leaders, did their best, till the end, to achieve their goal. People from other parts of India also thronged to the province for the same purpose. Even those who were not part of British India played a role, not only campaigning in favour of Pakistan but assisting materially as well. For instance, the ruler of Swat State gave an aid of 110,000 rupees in cash to the Muslim League to share the cost of the referendum, and sent his personal envoys to different parts of the Frontier to advise the people to cast their votes in favour of Muslim League, in other words in favour of joining Pakistan. Having *murid*s (disciples) of his grandfather in great numbers in certain areas, his message and instructions for the cause of the League worked towards the referendum going in Pakistan's favour.[40]

The Frontier Muslims were asked, by the League's leaders, to side with the Muslim League and favour its demand for Pakistan, as the province 'can prosper only...as a free partner in a progressive, democratic State' as they were 'sure Pakistan will be'.[41] A propaganda campaign, to encourage voting in favour of joining Pakistan, was carried out through public meetings, posters, and through visits to the rural areas. Arousing the sentiments of the Pukhtuns, they were reminded that on 15 August the British flag 'would be hauled down'. It was now up to them 'to decide whether they will like to replace it with the League's green and crescent, which stood for Muslim brotherhood and independence, or the Congress tri-colour, which stood for Hindu domination'.[42] Not only was the appointment of Muslim governors promised, but they were also told that it had been recommended to Jinnah[43] to rename the province 'Pathanistan', and that a vote for Pakistan was termed 'a vote for Islam'.[44] Ironically, after voting in favour of joining Pakistan and the emergence of Pakistan, neither was the province named Pathanistan (Pukhtunistan) nor was a Muslim governor installed. Instead, George Cunningham (a former British governor of the province) was recalled and appointed as the governor of the province.

Third Option Issue

As stated earlier, in Mountbatten's original plan for the transfer of power— sent to London for approval in the first week of May 1947—the provinces were given the right to determine their future, i.e., they could opt for freedom. Hence, 'the Frontier could opt out, it if so chose, outside of India or Pakistan'.[45] It was at the Congress, and especially Nehru's, reaction that the plan was redrafted; the option for freedom for the provinces was excluded from the redraft.[46] The Khudayi Khidmatgars, so closely knitted with the Congress and advocating a united free India in the preceding years, were not taken into confidence by the Congress leaders before taking the decision nor were they (the Khudayi Khidmatgars) prepared mentally—especially in the wake of their majority in the provincial legislature—for a referendum on the issue of whether the people of the province wanted to join India or Pakistan.

The redrafted plan, after approval from London, was presented 'before the principal Indian leaders' on 2 June 1947—later on, becoming known as the '3rd June Plan'. M.A. Jinnah, Liaquat Ali Khan, and Abdur Rab Nishtar represented the League, Jawaharlal Nehru, Sardar Patel, and Kripalani represented Congress, and Baldev Singh represented the Sikhs, at the meeting with Mountbatten. After rounds 'of interviews and meetings' with the leaders, Mountbatten presented his plan for the transfer of power, which included a referendum for the Frontier Province to decide its future course—to join the would-be dominion of either India or Pakistan. After giving copies of the plan to the Indian leaders, Mountbatten told them that he would meet them the next morning. He hoped that, before the next meeting, all the three parties would show 'their willingness to accept the Plan as a basis for a final' settlement of the Indian issue, and, in such a case, he, Nehru, Jinnah, and Baldev Singh would jointly announce their agreement to the world. He asked the leaders to let him know about their 'reaction to the plan by midnight'.[47]

On 3 June, at the Congress Working Committee's meeting, Sardar Patel and Rajagopalachari 'strongly favoured' holding a referendum in the Frontier Province.[48] Even Gandhi 'now spoke...in favour of partition'.[49] Abul Kalam Azad has narrated that Ghaffar Khan 'was completely stunned' at the Congress new stand 'and for several minutes he could not utter a word'.

> He then appealed to the Working Committee and reminded the Committee that he had always supported the Congress. If the Congress now deserted him, the reaction on the Frontier would be terrible. His enemies would laugh at him and even his friends would say that so long as the Congress needed the Frontier, they supported the Khudai Khidmatgars. When however the Congress wished to come to terms with the Muslim League, it gave up its opposition to partition without even consulting the Frontier and it leaders.[50]

Ghaffar Khan 'repeatedly said that the Frontier would regard it as an act of treachery if the Congress now threw the Khudai Khidmatgars to the wolves'.[51] At the committee's acceptance of the referendum proposal, Ghaffar Khan told its members that the Congress had deserted the Pukhtuns and 'thrown us to the wolves'. He stated that the Khudayi Khidmatgars would not agree to a referendum as the issue had been decided at the 1946 election, and declared: 'Now as India has disowned us, why should we have a referendum on Hindustan and Pakistan? Let it be on Pakhtunistan or Pakistan.'[52] But, according to Abul Kalam Azad, Dr Khan Sahib, who joined the meeting of the working committee at the later stage, could not object to the referendum proposal, being chief minister of the province. He, however, 'raised a new issue' by stating that 'if there was to be a plebiscite', the people of the province 'should have also the right to opt for Pakhtoonistan, a State of their own'.[53]

On the acceptance of Mountbatten's plan by the three major political parties of India, Olaf Caroe, governor of the province, informed the viceroy on 4 June that 'the Khudai Khidmatgars "will decline" to take part in the referendum'. Mountbatten invited Dr Khan Sahib to New Delhi for discussions and told him that the third option, i.e., of independence, was refused to the provinces 'on Congress insistence'. He also demonstrated his doubts about the viability of an independent Pukhtun state at that time. Although Dr Khan Sahib said that the Frontier Province 'would never join Pakistan', he assured Mountbatten that he would do his best to cooperate in the running of the referendum.[54]

However, the same day, Caroe informed Mountbatten 'that the provincial chief secretary "and other officials" held that "a peaceful referendum" was far more likely if the three issues—of Hindustan, Pakistan or Pathanistan—"could be put before the electors".'[55] Although the governor himself was doubtful about the League's agreement to the third option and also about the Frontier's ability to stand alone, he 'underlined that the case' of an independent Pukhtun state 'should be fully weighed'. He pleaded that a large number of its advocates were sincere: 'even some of those aligned with Jinnah were "not without sympathy" for this idea'.[56]

On the other hand, moved by Ghaffar Khan's appeal to the Congress Working Committee, Gandhi raised the Frontier issue with Mountbatten 'and told him that he would not be able to support' the partition plan unless satisfied of the League's fair deal with the Khudayi Khidmatgars.[57] Mountbatten, however, turned down the request for the third option 'in the proposed referendum "unless the Muslim League leadership

agreed to it", which, Nehru admitted, "was out of the question".'
Mountbatten reminded:

> Nehru that it was at 'his insistence' that he (Mountbatten) had 'renounced' the choice of independence in the case of Bengal as well as other provinces to avoid, what Nehru feared, would lead to 'Balkanisation'. It was a surprise to him that Nehru should have been a party to such a measure (viz., a third choice), more so as he (Nehru) admitted that the Frontier 'could not stand on its own'. In any case, the province would 'eventually' have to join with one side or the other.[58]

Congress leaders and Gandhi had different viewpoints about the referendum in the Frontier. Congress leaders were of the opinion that the Frontier Congress-Khudayi Khidmatgars might 'fight the referendum with all their might and win it. Otherwise the battle for the Frontier Province as a part of India was lost.'[59] Gandhi, however, did not believe so. Hence, in addition to pleading with Congress leaders, Gandhi met Mountbatten on 6 June to request him to ask Jinnah to spell out, to the Frontier Congress-Khudayi Khidmatgar leaders, the position of the Frontier in Pakistan and to convince them of the importance of the referendum. The same day, 'Sardar Patel complained to Gandhi that Nehru was "largely responsible" for the present situation in the Frontier, and also that Badshah Khan's influence was on the wane' but Gandhi repudiated his views.[60]

Nehru assessed the situation from his own perspective, which he elaborated in a memorandum. His analysis was that the referendum was 'a settled' fact; that the viceroy 'can only agree' to the third choice 'if the parties agree'; and that the third choice 'may also introduce an element of confusion in the voting'. At the same time, for his own reasons, he was not in favour of a boycott of the referendum.[61]

On 8 June, Ghaffar Khan informed Gandhi that he and his key workers were opposed to the referendum for it 'will lead to serious violence' and that 'we are also against Pakistan and we would like to have a free Pathan state within India'. On receiving Nehru's memorandum, another meeting of the Provincial Congress Committee, the Congress Parliamentary Party in the Frontier legislature, and the commanders of the Khudayi Khidmatgars was held on 11 June. After a lengthy debate, it was decided that they 'should not take part in the referendum' unless it was 'on the basis of Pakistan or free Pathan state'.[62] To reach an understanding and to have an amicable settlement between the Muslim League and the Frontier Congress-Khudayi Khidmatgars, Ghaffar Khan and Jinnah held a meeting in New Delhi on 18 June.

Abdul Ghaffar Khan informed Jinnah of the readiness of the Khudai Khidmatgars to join Pakistan provided Jinnah accepted: (a) complete provincial autonomy; (b) the right for the province to secede from Pakistan if it so desired; and (c) the right to admission to the NWFP of contiguous territories inhabited by Pashtoons. Jinnah asked them first to join the Constituent Assembly of Pakistan, and then to decide all these matters there with mutual understanding. Abdul Ghaffar Khan replied that after attending his party meeting at Bannu on 21 June he would inform Jinnah of the outcome.[63]

Many hopes were pinned on these meetings but to no avail. According to Abul Kalam Azad, it 'was not surprising' that the Jinnah-Ghaffar Khan 'talks were inconclusive'.[64] Parshotam Mehra is of the opinion that Jinnah viewed Ghaffar Khan's 'overtures as born out of his weakness, for he (Jinnah) was shrewd enough to see that he was in a winning position and would not yield. He certainly would not like to oblige his principal political antagonist in the Frontier by giving him back the power "he… was on the point of losing".'[65] Abul Kalam Azad asserts: 'Once the Congress had accepted partition, what future could there be for Khan Abdul Ghaffar Khan and his party?' Mountbatten's 'Plan was based on the principle that the Muslim majority provinces should be separated and formed into a separate State'. As the 'Muslims were in an overwhelming majority in the Frontier…it was bound to be included in Pakistan'.[66]

The decision to hold a referendum in the Frontier, and Congress' agreement, created a serious situation for the Frontier Congress and the Khudayi Khidmatgars because of their long-standing association with the Congress and also due to Congress' volte-face at this stage. In such a scenario, a combined meeting of the Provincial Jargah of the Frontier Congress and the Khudayi Khidmatgars, the members of the legislative assembly, the officers of the Khudayi Khidmatgars, and the Jargah of the Zalmay Pukhtun[67] was held on 21 June 1947 in Bannu under the presidentship of Khan Amir Muhammad Khan (Huti, Mardan). The session unanimously decided that an independent government of all the Pukhtuns should be established in this country, the constitution of which should be based on Islamic principles, democracy, equality, and social justice. The session appealed to all Pukhtuns to unite on one platform to achieve this supreme aim, and not to submit to anybody's rule save that of the Pukhtun.[68] Interestingly, the decision speaks not of an independent Pukhtun state (رياست) but government (حکومت). The poster announcing the decision was captioned:

پښتنو دَ خپل آزاد حکومت فیصله اوکړه ⁶⁹
پښتانه نه هندوستان غواړی نه پاکستان

Meaning: Pukhtuns have decided in favour of an independent government of their own: Pukhtuns neither want India nor Pakistan.

However, according to Tendulkar:

> After consulting all his Frontier colleagues Abdul Ghaffar intimated Jinnah of the following resolution: 'This meeting of the members of the Frontier Provincial Congress Committee, the Congress Parliamentary Party, the Khudai Khidmatgars and Zalme Pukhtuns held at Bannu on June 21, 1947, under the chairmanship of Khan Amir Mohammed Khan, President of the Frontier Provincial Committee, unanimously resolves that a free Pathan state of all the Pakhtuns be established. The constitution of the state will be framed on the basis of Islamic conception of democracy, equality and social justice. This meeting appeals to all the Pathans to unite for the attainment of this cherished goal and not to submit to any non-Pakhtun domination.'[70]

It may be underlined that the English rendering of the resolution, passed in Bannu, on 21 June, in the above-mentioned meeting, reproduced by most of the sources, e.g. D.G. Tendulkar,[71] Parshotam Mehra,[72] and S. Fida Yunus,[73] is flawed; but that of Erland Jansson[74] is up to the required mark.

The Frontier Congress-Khudayi Khidmatgars demanded that the option of an independent Pukhtun state must be included with the pre-existing two options of joining either India or Pakistan. Had the option of an independent Pukhtun state been included in the referendum, there were reasons that 'a large number of the Frontiermen might have voted for it' for 'they were afraid of being swallowed up by the Punjab and this fact alone might have swayed them to vote against Pakistan'.[75] However, neither Jinnah nor Mountbatten was 'prepared to accept this demand'. The viceroy 'made it clear that the Frontier could not form a separate and independent State, but must be included either in India or Pakistan'.[76] Interestingly enough, at the time of his press conference on 4 June 1947, regarding the 3rd June Plan, Mountbatten's reply to the question: 'Can... the Frontier people decide whether they wish to remain independent or whether they wish to join some Constituent Assembly?' was: 'If the Frontier were to vote for independence and if they can get the two High Commands [of the Congress and the League] to agree, I will, of course, agree. If, on the other hand, they want to join one of the two Constituent Assemblies, then we stick to what was originally agreed to.'[77]

Chaudhri Muhammad Ali contends that: 'The slogan of an independent frontier state or Pakhtoonistan had been provided for the Khan brothers by Gandhi. Behind this demand was the far-reaching strategy of reabsorbing the Province at a later stage after contiguity with it had been gained through the state of Jammu and Kashmir';[78] that: 'In a straight contest between Hindustan versus Pakistan, the verdict of the people, who were 92 percent [per cent] Muslims, would be in favor of Pakistan. Gandhi, therefore, conceived the idea of Pakhtoonistan or an independent North-West Frontier Province';[79] and that: 'At the same time Gandhi was also striving to avert a referendum in the North-West Frontier Province. On 8 May, he wrote to Mountbatten, "Referendum at this stage in the Frontier (or any Province for that matter) is a dangerous thing in itself. You have to deal with the material that faces you. In any case nothing should or can be done over Dr Khan Sahib's head".'[80] Contradictions are clearly evident from Chaudhri Muhammad Ali's statements.

The shift of the Khudayi Khidmatgars-Frontier Congress to an independent Pukhtun state was not abrupt. From the very beginning, the Khudayi Khidmatgars' aims included an independent Pukhtun state. Even before the League's Lahore Resolution of March 1940, Ghaffar Khan used to outline—during the course of his speeches—the blueprints of a Pukhtun state.[81] 'The report, entitled *Condition in India*, of the delegation sent out to India in 1932 by the India League of which the chairman was Bertrand Russell' also contained: 'It was also stated to us by a very high official that Abdul Ghaffar's real plan was to create a Pathanistan and not to work for Indian self-government.'[82] It was because of the very close association with the Congress that the same was not stressed later, and the province was tied to the tail of India.[83] However, when Congress did a volte-face, the old slogan was renewed with vigour. Interestingly, Qaiyum Khan, then a Congress member of the central legislative assembly from the Frontier, raised some questions in his book in 1945, which included: 'Would the Pathan homelands of the N.-W.F.P. and the Tribal Belt have the right to decide their own future? Would they have the right to join Hindustan, Pakistan or Afghanistan or even to form a State of their own if they so wished?'[84] Moreover, he asserted: 'We must have the right and freedom to determine our own political future. We will be a free sovereign unit, in alliance, however, with other sovereign units of Indian sub-nationalities, voluntarily surrendering a part of our sovereignty for common ends and the greater welfare of the country and reserving our right to walk out of the Indian Federation if we so desire.'[85] This, too, suggests that the idea of a separate independent Pukhtun state already existed in 1945.

Erland Jansson has made it clear that the demand for Pukhtunistan, as an independent Pukhtun state that could join other states on its own terms, was put forward by Dr Khan Sahib on 4 April 1946 during his meeting with the members of the Cabinet Mission; also, that he raised the issue during Mountbatten's visit to the Frontier in April 1947; and that it was on 13 May that Qazi Ataullah (provincial revenue minister), and later Dr Khan Sahib (the chief minister) and Yahya Jan (provincial education minister), openly spoke in this respect.[86] In Rittenberg's words:

> Initially, the demand for Pakhtunistan was a call for separatism. The party used it as no more than a shorthand for the right to join India or Pakistan while retaining complete internal autonomy... Thus, in terms of its actual content, the idea barely differed from the party's previous goals. The change was tactical, with the demand for autonomy being repackaged under a new, more appealing label. By mid-April, party leaders stopped talking about mere autonomy, substituting in its place a demand for sovereignty. But even at this point, they were not advocating a totally independent state.... The party did not abandon this position for complete separatism until Lord Mountbatten's partition plan forced them to do so.[87]

Whereas Tendulkar has stated that, in the course of the viceroy's meeting with the governor and the chief minister during his visit to the Frontier, when the chief minister, Dr Khan Sahib, 'turned to' the issue of Pukhtunistan, 'the discussion became explosive'.[88] And, it was on 22 May that 'Caroe made a mention' in his letter to John Colville of the Frontier Congress-Khudayi Khidmatgars' 'new Propaganda line' for a 'Pathan national province under a coalition if possible and making its own alliances as may suit it'.[89] Caroe's full statement, reproduced below, is interesting and revealing:

> The interesting local development in the political field is that my Ministry and Abdul Ghaffar Khan have started propaganda on a theme which I advised them to take up some months ago: that of Pathan National Province under a coalition if possible, and making its own alliances as may suit it. When I put it to them then they professed what amounted to fury at the mere suggestion. There is a good deal in the theme itself, and the appeal is a far more constructive one than that of Islam in danger. The switch-over has probably come too late, but to my mind it is a strength, and not a weakness, that Pathanistan cannot subsist financially or otherwise on its own legs. The weakness is that the Pathans have hitherto been too divided among themselves to set up a stable State, and where they have ruled they have ruled as conquerors of alien populations. They

themselves had always been in a state of anarchy right through history until we came and put them in order. (Afghanistan is not really a Pathan State at all).[90]

Erland Jansson, however, contends that 'the demand for Pakhtunistan was raised mainly for bargaining purposes and no real independence was envisaged'.[91] At this point, we are not deliberating on whether the demand for Pukhtunistan was simply a slogan that was raised as a bargaining tool or whether there was genuine belief in a real independent Pukhtun state. However, the demand was not accepted by the British or the Muslim League, and the Congress acceded to the 3rd June Plan, remaining deaf to the demands of their Frontier counterparts—except for a face-saving letter to the viceroy by its president, and Gandhi's limited support and outcry. Therefore, the Frontier Congress-Khudayi Khidmatgars decided to boycott the referendum—to be held in the province to determine whether the people of the province wanted to join India or Pakistan.[92] Ghaffar Khan announced that they would boycott the referendum, and, in a statement issued on 24 June, appealed to the 'Khudai Khidmatgars and others who believe in a free Pathan State not to participate in the referendum and keep away from it peacefully'.[93] At this, Jinnah charged that Gandhi and Ghaffar Khan's support for an independent Pukhtun state 'was "a direct breach" of the Congress acceptance of the 3 June plan'. He 'called the Pathanistan demand as both "insidious and spurious...a new stunt invented to mislead" the people' of the Frontier, and termed it the 'new volte-face' on the part of the Congress in the province which 'was "a piece of pure political chicanery and a manoeuvre intended to prop up the Khan clique in power". He charged Gandhi with giving the new move his "apostolic blessings".'[94] Moreover, he promised that in case they opted to join Pakistan, 'the Frontier would be' 'an autonomous unit of Pakistan'.[95]

THE REFERENDUM

The Khudayi Khidmatgars, 'although never communal...had always been almost exclusively a provincial organization'; and 'was a Pathan party first, a Congress faction second',[96] raised the slogan and demanded the inclusion of the choice of an independent Pukhtun state in the referendum. But, as the viceroy, and the leaders of the Muslim League and the Congress, did not accede to this, they decided to boycott the referendum. Not only was the viceroy not 'prepared to listen to any new demand', he also 'wanted to push through his scheme as fast as possible'. Hence, the question of a free Pukhtun state 'was not even discussed in detail'[97] and arrangements for conducting the referendum continued.

Ghaffar Khan 'denounced the British Government for refusing to include' the choice of an independent Pukhtun state 'in the referendum' and charged that 'they are bent upon thrusting Pakistan upon the N-WFP against the will of the Pathans, so as to establish military bases and landing grounds for themselves against Russia'.[98] Paying no heed to Ghaffar Khan and his associates' outcry, the viceroy went ahead with his plans for the referendum. As stated earlier, to avoid any sort of misunderstanding or charges of favouritism to any side, it was decided to hold the referendum under the viceroy's aegis with supervision provided by the armed forces personnel—and not under the aegis of either the provincial chief minister nor the governor. Hence, the viceroy had already informed Nehru to tell the chief minister that he was asking the commander-in-chief to provide nine British officers to help him in running the referendum.[99] Accordingly, Dr Khan Sahib, the chief minister, was provided with a list of fifteen suggested names of army officers to select any eight, but he raised no objections over any of them.[100] Consequent upon the chief minister's approval, Brigadier John Booth was appointed as the referendum commissioner; eight other senior officers were placed under him to conduct the referendum. All the lower staff, for this purpose, was also taken from the rank and file of the armed forces. However, the usual provincial election staff was also entrusted with performing 'the ordinary duties at the Polling Stations' as 'it was not possible to spare' and provide 'military officers for all the 460 polling stations'. So, the provincial election staff was placed under the members of the election commission—which comprised army officers,[101] for this referendum.

It was agreed upon, between the viceroy and the Indian leaders, that 'electioneering speeches' were to be avoided to the outmost for the referendum, as they would lead to bloodshed, and that 'the issue should' be 'clearly put before the voters'. So, it was suggested that 'electioneering speeches should by agreement between the parties, be banned' and 'election posters should be prepared' which should contain 'in very simple, improvocative and agreed language, the issue what the two future Dominions will be and the respective advantages they have to offer' to the province and 'a map would be printed showing the areas of the two Dominions'.[102]

The viceroy also instructed the governor that 'each side should have equal facilities in the matter of the supply of petrol' as requested by Jinnah, and that political prisoners should be granted amnesty except 'those charged with serious criminal offenses [offences]'.[103] The proposed poster was prepared, in which a short paragraph on the partition of India into two dominions of India and Pakistan and some 'explanation of the 3rd June Plan'—already accepted by the League and Congress leaderships—was discussed. Moreover, three parts were given in the proposed map: showing the areas that would join India (Hindustan) in red, the areas that were decidedly part of Pakistan in blue, and the areas yet to decide their future in white.[104]

To sensitise the Pukhtunistan issue, and to impress upon the people to refrain from voting in the referendum, the provincial Congress-Khudayi Khidmatgar leaders started to tour the province. Also, to lodge their protest against the non-inclusion of the Pukhtunistan option, the Provincial Congress Committee decided to observe 7 July as Pukhtunistan Day. The Khudayi Khidmatgars assembled in Peshawar, processions were taken out, and the people were asked not to vote in the referendum.[105]

Disapproving this state of affairs, and unhappy with the Congress-Khudayi Khidmatgars' tours, Mountbatten wrote to Gandhi to use his influence with Ghaffar Khan and his associates to ask them to refrain from the tours and anti-referendum campaign, as they 'would lead to violence' which would not be liked by either the viceroy or Gandhi.[106] Resultantly, not only did Gandhi ask Ghaffar Khan for 'no demonstration against the Muslim League' but also, 'Above all, every occasion for clash with the Muslim League members was to be avoided.' He enjoined:

Real Pathan bravery was now on its trial. It was to be shown by cheerfully meeting blows or even meeting death at the hands of the opponents without the slightest sort of retaliation. Boycott would certainly result in a legal victory for Pakistanis, but it would be a moral defeat, if without the slightest fear of violence from your side, the bulk of Pathans refrained in a dignified manner from participating in the referendum. There should be no fuss, no procession, and no disobedience of any orders from the authority.[107]

Interestingly, Ghaffar Khan stated to Gandhi that he and his workers were touring the villages to ask the people to be non-violent under all circumstances. He complained of the League's attitude and behaviour towards them, and stated that they were 'working under very difficult and trying circumstances' and that 'in a nut-shell, the Muslim Leaguers backed by officials are out to create disturbance', but for their part they were doing 'everything humanly possible to avoid a clash'.[108] Fraser Noble, however, 'stoutly denied...any "such organised conspiracy"',[109] of the officers, in collaboration with the Muslim League, against the Khudayi Khidmatgars as alleged by Ghaffar Khan.

In the meantime, due to mounting pressure from Congress, Olaf Caroe, who was alleged to have anti-Congress-Khudayi Khidmatgars and pro-Muslim League inclinations was replaced by Rob Lockhart as the new governor of the province on 18 June 1947. However, as noted earlier, the referendum was not held under the provincial chief minister nor the governor, but under the viceroy, in army's supervision—Brigadier John Booth was the referendum commissioner. Arrangements were made for polling to take place at different places on different dates; polling took place between 6 and 18 July 1947 in the then-six settled districts of the province.

The referendum took place amid the Frontier Congress-Khudayi Khidmatgars urging their adherents not to vote but to boycott the referendum, and the Muslim League's zealous, vigorous, and tireless campaign urging Muslims to vote for Pakistan. Of the total 572,798 registered votes, 292,118 votes—50.99 per cent—were cast, out of which 289,244 (50.49 per cent of the total registered votes but 99.01 per cent of the polled votes) were in favour of joining Pakistan and 2,874 (0.98 per cent of the cast votes but 0.5 per cent of the total registered votes) were in favour of joining India.[110]

Despite the dismissal of the referendum's result by the Frontier Congress-Khudayi Khidmatgars—terming it fraudulent and rigged—the viceroy expressed his satisfaction at the result and stated that his visit to the province had confirmed, for him, the view that the Frontier people 'would join Pakistan'. Therefore, he was 'particularly glad' that he 'insisted on the Referendum in spite of the strongest possible opposition up to the morning of the 3rd June from the Congress'. He further stated that the Congress 'prophesied…the most frightful rioting and bloodshed' if he 'insisted on the Referendum', and hence asserted: 'It is, therefore, all the more satisfactory to record the absence of any really serious disturbance during the ten days which the Referendum occupied.'[111]

However, the Khudayi Khidmatgars' charges of rigging, the use of fraudulent methods and means, and the casting of spurious votes in the referendum in favour of Pakistan,[112] were not completely baseless. According to Dr Sayed Wiqar Ali Shah:

> Surprisingly, the allegations of rigging and other fraudulent methods exercised by the Leaguers were confirmed by some prominent League leaders four decades after the actual event took place. In the absence of any scrutiny by

the Congress, they were free to do so, which they did, in most cases with the support of the Muslim polling staff. To deceive the general public, at each big polling booth a few votes were cast in support of India and the remainder went to Pakistan.[113]

It also has been argued:

> According to some estimates, about 25–30 per cent of bogus votes were cast in the referendum. It has been computed that if a conservative 15–17 per cent of the bogus votes were discounted from the total polled and then compared with the number registered in a normal election (65.6 per cent in 1946), the 'precarious nature of the League's victory' would be evident. It should not be forgotten either that in the final analysis, a little less than 10 per cent of the total population of the NWFP determined the fate of the province.[114]

However, the alleged rigging and other anti-referendum analysis has also been cited as 'biased Congress propaganda'. Sir Fraser Noble contended that the outcome, 'in any case, was "quite clear"', despite the Congress boycott'.[115] Abdul Ghaffar Khan laments Congress' policy, and the course adopted by it at the end in agreeing to the division of India and the referendum in the Frontier Province, and terms it a conspiracy by Mountbatten and Sardar Patel.[116]

Despite the allegations from the Congress-Khudayi Khidmatgars' camp, the result of the referendum was not affected by whether spurious votes had been polled or the referendum rigged. In the wake of the Khudayi Khidmatgars and their allies' boycott, and the Leaguers' rigorous campaign for voting in favour of Pakistan, a result favouring Pakistan was inevitable and logical. In such a situation, it was evident and natural that the result would be in favour of Pakistan—whatever the ratio of polled votes and of votes cast in favour of Pakistan—as also pointed out by Erland Jansson who states:

> On the basis of my sources it seems impossible to go any deeper into the question how far the referendum was affected by bogus votes and how far the boycott was effective. It would also be a somewhat futile exercise. The result was legally binding, no matter whether it resulted in a big or narrow victory and once the Congress had decided on a boycott, the outcome was certain.[117]

It is evident from the sources consulted that the Khan brothers—Dr Khan Sahib and Ghaffar Khan—were more focussed and stressed on the removal of Olaf Caroe from the governorship of the province. In other words, they were suffering from Caroe-phobia. They, and their associates in the Frontier, did not focus on the real issue and on striving to achieve their stand and objectives at that critical juncture in history: when the priorities and policies were rapidly altered by the Congress leadership and Mountbatten.[118] In this scenario, instead of blaming the Congress leadership, the British, and Muslim League for what happened to them and not achieving their cherished desires, they should have accepted responsibility for their own failure.

Not only was the referendum a blow to the Khudayi Khidmatgars and their political stand and future, but it also sealed the fate of the Frontier Province to be neither a part of India nor an independent Pukhtun state but an integral part of Pakistan.

Notes

1. Vidya Dhar Mahajan, *Constitutional History of India (including the National Movement)*, 5th edn., thoroughly rev. and enlarged (Delhi: SCC, 1962), 45.

2. Ibid.

3. Ibid., 46.

4. For the life sketch of A.O. Hume, his services and endeavours for an Indian organisation, and the consequent founding of the All India National Congress, see ibid., 555–8.

5. For details about the *khilafat* and *hijrat* movements, and the role of the province, see Sultan-i-Rome, 'The Role of the North-West Frontier Province in the Khilafat and Hijrat Movements', *Islamic Studies* (Islamabad), vol. 43 (No. 1, Spring 2004), 51–78.

6. For details, see chap. 9 of this book. Also see Sultan-i-Rome, 'The Khudai Khidmatgar Movement: From Genesis to Downfall', *Hamdard Islamicus* (Karachi), vol. 30 (No. 1, January–March 2007), 35–55.

7. See chap. 8 of this book. Also see Sultan-i-Rome, 'Constitutional Developments Relating to the North-West Frontier Province', *Journal of Law and Society* (Peshawar), vol. 30 (No. 43, January 2004), 79–100.

8. Stephen Alan Rittenberg, *Ethnicity, Nationalism, and the Pakhtuns: The Independence Movement in India's North-West Frontier Province* (Durham: CAP, 1988), 234.

9. Latif Ahmed Sherwani, *The Partition of India and Mountbatten* (Karachi: Council for Pakistan Studies, 1986), 140–1.

10. Rittenberg, *Ethnicity, Nationalism, and the Pakhtuns*, 234.

11. 'The 3rd June Plan (Extracts), North West Frontier Province' in Saleem Ullah Khan, comp., *The Referendum in N.W.F.P., 1947: A Documentary Record* (Islamabad: National Documentation Centre, 1995), 61; 'The Partition Plan, 3 June 1947' in Latif Ahmed Sherwani, ed., *Pakistan Resolution to Pakistan, 1940–1947: A Selection of Documents Presenting the Case for Pakistan*, with introduction by Ishtiaq Husain Qureshi (Karachi: National Publishing House Limited, 1969), 231–2.

12. D.G. Tendulkar, *Abdul Ghaffar Khan: faith is a battle* (Bombay: PP, 1967), 414.

13. Sayed Wiqar Ali Shah, *Ethnicity, Islam, and Nationalism: Muslim Politics in the North-West Frontier Province, 1937–1947* (Karachi: OUP, 1999), 216.

14. H.V. Hodson, *The Great Divide: Britain–India–Pakistan*, with epilogue written in 1985 which sums up the events since partition, and with new introduction, 7th impr. of the Jubilee Series edn., 1997 (Karachi: OUP, 2005), 284–5.

15. Syed Waqar Ali Shah, *Muslim League in N.W.F.P.* (Karachi: RBC, 1992), 152–3.

16. Ibid., 153.

17. Parshotam Mehra, *The North-West Frontier Drama, 1945–1947: A Re-Assessment*, edn. issued in Pakistan (Karachi: OUP, 2001), 173.

18. Ibid.

19. Ibid., 177. Also see Sherwani, ed., *Pakistan Resolution to Pakistan*, 225–7.

20. Mountbatten to Lord Ismay (via India Office), Telegram, R/3/1/170:ff 3–4, Important, Top Secret, New Delhi, 3 May 1947 in Khan, *The Referendum in N.W.F.P.*, 30. Also quoted in Juma Khan Sufi, *Bacha Khan, Congress and Nationalist Politics in NWFP* [henceforward Sufi, *Bacha Khan*] (Lahore: VB, 2005), 213.

21. Mehra, *The North-West Frontier Drama*, 174–5. Also see Sherwani, *The Partition of India and Mountbatten*, 145.

22. Mehra, *The North-West Frontier Drama*, 176. Also see 'Minutes of Viceroy's Tenth Miscellaneous Meeting (Extract)' in Khan, *The Referendum in N.W.F.P.*, 41–3.

23. See 'Minutes of Viceroy's Tenth Miscellaneous Meeting (Extract)' in Khan, *The Referendum in N.W.F.P.*, 41–4. Also see Mehra, *The North-West Frontier Drama*, 176.

24. Rittenberg, *Ethnicity, Nationalism, and the Pakhtuns*, 241–2.

25. Ibid., 235.

26. Sufi, *Bacha Khan*, 334.

27. See Abdul Ghaffar [Khan], *Zama Jwand aw Jidujahd* (Pukhtu) (Kabul: DM, 1983), 732–40; Tendulkar, *Abdul Ghaffar Khan*, 424–5; Khan Abdul Ghaffar Khan, *Ap Biti* (Urdu), repr. (Lahore: FH, 2004), 199–200; K.B. Narag, *My Life and Struggle: Autobiography of Badshah Khan as narrated to K.B. Narag*, with foreword by Jayaprakash Narayan, repr. (n.p.: DAT, 2008), 191–2.

28. For Wali Khan's contentions, see Abdul Wali Khan, *Rikhtya, Rikhtya di (Pirangay–Muslim League aw Mung)* (Pukhtu) (Kabul: Da Qaumunu aw Qabailu Wazarat, Da Nashratu Riyasat, 1987), 271–6; Abdul Wali Khan, *Facts are Sacred*, trans. Aziz Siddiqui (Peshawar: Jaun Publishers, n.d.), 109–12; Wali Khan, *Facts are Facts: The Untold Story of India's Partition*, trans. Syeda Saiyidain Hameed, repr. (Peshawar: Publication Cell, Baacha Khan Trust, 2006), 161–5. Also see Khan Abdul Wali Khan, *Bacha Khan aw Khudayi Khidmatgari* (Pukhtu), vol. 1 (Charsadah: WB, 1993), 488–94.

29. Sufi, *Bacha Khan*, 5.

30. Sayed Wiqar Ali Shah, 'Abdul Ghaffar Khan' in Parvez Khan Toru and Fazal-ur-Rahim Marwat, eds., *Celebrities of NWFP*, vol[s]. 1–2 (Pakistan Study Centre, University of Peshawar, 2005), 119–20; Shah, *Ethnicity, Islam, and Nationalism*, 219.

31. Sufi, *Bacha Khan*, 206.

32. Mehra, *The North-West Frontier Drama*, 175.

33. Shah, *Muslim League in N.W.F.P.*, 154.

34. Mehra, *The North-West Frontier Drama*, 180.

35. Shah, *Muslim League in N.W.F.P.*, 155.

36. See Mehra, *The North-West Frontier Drama*, 180.

37. Shah, *Muslim League in N.W.F.P.*, 155; Tendulkar, *Abdul Ghaffar Khan*, 425.

38. Shah, *Muslim League in N.W.F.P.*, 158.

39. 'Committee to Supervise Referendum (Press Report)', *Dawn*, Delhi, 18 June 1947 in Khan, *The Referendum in N.W.F.P.*, 94. Also in Mehra, *The North-West Frontier Drama*, 193.

40. See Muhammad Asif Khan, *Tarikh-i Riyasat-i Swat wa Sawanih-i Hayat Baniy-i Riyasat-i Swat Hazrat Miangul Gul Shahzadah Abdul Wadud Khan Badshah Sahib*, with *dibachah, hisah awal, saluramah hisah,* and *hisah pinzamah* by Muhammad Asif Khan (Pukhtu)

(Printed: Ferozsons Ltd., Peshawar, [1958]), 373–4. For the English translation of the account, see Muhammad Asif Khan, *The Story of Swat as told by the Founder Miangul Abdul Wadud Badshah Sahib to Muhammad Asif Khan*, with preface, introduction, and appendices by Muhammad Asif Khan, trans. preface and trans. by Ashruf Altaf Husain (Printed: Ferozsons Ltd., Peshawar, 1962), 126–7. The English translation of the account, done by Ashruf Altaf Husain (see ibid.), however, did not conform wholly to the original Pukhtu (Pashto) text. Also see Fredrik Barth, *The Last Wali of Swat: An Autobiography as told to Fredrik Barth*, repr. (Bangkok: White Orchid Press, 1995), 103; Sultan-i-Rome, 'Swat and the AIML', *JPHS* (Karachi), vol. 55 (Nos. 1–2, January–June 2007), 'All India Muslim League Centenary Special Number, Part I', 227.

41.   *The Pakistan Times*, 13 June 1947 quoted in Shah, *Ethnicity, Islam, and Nationalism*, 223.

42.   Ghazanfar Ali's speech at Abbottabad, 29 June 1947, *The Pakistan Times*, 1 July 1947 quoted in ibid.

43.   Feroz Khan Noon's speech at Dera Ismail Khan, 1 July 1947, *The Pakistan Times*, 3 July 1947, quoted in ibid.

44.   *The Pakistan Times*, 11 July 1947, quoted in ibid.

45.   Mehra, *The North-West Frontier Drama*, 177.

46.   See Rittenberg, *Ethnicity, Nationalism, and the Pakhtuns*, 240–1; Chaudhri Muhammad Ali, *The Emergence of Pakistan*, 5th impr. (Lahore: RSP, 1985), 138–9; Sherwani, ed., *Pakistan Resolution to Pakistan*, 225–7.

47.   Shah, *Muslim League in N.W.F.P.*, 154–5.

48.   Mehra, *The North-West Frontier Drama*, 177. Also see Narag, *My Life and Struggle*, 192.

49.   Abul Kalam Azad, *India Wins Freedom: An Autobiographical Narrative*, repr. (Bombay: OLL, 1964), 193.

50.   Ibid.; Tendulkar, *Abdul Ghaffar Khan*, 424.

51.   Azad, *India Wins Freedom*, 193; Tendulkar, *Abdul Ghaffar Khan*, 424.

52.   Tendulkar, *Abdul Ghaffar Khan*, 424. Also see Narag, *My Life and Struggle*, 192–3.

53.   Azad, *India Wins Freedom*, 194.

54.   Mehra, *The North-West Frontier Drama*, 179.

55.   Ibid.

56.   Caroe to Mountbatten, 5 June 1947, quoted in ibid.

57.   Azad, *India Wins Freedom*, 193.

58.   Mehra, *The North-West Frontier Drama*, 180–1. Also see Sherwani, *The Partition of India and Mountbatten*, 143.

59.   Tendulkar, *Abdul Ghaffar Khan*, 428.

60.   Mehra, *The North-West Frontier Drama*, 181–2. Also see Tendulkar, *Abdul Ghaffar Khan*, 428–9.

61.   For details, see Tendulkar, *Abdul Ghaffar Khan*, 429–32.

62.   Ibid., 433–4.

63.   Shah, *Ethnicity, Islam, and Nationalism*, 221–2.

64.   Azad, *India Wins Freedom*, 193.

65.   Mehra, *The North-West Frontier Drama*, 186. Also see Erland Jansson, *India, Pakistan or Pakhtunistan: The Nationalist Movements in the North-West Frontier Province, 1937–47* (Stockholm: AWI, 1981), 214.

66.   Azad, *India Wins Freedom*, 193.

67.   For the Zalmay Pukhtun see chap. 9 of this book.

68.   For the captioned poster, see *A Journal* (Pukhtu) with *sarizah* by Muhammad Gul (Jahangiri) (facts of publication have been torn but it was published in Afghanistan), p. in-between pp. 214–15. Also see ibid., 213–14; Jansson, *India, Pakistan or Pakhtunistan*, 213; S. Fida Yunas, *Abdul Ghaffar Khan: "Pushtunistan" and Afghanistan* (Peshawar: By the Author, n.d.), 21.

69. See the poster captioned so in *A Journal*, p. in-between pp. 214–15.
70. Tendulkar, *Abdul Ghaffar Khan*, 439. Also see Mehra, *The North-West Frontier Drama*, 186.
71. See Tendulkar, *Abdul Ghaffar Khan*, 439.
72. See Mehra, *The North-West Frontier Drama*, 186.
73. See Yunas, *Abdul Ghaffar Khan: "Pushtunistan" and Afghanistan*, 21.
74. See Jansson, *India, Pakistan or Pakhtunistan*, 213.
75. Azad, *India Wins Freedom*, 195. Also see Mehra, *The North-West Frontier Drama*, 179.
76. Azad, *India Wins Freedom*, 195.
77. Sherwani, ed., *Pakistan Resolution to Pakistan*, 244.
78. Ali, *The Emergence of Pakistan*, 164.
79. Ibid., 145.
80. Ibid., 146.
81. See Ghaffar, *Zama Jwand aw Jidujahd*, 527–8, 669–70. Also see chap. 9 of this book; Sultan-i-Rome, 'The Khudai Khidmatgar Movement: From Genesis to Downfall', 47–8.
82. Tendulkar, *Abdul Ghaffar Khan*, 152–3.
83. James W. Spain rightly has pointed out that since the Middle Ages, neither was the Frontier regarded as part of India nor did the Pukhtuns themselves ever consider themselves so. See James W. Spain, *The Pathan Borderland*, repr. (Karachi: IP, 1985), 162.
84. Abdul Qaiyum, *Gold and Guns on the Pathan Frontier* (Bombay: HK, 1945), 69.
85. Ibid., 72.
86. See Jansson, *India, Pakistan or Pakhtunistan*, 210; also n. 217.
87. Rittenberg, *Ethnicity, Nationalism, and the Pakhtuns*, 234.
88. Tendulkar, *Abdul Ghaffar Khan*, 413.
89. Caroe to Sir John Colville, 22 May 1947, quoted in Mehra, *The North-West Frontier Drama*, 192.
90. Olaf Caroe (NWFP) to J. Colville, 22 May 1947 (Extract) in Khan, *The Referendum in N.W.F.P. 1947*, 56.
91. For Erland Jansson's viewpoint, see Jansson, *India, Pakistan or Pakhtunistan*, 209.
92. See *A Journal*, 209–15; Ghaffar, *Zama Jwand aw Jidujahd*, 732–6.
93. Tendulkar, *Abdul Ghaffar Khan*, 441.
94. Mehra, *The North-West Frontier Drama*, 186.
95. Spain, *The Pathan Borderland*, 199; *Khaibar Mail*, 4 July 1947 quoted in Jansson, *India, Pakistan or Pakhtunistan*, 218.
96. Spain, *The Pathan Borderland*, 198.
97. Azad, *India Wins Freedom*, 194.
98. *New York Times*, 24 June 1947 quoted in Spain, *The Pathan Borderland*, 199. Also see Jansson, *India, Pakistan or Pakhtunistan*, 218.
99. Mountbatten to Nehru, 3 June 1947, TP, XI:101 quoted in Shah, *Muslim League in N.W.F.P.*, 157.
100. See Minutes of Viceroy['s] Forty First Staff Meeting (Extract), in Khan, *The Referendum in N.W.F.P.*, 70.
101. Shah, *Muslim League in N.W.F.P.*, 157.
102. The Viceroy's Meeting with Seven Indian Leaders, 13 June 1947, Quaid-i-Azam Papers, F.No. I, p. 6, National Archives, Islamabad, quoted in ibid.
103. Ismay to Jinnah, 22 June 1947, *NAI*, F.No. 2, p. 101 quoted in ibid., 158. Also see Mountbatten to Olaf Caroe (NWFP), Telegram, R/3/1/151, New Delhi, 13 June 1947 in Khan, *The Referendum in N.W.F.P.*, 79–80.
104. Eric Mieville to Jinnah, 27 June 1947, *NAI*, F.No. 2, pp. 77–8, quoted in Shah, *Muslim League in N.W.F.P.*, 158.

105. Shah, *Ethnicity, Islam, and Nationalism*, 223. Also see Jansson, *India, Pakistan or Pakhtunistan*, 218–21.

106. Mountbatten to Gandhi, 5 July 1947, TP, XI: 910–911 quoted in Shah, *Muslim League in N.W.F.P.*, 158.

107. Gandhi to Abdul Ghaffar Khan, 5 July 1947, quoted in Tendulkar, *Abdul Ghaffar Khan*, 445.

108. Abdul Ghaffar Khan to Gandhi, 12 July 1947 quoted in ibid., 445–6.

109. Mehra, *The North-West Frontier Drama*, 194.

110. See Jansson, *India, Pakistan or Pakhtunistan*, 222; Mehra, *The North-West Frontier Drama*, 194; Khan, *The Referendum in N.W.F.P.*, 241; Rittenberg, *Ethnicity, Nationalism, and the Pakhtuns*, 244; Amit Kumar Gupta, *North West Frontier Province: Legislature and Freedom Struggle, 1932–47* (New Delhi: ICHR, 1976), 200; Shah, *Muslim League in N.W.F.P.*, 159. Also see Khan, *Facts are Sacred*, 113; Khan, *Facts are Facts*, 166; Khan, *Rikhtya, Rikhtya di*, 278; Khan, *Bacha Khan aw Khudayi Khidmatgari*, vol. 1, 493.

111. Viceroy's Personal Report No. 14, 25 July 1947, L/PO/6/123:ff 196–203 in Khan, *The Referendum in the N.W.F.P.*, 241. Also quoted in Shah, *Muslim League in N.W.F.P.*, 160.

112. For such charges, also see Khan, *Facts are Sacred*, 112–13; Khan, *Facts are Facts*, 166; Khan, *Rikhtya, Rikhtya di*, 276–8; Khan, *Bacha Khan aw Khudayi Khidmatgari*, vol. 1, 492–3; Tendulkar, *Abdul Ghaffar Khan*, 446–8; Khan, *Ap Biti*, 176–7; Narag, *My Life and Struggle*, 168.

113. Shah, *Ethnicity, Islam, and Nationalism*, 226–7. Also see Khan, *Facts are Sacred*, 112–13; Khan, *Facts are Facts*, 166; Khan, *Rikhtya, Rikhtya di*, 276–8; Jansson, *India, Pakistan or Pakhtunistan*, 224–7; Gupta, *North West Frontier Province*, 200.

114. Mehra, *The North-West Frontier Drama*, 195. Also see Gupta, *North West Frontier Province*, 200 cf. Rittenberg, *Ethnicity, Nationalism, and the Pakhtuns*, 244–5.

115. Mehra, *The North-West Frontier Drama*, 195. However, Rittenberg's analysis shows a somewhat different picture (see Rittenberg, *Ethnicity, Nationalism, and the Pakhtuns*, 244–8).

116. See Ghaffar, *Zama Jwand aw Jidujahd*, 736–40; Tendulkar, *Abdul Ghaffar Khan*, 424–5; Khan, *Ap Biti*, 175–6, 199–200.

117. Jansson, *India, Pakistan or Pakhtunistan*, 226–7.

118. This is a testimony of the Khan brothers' lack of statesmanship and confirms the remarks of Dr Lala Baha, made in 1996, that while going through the archival records one wonders at the simple-mindedness of the Khan brothers (Dr Khan Sahib and Ghaffar Khan), their lack of awareness of what was going on behind their backs, and of the decisions and terms agreed to by and between the British, the Congress, and the Muslim League. This authenticates, to some extent, Juma Khan Sufi's remarks that Ghaffar Khan 'was just a camp follower [of Gandhi] knowing nothing about the real intentions of the Congress'. [Sufi, *Bacha Khan*, 334].

12 Tribal Administration

> Peace and progress on the Frontier were of little concern to the
> men who ruled India. Security was the all-important objective.
> – D.G. Tendulkar

V ERY LITTLE IS KNOWN, especially outside the area, about the tribal
areas adjoining the North-West Frontier Province of former British
India, now Pakistan, particularly about its mores and goods, people
and their way of life, beliefs and ideals, and the way the administrative
apparatus has operated there. For a judicious and proper understanding
and comprehension of the pattern of tribal administration that prevailed
till the area's merger in Khyber Pukhtunkhwa in May 2018, it is essential
to have a thorough knowledge of its historical background, constitutional
and legal status, and the all-embracing facets of the tribal society and the
people. As mentioned earlier, the tribal areas were merged, in May 2018,
in the province of Khyber Pukhtunkhwa; and their special status as tribal
areas brought to an end.

Being part, albeit loosely, of the then-Sikh kingdom of Punjab, the
settled areas of the present-day Khyber Pukhtunkhwa were annexed
by the Britons'[1] East India Company, into their Indian domain, by the
proclamation issued by the Governor-General, Lord Dalhousie, on 29
March 1849—on the defeat of the Sikhs in the Second Anglo-Sikh
War (1848–49). The area was made part of the province of Punjab and
administered along the same lines as the other parts of the province. But,
certain different laws and administrative tools were introduced and later
adopted, which continued to be enforced even after the area separated
from Punjab in 1901 and was formed into a separate province—the North-
West Frontier Province.

On the whole, the tribal areas—which in J.G. Elliott's words were
'stretches of inhospitable stony hills, the home of fiercely independent
tribesmen who bow to no man, not even their own elders; magnificent
fighting men who on their home ground are a match for any army in the
world'[2]—remained outside the domain, pale, and control of the colonial
government. Because, 'The north-western boundary of the new [Punjab]
province was drawn along the foothills as far as the line where the Sikhs,

and probably Durrani and Mogul [Mughal] before them, had claimed conquest and revenue.' And,

> No attempt was made to advance into the highlands, or even secure the main passages through the mountains such as the Khaibar Pass. As in the Peshawar valley, so in Bannu and the Derajat, the line of administration stopped like a tide almost at the first contour of rough country. Beyond that lay Yaghistan— the land of the rebels.[3]

The unruly and independent tribal areas remained a source of trouble for the colonial government because of regular raids into the British-administered and controlled areas that originated from these tribal areas. Therefore, initially, the main thrust of the British Frontier 'policy was to ensure law and order in the bordering districts', which they sought to achieve by 'securing **"pacification and contentment"** of the Frontier tribes'.[4] In view of this anomalous situation, special forces like the Punjab Frontier Force and the Punjab Border Military Police were created. The tribal territory, however, remained independent of the government and control of British India. With the passage of time, the colonial government attempted, mainly for strategic reasons, to bring these areas under its sphere of influence, as a protectorate of sorts.

With this objective in mind, most of the tribal territories were gradually brought under the British sphere of influence and protectorate during the years 1879 to 1895, by means of agreements with the tribesmen, the use of force, and the Durand Line Agreement. The areas were then formed into five political agencies, each headed by a political agent who looked after the affairs of the area, safeguarded British interest there, had a political and military check over the tribes, and communicated and dealt with the tribes. The independence and internal affairs of the tribes, however, were generally not interfered with, and they continued to enjoy their age-old independent status. It has aptly been stated in the 'Governor's Committee Report':

> The administration of tribal areas and formulation of tribal policy had constantly engaged attention of British Empire ever since the border alignment. From **'close door'** to **'forward'** policy, the British Empire carried out many moves in this direction supported by military expeditions, but kept its options open till finally evolving the policy of **'non-interference'** in accordance with the customs and traditions of tribal society and its governance through the tribal hierarchy of chieftains, Maliks and sectional elders by entering into treaties with the tribes. The Crown strengthened its hold through an evolutionary

process of making inroads into the tribal society and expanded its area of influence by establishing communication links in closed areas and studded them with posts, picquets and forts at strategic points.[5]

'The Frontier Regions', or the tribal areas that 'remained attached to the adjoining districts ever since...enjoyed the status of "**centrally administered**" area in respect of which the Home Government at London was always taken into confidence in all policy decisions' owing 'to the sensitivity of lengthy unmanned border with Afghanistan and long history of incursions of foreign as well as local invaders through its passes', and also because 'it had a direct link with the "**British external policy and defence**" of its possessions in the Sub-Continent'.[6]

The creation of the political agencies in the 1870s and 1890s, and the appointment of 'political agents responsible only for tribal affairs resulted in a far clearer understanding of the problems involved'.[7] When the separate Frontier Province was created, the situation remained unchanged. The tribal areas, D.G. Tendulkar states, still 'constituted a no man's land'. Although a 'part of India on the map', it was not so 'in fact'.

> Its residents did not owe any direct allegiance to the British Crown...Beyond the military roads, the tribesmen did what was right in their own eyes.... They were not to be treated as British subjects but British protected persons, independent as long as they remained passive but subject to 'protection' as soon as they became active.[8]

The tribal areas, although little known to the outside world, were, and still are, 'a focal point in international strategy'. 'British attitude towards this area was completely different' from its attitude elsewhere—it was looked upon 'primarily as [a] strategic area', to be controlled 'for the defence of their empire in India'.[9] British policy and attitude, however, changed over the course of time. Nevertheless, 'because of their global strategy', they 'could never tackle the problem of tribal control by isolating it'. However, 'the immediate requirements of the local situation often made the frontier problem more complex'. Therefore, 'Expedition...after expedition was necessary to show each tribe, in turn, the strength of the British Government and the folly of resisting it by force of arms.' But, at the same time, 'no effort was spared to encourage friendly feelings and to show the tribesmen that all the British Government, insisted upon was peace on the border'.[10] The British practised a 'Policy of Pacification and Contentment' till the end of their rule.[11]

The British followed a policy of 'indirectly governing the tribal area', which meant non-interference in the internal affairs of the tribes, allowing them self-rule or governance in conformity with their customary laws or *riwaj*. However, they ensured protection of their own interests, roads, and government installations through the treaties they concluded with the tribes, making them responsible under the rule of tribal and territorial responsibility. Although not fool-proof, the system was largely 'economical and effective'.[12] The British were not interested in the development of the tribal areas for their own reasons.

After the emergence of Pakistan, the Pakistan government followed the British policy, and the status quo continued, to a great extent, until the end of the 1960s. The Pakistan government, however, changed its policy in the 1970s and initiated 'a deliberate policy of development', to achieve integration of the tribal areas 'through development in communication infrastructure and other social sectors like education, health etc.'; and with an 'increase in concessions in border trade' (now called smuggling). The concessions given under this policy were:

i.   Alluring tribesmen to develop business stakes in administered areas of FATA and settled districts;
ii. Reservation of quotas in services and educational institutions with emphasis on professional education;
iii. Scholarships and stipends to tribal students;
iv. Imparting technical education in various trades for availing labour opportunities in Pakistan and abroad;
v.   Recruitment in Civil Armed Forces on the basis of tribal identity and assigning platoon strengths to various tribes;
vi. Supply of electricity at subsidized fixed rates;
vii. Telephone and telegraph network; and
viii. Non-extension of any corporate or tax-based laws.[13]

According to the Governor's Committee report, the above-mentioned 'policy of peaceful penetration and integration' was 'highly successful'.[14]

The British demonstrated no major concern for the educational, economic, or social development of the tribal areas, terming it 'unnecessary interference' which was to be avoided. Pakistan inherited this situation and renewed the treaties with the tribes—the ones they had previously concluded with the British. To win the tribesmen over and to create a sense of ownership, the Pakistan government withdrew the army. The local khasadars were made 'fully responsible for [the] civil administration'; the scouts and militia, recruited from among the tribesmen, performed the duty of the army. Although not real or adequate, some sort of socio-economic programmes were begun. Schools and colleges were opened, and tribal students were 'given special privileges for admission' to professional and technical colleges and universities, as well as financial assistance. Quotas were fixed for them in different government-run educational institutions, and services and trade privileges were afforded to them. They were granted representation in the National Assembly (and Senate with, at first, the right of vote to a limited section—*malak*s (in Pukhtu: *malakan/malakanan*) and *lungi* (in Pukhtu: *lungai*) holders—which was extended to adult franchise in 1997 and agency councils in 2001. The agency councils, however, practically remained non-operational). With the passage of time, they have gained opportunities in trade and industry, business and commerce, and other spheres of life; the whole country is now open to them for these purposes.[15]

It is worth mentioning that it was in 1944 that 'the Commander in Chief appointed a committee to review future defence policy on the frontier'. The committee 'recommended the withdrawal of the regular army from [the] tribal territory to the administrative border, and the better equipment of the Frontier Corps (or Scouts) on whom in the first instance the main burden of dealing with trouble should in future fall'.[16] The recommendation was implemented after the departure of the British when, 'in September 1947 the Pakistan Government ordered this policy to be put into effect'[17] and the regular army was withdrawn from the tribal areas.

Types of Tribal Areas

FATA: During the British period, the tribal areas were administratively divided into two types, i.e. Political Agencies and Frontier Regions (FRs). Although both were, on the whole, administered by the same laws, rules, and procedures, the political agencies were headed by political agents, with their own type of administrative hierarchy (detailed later). As the Frontier Regions were linked to the neighbouring settled districts for administrative purposes, the deputy commissioners of the respective districts were in-charge and headed the administration of the Frontier Regions. The Frontier Region of FR Kurram was an exception as it was linked to the Kurram Agency; hence, the political agent of the agency also headed the administration of this Frontier Region. Even with the departure of the British and the emergence of Pakistan, the same categorisation of the tribal areas and administrative apparatuses continued. When the

British departed, there were five political agencies—the Agency of Dir, Swat and Chitral (commonly referred to as the Malakand Agency [created in 1895]), the Khyber Agency (created in 1879), the Kurram Agency (created in 1892), the North Waziristan Agency (created in 1895), and the South Waziristan Agency (created in 1896)—ranging from the north to the south of the area. Subsequently, the Pakistan government created three more agencies—Muhmand Agency (created in 1951), Bajawar Agency (created in 1973), and Urakzai Agency (created in 1973)—out of the tribal areas. The Frontier Regions, later, were FR Peshawar, FR Kuhat, FR Kurram (later termed Central Kurram), FR Bannu, FR Lakki Marwat, FR Tank, and FR Dirah Ismail Khan, from the north to the south. These tribal areas were termed the Federally Administered Tribal Areas (FATA) under the Pakistan Constitution of 1973.[18]

PATA: There was another type of tribal area called the Provincially Administered Tribal Areas (PATA). The jurisdiction of the Agency of Dir, Swat and Chitral was spread over the Malakand Protected Area, Bajawar, Utman Khail, and the territories of the Indian States/Princely States of Chitral, Dir and the later-emerged Swat State. Although the political agent in Malakand—the agency headquarter—had no direct say or role in the internal affairs of the princely states, the British conducted all their dealings with the rulers through the political agent, who was the head of administration for the Malakand Protected Area, Bajawar and Utman Khail—like the political agents of the other agencies. After the departure of the British, the Pakistan government continued to conduct dealings with the rulers of the princely states through the political agent in Malakand, who continued to head the administration of the Malakand Protected Area, Bajawar and Utman Khail, like the political agents of the other agencies.

Although arrangements remained the same for Swat State, the situation in Dir and Chitral states changed later; the political authorities of the agency were given a say and role in their internal administration. However, there too, the separate constitutional status of 'special areas' and 'tribal areas' of the areas linked with the Agency of Dir, Swat and Chitral was kept intact. The three states ceased to exist in 1969, and each formed a separate district, but the special status of once been a tribal area was retained (details in chapter 8).

Under the Province of West Pakistan (Dissolution) Order of 1970 (P.O. No. 1 of 1970), the territories of the former states of Amb, Chitral, Dir, and Swat as well as the Malakand Protected Area, and the tribal area adjoining Hazarah District were incorporated in the North-West Frontier Province (now Khyber Pukhtunkhwa). Thus, the area that formerly comprised the Agency of Dir, Swat and Chitral—commonly referred to as Malakand Agency—excluding the Bajawar and Utman Khail areas, was made part of the Frontier Province and placed under its provincial government.

In the Interim Constitution of 1972, a new type of tribal area called Provincially Administered Tribal Areas (PATA) was created; article 260 (b) i, which was related to PATA of NWFP, defined them as 'the districts of Chitral, Dir and Swat (which includes Kalam), Malakand Protected Area, the Tribal Area adjoining Hazara district and the former State of Amb'. No law or Act, passed by the central or provincial legislatures, was automatically applicable to the area, as special procedures were provided under article 261 for the extension of these laws to PATA.[19] The same status and position was retained under article 246 and 247 of the Constitution of 1973.[20] However, being part of the province, unlike FATA which had representation only in the National Assembly and Senate, PATA had representation in the provincial legislature as well. Special procedures were provided for the extension of any law to PATA, under article 247 of the Constitution of 1973, and different sets of laws were given to the people from time to time.

As stated in Chapter 8, the special constitutional status of the tribal areas was brought to an end through the Constitution (25th Amendment) Act, 2018. Therefore, the distinct administrative pattern and apparatus in place in the area is changed and is brought in line with that in the settled areas, or districts, of the province. However, being operative for more than a century and being a significant part of history, the pattern and apparatus of tribal administration is retained and dealt with in this book which is restricted to the now former, or erstwhile, tribal areas called FATA and only the Malakand Protected Area (Malakand Agency) of PATA. The administration system of the rest of the now former PATA areas, with the exception of the Tur Ghar or Kala Dhakah (Black Mountain) and former Amb State area, was not distinctive but was the same as in the other settled areas or districts, except the judicial aspect. The Tur Ghar or Kala Dhakah (Black Mountain) and former Amb State area were administered on the pattern of the now former, or erstwhile, Frontier Regions. The Tur Ghar or Kala Dhakah (Black Mountain) area was granted the status of a district, in 2011, and named Tur Ghar District; hence its administrative apparatus changed to that of the other districts of PATA. However, the Malakand Protected Area (commonly called Malakand Agency) was headed by a political agent instead of a deputy commissioner but, after the introduction of the local government system in 2001, a district coordination officer (DCO) headed the area till 2012. Now in 2021, the administrative apparatus in use in the Malakand Protected Area, now also called Malakand District, is the one practically followed in the other districts. However, instead of police, the levy still operates and the deputy commissioner at Malakand heads the levy as a commandant of the force, as in 2013 the district coordination officers were again replaced with deputy commissioners. However, the levy will be replaced with the police after the Constitution (25th Amendment) Act, 2018.

CONSTITUTIONAL STATUS

In the Government of India Act, 1935, 'tribal area' was defined as 'the areas along the Frontier of India or in Balochistan which are not part of British India or of Burma or of any Indian State or of any Foreign States'.[21] The British did not make the tribal areas, situated on the North-West Frontier, part of British India because the control and jurisdiction of the British Empire, in the tribal areas, 'was not acquired through conquest or cessation but through treaty rights or capitulation or grant of usage or sufferance etc.'.[22] As the British had concluded treaties with the tribes, they granted, and maintained, the special constitutional status of the North-West Frontier tribal areas till the end of their rule.[23]

As the tribal areas were not part of any of the provinces that would form Pakistan, they were not included in the dominion of Pakistan under the Indian Independence Act, 1947. It was left for Pakistan 'to enter into such arrangements with the Tribal Area' as they had with the departing British power, which would lapse on 15 August 1947.[24] Therefore, Muhammad Ali Jinnah, Governor-General of Pakistan, assured the tribesmen, both in the pre- and post-Partition days, of maintaining the treaties they had concluded with the British and also of their special status. Consequently, the tribesmen and Pakistan ratified the terms of the treaties previously concluded between the tribes and the British.[25]

Therefore, in the subsequent constitutional documents and develop-ments in the country, the special status of the tribal areas, which existed under the Government of India Act, 1935, was retained except that the areas were made an 'integral part of the dominion of Pakistan' with effect from 15 August 1947, by a notification of the Governor-General of Pakistan issued on 27 June 1950.[26] Although the 'Establishment of West Pakistan Act, 1955' incorporated the tribal areas in the Province of West Pakistan, their special status was retained by making them part of the 'specified territories' under section 2 (1) iv. Section 2 (3) envisaged: 'Nothing in this Act shall authorise any change in the internal administration of the Tribal Areas of Baluchistan and the North-West Frontier or the States of Amb, Chitral, Dir and Swat (hereinafter referred to as the "special areas") except in accordance with this subsection and the following provisions shall apply to the special areas'. Provisions (a) to (c) of section 2 (3) dealt with the procedures through which any law was to be extended, or regulation made, for the 'specified territories' and directions given by the governor-general to the governor regarding tribal areas. However, provision (d) of section 2 (3) authorised the governor-general to change the special status of the tribal areas: 'Provided that before making such an order the Governor-General shall ascertain, in such manner as he considers appropriate, the views of the people of the special area or areas concerned.'[27]

The special status of the tribal areas and the Princely States (now also called the Frontier States) was retained under the Constitution of 1956. Article 218 of the constitution defined the 'Special Areas'; and article 104, clauses (1) to (3), dealt with the procedures through which any law was to be extended, or regulation made, for the 'Special Areas', and directions given to the governor by the president. Clause (4) of the same article 104 authorised the president, conditionally, to change the special status of the 'Special Areas' or part thereof by stating:

> The President may, at any time, by order, direct that the whole or any part of a Special Area shall cease to be a Special Area, and any such order may contain such incidental and consequential provisions as appear to the President to be necessary and proper:
>
> Provided that before making any Order under this clause, the President shall ascertain, in such manner as he considers appropriate, the views of the people of the area concerned.[28]

In the Constitution of 1962, the tribal areas of the North-West Frontier, as they were on 13 October 1955, and the states of Amb, Chitral, Dir, and Swat, along with the tribal areas of Baluchistan and Punjab, were defined as 'Tribal Areas', under article 242. And clauses (1) and (2) of article 223 dealt with the procedures through which any law could be extended or regulation made for the 'Tribal Areas'. Clause (3) of article 223 gave the president the same powers as were given in clause (4) of article 104 of the Constitution of 1956, reproduced above, in respect of the 'Tribal Areas' but with restrictions. However, clause (4) of the same article added: 'This Article shall not be construed as limiting in any way the executive authority of the Republic or of a Province in relation to a Tribal Area.'[29]

As stated earlier, the tribal areas were divided into two types—Provincially Administered Tribal Areas (PATA) and Centrally Administered Tribal Areas—under article 260 of the Interim Constitution of 1972. The 'districts of Chitral, Dir and Swat (which includes Kalam), Malakand Protected Area, the Tribal Area adjoining Hazara district and the former State of Amb' of the Frontier Province were made PATA and the rest of the tribal areas adjoining the province—the political agencies and Frontier Regions—were made Centrally Administered Tribal Areas. Article 261, clause (1) extended the executive authority of the Federation and Provinces to the respective tribal areas; and clauses (2) to (5) gave the procedures required to be adopted for the extension of laws made, and acts passed, by the central and provincial legislatures; and the making of regulations and status of the directions of the president to the governor relating to the tribal areas. And clause (6) of article 261 granted the president the same power as was previously given in clause (4) of article 104 of the Constitution of 1956, and clause (3) of article 223 of the Constitution of 1962, but with the difference that the president should ascertain the views of the people of the concerned area before withdrawing its tribal status 'as represented in jirga'. The full text of article 261, clause (6) is:

> The President may at any time by Order, direct that the whole or any part of a Tribal Area shall cease to be a Tribal Area, and such Order may contain such incidental and consequential provisions as appear to the President to be necessary and proper:
> Provided that before making any Order under this clause, the President shall ascertain, in such manner as he considers appropriate, the views of the people of the area concerned, as represented in jirga.[30]

All the aforesaid—envisaged in articles 260 and 261 of the Interim Constitution of 1972—were retained under articles 246 and 247 of the Constitution of 1973, with the difference that the name 'Centrally Administered Tribal Areas' was replaced by 'Federally Administered Tribal Areas'.[31]

The special status thus given to the tribal areas in the British days, and acceded to and maintained by Pakistan, can only be changed under article 247, clause (6) of the constitution—with the consent of the people represented in tribal *jargah*. But the Governor's Committee—constituted as per the decision of the federal cabinet's special meeting held on 23 August 1997 and headed by Governor NWFP, the first issue of the terms of reference of which was to study in-depth the '**justification for**

retention of special status of FATA and PATA of NWFP and Class-A and Class-B Areas of Balochistan'—has stated that 'the existing situation does not warrant any adventurism of even broaching such an overture', i.e., for changing the existing constitutional status. Because, 'it will give rise to fears and apprehensions and all efforts made in the last fifty years to integrate tribal population in national polity would fall apart resulting in an un-retrievable situation';[32] and that the treaties entered into with the tribes in the past 'can not be over ruled or ignored without serious socio-political repercussions'.[33]

The Governor's Committee further stated that, often, 'law and order issues are linked with ill-conceived ideas like discarding special status of FATA' and asserted that 'these are, of course, law and order issues of great importance, but most of these were there in one form or another throughout the long history of the borderland' and hence was of the opinion:

> Whereas there is a dire need to tone up the Political Administration to deal with law and order issues the present status of FATA should not be tampered with and the present policy of peaceful penetration in inaccessible tribal areas and integration of tribal society with the mainstream of national polity should continue. Moreover, demands like introduction of local self government, and legal reforms within the existing tribal system could be considered in real earnest.[34]

About the proposal for a change in the special status of PATA, the committee concluded: 'We need not meddle with its status, because the consent of the people is necessary under the Constitution which will not be forthcoming in the existing conditions.' 'As far as' the FATA 'is concerned even slight indication of merger with settled areas may lead to mass uprising. The policy makers should not be carried away by the slogans of reforms raised by a few tribesmen who have settled down in NWFP and elsewhere. No doubt the tribesmen raise demands for legal and administrative reforms but by no mean they are ready to barter away their special status.'[35] And while dealing with policy options, the committee stated: 'A sudden change in the status of FATA neither appears to be possible nor advisable.' The committee, moreover, assessed the factors in favour of and against a change to the current constitutional status, and favoured gradual integration by way of socio-political changes.[36]

The situation and environment changed drastically since the committee's work and report in 1997, following the US invasion of Afghanistan in 2001, the deployment of Pakistani armed forces in the tribal areas and along the border with Afghanistan, and also as a result of the military actions and operations in the tribal areas.

Despite all that has been previously said—as stated in detail in chapter 8—in May 2018 the existing special constitutional status of the FATA was brought to an end and the areas were made an integral part of the Khyber Pukhtunkhwa province, through the Constitution (25th Amendment) Act, 2018, and the existing special constitutional status of the PATA of the province also came to an end.

ADMINISTRATION HIERARCHY

During the British rule in India, the Foreign and Political Department of the Government of India exercised overall administration of the tribal areas. Executive authority rested with the Punjab governor, as Agent to the governor-general, for the agencies of Khyber, Kurram, North Waziristan, and South Waziristan, and directly with the governor-general for the Agency of Dir and Swat (later Dir, Swat and Chitral). After the creation of the separate Frontier Province in 1901, executive authority for all five agencies rested with the head of the province—initially the chief commissioner and agent to the governor-general, and later the governor and agent to the governor-general—in his capacity as Agent to the governor-general for these areas.[37]

After the emergence of Pakistan, overall administration of these tribal areas was exercised at the federal level by SAFRON, formerly a separate ministry known as the Ministry of States and Frontier Regions, and later part of the Ministry of Kashmir and Tribal Areas.[38] However, executive authority rested with the governor of the province, formerly as Agent to the Governor-General of Pakistan and later as Agent to the President of Pakistan. At the provincial level, the Home Ministry was in-charge of tribal administration, under the governor; the Secretary of Home and Tribal Affairs, at the provincial secretariat, conducted tribal matters. But, following the post-2001 US invasion of Afghanistan and military action in the tribal areas by the Pakistan government, a special secretariat—the FATA Secretariat—was established and tribal affairs were conducted through that secretariat under the governor of the Frontier Province. The administrative apparatus at the local/agency level is dealt with below.

The tribal areas—later called FATA—were divided into political agencies for administration purposes; every agency was an administrative unit with its territorial limits. The administration skeleton at the agency level comprised a political agent at the top, under whom were an assistant political agent and one or more assistant political officers, under whom were two or more *naib tahsildar*s (in Pukhtu: *naib tahsildaran*) or one *tahsildar* and one or more *naib tahsildar*s. The post of assistant political agent was usually filled by a superior service officer understudy. By virtue of his office, the political agent was the head of all the nation-building or line departments working within the agency; hence, he was the head and in-charge of all the officers of these departments in the agency. He was to coordinate the work of the line departments.[39]

As 'pivot of the entire administrative set-up' of the agency, the political agent was 'to control the tribes by his constant vigilance' and was 'to have a close eye over a particular ebb and flow of tribal opinion'. He, however, 'least' interfered 'with [the] domestic [or internal] affairs of the tribes who' were 'regulated by a tough unwritten code of conduct or better said "code of honour".'[40]

The agency's administration and all administrative affairs in the agency revolved around the political agent. He was to administer the area through 'his personal relations with the tribes', and, hence, was 'to win the confidence of the tribes and ensure that they have faith in his sincerity'. He was to command respect in the area through his virtues and fairness, 'so that [the] people bring their problems and disputes to him for settlement and arbitration'. As the tribesmen associated 'the entire Government with' the person of the political agent, a good political agent always meant good government to the tribesmen and vice versa. As stated earlier, the political agent headed all the line departments within the agency, due to which his duties were 'manifold and all embracing' as he needed to be the magistrate, director of health and education, chief engineer, and head of employment and so forth.[41]

LAW AND ORDER

Certain traits of the tribesmen, and of tribal life, affected not only the day-to-day activities of the people but were responsible, in their own way, for the law and order situation and its maintenance in the agencies. Most of these have already been dealt with in chapter 3.[42] A further trait and custom was *itbar* (trust), but in the context of administration and law and order it also referred to 'voluntary surrender on safe conduct'. 'Any infringement' of *itbar* was contrary to one's 'sense of honour', and left 'a permanent stain' on the breaker's reputation. Because it applied to 'dishonourable conduct', no explanation of, or justification for, it was acceptable.[43]

TRIBAL AND TERRITORIAL RESPONSIBILITY OR COLLECTIVE TRIBAL RESPONSIBILITY

Tribal and territorial responsibility was an important organ and 'corner stone' of tribal administration. Under the obligation of tribal responsibility, a tribe or sub-tribe was collectively responsible for the offences or crimes committed by any of its members or individuals; under the obligation of territorial responsibility, the tribe or sub-tribe was collectively responsible for the offences or crimes committed within its territorial jurisdiction— no matter whether or not the offender or culprit belonged to the tribe or sub-tribe. These were collective or joint responsibilities, enforced through tribal *jargahs* (in Pukhtu: *jargay*) and by the political authorities. Under these obligations, in case of the imposition of a fine, the share of an individual was determined by the system of *nikat* and *wurbal* or *lugay* (*logay*).[44] Both of these collective responsibilities were 'the two main principles of dealing with the tribes in regard to the maintenance of peace both within their own territory and on the border with the settled districts'.[45]

NIKAT AND URBAL

Nikat was 'the close and detailed organization based on heredity in a tribe'. It fixed 'the share of each class [clan] and sub-section, even of each family in all tribal loss and gain—benefits' were 'distributed and liabilities apportioned'. It regulated 'shares in allowances from the government, or booty from a raid and equally the amount due in fine under any settlement either with the government or with contending sections'.[46] *Nikat* even determined the share or proportion of each section or sub-section in the government services—especially in the forces. A 'raison d'être of the tribal system', *nikat* was 'no less than a temporal command' which was non-negotiable in spite 'of intervening demographic changes'. And, 'any deviation' from it invited 'serious trouble and no Political Administration' was to 'venture to enter into this forbidden area'. The 'rigidity' with which this rule was stuck to and followed 'could be imagined from the fact that in some Agencies even the ration and development outlay' was 'based on the dictates of shares contrived under "Nikat".'[47]

Sometimes, problems were created for the government when the tribes rigidly stuck to the principle of *nikat*, especially in cases of promotion in the army and Frontier Corps, and rewards for good services or penalties for misconduct. However, with the passage of time, due to the spread of education, travelling around the country, and increased migration for economic reasons, 'adherence to Nikat' became 'softened down in cases of outstanding merit or of penalty to a person with established guilt'.[48]

Urbal was followed, instead of *nikat*, in cases where a small number of tribesmen were involved in sharing the fines due or distributing the amount received. *Urbal* is the method or custom through which benefits and losses are shared on a household basis.[49] Households are ascertained, or counted, by the number of fires lit for cooking food at the end of the day; if they are counted by the columns of smoke rising from the houses, it is called *lugay*. In *urbal* and *lugay*, the fires lit or columns of smoke rising are not counted as a one-off but on a permanent basis. Under this rule, although a number of families may live in a single house, but if they cook collectively and, hence, light a single fire in the house, they are counted as one household. On the same token, if people living in one house permanently light different fires for cooking, each column of smoke is considered a different household in spite of living in one house.

Temporary Cessation of Hostilities

Pukhtu—the Pukhtun code of life—and the tribal system have a built-in procedure for the temporary cessation of hostilities, to give peace a chance and an opportunity for a permanent peaceful solution. Normally, 'disputes' were 'solved by mutual consultation' or 'through arbitration by impartial parties' or persons. In cases where third parties were involved in the solution, consensus of the involved parties was obtained. Sometimes, the political authorities were required to intervene in case the dispute disturbed the 'tranquillity of the area'. In such a situation, a temporary truce was struck between the parties—symbolised by placing a stone called *tigah* or *kunrah* (*kanray*)—whereby there was a cessation of hostilities and 'forgetting of the dispute by both the sides till tempers cool [down] and sanity returns' and the matter 'decided on principles of justice and fairplay, to the satisfaction of both the sides'.[50]

The government guaranteed the maintenance of such a truce; its violation was 'punishable' according to the terms agreed upon, and 'often there' was 'a provision of a substantial fine or forfeiture of a right'. In the event that the political authorities were 'party to the truce', the violation also resulted in their displeasure—they, who were entitled in such a situation, were 'to suspend any of the economic benefits enjoyed by the offending party'. A wise political agent could save 'an ugly situation' by tactful use of this indigenous solution and article of the Pukhtun code of conduct.[51] Besides the other components and commandments of Pukhtu—outlined in Chapter 3—the aforementioned were the salient features of the tribal mores and customs, which played their due role in the maintenance of law and order in the tribal areas as, in Izzat Awan's words:

> As a race, tribesmen are never constant in respect for authority as such, and never forget a slight on them as they see it. Such men can only be held in a bond of loyalty which is personal and which is offered specifically to the tribe or tribes. Even today the Pathans will chafe under authority and the slightest affront would rouse the instinct of the tribesmen to get free, to strike off every bond, obeying only the 'nang', the honour.[52]

Punjab Frontier Force

The internal administration of the British-occupied territories remained the same as in the other parts of Punjab, 'but to maintain the peace of the border' with the tribes, 'a special force—the Punjab Frontier Force—was raised under the direct orders of the Board' of Administration in Lahore. The force, at first, consisted 'of 5 regiments of cavalry, the Corps of Guides, 5 regiments of infantry, 3 light field batteries, 2 garrison batteries, 2 companies of sappers and miners, and the Sind Camel Corps'. However, 'various changes were made in its composition', and in 1886 it was detached from the Punjab government's control and 'amalgamated with the regular army'.[53]

Role of Frontier Corps

The Frontier Corps is different from the army though it, too, is an organised force with the same standard of discipline and is built along a similar pattern. The Corps is divided into the militia, scouts, and rifles, etc. according to the term assigned to it in the specific agency and area.

Militia: It is derived from the Latin word *miles*, which 'means a soldier and Militia means force on military service comprising of soldiers'. Militia is a type of Frontier Corps and 'a body of men specially raised from among civil population', 'drilled as soldiers' and 'liable to home service only', but 'in case of emergency, assist the regular army in operations'. The Turi Militia was the first of its kind, raised out of the Turi tribe—'who volunteered to serve under the British in their own area'—of the Kurram Valley in 1892, who were later named the Kurram Militia. Later, many other militias were also raised in the other areas by enrolling the local tribesmen as soldiers, such as the North Waziristan Militia, the South Waziristan Militia, the Mohmand Militia. The militias' 'knowledge of their own' areas greatly assisted and facilitated the British during the course of their expeditions against the tribes.[54]

Scouts: The word scouts is derived from the Latin word *auscultare* meaning listening; 'scouting', in the context of the Scout force, as used by the British, stands for 'spying, watching or observation'. As the British needed 'to use force against' the tribes for a number of problems and factors, instead of using British or Indian forces, they used the militia to gather information and carry out small actions both at the front and the flank. This changed the role of the militia to picqueting and guarding routes before military action could begin—because of which, the name 'militia lost its practical meaning and the Corps' was named the scouts. Hence, the North and South Waziristan militias were renamed the scouts; later, other scouts Corps were also raised, such as the Chitral Scouts, the Dir Scouts, the Bajawar Scouts, the Tal Scouts.[55]

Rifles: 'The units whose troops were armed with rifles were named as rifles.' The rifles' basic organisation was laid on the *qaum* or tribe basis. With the passage of time, many Corps named Rifles were raised—such as the Khyber Rifles, the Mohmand Rifles, the Shawal Rifles—that have also been part of the Frontier Corps. However, the 'Samana Rifles which existed in Kohat district and named after the famous Samana valley, was border military police force and in no way part of the Frontier Corps'.[56]

Thus, 'Corps or units in the Frontier Corps existed under the names' militia, rifles, and scouts, with the same 'organization and role'. 'Organized into various wings' and *qaumi* platoons, these Corps worked, 'on the famous customs of the militia'. They were later equipped with 'modern weapons and equipment'.[57]

Later governed by the Frontier Corps Ordinance, 1959, 'the Frontier Corps' acted 'as an arm of the Political Agent' and of the deputy commissioner (district coordination officer from 2001 till 2012 CE)— where the Frontier Region was linked with the district for administrative purposes—'in maintaining law and order in tribal areas besides its role of guarding the Frontiers'. As it was 'necessary that the Frontier Corps' was always to be 'on the beck and call of the Political Agent', and the deputy commissioner, 'without seeking prior orders from the Headquarters', section 7 (2) of the Frontier Corps Ordinance, 1959, provided this power by ordaining: '*Every Frontier Corps and the Commandant of every Unit of Frontier Corps shall, in time of peace, be subject save in respect of administration, internal economy and training to the directions of the*

*Political Agent or the Deputy Commissioner of the area within [which]
the headquarters of the Frontier Corps are located.*[58]

The Frontier Corps has been 'specially effective for "Guerrilla" type of warfare', and as the army was withdrawn from the tribal areas after the emergence of Pakistan, the defence of the border rested 'with the Frontier Corps'. An army officer of the rank of brigadier commands the force, the commanding officer of each unit is a Lt. Colonel, and the second-in-command is of the rank of a major in the army. Although a number of officers 'have been promoted' from the rank and file of the force, the officers mostly come from the army. Recruitment has been 'from the tribal areas, on [a] tribal and sectional basis' or according to the rule of *nikat*. The applicants have to fulfil the standards or requirements laid down for the army, in all respects, before they being recruited. Not only does the Frontier Corps solved the issue of employment for the tribesmen and provided 'prestigious source of livelihood' to them, it also provided an efficient and effective force for the government, which not only relieved the army from the tribal areas but also assisted it elsewhere in times of emergency.[59]

The Frontier Corps has served within the tribal areas and along the border with Afghanistan until the army was once again deployed—after 11 September 2001 incident in USA and the consequent hunt for Al-Qaida and Taliban members—along the border and inside the tribal areas. The Frontier Corps, however, carries on its other duties as before.

ROLE OF LEVIES AND KHASADARS

Levies and khasadars have been 'a sort of police' force, at the disposal of the political agents of the tribal agencies—Malakand Levies and Bitani Levies are examples of the levies force—who have played their role in the tribal or agency administration. They have been 'responsible for [the] maintenance of law and order in [their] respective areas' in the agencies. Raised from the tribes—on the basis of a fixed quota for each tribe and section—the khasadars are paid by the government but carry 'their own weapons'.[60] 'The main difference between [the] Khasadars and the Levies is that whereas the Khasadari is hereditary and the incumbent supplies his own weapon, the Government provides service rifles to the Levies and they can be replaced by selection.'[61] Except for this, the khasadars and the levies are similar forces that have the same duties, responsibilities, and obligations.

Not only does the khasadari system, introduced in 1921, placed 'responsibility for [the] maintenance of law and order' on the tribesmen themselves but it also has been the most inexpensive way of dealing with the tribes while at the same time bolstering the power and influence of the *malak*s, which in turn was to serve the government's cause. Not only does this decreased military commitment and responsibility in the tribal areas, it also extended government's control by placing responsibility for maintaining law and order and enforcing the government's writ on the tribes by the tribesmen themselves. The khasadars being recruited—on the basis of *nikat* or quota—by the tribal *malak*s, the khasadari system has been a corollary to the *malaki* system, and hence 'has often been termed as a colossal favour to the Maliks or even blackmail'. Sher Muhammad Mohmand, however, contends that 'this is an unfair criticism', because the khasadars have been 'used as tribal police force to back the authority of the Maliks when they' have to act 'as agents to the Government, in maintaining Law and Order and protecting roads, buildings, and other installations and properties of the Government'.[62]

The 'duties and responsibilities' of the khasadars 'in the tribal structure' classified 'them as the instrument of the tribal will'. As Bruce points out, 'though paid by the Government', the khasadars are 'not the servants of the Government' but of the tribe. The collective local responsibility has been 'an important feature' of the khasadari system from many aspects: their 'selection through tribal consultation'; khasadars' liability to punishments—such as fines, suspension of pay, arrest—for 'misbehaviour on the part of the [concerned] tribe'; the *malak*s and even the tribe which is answerable to the government for the khasadars' absence from duty; and the khasadars' liability for punishment under their territorial responsibility for offences occurring in their areas of jurisdiction.[63]

The khasadars were supposed to protect their territorial jurisdiction from raids and offences; to provide escort to government officials and protect government property; to investigate reports and provide correct information about activities and intentions of anti-government elements; to trace the whereabouts of, and recover, kidnapped persons—whether kidnapped from settled districts, government roads, or tribal areas; to report incidents that have occurred in their territorial jurisdiction; to summon and provide safe passage to people as required; and to perform other general duties.[64]

The duties of the khasadars have been similar to those of the police force in the settled districts. J.G. Elliott points out that the khasadars are 'by no means the figures of fun' as they have 'often made out to be—one of them was given the posthumous award of the George Cross'. But, being 'recruited, trained and administered entirely under tribal arrangements', it has been 'obviously impossible to count on their services if things' go 'badly'.[65]

Organised into companies, 'each under the command of a subedar', the khasadars have 'their own uniform' in different agencies. At the agency level, a khasadar officer, under the political agent, oversaw the affairs of the khasadars, their 'training, discipline, performance of duty, pay and administration'. Their posts are established at various important locations and along the road-side; and their companies transferred, from one place to another, at regular intervals. Their companies, having 'a tribal and sectional basis' are 'usually employed in their own areas'. Divided into two, the companies are on duty at their posts 'on alternate months'. For the month when they are not on active duty, they return to their homes, but are still supposed to be on duty and hence are 'liable to checking and responsibility, both tribal and territorial'. This privilege was granted to them in lieu of lesser pay, but the alternate months during which they remain at home are 'considered as privileged leave with full pay'.[66]

ROLE OF FRONTIER CONSTABULARY

After the occupation of the settled districts of the Frontier, the British felt the need for a special force to pursue the ordinary raiding gangs and to take action against a section of a tribe within the district border— because military aid was not always forthcoming for such matters. As the tribesmen 'were armed to the teeth', Olaf Caroe contends, 'and were the most notorious raiders and plunderers', 'it was clearly necessary to build up a force which should be more mobile than regular soldiers and act under the civil authority'.[67]

As the Guides were the model of such a force, a militia named Punjab Irregular Force—also called the Piffers—was raised on this model. This Frontier force, which at first operated as the Border Military Police, 'were not employed as policemen on the investigation or control of crime'.[68] In 1913, they were 'reorganized on a more efficient footing as the Frontier Constabulary, with officers seconded from the Indian Police'[69] for the purpose previously served by the Border Military Police. They formally came into being, as a new force, under FC Act No. XIII of 1915, and were reorganised in 1926. The Frontier Constabulary is now an independent civil armed force by virtue of its organisation, control, and officers.[70]

The personnel of the Frontier Constabulary were recruited from among the tribesmen and staffed by officers of the Indian Police, later the Pakistan Police Service. The force is now commanded by a commandant at its headquarter in Peshawar, with its own divisions commanded by its own district officers. Its district officer is equal in rank to that of superintendent of police; large districts also have assistant district officers of the Frontier Constabulary. The junior commissioned and non-commissioned officers in the Frontier Constabulary are similar to those in the army. The force has been organised on a platoon-basis; being recruited from tribesmen, the platoons are formed on a 'tribal and sub-tribal basis'.[71]

Although recruited from the tribal areas, the Frontier Constabulary has been stationed in the settled districts. Its posts are situated close to the borders with the tribal areas, in places that are suitable 'for watch and ward duties'—as it has to perform its duties mainly along the borders with the tribal areas. It normally patrols along the borders of the tribal and settled areas, to prevent raids from the tribal areas and to check smuggling. However, being 'a mobile force', it is despatched 'wherever the need arises', even inside the districts. Although 'not trained strictly in the military sense', they possess 'a fair knowledge of guerrilla warfare and make effective use of the ground with which they are familiar as having been born in the locality and neighbourhood'. They carry out surveillance patrols from their posts, both during the day as well as in the night—the number 'depends on the local conditions'.[72]

The Frontier Constabulary 'led a life of Spartan simplicity manning small forts and piquets in remote, inaccessible spots, constantly on the move and always ready to concentrate to meet a major threat.'[73] 'They numbered in their ranks many remarkable characters, none more famous than Handyside who was their commandant for five years from 1921', who 'was killed leading an attack on a village house occupied by a raiding gang'. Therefore, 'an arch was erected over the road at the summit of the Kohat Pass', 'as a tribute to his fearlessness, tenacity and almost quixotic bravery, which gained him the name of Kishn Sani—Mackeson the Second'.[74]

Not only does the force provide jobs with lucrative opportunities for promotion and benefits to a large number of tribesmen, but its thoroughness, discipline, efficiency, and efficacy has also been commendable.

POLICE FORCE'S ROLE IN RELATION TO TRIBAL AREAS

The police force has no direct role in the tribal administration and the tribal affairs. However, tribesmen from neighbouring tribal areas used to come to the settled areas on a daily basis, and a significant number of them took up permanent abode in the settled areas—to work and run their businesses. This brought these tribesmen within the pale and domain of the police force, as far as their affairs were concerned in the settled areas. It not only increased the responsibilities of the police but also created problems for them—when culprits and offenders hailing from the tribal areas committed crimes and offences in the settled areas and then fled or absconded to the tribal areas.[75]

Sometimes, the tribesmen hijacked vehicles and persons from the settled areas for ransom; and criminals hailing from the settled areas sometimes also took shelter and abode in the tribal areas. In all such circumstances, 'the police' invoked 'the relevant provisions' of the law 'regarding issuance of proclamation and attachment/confiscation of [the] offenders [offenders'] property', and sought the cooperation of the Frontier Constabulary and political authorities of the tribal agencies. In case this did not 'work in bringing the offenders back, a perpetual warrant of arrest' was 'issued by the Court against the offenders'. The Frontier Crimes Regulation, 1901, being in force in the tribal areas, meant the political authorities were empowered 'to take effective action' in the tribal areas against such wanted persons and to bring them to book and to face the law. They also used other methods such as collective responsibility and economic pressure by different means.[76]

Likewise, when offenders, criminals, and persons wanted by the political authority and government, for acts committed in the tribal areas, fled or absconded and took shelter in the settled areas, the political authorities and their forces, who had no jurisdiction and power in the settled areas, sought the cooperation and assistance of the police and administration of the settled areas.

Hence, full cooperation between the political authorities of the tribal areas, and their forces, and the administration of the settled districts, and their police force, was vital and unavoidable. This cooperation, between the political and district authorities and the police, ensured the smooth working of the administration, maintenance of law and order, and protection of the people, both in the tribal and settled areas, to a considerable degree.[77]

After the merger of FATA in Khyber Pukhtunkhwa, the regular police system, like in other parts of the province, was to be introduced in the area. For this purpose, the sub-divisions Hassan Khail (ex-FR Peshawar), Darah Adam Khail (ex-FR Kuhat), Wazir (ex-FR Bannu), Bitani (ex-FR Lakki Marwat), Darazanda (ex-FR Dirah Ismail Khan), and Jandula (ex-FR Tank) were made part of the Police Districts of Peshawar, Kuhat, Bannu, Lakki Marwat, Dirah Ismail Khan, and Tank, respectively.[78] Whereas the merged districts of South Waziristan, North Waziristan, Urakzai, Kurram, Khyber, Muhmand and Bajawar were made part of the Police Regions of Dirah Ismail Khan, Bannu, Kuhat, Peshawar, Mardan and Malakand, respectively.[79] It is to be noted that both the Urakzai and Kurram were made part of the Kuhat Region.

MALAKI AND MUAJIBS

During the British period, the political officers dealt with the 'tribes through their elders' and, as a result of their past experiences, they 'started formally enlisting Maliks', so evolving into the institution of *malaki* that was 'synonymous with the system of tribal administration'. Besides those 'previously in the pay of Afghanistan, fresh registration of tribal elders [*malak*s; in Pukhtu: *malakan/malakanan*] on the basis of house hold strength was made'. These *malak*s were also called *lungi* (in Pukhtu: *lungai*) holders, and were paid *lungi* allowance, locally called *muajib* (*majab*; *muwajib*), for their 'political services' to the government. The *lungi* or *malaki* was terminated on the death of the *malak* or *lungi* holder, but as the system involved his family deeply in services to the government, the political agent held the authority to designate his eldest son as the *malak* and allow continuation of the *lungi* allowance or *muajib* in his favour. This provided continuity, not only 'in the allegiance of the family' to the government but also in rendering political services. This institution continued, and has carried on into the post-1947 days as well.[80]

Besides the above-mentioned allowances paid to the *lungi* holders or tribal *malak*s, other kinds of *muwajib* or allowances are paid to the tribesmen. These *muajib*s are mostly paid either in lieu of permanent losses incurred by the tribes—for giving up their rights to water, for handing over possession of land to the government to meet the government's needs, for rendering services such as the khasadari, and for giving up traditional sources of revenue in favour of the government, such as *rahdari*s and tolls on passages passing through their territories and jurisdictions.[81] The *muajib*s (allowances) paid to the tribesmen have remained 'the most mis-understood part of the tribal administration', Izzat Awan contends. These have sometimes been termed as 'dole-money', which is not appropriate. Izzat Awan illustrates the point:

> If one travels through the tribal areas, one will at once realize that the best cultivable land or land with water facilities was taken over by the British for an Army camp or for a post or for a road or for an air-field. In a mountaneous area where plain land is difficult to find and where water facilities are practically non existent, it was indeed a great hardship for the tribes who were deprived of these. One must not forget that in these inhospitable areas there are no alternative means of livelihood. So the British, in order to secure the goodwill of the people, arranged a fixed annual payment for the things taken rather than making an outright lumpsum payment as compensation.[82]

Olaf Caroe has dealt with the issue of *muajib*s, paid to the tribes, from another perspective. He points out that 'the application of force by the army or civil power' to restrain the tribesmen from carrying out raids and depredations, and keeping them passive 'was the negative side of the coin', and that the British 'administrators were not without positive ideas. The most obvious of these [ideas] were written agreements and allowances.' Therefore, 'during the first twenty years' of their coming to the area, 'signed agreements were negotiated with every tribe up and down the Frontier and secured, on paper, everything that the government needed'. A clause of these agreements guaranteed 'an annual allowance contingent' to the tribes called *muajib* but it was subject to their 'good behaviour' and their abiding by the terms of the treaty.[83] Besides,

> These payments might be in the form of compensation for roads through their country, or in recognition of some special service. A good example is that of the Khaibar Afridis, whose original allowances were granted in lieu of the tolls which the tribe itself formerly levied by force on all traffic through the pass. Subsequent increases were made to the Afridi allowances as rewards for the signal service rendered by the tribe in remaining staunch through World War I, and as compensation for roads, railways and camps.[84]

Caroe, in the strongest words, negates the arguments and objections of those who have termed the *muajib*s 'blackmail' and, besides other arguments, concludes:

> All allowances, for whatever reason given, are conditional on good behaviour and liable to suspension, or forfeiture, in part or in whole, if the tribe breaks an agreement or commits offences. Such suspension is one of the most effective

weapons of retaliation upon a lawless tribe, and the value of the allowance system is best shown by government's comparative impotence in dealing with a tribe not so subsidized.[85]

'There is no doubt', J.G. Elliott observes, 'that over the years these allowances achieved a considerable degree of success but they were a palliative and not a cure, and on occasion they could be the cause of trouble when those who were receiving what they felt to be less than their fair share stirred up trouble to discredit those through whom the political agent dealt when making the payments'.[86] Dr Muhammad Anwar Khan clarifies the position in another way when he states:

> While the settled area contributed, though marginal to the revenue income of the state, the tribal belt remained exempt from all kind of taxes, rather some public monetary assistance, though nominal, was extended to the Maliks, tribes and individuals. *Lungi* went to the Malik, *muajib* for the tribe and *kharcha* [expenditures' sum, or pocket money, or sum for the expenditures incurred] to the worker. In return the tribesmen protected the security infrastructure in their area and helped in maintenance of peace against raids and dacoity in the settled districts.[87]

BANDISH AND BARAMTAH

Besides the punitive expeditions and stoppage of allowances (*muajibs*), 'for controlling tribal depredation on the [settled] districts', *bandish* (blockade) and *baramtah* were also used. *Bandish* or 'blockade is a means of exerting economic pressure by excluding a tribe from markets, land, or grazing in the neighbouring district'. *Baramtah* means 'the seizure of persons, animals or property belonging to a tribe or an individual at fault, in order to bring pressure for restitution'. *Bandish* and *baramtah* were part of both the individual and collective tribal responsibility, of which the latter 'weapon' worked 'best when enforced against the tribal section actually responsible, or to which the aggressors actually belong[ed]; the smaller the section on which pressure can be brought, the more likely' was the 'restitution'.[88]

SECRET SERVICE AND ENTERTAINMENT FUNDS

Despite the difference in their nature and methods, a secret service always remains an integral and established part of an administration, irrespective of the pattern or system of government. The same was also applicable to the tribal areas, and, hence, it has remained part of tribal administration. The political authorities of the political agencies were granted funds for the purpose, the utilisation and disbursement of which remained at their disposal. Izzat Awan contends that 'in present monetary terms' the amount under this head at the disposal of the political agents 'are small' and that these funds 'are as much accountable as the funds for entertainment or any other fund for that matter'.[89] It, however, has been commonly believed that the opposite has remained the case. Besides, as stated earlier, the khasadars also performed secret service and intelligence work.

A political agent also had an entertainment fund at his disposal, the purpose of which was 'partly to meet the food and lodging expenses' of the tribesmen, 'in order to induce' them to leave their homes and 'come to the agency's headquarters and apprise the Political Agent' of their and their tribes' 'problems or difficulties'. Because most of the tribesmen were poor and lived in remote areas that had no roads or other means of communication—as are available to them now—this allowance was to induce them to come and apprise the political authorities of any problems faced by their people or of any calamity occurring in their areas, without the anxiety of having to bear the expenses incurred from their own resources. Had this tool and technique not been devised and used, they most probably would not have carried out this service and assistance. For instance, 'a tribesman may have come a long distance to tell the government that small-pox' had 'broken out in his area' and that they needed an urgent visit from 'a doctor and a vaccinator'.[90] This was the *kharchah* (expenditure or pocket money or amount for the expenditures incurred) referred to in the section '*Malaki* and *Muajib*s'.

But, entertainment funds were later mostly used for other purposes, such as entertaining the *malak*s and other tribal dignitaries when they visited the political agents, granting them pocket money at their visits to the political agents—commonly considered greasing their palms—and similar purposes at the discretion of the political agents, which—whether advertently or inadvertently—are not mentioned by Izzat Awan and other writers who hail from the civil services. In the post-2001 scenario, the situation greatly changed in this respect as well.

LAW: *RIWAJ* AND FRONTIER CRIMES REGULATION

During the British era, the tribal areas were granted special status and were governed by special laws under the governor of the province—first of Punjab and then of the Frontier Province—in his role as Agent to the governor-general. In Pakistan, too, they were granted a special legal-administrative status.

Tribal society was governed by its own customs and traditions, and the governments interfered as little as possible in the internal affairs of the tribes. The cases and disputes were generally decided by the *jargahs* (in Pukhtu: *jargay*) as per customary law or *riwaj*. The decision of the *jargahs* were binding; the violator remained liable to a penalty that varied according to the gravity and nature of the offence—the penalty was to be as severe as his house being burnt down or his *sharuntya* (exile or banishment from the tribe or home place) for a specific period or forever. The significant aspect in deciding cases and disputes in *jargahs* is not to pronounce guilt and punish the aggressor but to satisfy the aggrieved. Olaf Caroe rightly states:

> The point to realize is this. Pathan custom requires the satisfaction of the aggrieved rather than the punishment of the aggressor. The law as we understand it concentrates against the aggressor, and compensation for the aggrieved hardly enters the picture. The Pathan in fact treats crime as a kind of tort.[91]

In case the parties, by consensus, brought their disputes to the political agent, he, too, was supposed to settle them in accordance with the local customs or *riwaj*. Izzat Awan claims, in the early 1970s, that 'the "Rewaj" is being replaced by the Shariah laws'[92] but, on the whole, this was not the case. Shariah laws gained a foothold, especially as a result of the anti-Soviet war in Afghanistan which was fought in the name of Islam; cases were decided according to Shariat, but with the consent of the parties. Although not found in a codified form in most of the tribal areas, each and every individual knew the customary laws or *riwaj*. However, the Turi tribe of the Kurram Agency codified their customary law called *Turizuna*; and the *riwaj* of Malakand Agency (Malakand Protected Area) was also codified, titled *Riwaj Namah Malakand Agency*.[93] References were made to these codified customary laws, as the Penal Code, in deciding the cases.

In 1939, 'the administration of justice' in the tribal areas 'was brought under the procedural realm of Frontier Crimes Regulation, 1901[,] and the Criminal Procedure Code 1898. Concurrently, the Indian Penal Code 1860 was extended alongwith the Frontier Murderous Outrages Regulation, 1901.'[94]

The Frontier Crimes Regulation (FCR)—the first set of which 'was promulgated in 1872', 'revised in 1887', and the third set was enacted in 1901 after the formation of the NWFP[95] and, hence, thereafter called the Frontier Crimes Regulation, 1901—was in force in the tribal areas for the administration of or administering justice. Olaf Caroe terms the introduction of FCR in 1872, 'a positive attempt' because it authorised the settlement of disputes—'arising out of the blood-feud, of disputes about women, and questions generally affecting Pathan honour'[96]—by a customary method. He, however, was critical of the practical method used, as he contends that it 'was a failure, for, as so operated, it satisfied neither the law nor the custom. It became merely an easy means of punishing crime as from the State, without being a recognition of the Pathan idea. It failed to administer custom on the basis of local tradition, and it fell between two stools.'[97] Nevertheless, he asserts that when, in the 1890s, 'a loose administration in certain tribal areas' was imposed, the regulation showed positive results 'in these places' as here it 'was operated not as a parallel system, to be applied when the ordinary process of law was expected to fail, but as the sole and substitute code, whenever the parties were tribesmen'. The regulation 'was indeed in these' tribal 'territories regarded mainly as a means of adjudication on custom, and not as a procedure for enforcing the sanctions of the State. Thus in a criminal case[,] penalties would ordinarily not exceed those imposed by custom, unless the crime had outraged both custom and the authority of the government.'[98]

Infamous and repressive in certain aspects, the FCR was followed in FATA and worked well to a great extent. Applicable to the whole of FATA, the FCR had its own system and provisions for trials, on the whole in-keeping with tribal traditions. It also contained a set of provisions that suited and safeguarded government interest in relation to affairs related to law and order and other spheres. Although amendments were made to the FCR in 1997, there was still a hue and cry, in some circles, against the regulation: especially its preventive sections which grant unfettered powers to the political authorities, the fines imposed in case of failure to fulfil obligations of territorial responsibility, bulldozing houses of offenders and their nearest relatives, subservience of the political authorities-appointed *jargah* members to the concerned authorities' dictates when they had to deal with criminal cases, and the negative attitude of the political authorities in granting bail to those arrested under section 40 of the regulation. These, however, have been 'some of the ground realities', Sher Muhammad Mohmand asserts, 'that are not looked at righteously by the public at large and condemned outright by terming it as Black Law, unjudicious and against the spirit of Islam and Sharria'.[99] He, moreover, contends:

> To many a lawyer, the FCR may be a 'black law' but to victims of violent crime, nothing provides justice more readily and never is the guilty so adequately punished as under it. Those having an intimate knowledge of the actual workings of the civil and criminal jirga trials would readily conclude that if the Political Officers act honourably, no system of justice is cheaper, quicker or more deterrent.
>
> The fact that the law and order and the crime situation in the Tribal Area is invariably better than the Settled Districts, is because of the efficacy of the FCR.[100]

And that:

> Of course, a suggestion can be made that in order to further improve the law and order situation in the Settled Districts, a limited applicability of the FCR be considered at least in murder, kidnapping, abduction, dacoity and robbery cases where direct evidence is not readily forthcoming.[101]

Further amendments were made to the FCR in 2011, but that too did not satisfy the critics.

Any Act and law passed by the parliament did not apply to FATA, unless specially extended by the president, as ordained in article 247 of the Constitution of 1973. The article also authorised the president to 'make regulations for the peace and good government of a Federally Administered Tribal Area or any part thereof'—'with respect to any matter'.[102]

However, offences committed on the roads, camps, and other government property were 'dealt with under the normal law', and many Pakistani laws were extended to the areas.[103]

At this point, it is pertinent to mention that with bringing an end to the special tribal status of FATA, under the Constitution (25th Amendment), Act, 2018, the existing seven tribal agencies were granted the status of one district each and the existing six Frontier Regions were made sub-divisions of the adjacent former districts. Consequently, the new districts, namely Bajawar, Muhmand, Khyber, Urakzai, Kurram, North Waziristan and South Waziristan, were declared Session Divisions; and the newly sub-division, namely Hassan Khail, Darah Adam Khail, Wazir, Bitani, Darazanda and Jandula, were declared sub-divisions of the District/Session Divisions of Peshawar, Kuhat, Bannu, Lakki Marwat, Dirah Ismail Khan and Tank, respectively.[104] Besides, a 'steering committee' was constituted 'tasked in establishing regular courts for the erstwhile FATA now merged in Khyber Pakhtunkhwa Province'.[105] However, 'The Khyber Pakhtunkhwa Continuation of Laws in Erstwhile Federally Administered Tribal Areas Bill, 2019 (Khyber Pakhtunkhwa Act No. XXIV of 2019)', passed by the provincial assembly on 29 April 2019 and assented to by the governor of the province on the same day, ordains:

> 3. **Continuation of laws.**---(1) Notwithstanding anything contained in any other law, for the time being in force, all the laws, Regulations, rules, notifications and bye-laws, including Actions (in Aid of Civil Power) Regulation, 2011, or any other legal instrument, applicable in the erstwhile Federally Administered Tribal Areas and having had the force of law, under or in pursuance of Article 247 of the Constitution of the Islamic Republic of Pakistan and now omitted vide the Constitution (Twenty-fifth Amendment) Act, 2018 (Act No. XXXVII of 2018), shall continue to remain in force until altered, repealed or amended by the competent authority:
>
> Provided that anything done, action taken, rules made and notifications or orders issued by the law enforcement agencies in their discharge of official duties under any regulations, laws, rules, orders shall be deemed to be valid and the same shall not be called in question in any court of law and shall also be deemed to have done, taken, made or issued under this Act.
>
> (2) The provision of sub-section (1) shall not be applicable to the Federally Administered Tribal Areas Interim Governance Regulation, 2018 and Frontier Crimes Regulation, 1901.[106]

A loophole in this Act is the statement in section 1, sub-section (3) which states: 'It shall come into force at once.' As this was passed and ascended to on 29 April 2019, and the Constitution (25th Amendment) Act, 2018, received the assent of the President on 31 May 2018, no legal cover or constitutional backing is provided to what has been referred to in the above quoted section 3, subsection (1), and done after 31 May 2018 till 29 April 2019.

LINE DEPARTMENTS

The writings of those who stayed on in the Pakistan administration demonstrate that the British did not work sufficiently in other spheres such as education, communication, health, and agriculture. The British position in the tribal areas, the attitude of the tribesmen towards them, and the physical nature of the area, cannot be underestimated. Therefore, whatever work they did should be considered to be, at least, the foundation that was laid for future progress.

The Pakistan government's attitude and progress in this respect, too, was not initially up to the mark. However, the policy of peaceful penetration worked to an extent and much headway was made. The policy and course adopted by the Pakistan government in 1970s, proved a great success. But, much still needed to be done. The administration and developmental functions were carried out by the concerned line departments of the Frontier Province, but 'under overall policy directions and controls of the Federal Government'.[107]

Officers and staff of the Frontier Province's line departments, which also have tribesmen among their rank and file, manned the line departments in the tribal areas. However, as also stated earlier, the political agent of each agency supervised and coordinated the work of all the line departments in the agency.[108]

COST EFFECTIVENESS

The Governor's Committee looked into the cost effectiveness of the tribal administration. Stating that 'the FATA Administration under a political representative of the Government is most suited to the genius of the people', the committee has asserted that 'its cost on administrative structure is minimal as compared to settled districts, with one Political Agent, assisted by a couple of Assistant Political Agents, a few Tehsildars, a small outfit of Khasadars and Levies. Similarly, the strength of [the] Attached Departments is also negligible as compared with [the] settled districts.'[109] The committee has, moreover, drawn 'a random comparison' between four districts and agencies 'as an illustration'—which is given below:[110]

District[s]		Agencies	
Swat	11.725 M	S.W. Agency	4.920 M
Abbottabad	8.483 M	Khyber Agency	3.840 M
Swabi	8.570 M	Bajaur Agency	3.789 M
Haripur	5.712 M	Orakzai Agency	2.294 M

On the basis of this comparison, the committee states that 'the present cost effectiveness of these agencies is more than half of the expenses incurred on the Administration of the District'. Moreover, it contended that 'this is true of entire FATA when compared with [the] settled districts'.[111]

The difference in the cost of administration in the settled districts and in the tribal agencies may also have been because all the areas of the agencies were not open to administration; hence, no expenditures were incurred in those areas on administrative measures or on education, health, communication, agriculture, and so forth. As the number of educational institutions, health facilities—such as hospitals, basic health units, and dispensaries—roads, irrigation canals, and so forth in the tribal areas were fewer, as compared to the districts, not only were there comparatively fewer employees in the line departments in the agencies—which has an impact on the budget vis-à-vis salaries etc.—but other developmental and non-developmental costs incurred by the agencies were also smaller.

While the above is the main blueprint of the pattern of administration that was in practice in the tribal areas, there was a slight variation in the way it operated in different areas and agencies. Interestingly, the system was both simple and yet complex.

The constitution guaranteed and maintained the special status, and mode of governance and administration, in the tribal areas. Barring the jurisdiction of the supreme court in FATA, the constitution also stipulated non-interference with the special status of the tribal areas without ascertaining the prior consent of the people concerned, and retained the areas outside the domain of the laws made and passed by the legislature—which could be extended only through a special procedure under article 247. However, as stated earlier, this was brought to an end through the Constitution (25th Amendment) Act, 2018.

'The system of Khassadaris, FC [Frontier Corps] and Levies for controlling law and order in the Agency together with [the] FCR had stood the test of time', Sher Muhammad Mohmand asserts, 'and despite its inherent weaknesses, it has proved an effective means of enforcing Government will in the interior of the Agency and in [the] areas which are not easily accessible to officials'. He, however, has acceded that 'the system is not fool proof and there is great scope for improving and building on what presently exists'.[112]

The efficacy of the tribal administration, evolved by the British and followed and maintained by Pakistan, has been referred to—in different unfavourable contexts ranging from 1961 until the late 1990s—and highlighted by the Governor's Committee in its report in 1997. The committee has expressed the view that 'it was the efficacy of the system of administration [in practice] which withstood all the pressures and no military solution was resorted to', and has asserted that 'we can ill-afford any move which weakens or disrupts the erstwhile policy of indirect dealing with [the] tribes through [the] Political Administration'.[113] The committee has also stated that the 'policy of integration' adopted by Pakistan government, 'by development and alluring [the] tribesmen to develop business stakes in [the] settled areas' has 'proved highly successful and now more than 70% of [the] tribal area is open to tribal administration as compared to about 30% during the British Rule'.[114]

The wisdom and aptness of the view held by the Governor's Committee—advising indirect dealing with the tribes through the political administration and the avoidance of direct intervention and military action—was borne out by the results of military intervention and the use of force in the post-US invasion of Afghanistan (2001) scenario: the resultant casualties on both the security forces and the tribal people's sides, the destruction and devastation of the area, the treaties that were devised with the tribesmen to allow face-saving retreats, and the greatest disaffection and disgruntledness of the tribal people as well as the financial expenses and burden that was borne.

Notes

1. For note about the 'Britons', see chap. 4, n. 6.
2. J.G. Elliott, *The Frontier, 1839–1947: The Story of the North-West Frontier of India*, with preface by Olaf Caroe (London: Cassell & Company Ltd, 1968), 4.
3. Ibid., 87.
4. *Tribal Areas: Status, Border Control and Policy; Governor's Committee Report* [henceforward *Tribal Areas*] (Unpublished) (Government of North-West Frontier Province, Home and Tribal Affairs Department, September–October 1997), 55.
5. Ibid., 10.
6. Ibid., 55.
7. Elliott, *The Frontier*, 93.
8. D.G. Tendulkar, *Abdul Ghaffar Khan: faith is a battle* (Bombay: PP, 1967), 3.
9. Izzat Awan, *Pattern of Administration in the Tribal Areas of Pakistan* (Peshawar: Provincial Civil Services Academy, 1972), 7–8.
10. Ibid., 14.
11. *Tribal Areas*, 56.
12. Ibid., 11.
13. Ibid., 11–12.
14. For the claimed successful results of the policy, see ibid., 12–13.
15. Also see Awan, *Pattern of Administration in the Tribal Areas of Pakistan*, 15–17.
16. F.A.K. Harrison, 'The British Interest in the North West Frontier', *Peshawar University Review* (Peshawar), vol. 1 (No. 1, 1974–75), 55.
17. Ibid.
18. Dr Muhammad Anwar Khan has mistaken the Frontier Regions for the Provincially Administered Tribal Areas (PATA), and hence has stated: 'The provincial administered area [Provincially Administered Tribal Areas] (PATA), also called Frontier Region are

tribes and clans contiguous or lying within a district. These regions are four in number and are administered by the deputy commissioner of the district. They are (i) F.R. Peshawar concerned with Mohmand and Afridis (ii) F.R. Kohat dealing with Afridis of Dara Adam Khel (iii) F.R. Bannu governing Bhittani, and Wazir tribes of the district and (iv) F.R. Dera Ismail Khan relating to Bhittani and Sherani tribesmen. In a way the provincial chief minister is concerned with the Frontier Region tribes, while the governor carries responsibility for the tribal belt located on the Durand border.' Muhammad Anwar Khan, *The Role of N.W.F.P. in the Freedom Struggle* (Lahore: RSP, 2000), 11.

19. See 'The Interim Constitution of the Islamic Republic of Pakistan [1972]' in *The All Pakistan Legal Decisions* [henceforward *PLD*], vol. 24 (1972), Central Statutes, 579–80.

20. See Muhammad Munir, *Constitution of the Islamic Republic of Pakistan: Being a Commentary on the Constitution of Pakistan, 1973*, ed. Mian Bashir Ahmad, vol. 2, *[Art. 185–Subject Index]* (Lahore: P.L.D. Publishers, 1996), 1359–62; Safdar Mahmood, *Constitutional Foundations of Pakistan (Revised and Enlarged)* (Lahore: Jang Publishers, 1997), 969–71.

21. *PLD*, vol. 59 (2007), Peshawar, 45–6.

22. Ibid., 49. Also see 46.

23. Also see ibid., 45–9.

24. Ibid., 49.

25. Also see *Tribal Areas*, 11, 15, 60–1.

26. *PLD*, vol. 59 (2007), Peshawar, 50.

27. See 'Establishment of West Pakistan Act, 1955' in *PLD*, vol. 7 (1955), Central Acts and Notifications, 273–4. Also see *PLD*, vol. 59 (2007), Peshawar, 51.

28. See 'The Constitution of the Islamic Republic of Pakistan [1956]' in *PLD*, vol. 8 (1956), Central Acts and Notifications, 120–1, 88–9. Also see Mahmood, *Constitutional Foundations of Pakistan (Revised and Enlarged)*, 307–8, 275.

29. See 'Constitution of the Republic of Pakistan, 1962' in *PLD*, vol. 14 (1962), Central Statutes, 206, 215. Also see Mahmood, *Constitutional Foundations of Pakistan (Revised and Enlarged)*, 620, 608.

30. See 'The Interim Constitution of the Islamic Republic of Pakistan [1972]' in *PLD*, vol. 24 (1972), Central Statutes, 579–80. Also see Mahmood, *Constitutional Foundations of Pakistan (Revised and Enlarged)*, 752–3.

31. See Munir, *Constitution of the Islamic Republic of Pakistan*, vol. 2, 1359–62. Also see Mahmood, *Constitutional Foundations of Pakistan (Revised and Enlarged)*, 969–71.

32. *Tribal Areas*, 13.

33. Ibid., 15.

34. Ibid., 16.

35. Ibid., 17.

36. See ibid., 18–19.

37. This assertion of Dr Muhammad Anwar Khan's, that 'Malakand agency since placed inside the N.W.F.P. remained provincial subject while those located on the border, termed Durand Line since 1893, became part of the Indian foreign affairs concern and treated as central government issue' (Khan, *The Role of N.W.F.P. in the Freedom Struggle*, 5) did not stand up to review.

38. Also see Sher Muhammad Mohmand, *FATA (Federally Administered Tribal Areas of Pakistan): A Socio-Cultural and Geo-Political History* [henceforward Mohmand, *FATA*] (n.p., n.d.), ii–iii.

39. Also see Awan, *Pattern of Administration in the Tribal Areas of Pakistan*, 29–31.

40. Mohmand, *FATA*, iii.

41. Awan, *Pattern of Administration in the Tribal Areas of Pakistan*, 30–1.

42. Also see Sultan-i-Rome, '*Pukhtu*: The *Pukhtun* Code of Life', *Pakistan Vision* (Lahore), vol. 7 (No. 2, December 2006), 1–30.

43. Awan, *Pattern of Administration in the Tribal Areas of Pakistan*, 18.

44. See *Tribal Areas*, 65; Awan, *Pattern of Administration in the Tribal Areas of Pakistan*, 20.

45. Mohmand, *FATA*, iv.

46. Awan, *Pattern of Administration in the Tribal Areas of Pakistan*, 20.

47. *Tribal Areas*, 64.

48. Awan, *Pattern of Administration in the Tribal Areas of Pakistan*, 20–1.

49. Ibid., 20.

50. Ibid., 21.

51. Ibid., 21–2.

52. Ibid., 22.

53. *Administration Report of the North-West Frontier Province from 9th November 1901 to 31st March 1903* (Peshawar: Printed at the North-West Frontier Province Government Press, 1903), 6. Also see C. Collin Davies, *The Problem of the North-West Frontier, 1890–1908: With a survey of policy since 1849*, 2nd edn., rev. and enlarged (London: CPL, 1975), 24.

54. Mohmand, *FATA*, vi–vii. For the formation, structure, and role of the militias, also see Elliott, *The Frontier*, 95–6.

55. Mohmand, *FATA*, vii-viii. For instances of the scouts mobility, success, and working, also see Elliott, *The Frontier*, 96.

56. Mohmand, *FATA*, viii–ix.

57. Ibid., ix.

58. *Tribal Areas*, 66–7.

59. Awan, *Pattern of Administration in the Tribal Areas of Pakistan*, 23–4.

60. Mohmand, *FATA*, x.

61. *Tribal Areas*, 65.

62. Mohmand, *FATA*, x–xi.

63. Ibid., xi.

64. Ibid., xi–xii.

65. Elliott, *The Frontier*, 96–7.

66. Mohmand, *FATA*, xii–xiii.

67. Olaf Caroe, *The Pathans: 550 B.C.–A.D. 1957*, repr. (Karachi: OUP, 1976), 348.

68. Ibid.

69. Elliott, *The Frontier*, 94.

70. Awan, *Pattern of Administration in the Tribal Areas of Pakistan*, 24–5.

71. Ibid., 25.

72. Ibid., 25–6.

73. Elliott, *The Frontier*, 94–5.

74. Ibid., 95.

75. See Awan, *Pattern of Administration in the Tribal Areas of Pakistan*, 28.

76. Ibid., 29.

77. Also see ibid.

78. Notification, No. 1117/Legal, Peshawar, dated 6 March 2019, Extraordinay, Registered No. P.III, Government Gazette, Published by Authority, Peshawar, Friday, 8 March 2019, Office of Provincial Police Officer, Khyber Pakhtunkhwa.

79. Notification, No. 1114/Legal, Peshawar, dated 6 March 2019, Extraordinay, Registered No. P.III, Government Gazette, Published by Authority, Peshawar, Friday, 8 March 2019, Office of Provincial Police Officer, Khyber Pakhtunkhwa.

80. *Tribal Areas*, 64–5.

81. See Awan, *Pattern of Administration in the Tribal Areas of Pakistan*, 33. Also see Elliott, *The Frontier*, 71; Arthur Swinson, *North-West Frontier: People and Events, 1839–1947* (London: Hutchinson & Co (Publishers) Ltd, 1967), 251.

82. Awan, *Pattern of Administration in the Tribal Areas of Pakistan*, 33.

83. Caroe, *The Pathans*, 349. For instances of such agreements, see S. Fida Yunas and Sher Zaman Taizi, eds., *Treaties, Engagements and Sanads Relating to the North West Frontier Province: Covering the Period upto 1930 based on the Mr C.W. Aitchison's Compilation (Reprint of Relevant Portions)* (Peshawar: Area Study Centre (Russia, China & Central Asia), University of Peshawar, n.d.), passim.

84. Caroe, *The Pathans*, 349–50. For instances of such treaties, see Yunas and Sher Zaman Taizi, eds., *Treaties, Engagements and Sanads Relating to the North West Frontier Province*, passim. Also see Elliott, *The Frontier*, 71; Davies, *The Problem of the North-West Frontier*, 139.

85. Caroe, *The Pathans*, 350.

86. Elliott, *The Frontier*, 71.

87. Khan, *The Role of N.W.F.P. in the Freedom Struggle*, 7.

88. Caroe, *The Pathans*, 350.

89. Awan, *Pattern of Administration in the Tribal Areas of Pakistan*, 34.

90. Ibid.

91. Caroe, *The Pathans*, 355. Also see Elliott, *The Frontier*, 77; Swinson, *North-West Frontier*, 251; Harrison, 'The British Interest in the North West Frontier', 48.

92. Awan, *Pattern of Administration in the Tribal Areas of Pakistan*, 39.

93. See Khan Zafar Ali Khan, Khan Abdul Aziz Khan, and Ghulam Habib Khan, *Riwaj Namah Malakand Agency* (Urdu) (Peshawar: Manzur-i Aam Press, 1964). A customary law book of the former Swat State (1915–1969 CE) areas was also compiled by Ghulam Habib Khan (Superintendent, Deputy Commissioner Office, Swat), in 1973, entitled *Riwaj Namah-i Swat* (customary law book of Swat), which according to Muhammad Asif Khan, is not *Riwaj Namah* (customary law book) but *Mizaj Namah* (temperament law book) as it contains the decisions/verdicts/orders that the Wali Sahib (Miangul Jahanzeb, ruler of Swat State, who ruled from 12 December 1949 till 15 August 1969) made according to his temperament. (Muhammad Asif Khan, interview by the author, at Saidu Sharif, Swat, 24 May 1998).

94. *Tribal Areas*, 58.

95. James W. Spain, *The Pathan Borderland*, repr. (Karachi: IP, 1985), 145. For details about the set or series of the Frontier Crimes Regulation and the correspondence in this respect, see Robert Nichols, ed., *The Frontier Crimes Regulation: A History in Documents* (Karachi: OUP, 2013).

96. Caroe, *The Pathans*, 353.

97. Ibid., 354.

98. Ibid.

99. Mohmand, *FATA*, xvi.

100. Ibid., xvii.

101. Ibid.

102. See Munir, *Constitution of the Islamic Republic of Pakistan*, vol. 2, 1361–2. Also see Mahmood, *Constitutional Foundations of Pakistan (Revised and Enlarged)*, 970.

103. Awan, *Pattern of Administration in the Tribal Areas of Pakistan*, 32.

104. Notification, No. SO(J)HD/3-71/2019, dated Peshawar 29 January 2019, Home & Tribal Affairs Department, Government of Khyber Pakhtunkhwa.

105. Order, No. SO (Judl)/HD/2019/Vol-I, dated Peshawar 21 February 2019, Home & Tribal Affairs Department, Government of Khyber Pakhtunkhwa.

106. 'The Khyber Pakhtunkhwa Continuation of Laws in Erstwhile Federally Administered Tribal Areas Bill, 2019 (Khyber Pakhtunkhwa Act No. XXIV of 2019)', Gazette of the Khyber Pakhtunkhwa, Extraordinary, dated 3 May 2019.
107. Mohmand, *FATA*, iii.
108. For details about aspects such as education, health, communication, and agriculture, see Mohmand, *FATA*.
109. *Tribal Areas*, 67.
110. Ibid.
111. Ibid.
112. Mohmand, *FATA*, xiii.
113. *Tribal Areas*, 14–15.
114. Ibid., 2.

13 Role of Sahibzadah Abdul Qayyum in Politics and Promotion of Education

Sir Abdul Qayyum was certainly the first statesman of his time in NWFP.
– George Cunningham

Sir Sahibzada Abdul Qaiyum, [was] a clear-headed moderate statesman, a man gifted with vision and foresight, and withal a man of singularly charming manners.
– Abdul Qaiyum [Khan]

SAHIBZADAH (commonly spelled as Sahibzada) Abdul Qayyum was a descendant of Ibrahim Ludi's family. When Ibrahim Ludi (Lodi) was defeated by Zahiruddin Babur at the First Battle of Panipat in 1526, some of his family members went to Afghanistan and settled there. Abdul Karim, a scion of the family, accompanied Ahmad Shah Abdali on his Indian campaign in 1758, and stayed behind, settling on the bank of Indus. He later moved and settled in the village of Tupai (Topai) in the Swabi (Swabai) area. Being a religious figure, he became well known in the surrounding areas and his descendants were given the title of Sahibzadah. Some prominent religious figures have emerged among his descendants, one of whom was Sahibzadah Abdur Rawuf.[1]

Abdur Rawuf married the daughter of his maternal uncle, a prominent religious figure of the Frontier—Syed Amir of Kutah, Swabi. A son was born to them in 1863 and was named Sahibzadah Abdul Qayyum. Abdul Qayyum was three years old when his mother died, and so was brought up by his sister. On 19 August 1873, his father was stabbed to death, and, hence, his maternal uncle, Syed Ahmad, brought both Sahibzadah Qayyum and his sister to his home in Kutah. Sahibzadah Abdul Qayyum was admitted to the primary school in Kutah, where his maternal uncle himself was a teacher; attention was paid to his education and training. On completing his primary education, Sahibzadah Abdul Qayyum was appointed as a teacher at the primary school in Marghuz. However, he left the service and went to Peshawar for higher education, on the advice, and promise of help, of a Christian missionary and priest, Hughes.[2]

In Peshawar, at first, he lived in Upper Tahkal with a disciple of his father, and received religious education from him for some time. He then moved to Yakatut, where he stayed with Mawlana Ghulam Hasan, followed by some time in Darbangi. While a student at the Mission School in Peshawar—to which he was admitted with Hughes' help—he would visit Muslim scholars after school for further religious education. Hughes stayed in touch, visiting him regularly and constantly encouraging him in his endeavours. A number of other people also assisted the Sahibzadah, in their own ways, during his studies in Peshawar—these included Mawlana Ghulam Hasan Niyazi (Niazi), Mawlana Nurul Hasan, Mawlwi Nur Muhammad, Arbab Saadat Ali Khan (Arbab Sikandar Khan Khalil's father), and Mirza Muhammad Ismail.[3]

Sahibzadah Qayyum was selected for the course of *naib tahsildar*, on 3 December 1887, after passing the secondary school exam from the Mission School. On completion of the course, he was appointed to the commissioner's office in Peshawar. Because of his fluency in translating from English to Pukhtu and vice versa, he gained prominence in the commissioner's office. He worked under the Deputy Commissioner Hazarah, Mr Udney, at the time of the Black Mountain expedition of 1888; and having served meritoriously, he was posted as superintendent in the commissioner's office at the end of the expedition.[4]

On 21 January 1890, he was selected for a course on land settlement in the revenue department, and was sent to Sialkot for three months' training. On completion of the course, he was appointed *girdawar* in Kuhat, and was later made *naib tahsildar* in Miranzai in 1891, at the time of the Samana War. Following meritorious service during the Samana expedition, he served in the Kurram Agency as settlement *tahsildar*, revenue officer, and accounts officer, playing a vital role in defusing anti-British sentiment in the area. During this period, he developed friendship with Roos-Keppel,[5] a British officer in the Frontier.

He also worked as assistant political agent in the Afghan Boundary Commission at the time of the Durand Line demarcation, and later as superintendent and political assistant with Sir Richard Edney for the demarcation of the boundary at Asmar. On completion of the Boundary Commission's work, he was, again, appointed as superintendent in the commissioner's office in Peshawar. He defused tensions and normalised relations between the British and the Muhmand, and the British and the

Afridi. During this period, he received recognition for his services to the British; the title of Khan Bahadar was bestowed on him for his services at the time of the Tirah expedition of 1897.[6]

Although he was transferred to the Punjab area in 1898, Sahibzadah Abdul Qayyum was soon appointed as the assistant political agent of Khyber Agency, where his close friend Roos-Keppel was the political agent. Sahibzadah Abdul Qayyum remained in the service of the British, in the last years of his career in the capacity of political agent, Khyber Agency, until his retirement in 1919.[7] He was 'a clear-headed moderate statesman, a man gifted with vision and foresight, and withal a man of singularly charming manners'.[8]

ROLE IN POLITICS

Sahibzadah Abdul Qayyum, who served the British colonial[9] government for many years in various capacities, retired from their service in 1919. During his service tenure, he indirectly played a part in politics. For instance, when 'in 1914, the Muslim Educational Conference, originally planned for Peshawar held its sitting...in Rawalpindi', he was among those who 'are reported to have participated in it' from the Frontier.[10] However, his active and direct political role started after his retirement.

It was under his leadership that the Muslim Association was founded in the Frontier, in 1922, through which the struggle for the extension of political reforms to the province began.[11] When members of the Bray Committee visited the Frontier Province in May 1922, to interview people and inquire about the various issues of the province, Sahibzadah Abdul Qayyum was among those who were consulted. He, 'like some other Muslim elite of the area wanted share [for the Frontier]...in the forthcoming reforms',[12] and pleaded for the same before the Bray Committee as well. He was nominated as a member of the central legislature of India, from the Frontier, in 1924 and retained the position till 1932. Diwan Chand Obhrai admits: 'He was one of the leading members of the Central Legislative Assembly when representing the N.-W. F. Province as its sole nominated member.'[13] In this capacity, he strived for the extension of reforms to the Frontier Province, voiced the rights of the province, and played a role at an all-India level.

He 'often advocated in the legislature the cause of the extension of constitutional reforms to N. W. F. P'.[14] When, on 16 February 1926, Sayyad Murtaza Bahadur presented a resolution in the central legislature of India, asking the colonial government to extend some provisions of the

Government of India Act of 1919 to the Frontier Province—to grant the province the right to form a legislative council and cabinet—Sahibzadah Qayyum spoke in its favour when it was put up for discussion in the assembly in March, pleading the case of the province in the strongest words and a logical manner.[15]

In 1926, Sahibzadah Abdul Qayyum was among the fourteen-member central committee of All India Muslim League, at the same time being a member of its provincial committee.[16] The *khilafatists* invited Jamiat-ul-Ulamay-i Hind to hold its annual session in Peshawar at the end of 1927. To make the meeting a success, the organisers searched for a person who could become president of the welcoming committee and also be a bridge between the colonial British government and the Jamiat. They selected Sahibzadah Qayyum, to be the president, and he performed his duties efficiently and effectively.[17]

He pleaded the case of the Frontier Province at each and every forum, particularly for granting reforms and bringing the province on a par with the other provinces of British India. In Olaf Caroe's words:

> In season and out, Abdul Qayyum pressed for recognition of his point that the Pathan province, if to remain as part of an all-India polity, must share in the general measures for the extension of responsible government. He never tired of saying that, far from being behind other peoples in the sub-continent in their understanding of political and egalitarian concepts, they were in fact in advance. They had their own indigenous system by which they chose representatives and ordered their affairs.[18]

Sahibzadah Abdul Qayyum was nominated as the sole member to represent the Frontier Province at the Round Table Conferences, arranged in London, to seek solutions for Indian constitutional problems in a manner that would be acceptable to all the stakeholders and parties. He, 'apart from the intensive lobbying in London',[19] also pleaded the case of the Province efficiently and effectively. When, against the extension of reforms to the Frontier, it was argued that 'the province was too small for representative institutions', his reply, 'in his inimitable way', included the remark, 'a flea might be a small creature, but in his country they found it very inconvenient inside their trousers'.[20]

He cleared obstacles, in the way of the extension of reforms and the granting of responsible government to the province, by effectively participating in the proceedings at all the forums of the First Round Table Conference—where the issue of the Frontier Province was addressed. He was nominated as a member of the Frontier Subject Committee, formed in

1931 following the decision of the Round Table Conference to determine the spheres of the centre and the province in accordance with the decision of Sub-Committee No. 5 at the First Round Table Conference. He again represented the province at the Second Round Table Conference, where he once again skilfully pleaded the case of the province.[21]

In light of the recommendations of the Franchise Committee of the Second Round Table Conference, a committee was formed to submit a comprehensive report to the British parliament about electoral procedures, criteria for voters, and allocation of seats in the assemblies in India; when a provincial committee was formed in the Frontier Province to facilitate the work of the British committee, Sahibzadah Qayyum was nominated to be its member.[22]

As a result of the struggles of Sahibzadah Abdul Qayyum and others at the various forums, the status of the Frontier Province was raised to that of a full-fledged or governor province in 1932, thus bringing the province on a par with the other provinces of British India from the constitutional and political stand-points. On raising the status of the province to a governor province, elections to the provincial legislative council were held in 1932. Not only did Sahibzadah Qayyum win the seat on the legislative council unopposed, he was also appointed the sole in-charge minister of the transferred departments. He served in this capacity until 1936, and, hence, had the privilege of being the first minister of the province.

The members of the legislative council were divided into four groups— Liberal Party, Progressive Party, Azad Party, and Hindu Sikh Party; Sahibzadah Abdul Qayyum headed the progressive element.[23] Although they had boycotted the election for the provincial legislative council, the Khudayi Khidmatgars-Congress decided to contest the elections for the provincial elected member seat in the central legislature, under the Government of India Act of 1919. In spite of certain failure, Sahibzadah Qayyum's party in the council decided to contest the election against Dr Khan Sahib—the Khudayi Khidmatgars-Congress nominee—so that Dr Khan Sahib would not succeed unopposed, and so nominated Raja Haidar Zaman Khan.[24]

Muhammad Shafi Sabir states that the province was raised to the status of a full-fledged province on 31 December 1931, that Sahibzadah Qayyum was elected the first chief minister of the province after the election for the legislative council, and that in 1936 he became the chief minister of the province for the second time.[25] In fact, the province was raised to the status of a full-fledged province in 1932, and Sahibzadah Qayyum became the sole minister of the transferred departments after the election for the legislative council. Also, there was no chief minister in the legislative councils under the Government of India Act of 1919.[26]

While he was minister in-charge of the transferred departments, Sahibzadah Qayyum 'moved a resolution in the [legislative] Council on 12 November 1936 for the withdrawal of prohibitory orders on Abdul Ghaffar Khan'. He asked the colonial British government, 'whether the aspiration of a country for independence is to be considered a crime'. And reminded them that 'each and every *Khudai Khidmatgar* in this province...each and every inhabitant of this province has that aspiration in his heart'.[27]

During this period, the council dealt with problems, provided a basis for development, abolished social evils, and worked towards economic rather than cultural development—as is apparent on comparison of the proceedings of the budget sessions for the years 1932 and 1936.[28]

Sahibzadah Abdul Qayyum formed the Muslim Independent Party, which was joined by some prominent figures from different parts of the province. The party invited Muhammad Ali Jinnah, president of the All India Muslim League, to visit Peshawar. He came to the province on a week-long visit in October 1936. During his visit, the Sahibzadah provided him with a car for his use and invited him to stay at his house in Yakatut, Peshawar.[29] When Jinnah suggested that he contest the elections of 1937 on party basis, i.e. from the Muslim League platform, Sahibzadah Abdul Qayyum told him that, in that case, it would first be necessary to organise the party in the province—which was not possible in the three months left before the elections. However, he said, in the event that the Frontier Muslims contested the election from the League's platform, he would support the League.[30]

In the elections held in the province in February 1937, under the Government of India Act of 1935, Sahibzadah Qayyum contested from two constituencies—one, his home constituency of Tupai, Swabi, and the other that of Khanpur, Hazarah. His rival Khudayi Khidmatgar-Congress candidate beat him in his home constituency, but he defeated the Khudayi Khidmatgar-Congress candidate on the Khanpur seat and became an independent member of the provincial legislature.[31]

Although they did not have absolute majority, the Khudayi Khidmatgars-Congress emerged as the largest party in the provincial legislature. However, they failed to form the government because of deadlock with the colonial government over certain aspects of the Government of India Act of 1935. Although Sahibzadah Abdul Qayyum had won the election as independent candidate, he formed a party in the assembly called the United Muslim Nationalist Party, with the overt goal of 'complete independence by all constitutional means'. Its members, however, had 'no common programme' and joined him 'for the sake of office and power'.[32] With the assistance of the provincial governor, he succeeded in winning the support of the Hindu-Sikh Nationalist Party on their terms, and also of some independent members, and formed the government, which he headed as the chief minister. The ministers took oath of office of their portfolios on 1 April 1937.[33] Sahibzadah Qayyum, thus, became the first chief minister of the province. Allah Bakhsh Yusufi has referred to the party—the Mutahidah Muslim Taraqi Pasand or the United Muslim Progressive Party—formed by Sahibzadah Abdul Qayyum in the assembly, as the Nawab Party. The party had the support of sixteen members in the legislature.[34]

Sahibzadah Abdul Qayyum, however, 'was unable to improve his position in the five months before the next assembly session, even with the active assistance of Cunningham [the governor] and the permanent administration'.[35] On the other hand, All India National Congress and the colonial authorities came to an understanding on an all-India level due to which Congress formed ministries in provinces where they held the majority in the provincial legislatures, and tried to do the same in the Frontier Province. Erland Jansson, on the authority of the 'Governor's Report', states that when the colonial authorities and Congress came to terms, Sahibzadah Qayyum 'considered tendering his resignation without even facing the assembly, but encouraged by the governor he decided to battle on'.[36] On reaching an understanding with the Hindu-Sikh Nationalist Party and the Hazarah group of the Hazarah Democratic Party, a no-confidence motion was sent to the governor, against the ministry, by the opposition leader Dr Khan Sahib (Sayb, Saib). Sahibzadah Qayyum 'made last minute efforts and met some members of the Khudai Khidmatgar[s] and reminding them of his past services for the welfare of the Pashtoons, tried to dissuade them from moving a vote of no-confidence',[37] but to no avail. Allah Bakhsh Yusufi contends that despite being aware of his weak position in the assembly, after Congress came to terms with other groups/parties/members, Sahibzadah Abdul Qayyum refused to resign. He preferred to face a no-confidence motion to identify those who were overtly demonstrating loyalty to him but had covertly made terms with the Congress.[38] Interestingly, it was Sahibzadah Abdul Qayyum who, on 22 August 1937, had 'lifted all restrictions' on the 'political activities' of the Frontier Congress-Khudai Khidmatgars and 'allowed Abdul Ghaffar Khan to return to the province'.[39]

On 3 September 1937, the motion was placed before the assembly; only the opposition leader, Dr Khan Sahib, and the leader of the house, Sahibzadah Abdul Qayyum, spoke over the subject. In his speech on the no-confidence motion, among his other points, the Sahibzadah said:

> Times were when waves from the cool north swept over the country to the south thereby lending fresh vigour to the old and rather worn out culture and civilisation of India, but my friends would now have me believe that we must henceforth draw our inspiration from the torrid south which will in its turn send its monsoons of modern conceptions of social and economic values and of new tendencies towards the centralization of authority and a blending of culture.[40]

The motion was passed by 27 votes to 22[41] the same day, with which his ministry came to an end. However, not only was Congress' justification for accepting the 'office without a clear elected majority' of its own, 'on grounds of "special circumstances",' questionable[42] but also the manner in which the support of the majority of the members was achieved.

In the short period of his chief ministership, Sahibzadah Qayyum abrogated the infamous Frontier Crimes Regulation, 1901,[43] except for a few articles. In dealing with political prisoners, those under surveillance, and the exiled and different political parties, his ministry—despite been considered loyal to the British—did not lag behind the Congress ministries. It took the bold steps of lifting 'the ban on political externees, including Abdul Ghaffar Khan and Allama Mashriqi, and withdrew all notices under the Public Tranquillity Act... The ban on *Naujawan Bharat Sabha* was also lifted.'[44]

Before the fall of his ministry, having noted Congress' manoeuvrings against him, Sahibzadah Qayyum endeavoured to organise the Muslim League in the province. He deliberated with the members of the Muslim Association, and decided to initiate the work from Abbottabad, and not from the assembly members but from the masses. He sent Qazi Abdul Hakim, a contractor from Jaluzai, to Peshawar to summon prominent religious figures to Abbottabad for the purpose. Qazi Hakim returned with Mawlana Muhammad Shuaib, Abdul Khaliq Khaleeq, Sultan Shah, and Mawlana Shakirullah. And so, with the full support of Sahibzadah Qayyum, some prominent *ulama* from Peshawar, Mardan, and Hazarah, and other people gathered in the hall of Islamia High School, Hazarah. A meeting was held, chaired by Abdul Khaliq Khaleeq, at which members of the Muslim League's provincial organisation were elected, and an action plan for the provincial elections and to organise the League at district levels was chalked out. Sahibzadah Abdul Qayyum met, from his own pocket, all the expenses of those brought to Abbottabad, from Peshawar, Mardan, and Nawkhar (Nawshirah, Nowshera), to organise the League.[45]

Sahibzadah Abdul Qayyum asked his friends and members of the Muslim Association to extend their cooperation in organising the League. It was decided to send invitations, to attend the League conference in Peshawar, to prominent figures in the province; Mian Ziauddin was authorised to make the arrangements for the conference and to announce its date and venue. Initial arrangements were in progress when Sahibzadah Qayyum fell seriously ill. But, following his instructions, a meeting of some of the prominent figures of the province was held at the residence of Mian Ziauddin, at which a date for the proposed meeting to organise the League was fixed. Sahibzadah Qayyum was informed of the proceedings of the meeting. However, he died on 4 December 1937, before the scheduled date of the meeting.[46] 'His death left the Congress the "virtual masters of the province",' reported the daily *Khyber Mail*.[47]

Sahibzadah Abdul Qayyum had guided and instructed even those with whom he had no outward links, when he deemed it to be in the interest of the province and its progress, and thus played an indirect role in the province's politics as well. For instance, the government arranged a warm reception for the Prince of Wales (Edward—the future Edward VIII) on 6 May 1922 during his visit to Peshawar. However, adherents of the *khilafat* movement resolved to make it a failure and, hence, chalked out a programme for a general strike in the city on that day. Sahibzadah Qayyum secretly told the *khilafatist* leaders of the city that if they were sure of a successful strike, well and good, otherwise they should not waste their power and energy. Although he outwardly asked the leaders not to go on strike, in fact, he wished a successful strike, claims Allah Bakhsh Yusufi, as it would be beneficial to the province.[48] He even apprised the Khudayi Khidmatgars in 1930 of the whims and ill intentions of the colonial government and asked them to join the Congress.[49] And when, in 1931, the colonial government, after making terms with Gandhi, wanted to make separate terms with the Khudayi Khidmatgars, he told them to refuse and to tell the government that Gandhi was the leader of all India and that they had trust in him.[50] Besides—as stated earlier in Chapter 9—when it was propagated that Ghaffar Khan was parting ways with the Congress, he sent an envoy to Lahore to ask him not to do so because the British would then give nothing to the Frontier Province.[51]

ROLE IN PROMOTION OF EDUCATION

A 'great educationist of the Province', asserts Qaiyum Khan, Sahibzadah Abdul Qayyum 'was the first to realize that without education the Pathans would be nowhere in a world fast moving ahead'.[52] Sahibzadah Qayyum's educational services started when he, along with Qazi Abdul Ghani, assisted Roos-Keppel in writing a Pukhtu manual of grammar in 1898, which was published in 1901. Sahibzadah Qayyum was still in the service of the colonial government when the British government denied the constitutional reforms of 1909 to the Frontier Province on the plea that the people of the Frontier were backward and uneducated. He, therefore, endeavoured to educate the people of the province on modern lines, so that they would qualify for the reforms and rights from the British. For this purpose, he asked George Roos-Keppel—now the chief commissioner of the province, who himself wished to educate the people of the Frontier along modern lines—to strive, on an official level, to establish a Darul Ulum (college) in the Frontier.[53]

On 9 August 1909, the annual meeting of the Anjuman Himayat-ul-Islam was held at Islamia High School Peshawar, presided over by the Chief Commissioner—Roos-Keppel. The audience appealed to Roos-Keppel to pursue, on an official level, the establishment of the Darul Ulum in the province so that the children of the Frontier could also have access to higher education. Responding to their appeal, Roos-Keppel assured the audience that he would consider their request sympathetically but, at the same time, told them that the opinion of the people of the Frontier may be sought lest the establishment of the college create troubles for the government, as the people were allergic to modern education. Hence, Qazi Muhammad Akbar, Secretary of Anjuman Himayat-ul-Islam, issued an appeal to the people of the Frontier asking them to assist fully in establishing the college for higher studies. The response was positive, and people from all corners of the province promised assistance. The landlords even demonstrated a willingness to pay an extra tax of one *anna* (*anah*) per rupee (1/16 rupee) to the land revenue, for the establishment of the Darul Ulum.[54]

In the meantime, students from the Frontier studying at Aligarh College invited Roos-Keppel and Sahibzadah Abdul Qayyum to a function, when the latter were en route to Calcutta (Kolkata). The students collected a donation of 100 rupees, and handed it to Roos-Keppel and Sahibzadah Qayyum, with the request that a hostel be constructed in Aligarh for students from the Frontier, or a Darul Ulum be established in the Frontier so that students from the Frontier would not have to face any problems when they have to travel far from home to study. Roos-Keppel assured them that he was already striving to establish the Darul Ulum in the Frontier. At the same time, Mr Merk, the acting chief commissioner, was informed of the people's positive response to Qazi Muhammad Akbar's appeal and was asked to extend all possible help from the government. The preliminary arrangements for the Darul Ulum began. Dr Ansari, teacher of Islamic Studies at Aligarh Muslim College, went to Peshawar on 18 January 1910, to discuss the Islamic Studies course of the Darul Ulum. The chief commissioner told Dr Ansari, at a meeting with him, that first the land will have to be acquired for the Darul Ulum, after which construction, and other details could be chalked out. The proposal was agreed to by the delegation accompanying Dr Ansari, and efforts began to acquire the land. Different sites were considered but were not selected or acquired for one reason or the other. At last, a committee was formed to manage the acquisition of the land and construction of the college. Sahibzadah Qayyum was made honorary secretary of the committee.[55]

A meeting of the notables of Peshawar, chaired by Sahibzadah Qayyum, was held at the residence of Abdul Karim, a contractor of Peshawar, after the formation of the committee. The meeting appealed for donations to meet the initial expenses of the construction of the Darul Ulum. The response was positive from the audience. In 1911, an open plain in Upper Tahkal was selected for the building, for which the owners demanded 30,166 rupees for the 916 kanal and 17 marla (marlah) land. The response to the appeal, for donations to purchase the land, was excellent—812,466 rupees, 5 anahs (in Pukhtu: anay), and 2 paisas (paisahs; in Pukhtu: paisay) were collected by May 1912.[56] Interestingly, the Nawab of Dir, Aurangzeb Khan (also known as Bacha Khan and Chara Nawab), who ignored education in his own state, also announced a donation of 150,000 rupees for the Darul Ulum.[57]

In the meantime, Sahibzadah Qayyum was posted at Chitral in 1910, but because of his efforts towards the construction of the Darul Ulum, Roos-Keppel soon posted him at the Khyber Agency as political agent. On 29 May 1911, caretaker members were selected for the establishment and construction of the Darul Ulum, at a meeting held at the Victoria Memorial Hall of the current Peshawar Museum; 21 March 1912 was fixed as the date for laying the foundation stone. People from different segments and walks of life were invited—about 30,000 people assembled at the appointed day and place. After the initial proceedings, at the request of Sahibzadah Qayyum, Fazl-i Wahid (also known as Haji Sahib of Turangzi)—a renowned religious figure of the Frontier Province—laid the inscription at the appointed place and all the other *ulama* and *mashaikh* laid a brick each on the foundation, as per the request of the Sahibzadah.[58] However, on the arrival of Roos-Keppel and other British officers at this juncture, Haji Sahib of Turangzi expressed his disapproval and left the site in protest along with his disciples. After the ceremony, Sahibzadah Qayyum handed over the design of the Darul Ulum to the engineer, and the colonial government granted 200,000 rupees for the purpose of construction.[59] However, Dr Lal Baha—who was working on a book on Islamia College—contended that Haji Sahib of Turangzi laid the foundation stone of the mosque of the Islamia College, Roos-Keppel (chief commissioner, NWFP) laid the foundation stone of the college building, and Butler (education member of the viceroy's council) laid the foundation stone of the Islamia Collegiate School.[60]

Due to the status and influence of both Roos-Keppel and Sahibzadah Qayyum—the people behind the college scheme—the colonial government did not impose strict or hard conditions for its financial support of the Darul Ulum, except that the deputy commissioner Peshawar, inspector-general police, chief commander, royal engineers, chief medical officers, etc. should be included in its organising committee.[61] On 23 May 1912, the organising committee of the Darul Ulum held its meeting at which an appeal was made to the government, through a resolution, to grant more funds for the college expenses; in another resolution, Sahibzadah Qayyum was thanked for all the considerable efforts he undertook on an honorary basis for the Darul Ulum.[62] Sahibzadah Qayyum later stated in a speech that he had inherited the idea of the establishment of the Islamia College, from the Christian missionaries' passion for service, during his student life.[63] According to Olaf Caroe, Roos-Keppel

> had his dreams, and the greatest of them, the Islamia College, saw the light of day. In this creative effort—perhaps his only labour of love—as in his paternal dealings with the Afridis in the Khaibar, he found an unfailing helper in Sahibzada Abdul Qayyum…, his chosen interpreter and at one time almost his second self.[64]

At first, the name of the college was Darul Ulum Islamia Sarhad but it later came to be known as the Islamia College. Sahibzadah Abdul Qayyum, who remained its honorary secretary until his death, continuously struggled for its development.[65] On the completion of the construction work of Islamia Collegiate School and the college buildings in 1913, regular classes were started, both at the school and the college, at the start of the school and college sessions.[66]

In his account of Roos-Keppel and Sahibzadah Abdul Qayyum, Caroe further states:

> Together they created the Islamia College, now grown into the University of Peshawar. That is their joint and visible monument, the tribute to their foresight and wisdom. No man who was not great, whose imagination did not soar, would have founded a great place of learning on the very margin of the cultivated lands, overlooked by the black jaws of Khaibar, open maybe to raiders, on the very site of the furious battle between Akbar Khan and Hari Singh. Yet this is what they did, and they planned well. The white mosque, the centre of a cluster of russet buildings, proclaims a sanctuary that no raider dare violate. Since R-K's [Roos-Keppel's] day that mosque, once seen as soon as the traveller turns the last curve of Khaibar, has come to be embowered in groves of cypress and other trees, but it remains the symbol of an inspiration that has finally given birth to a university.[67]

Interestingly, to some anti-British elements, the establishment of Islamia College Peshawar meant a nest to produce British loyalists. They thought of the college, 'to all intents and purposes', as 'a political college having a body of European civil and military officers including the Inspector General of Police in the Committee. With Khan Bahadur Sahibzada Abdul Qayooum Khan, Assistant Political Officer of the Khyber Pass, as official secretary.' The Muslim members of its committee, in their opinion, were 'only two bankers after titles (a pleader and a Barrister), the rest being tehsildars, E.A.C. and men in service'. They held the view that the college 'will educate people; but it has stopped people from going to Aligarh, and other places' and expressed the fear that 'thus free education will disappear'.[68] Dr Muhammad Anwar Khan asserts:

> Roos-Keppel always thought that [the] Frontier was north-westerly and not south-easterly in its outlook and the Pathan could only be tamed to civility with greater watch. The foundation of Islamia collegiate school and college in concert with Sahibzada Abdul Qayyum was one of those taming efforts.[69]

Sahibzadah Abdul Qayyum was twice offered the vice-chancellorship of Aligarh Muslim University after his retirement from the service, but he refused both the times stating that he wished to remain in the Frontier and ameliorate the educational conditions of the province. He continued his efforts for the educational uplift of the people of the Frontier, even after his retirement from the colonial government service. Being nominated as member of the central legislative assembly, he always stressed on the colonial government, at the time of the budgets, to allocate more funds for the Frontier. He wished for progress in the field of education in the tribal areas as well as the settled areas.[70] He argued with the British, in the central legislature of India, that instead of spending huge amounts on military expeditions into the tribal areas, they should spend it on educational advancement in the settled and tribal areas. The establishment of a university in Peshawar was his greatest and most cherished desire and design.[71] It was because of his endeavours and services in the field of education in the Frontier that 'he was selected to preside over the All-India Mohammedan Educational Conference, when' it 'was celebrating its Golden Jubilee in 1925'.[72]

When the province was raised to the status of a full-fledged province in 1932 and he became the sole minister of the transferred departments, although the governor was in-charge of the government, he strived till the end of 1936 for a greater portion of the budget to be allocated for the establishment of more educational institutions for both the genders. Due to his efforts, some schools were upgraded, the Islamia schools were granted considerable official financial assistance, extensions to the Islamia Collegiate School and Islamia College were constructed, uniformity of syllabus was introduced, the best text books were introduced in the Frontier schools, and seventy-one new schools—forty-six primary, four lower middle, one middle, and two high schools for boys; twelve primary, two lower middle, three middle, and one high school for girls— were opened in the settled and tribal areas of the province. In addition, he approved a boarding house for girls in Abbottabad.[73]

Sahibzadah Abdul Qayyum endeavoured to establish a university in the Frontier but, allegedly, did not succeed due to opposition from the Congress.[74] Qaiyum Khan's statement, that 'some time back a resolution recommending the conversion of this college [Islamia College, Peshawar] into a University was unanimously carried in the Central Legislative Assembly, but so far there has been no practical response from the powers that be',[75] however, negates the contention that Congress was opposed to the establishment of a university in the Frontier Province or to raising the status of the Islamia College Peshawar to that of a university. Sahibzadah Qayyum wished to establish a unique university in the province, different from all the universities of India, the blueprint of which was evident from his speech on the subject, as minister of the transferred departments, in the Frontier legislative council in 1936.[76]

He was of the opinion that education must be in the mother-tongue. When he was minister-in-charge of the transferred departments, it was decided in 1935 that the medium of education in the first and second classes in schools in the Pukhtu speaking areas was to be Pukhtu, but due to unknown reasons it was not implemented.[77] During his short tenure as chief minister of the province, he made compulsory the study of the series of books *Silsilah Talim-i Islami*, by Mufti Kifayatullah (President Jamiat-ul-Ulamay-i Hind) until the seventh class in government schools.[78] He also was of the view that the culture of the people of the Frontier must be protected, which he considered better than that of the people of the Punjab.[79] He strived, till his death, for the educational advancement of the Frontier, and used to pay scholarships, from his own pocket, to a large number of poor students studying in different areas of India.[80] He was in-charge of the education department from 1932 till 1936 as the sole minister of the transferred departments; as chief minister too, in 1937, he held the portfolio of education in his own hands.

Sahibzadah Abdul Qayyum did his best, and strived hard, for the cause of the Frontier Province on different fronts and forums, especially for the advancement and uplift of the province's Muslims. It, however, is an irony of fate that he agreed to terms with the Hindu-Sikh members of the Frontier legislature in 1937, in order to form the government, that were contrary to the interests of the Muslims and 'highly advantageous to the Hindu and Sikh communities'.[81] For instance, in spite of the Hindus-Sikhs amounting to only 7 per cent of the population of the province, the terms agreed with them included that 'the Hindi-Gurmukhi Circular should be withdrawn', which he himself had issued as minister of the transferred departments; and:

> Grants to educational institutions should be maintained in their existing form, and no discrimination should be made against Hindu institutions; 25 per cent of the admissions to technical and professional schools and colleges should be reserved for Hindus and Sikhs; 25 per cent of the appointments to the public services should be given to Hindus and Sikhs.[82]

Reserving such a big chunk in the services and educational institutions for the Hindus and Sikhs—only seven per cent of the population—for political reasons was a great backtrack on his part.

He, however, has rightly been termed Sir Sayyad-i Sarhad for his educational services to the people of the Frontier,[83] and 'will be for ever remembered as the foremost politician of his age, and one of the greatest benefactors of his community'.[84] According to Abdul Khaliq Khaleeq, he was clever and worthy of respect among the loyalists of the colonial government and, unlike the other titleholder *khans* (in Pukhtu: *khanan*), he was not an enemy of his own nation,[85] impliedly the Pukhtuns or the people of the Frontier.

Notes

1. Aziz Javaid, *Sarhad ka Ayini Irtiqa* (Urdu) (Peshawar: Idarah Tahqiq wa Tasnif, 1975), 330–1.
2. Ibid., 331–4. Mir Abdu-Samad Khan, however, has stated the year of his birth as 1862 [see Mir Abdu-Samad Khan, *Luy [Loi; Loy] Pukhtun: Sir Sayyad-i Sarhad Sahibzadah Abdul Qayyum Khan* (Urdu) (Peshawar: UBA, n.d.), 39]. According to Naushad Khan and Noor-ul-Amin, he 'was born on December 4, 1866' [Naushad Khan and Noor-ul-Amin, 'Sahibzada Abdul Qaiyum Khan' in Parvez Khan Toru and Fazal-ur-Rahim Marwat, eds., *Celebrities of NWFP*, vol[s]. 1–2 (Peshawar: Pakistan Study Centre, University of Peshawar, 2005), 17]. Whereas, according to S.M. Ikram, he 'was born on 12 December 1863' [S.M. Ikram, *Modern Muslim India and the Birth of Pakistan*, repr. (Lahore: IIC, 2016), 349].
3. Javaid, *Sarhad ka Ayini Irtiqa*, 334–5.
4. Ibid., 335. Aziz Javaid frequently refers to the chief commissioner's office, but there was no chief commissioner in Peshawar for the area during this period, as it was part of the province of Punjab from 1849 till 1901.
5. Ibid., 336.
6. See ibid., 336–7. Also see Khan, *Luy Pukhtun*, 40.
7. Javaid, *Sarhad ka Ayini Irtiqa*, 337, 346.
8. Abdul Qaiyum, *Gold and Guns on the Pathan Frontier* (Bombay: HK, 1945), 22.
9. For the 'colonial' and 'colonialist', see note 29 in chap. 6.
10. Muhammad Anwar Khan, *The Role of N.W.F.P. in the Freedom Struggle* (Lahore: RSP, 2000), 47.
11. Javaid, *Sarhad ka Ayini Irtiqa*, 37.
12. Khan, *The Role of N.W.F.P. in the Freedom Struggle*, 45.
13. Diwan Chand Obhrai, *The Evolution of North-West Frontier Province: Being a Survey of the History and Constitutional Development of N.-W. F. Province, in India*, repr. (Peshawar: SBB, n.d.), 297.
14. Amit Kumar Gupta, *North West Frontier Province: Legislature and Freedom Struggle, 1932–47* (New Delhi: ICHR, 1976), 20.
15. For details, see Javaid, *Sarhad ka Ayini Irtiqa*, 89–104; Khan, *Luy Pukhtun*, 68–72; Allah Bakhsh Yusufi, *Sarhad aur Jidujahd-i Azadi, tarmim wa izafah shudah edn.* (Urdu), (Karachi: Nafees Academy, 1989), 467–76; Ikram, *Modern Muslim India and the Birth of Pakistan*, 346; Himayatullah, 'Jinnah, Muslim League and Constitutional Reforms in the N.W.F.P.', *JPHS* (Karachi), vol. 55 (Nos. 1–2, January–June 2007), 'All India Muslim League Centenary Special Number, Part I', 149–50.
16. See Khan, *The Role of N.W.F.P. in the Freedom Struggle*, 57.
17. See Yusufi, *Sarhad aur Jidujahd-i Azadi*, 499–500. Also see Abdul Khaliq Khaleeq, *Zah aw Zama Zamanah* (Pukhtu) (Pikhawar: IIS, 1968), 42 n. 1.
18. Olaf Caroe, *The Pathans: 550 B.C.–A.D. 1957*, repr. (Karachi: OUP, 1976), 430–1.
19. Gupta, *North West Frontier Province*, 22.
20. Caroe, *The Pathans*, 431.

21. For details, see Javaid, *Sarhad ka Ayini Irtiqa*, 185–215.
22. Ibid., 215–16.
23. See Yusufi, *Sarhad aur Jidujahd-i Azadi*, 656.
24. See ibid., 662–5.
25. See Muhammad Shafi Sabir, *Shakhsiyat-i Sarhad* (Urdu) (Peshawar: UBA, n.d.), 392.
26. Also see Yusufi, *Sarhad aur Jidujahd-i Azadi*, 679.
27. Gupta, *North West Frontier Province*, 57.
28. Khan, *Luy Pukhtun*, 291.
29. Syed Waqar Ali Shah, *Muslim League in N.W.F.P.* (Karachi: RBC, 1992), 26–7.
30. Javaid, *Sarhad ka Ayini Irtiqa*, 351.
31. Ibid., 352.
32. Erland Jansson, *India, Pakistan or Pakhtunistan: The Nationalist Movements in the North-West Frontier Province, 1937–47* (Stockholm: AWI, 1981), 73.
33. See Shah, *Muslim League in N.W.F.P.*, 29–30; Jansson, *India, Pakistan or Pakhtunistan*, 74–5; Gupta, *North West Frontier Province*, 70–1; Stephen Alan Rittenberg, *Ethnicity, Nationalism, and the Pakhtuns: The Independence Movement in India's North-West Frontier Province* (Durham: CAP, 1988), 141.
34. See Yusufi, *Sarhad aur Jidujahd-i Azadi*, 674. For the names of the members of the United Muslim Nationalist Party, also see Obhrai, *The Evolution of North-West Frontier Province*, 304.
35. Rittenberg, *Ethnicity, Nationalism, and the Pakhtuns*, 142.
36. Jansson, *India, Pakistan or Pakhtunistan*, 76. Also see Sayed Wiqar Ali Shah, *Ethnicity, Islam, and Nationalism: Muslim Politics in the North-West Frontier Province, 1937–1947* (Karachi: OUP, 1999), 60 cf. Yusufi, *Sarhad aur Jidujahd-i Azadi*, 688–90.
37. Shah, *Ethnicity, Islam, and Nationalism*, 60.
38. See Yusufi, *Sarhad aur Jidujahd-i Azadi*, 688–91.
39. Rittenberg, *Ethnicity, Nationalism, and the Pakhtuns*, 148.
40. Shah, *Ethnicity, Islam, and Nationalism*, 262. Also see Khan, *Luy Pukhtun*, 376 cf. Yusufi, *Sarhad aur Jidujahd-i Azadi*, 691; Javaid, *Sarhad ka Ayini Irtiqa*, 353–4.
41. Jansson, *India, Pakistan or Pakhtunistan*, 76. Also see Shah, *Muslim League in N.W.F.P.*, 31; Gupta, *North West Frontier Province*, 77.
42. Gupta, *North West Frontier Province*, 77–8.
43. Khan, *Luy Pukhtun*, 371.
44. Gupta, *North West Frontier Province*, 76. Also see Khan, *Luy Pukhtun*, 374.
45. Javaid, *Sarhad ka Ayini Irtiqa*, 354. For details about the formation of the League in the Frontier, and Sahibzadah Abdul Qayyum's endeavours in this respect, see chap. 10 of this book.
46. Ibid., 355.
47. *Khyber Mail*, 5 December 1937, quoted in Shah, *Ethnicity, Islam, and Nationalism*, 61.
48. See Yusufi, *Sarhad aur Jidujahd-i Azadi*, 319–26.
49. See Abdul Khaliq Khaleeq, *Da Azadai Jang: Sah Lidali aw sah Awridali* (Pukhtu), 2nd edn. (Pikhawar: IIS, 1972), 89–90; Khaleeq, *Zah aw Zama Zamanah*, 77 n. 1.
50. See Khaleeq, *Da Azadai Jang*, 94–5; Khaleeq, *Zah aw Zama Zamanah*, 77 n. 1.
51. See Abdul Ghaffar [Khan], *Zama Jwand aw Jidujahd* (Pukhtu) (Kabul: DM, 1983), 486; Khan Abdul Ghaffar Khan, *Ap Biti* (Urdu), repr. (Lahore: FH, 2004), 133. Also see Khaleeq, *Da Azadai Jang*, 111.
52. Qaiyum, *Gold and Guns on the Pathan Frontier*, 22.
53. Javaid, *Sarhad ka Ayini Irtiqa*, 338–9.
54. Ibid., 339. Also see Lal Baha, *N.-W.F.P. Administration under British Rule, 1901–1919* (Islamabad: NCHCR, 1978), 208.
55. Javaid, *Sarhad ka Ayini Irtiqa*, 339–41.

56. For details, see ibid., 341–2. Also see Baha, *N.-W.F.P. Administration under British Rule*, 209–10.

57. See Javaid, *Sarhad ka Ayini Irtiqa*, 342.

58. Muhammad Shafi Sabir has spoken of the laying of the foundation stone of the mosque of the college on 31 March 1913 (see Sabir, *Shakhsiyat-i Sarhad*, 392); Allah Bakhsh Yusufi has stated that the college's construction work began in 1913 and that its foundation stone was laid by the Haji Sahib of Turangzi [see Yusufi, *Sarhad aur Jidujahd-i Azadi*, 128]. In S.M. Ikram's words: 'Originally, the Sahibzadah set up a committee for running an Islamia High School, and in 1912...laid the foundation of a proper residential college. A fund of Rs 15 lakhs was collected, 200 acres of land purchased and in 1913 construction of well-planned buildings began on lines which made Islamia College, Peshawar, "a garden-town of learning".' [Ikram, *Modern Muslim India and the Birth of Pakistan*, 349]. And, in Dr Muhammad Anwar Khan's words: The Haji Sahib Turangzi 'was invited to lay foundation stone of the first building (mosque) of Islamia College complex on March 12, 1912 by Sahibzada Abdul Qayyum Khan to win local support for a European model schooling on the confluence of the settled-tribal land in the Khyber area' [Khan, *The Role of N.W.F.P. in the Freedom Struggle*, 30]. Abdul Khaliq Khaleeq has said that the Haji Sahib of Turangzi was invited for the laying of the foundation stone of Islamia College but instead he laid the foundation stone of the mosque of the college (see Khaleeq, *Da Azadai Jang*, 7–8). However, Dr Lal Baha has stated that 'the foundation stone' of the mosque 'was laid on 21 March 1912' and 'the building of both College [the Islamia College] and School [the Islamia Collegiate School] began in October 1912' (Baha, *N.-W.F.P. Administration under British Rule*, 211, 215).

59. For details, see Javaid, *Sarhad ka Ayini Irtiqa*, 342–4.

60. Dr Lal Baha, interview by the author, at Peshawar, verbal, 22 June 2009.

61. Yusufi, *Sarhad aur Jidujahd-i Azadi*, 128.

62. Javaid, *Sarhad ka Ayini Irtiqa*, 344.

63. Khan, *Luy Pukhtun*, 132.

64. Caroe, *The Pathans*, 424.

65. Javaid, *Sarhad ka Ayini Irtiqa*, 344–5.

66. Dr Lal Baha, interview by the author, at Peshawar, verbal, 22 June 2009. Also see Baha, *N.-W.F.P. Administration under British Rule*, 216.

67. Caroe, *The Pathans*, 424.

68. Ali Abbas Bukhari to Syed Wazir Hasan, 23 June 1914 *AFM*, Vol. 206 quoted in Shah, *Muslim League in N.W.F.P.*, 21. Dr Lal Baha has stated that 'the private correspondence of Hardinge, Roos-Keppel, and Harcourt Butler...provides clear proof of the policy of the [colonial] Government' that, through the establishment of the Islamia College, in addition to the educational advancement of the people of the Frontier and the achieving of other goals, they wished to create a barrier between Aligarh and its Indian political sentiments and the inhabitants of the Frontier (see Baha, *N.-W.F.P. Administration under British Rule*, 213–14). This is testament to the fact that the apprehensions of the anti-British elements were not unfounded.

69. Khan, *The Role of N.W.F.P. in the Freedom Struggle*, 43.

70. Javaid, *Sarhad ka Ayini Irtiqa*, 364–5, 379.

71. Ibid., 383.

72. Ikram, *Modern Muslim India and the Birth of Pakistan*, 349.

73. Javaid, *Sarhad ka Ayini Irtiqa*, 379–82.

74. Ibid., 382–3.

75. Qaiyum, *Gold and Guns on the Pathan Frontier*, 23.

76. See Khan, *Luy Pukhtun*, 133–4, 325–8.

77. Ibid., 382–3.

78. Ibid., 371.
79. Ibid., 326.
80. Javaid, *Sarhad ka Ayini Irtiqa*, 382.
81. Jansson, *India, Pakistan or Pakhtunistan*, 74. Also see Khaleeq, *Da Azadai Jang*, 129.
82. Jansson, *India, Pakistan or Pakhtunistan*, 74–5. Also see Shah, *Muslim League in N.W.F.P.*, 30.
83. See Khan, *Luy Pukhtun*, title, 47–67; Yusufi, *Sarhad aur Jidujahd-i Azadi*, 127.
84. Obhrai, *The Evolution of North-West Frontier Province*, 298.
85. Khaleeq, *Da Azadai Jang*, 111.

14 Role of Abdul Ghaffar Khan in Politics and Promotion of Education

> Abdul Ghaffar Khan is one of the victims of unfair treatment at the hands of his adversaries as well as his admirers.
> – M.S. Korejo

> Bacha Khan will remain part and parcel of Pukhtoon history despite his failures and shortcomings.
> – Juma Khan Sufi

ABDUL GHAFFAR (popularly known as Abdul Ghaffar Khan, Khan Abdul Ghaffar Khan, Ghaffar Khan, Bacha Khan, Badshah Khan, Sarhadi Gandhi, and the Frontier Gandhi) remained an outstanding personality during the twentieth century due to his ideas, and his role and struggle both in the pre- and post-independence periods, not only in the Frontier Province (now Khyber Pukhtunkhwa) but also in the subcontinent as a whole. He possessed 'an idealist bent of character and a gift for communicating with the common man'.[1] As his early life has already been outlined in chapter 9, his role in politics and promotion of education is being dealt with in this chapter.

ROLE IN POLITICS

Abdul Ghaffar Khan's political carrier began with his participation in the annual session of the All India Muslim League, held in Agra in 1913, followed by his visit to Deoband in 1914 where he was assigned the task of selecting a suitable place for establishing a centre and base in Bajawar for the liberation of India from the British yoke.[2] Although the scheme visualised from Deoband did not succeed, due to the outbreak of World War I and other developments on the local and all-India scene, Ghaffar Khan's links and association with the leaders of the Deoband school of thought, and the task assigned to him, proved a milestone in his political life, as they firmly established him in the anti-British camp.

As in the other parts of India, the Rowlatt Act of 1919 created a stir in the Frontier Province, and Ghaffar Khan joined the rank and file of the agitators. His role and participation in the anti-Rowlatt Act agitation earned him the title of Bacha Khan/Badshah Khan and also put him behind bars for the first time.[3] He was now 'immersed in public activities and his jail experiences drew him more to politics'.[4] In 1920, he went to Delhi to participate in the *khilafat* conference, which was also attended by all-India leaders of towering stature like Mohandas Karamchand Gandhi (popularly known as Gandhi, Mahatma Gandhi, and Gandhi-ji), Abul Kalam Azad, Hakim Ajmal Khan, the Ali brothers (Muhammad Ali Jauhar and Shaukat Ali), and many others. The *khilafat* movement resulted in the *hijrat* movement to Afghanistan, and, although not in favour, Ghaffar Khan, compelled by circumstances, migrated to Afghanistan. He was made a member of the committee, formed in Afghanistan, to look into the affairs of the migrants in that country. Although it ultimately met with failure, the *hijrat* movement positively affected Ghaffar Khan's ideas and ideals.[5]

In 1921, he and his colleagues founded the Anjuman Islah-ul-Afaghinah. The aims and objectives of the association 'were economic and social' and, according to D.G. Tendulkar, 'non-political and purely missionary'.[6] Its objectives included infusing a spirit and love of nationhood in the Pukhtuns.[7] Ghaffar Khan also became president of the provincial *khilafat* committee. He was sentenced to three years' rigorous imprisonment for his activities and for his refusal to give a surety for the *khilafat* committee and the schools established by him and his colleagues. On being set free in 1924, the Anjuman Islah-ul-Afaghinah organised a large public meeting in his honour, during which he was further honoured with an address in his honour, a medal and robe, and the title 'Fakhr-i Afghan' (Pride of the Afghans).[8] Furthermore, at the time of his visit to the Frontier in 1937, Nehru remarked that he 'was not only "Fakhr-e-Afghan" but it was right to call him "Fakhr-e-Hind" [Fakhr-i Hind: Pride of India].'[9]

In 1925–26, he was invited to, and participated in, the conference of the Jamiat-ul-Ulamay-i Hind in Peshawar.[10] In Tendulkar's words:

The period between 1924 and 1929 was a hard testing in the struggle for independence. The communal passions mounted high and many lost their moorings. Abdul Ghaffar kept himself severely aloof from all activities of a narrow communal type and refused to be drawn into the surging communal passion.[11]

In 1928, the Afghan monarch, Amanullah Khan, lost the throne and Bacha Saqau (also Bachah Saqah) occupied it. Ghaffar Khan struggled and strived in Amanullah Khan's favour but to no avail. Although Bacha Saqau was removed from power (in 1929), Nadar Khan assumed power (instead of handing it over to Amanullah Khan)—which did not please Ghaffar Khan.[12] Ghaffar Khan endeavoured to start the first journal in the Pukhtu language, titled *Pukhtun*; its first issue was published in 1928. Although it could not be published regularly due to his imprisonment and exile from the province, the journal did well, helping raise political awareness among the Pukhtuns in the Frontier Province and further afield.[13] In Qaiyum Khan's words: 'Patriotic poems and articles in Pushtu, inculcating love of freedom, and aiming at social reform, were a notable feature of this journal.'[14]

In 1929, Ghaffar Khan and his associates founded another organisation, the Khudayi Khidmatgar.[15] Qaiyum Khan asserts: 'This remarkable organization, unique in many respects, bears testimony to Abdul Ghaffar's wonderful genius for organizing his people.'[16] 'It was a completely non-political organization, but the British policy of oppression compelled it to participate in politics.'[17] The foundation of the Khudayi Khidmatgar Organisation, which was not only an organisation but a movement as well, gave a new boost and further ground to Ghaffar Khan's struggle. In December 1929, he and his associates attended the annual session of the All India National Congress, held at Lahore, which changed their outlook and gave a political perspective to their views and struggle. D.G. Tendulkar claims: 'Abdul Ghaffar resigned from the Khilafat Committee, because that body had become anti-Congress';[18] and: 'It was after the Lahore Congress that Abdul Ghaffar decided to turn the small body of workers into a full-fledged organization to carry out the programme of the Congress.'[19] Ghaffar Khan later came closer to the Congress, was made a member of its working committee, and its presidentship was also offered to him but, although impressed by the struggle and successes of the Congress, at least at this stage, his focus was on the Frontier not on all-India politics.

The All India National Congress started the *satyagraha* and non-cooperation movement on an all-India level. The Frontier Congressmen followed suit and invited Ghaffar Khan to visit them and participate in their civil disobedience. He accepted the invitation but, while on his way, was arrested by the colonial government. A number of other Khudayi Khidmatgars were also arrested. In the meantime, the Qisah Khwani incident and massacre occurred (when the British soldiers opened fire on the people protesting against the arrest of their leaders), which further aggravated the situation in the province. Not only did the colonial government declare martial law, but it also carried out a blockade of the province and resorted to atrocities. At their refusal to submit surety to the colonial British government, Ghaffar Khan and the others were sentenced to three years' rigorous imprisonment.[20] These measures resulted in an affiliation between the Khudayi Khidmatgar movement and the Congress, which proved to be a turning point in Ghaffar Khan's career, as thereafter he became a leader of an all-India stature; slowly and gradually his endeavours shifted from social, economic, and educational aspects to political one.

Jawaharlal Nehru admitted that the Frontier Province 'played a leading and remarkable part' in the civil disobedience movement of 1930; and 'this was largely due to the work and personality of Khan Abdul Ghaffar Khan, the unquestioned and beloved leader of the Pathans in this province'.[21] By the end of 1930, he had become the undisputed leader of the Pukhtun masses in the then-Peshawar district—present-day (2021) Peshawar, Charsadah, Nawshihrah (Nowshera), Mardan, and Swabi districts. The scope of his leadership, however, soon spread to the other districts of the province. 'The initiative of mass political struggle in the history of' the Frontier Province 'lies with him'.[22]

Consequent upon the Irwin-Gandhi Pact, he was released from jail in March 1931. He, however, termed the 'pact as a temporary truce' and asked the people 'to raise the number of Khudai Khidmatgars to a hundred thousand'. Convinced that the truce was short lived, he embarked on tours to organise the movement, in the course of which he remarked in his speeches:

One horn of the Firangi is already broken. Now you arise and get ready to break the other horn. This is your land, God has ordained it to you, but owing to your disunity, the Firangis are occupying your land. Your children die of hunger and thirst, while their children are enjoying everything they want.[23]

In his speeches, he emphasised, the importance of the alliance with the Congress and of 'forging the unity of the people. "The Congress is a national and not a Hindu body", he asserted, "it is a *Jirga* composed of Hindus, Jews, Sikhs, Parsis, Christians and Muslims".'[24] In addition to touring the different parts of the province, he led a delegation of Khudayi Khidmatgars to the Congress public meeting in Karachi, and also participated in the annual session of the Jamiat-ul-Ulamay-i Hind—also in Karachi—before going on to India.[25]

In addition to being made a member of the Congress Working Committee—the highest and most powerful body of the Congress—the presidentship of Congress was also offered to him in October 1934 and in 1937, but he declined at both the instances.[26] In 1934, 'the main pavilian' of the Congress annual session in Bombay 'was named after him'.[27] It is to be noted that S.M. Ikram states the year as '1935'.[28] S.M. Ikram states the name as 'Ghaffar Nagar', while Abdul Khaliq Khaleeq refers to it as 'Abdul Ghaffar Khan Nagar'.[29] Juma Khan Sufi—Ghaffar Khan's fan-turned-critic—concedes to his popularity in the Frontier in 1934 by stating: 'Bacha Khan was made a member of the Central Working Committee in 1934, *not because he was a true disciple of Gandhi* [italics mine], but because he really had the Frontier behind him.'[30]

On various occasions, he had to explain his reasons for becoming allied to the Congress. When faced with objections and resentment from some Khudayi Khidmatgars, he assured them that he would sever his connections with the Congress if the union 'was, in any way, going to prove disadvantageous to the Pathans or to the faith', and that he 'would be the first person to declare a peaceful war against the whole world for safeguarding the interests of the Pathans'.[31] Although released from jail on 27 August 1934, he was prohibited from entering the provinces of the Frontier and Punjab. Therefore, he toured around, and played a role in, the other provinces of India.[32] He was imprisoned, once again, in December 1934; and, once again, on his release in 1936, was banned from entering the provinces of Punjab and the Frontier.[33]

Ghaffar Khan believed in non-violence. Although, in his speeches, he frequently spoke of foreign rule, the curse of foreign domination, slavery and tyranny, and stressed the need for the people to unite and struggle to be rid of oppression and to achieve independence—and later provincial autonomy as well—he neither advocated, nor did he incite, violence. Rather, he abhorred it and asked his fellows and adherents to avoid and reject it. Even in politics, he mostly preferred to follow the rules of the game—a rare phenomenon in the region, both at the time and later. This is borne out by his response to the outcome of the election of 1937—when the governor invited Sahibzadah Abdul Qayyum to form the ministry, in spite of the Khudayi Khidmatgars-Congress being the largest party in the assembly, Ghaffar Khan remarked to some of his colleagues that he 'do not feel dejected over the action of the Governor in offering' the chief ministership to the Sahibzadah; because, 'If you could not return your men in a large majority, you should not have any cause of complaint if the chief ministership did not come to you.' And, as the focus of his politics was not about simply having governing powers, but about serving the people, he asked his colleagues: 'Whatever might have been your success or failure, go ahead with your constructive programme with redoubled energy.'[34]

When the Congress Working Committee discussed the issue of rejecting the policy of non-violence, during its emergency meeting in Delhi on 3 July 1940, Ghaffar Khan not only voted against it but also resigned from the working committee as he believed that the committee's decision was contrary to his faith and a deviation from the righteous path.[35] However, when in September 1940 the All India Congress Committee cancelled its previous decision and adopted a resolution to return to its policy of non-violence, he 'withdrew his resignation from the Working Committee to participate in the Congress activities as before'.[36] After Japan's joining the World War II in 1941, when the All India Congress Committee renounced its policy of non-violence, in its meetings at Barduli and Wardha, in mid-January 1942, by resolving to join the war once again, Ghaffar Khan resigned from the working committee and from the Congress over policy differences related to non-violence.[37] However, he stated: 'I will better be able to carry on the message of non-violence to the Pathan mind if I am detached officially from the Congress whose policy can vary according to the exigencies as they may arise from time to time. My bond with the Congress will thus be richer than hitherto.'[38] 'By his resignation', Dr Sayed Wiqar Ali Shah claims, he 'proved himself to be a firm believer in non-violence. Moreover, this also proved that being a man of strict principles, in no way he was ready even to follow Gandhi blindly.'[39]

He detested violence to the extent that, at the time of the communal violence and riots in Bihar, he toured Bihar to try to bring the people to their senses and to end the riots. He wrote to Gandhi in March 1947: 'You are right. Our ahimsa is on test. When I see the politicians surrounding us wrongly using the name of God and religion to propagate hatred, I begin to hate politics.'[40] At the time of the Muslim League's agitation and disturbances in 1947, in the Frontier, he expressed the view: 'I hope and trust that God will help us in the sacred mission and people will recognize that the essence of love, truth and non-violence is the hall-mark of every good, free and prosperous society.'[41]

Rajmohan Gandhi, however, concludes after citing two events relating to Nehru's visit to the Frontier in 1946: 'Badshah Khan's nonviolence was thus clearly pragmatic and not limitless; he had no hesitation in asking for soldiers and guns, or, later, in lauding his brother for threatening to use the revolver.'[42] His tacit approval of Zalmay Pukhtun—the Khudayi Khidmatgars' support organisation, which was armed and believed in violence and the use of force[43]—is also testimony that his belief in non-violence was not limitless.

Whether Ghaffar Khan's creed of non-violence was his own, or he got it from Gandhi, has not been agreed upon by sources that were consulted for the writing of this book. Although he himself, on occasion, claimed that it was derived from Prophet Muhammad's (s.a.w.) life in Makkah and Islam, D.G. Tendulkar, Eknath Easwaran, M.S. Korejo, and Juma Khan Sufi's writings suggest that he was impressed by Gandhi's thinking, philosophy, and manner of politics and, hence, moulded his thoughts and philosophy accordingly.[44] Dr Sayed Wiqar Ali Shah, however, contends that he had 'developed his own perception of adopting non-violence since early 1910s', and that his 'biographers...wrongly attributed it to the non-violence of Gandhi, and argue that it was a variant of the same non-violence preached by Gandhi in the rest of India'. He tries to negate the aforementioned viewpoint of Ghaffar Khan's biographers, and to prove that Ghaffar Khan's non-violence was based on his own creed.[45] Jawaharlal Nehru contends:

> Of all the remarkable happenings in India in recent times, nothing is more astonishing than the way in which Abdul Ghaffar Khan made his turbulent and quarrelsome people accept peaceful methods of political action, involving enormous suffering. That suffering was indeed terrible and has left a trail of bitter memories; and yet their discipline and self-control were such that no act of violence was committed by the Pathans against the Government forces or others opposed to them. When it is remembered that a Pathan loves his gun more than his brother, is easily excited, and has long had a reputation for killing at the slightest provocation, this self-discipline appears little short of miraculous.[46]

'Although factionalism was endemic in the Frontier Congress, it rarely involved Abdul Ghaffar Khan.'[47] He was the main prop of the Congress-Khudayi Khidmatgars' influence in the Frontier Province, which was understood by Gandhi as well. Therefore, while negating the Congress leaders' view of a decrease in his influence in the Frontier in 1947, Gandhi wrote to Nehru, after his meeting with Sardar Patel:

> He [Patel] is of the opinion that Badshah Khan's influence is on the wane. Badshah Khan has not left any such impression on me. Whatever he is today, he was always. There is undoubtedly more steadiness today than before. I also

feel that Dr Khan Sahib and his colleagues would be nowhere without the Badshah. He alone counts in so far as the Congress influence is concerned.[48]

Olaf Caroe has also observed that 'like Gandhi in India', although he 'remained outside' the ruling power, Ghaffar Khan was 'the recognized leader of the Frontier Congress [Khudayi Khidmatgars] in the villages. He had chosen the role of power without responsibility.'[49] And, in Rittenberg words: 'Abdul Ghaffar Khan's power rested on two institutional bases. First, he controlled the Khudai Khidmatgars, the more popular wing of the party... Second, he served as a member of the All-India Congress Working Committee.'[50]

When the Congress adopted the 'Quit India' resolution, Ghaffar Khan pledged his full support to it and took the movement to heart—leading to his imprisonment.[51] However, although 'violence erupted all over India' during the course of the movement, 'the Frontier remained nonviolent. The picketing and "raids" continued, but there was no sabotage' because of his 'unrelenting nonviolence'.[52] He was one of the four Congress-nominated representatives who participated at the conference, with the British Cabinet Mission and Muslim League members, in Simla in May 1946.[53] He tried to persuade Gandhi to head the government himself, like Lenin, at that critical juncture in India's independence in order to avert crisis and riots, but to no avail.[54]

He was opposed to the Partition of India, into Muslim and Hindu majority dominions, and favoured a united India after the departure of the British. He, and 'his compatriots', 'cast their lot' with the Congress, 'often in opposition to the League'. For him, partition meant 'abandonment' and the placing of 'the Frontier Province under' the League, 'which had battled' him and 'the Khudai Khidmatgars for a decade'.[55]

Ghaffar Khan's stand on the Pukhtunistan issue took different twists on different occasions and in different circumstances. For instance, after the passage of the Bannu Resolution on 21 June 1947, in which an independent Pukhtun state/government was asked for, his statement, issued on 24 June, included: 'Our struggle all along had been for the freedom of India and more especially of the Pathans. We want complete freedom. That ideal of ours still remains with us and we shall work for it.' Commenting on the 3rd June Plan, he stated: 'This limits our choice to two alternatives, neither of which we are prepared to accept. We cannot vote as we want to vote for a free Pathan state.'[56] He maintained: 'It is necessary to provide an opportunity for us to vote in the referendum for a free Pathan state.'[57] He asserted: 'I maintain that a great majority of the

Pakhtuns are for the establishment of a free Pathan state. With a view to ascertain the will of the people in this respect, I am prepared for holding a referendum or the general election.'[58] Continuing on, he put the question: 'What are we to do in these circumstances?'[59] He subsequently asserted:

> I would appeal to all Khudai Khidmatgars and others who believe in a free Pathan State not to participate in the referendum and keep away from it peacefully.
>
> But this does not mean that we should sit still. A new struggle has been forced upon us.[60]

'Addressing a meeting on 27 June', he said: 'We have decided to establish Pathanistan, which will be an independent state of all the Pathans.... Let us organize for freedom from any domination. After that we can keep brotherly relations with the other Muslim countries in the interests of both.'[61]

At the gathering arranged at Sardaryab on 3–4 September 1947—attended by the Provincial Jargah, the Parliamentary Party, the Zalmay Pukhtun, Khudayi Khidmatgars, and representatives from the tribal areas—he once more re-affirmed his demand of a 'new [Pukhtun] state' which 'will comprise the present six Settled Districts of the North-West Frontier Province and all such other contiguous areas inhabited by the Pakhtuns which may wish to join the new state of their own free will. The state will enter into agreement on defence, external affairs, and communications with Pakistan.' Ghaffar Khan asserted: 'I have been working for the establishment of Pakhtunistan all my life.' And, 'It was for the purpose of achieving unity among the Pakhtuns that the Khudai Khidmatgar organization was started in 1929, and I stand for those principles today. My path is, therefore, quite clear. I will not forsake it even if I stand alone in the world.'[62] This claim, however, is in contrast to, and is negated by, his stand against Partition and him been in favour of a united India. He was not for an independent Pukhtun State if India had to remain united, and advocated an independent Pukhtun State only in case of the division of India.[63] Therefore, Juma Khan Sufi's assertion that 'an Indian nationalist by choice, Bacha Khan became a Pukhtoon nationalist by default when Congress left him in wilderness'[64] carries *some* weight. If he 'had really aroused Pukhtoons' nationalist feelings before the Muslim League rode on the chariot of 'Islam in danger',' Juma Khan Sufi asserts,

> he would have won the sympathies of all Pukhtoons, including the tribes, and even the British Government could have been forced to submit to their

aspirations of freedom and reunification in the end. The Pukhtoons were not Sikhs sandwiched between the devil and the deep blue sea, whose options were limited. They could have easily achieved independence and even rejoined Afghanistan in a federal or confederal arrangement had they played their cards well. But Bacha Khan was blind to the emerging realities of Indian politics and those on whom he had reposed most of his trust betrayed him in the end.[65]

To put the record straight, Ghaffar Khan aroused the Pukhtuns' nationalist feelings by, at first, frequently urging them to work for *qaam* and *watan*—impliedly the Pukhtun nation and homeland. This, however, went into the background later as they became closer to Congress—discussed earlier in chapters 9 and 11.

However, his stance on Pukhtunistan changed after the emergence of Pakistan: from a call for an independent Pukhtun state to 'an autonomous unit in Pakistan'; for the name of the province to be changed to Pukhtunistan; and he 'categorically denied as baseless the charge that he wanted to truncate Pakistan by forging an independent sovereign state of Pakhtunistan. The very fact that he would be taking the oath of allegiance to the constitution of Pakistan ought to give a lie to that allegation.'[66] Thus, his focus was now on something that neither he nor his organisation had voiced earlier—the renaming of the province—a change he tried to defend.[67]

As he was elected a member of the central legislative assembly of India, from the Frontier Province, in 1946, he became a member of the Pakistan's parliament or central legislative assembly at the birth of Pakistan. Being a member of Pakistan's parliament, he took an oath of allegiance to Pakistan, on 23 February 1948, in Karachi at the session of the parliament. Muhammad Ali Jinnah, Governor-General of Pakistan, met him, and Ghaffar Khan invited him to visit the Frontier, which he accepted. On 5 March 1948, Ghaffar Khan, in the new scenario, tried to make the position of the League's Frontier provincial government clear, on the floor of the parliament, and also his own and his organisation's positions. In his speech, while discussing Pukhtunistan, he contended that renaming the province as Pukhtunistan would represent the people who inhabited the land, as was already the case with Sindh, Punjab, and Bengal.[68] Abul Kalam Azad rightly observes that, after the Partition, Ghaffar Khan's attitude changed 'in conformity with the demands of the situation'. And so, it was declared that the 'demand for a free Pakhtoonistan did not mean the creation of a separate State but the recognition of full autonomy for the Frontier as a unit of Pakistan'.[69]

In the pre-Partition days, at times, he had tried to create working relations and alliances with the League and Leaguers,[70] but he was now so dejected that he did not come to an agreement with them. He met Jinnah in Peshawar, at the time of the latter's official visit to the province, but attempts at a settlement and amicable relations, or a merger of the Khudayi Khidmatgars with the League, did not succeed for a variety of reasons. He turned down Jinnah's proposal to join the League and instead invited him to head the Khudayi Khidmatgars.[71] He even proposed disbanding the League, as it had achieved its goal of creating Pakistan, and advocated the founding of new parties with new objectives in the new and changed scenario.[72]

Ghaffar Khan was averse to the domination of Punjab. He demonstrated his reservations about it and struggled against it both before and after the partition of India and the emergence of Pakistan. He, therefore, 'opposed the compulsory grouping' of the provinces as suggested by the Cabinet Mission in 1946, 'as it would force them to join the Punjab' in which case the Frontier Province will 'remain under the Punjab's domination forever'. Although he and his organisation were ready to 'join Group B', on Punjab's assurances of 'better treatment', the best alternative to him was to 'leave them alone' as they were happy in framing their own destiny by themselves.[73]

In March 1948, he, along with G.M. Sayyad, a former Leaguer, founded a new party, Jamiat-ul-Awam or the People's Party, of which he was elected the president. On 13 May 1948, he announced his decision to extend the Khudayi Khidmatgar movement to all the provinces of Pakistan and announced that it 'would serve as a volunteer corps' of the newly founded party. The Pakistani authorities did not like the foundation of this new party which was 'a non-communal organization, inclusive of progressive sections in Pakistan, and stood for liberal and democratic ideals', and dubbed Ghaffar Khan an 'arch disruptionist'.[74]

He returned from Karachi in the third week of May 1948 and started a tour of the Frontier Province, to place the programme of the new party—Jamiat-ul-Awam or People's Party—before the people. While, he had forbidden any comments against Jinnah in the pre-Partition days, and tried to reconcile with him in the post-Partition days, now he 'did not spare even Jinnah' in his speeches. He warned the Pukhtuns that they were partners in Pakistan and 'entitled to a one-fourth share'. He urged them to strive for their due share and rights, and said: 'We will not rest content till we succeed in establishing *Pakhtunistan—rule of the Pakhtuns, by the Pakhtuns, and for the Pakhtuns* [italics mine].' While on tour, he was arrested on 15 June 1948 under the North-West Frontier Province Safety Ordinance and 'charged with "sedition" and "intended collaboration with the hostile Fakir of Ipi".' At a summary trial, when he refused to defend himself or produce security, 'he was awarded three years' rigorous imprisonment' by the deputy commissioner Kuhat and sent to Montgomery jail in Punjab.[75]

On expiry of his three years of imprisonment, instead of being released, he 'was held as a detenu under Bengal Regulation of 1818' and the period was extended after every six months.[76] When asked, after his release on 5 January 1954, whether 'he would resume' politics in the Frontier Province, he said: 'I am not a politician, I am a soldier. My job is service to mankind and I shall continue to do that.'[77] Although released from jail, he was placed under house-arrest at the circuit house. In March 1954, he was allowed to attend the budget session of the Pakistan parliament in Karachi, where he took an active part in the session, putting his position and viewpoint before the house. He also tabled a motion to postpone consideration of the Basic Principles Committee Report.[78] After the lifting of the ban on his entering the Frontier Province, in July 1955, and his subsequent entry, 'when asked':

> whether he still persisted in his demand for Pakhtunistan and what was the difference between the conception of Pakhtunistan as demanded by Afghanistan and himself, he replied that he was not concerned with Afghan demand, but his conception was of a Pakhtunistan province, which would be an integral part of Pakistan.[79]

The Pakistan government's efforts to induce him to agree to the one-unit scheme failed, and he continued his anti-one-unit struggle. In his campaign, Ghaffar Khan also said that 'my elder brother'—who favoured the one-unit scheme and became the first chief minister of the united province of West Pakistan—'is the Prime Minister of West Pakistan, and among the Pakhtuns the elder brother is given the position of the father. But then I have dared to disagree with him on the issue of one unit because I see great harm in it for my people.'[80] He was arrested again in July 1956,[81] basically for his disagreement with the One Unit and the struggle against it.

On 27 January 1957, 'he announced his decision to join the Pakistan National Party', which had been formed through 'the merger of six opposition parties'. He continued a vigorous anti-One Unit campaign and, in July 1957, along with Abdul Hamid Bashani, G.M. Sayyad, and

Mian Iftikhar-ud-Din founded the National Awami Party (NAP) in Dacca (now Dhaka)—a country-wide organisation. However, he was put behind bars time and again, and also 'disqualified from being a member of any elective body until the end of 1966'.[82] He started a campaign against his disqualification, during the course of which he was detained again. President Ayub Khan alleged, in a press conference: 'Abdul Ghaffar Khan wanted the Frontier area to become a part of India. Having failed in this venture, he demanded a separate province in Pakistan, where he wanted to be the king. Later, he wanted to make this Frontier region a part of Afghanistan.'[83]

Ghaffar Khan's detention period was extended every six months. However, he was allowed to go to England for medical treatment in September 1964. From there, he went to Cairo; and then, in December 1964, to Afghanistan purportedly for medical purposes, but subsequently refused to return to Pakistan in spite of the authorities' assurances of assistance with his medical treatment, as he feared he would be jailed again. In Kabul, in response to a query about the 'prospect of a reconciliation with Pakistan', he expressed the view that he 'had tried every means' but in vain. As 'his faith' in such a reconciliation 'had been completely shattered', he 'wished to have nothing whatsoever to do with Pakistan. He would do or die—either achieve Pakhtunistan or die fighting for it.'[84]

Speaking on the occasion of Pukhtunistan Day in Kabul on 31 August 1965, at a gathering of about 50,000 people, he said: 'Pakistan is created by us... It is created by the blood of the Pathans. We want to be friendly with Pakistan. The Pathans are demanding only the right to build their own home.'[85] Concluding his address, 'he said that Pakhtuns will continue their struggle until their aim is achieved'.[86] However, in his speech on Pukhtunistan Day in 1967, he said: 'We want a name, a room in the same house, but we want to be masters of the room.'[87] According to Huseyn Shaheed Suhrawardy, 'the autonomous province of Pakhtunistan which he visualized was to remain an integral part of Pakistan'.[88] Sher Zaman Taizai contends that though he 'demanded an autonomous status for [the] Pakhtuns', 'in not a single speech did he express any desire for a separate and independent state' for them out of Pakistan.[89]

However, when riots erupted in East Pakistan in 1971, while he was in exile in Afghanistan, he offered to go to East Pakistan, with a few of the other elders from the four provinces of West Pakistan, to 'try to settle' the issue with Sheikh Mujib, for 'the solidarity of the country'—if permitted to do so by the Pakistan government—but his offer was not accepted.[90] He returned to Pakistan in December 1972, following which he was arrested a number of times by the Bhutto regime.

He, again, went to Afghanistan in 1978. Despite his ill-health and hospitalisation in 1984 in Afghanistan, the Indian diplomat Dixit considered him 'politically alive and sharp'.[91] Although he had initially welcomed Soviet intervention in Afghanistan in 1979, because of Hafizullah Amin's atrocities, he had become a sharp opponent of the Soviet presence in Afghanistan 'by the end of 1981'. He was of the view that the 'Afghans, Pashtoons will never accept Communism or Russia. They will just die. Those who can will leave the country.' Also, that 'the Communists…are not only destroying people but trees in Afghanistan. The revolution had become oppression.'[92] He urged the Indian Prime Minister, Indira Gandhi, and the Afghan President, Babrak Karmal, to arrange for him to meet with the Soviet President, Leonid Brezhnev, so that he could ask him to withdraw the Soviet troops from Afghanistan. But when he finally visited Moscow after a great effort, Brezhnev did not meet him, which angered him considerably.[93]

Ghaffar Khan returned to Pakistan when work on the Kalabagh Dam project was about to start. Deeming the dam to be against the interest of the Frontier Province, he not only opposed its construction, but also launched a vigorous campaign against it—despite being wheelchair-bound—in the course of which he toured the Frontier Province and Karachi addressing large public meetings. While he was detained during the course of his anti-Kalabagh Dam campaign, his struggle continued—which put the dam in limbo and also provided the Awami National Party (ANP) with an issue.

Ghaffar Khan's greatest achievement and role in politics was to inculcate a spirit of non-violence, and strict and rigid adherence to it—despite the display and use of force by the British and later Pakistani sides—in a nationalist movement, and in an area where arms were so readily obtainable and openly owned, and also in a people who were used to resorting to violence at the slightest provocation, disgrace, or repression. He linked non-violence to Islam. In the words of his fan-turned-critic, Juma Khan Sufi: 'The credit definitely goes to Bacha Khan for starting the first ever-pure [first-ever pure] political movement on Pukhtoon soil. Before him all movements were basically religious in character, calling people to armed *jihads* and were thus retrogressive in nature and outlook.'[94] Although he neither waged nor advocated armed *jihad*, in fact his movement had a religious inclination as well. He claimed to have derived his guidelines from Islam, and that he and his associates were to serve only for the Almighty's sake—a religious claim.

His views and doctrine seemingly changed from pan-Pukhtunism to Indian nationalism in the 1930s, and then, in the post-Partition days, to Pukhtun nationalism compatible within the Pakistan framework. The focal point of his politics in the post-Partition days was the Frontier Province and getting a special status for it. Hence, 'While denying that he had ever supported an independent "Pukhtunistan", he continued to insist that the Frontier must have some special autonomous status.'[95] He 'will remain part and parcel of Pukhtoon history despite his failures and shortcomings'.[96]

Scottish scholar, Erland Jansson, stresses that Ghaffar Khan's son, Ghani Khan had observed that Ghaffar Khan was 'not an intellectual' but 'an instinctive man'. He further says:

> Moreover, he addresses himself to an overwhelmingly illiterate population. His speeches and writings are intended to move the masses, not to convince intellectuals. They are meant to make sense politically in specific political situations but were not conceived with a view to logical consistency. Often they are confused and contradictory, which his more sophisticated opponents have been quick to point out. Many an official has regarded Ghaffar Khan either as a simpleton or a hypocrite... This is unfair. In fact, his political writings and activities have shown remarkable consistency over the years and his perspicacity has often been striking.[97]

Ghaffar Khan did not regard himself as a politician—as he said in 1946: 'I must own that I am no politician.... I do not understand legalities. I know nothing of diplomacy. I want the freedom of India, and with me non-violence is not a policy but a permanent creed'.[98] One may disagree with his stand over, and role at, different issues and occasions, but he no doubt played a great role in politics (both direct and indirect) for most of his life, since he was in his 20s. And, 'the record of his sacrifices', Qaiyum Khan contends, 'is incomparable'.[99] M.S. Korejo, one of his critics, asserts:

> As a Congressman Ghaffar Khan participated in the battle of independence, in the battle against partition, and in the struggle against referendum. Some battles were won, others were lost. These experiences, along with long periods of imprisonments, strengthened his resolve and hardened his convictions. He never surrendered, nor compromised.[100]

His political ideals and role in politics continue to play a role in Pakistani politics, in spite of his death on 20 January 1988.

ROLE IN PROMOTION OF EDUCATION

As stated earlier, in chapter 9, Abdul Ghaffar Khan was admitted to the Edwardes Memorial Mission High School in Peshawar, where he was very impressed by the selfless services of the headmaster of the school, E.F.E. Wigram, and of his younger brother, Dr Wigram, who headed the Mission Hospital in Peshawar.[101] Their selflessness induced Ghaffar Khan to serve the Pukhtuns and his homeland. There was a lack of awareness and literacy in the province, leading to miserable conditions for the people, but neither the colonial[102] British government made proper arrangements to educate the people nor they themselves made any efforts. If a primary school was established anywhere in the province, the *mula*s (in Pukhtu: *mulan/mulyan*) would create a hurdle.[103] Commenting on the situation, Ghaffar Khan states:

> It is most regrettable…that the British had established no schools for us, and if there was any, the mullahs were set behind us to propagate that it was a sin to learn. They wanted the Pakhtuns to remain illiterate and ignorant. That is why the Pathans remained the most backward community throughout India.[104]

In addition to other points raised by the *mula*s, when propagating against modern or school-education, they said:

سبق د مدرسی وئ   دپاره د پیسی وئ[105]

جنت کښی به یی ځای نه وی   په دوزخ کښی به کسی وهی

Meaning: Those who learn at school (get modern education) do so just for earning money. They will have no place in the Heaven and will be tortured in Hell.

At an early age, Ghaffar Khan endeavoured to reason with the *mula*s, to convince them of the need for modern education, but it proved to be of no use. Convinced of its significance himself, he wanted to strive to establish *madrasah*s (in Pukhtu: *madrasay*; schools) to educate the Pukhtun children. He and his colleagues founded a Darul Ulum at Gaddar, under the patronage of the Haji Sahib of Turangzi; Mawlwi Taj Muhammad was made its head. The function of the Darul Ulum 'was to popularize education and to open schools in the villages'.[106] Eknath Easwaran, however, stated that the Gaddar school was 'for older boys'.[107] In 1910, Ghaffar Khan, only 20 years old, and Mawlwi Abdul Aziz established a *madrasah* (school) in Utmanzi, and began visiting other areas with a view to establishing more *madrasah*s. According to Rajmohan Gandhi: 'Taking a cue from the example of his former headmaster [E.F.E. Wigram], Ghaffar Khan and a friend opened a school in Utmanzai in 1910 and sought to enlist support for a network of schools elsewhere.'[108] He directed the people's attention towards modern education, and created a sense of its need and importance among the Pukhtuns. In this way, work on setting up *madrasah*s began and a number of them were established in a short time.[109] In Easwaran's words:

> Ghaffar's school had been an instant success. The mullahs had always urged villagers to boycott the British schools, but they had offered no real alternative. The more liberal Pathans began to take notice of the school in Utmanzai. [Ghaffar] Khan and his co-worker, Abdul Aziz, started several more like it in surrounding villages, and in a short time they had enrolled a large number of students.[110]

Both modern and religious education was imparted to the students at these *madrasah*s, to prepare them to meet the challenges of the time efficiently and effectively. The *mula*s were not happy about this, as they had never considered or acknowledged modern education as education. Ghaffar Khan has narrated that once, when they were in Muftiabad—a place near his home village—in connection with establishing a new *madrasah*, a *mula*, known as Chatralay Mula, came with a gun and books and said that he did not acknowledge that the education started by Ghaffar Khan was education. Also, that the books taught in these *madrasah*s contain 'ایک کٹ بھونکتا ہے' (a dog is barking) and 'A big fig'. He asked: Is this education (knowledge)?[111]

Despite their imparting religious education as well, the *mula*s opposed the *madrasah*s. To counter their opposition, Haji Sahib of Turangzi was made the patron of the *madrasah*s. This somewhat dampened the *mula*s' machinations and allowed the scheme to progress. Ghaffar Khan alleges that the British were also involved in the anti-*madrasah*s campaign.[112] Rajmohan Gandhi asserts that, in his 'venture' of schools, Ghaffar Khan 'received encouragement from Haji Fazli Wahid Sahib of the village of Turangzai, which was a mile away. Enjoying a high reputation in the Pakhtun country, the Haji also wanted to set up schools.' Both Ghaffar Khan and Haji Sahib envisioned 'schools that would promote not only reform among the Pakhtuns—the ending of feuds and of wasteful expenditure on weddings and funerals—but also autonomy vis-à-vis the British. These would be *azad madrassas*, independent Islamic schools.'[113]

Although 'no details are available about the exact number of these Madarris, the number of students, teachers and their source of income',[114] the 'main source of funding' was from the members of the Anjuman Islah-ul-Afaghinah, 'who contributed enormously'.[115]

The *madrasah*s were a success story. *Madrasah*s were established at a number of places and the children enrolled with great enthusiasm. However, a proportionate increase in financial resources was required for the progress and running of the institutions. To raise funds, tours were undertaken and people were asked to give alms in the form of raw material and cash instead of cooked food. Ways and means to meet the financial needs of the educational programme were worked at.[116]

Haji Sahib of Turangzi's patronage contributed towards countering the opposition of the *mula*s, and to the progress of the educational scheme for the time being, but it later proved to be a great set-back. Being anti-British, and associated with those who were struggling for the freedom of India, Haji Sahib of Turangzi made a *hijrat* (migration) to Bunair—part of the then-independent Pukhtun tribal tract known as Yaghistan (land of the unruly; land of those not subservient to any ruling authority; the land of rebels)—on the directives of Mahmud-ul-Hasan and Ubaidullah Sindhi, to start *jihad* against the British. This attempt proved to be a failure and provided an opportunity to the colonial British government to close the *madrasah*s. Ghaffar Khan argue that though the *madrasah*s did not belong to the Haji Sahib, and that he had been made the patron only to silence the opposition of the *mula*s, they were closed by the colonial government because of Haji Sahib's anti-British activities and because the *madrasah*s were considered a thorn in the side of the British. Moreover, the teachers, the workers, those who used to collect donations for the *madrasah*s, and those who looked after the *madrasah*s were also arrested. They were jailed, tortured, tyrannised, and ill-treated. Irreligious works were taken away from them, their beards were shaved, and they were beaten, disgraced, and treated inhumanly.[117] Although they were released after a year, the *madrasah*s received a blow that they did not recover from for years.

An offshoot of World War I was the *khilafat* and *hijrat* movements. Ghaffar Khan also felt compelled to resort to *hijrat* (migration) to Afghanistan. Because of the failure of the *hijrat* movement, he toured some of the tribal areas to establish *madrasah*s there, 'but, persuaded by the British Political Agent, the tribal chiefs' in Bajawar 'denied support' to him to open schools there and hence 'was obliged to return to Utmanzai'.[118] During the course of these visits, a *madrasah* was established in the village of Khalunah in Dir. It grew rapidly, to 400 students in a short time, but was later demolished and set on fire by the Nawab of Dir (Shah Jahan Khan) at the behest and instigation of the British political agent in Malakand.[119] Interestingly, the Political Agent, E.H.A. Cob, told the Nawab to observe the situation in the areas under British control—where they had provided some education facilities—as the agitation raging there at the time was sphere-headed by the modern-educated, and told him that 'all this education is creating endless trouble for us. If you want to avoid getting yourself into difficulties, you'd better see that this school is destroyed as soon as possible.'[120]

Observing the situation in Afghanistan and the tribal area, and having struggled in British India, for fifteen years, Ghaffar Khan was now convinced that revolution was neither easy nor it could be achieved in a hurry. He believed that one of the pre-requisites for revolution was education and knowledge, and the scholars and the learned—to encourage and guide the people towards revolution; also, that revolutions need personalities. Hence, he resolved to establish national schools (*qaumi madrasay*), to educate and train the revolutionaries, and so returned to Utmanzi after the *hijrat* and worked to re-open the *madrasah*s that had been closed by the colonial administration during World War I.[121]

Towards the end of 1920, Ghaffar Khan, along with Qazi Ataullah, went to Aligarh to participate in a function at the Aligarh Muslim University. There, they shared their views with students from the Frontier Province, among whom were those who had left college because of the non-cooperation programme that had been launched in India.[122]

In 1921, he founded, or in other words re-opened (because, as stated earlier, it was first opened in 1910 but closed by the British colonial government during World War I), the Azad Madrasah (Azad School) in Utmanzi with the support of his friends. Qazi Ataullah, Mian Ahmad Shah, Haji Abdul Ghaffar Khan, Muhammad Abbas Khan, Khan Ahmad Khan, Abdul Akbar Khan, Taj Muhammad Khan, Abdullah Shah, and Khadim Muhammad Akbar were his associates and were on the *madrasah*'s staff. Due to a shortage of both teachers and funds, Ghaffar Khan personally taught the students. Amir Mukhtar Khan of village Mira Khail, Bannu, sent his two sons, Amir Mumtaz Khan and Maqsud Jan, to teach at the Azad Madrasah, Utmanzi. The two brothers were students at the Islamia College Peshawar but left the college during the *tark-i mawalat* movement. Maqsud Jan became the first headmaster of the Azad Madrasah; when he rejoined Islamia College, he was replaced by Amir Mumtaz Khan.[123] According to Rajmohan Gandhi: 'Returning to the Frontier, he raised the Utmanzai school to high-school level. Talented teachers joined him in instructing pupils in a range of subjects including Pakhtun history and Islam. Pakhto was the language of instruction.'[124] The curriculum not only 'included teaching of Holy Quran and *Hadith*, *Fiqha* [*fiqah*], Islamic history, Pashto, Mathematics, English and Arabic' but 'vocational skills like carpentry, weaving and tailoring were also introduced in the school'.[125] Not only were new *madrasah*s opened, but the old ones were also re-opened. In Easwaran's words: 'He stormed the Pathan villages, reopening schools, starting new ones, and urging villagers to improve their lot.'[126]

The colonial authorities did not like the Azad Madrasah. They tried, in one way or another, to dissuade the teachers from teaching there. They 'tried to frighten the teachers who joined' the school, and also 'to entice them' away by offering them high-paying jobs or by constantly harassing the new teachers.[127] Eknath Easwaran comments: 'Activities and ideas which could be tolerated and even encouraged in greater India alarmed the military officials of the Frontier. As the Frontier went, its officials argued, so did India.'[128] The Chief Commissioner, Hamilton Grant, called Ghaffar Khan's father and asked him what his son was doing. Grant told him that while the people were living quietly and peacefully, his son was establishing *madrasah*s and instigating the people against the British; he warned him to stop his son. Grant's Secretary, Sadullah Khan of Umarzi, also told Ghaffar Khan's father that the chief commissioner gave him respect and honoured him; in return, he had to ask his son (Ghaffar Khan) to stop his activities of educating the people—in consideration of the chief commissioner. Hence, Ghaffar Khan's father asked him to stop his mission as the colonial British government did not like it and that, if others were not spreading education, why was he? Ghaffar Khan replied that he would do so, but as a lot of people had stopped offering their prayers, he would also do so, and that his father would not then question him. His father retorted that prayers are obligatory (*farz*). Ghaffar Khan replied that education is also obligatory—at which his father told him to continue with his mission. Moreover, Ghaffar Khan's father went to the chief commissioner and told him that they would not give up their religion to please the British.[129] And, 'when a British officer directly confronted Ghaffar Khan, the latter answered that he wanted his schools to be like the missionary school he had attended. "This is not service but rebellion", he [Ghaffar Khan] was told',[130] by the officer.

During this time, a rift started among the Frontier exponents of the *khilafat*. It became routine that one group would announce a person as the president of the provincial *khilafat* committee one day, and the next day the other group would announce another person as the president. This state of affairs adversely affected the *khilafat* movement in the province. To solve the problem, both the groups asked Ghaffar Khan to become the president of the provincial *khilafat* committee. He accepted, on their insistence, but on the condition that the subscriptions collected in the Frontier Province would not be sent to Punjab but would be spent on education in the province. He also went on tours to achieve his purpose.[131] This demonstrates the extent to which he was concerned about the spread of education in the province. In Tendulkar's words: 'The spread of education was a passion with him and he bent his energies to make it a success. He started on a tour to renew his contacts with the people and to restart the defunct schools which had attracted children of the tribesmen from the contiguous areas of Malakand, Bajaur and Swat.'[132]

However, he was imprisoned on 17 December 1921, under section 40 of the Frontier Crimes Regulation, 1901, for his association with the *khilafat* movement and the establishment of the Azad *madrasah*s. The deputy commissioner sentenced him to three years' rigorous imprisonment. The colonial government offered to release him and permit him to run the *madrasah*s, but on the condition that he would not go on his tours. He declined this offer.[133] And the Azad School 'flourished during the incarnation' of Ghaffar Khan and 'the imprisonment...popularized his cause'.[134] His imprisonment made the people 'more sympathetic to' the 'Azad school and they gave larger aid'.[135] On his release from jail, after three years, he took on the work of the *madrasah*s and the reform of the Pukhtuns. He was so focussed that he asked all those who wished to offer him hospitality, according to Pukhtun traditions, to give the amount they would have spent on the hospitality to him in cash—to be utilised for education and education-oriented work.[136] He stressed the need for change in the method of alms-giving; instead of distributing money in kind among the people, he gave 2,000 rupees to the village school—in memory of his father who had passed away.[137] However, as stated earlier, the main source of funding for these schools came from the members of the Anjuman Islah-ul-Afaghinah, who 'contributed generously to finance them'.[138]

The colonial British authorities endeavoured to make a failure of the reform and education movement but to no avail. Although Ghaffar Khan was imprisoned, a number of *madrasah*s were opened in different parts of the province through the efforts of the Anjuman Islah-ul-Afaghinah and the great enthusiasm of the people for their children's education. After his release, Ghaffar Khan and Khadim Muhammad Akbar started touring and inspecting the *madrasah*s. During their tours, Khadim Muhammad Akbar conducted examinations while Ghaffar Khan discussed affairs with the people. The visits were successful; they not only visited the *madrasah*s of Ashnaghar, Duwawa (Doaba), Mardan, and Swabi regions, as well as visited Peshawar, Kuhat, and Bannu districts, but two more *maktab*s (lower schools) were also opened in Bannu with the cooperation of the *mula*s.[139] Although an accurate figure is not available about the number of Azad schools, 'a careful study suggests' it to be seventy.[140] However, according to Rittenberg:

> The *Azad* schools were, for the most part, *ad hoc* bodies which were strapped for funds, lacked qualified staff, and had no fixed curriculum. According to a 1922 government report, '. . . no regular scheme of instruction appears to be followed. Schools open, exist for a few months and then close. Their pupils have then to shift for themselves. . . .' . . . The exception to this pattern was the original school in Utmanzai, which was affiliated with Jamia Millia in Delhi and prepared its pupils for the matriculation exam of the Punjab University. The main goals of even that *Azad* school, however, were to offer instruction in Islam, foster Pashtu culture, and promote a sense of ethnic self-awareness and pride.[141]

Ghaffar Khan's love and passion for modern education was not restricted to men; he wanted Pukhtun 'women to study'[142] as well; not only did he do his best to educate his sons abroad to a high standard, but 'in 1932' also 'sent his daughter Mehr Taj, who had just entered her teens, to study in England'.[143] When she was 14, she was brought back from England 'to join the Kanya Ashram, a girls' institute at Wardha'.[144] He asked Gandhi to assist him in his struggle for women's education, and so 'Gandhi first sent Mirabehn and then Bibi Amtus Salam', for the purpose.[145] Ghaffar Khan and his colleagues established 'a girls' school' which, according to Mary Barr, an English missionary teacher, was 'a rare thing in the Muslim North'.[146]

When the journal *Pukhtun* was re-started and there was a lack of encouraging responses to articles on women's problem, written by women themselves, Ghaffar Khan expressed dissatisfaction over this state of affairs in a column in the *Pukhtun*:

> It seems to me that none is interested in raising the status of their sisters and daughters. Here, I want to draw the attention of my Pakhtun brethren to the fact that unless the women are enlightened, no community in the world can be truly enlightened. The community in which the women are not well trained,

can never enjoy freedom. Men and women are like two wheels of a cart. A cart with one wheel cannot move. The mother's lap is the first training-school for a child. And the child, indeed, constitutes the community. A worthy mother rears a worthy child, and an educated mother an educated child. A father does not influence a child to the extent the mother does. I laugh at the ways of most of the educated families today. Their women folk are illiterate. Civilization and culture of a community depend to a large extent on the help rendered to it by its women folk.[147]

Ghaffar Khan's desire to educate both genders of the province was constantly on his mind. In 1931, when Jawaharlal Nehru told him that the Congress was going to increase the Peshawar Congress Committee's monetary assistance from 500 rupees to 1,000 rupees per month; he refused to accept the offer and told Nehru: 'If you want to help us then build a girls' school and a hospital for our women.'[148] During an interview with the chief commissioner of the province, Ralph Griffith, Ghaffar Khan told him: 'Schools should be built in the tribal area for helping the children to lead a new life. Hospitals should be opened for their succour. Such facilities will enable these chivalrous and brave people to become useful members of the Pakhtun society.'[149]

However, because of Ghaffar Khan and his associates' increasing occupation with other matters—such as the founding of the Khudayi Khidmatgar movement, their association with the Congress, and other developments—their endeavours for the spread and promotion of education received a great set-back, and ultimately faded away. Nevertheless, his role in introducing, familiarising, and spreading modern education in the Frontier Province cannot be underestimated.

Ghaffar Khan, convinced of the need for, and significance of, modern education established the *madrasah* (school), for the first time, in Utmanzi in 1910, and later endeavoured to extend the chain to other parts of the province. Like Sir Sayyad Ahmad Khan, he and his associates established institutions where both modern and religious education was imparted. He might have surpassed Sir Sayyad Ahmad Khan in the service of education had his own and his associates' activities not taken a political anti-British turn, which greatly hampered their educational endeavours—because of the British government's fears and apprehensions and because of Ghaffar Khan and his associates' occupation in other matters at an all-India level. His contribution in providing education to the people was no less than that of Sir Sayyad Ahmad Khan or Sir Sayyad-i Sarhad (Sahibzadah Abdul Qayyum), nor can the contribution of his associates be ignored or underestimated.

Ghaffar Khan surpassed Sahibzadah Abdul Qayyum in the service and promotion of education in the Frontier Province, as he—along with his associates—established educational institutions on his/their own initiative. While Sahibzadah Abdul Qayyum demonstrated his own initiative, and the interest demonstrated by Roos-Keppel, he was persuaded, to promote education in the Frontier, by the students of Aligarh College among others. Moreover, Ghaffar Khan and his associates did not have the support of the colonial British government, but had to face opposition and hurdles from that quarter; Sahibzadah Abdul Qayyum, on the other hand, enjoyed the colonial British government's full support, assistance, and blessings: both the opposition, and the blessings, of the colonial government had significant favourable and unfavourable repercussions and consequences, respectively, in that scenario and environment.

Notes

1. Amit Kumar Gupta, *North West Frontier Province: Legislature and Freedom Struggle, 1932–47* (New Delhi: ICHR, 1976), 14.

2. For details, see Abdul Ghaffar [Khan], *Zama Jwand aw Jidujahd* (Pukhtu) (Kabul: DM, 1983), 84–113; D.G. Tendulkar, *Abdul Ghaffar Khan: faith is a battle* (Bombay: PP, 1967), 24–5; Khan Abdul Ghaffar Khan, *Ap Biti* (Urdu) (Lahore: FH, 2004), 26–30.

3. For details, see Ghaffar, *Zama Jwand aw Jidujahd*, 135–60; Khan, *Ap Biti*, 35–40. Abdul Ghaffar Khan's own, and others', versions vary about how and why he was given the title/epithet of Bacha Khan/Badshah Khan. See Ghaffar, *Zama Jwand aw Jidujahd*, 136–7 cf. Tendulkar, *Abdul Ghaffar Khan*, 26; and Eknath Easwaran, *A Man to Match His Mountains: Badshah Khan, Nonviolent Soldier of Islam*, with afterword by Timothy Flinders, 2nd print (California: Nilgiri Press, 1985), 79.

4. Tendulkar, *Abdul Ghaffar Khan*, 32.

5. See ibid., 31–3; Khan, *Ap Biti*, 43–8; Ghaffar, *Zama Jwand aw Jidujahd*, 170–83.

6. Tendulkar, *Abdul Ghaffar Khan*, 36. Also see Abdul Khaliq Khaleeq, *Da Azadai Jang: Sah Lidali aw sah Awridali* (Pukhtu), 2nd edn. (Pikhawar: IIS, 1972), 23.

7. Ghaffar, *Zama Jwand aw Jidujahd*, 183–4.

8. See ibid., 186–309; Tendulkar, *Abdul Ghaffar Khan*, 36–46; Khan, *Ap Biti*, 49–78.

9. Tendulkar, *Abdul Ghaffar Khan*, 220.

10. Ghaffar, *Zama Jwand aw Jidujahd*, 320.

11. Tendulkar, *Abdul Ghaffar Khan*, 48.

12. For details, see Ghaffar, *Zama Jwand aw Jidujahd*, 339–52; Tendulkar, *Abdul Ghaffar Khan*, 56–8; Khan, *Ap Biti*, 86–93. Also see Khaleeq, *Da Azadai Jang*, 53–4.

13. For details, see Ghaffar, *Zama Jwand aw Jidujahd*, 333–5; Tendulkar, *Abdul Ghaffar Khan*, 50–5; Khan, *Ap Biti*, 85–6.

14. Abdul Qaiyum, *Gold and Guns on the Pathan Frontier* (Bombay: HK, 1945), 24.

15. For some details about the Khudayi Khidmatgar Organisation, see chap. 9 of this book. Also see Sultan-i-Rome, 'The Khudai Khidmatgar Movement: From Genesis to Downfall', *Hamdard Islamicus* (Karachi), vol. 30 (No. 1, January–March 2007), 35–55.

16. Qaiyum, *Gold and Guns on the Pathan Frontier*, 42.

17. Tendulkar, *Abdul Ghaffar Khan*, 59.

18. Ibid., 62.

19. Ibid., 63.

20. See Ghaffar, *Zama Jwand aw Jidujahd*, 370–4; Khan, *Ap Biti*, 99–100.

21. Jawaharlal Nehru, *The Discovery of India*, 12th impr. (New Delhi: JNMF, 1992), 381.

22. Juma Khan Sufi, *Bacha Khan, Congress and Nationalist Politics in NWFP* [henceforward Sufi, *Bacha Khan*] (Lahore: VB, 2005), 329.

23. Tendulkar, *Abdul Ghaffar Khan*, 78. For his tours, also see Easwaran, *A Man to Match His Mountains*, 131–6; Ghaffar, *Zama Jwand aw Jidujahd*, 416–18, 451–8; Khan, *Ap Biti*, 119–21, 125.

24. Gupta, *North West Frontier Province*, 26.

25. See Tendulkar, *Abdul Ghaffar Khan*, 79–100; Ghaffar, *Zama Jwand aw Jidujahd*, 418–39; Khan, *Ap Biti*, 123–33.

26. Ghaffar, *Zama Jwand aw Jidujahd*, 566, 583. Also see Easwaran, *A Man to Match His Mountains*, 146.

27. Easwaran, *A Man to Match His Mountains*, 146; Ghaffar, *Zama Jwand aw Jidujahd*, 566–7; S.M. Ikram, *Modern Muslim India and the Birth of Pakistan*, repr. (Lahore: IIC, 2016), 351. Also see Khaleeq, *Da Azadai Jang*, 122–3.

28. See Ikram, *Modern Muslim India and the Birth of Pakistan*, 351.

29. See ibid.; Khaleeq, *Da Azadai Jang*, 122–3.

30. Sufi, *Bacha Khan*, 47.

31. Tendulkar, *Abdul Ghaffar Khan*, 123. Also see Khan, *Ap Biti*, 135.

32. See Ghaffar, *Zama Jwand aw Jidujahd*, 567–70, 578–610; Khan, *Ap Biti*, 149–51.

33. See Khan, *Ap Biti*, 151–3; Ghaffar, *Zama Jwand aw Jidujahd*, 570–9; Tendulkar, *Abdul Ghaffar Khan*, 193–216.

34. Tendulkar, *Abdul Ghaffar Khan*, 218.

35. Easwaran, *A Man to Match His Mountains*, 167–8. For the date and detail of the meeting, see Tendulkar, *Abdul Ghaffar Khan*, 315–28.

36. Tendulkar, *Abdul Ghaffar Khan*, 332. For detail of the meeting, see ibid., 329–32.

37. See Ghaffar, *Zama Jwand aw Jidujahd*, 651–4. Also see Khan, *Ap Biti*, 156; K.B. Narag, *My Life and Struggle: Autobiography of Badshah Khan as narrated to K.B. Narag*, with foreword by Jayaprakash Narayan, repr. (n.p.: DAT, 2008), 150; Tendulkar, *Abdul Ghaffar Khan*, 341–3.

38. Tendulkar, *Abdul Ghaffar Khan*, 343.

39. Sayed Wiqar Ali Shah, 'Abdul Ghaffar Khan' in Parvez Khan Toru and Fazal-ur-Rahim Marwat, eds., *Celebrities of NWFP*, vol[s]. 1–2 (Peshawar: Pakistan Study Centre, University of Peshawar, 2005), 116; Sayed Wiqar Ali Shah, *North-West Frontier Province: History and Politics* (Islamabad: NIHCR, 2007), 75.

40. Tendulkar, *Abdul Ghaffar Khan*, 403.

41. Ibid., 406.

42. Rajmohan Gandhi, *Ghaffar Khan: Nonviolent Badshah of the Pakhtuns* (New Delhi: Penguin Books India (Pvt) Ltd., 2008), 163. For the events, Ghaffar Khan's asking for soldiers, the use of force, lauding his brother's act of threatening to use a revolver, and the people taking up arms, see Khan, *Ap Biti*, 183–7; Tendulkar, *Abdul Ghaffar Khan*, 387–9; Ghaffar, *Zama Jwand aw Jidujahd*, 711–16; Narag, *My Life and Struggle*, 175–81.

43. See Tendulkar, *Abdul Ghaffar Khan*, 418; Ghaffar, *Zama Jwand aw Jidujahd*, 687–8; Khan, *Ap Biti*, 197. Also see chap. 9 of this book.

44. For instances, see Tendulkar, *Abdul Ghaffar Khan*, 35; Easwaran, *A Man to Match His Mountains*, 78–9, 170; MS Korejo, *The Frontier Gandhi: His Place in History*, 2nd edn. (Karachi: OUP, 1994), 49; Sufi, *Bacha Khan*, 15–16.

45. See Shah, 'Abdul Ghaffar Khan' in Toru and Fazal-ur-Rahim Marwat, eds., *Celebrities of NWFP*, vol[s.] 1–2, 110–11. Also see Shah, *North-West Frontier Province*, 68.

46. Nehru, *The Discovery of India*, 381.

47. Stephen Alan Rittenberg, *Ethnicity, Nationalism, and the Pakhtuns: The Independence Movement in India's North-West Frontier Province* (Durham: CAP, 1988), 150.

48. Tendulkar, *Abdul Ghaffar Khan*, 429.

49. Olaf Caroe, *The Pathans: 550 B.C.–A.D. 1957*, repr. (Karachi: OUP, 1976), 433.

50. Rittenberg, *Ethnicity, Nationalism, and the Pakhtuns*, 150.

51. See Ghaffar, *Zama Jwand aw Jidujahd*, 666–71; Tendulkar, *Abdul Ghaffar Khan*, 353–5; Khan, *Ap Biti*, 157–61.

52. Easwaran, *A Man to Match His Mountains*, 172. Also see Ghaffar, *Zama Jwand aw Jidujahd*, 666–74, 684–5.

53. See Ghaffar, *Zama Jwand aw Jidujahd*, 698–700; Tendulkar, *Abdul Ghaffar Khan*, 369–70; Khan, *Ap Biti*, 179–80.

54. See Ghaffar, *Zama Jwand aw Jidujahd*, 701. Ghaffar Khan has contended that if Gandhi had headed the government, there would never have been the catastrophe and destruction that occurred in India in 1947 as a result of the partition; in case of his being uneasy with the power, he would have given it away after completing the task—as Mao did (see ibid.).

55. Easwaran, *A Man to Match His Mountains*, 176.

56. Tendulkar, *Abdul Ghaffar Khan*, 439.

57. Ibid., 440.

58. Ibid., 440–1.

59. Ibid., 441.

60. Ibid.

61. Ibid., 441; also see ff. (viz. the pages following p. 441).

62. Ibid., 451.

63. For his such a stand, see ibid., 424–5; Ghaffar, *Zama Jwand aw Jidujahd*, 732–8; Khan, *Ap Biti*, 199–200; Narag, *My Life and Struggle*, 165–7.

64. Sufi, *Bacha Khan*, 347.

65. Ibid., 359.

66. Tendulkar, *Abdul Ghaffar Khan*, 451.

67. For his defence of his new stand, see ibid., 451–3.

68. See ibid., 453–8.

69. Abul Kalam Azad, *India Wins Freedom: An Autobiographical Narrative*, repr. (Bombay: OLL, 1964), 195.

70. For instances of such claims by Ghaffar Khan, see Ghaffar, *Zama Jwand aw Jidujahd*, 479–80, 695–6, 726–7; Khan, *Ap Biti*, 107.

71. See Tendulkar, *Abdul Ghaffar Khan*, 460–3.

72. Ibid., 457.

73. Shah, 'Abdul Ghaffar Khan' in Toru and Fazal-ur-Rahim Marwat, eds., *Celebrities of NWFP*, vol[s]. 1–2, 117–18. Also see Sayed Wiqar Ali Shah, *Ethnicity, Islam, and Nationalism: Muslim Politics in the North-West Frontier Province, 1937–1947* (Karachi: OUP, 1999), 173; Shah, *North-West Frontier Province*, 76–7.

74. Tendulkar, *Abdul Ghaffar Khan*, 460, 463.

75. Ibid., 464–5. Also see Narag, *My Life and Struggle*, 195.

76. Tendulkar, *Abdul Ghaffar Khan*, 471. Also see Narag, *My Life and Struggle*, 195–6.

77. Tendulkar, *Abdul Ghaffar Khan*, 475.

78. See ibid., 476–80.

79. Ibid., 487.

80. Ibid., 490.

81. See ibid., 490–504.

82. See ibid., 505–16.

83. Ibid., 516–18.

84. Ibid., 520–7.

85. Ibid., 11, 528.

86. Ibid., 529.

87. Ghaffar Khan, *My Life and Struggle*, 243–4 quoted in Gandhi, *Ghaffar Khan*, 243. Also see Narag, *My Life and Struggle*, 229.

88. Mohammed Talukdar, ed., *Memoirs of H.S. Suhrawardy* (Dhaka: University Press, 1987), 99 quoted in Gandhi, *Ghaffar Khan*, 244.

89. Sher Zaman Taizi, *Bacha Khan in Afghanistan: A Memoir* (*June 2002*, in www. asianreflection.com edited by Damon Lynch, August 2002) quoted in Gandhi, *Ghaffar Khan*, 243.

90. S. Fida Yunas, *Abdul Ghaffar Khan, "Pushtunistan" and Afghanistan* (Peshawar: By the Author, n.d.), 68–9; Sher Zaman Taizi, *Bacha Khan in Afghanistan* quoted in Gandhi, *Ghaffar Khan*, 250–1.

91. Gandhi, *Ghaffar Khan*, 262.

92. J.N. Dixit, *An Afghan Diary: Zahir Shah to Taliban* (New Delhi: Konark, 2000), 30–1 quoted in Gandhi, *Ghaffar Khan*, 254–5. Also see Sufi, *Bacha Khan*, 340–1.

93. See Gandhi, *Ghaffar Khan*, 255–9; Sufi, *Bacha Khan*, 341–2.

94. Sufi, *Bacha Khan*, 331.

95. James W. Spain, *The Pathan Borderland*, repr. (Karachi: IP, 1985), 226.

96. Sufi, *Bacha Khan*, 336.

97. Erland Jansson, *India, Pakistan or Pakhtunistan: The Nationalist Movements in the North-West Frontier Province, 1937–47* (Stockholm: AWI, 1981), 49.

98. Andre Singer, *Lords of the Khyber: The Story of the North-West Frontier* (London: FFL, 1984), 206.

99. Qaiyum, *Gold and Guns on the Pathan Frontier*, 44.

100. Korejo, *The Frontier Gandhi*, 195.

101. See Tendulkar, *Abdul Ghaffar Khan*, 21; Ghaffar, *Zama Jwand aw Jidujahd*, 65–6; Easwaran, *A Man to Match His Mountains*, 55; Khan, *Ap Biti*, 23–4.

102. For the 'colonial' and 'colonialist', see note 29 in chapter 6.

103. Ghaffar, *Zama Jwand aw Jidujahd*, 65–6; Khan, *Ap Biti*, 23–4; Narag, *My Life and Struggle*, 3–5.

104. Tendulkar, *Abdul Ghaffar Khan*, 15; Narag, *My Life and Struggle*, 3.

105. Ghaffar, *Zama Jwand aw Jidujahd*, 15; Narag, *My Life and Struggle*, 5.

106. Tendulkar, *Abdul Ghaffar Khan*, 22. Also see Khan, *Ap Biti*, 24–5; Narag, *My Life and Struggle*, 20.

107. Easwaran, *A Man to Match His Mountains*, 67.

108. Gandhi, *Ghaffar Khan*, 46. Also see Khan, *Ap Biti*, 24.

109. Ghaffar, *Zama Jwand aw Jidujahd*, 66; Khan, *Ap Biti*, 25.

110. Easwaran, *A Man to Match His Mountains*, 66.

111. See Ghaffar, *Zama Jwand aw Jidujahd*, 66–7.

112. See ibid., 68–70.

113. Gandhi, *Ghaffar Khan*, 47.

114. Shah, 'Abdul Ghaffar Khan' in Toru and Fazal-ur-Rahim Marwat, eds., *Celebrities of NWFP*, vol[s]. 1–2, 104. Also see Shah, *Ethnicity, Islam, and Nationalism*, 18.

115. Shah, *North-West Frontier Province*, 63.

116. See Ghaffar, *Zama Jwand aw Jidujahd*, 89–92.

117. See ibid., 107–17. Ghaffar Khan's own account contends that the Haji Sahib of Turangzi was made patron later, to counter and silence the *mulas*' propaganda and opposition, but D.G. Tendulkar's statement gives the impression that the Haji Sahib was associated with

Ghaffar Khan in the establishment of the *madrasah*s (schools) from the start (see Tendulkar, *Abdul Ghaffar Khan*, 22. Also see Shah, *Ethnicity, Islam, and Nationalism*, 18; Shah, 'Abdul Ghaffar Khan' in Toru and Fazal-ur-Rahim Marwat, eds., *Celebrities of NWFP*, vol[s]. 1–2, 104).

118. Gandhi, *Ghaffar Khan*, 60.
119. See Ghaffar, *Zama Jwand aw Jidujahd*, 178–9. Also see Tendulkar, *Abdul Ghaffar Khan*, 33; Khan, *Ap Biti*, 47; Narag, *My Life and Struggle*, 44–5.
120. Easwaran, *A Man to Match His Mountains*, 78; Narag, *My Life and Struggle*, 44–5; Khan, *Ap Biti*, 47.
121. See Ghaffar, *Zama Jwand aw Jidujahd*, 182–3; Khan, *Ap Biti*, 47.
122. See Ghaffar, *Zama Jwand aw Jidujahd*, 183; Khan, *Ap Biti*, 47–8; Narag, *My Life and Struggle*, 45.
123. Ghaffar, *Zama Jwand aw Jidujahd*, 183–5; Khan, *Ap Biti*, 48–9; Tendulkar, *Abdul Ghaffar Khan*, 36. Also see Khaleeq, *Da Azadai Jang*, 23–4; Narag, *My Life and Struggle*, 46–7.
124. Gandhi, *Ghaffar Khan*, 61.
125. Shah, 'Abdul Ghaffar Khan' in Toru and Fazal-ur-Rahim Marwat, eds., *Celebrities of NWFP*, vol[s]. 1–2, 107; Shah, *Ethnicity, Islam, and Nationalism*, 23; Shah, *North-West Frontier Province*, 63.
126. Easwaran, *A Man to Match His Mountains*, 77.
127. Tendulkar, *Abdul Ghaffar Khan*, 36.
128. Easwaran, *A Man to Match His Mountains*, 83.
129. Ghaffar, *Zama Jwand aw Jidujahd*, 185–6. Also see Tendulkar, *Abdul Ghaffar Khan*, 37; Easwaran, *A Man to Match His Mountains*, 83–4; Khan, *Ap Biti*, 51–2; Narag, *My Life and Struggle*, 49–50. Eknath Easwaran and D.G. Tendulkar had given the name of the chief commissioner as John Maffey, but Ghaffar Khan himself has referred to him as Hamilton Grant.
130. Gandhi, *Ghaffar Khan*, 62. Also see Easwaran, *A Man to Match His Mountains*, 84.
131. See Ghaffar, *Zama Jwand aw Jidujahd*, 186–7; Tendulkar, *Abdul Ghaffar Khan*, 36–7; Khan, *Ap Biti*, 51; Narag, *My Life and Struggle*, 48–9.
132. Tendulkar, *Abdul Ghaffar Khan*, 37.
133. Ghaffar, *Zama Jwand aw Jidujahd*, 190–3; Easwaran, *A Man to Match His Mountains*, 84–7. Also see Gandhi, *Ghaffar Khan*, 62–3, 66.
134. Gandhi, *Ghaffar Khan*, 74. Also see Khan, *Ap Biti*, 71.
135. Tendulkar, *Abdul Ghaffar Khan*, 45. Also see Khan, *Ap Biti*, 78.
136. Ghaffar, *Zama Jwand aw Jidujahd*, 307–8.
137. Tendulkar, *Abdul Ghaffar Khan*, 47.
138. Shah, *Ethnicity, Islam, and Nationalism*, 23. Also see Shah, 'Abdul Ghaffar Khan' in Toru and Fazal-ur-Rahim Marwat, eds., *Celebrities of NWFP*, vol[s]. 1–2, 107; Shah, *North-West Frontier Province*, 63.
139. Ghaffar, *Zama Jwand aw Jidujahd*, 311–16.
140. Shah, 'Abdul Ghaffar Khan' in Toru and Fazal-ur-Rahim Marwat, eds., *Celebrities of NWFP*, vol[s]. 1–2, 106–7; Shah, *Ethnicity, Islam, and Nationalism*, 23.
141. Rittenberg, *Ethnicity, Nationalism, and the Pakhtuns*, 70.
142. Gandhi, *Ghaffar Khan*, 3.
143. Ibid.
144. Tendulkar, *Abdul Ghaffar Khan*, 195; Easwaran, *A Man to Match His Mountains*, 145.
145. Tendulkar, *Abdul Ghaffar Khan*, 289.
146. Easwaran, *A Man to Match His Mountains*, 169.
147. Tendulkar, *Abdul Ghaffar Khan*, 289–90.
148. Ibid., 125. Also see Khan, *Ap Biti*, 124; Narag, *My Life and Struggle*, 121.
149. Tendulkar, *Abdul Ghaffar Khan*, 133; Khan, *Ap Biti*, 136.

Bibliography

UNPUBLISHED OFFICIAL RECORD

District Record Room, at Gulkadah, Swat

Record of Swat State/District Swat

District/Sadar Qanungu Office, at Gulkadah, Swat

Settlement Record of District Swat

National Documentation Centre, Cabinet Division, Islamabad

India Office Record (Microfilm Copies)

Personal Collection of the Author (Sultan-i-Rome), Hazarah, Swat

Miscellaneous

Provincial Archives, NWFP (Khyber Pukhtunkhwa) at Peshawar (Record Section)

Files of Chief Commissioner Office, Peshawar
Files of Commissioner Office, Peshawar
Files of Deputy Commissioner Office, Peshawar
Files of Inventories of Documents
Files of Special Branch Police NWFP
Files of Tribal Research Cell (Agencies)

Tribal Affairs Research Cell, NWFP (Khyber Pukhtunkhwa), at Peshawar

Dir Distt:/State Files
Swat Files

INTERVIEWS

Dr Lal Baha (died on 4 February 2011). Peshawar, verbal, 22 June 2009.
Muhammad Asif Khan (died 2002). Writer of the autobiography of Miangul Abdul Wadud (ruler of Swat State, 1917–1949), with *dibachah*, *hisah awal*, *saluramah hisah*, and *hisah pinzamah* by him. A learned person with analytical ability and critical perception but fell prey to distorting facts being court writer, a fact he admitted in the course of his interview. Saidu Sharif, Swat, verbal, 24 May and 14 June 1998.

UNPUBLISHED WORKS

Hassan, Syed Minhaj ul. 'NWFP Administration under Abdul Qaiyum Khan, 1947–53.' PhD Dissertation, Department of History, University of Peshawar, 2003.
Jadoon, Muhammad Mushtaq. 'Note on Durand Line Issues' (June 2003). Tribal Affairs Research Cell, Home and Tribal Affairs Department, North-West Frontier Province, Peshawar, Book No. 988.

Khan, Muhammad Nasir. 'History of Constitutional Development in N-W.F.P. (1901–1932).' MPhil Thesis, Department of History, University of Peshawar, [1999].

Khan, Munir. 'The Khudai Khidmatgar Movement.' A Term Paper Submitted to the Department of History, University of Peshawar, 1994.

Sultan-i-Rome. 'Swat State under the Walis (1917–69).' PhD Dissertation, Department of History, University of Peshawar, 2000.

Tribal Areas: Status, Border Control and Policy; Governor's Committee Report. Government of North-West Frontier Province, Home and Tribal Affairs Department, September–October 1997.

CONFIDENTIAL OFFICIAL REPORTS

Administration Reports of the North-West Frontier Province

Administration Reports of the North-West Frontier Province: From 9 November 1901 to 31 March 1903; and for the years: 1921–22, 1922–23.

Punjab Frontier Administration Reports

Punjab Frontier Administration Reports for the Years: 1893–94, 1894–95.

Reports on the Administration of the Border of the North-West Frontier Province

Reports on the Administration of the Border of the North-West Frontier Province for the years: 1901–02, 1902–03, 1906–07, 1907–08, 1909–10, 1910–11, 1911–12, 1912–13, 1913–14, 1914–15, 1915–16, 1916–17, 1917–18, 1918–19, 1919–20, 1921–22, 1922–23, 1924–25, 1925–26, 1926–27, 1929–30, 1935–36, 1938–39.

Reports on the Administration of the 'Frontier Regions'

Report on the Administration of the "Frontier Regions" for the year 1948–49.

Reports on the Administration of the Punjab and its Dependencies

Reports on the Administration of the Punjab and its Dependencies for the years: 1875–76, 1876–77, 1877–78, 1878–79, 1879–80, 1880–81, 1881–82, 1882–83, 1883–84, 1884–85, 1886–87, 1887–88, 1888–89, 1889–90, 1890–91, 1891–92, 1892–93, 1893–94, 1895–96, 1896–97, 1897–98, 1898–99.

Summary of Events in North-West Frontier Tribal Territory

Summary of Events in North-West Frontier Tribal Territory: 1 January 1923 to 31 December 1923; 1 January 1924 to 31 December 1924; 1 January 1925 to 31 December 1925; 1 January 1926 to 31 December 1926; 1 January 1927 to 31 December 1927; 1 January 1928 to 31 December 1928; 1 January 1930 to 31 December 1930.

The North-West Frontier of Pakistan: Reports on the Administration

The North-West Frontier of Pakistan: Reports on the Administration for the years: 1953–54; 1954–55; 1955–56.

The North-West Frontier of Pakistan: Reports on the Administration of Tribal Areas of Peshawar and D.I. Khan Divisions

The North-West Frontier of Pakistan: Reports on the Administration of Tribal Areas of Peashawar and D.I. Khan Divisions for the years: 1956–57; 1957–58; 1958–59.

The North-West Frontier of Pakistan: Reports on the Border Administration

The North-West Frontier of Pakistan: Reports on the Border Administration for the years: 1949–50; 1950–51; 1951–52.

CENSUS REPORTS

Census of India, 1941. Vol. 10-Appendix, *Trans-Border Areas: Report and Tables*. By I.D. Scott. Delhi: Manager of Publications, 1942.

Census of Pakistan, 1951. Vol. 4. *North-West Frontier Province, Reports & Tables*. Karachi: Manager of Publications, Government of Pakistan, n.d.

Population Census of Pakistan 1961: Census Report of Tribal Agencies. Parts I–III. *General Description, Population Tables and Village Statistics*. Karachi: Manager of Publications, Government of Pakistan, n.d.

OFFICIAL/SEMI OFFICIAL WORKS

(Confidential), Central Asia. Part I. *A Contribution towards the Better Knowledge of the Topography, Ethnography, Statistics, & History of the North-West Frontier of British India*. Vol. 3. Compiled for Military and Political Reference by C.M. MacGregor. Calcutta: Office of the Superintendent of Government Printing, 1873.

Confidential, Gazetteer of the North-West Frontier: From Bajaur and the Indus Kohistan on the North to the Mari Hills on the South. Vols. 1 & 4. Compiled for Political and Military Reference in the Intelligence Branch of the Quarter Master General's Department in India. Completed and edited by A.L'e. Holmes. Simla: Printed at the Government Central Branch Press, 1887.

"Extract from Civil and Mily: Gaz: dated 6 March 1898, 'The Rising in Swat'." *Civil & Military Gazette*, 1898.

Khan, Khan Zafar Ali, Khan Abdul Aziz Khan, and Ghulam Habib Khan. *Riwaj Namah Malakand Agency*. Peshawar: Manzur-i Aam Press, 1964.

List of Members of the Constituent Assembly of Pakistan. n.p., n.d.

List of Members of the Constituent Assembly of Pakistan (Showing Permanent Addresses). n.p., 8 December 1955.

McMahon, A.H. and A.D.G. Ramsay. *Report on the Tribes of the Malakand Political Agency (Exclusive of Chitral)*. Revised by R.L. Kennion. Peshawar: Government Press, North-West Frontier Province, 1916.

Notification, No. 23501/Rev-VI, Peshawar dated 10 December 1990, Revenue Department, Government of N.W.F.P.

Notification, No. Rev:VI/Creation of New Distt:/Kolai Pallas.Kohistan/16361, dated Peshawar 10 August 2017, Board of Revenue, Revenue & Estate Department, Government of Khyber Pakhtunkhwa.

Notification, No. SO(J)HD/3-71/2019, dated Peshawar 29 January 2019, Home & Tribal Affairs Department, Government of Khyber Pakhtunkhwa.

Notification No. 1114/Legal, dated Peshawar 6 March 2019, Office of Provincial Police Officer, Khyber Pakhtunkhwa, Extraordinary, Registered No. P.III, Government Gazette, Published by Authority, Peshawar, Friday, 8 March 2019.

Notification No. 1117/Legal, dated Peshawar 6 March 2019, Office of Provincial Police Officer, Khyber Pakhtunkhwa, Extraordinary, Registered No. P.III, Government Gazette, Published by Authority, Peshawar, Friday, 8 March 2019.

Order, No. SO(Judl)/HD/2019/Vol-I, 21 February 2019, Home & Tribal Affairs Department, Government of Khyber Pakhtunkhwa.

Pakistan Information 1956–57. Reference Series No. 2. Karachi: Press Information Department, Government of Pakistan, n.d.

Riwaj Namah-i Swat. Compiled by Ghulam Habib Khan, Superintendent, Deputy Commissioner Office, Swat. n.p., n.d. [1973].

'Constitution (Twenty-fifth Amendment) Act, 2018', Registered No. M - 302/L.-7646, The Gazette of Pakistan, Extraordinary, Published by Authority, Islamabad, Tuesday, June 5, 2018.

The Khyber Pakhtunkhwa Continuation of Laws in the Erstwhile Provincially Administered Tribal Areas Act, 2018 (Khyber Pakhtunkhwa Act No. III of 2019), Gazette of the Khyber Pakhtunkhwa, Extraordinary, dated 10 January 2019.

The Khyber Pakhtunkhwa Continuation of Laws in Erstwhile Federally Administered Tribal Areas Bill, 2019 (Khyber Pakhtunkhwa Act No. XXIV of 2019), Gazette of the Khyber Pakhtunkhwa, Extraordinary, dated 3 May 2019.

Year Book of the North-West Frontier Province 1954. Peshawar: Secretary to Government, N.W.F.P., Information Department, n.d.

Year Book of the North-West Frontier Province, 1955, n.p., Secretary to Government, N.W.F.P., Information Department, Peshawar, n.d.

OFFICIAL WORKS PRIVATELY PUBLISHED

'Chief Executive's Order 24 of 2002, Legal Framework Order, 2002.' *The All Pakistan Legal Decisions*. Vol. 54 (2002), Central Statutes, pp. 1604–19.

'Chief Martial Law Administrator's Order 1 of 1977, Laws (Continuance in Force) Order, 1977.' *The All Pakistan Legal Decisions*. Vol. 29 (1977), Central Statutes, pp. 327–8.

'Constitution of the Islamic Republic of Pakistan [1956].' *The All Pakistan Legal Decisions*. Vol. 8 (1956), Central Acts and Notifications, pp. 54–144.

'Establishment of West Pakistan Act, 1955.' *The All Pakistan Legal Decisions*. Vol. 7 (1955), Central Acts and Notifications, pp. 273–89.

Frontier and Overseas Expeditions from India. 3 Vols. 2nd edn. published in Pakistan, Quetta: Nisa Traders, 1982.

Gazetteer of the Peshawar District, 1897–98. Reprint, Lahore: Sang-e-Meel Publications, 1989.

Imperial Gazetteer of India: Provincial Series; North-West Frontier Province. Reprint, Lahore: Sang-e-Meel Publications, 1991.

Mutiny Reports from Punjab & N.W.F.P. Vol. 2. Reprint, Lahore: Al-Biruni, n.d.

'President's Order No. 1 of 1970, Province of West Pakistan (Dissolution) Order, 1970.' *The All Pakistan Legal Decisions*. Vol. 22 (1970), Central Statutes, pp. 218–29.

'President's Order No. 2 of 1970, Legal Framework Order, 1970.' *The All Pakistan Legal Decisions*. Vol. 22 (1970), Central Statutes, pp. 229–44.

'President's Order 14 of 1985, Revival of the Constitution of 1973 Order, 1985.' *The All Pakistan Legal Decisions*. Vol. 37 (1985), Central Statutes, pp. 456–98.

'Proclamation of Martial Law, Gazette of Pakistan, Extraordinary, Part I, 5th July 1977.' *The All Pakistan Legal Decisions*. Vol. 29 (1977), Central Statutes, p. 326.

'Province of West Pakistan (Dissolution) Order, 1970 (*Date of enforcement*).' *The All Pakistan Legal Decisions*. Vol. 23 (1971), Central Statutes, p. 48.

'Provisional Constitution Order.' *The All Pakistan Legal Decisions*. Vol. 21 (1969), Central Statutes, pp. 41–2.

'Provisional Constitution Order, 1 of 1999.' *The All Pakistan Legal Decisions*. Vol. 51 (1999), Central Statutes, pp. 446–7.

'The Constitution of the Republic of Pakistan [1962].' *The All Pakistan Legal Decisions*. Vol. 14 (1962), Central Statutes, pp. 143–223.

The Indian Independence Act, 1947 and Orders Issued Thereunder, n.p., n.d.

'The Interim Constitution of the Islamic Republic of Pakistan, [1972].' *The All Pakistan Legal Decisions*. Vol. 24 (1972), Central Statutes, pp. 505–611.

ORGANIZATIONS' WORKS

Muslim League's Documents

All India Muslim League, Central Board, Policy and Programme. n.p., n.d.

Constitution & Rules of the Pakistan Muslim League. Karachi: Qazi Mohammad Isa, Honorary General Secretary, Pakistan Muslim League, n.d.

Constitution & Rules of the Pakistan Muslim League. Karachi: Mohammad Yusuf Khattak, General Secretary, Pakistan Muslim League, n.d.

Resolutions of the All India Muslim League: From December 1938 to March 1940. (Nawabzada) Liaqat Ali Khan, Honorary Secretary: All India Muslim League, n.d.

The Constitution and Rules of the All India Muslim League. Nawabzada Liaqat Ali Khan, Honorary Secretary, All India Muslim League, n.d.

The Constitution and Rules of the All-India Muslim League (as amended up to date) [1924]. n.p., n.d.

The Constitution and Rules of the All-India Muslim League (as amended upto the end of 1919). Syed Zahur Ahmad, Honorary Secretary, 1920.

The Constitution and Rules of the All-India Muslim League: Passed at the session at Lucknow on the 18th October, 1937. n.p., n.d.

The Constitution and Rules of the Frontier Muslim League (Provincial Muslim League N.W.F.P.). Published for the League by: Mohammad Ismail Khan Ghaznavi, Barrister-at-Law, Honorary Secretary, n.d.

RELIGIOUS SCRIPTURES

Qur'an Majeed: The Meaning of the Glorious Qur'an; An explanatory translation by Marmaduke Pickthall. Delhi: Taj Company, 1981.

Roman Translation of the Holy Quran with full Arabic Text: English translation by Abdullah Yusuf Ali. Lahore: Sh. Muhammad Ashraf, 1979.

The Hymns of the Rigveda, Eng. trans. Ralph T.H. Griffith, 2nd edn. (Kotagiri (Nilgiri), 1896), downloaded in pdf form from http://www.sanskritweb.net; accessed also on http://www.hinduwebsite.com/sacredscripts/rigintro.htm on 20/8/2019.

BOOKS IN ENGLISH

Abid, Massarrat and Qalb-i-Abid, eds. *South Asia: Politics, Religion and Society*. Lahore: Pakistan Study Centre, 2008.

Abu-l-Fazl. *The Akbar Nama of Abu-l-Fazl (History of the Reign of Akbar Including an Account of His Predecessors)*. Translated from the original Persian by H. Beveridge. Vol. 3. Reprint, Lahore: Sang-e-Meel Publications, 2005.

Adamec, Ludwig W. *Afghanistan, 1900–1923: A Diplomatic History*. Berkeley: University of California Press, 1967.

Adamson, Hilary and Isobel Shaw. *A Traveller's Guide to Pakistan*. Islamabad: The Asian Study Group, 1981.

Adye, John. *Sitana: A Mountain Campaign on the Borders of Afghanistan in 1863*. East Sussex: The Naval & Military Press Ltd, 2004.

Afridi, A. Qayyum. *The Hill Tribes (Along the Eastern side of Durand Line): Origin & Social Structure, Customs & Traditions and Problems & Solutions*. Peshawar: By the Author, 2003.

Afridi, Omar Khan. *Pukhtanah: A Concise Account*. Karachi: Pakistan Law House, 2014.

Afzal, M. Rafique. *Political Parties in Pakistan, 1947–1958*. Vol. 1. 9th edn., Islamabad: National
   Institute of Historical and Cultural Research, 2013.
Ahmad, Khwajah Nizamuddin. *The Tabaqat-i-Akbari of Khwajah Nizamuddin Ahmad: (A History
   of India from the Early Musalman Invasions to the Thirty-eight year of the Reign of Akbar)*.
   Vol. 2. Translated by Brajendra Nath De. Revised and edited by Baini Prashad. Delhi: Low
   Price Publications, 1992.
Ahmad, Makhdum Tasadduq. *Social Organization of Yusufzai Swat: A Study in Social Change*.
   Lahore: Panjab University Press, 1962.
Ahmad, Qeyamuddin. *The Wahabi Movement in India*. Reprint, Islamabad: National Book
   Foundation, n.d.
Ahmad, Riaz, ed. *The Frontier Muslim League, 1913–1947: Secret Police Abstracts*. Islamabad:
   National Institute of Historical and Cultural Research, 2008.
Ahmed, Akbar S. *Millennium and Charisma among Pathans: A Critical Essay in Social
   Anthropology*. London: Routledge & Kegan Paul Ltd, 1976.
Ahmed, Akbar S. *Social and Economic Changes in the Tribal Areas, 1972–1976*. With Foreword
   by Nasirullah Khan Babar. Karachi: Oxford University Press, 1977.
Ahmed, Akbar S. *Pukhtun economy and society: Traditional structure and economic development
   in a tribal society*. London: Routledge & Kegan Paul Ltd, 1980.
Ahmed, Akbar S. *Religion and Politics in Muslim Society: Order and Conflict in Pakistan*. 1st
   Pakistani edn., Karachi: Royal Book Company, 1987.
Ahmed, Akbar S., ed. *Pakistan: The Social Science Perspective*. Karachi: Oxford University
   Press, 1990.
Ahmed, Mutahir. *Pak-Afghan Security Dilemma: Imperfect Past and Uncertain Future*. Lahore:
   Tarikh Publications, 2014.
Ahsan, Aitzaz. *The Indus Saga and the Making of Pakistan*. 6th Nehr Ghar Print, Lahore: Nehr
   Ghar Publications, 2001.
al-Mujahid, Sharif. *Quaid-i-Azam Jinnah: Studies in Interpretation*. 2nd revised edn., Karachi:
   Quaid-i-Azam Academy, 1981.
Ali, Chaudhri Muhammad. *The Emergence of Pakistan*. 5th Impression, Lahore: Research Society
   of Pakistan, 1985.
Ali, Ishfaq. *Laws Extended to the Tribal Areas with Jirga Laws*. 3rd edn. *(With all Amendments
   and up-to-date Case Laws)*. Lahore: Al-Shammas Law House, 2009.
Ali, Mehrunnisa, ed. *Pak-Afghan Discord: A Historical Perspective (Documents 1855–1979)*.
   Karachi: Pakistan Study Centre, University of Karachi, 1990.
Ali, Mohammad. *...And Then the Pathan Murders*. Peshawar: University Book Agency, 1966.
Ali, Mohammed. *Guide to Afghanistan*. With Maps and Illustrations. Kabul, 1938.
Ambedkar, B.R. *Pakistan or the Partition of India*. 1st Pakistani edn., Lahore: Book Traders, 1976.
Asar, Idrees. *Pakhtoonwalee: Code of Love & Peace*. Peshawar: Printed at Danish Book Store,
   2005.
Atayee, M. Ibrahim. *A Dictionary of the Terminology of Pashtun's Tribal Customary Law and
   Usages*. Translated into English by A. Mohammad Shinwary. Edited by A. Jabar Nader. Kabul:
   International Centre for Pashto Studies, 1979.
Awan, Izzat. *Pattern of Administration in the Tribal Areas of Pakistan*. Peshawar: Provincial Civil
   Services Academy, 1972.
Azad, Abul Kalam. *India Wins Freedom: An Autobiographical Narrative*. Reprint, Bombay:
   Orient Longmans Ltd, 1964.
Aziz, K.K., ed. and comp. *The All India Muslim Conference, 1928–1935: A Documentary Record*.
   Karachi: National Publishing House Ltd, 1972.
Baha, Lal. *N.-W.F.P. Administration under British Rule, 1901–1919*. Islamabad: National
   Commission on Historical and Cultural Research, 1978.

Baig, M. Azam, comp. *Pukhtunkhwa today*. With Preface by Fazal-ur-Rahim Marwat. Peshawar: DUNYA (Pvt) Limited, 2009.

Baig, Rahmat Karim. *Hindu Khush Study Series*. Vol. 1. Printed at Rehmat Printing Press, Peshawar, 1994.

Bakhshi, Nizam-ud Din Ahmad. *Tabakat-i Akbari*. Ttranslated and edited by H.M. Elliot and John Dowson. Reprint, Lahore: Sang-e-Meel Publications, 2006.

Balneaves, Elizabeth. *The Waterless Moon*. Reprint, Karachi: Indus Publications, 1977.

Banerjee, Mukulika. *The Pathan Unarmed*. Karachi: Oxford University Press, 2000.

Bangash, Salman. *The Frontier Tribal Belt: Genesis and Purpose under the Raj*. Karachi: Oxford University Press, 2016.

Barth, Fredrik. *Indus and Swat Kohistan: An Ethnographic Survey*. Oslo: Forenede Trykkerier, 1956.

Barth, Fredrik. *Political Leadership among Swat Pathans*. London: The Athlone Press, 1959.

Barth, Fredrik. *The Last Wali of Swat: An Autobiography as told to Fredrik Barth*. Reprint, Bangkok: White Orchid Press, 1995.

Bates, Crispin, ed. *Mutiny at the Margins: New Perspectives on the Indian Uprising of 1857*. Vol. 1. *Anticipations and Experiences in the Locality*. New Delhi: SAGE Publications India Pvt Ltd, 2013.

Bellew, H.W. *An Inquiry into the Ethnography of Afghanistan*. Reprint, Karachi: Indus Publications, 1977.

Bellew, H.W. *The Races of Afghanistan: Being a Brief Account of the Principal Nations Inhabiting that Country*. Reprint, Lahore: Sh. Mubarak Ali, n.d.

Bellew, H.W. *A General Report on the Yusufzais*. 3rd edn., Lahore: Sang-e-Meel Publications, 1994.

Bellew, H.W. *Afghanistan and the Afghans: Being a Brief Review of the History of the Country and Account of its People with a Special Reference to the Present Crisis and War with the Amir Sher Ali Khan*. Reprint, Lahore: Sang-e-Meel Publications, 1979.

Biddulph, John. *Tribes of the Hindoo Koosh*. Preface to the 1971 edition by Karl Gratzl. Reprint, Lahore: Ali Kamran Publishers, 1986.

Bokawee, Mohammad Afzaul Shah. *The Pukhtoons*. n.p.: By the Author, 2006.

Bokhari, Syed Abid, ed. and comp. *Through the Centuries: North West Frontier Province*. Quetta: Mr Reprints, 1993.

Bridget and Raymond Allchin. *The Rise of Civilization in India and Pakistan*. Special Edition for sale in South Asia only. Reprint, New Delhi: Cambridge University Press India Pvt. Ltd., 2008.

Brohi, Nazish. *The MMA Offensive: Three Years in Power, 2003–2005*. Islamabad: ActionAid International-Pakistan, 2006.

Bruce, Richard Isaac. *The Forward Policy and its Results or Thirty-Five Years work amongst the Tribes on Our North-Western Frontier of India*. With Illustrations and a Map. 2nd edn. in Pakistan, Quetta: Nisa Traders, 1979.

Caroe, Olaf. *The Pathans: 550 B.C.–A.D. 1957*. Reprint, Karachi: Oxford University Press, 1976.

Chandra, Moti. *Trade and Trade Routes in Ancient India*. New Delhi: Abhinav Publications, 1977.

Chauhan, Rana Ali Hasan. *A Short History of the Gujars (past and present)*. Gujranwala: Chauhan Publications, 1998.

Churchill, Winston S. *The Story of the Malakand Field Force: An Episode of Frontier War*. Reprint, London: Leo Cooper, 2002.

[Cunningham, Alexander]. *Cunningham's Ancient Geography of India*. Edited with Introduction and Notes by Surendranath Majumdar Sastri. Calcutta: Chuckervertty, Chatterjee & Co. Ltd., 1924.

Dani, Ahmad Hasan. *History of Northern Areas of Pakistan (Upto 2000 AD)*. Revised 1st edn., Lahore: Sang-e-Meel Publications, 2001.

Dani, Ahmad Hasan. *Peshawar: Historic City of the Frontier*. [2nd edn.], Lahore: Sang-e-Meel Publications, 1995.

Davies, C. Collin. *The Problem of the North-West Frontier, 1890–1908: With a survey of policy since 1849*. 2nd edn. revised and enlarged, London: Curzon Press Ltd, 1975.

d'Auvergne, V. *Zindari: A Daughter of the Indian Frontier and other Thrilling Tales of the Indian Frontier*. Reprint, Karachi: Indus Publications, 1982.

Dichter, David. *The North-West Frontier of West Pakistan: A Study in Regional Geography*. London: Oxford University Press, 1967.

Douie, James. *The Panjab, North-West Frontier Province and Kashmir*. Reprint, Delhi: Low Price Publications, 1994.

Dupree, Louis. *Afghanistan*. Princeton: Princeton University Press, 1973.

Durand, Algernon. *The Making of a Frontier: Five Years' Experiences and Adventures in Gilgit, Hunza, Nagar, Chitral, and the Eastern Hindu-Kush*. With Introduction by Oliver Forster. Reprint, 2nd Impression, Karachi: Oxford University Press, 2004.

Eade, Charles, ed. *Churchill: By his Contemporaries*. Reprint, London: Hutchinson & Co. (Publisher) Ltd., 1954.

Easwaran, Eknath. *A Man to Match His Mountains: Badshah Khan, Nonviolent Soldier of Islam*. With Afterword by Timothy Flinders. 2nd Print, California: Nilgiri Press, 1985.

Elliott, J.G. *The Frontier, 1839–1947: The Story of the North-West Frontier of India*. With Preface by Olaf Caroe. London: Cassell & Company Ltd, 1968.

Elphinstone, Mountstuart. *An Account of the Kingdom of Caubul*. With New Introduction by Olaf Caroe. 2 Vols. Karachi: Oxford University Press, 1972.

Embree, Ainslie T., ed. *Pakistan's Western Borderlands: The Transformation of a Political Order*. Reprint, New Delhi: Vikas Publishing House Pvt. Ltd, 1985.

Ewart, J.M. and E.B. Howell. *Story of the North West Frontier Province*. Reprint, Lahore: Sang-e-Meel Publications, 2009.

Eyre, Vincent. *The Military Operations at Kabul, which ended in the Retreat and Destruction of the British Army, January 1842*. With Journal of Imprisonment in Afghanistan. Peshawar: Qami Maktaba, Khyber Bazaar, n.d.

Fairley, Jean. *The Lion River: The Indus*. With Introduction by Monte Porzio. 1st edn. in Pakistan, Lahore: S.I. Gillani, 1979.

Faiz, Ashraf. *The Parachgan*. Lahore: The Frontier Post Publications, 1994.

Fakhr-ul-Islam. *Khyber Pakhtunkhwa: A Political History (1901–1955)*. Islamabad: National Institute of Historical and Cultural Research, 2014.

Feldman, Herbert. *The Land and People of Pakistan*. With Fifteen Photographs and a Map. London: Adam and Charles Black, 1958.

Ferishta, Mahomed Kasim [Muhammad Qasim]. *History of the Rise of the Mahomedan [Muhammadan] Power in India, till the year A.D. 1612*. Translated from the original Persian of Mahomed Kasim Ferishta by John Briggs. 2 Vols. Reprint, Lahore: Sang-e-Meel Publications, 1977.

Fraser-Tytler, W.K. *Afghanistan: A Study of Political Developments in Central and Southern Asia*. 2nd edn., London: Oxford University Press, 1953.

Gandhi, Rajmohan. *Ghaffar Khan: Nonviolent Badshah of the Pakhtuns*. New Delhi: Penguin Books India Pvt. Ltd., 2008.

Gohar, Ali. *Who learns from whom?: Pukhtoon Traditions in Modern Perspective*. n.p.: Just Peace International, n.d.

Gokalp, Zia. *Turkish Nationalism and Western Civilization: Selected Essays of Zia Gokalp*. Translated and edited with Introduction by Niyazi Berkes. London: George Allen and Unwin Ltd, 1959.

Gregorian, Vartan. *The Emergence of Modern Afghanistan: Politics of Reforms and Modernization, 1880–1946*. California: Stanford University Press, 1969.

Gupta, Amit Kumar. *North West Frontier Province: Legislature and Freedom Struggle, 1932–47*. New Delhi: Indian Council of Historical Research, 1976.

Habib, Mohammad. *Sultan Mahmud of Ghaznin*. 2nd edn., Delhi: S. Chand & Co., n.d.

Hamid, Abdul. *Muslim Separatism in India*. n.p., n.d.

Hamilton, Agnus. *Afghanistan*. With a Map and Numerous Illustrations. London: William Heinemann, 1906.

Haq, Syed Moinul. *The Great Revolution of 1857*. Karachi: Pakistan Historical Society, 1968.

Haq, Syed Moinul. *Islamic Thought and Movements in the Subcontinent (711–1947)*. Karachi: Pakistan Historical Society, 1979.

Haq, Syed Moinul, ed. *A History of the Freedom Movement*. Vol. 4. *1936–1947*, Parts I & II. Karachi: Pakistan Historical Society, 1970.

Haque, Mian Manzoorul. *Around Khyber: A Brochure on the Physical, Economic, Agricultural, Industrial, Social and Cultural aspects of the North-West Frontier Province, the Frontier States & the Tribal Areas*. n.p., A Pie Publication, n.d.

Haroon, Sana. *Frontier of Faith: A History of Religious Mobilisation in the Pakhtun Tribal Areas c. 1890–1950*. First Published in Pakistan, Karachi: Oxford University Press, 2011.

Harwi, Khwajah Nimatullah. *History of the Afghans: Translated from the Persian of Neamet Ullah*. Translated by Bernhard Dorn. 3rd edn., Karachi: Indus Publications, 2001.

Hassan, Syed Minhajul. *The Dawn of New Era in Khyber Pakhtunkhwa: Abdul Qaiyum Khan Chief Ministership, 1947–53*. Islamabad: National Institute of Historical and Cultural Research, 2016.

Hell, Joseph. *The Arab Civilization*. Translated by S. Khuda Bakhsh. Reprint, Lahore: Sh. Muhammad Ashraf, 1969.

Hensman, Howard. *The Afghan War of 1879–80*. 1st edn. published in Pakistan, Lahore: Sang-e-Meel Publications, 1978.

Hodson, H.V. *The Great Divide: Britain-India-Pakistan*. With Epilogue written in 1985 which sums up the events since partition, and with new Introduction. 7th Impression of the Jubilee Series edition, 1997, Karachi: Oxford University Press, 2005.

Holdich, Thomas. *The Gates of India: Being an Historical Narrative*. 1st edn. published in Pakistan, Quetta: Gosha-e-Adab, 1977.

Holdich, T. Hungerford. *The Indian Borderland, 1880–1900*. 1st reprint in India, Delhi: Gian Publishing House, 1987.

Hopkins, Benjamin D. and Magnus Marsden, eds. *Beyond Swat: History, Society and Economy along the Afghanistan-Pakistan Frontier*. London: C. Hurst & Co. (Publishers) Ltd., 2013.

Hunter, W.W. *The Indian Musalmans*. With Introduction by Bimal Prasad. Reprint, New Delhi: Rupa & Co, 2002.

Husain, Farrukh. *Afghanistan in the Age of Empires: The Great Game for South and Central Asia*. n.p.: Silk Road Books, 2018.

Hussain, Zahid. *Frontline Pakistan: The Struggle with Militant Islam*. New Delhi: Penguin Books India Pvt. Ltd, 2007.

Ibbetson, Denzil. *Punjab Castes*. Reprint, Delhi: Low Price Publications, 1993.

Ikram, S.M. *Modern Muslim India and the Birth of Pakistan*. Reprint, Lahore: Institute of Islamic Culture, 2016.

Ikram, S.M. *A History of Muslim Civilization in India and Pakistan: A Political and Cultural History*. 6th edn., Lahore: Institute of Islamic Culture, 1994.

Jalal, Ayesha. *The Sole Spokesman: Jinnah, the Muslim League and the Demand for Pakistan*. Cambridge: Cambridge University Press, 1985.

Janjua, Zia-ul-Islam. *The Jirga Laws*. Lahore: Lahore Law Times Publications, n.d.

Jansson, Erland. *India, Pakistan or Pakhtunistan: The Nationalist Movements in the North-West Frontier Province, 1937–47*. Stockholm: Almqvist & Wiksell International, 1981.

Kakar, M. Hasan. *Afghanistan: A Study in International Political Developments, 1880–1896*. Kabul, 1971.

Kasi, Abdul Malik. *Aryana: Accounts of the Important Religious-Politcal and Social Movements in Ancient and Modern Afghanistan and Pakistan*. Quetta: United Printers, n.d.

Kaura, Uma. *Muslims and Indian Nationalism: The Emergence of the Demand for India's Partition, 1928–40*. Lahore: Book Traders, n.d.

Kazimi, Muhammad Reza, ed. *Jinnah-Liaquat Correspondence*. Karachi: Pakistan Study Centre, University of Karachi, 2003.

Keay, John. *The Gilgit Game: The Explorers of the Western Himalayas, 1865–95*. Reprint, Karachi: Oxford University Press, 1993.

Keen, W.J. *The North-West Frontier Province and the War*. Peshawar, 1928.

Kennedy, Charles H., Kathleen McNeil, Carl Ernst, and David Gilmartin, eds. *Pakistan at the Millennium*. Karachi: Oxford University Press, 2003.

Keppel, Arnold. *Gun-Running and the Indian North-West Frontier*. Reprint, Lahore: Sang-e-Meel Publications, 2004.

Khalil, Hanif. *Pakhtun Culture in Pashto Tappa*. Islamabad: National Institute of Historical and Cultural Research, 2017.

Khan, Abdul Wahab, Bakht Jehan, and M. Usman, eds. *The River Swat: Experiences of River Swat Conservation Project*. Saidu Sharif, Swat: Environmental Protection Society (EPS), 2003.

Khan, Abdul Wali. *Facts are Sacred*. Translated by Aziz Siddiqui. Peshawar: Jaun Publishers, n.d.

Khan, Abdul Wali. *Facts are Facts: The Untold Story of India's Partition*. Translated by Syeda Saiyidain Hameed. Reprint, Peshawar: Publication Cell, Baacha Khan Trust, 2006.

Khan, Azmat Hayat. *The Durand Line—Its Geo-Strategic Importance*. Edited by M.Y. Effendi. 3rd edn., Peshawar: Area Study Centre, University of Peshawar, 2005.

Khan, Ghani. *The Pathans: A Sketch*. Reprint, Islamabad: Pushto Adabi Society (Red), 1990.

Khan, Mohammad Afzal. *Chitral and Kafiristan—A Personal Study*. Peshawar: Reprinted at Printing Corporation of Frontier Ltd., 1980.

Khan, Mohammad Anwar. *England, Russia and Central Asia (A Study in Diplomacy), 1857–1878*. Peshawar: University Book Agency, n.d.

Khan, Mohammad Anwar. *The Role of N.W.F.P. in the Freedom Struggle*. Lahore: Research Society of Pakistan, 2000.

Khan, Mohammad Said. *The Voice of the Pukhtoons*. n.p., n.d. (Printed at Ferozsons Limited, Lahore).

Khan, Mohd. Ayub. *The Evolution of Judicial Systems and Law in the Sub Continent*. n.p., 1987. (Printed by Universal Printers Peshawar).

Khan, Muhammad Asif. *The Story of Swat as told by the Founder Miangul Abdul Wadud Badshah Sahib to Muhammad Asif Khan*, With Preface, Introduction and Appendices by Muhammad Asif Khan. Preface to the Translation and Translation by Ashruf Altaf Husain. Printed by: Ferozsons Ltd., Peshawar, 1962.

Khan, Muhammad Hayat. *Afghanistan and its Inhabitants: Translated from the Hayat-i-Afghani of Muhammad Hayat Khan*. Translated by Henry Priestley. Reprint, Lahore: Sang-e-Meel Publications, 1999.

Khan, Muhammad Nawaz. *Pakistan: The Evolution of N.W.F.P. and the "Tribal Area" (In Historical, Constitutional, Judicial Retrospect): Also Containing Studies in the PATA (Nifaz-e-Nizam-e-Shariah) Regulation 1994 with Act IV 1995*. Mardan: Radiant Publishers, 1996.

Khan, Munawwar. *Anglo-Afghan Relations, 1798–1878: A Chapter in the Great Game in Central Asia*. Peshawar: University Book Agency, n.d.

Khan, Saleem Ullah, comp. *The Referendum in N.W.F.P. 1947: A Documentary Record*. Islamabad: National Documentation Centre, 1995.

Khan, Sultan Mahomed, ed. *The Life of Abdur Rahman: Amir of Afghanistan*. With New Introduction by M.E. Yapp. Vol. 2. Reprint in Pakistan, Karachi: Oxford University Press, 1980.

Khattak, Khushhal Khan. *Dastar Nama of Khushal Khan Khattak*. Translated by Arif Naseem. With Preface by Salma Shaheen. Peshawar: Pashto Academy, 2007.

Khilji, Jalaluddin, ed. *Muslim Celebrities of Central Asia*. Peshawar: Area Study Centre (Central Asia), University of Peshawar, n.d.

Knight, E.F. *Where Three Empires Meet: A Narrative of Recent Travel in Kashmir, Western Tibet, Gilgit, and the Adjoining Countries*. Reprint, Lahore: Sang-e-Meel Publications, 1996.

Korejo, MS. *The Frontier Gandhi: His Place in History*. 2nd edn., Karachi: Oxford University Press, 1994.

Lal, Kishori Saran. *History of the Khaljis: A.D. 1290–1320*. Karachi: Union Book Stall, n.d.

Linck, Orville F. *A Passage Through Pakistan*. Detroit: Wayne State University Press, 1959.

Lindholm, Charles. *Generosity and Jealousy: The Swat Pukhtun of Northern Pakistan*. New York: Columbia University Press, 1982.

Lindholm, Charles. *Frontier Perspectives: Essays in Comparative Anthropology*. Karachi: Oxford University Press, 1996.

Loude, Jean-Yves and Viviane Lievre. *Kalash Solstice: Winter Feasts of the Kalash of North Pakistan*. Translated from the French by Grahame Romaine and Mira Intrator. Photographs and Drawings by Herve Negre. Islamabad: Lok Virsa Publishing House, n.d.

Lumby, E.W.R. *The Transfer of Power in India, 1945–7*. London: George Allen & Unwin Ltd., 1954.

Macmunn, George. *The Romance of the Indian Frontiers*. 1st Pakistani edn., Quetta: Nisa Traders, 1978.

Macmunn, George. *Afghanistan: From Darius to Amanullah*. Reprint, Lahore: Sang-e-Meel Publications, 2002.

Macmunn, George. *The Martial Races of India*. 2nd Pakistani edn., Quetta: Nisa Traders, 1982.

Macmunn, George. *Vignettes from Indian Wars*. Reprint, Quetta: Nisa Traders, 1982.

Mahajan, Vidya Dhar. *Constitutional History of India (including the National Movement)*. 5th edn., Thoroughly revised and enlarged, Delhi: S. Chand & Co., 1962.

Mahmood, Safdar. *Constitutional Foundations of Pakistan*. Lahore: Publishers United Ltd., n.d.

Mahmood, Safdar. *Constitutional Foundations of Pakistan (Enlarged and Revised)*. Lahore: Jang Publishers, 1997.

Majumdar, R.C., H.C. Raychaudhuri, and Kalikinkar Datta. *An Advanced History of India*. Reprint, Lahore: Famous Books, 1992.

Mallam, Leslie. *Thirty Years on the North-West Frontier; Recollections of a Frontiersman*. Karachi: Oxford University Press, 2011

Malik, Salahuddin. *1857: War of Independence or Clash of Civilizations?: British Public Reactions*. Karachi: Oxford University Press, 2008.

Marsden, Magnus. *Living Islam: Muslim Religious Experience in Pakistan's North-West Frontier*. South Asian Edition, New Delhi: Cambridge University Press, 2008.

Marsden, Magnus and Benjamin D. Hopkins. *Fragments of the Afghan Frontier*. Karachi: Oxford University Press, 2013.

Marsh, John. *The Young Winston Churchill*. London: World Distributors, 1962.

Marwat, Fazal-ur-Rahim and Sayed Wiqar Ali Shah Kakakhel, eds. *Afghanistan and the Frontier*. Peshawar: Emjay Books International, 1993.

Marwat, Fazal-ur-Rahim and Parvez Khan Toru. *Talibanization of Pakistan (A Case Study of TNSM)*. Peshawar: Pakistan Study Centre, University of Peshawar, 2005.

Mathur, Y.B. *Quit India Movement*. 1st Published in Pakistan, Lahore: Book Traders, 1979.

Mathur, Y.B. *Growth of Muslim Politics in India*. 1st Published in Pakistan, Lahore: Book Traders, 1980.

Matthews, Matt M. *An Ever Present Danger: A Concise History of British Military Operations on the North-West Frontier, 1849–1947.* Occasional Paper 33. Kansas: Combat Studies Institute Press, 2010.

Mayne, Peter. *The Narrow Smile: A Journey back to the North-west Frontier.* London: John Murray (Publishers) Ltd., 1955.

McMahon, A.H. and A.D.G. Ramsay. *Report on the Tribes of Dir, Swat and Bajour* [Bajawar] *together with the Utman-Khel and Sam Ranizai.* Reprint, edited with Introduction by R.O. Christensen. Peshawar: Saeed Book Bank, 1981.

Mehra, Parshotam. *The North-West Frontier Drama, 1945–1947: A Re-Assessment.* Edition issued in Pakistan, Karachi: Oxford University Press, 2001.

Miller, Charles. *Khyber: British India's North-West Frontier; The Story of an Imperial Migraine.* London: Macdonald and Jane's Publishers Limited, 1977.

Mills, H. Woosnam. *The Pathan Revolt in North-West India.* Reprint, Lahore: Sang-e-Meel Publications, 1996.

Mishra, Yogendra. *The Hindu Sahis of Afghanistan and the Punjab, A.D. 865–1026.* Patna: Vaishali Bhavan, 1972.

Mohmand, Sher Muhammad. *FATA (Federally Administered Tribal Areas of Pakistan): A Socio-Cultural and Geo-Political History.* n.p., n.d.

Mohmand, Sher Muhammad. *The Pathan Customs.* n.p., n.d.

Moon, Penderel, ed. *Wavell: The Viceroy's Journal.* Reprint, Karachi: Oxford University Press, 1997.

Morgenstierne, Georg. *Report on a Linguistic Mission to North-Western India.* Reprint, Karachi: Indus Publications, n.d.

Mughal, Munir Ahmad, Muhammad Khurram, and Muhammad Hammad Munir. *The Constitution (Eighteenth Amendment) Act, 2010.* Lahore: Muneeb Book House, 2010.

Muhammad, Taj. *The Pashtuns of Waziristan and the Custom Based Wazairi Law from Sharia Perspective.* Translated by Muhammad Umer Dar. Reviewed by Ahsan-ur-Rehman. Islamabad: Mithaq Enterprises, 2015.

Munir, Muhammad. *From Jinnah to Zia.* 2nd edn., Lahore: Vanguard Books Ltd., 1980.

Munir, Muhammad. *Constitution of the Islamic Republic of Pakistan: Being a Commentary on the Constitution of Pakistan, 1973.* Edited by Mian Bashir Ahmad. Vol. 2, [*Art. 185-Subject Index*]. Lahore: P.L.D. Publishers, 1996.

Narang, K.B. *My Life and Struggle: Autobiography of Badshah Khan as narrated to K.B. Narang.* With Foreword by Jayaprakash Narayan. Reprint, n.p., Daily Afghanistan Times, 2008.

Narain, A.K. *The Indo-Greeks.* Reprint, Oxford: At the Clarendon Press, 1962.

Nawaz, Mohammad. *The Guardians of the Frontier: The Frontier Corps NWFP.* Peshawar: The Frontier Corps North-West Frontier Province, 1994.

Nazim, Muhammad. *The Life and Times of Sultan Mahmud of Ghazna.* With Foreword by Thomas Arnold. Cambridge: At the University Press, 1931.

Nehru, Jawaharlal. *The Discovery of India.* 12th Impression, New Delhi: Jawaharlal Nehru Memorial Fund, 1992.

Nehru, Jawaharlal. *Glimpses of World History: Being Further Letters to His Daughter, Written in Prison, and Containing a Rambling Account of History for Young People*, With 50 Maps by J.F. Horrabin, New Delhi: Penguin Books, 2004.

Nevill, H.L. *Campaigns on the North-West Frontier.* Reprint, Lahore: Sang-e-Meel Publications, 2003.

Nichols, Robert. *Settling the Frontier: Land, Law, and Society in the Peshawar Valley, 1500–1900.* 2nd edn., Karachi: Oxford University Press, 2017.

Nichols, Robert, *A History of Pashtun Migration, 1775–2006.* Karachi: Oxford University Press, 2008.

Nichols, Robert, ed. *Colonial Reports on Pakistan's Frontier Tribal Areas*. Karachi: Oxford University Press, 2005.

Nichols, Robert, ed. *The Frontier Crimes Regulation: A History in Documents*. Karachi: Oxford University Press, 2013.

Obhrai, Diwan Chand. *The Evolution of North-West Frontier Province: Being a Survey of the History and Constitutional Development of N.-W. F. Province, in India*. Reprint, Peshawar: Saeed Book Bank, n.d.

Oliver, Edward E. *Across the Border or Pathan and Biloch*. Reprint, Lahore: Sang-e-Meel Publications, 2000.

Pennell, T.L. *Among the Wild Tribes of the Afghan Frontier: A Record of Sixteen years close Intercourse with the Natives of the Indian Marches*. With Introduction by Earl Roberts, and with 37 Illustrations & 2 Maps. London: George Bell & Sons, 1909.

Philips, C.H. and Mary Doreen Wainwright. *The Partition of India: Policies and Perspectives, 1935–1947*. London: George Allen and Unwin Ltd, 1970.

Popowski, Josef. *The Rival Powers in Central Asia*. Translated by Arthur Baring Brabant. Edited with Introduction by Charles E.D. Black. 1st edn. in Pakistan, Quetta: Gosha-e-Adab, 1977.

Powell-Price, J.C. *A History of India*. London: Thomas Nelson and Sons Ltd., 1955.

Qadir, Altaf. *Reforming the Pukhtuns and Resisting the British: An Appraisal of the Haji Sahib Turangzai's Movement*. Islamabad: National Institute of Historical and Cultural Research, 2015.

Qaiyum, Abdul. *Gold and Guns on the Pathan Frontier*. Bombay: Hind Kitabs, 1945.

Quddus, Syed Abdul. *The Pathans*. Lahore: Ferozsons (Pvt.) Ltd., 1987.

Quddus, Syed Abdul. *The Cultural Patterns of Pakistan*. Lahore: Ferozsons (Pvt.) Ltd., 1989.

Quddus, Syed Abdul. *The North-West Frontier of Pakistan*. Karachi: Royal Book Company, 1990.

Quddus, Syed Abdul. *Pakistan from Khyber to Karachi*. Lahore: Islamic Book Centre, n.d.

Qureshi, Ishtiaq Husain. *The Struggle for Pakistan*. Reprint, Karachi: University of Karachi, 1982.

Qureshi, Ishtiaq Husain, ed. *A Short History of Pakistan; Books One to Four*. 2nd edn., Karachi: University of Karachi, 1984.

Rana, Muhammad Amir and Rohan Gunaratna. *Al-Qaeda Fights Back Inside Pakistani Tribal Areas*. Lahore: Pakistan Institute for Peace Studies (PIPS), 2007.

Rashid, Abdur. *Civil Service on the Frontier*. n.p., n.d.

Rashid, Haroon. *History of the Pathans*. Vol. 1. *The Sarabani Pathans*. Islamabad: By the Author, 2002.

Raverty, Henry George. *Notes on Afghanistan and Baluchistan*. 2 Vols. 2nd edn. in Pakistan, Quetta: Nisa Traders, 1982.

Reeves, Richard. *Passage to Peshawar: Pakistan—Between the Hindu Kush and the Arabian Sea*. New York: Simon and Schuster, 1984.

Rehman, Abdur. *The Last Two Dynasties of the Sahis (An analysis of their history, archaeology, coinage and palaeography)*. Islamabad: Director, Centre for the Study of the Civilizations of Central Asia, 1979.

Reventlow, Count Ernst Zu. *India: Its importance for Great Britain, Germany and the future of the world*. Translated into English in Central Intelligence Office, Simla, 1918.

Richards, D.S. *The Savage Frontier: A History of the Anglo-Afghan Wars*. London: Macmillan London Limited, 1990.

Rittenberg, Stephen Alan. *Ethnicity, Nationalism, and the Pakhtuns: The Independence Movement in India's North-West Frontier Province*. Durham: Carolina Academic Press, 1988.

Roberts, Lord. *Forty-one Years in India: From Subaltern to Commander-in-Chief*. New edition in one volume, with forty-four Illustrations. London: Macmillan and Co., Limited, 1898.

Roberts, P.E. *History of British India under the Company and the Crown*. 3rd edn. Completed by T.G.P. Spear. Reprint, London: Oxford University Press, 1952.

Robertson, Charles Gray. *Kurum, Kabul & Kandahar: Being a Brief Record of Impressions in Three Campaigns under General Roberts*. Reprint, Lahore: Sang-e-Meel Publications, 1979.

Robertson, George S. *Chitral: The Story of a Minor Siege*. 2nd edn., London: Methuen & Co., 1899.

Rose, H.A., comp. *A Glossary of the Tribes and Castes of the Punjab and North-West Frontier Province. Based on the Census Report for the Punjab, 1883, by Denzil Ibbetson; and the Census Report for the Punjab, 1892, by E.D. MacLagan*. Vol. 3. 1st Pakistani edn., Lahore: Aziz Publishers, 1978.

Sabir, Mohammad Shafi. *Story of Khyber*. Peshawar: University Book Agency, n.d.

Said, Hakim Mohammed, S. Moinul Haq, Shariful Mujahid, and Ansar Zahid Khan., eds. *Road to Pakistan: A comprehensive history of the Pakistan Movement-1947*. Vol. 1. *712–1858*. Karachi: Hamdard Foundation Pakistan, and Pakistan Historical Society, 1990.

Scott, George B. *Afghanistan and Pathan: A Sketch*. London: The Mitre Press, 1929.

Sethi, R.R. and Vidya Dhar Mahajan. *Constitutional History of India*. 2nd edn., revised and enlarged, Delhi: S. Chand & Co., 1954.

Shah, Sayed Wiqar Ali. *Ethnicity, Islam, and Nationalism: Muslim Politics in the North-West Frontier Province, 1937–1947*. Karachi: Oxford University Press, 1999.

Shah, Sayed Wiqar Ali. *North-West Frontier Province: History and Politics*. Islamabad: National Institute of Historical and Cultural Research, 2007.

Shah, Sirdar Iqbal Ali. *Afghanistan of the Afghans*. With numerous Illustrations and a Map. First edition published in Pakistan, Quetta: Gosha-e-Adab, 1977.

Shah, Syed Waqar Ali. *Muslim League in N.W.F.P.* Karachi: Royal Book Company, 1992.

Shakib, Siba. *Afghanistan, Where God only Comes to Weep: A woman's story of courage, struggle and determination*. London: Century, 2002.

Shaw, Isobel. *Pakistan: Handbook*. Hong Kong: The Guidebook Company Limited, 1989.

Sherwani, Latif Ahmed. *The Partition of India and Mountbatten*. Karachi: Council for Pakistan Studies, 1986.

Sherwani, Latif Ahmed, ed. *Pakistan Resolution to Pakistan, 1940–1947: A Selection of Documents Presenting the Case for Pakistan*. With Introduction by Ishtiaq Husain Qureshi. Karachi: National Publishing House Limited, 1969.

Siddique, Abubakar. *The Pashtuns: An Unresolved Key to the Future of Pakistan and Afghanistan*. Gurgaon: Random House Publishers India Private Limited, 2014.

Singer, Andre. *Lords of the Khyber: The Story of the North-West Frontier*. London: Faber and Faber Limited, 1984.

Singer, Andre, et.al. *Guardians of the North-West Frontier?: The Pathans*. Reprint, Karachi: Liberty Books (Private) Limited, 1991.

Singh, Ganda. *Ahmad Shah Durrani: Father of Modern Afghanistan*. Bombay: Asia Publishing House, 1959.

Skeen, Andrew. *Passing it on: Short Talks on Tribal Fighting on the North West Frontier of India*. With Foreword by Philip W. Chetwode. 1st Pakistani edn., Lahore: Aziz Publishers, 1978.

Smith, Vincent A. *Akbar: The Great Mogul* [Mughal], *1542–1605*. 2nd edn., revised. Indian reprint, Delhi: S. Chand & Co., 1958.

Spain, James W. *The People of the Khyber: The Pathans of Pakistan*. New York: Frederick A. Praeger, Inc. Publisher, 1963.

Spain, James W. *The Pathan Borderland*. Reprint, Karachi: Indus Publications, 1985.

Spain, James W. *The Way of the Pathans*. 7th Impression, Karachi: Oxford University Press, 1994.

Spain, James W. *Pathans of the Latter Day*. Karachi: Oxford University Press, 1995.

Stephens, Ian. *Horned Moon: An account of a Journey through Pakistan, Kashmir, and Afghanistan*. Bloomington: Indiana University Press, 1955.

Stocqueler, J.H. *Memorials of Affghanistan: Being State Papers, Official Documents, Dispatches, Authentic Narratives, etc.; Illustrative of the British Expedition to, and Occupation of,*

Affghanistan and Scinde, Between the years 1838 and 1842. Reprint, Peshawar: Saeed Book Bank, 1983.

Sufi, Juma Khan. *Bacha Khan, Congress and Nationalist Politics in NWFP.* Lahore: Vanguard Books, 2005.

Sultan-i-Rome. *Swat State (1915–1969): From Genesis to Merger; An Analysis of Political, Administrative, Socio-Political, and Economic Developments.* Karachi: Oxford University Press, 2008.

Swami, Praveen. *India, Pakistan and the Secret Jihad: The covert war in Kashmir, 1947–2004.* 1st Indian Reprint, Pondicherry, India: Integra Software Services Pvt. Ltd, 2007.

Swinson, Arthur. *North-West Frontier: People and Events, 1839–1947.* London: Hutchinson & Co. (Publishers) Ltd., 1967.

Tahir, Madiha R., Qalandar Bux Memon, and Vijay Prashad, eds. *Dispatches from Pakistan.* New Delhi: LeftWord Books, 2012.

Tarn, W.W. *The Greeks in Bactria & India.* Reprint, Cambridge: At the University Press, 1966.

Tendulkar, D.G. *Abdul Ghaffar Khan: faith is a battle.* Bombay: Popular Prakashan, 1967.

Thomson, H.C. *The Chitral Campaign: A Narrative of Events in Chitral, Swat, and Bajour.* Reprint, Lahore: Sang-e-Meel Publications, 1981.

Thomson, H.C. *A Narrative of Events in Chitral, Swat and Bajour: Chitral Campaign.* Reprint, Lahore: Sang-e-Meel, 1981.

Toru, Parvez Khan and Fazal-ur-Rahim Marwat, eds. *Celebrities of NWFP.* Vol[s]. 1–2. Peshawar: Pakistan Study Centre, University of Peshawar, 2005.

Trench, Charles Chenevix. *The Frontier Scouts.* With Foreword by Philip Mason. Reprint, London: Jonathan Cape Ltd, 1986.

Trotter, Lionel J. *The Life of John Nicholson: Soldier and Administrator; Based on Private and Hitherto Unpublished Documents.* 1st edn. in Pakistan, Karachi: Karimsons, 1978.

Verma, H.C. *Medieval Routes to India: Baghdad to Delhi; A Study of Trade and Military Routes.* Lahore: Book Traders, n.d.

Warburton, Robert. *Eighteen Years in the Khyber, 1879–1898.* Reprint, 3rd Impression, Karachi: Oxford University Press, 1975.

Wazir, Badshah Gul and Jehangir Khan Mohmand. *Futuristics of Tribal Administration.* Peshawar: Pakistan Academy for Rural Development, 1995.

Wilcox, Wayne Ayres. *Pakistan: The Consolidation of a Nation.* New York: Columbia University Press, 1963.

Williams, L.F. Rushbrook. *The State of Pakistan.* With Maps by N.S. Hyslop. London: Faber and Faber Limited, 1962.

Woodcock, George. *The Greeks in India.* London: Faber and Faber Ltd., 1966.

Wylly, H.C. *The Borderland: The Country of the Pathans.* [First published under the title *From the Black Mountains to Waziristan*, 1912]. Reprint, Karachi: Indus Publications, 1998.

Wylly, H.C. *From the Black Mountain to Waziristan.* Reprint, Lahore: Sang-e-Meel Publications, 2003.

Yaqubi, Himayatullah. *Mughal-Afghan Relations in South Asia: History and Developments.* Islamabad: National Institute of Historical and Cultural Research, 2015.

Younghusband, G.J. and Francis Younghusband. *The Relief of Chitral.* With Map and Illustrations. Reprint, Rawalpindi: English Book House, 1976.

Yousaf, Mohammad and Mark Adkin. *Afghanistan: The Bear Trap; The Defeat of a Superpower.* New Delhi: Bookwise (India) Pvt. Ltd., 2007.

Yousufzai, Hassan M. and Ali Gohar. *Towards Understanding Pukhtoon Jirga: An indigenous way of peacebuilding and more....* Peshawar: Just Peace International, 2005.

Yunas, S. Fida. *Abdul Ghaffar Khan: "Pushtunistan" and Afghanistan.* Peshawar: By the Author, n.d.

Yunas, S. Fida. *The Afghans (Pashtuns/Non-Pashtuns): Ethnic Groups/Tribes.* Peshawar: By the Author, 2011.

Yunas, S. Fida and Sher Zaman Taizi, eds. *Treaties, Engagements and Sanads Relating to the North West Frontier Province: Covering the Period upto 1930 based on the Mr C.W. Aitchison's Compilation (Reprint of Relevant Portions).* Peshawar: Area Study Centre (Russia, China & Central Asia), University of Peshawar, n.d.

Yunus, Mohammad. *Frontier Speaks.* With Foreword by Jawahar Lal [Jawaharlal] Nehru; Preface by Khan Abdul Ghaffar Khan; Maps by Sardar Abdur Rauf. Lahore: Minerva Book Shop, n.d.

Yusufi, Allah Bukhsh. *The Frontier Tragedy.* 2nd edn., Karachi: Mohammed Ali Education Society, 1986.

A Glossary of the Tribes and Castes of the Punjab and North-West Frontier Province. 3 Vols. Reprint, Lahore: Aziz Publishers, 1978.

Durand Line. n.p., n.d.

Guide to Pakistan. Karachi: Ferozsons Limited, n.d.

Jinnah: Speeches and Statements, 1947–1948. With Introduction by S.M. Burke. The Millennium Series. Karachi: Oxford University Press, 2000.

Longmans' History of India (From the Beginning to A.D. 1526). 3rd edn., Bombay: Longmans, Green and Co. Ltd., 1947.

Pakhtunkhwa: A Development Framework. n.p.: National Democratic Consultative Process, 2003.

Pakistan Miscellany. Vol. 2. Karachi: Pakistan Publications, 1958.

Struggle for Independence, 1857–1947: A Pictorial Record. Karachi: Pakistan Publications, 1958.

The Cambridge History of India. Vol. 1. *Ancient India.* Edited by E.J. Rapson. 1st Indian reprint, Delhi: S. Chand & Co., 1955.

The Cambridge History of India. Vol. 6. *The Indian Empire, 1858–1918, with chapters on the development of Administration 1818–1858.* Edited by H.H. Dodwell. *And the Last Phase 1919–1947* by R.R. Sethi. Published in India, Delhi: S. Chand & Co., 1964.

The Risings on the North-West Frontier (Compiled from the Special War Correspondence of the "Pioneer"). Allahabad: Printed and Published at the Pioneer Press, 1898.

BOOKS IN PERSIAN

Darwizah, Akhun. *Tazkiratul Abrar-i wal Ashrar.* Peshawar: Islami Kutub Khanah, n.d.

Kuhzad, Ahmad Ali. *Tarikh Afghanistan*, Vol. 1, *Az Adwar Qabal al-Tarikh ta Saqut Sulta* [sic; *Sultanat*] *Mauriya, Hisah Awal Fasl Fanjum 'Lashkar Kashihayi Iskandar': Az Safhah 364 ta 426* by Muhammad Usman Sadafi. Facts of Publication torn out.

BOOKS IN PUKHTU (PASHTO)

Abdali, Ahmad Shah. *Diwan Ahmad Shah Abdali.* Compiled by Qazi Hidayatullah, With *Pijandgalu* by Mawlana Abdul Qadir. Pikhawar: Pukhtu Academy, 1963.

Ahmad. *Khudayi Khidmatgar Tahrik.* With *Sarizah* by Khan Abdul Wali Khan. Vol. 1. Peshawar: University Book Agency, 1991.

Ahmad. *Khudayi Khidmatgar Tahrik.* With *Sarizah* by Khan Abdul Wali Khan. Vol. 2. n.p., n.d.

Barq, Sadullah Jan. *Da Pukhtanu Asal Nasal.* Vol. 1. n.p.: By the Author, 2008. Vol. 2. Pikhawar: University Book Agency, 2009. Vol. 3. Pikhawar: University Book Agency, 2010.

Barq, Sadullah Jan. *Pukhtun: Qam ya Nasal? (Tazah Tarin Tahqiq).* n.p., Printed by Araf Printers, Pikhawar, 2018.

Churchill, Winston S. *Malakand Field Force.* Translated by Shabaz Muhammad. n.p., n.d.

Darwizah, Akhun. *Makhzan.* With *Muqadimah* by Sayyad Muhammad Taqwim-ul-Haq Kaka Khail. 2nd Impression, Pikhawar: Pukhtu Academy, 1987.

Falsafi, Liwanay [Abdul Ghani Khan]. *Gaday Waday*. With *Muqadimah, Hashyah aw Latun* by Sayyad Iftikhar Husain. Pikhawar: Pakistan Studies Centre, University of Peshawar, n.d.

Ghaffar [Khan], Abdul. *Zama Jwand aw Jidujahd*. Kabul: Dawlati Matbah, 1983.

Habibi, Abdul Hai. *Pukhtanah Shuara: Hisah Awal*. Pikhawar: Idarah Ishaat-i Sarhad, n.d.

Hai, Abdul. *Afghanistan aw Sarhad: Yawah Tarikhi Jayizah*. Peshawar: Haji Faqir Muhammad and Sons, 1988.

Hamdani, Raza, comp. and trans. *Razmiyah Dastanayn*. Pukhtu with Urdu translation by Raza Hamdani. Islamabad: Lok Virsay ka Qaumi Idarah, 1981.

Isafzay, Ayaz. *Khpal Atlan Wapijanai*. Vol. 1. Pikhawar: Mangal Kitabkur, 2019.

Kaka Khail, Sayyad Bahadar Shah Zafar. *Pukhtanah da Tarikh pah Ranra kay*. Pikhawar: University Book Agency, n.d.

Khaleeq, Abdul Khaliq. *Zah aw Zama Zamanah*. Pikhawar: Idarah Ishaat-i Sarhad, 1968.

Khaleeq, Abdul Khaliq. *Da Azadai Jang: Sah Lidali aw sah Awridali*. 2nd edn., Pikhawar: Idarah Ishaat-i Sarhad, 1972.

Khalil, Hamish, comp. *Da Charbaitay Pakhwani Shairan*. Pikhawar: Pukhtu Academy, 2008.

Khalil, Hamish, comp. and trans. *Jangi Charbaytay*. Pashto with Urdu translation by Hamesh Khalil. Peshawar: Pashto Academy, 2008.

Khan, Abdul Qaiyum. *Zar aw Zur da Pukhtun pah Pulah*. Translated by Yasin Iqbal Yusufzay. Pikhawar: University Book Agency, 2008.

Khan, Abdul Wali. *Rikhtya, Rikhtya di (Pirangay-Muslim League aw Mung)*. Kabul: Da Qaumunu aw Qabailu Wazarat, Da Nashratu Riyasat, 1987.

Khan, Khan Abdul Ghani. *Da Ghani Kulyat: Da Panjray Chaghar, Palwashay aw Panus*. Afghanistan: Da Qaumunu aw Qabailu Wazarat, Da Nashratu Riyasat, 1985.

Khan, Khan Abdul Wali. *Bacha Khan aw Khudayi Khidmatgari*. Charsadah: Wali Bagh: Vol. 1, 1993; Vol. 2, 1994; Vol. 3, 1998; Vol. 4, 1999.

Khan, Muhammad Afzal Khan. *Pukhtun Qami Wahdat*. Peshawar: Pukhtunkwa Publications, 1996.

Khan, Muhammad Afzal Khan, comp. *Da Durand Karkhah: Pah Pikhawar kay da Shawi Seminar da Maqalu aw Wainaganu Tulgah*. n.p., 2004.

Khan, Muhammad Asif. *Tarikh-i Riyasat-i Swat wa Sawanih-i Hayat Baniy-i Riyasat-i Swat Hazrat Miangul Gul Shahzadah Abdul Wadud Khan Badshah Sahib*. With *Dibachah, hisah awal, saluramah hisah*, and *hisah pinzamah* by Muhammad Asif Khan. Printed by Ferozsons Ltd., Peshawar, [1958].

Khan, Muhammad Nawaz. *Tarikhi Tapay*. Pikhawar: University Book Agency, 2004.

Khan, Muhammad Nawaz. *Malakand da Tarikh pah Ranra kay*. Translated by Shabaz Muhammad. Mingawarah: Shoaib Sons Publishers & Booksellers, 2010.

Khan, Qazi Ataullah. *Da Pukhtanu Tarikh*. 3rd impression, Pikhawar: University Book Agency, 2012.

Khattak, Afzal Khan. *Tarikh Murasa*. Muqabilah, Tashih aw Nutunah lah Dost Muhammad Khan Kamil Momand. Pikhawar: University Book Agency, 2006.

Khattak, Khushal Khan. *Kulyat-i Khushal Khan Khattak: Sarah da Muqadimay aw Hashyay da Dost Muhammad Khan Kamil (Momand)*. 2nd edn., Pikhawar: Idarah Ishaat-i Sarhad, 1960.

Khattak, Khushal Khan. *Kulyat-i Khushal Khan Khattak*. Vol. 1. *Ghazliyat*. *Muratabah* and with *Da Khushal pah Haqlah* by Sher Shah Tarkhawi. Pikhawar: Azeem Publishing House, n.d.

Khattak, Khushal Khan. *Kulyat-i Khushal Khan Khattak*. Vol. 2. *Qasaid, Rubaiyat, Qitat aw Mutafariqat*. Pikhawar: Azeem Publishing House, n.d.

Khattak, Khushal Khan. *Da Khushal Khan Khattak Kulyat*. *Audanah, Partalanah, Samun aw Wibpangah* by Abdul Qayum Zahid Mishwanri. 3rdn. edn., n.p., Danish Khparanduyah Tulanah, 2013.

Khattak, Khushal Khan. *Dastar Namah*. With *Pishlafz* by Muhammad Nawaz Tair, *Pijandgalu* by Purdal Khan Khattak. Pikhawar: Pukhtu Academy, 1991.

Khattak, Raj Wali Shah. *Da Pukhtu Adabi Tahrikunah.* 2nd impression, Peshawar: Pukhtu Academy, 2018.

Khidmatgar, Abdullah Bakhtani. *Da Suli aw Azadai Qaharman Khan Abdul Ghaffar Khan (Landah Biography).* Kabul: Da Qaumunu aw Qabailu da Charu Wazarat, Da Nashratu aw Farhangi Charu Riyasat, 1366 [Hijri Shamsi].

Khidmatgar, Abdullah Bakhtani, comp. *Da Khan Abdul Ghaffar Khan Likunah.* 2nd edn., n.p.; Da Afghanistan da Kalturi Waday Tulanah, Germany, 2008.

Khybari, Ghaus. *Pukhtanah da Barhama, Zardakht, Buda aw Islam pah Pirunu kay.* n.p., Danish Khparanduyah Tulanah, 2012.

Layaq, Murad. *Aimal Khan Baba (Tahqiqi aw Tanqidi Jayizah).* Mumandrah: Shamshad Adabi Bahir, 1391 Hijri Shamsi.

Liwanay, Akmal, comp. *Da Nan Mazmun Da Nan Unwan Bacha Khan.* Mardan: Katlang Pukhtu Adabi Jargah, 2013.

Mangal, Asir. *Da Kurmay aw Tal Tarikh.* Peshawar: Pukhtu Alami Convention, 2011.

Mian, Akbar Shah. *Da Azadai pah Talash.* n.p., n.d.

Mehsud, Ali Khan. *Lah Pir Rukhanah tar Bacha Khan Puray: Da Pukhtanu Mili Mubarizay tah Katanah.* Pikhawar: Da Danish Khparanduyay Tulanay Takhniki Sangah, n.d.

Muhammad, Shabaz. *Da Malakand Ghazaganay.* Chakdarah: Pukhtu Sangah, Malakand Puhantun, 2016.

Muslim Dust, Abdur Rahim and Badr-ul-Zaman Badar. *Da Gwantanamu Matay Zawlanay.* n.p., 'Khilafat' Khparanduyah Tulanah, 1385 Hijri Shamsi.

Qadir, Abdul. *Da Fikar Yun: Da Mawlana Abdul Qadir da Mazmununu Majmuah.* Compiled by Abdur Rahman Shabab. 2nd edn., Pikhawar: University Book Agency, 1997.

Rome, Badshah-i. *Pukhtanah aw Tawahumat (Kaganay Angiranay).* Amandarah: Hamishah Pukhtu Adabi Tulanah (Registered), 2019.

Saqi, Fazlur Rahim. *Da Khudayi Khidmatgarai pah Tahrik kay Zama Jwandun.* n.p.: Yusuf Lodi, n.d.

Sayal, Khwajah Muhammad. *Khushalyat aw Haqayaq (Intiqadi Jaaj).* n.p.: By the Author, 2006.

Shah, Pir Muazam Shah. *Tawarikh Hafiz Rahmat Khani.* With *Dibachah* by Muhammad Nawaz Tair. 2nd Impression, Pikhawar: Pukhtu Academy, 1987.

Shaheen, Salma, collector, compiler and researcher. *Ruhi Sandaray (Tapay).* [Vol. 1.] With *Maqalah Khususi* by Muhammad Nawaz Tair. Pikhawar: Pukhtu Academy, 1984.

Shaheen, Salma. *Ruhi Sandaray (Tapay).* Vol. 2. With *Pishlafz* by Muhammad Nawaz Tair. Pikhawar: Pukhtu Academy, 1994.

Shalman, Fazali Zaman. *Mawlawi Fazal Mahmud Makhfi.* n.p., n.d. (Printed by Amir Print and Publishers Pikhawar).

Shalmani, Arshad Karim. *Shalmani (Yawah Siranah).* n.p.: Tanrah Adabi Tulanah Malakand, 2019.

Shinwari, Amir Hamzah Khan. *Ghazawanay.* 14th edn., n.p.: Hamzah Academy, 2010.

Stori, Kabir. *Zabsapohana.* Pikhawar: Da Pukhtunkhwa da Puhanay Dirah, 2000.

Sultan-i-Rome. *Matalunah.* Mingawarah: Shoaib Sons Publishers & Booksellers, 2013.

Sultan-i-Rome. *Tapay.* Mingawarah: Shoaib Sons Publishers & Booksellers, 2018.

Swati, Saranzeb. *Tarikh Riyasat-i Swat.* Pikhawar: Azeem Publishing House, 1984.

Tair, Muhammad Nawaz. *Tapah aw Jwand.* Pikhawar: Pukhtu Academy, 1980.

Tair, Muhammad Nawaz. *Ruhi Saqafat: Tapah aw Jwand.* n.p.: Hukumat-i Khyber Pukhtunkhwa, 2012.

Yusafzai, Fatehul Mulk Nang. *Tur Makhunah, Spin Pukhunah.* Vol. 1. n.p.: By the Author, 2002.

Zaibsar, Taj Muhammad Khan, *Uruj-i Afghan* (verse), Vol. 1: Printed at Manzur-i Aam Press, Peshawar, 1360 AH; Vol. 2: Riyasat-i Swat, 1361 AH.

Zaif, Abd-us-Salam. *Da Guntanamu Inzur.* n.p., n.d.

Zyar, Mujawar Ahmad. *Pukhtu aw Pukhtanah da Jabpuhanay pah Ranra kay (Lah Saki Makhinay Sarah).* Pikhawar: Da Sapi Pukhtu Siranu aw Parakhtya Markaz, 2001.

BOOKS IN URDU

Abidi, Raza Ali. *Shir Darya*. Lahore: Sang-e-Meel Publications, 1998.

Adrawi, Asir. *Tarikh Jamiyat-i Ulamay-i Hind*. New Delhi: Shubah-i Nashr-u-Ishaat, Jamiyat-i Ulamay-i Hind, 1403 AH.

Ahmad, Mir. *Tarikh-i Sarhad*. Lahore: Maktabah-i Jamal, 2010.

Ahmad, Qeyamuddin. *Hindustan mayn Wahabi Tahrik*. Translated by Muhammad Muslim Azeemabadi. 2nd edn., Karachi: Nafees Academy, 1976.

Akhtar, Muhammad. *Tajak Swati wa Mumlikat-i Gabar Tarikh kay Ayinah mayn*. Abbottabad: Sarhad Urdu Academy, 2002.

Albiruni, Abu Rehan. *Hindu Dharam: Hazar Baras Pihlay*. Lahore: Nigarishat, 2000.

Ashraf, Sahibzadah Muhammad. *Khyber Pukhtunkhwa ka Azim Insan: Halat-i Zindagi Sir Sahibzadah Nawab Abdul Qayyum Khan*. Kutah, Swabi: Sahibzadah Book Foundation, n.d.

Aslam, Shaikh Navid. *Shimali Alaqajat aur Pakistan*. Lahore: Sang-e-Meel Publications, 2000.

Azad, Abul Kalam. *Masalah-i Khilafat*. Lahore: Maktabah-i Jamal, 2004.

Barq, Sadullah Jan. *Khidmatgari say Fawajdari Tak*. Peshawar: University Book Agency, 2012.

Barq, Sadullah Jan. *Pushtunistan ka Muqadimah (Pushtun banam Mazhab)*. n.p., 2019.

Bon, Gustav le [Mr le Bon]. *Tamadun-i Hind*. Translated by Sayyad Ali Bilgrami. With *Muqadimah* by Rais Ahmad Jafri. Lahore: Maqbul Academy, n.d.

Bukhari, Farigh. *Bacha Khan (Khan Abdul Ghaffar Khan kay Sawanih Hayat)*. Peshawar: Naya Maktabah; Lahore: Gushah-i Adab, 1957.

Bukhari, Farigh and Raza Hamdani, eds. *Attak kay us Par*. Lahore: Gushah-i Adab, n.d.

Caroe, Olaf. *Pathan*. Translated by Sayyad Mahbub Ali. With *Muqadimah* by Mawlana Abdul Qadir, *Pishlafz* by Raj Wali Shah Khattak and *Ikhtitamiyah* translated by Ashraf Adeel. 3rd edn., Peshawar: Pashto Academy, 2000.

Chauhan, Ali Hasan. *Tarikh Gurjar (Halat-i Hazirah)*. Part 4. n.p., n.d.

Dani, Ahmad Hasan. *Shah Rais Khan ki Tarikh-i Gilgit*. Lahore: Sang-e-Meel Publications, 2000.

Danishwar, Mahmud. *Kafiristan aur Chitral-Dir-Swat ki Sayahat*. Translated by Khalil Ahmad. 2nd revised edn., Lahore: West Pak Publishing Company Limited, October 1953.

Harwi, Khwajah Nimatullah. *Tarikh Khan Jahani wa Makhzan-i Afghani*. Translated by Muhammad Bashir Husain. Lahore: Markazi Urdu Board, 1978.

Hasan, Sibte. *Musa say Marx tak*. 7th edn., 8th Impression, Karachi: Maktabah Danyal, 1986.

Hunter, W.W. *Hamaray Hindustani Musalman*. Translated by Sadiq Hussain. Lahore: Qaumi Kutub Khanah, n.d.

Iqbal, Qari Javaid. *Saqafat-i Sarhad: Tarikh kay Ayinay mayn*. Islamabad: Lok Virsa ka Qaumi Idarah, and Lahore: Al-Faisal Nashiran, 2002.

Jafar, Sardar Haidar. *Mujahidat-i Subah Sarhad: Tahrik-i Pakistan ki Numayan Khawatin Karkun*. Peshawar: Syndicate of Writers Pakistan (Registered), n.d.

Jafri, Rais Ahmad, comp. *Awraq-i Gumgashtah*. Lahore: Muhammad Ali Academy, 1968.

Javaid, Aziz. *Sarhad ka Ayini Irtiqa*. Peshawar: Idarah Tahqiq wa Tasnif, 1975.

Javaid, Aziz. *Quaid-i Azam aur Sarhad*. 2nd edn., Peshawar: Idarah Tahqiq wa Tasnif, Pakistan, 1977.

Kaka Khail, Sayyad Bahadar Shah Zafar. *Pushtun Tarikh kay Ayinay mayn (550 q.m. say 1964 tak*. Translated by Sayyad Anwarul Haq. Peshawar: University Book Agency, n.d.

Kaka Khail, Sayyad Bahadar Shah Zafar. *Pushtun: Apni Nasal kay Aayinay mayn*. Peshawar: University Book Agency, 1994.

Kamran, Tahir. *Pakistan mayn Jamhuriat aur Governance*. Lahore: South Asia Partnership, Pakistan, 2008.

Khan, Khan Abdul Ghaffar. *Ap Biti*. Reprint, Lahore: Fiction House, 2004.

Khan, Khan Abdul Wali. *Bacha Khan aur Khudayi Khidmatgari (Taqsim-i Hind ya Taqsim-i Musalmanan)*. Vol. 1. Peshawar: Bacha Khan Research Centre, 2009.

Khan, Khan Abdul Wali. *Asal Haqyaq yay Hayn*. Karachi: Shibal Publications, 1988.

Khan, Mir Abdu-Samad. *Luy Pukhtun: Sir Sayyad-i Sarhad Sahibzadah Abdul Qayyum Khan*. Peshawar: University Book Agency, n.d.

Khan, Khan Roshan. *Tazkirah (Pathanu ki Asliyat aur un ki Tarikh)*. 4th impression, Karachi: Roshan Khan and Company, 1983.

Khan, Khan Roshan. *Yusufzai Qaum ki Sarguzasht*. Karachi: Roshan Khan and Company, 1986.

Khan, Muhammad Irshad Khan. *Tarikh-i Hazarah: Turku ka Ahad*. Peshawar: Ahbab Printers and Publishers, 1976.

Khan, Sultan Muhammad. *Pukhtunu ka Tarikhi Safar: Bani Israel kay Tanazur mayn*. Karachi: Pakistani Adab Publications, 1997.

Khattak, Afrasiyab. *Sarhad: Tarikhi Khakah*. Lahore: South Asia Partnership, Pakistan, 2000.

Khattak, Khushal Khan. *Dastar Namah*. Translated by Khatir Ghaznawi, Review by Purdal Khan Khattak, With *Pishlafz* by Muhammad Nawaz Tair, *Dibachah* by Preshan Khattak. Peshawar: Pashto Academy, 1980.

Khattak, Preshan. *Pushtun Kaun? (Tarikh, Tahqiq, Tanqid)*. Revised by Muhammad Nawaz Tair and Jahanzeb Niyaz. Peshawar: Pashto Academy, 1984.

Khattak, Qabil Khan. *Samah aur Swat*. n.p., 1992.

Kiwhur, Nawshirawan. *Turwal kay Qabail*. Peshawar: Gandhara Hindku Academy, 2017.

Lane-Poole. *Farmanrawayan-i Islam*. Translated by Ghulam Jilani Barq. Lahore: Shaikh Ghulam Ali and Sons, 1968.

Macmunn, George. *Shimal Maghribi Pakistan aur Bartanawi Samraj*. Translated by M. Anwar Roman. Quetta: Nisa Traders, 1979.

Mahmood, Safdar. *Pakistan: Muslim League ka Daur-i Hukumat, 1947–1954*. Lahore: Sang-e-Meel Publications, 1986.

Mangluri, Sayyad Tufail Ahmad. *Musalmanu ka Rushan Mustaqbil*. Reprint, Lahore: Himadul Kutbah, n.d.

Panni, Sher Bahadar Khan. *Tarikh Hazarah*. 3rd edn., Lahore: Maktabah Rahmaniyah, 2001.

Qadiri, Muhammad Amir Shah. *Tazkirah Ulama wa Mashaikh-i Sarhad*. Vol. 1. Peshawar: Maktabah al-Hasan, n.d.

Qasuri, Muhammad Ali. *Mushahidat-i Kabul wa Yaghistan*. Karachi: Anjuman Taraqi Urdu (Pakistan), n.d.

Qayyum, Abdul. *Mashahir-i Sarhad*. 2nd edn., Lahore: Ferozsons Limited, 2006.

Quraishi, Muhammad Faruq. *Wali Khan aur Qararadad-i Pakistan*. Enlarged edn., Lahore: Fiction House, 1997.

Rahman, Fuyuzur. *Mashahir Ulama-i Sarhad*. Karachi: Majlas-i Nashriyat-i Islam, 1998.

Rashid, Ahmad. *Taliban: Islam, Til aur Wast-i Asia mayn Sazashu ka Naya Khayl*. Translated by Hamid Jehlami. Lahore: Mashal, 2001.

Sabir, Muhammad Shafi. *Dastan-i Khyber*. Peshawar: University Book Agency. n.d.

Sabir, Muhammad Shafi. *Quaid-i Azam aur Subah Sarhad*. Peshawar: University Book Agency, n.d.

Sabir, Muhammad Shafi. *Shakhsiyat-i Sarhad*. Peshawar: University Book Agency, n.d.

Sabir, Muhammad Shafi. *Tarikh Khyber Pukhtunkhwa (Sabiqah Subah Sarhad)*. 2nd edn., Peshawar: University Book Agency, 2019.

Sabir, Muhammad Shafi. *Tahrik-i Pakistan mayn Subah Sarhad ka Hisah*. Peshawar: University Book Agency, 1990.

Sabir, Muhammad Shafi. *Tazkirah Sarfarushan-i Sarhad*. Peshawar: University Book Agency, n.d.

Sabur, Abdul. *Pushtun Bani Ishaq*. Tadwin wa Hawashi by Ismail Gauhar. Islamabad: Sangar Publications Mardan, 2015.

Sarhadi, Abdul Naeem. *Bacha Khan aur Tahrik Azadi kay Hiruz*. Peshawar: Naeem Sarhadi Publications, 2018.

Shah, Pir Muazam. *Tawarikh Hafiz Rahmat Khani: Afghan Qabail aur un ki Tarikh*. *Tartib wa Hawashi* by Khan Roshan Khan. 2nd impression, Peshawar: Pashto Academy, 2017.

Saulat, Sarwat. *Millat-i Islamiyah ki Mukhtasar Tarikh*. Part 2. 4th edn., Lahore: Islamic Publications (Private) Limited, 1988.

Sidiqi, Javaid Ahmad. *Wali Khan Aaj aur Kal*. Karachi: Shibal Publications Limited, 1986.

Sufi, Juma Khan. *Farib-i Natamam (Yadayn aur Yadashtayn)*. *Izafah shudah* edition, Islamabad: Mister Books, 2016.

Sufi, Mir Ahmad Khan. *Ghazi Pir: Sayyad Muhammad Aminul Hasanat Manki Sharif*. Pabi: Sufi Medical Hall, 1987.

Taji, Habibullah. *Pushtun*. Translated by Shaukat Tarin. Quetta: Ghaznawi Khparanduyah Tulanah, 2004.

Tarin, Abdul Hamid. *Faqir Ipi*. Karachi: Taj Company Limited, 1984.

Yusufi, Allah Bakhsh. *Yusufzai*. Karachi: Muhammad Ali Educational Society, 1960.

Yusufi, Allah Bakhsh. *Afghan ya Pathan*. With *Pishlafz* by Shaikh Muhammad Shafi. 3rd edn., Karachi: Muhammad Ali Educational Society, 1960.

Yusufi, Allah Bakhsh. *Azad Pathan*. Vol. 1. *Khyber Agency*. Karachi: Sarhad Syndicate, Tin Hatti, Karachi, n.d.

Yusufi, Allah Bakhsh. *Tarikh-i Azad Pathan*. Vol. 2. With *Pishlafz* by Habibur Rahman. Karachi: Muhammad Ali Educational Society, 1959.

Yusufi, Allah Bakhsh. *Sarhad aur Jidujahd-i Azadi*. *Tarmim wa Izafah Shudah edn.*, Karachi: Nafees Academy, 1989.

Yusufzai, Aqeel. *Talibanization: Afghanistan say Fata, Swat aur Pakistan tak*. Lahore: Nigarishat Publishers, 2009.

Yusufzai, Nurul Amin. *Pukhtu, Pukhtun aur Pukhtunwali: Pukhtu Zaban, Adab, Pukhtun Tarikh aur Saqafat kay Hawalay say Mazamin ka Majmuah*. Swabi: Qam Qalam Swabi, 2015.

Yusufzay, Muhammad Jameel. *Pushtunu ki Jarayn*. 2nd edn., n.p.: Printed by Aks Printing Press Batkhilah, 2018.

JOURNAL ARTICLES

English

Baha, Lal. 'Khilafat Movement and the North-West Frontier Province.' *Journal of the Research Society of Pakistan*, (Lahore). Vol. 14 (No. 3, July 1979), pp. 1–22.

Baha, Lal. 'The Hijrat Movement and the North-West Frontier Province.' *Islamic Studies* (Islamabad). Vol. 18 (No. 3, Autumn 1979), pp. 231–42.

Dar, Farooq Ahmad. 'Jinnah and Pakistan's Independence Ceremonies'. *Journal of the Pakistan Historical Society* (Karachi). Vol. 62 (No 2, April–June 2014), pp. 57–76.

Fahim, Mohammad. 'Afghanistan and World War-I.' *Journal of the Pakistan Historical Society* (Karachi). Vol. 24 (Part 2, April 1978), pp. 107–15.

Harrison, F.A.K. 'The British Interest in the North West Frontier.' *Peshawar University Review* (Peshawar). Vol. 1 (No. 1, 1974–75), pp. 46–56.

Hassan, Syed Minhajul. 'The Impact of Mountbatten-Nehru Relationship on the Partition of India.' *Journal of the Pakistan Historical Society* (Karachi). Vol. 44 (Part 3, July 1996), pp. 229–42.

Hassan, Syed Minhajul. 'Tribal Areas of NWFP (Pakistan): Land and People.' *Al-Siyasa* (Lahore). Vol. 6 (Winter 2004), pp. 59–75.

Himayatullah. 'Jinnah, Muslim League and Constitutional Reforms in the N.W.F.P.' *Journal of the Pakistan Historical Society* (Karachi). Vol. 55 (Nos. 1–2, January–June 2007), 'All India Muslim League Centenary Special Number, Part I', pp. 141–57.

Himayatullah. 'Religious Transformation and Development among the Pakhtuns: A Historical and Analytical Study.' *Pakistan Journal of History and Culture* (Islamabad). Vol. 28 (No. 2, July–December 2007), pp. 129–50.

Jaffar, Ghulam Muhammad. 'The Ambella Campaign and the Followers of Sayyid Ahmad.' *Journal of the Pakistan Historical Society* (Karachi). Vol. 40 (Part 3, July 1992), pp. 289–97.

Kaka Khel, Sayed Wiqar Ali Shah. 'N.-W.F.P. and the Khilafat & Hijrat Movements.' *Central Asia* (Peshawar). No. 20 (Summer 1987), pp. 121–41.

Khan, Munawwar. 'Swat in History.' *Peshawar University Review* (Peshawar). Vol. 1 (No. 1, 1973), pp. 51–63.

Khan, Munawwar. 'Swat: Second Instalment.' *Peshawar University Review* (Peshawar). Vol. 1, (No. 1, 1974–75), pp. 57–77.

Khurshid. 'Sandakai Mullah: Career and Role in the Formation of Swat State, Pakistan.' *Journal of the Pakistan Historical Society* (Karachi). Vol. 47 (No. 2, April–June 1999), pp. 77–81.

Menon, M.M. 'Swat: Some Aspects of its Geography.' *Pakistan Geographical Review* (Lahore). Vol. 12 (No. 1, 1957), pp. 58–64.

Niazi, Shaheer. 'The Origin of the Pathans.' *Journal of the Pakistan Historical Society* (Karachi). Vol. 18 (Part 1, January 1970), pp. 23–38.

Stein, Aurel. 'From Swat to the Gorges of the Indus.' *The Geographical Journal* (London). Vol. 100 (No. 2, August 1942), pp. 49–56.

Sultana, Razia. 'Pukhtoons Settlement in the Peshawar Valley: An Appraisal.' *Journal of the Pakistan Historical Society* (Karachi). Vol. 50 (No. 4, October–December 2002), pp. 63–75.

Sultan-i-Rome. 'Abdul Ghaffur (Akhund), Saidu Baba of Swat: Life, Career and Role.' *Journal of the Pakistan Historical Society* (Karachi). Vol. 40 (Part 3, July 1992), pp. 299–308.

Sultan-i-Rome. 'The Sartor Faqir: Life and Struggle against British Imperialism.' *Journal of the Pakistan Historical Society* (Karachi). Vol. 42 (Part 1, January 1994), pp. 93–105.

Sultan-i-Rome. 'The Malakand Jihad (1897): An Unsuccessful Attempt to oust the British from Malakand and Chakdarah.' *Journal of the Pakistan Historical Society* (Karachi). Vol. 43 (Part 2, April 1995), pp. 171–86.

Sultan-i-Rome. 'Constitutional Developments Relating to the North-West Frontier Province.' *Journal of Law and Society* (Peshawar). Vol. 30 (No. 43, January 2004), pp. 79–100.

Sultan-i-Rome. 'The Role of the North-West Frontier Province in the Khilafat and Hijrat Movements.' *Islamic Studies* (Islamabad). Vol. 43 (No. 1, Spring 2004), pp. 51–78.

Sultan-i-Rome. 'The Durand Line Agreement (1893): Its Pros and Cons.' *Journal of the Research Society of Pakistan* (Lahore). Vol. 41 (No. 1, July 2004), pp. 1–25.

Sultan-i-Rome. 'Geography of North-West Frontier Province in Historical Perspective.' *Pakistan Perspectives* (Karachi). Vol. 11 (No. 1, January–June 2006), pp. 113–32.

Sultan-i-Rome. 'Origin of the Pukhtuns: The Bani Israelite Theory.' *Journal of the Pakistan Historical Society* (Karachi). Vol. 54 (No. 4, October–December 2006), pp. 73–104.

Sultan-i-Rome. '*Pukhtu*: The *Pukhtun* Code of Life.' *Pakistan Vision* (Lahore). Vol. 7 (No. 2, December 2006), pp. 1–30.

Sultan-i-Rome. 'The Khudai Khidmatgar Movement: From Genesis to Downfall.' *Hamdard Islamicus* (Karachi). Vol. 30 (No. 1, January–March 2007), pp. 35–55.

Sultan-i-Rome. 'Swat and the AIML.' *Journal of the Pakistan Historical Society* (Karachi). Vol. 55 (Nos. 1–2, January–June 2007), 'All India Muslim League Centenary Special Number, Part I', pp. 225–30.

Sultan-i-Rome. 'Pattern of the Tribal Administration System.' *Pakistan Perspectives* (Karachi). Vo. 12 (No. 1, January–June 2007), pp. 15–49.

Sultan-i-Rome. 'The Uprising of 1897: An Appraisal of the Tribals Attempt against the Mighty British Power on the North-West Frontier of British India.' *Pakistan Perspectives* (Karachi). Vol. 12 (No. 2, July–December 2007), pp. 157–97.

Sultan-i-Rome. 'The Formation of North-West Frontier Province.' *Afghan Research Journal* (Lahore). Vol. 1 (No. 1, January 2008), pp. 1–34.

Sultan-i-Rome. 'Origin of the Pukhtuns: The Aryan Race Theory.' *Journal of the Pakistan Historical Society* (Karachi). Vol. 56 (No. 3, July–September 2008), pp. 35–62.

Sultan-i-Rome. 'The Referendum in N.W.F.P. in 1947.' *Afghan Research Journal* (Lahore). Vol. 2 (No. 1, January 2009), pp. 28–64.

Sultan-i-Rome. 'Origin of the Pukhtuns: The Mixed Race Theory.' *Journal of the Pakistan Historical Society* (Karachi). Vol. 57 (No. 3, July–September 2009), pp. 27–45.

Sultan-i-Rome. 'Khushhal Khan Khattak. 'An Afghan Nationalist or a Mughul Loyalist?.' *Journal of the Pakistan Historical Society* (Karachi). Vol. 64 (No. 3, July–September 2016), pp. 61–94.

Journal of the Pakistan Historical Society (Karachi). Vol. 55 (Nos. 1–2 January–June and Nos. 3–4, July–December 2007), All India Muslim League Centenary Special Number, Parts I and II.' *Hamdard Islamicus* (Karachi). Vol. 30 (No. 1, January–March 2007).

Pukhtu (Pashto)

A Journal with '*Sarizah*' by Muhammad Gul (Jahangiri). Facts of publication have been torn out, but was published from Afghanistan.

Ajmali, Muhammad Islam. 'Saidu Babaji nah tar Wali Swat Puray.' *Pukhtu* (Pikhawar). Vol. 29 (Nos. 7–8, July–August 1997), pp. 171–5.

Barq, Sadullah Jan. 'Da Pukhtanu Asal Nasal (Trikh Tarikh).' *Pukhtu* (Pikhawar). Vol. 29 (Nos. 9–10, September–October 1997), pp. 26–41.

Barq, Sadullah Jan. 'Da Pukhtanu Asal Nasal: Da Qays Abdur Rashid Qisah.' *Pukhtu* (Pikhawar). Vol. 30 (Nos. 1–2, January–February 1998), pp. 45–7.

Barq, Sadullah Jan. 'Da Pukhtanu Asal Nasal: Da Jinnatu Masalah, Trikh Tarikh.' *Pukhtu* (Pikhawar). Vol. 30 (Nos. 5–6, May–June 1998), pp. 7–13.

Barq, Sadullah Jan. 'Da Pukhtanu Asal Nasal: Pukhtanah Arya Di?; Trikh Tarikh.' *Pukhtu* (Pikhawar). Vol. 30 (Nos. 7–8, July–August 1998), pp. 7–12.

Dawud, Dawar Khan. 'Pukhtanah aw Ghwaryakhail Momand.' *Pukhtu* (Pikhawar). Vols. 36–37 (Nos. 10–12, October–December 2006, Nos. 1–3, January–March 2007), pp. 58–72.

Liaqat, Farkhanda. 'Da Abdul Akbar Khan Akbar da Jwand Halat.' *Quarterly Tatara* (Pikhawar). Vol. 10 (No. 1, January–March 2006), pp. 65–77.

Shaheen, Muhammad Parwaish. 'Da Swat Ghrunah aw kah da Azadai da Tarikh Babunah.' *Pukhtu* (Pikhawar). Vol. 29 (Nos. 7–8, July–August 1997), pp. 284–9.

Shalman, Fazli Zaman. 'Da Pakistan da Juridu Panzuskalanah aw da Qabailu da Ghazaganu Salkalanah.' *Pukhtu* (Pikhawar). Vol. 30 (Nos. 9–10, September–October 1998), pp. 41–51.

Sultan-i-Rome. '"Da Saidu Babaji nah tar Wali Swat Puray": Yawah Tanqidi Jaizah.' *Pukhtu* (Pikhawar). Vol. 29 (Nos. 11–12, November–December 1997), pp. 12–23.

Sultan-i-Rome. ' "Da Swat Ghrunah aw kah da Azadai da Tarikh Babunah": Yawah Tajziyah.' *Pukhtu* (Pikhawar). Vol. 30 (Nos. 11–12, November–December 1998), pp. 44–57.

LAW JOURNALS

The All Pakistan Legal Decisions (P.L.D.). Lahore: P.L.D. Publications.

NEWSPAPERS

Ayaz, Gul. '*Swara*: Stigma on Pukhtun Social Code.' *Statesman*, Peshawar, 6 May 2002.

Effendi, Aslam. 'Durand Line and the elephant.' *The News International*. Islamabad/Rawalpindi, 2 January 2004.

Hastings, Max. 'Did Chinese discover America?.' *The Guardian*. Urdu trans. '*Amrica Chiniyu nay Daryaft kiya*?' Translated by Muhammad Sharif Shakib. *Roznamah Aaj Peshawar* (Urdu, daily), 7 May 2005.

Jillani, Anees. 'Forgotten Tribal Areas.' *The News International*. Islamabad/Rawalpindi, 4 August 1998.

Khan, Amir Zaman. 'Law that Governs the People of Malakand Division.' *The Frontier Post*, '*Weekend Post*.' Peshawar, 15 July 1988.

Khan, Munawwar. 'Chitral Expedition & the 1897 Uprising-I.' *The Frontier Post*. Peshawar, 15 March 1995.

Yusufzai, Rahimullah. 'It's Durand Line again.' *The News International*. Islamabad/Rawalpindi, 4 January 2003.

Dawn, The Internet Edition.

The News International (Islamabad/Rawalpindi edition).

The Frontier Post (Peshawar edition).

Ruznamah Aaj Peshawar (Urdu daily).

Ruznamah Mashriq (Urdu daily, Peshawar edition).

WEBSITES

BBC URDU.com, Wednesday, 7 February 2007, 11:57 GMT 16:57 PST, www.bbc.co.uk/urdu/ pakistan/story/2007/02/printable/070207_mullah_zaeef_part2_rs. Accessed: 14 November 2007.

www.bbc.com/urdu/regional-44440204, Accessed: 13 June 2018.

www.bbc.com/urdu/pakistan-48866470, Accessed: 17 August 2019.

www.bbc.com/urdu/pakistan-53482078, Accessed: 29 July 2020.

https://www.bbc.com/urdu

http://www.valleyswat.net/

www.ipcs.org

Index

1st Punjab Infantry, 165
1st Sikhs Infantry, 165
3rd June Plan, 330, 331, 334, 336, 340, 343, 345, 416
24th Punjab Infantry, 167
25th Amendment in the Constitution of Pakistan, 1973, 2, 4, 126, 186, 242, 252, *see also* Constitution (Twenty-fifth Amendement) Act, 2018
35th Sikhs regiment, 167
38th Dogra regiment, 167
45th Sikhs, 166

A

Aaj (Urdu daily, Peshawar), 243
Abasin (Indus) Kuhistan, 17
Abbasi, Sardar Mehtab Khan, 318
Abbottabad, 203, 207, 298, 299, 320 n., 397, 398, 403; District, 5, 383; League, 300; *tahsil*, 203
Abdali (tribe), 78
Abdali, Ahmad Shah, 17, 46, 68, 90 n., 120, 121, 128 n., 390
Abdali, Sarmast Khan, 40
Abdul Ghaffar Khan Nagar, 413
Abd-ur-Rahman/Abdurrahman (Abdur Rahman), 137, *see also* Rahman, Amir Abdur
Abraham (AS), Prophet, 25, *see also* Ibrahim (AS), Prophet
Abu Klea, 173
Achaemenian Empire, 71, 74; ruler, 75
Acharia, Rajagopal, 333, *see also* Rajagopalachari
Actions (in Aid of Civil Power) Regulations of 2011, 242, 282
Adam (AS), 26, 30
Adamec, L.W., 143
Adams, Lieutenant-Colonel, 193 n.
Administration Report on the North-West Frontier Province, 155, 157
Advisory Council, 218, 220
Af, 36
Afghan (Talut's son), 32, 40
Afghan (title), 36; name/nomenclature, 37, 39, 46, 47; term, 41, 45, 47, 49
Afghan(s), 15, 22 n., 24, 25, 26, 30, 31, 32, 33, 34, 36, 40, 41, 42, 43, 45, 47, 48, 49, 57, 58, 59, 62, 63, 64, 65, 69, 70, 71, 72, 73, 75, 77, 78, 79, 81, 82, 84 n., 86 n., 89 n., 122, 131, 133, 136, 143, 144, 147, 150, 158, 162, 267, 422; aggression, 145; agreements, 148; Ambassador, 148; Amir(s), 123, 125, 130, 131, 133, 145, 156, 159, 162, 175; ancestry, 43; areas, 57; authorities, 149; Boundary Commission, 391; claim, 149; courtiers, 43; customary law, 211; delegation, 45; demand, 146, 147, 420; ethnicity/origin/race, 24, 49, 82; factor, 161, 162; First War, 124; forces/authorities,

20; frontier, 145; general, 145; government(s), 65, 144, 145, 146, 147, 148, 149, 268, 274; hands, 134; head, 47; historians, 150; independence, 145; interest, 269; intrigues, 163; invader, 89 n.; issues, 149; kingdom, 132; land, 46, 79; *malik*s, 33; masses, 131; military commanders, 149; *millat*, 65; monarch, 268, 411; *nang*, 46; nation, 25, 78; National Assembly, 147; nomenclature, 73; officials, 159; outpost, 139; people's issue, 148; president, 148, 422; proper, 78; representation, 146; scholar, 65; Second War, 125, 135; side, 149; *sipah salar*, 159, 161, 162; soldiers, 133, 159; stock, 82; territory/territories, 14, 132, 135, 149; Third War, 145; women, 33; Youth League, 254, 265; non-Afghan historians, 65
Afghana (Armya's son), 29, 30, 33, 38, 39, 41, 45; descendants (children) of, 30
Afghani (language), 45, 46, 48; head, 48
Afghani tahzib (Afghani civilisation), 48
Afghanistan, 2, 4, 7, 8, 10, 11, 13, 14, 18, 20, 24, 40, 41, 45, 48, 50, 51, 52, 53, 57, 65, 68, 71, 75, 77, 104, 107, 120, 121, 125, 126, 130, 131, 132, 133, 134, 135, 136, 138, 139, 140, 141, 142, 143, 144, 145, 146, 147, 148, 149, 150, 155, 156, 161, 162, 212, 243, 253, 283, 341, 342, 355, 364, 370, 375, 379, 390, 410, 418, 420, 421, 422, 426, 427; Foreign Minister of, 48; ant-Soviet proxy war in, 18; Soviet intervention in (1979), 422; USA invasion of (2001), 104, 385
Afghanistan (book), 150
Africa, 118
Afridi(s) (tribe), 15, 16, 55, 72, 76, 78, 91 n., 159, 163, 168, 169, 170, 171, 174, 176, 177, 181, 182, 183, 191 n., 193 n., 376, 386 n., 392, 401; allowances, 376; country/territory, 14, 125, 141, 182; rising/uprising, 169, 191 n.; valleys, 182
Afzal, M. Rafique, 317
Afzal, Sher, 126, 160
Agency of Dir and Swat, 20 n., 126, 364
Agency of Dir, Swat and Chitral, 3, 5, 7, 8, 20 n., 126, 198, 201, 203, 204, 206, 207, 358, 359, 364, *see also* Dir, Swat and Chitral Agency
Agent to the government/governor-general, 206, 208, 216, 219, 226, 364, 378, 379
Agent to the president, 364
Agnew, Vans, 122
Agra, 252, 409
Ahadith, 45
Ahimsa, 276, 414
Ahmad, Barrister Aziz, 295, 296
Ahmad, Malak (Yusufzi's chief), 107
Ahmad, Qazi Mir, 295, 296
Ahmad, Syed, 390
Ahmad Khail, 14
Ahmed, Akbar S., 186